Appealing for Liberty

Appealing for Liberty

Freedom Suits in the South

LOREN SCHWENINGER

OXFORD
UNIVERSITY PRESS

OXFORD
UNIVERSITY PRESS

Oxford University Press is a department of the University of Oxford. It furthers
the University's objective of excellence in research, scholarship, and education
by publishing worldwide. Oxford is a registered trade mark of Oxford University
Press in the UK and certain other countries.

Published in the United States of America by Oxford University Press
198 Madison Avenue, New York, NY 10016, United States of America.

Library of Congress Cataloging-in-Publication Data
Names: Schweninger, Loren, author.
Title: Appealing for liberty : freedom suits in the South / Loren Schweninger.
Description: New York, NY : Oxford University Press, [2018] |
Includes bibliographical references and index.
Identifiers: LCCN 2018000828 (print) | LCCN 2018002025 (ebook) |
ISBN 978-0-19-066429-9 (updf) | ISBN 978-0-19-066430-5 (epub) |
ISBN 978-0-19-066428-2 (hardback : alk. paper)
Subjects: LCSH: Slaves—Legal status, laws, etc.—Southern States. |
Slavery—Southern States—Legislative history. | Southern States—Race relations—History. |
Southern States—History—1775-1865.
Classification: LCC KF482 (ebook) | LCC KF482 .S39 2018 (print) |
DDC 342.7308/7—dc23
LC record available at https://lccn.loc.gov/2018000828

1 3 5 7 9 8 6 4 2

Printed by Sheridan Books, Inc., United States of America

A revised and updated version of "Freedom Suits, African American Women, and the Genealogy of Slavery,"
1, 3rd ser., January 2014, in the *William and Mary Quarterly*, is published here courtesy of the Omohuundro
Institute of Early American History and Culture.

A revised and update version of "The Vass Slaves: County Courts, State Laws and Slavery in Virginia, 1831–
1861," 114, no. 4, 2006, in the *Virginia Magazine of History and Biography*, is published here courtesy of the
Virginia Magazine.

For
Mark
Ann
Lee
Jan
Lauren
Elijah Franklin
Helen Jean
George Franklin
Family members all

CONTENTS

ACKNOWLEDGMENTS

Much of the documentary evidence contained in this study comes from the Race and Slavery Petitions Project at the University of North Carolina at Greensboro. Although their numbers are far too great to cite individually, it is a pleasure to acknowledge the archivists, librarians, clerks of court, and staff people at various courthouses across the South who generously assisted the Project Director in locating, photocopying, and microfilming relevant documents. Also helpful were several directors and numerous staff members of fourteen southern state archives and the National Archives. A number of graduate research assistants and Project employees checked and rechecked names and dates and other information, entering the information into the Project's database. They included Tonya Blair; Chad Bowser (assistant editor); James Broomall; Jennifer Burns; Brian Candler; Sallie Clotfelter; Janie Copple; Nicole Corlew; Jennifer Dorsey (postdoctoral fellow); Denise Ettenger; Brad Foley; Melissa Garrison; Jim Giesen; Kori Graves; David Herr; Chuck Holden; Greg Houle; Mike Huber; Kate Knight; Denise Kohn; Dave MacWilliams; Ka'Mal McClarin; Lisa Marshall; Lisa Maxwell (assistant editor); Diane Mead; Adrienne Middlebrooks; Courtney Moore; David Norton; Rebecca Parker; Fate Passmore; Brenda Rice; Patrick Richard; James, John, and, Michael Schweninger; Michiko Savert; Julia Skaggs; Robert Shelton (assistant editor); Janice Sniker; Diana Sweatt; Jon Walker; Carlos Watson; Joy Watson; Laurette Wharton; Matisha Wiggs; Kellie Wilson-Buford; Jeff Winstead; and Catherine Wright. Associate editor Marguerite Ross Howell and assistant editor Nicole Mazgaj deserve special recognition for their loyalty and expertise over many years. The University's Chancellor Emeritus William E. Moran supported our work from its inception, and the work could not have been completed without the foresight and generosity of Mott Foundation president Bill White. The analysis of slaveholding among lawyers and the chapter on legal counsel were greatly enhanced by the Excel file created by Denise Johnson. I owe her a special debt of gratitude. The author thanks Allison Seyler of the Maryland State Archives for providing pertinent information on the Ogleton family. Peter Skutchens brought his remarkable editorial talents to the final draft of the manuscript and deserves very special thanks. Historians Kelly Kennington, who kindly shared with me her results of Missouri freedom suits, and Richard Paul Fuke, who critiqued an early version of chapter 1, have my gratitude. Also reading and critiquing a draft of chapter 1 were my wife, Patricia, and daughter, Emily Schweninger, who provided a good perspective and useful comments. I am especially grateful to the two anonymous reviewers chosen by Oxford University Press for their detailed, critical, yet constructive reports. The manuscript was substantially revised and greatly improved as a result. The memory of the late John Hope Franklin remains a source of strength and inspiration. Any errors or mistakes in this study, however, are the author's alone.

Introduction

Shortly before daylight on an icy cold morning of sleet, rain, and snow in February 1837, a constable in York County, Pennsylvania, and several men from Harford County, Maryland, entered the home of free blacks Jerry and Margaret Morgan and their children. The constable arrested them under a warrant issued by a justice of the peace and procured by Harford County slave-catcher Edward Prigg, who claimed that the family members were fugitive slaves who had fled to the North. Allowing the family to take only the clothes they wore, the men transported the Morgans in an open wagon about ten miles to the home of Thomas Henderson, the justice of the peace. Jerry Morgan immediately explained that he could prove his free status: one of the children had been born free in Pennsylvania, and Margaret had acted as a free black for many years. She was born about 1800 in Harford, Maryland, on the farm of John Ashmore, who had freed her parents but had failed to formalize the manumissions with an appropriate deed. In 1832, in the wake of new restrictive laws against free blacks in Maryland, including one that required free black families to register with the orphans' court or leave the state, the family decided to cross the state line into York County, Pennsylvania.

Even though Henderson issued the warrant, he now had qualms about the arrest, capture, and transportation of the Morgan family. He decided to release the husband, as the evidence showed he was in fact free. But he was concerned about Priggs's insistence that he was acting on behalf of the Maryland slave owner Margaret Ashmore for a return of her fugitives, so he waited to make a decision about Margaret and their children. As night fell, the Maryland men decided to take matters into their own hands and took the mother and children back into their state without legal authorization. It was still bitterly cold and sleeting when the men crossed the border with their captives, and at morning light Prigg and the others sold the mother and her children to a slave trader, who, in turn, put them in jail and readied them for shipment out of the state.

The family tragedy was compounded when Jerry Morgan, on a return boat trip from Harrisburg, where he had sought help from the governor of Pennsylvania, was accused of stealing a jacket and threatened by the crew and passengers. The lone black person on the boat, fearing for his life, he jumped overboard and disappeared in the fast-moving water. Meanwhile, as news of the events became public in Maryland, Margaret and her children were saved from their misfortune. Residents of York County, outraged by the kidnapping, complained to the governor of Pennsylvania, who contacted the governor of Maryland concerning a violation of Pennsylvania law. Eventually, Prigg was indicted for kidnapping and for violating Pennsylvania's personal liberty law of 1826, which had been enacted to protect people like the Morgans. Margaret, however, remained in jail, although she was allowed to see her children. Eventually, she filed a freedom suit in the Harford County Court on the grounds that she and her parents had always acted as free persons, even while living on the property of John Ashmore. In the spring of 1839, responding to a freedom suit, Judge Stevenson Archer of the Harford County Court ruled that Margaret and her children were fugitive slaves. As such, since their former owner did not wish to claim them, they were sold into slavery.

The tragedies that befell the Morgan family are well known to historians. Five years after the abduction, in one of the most significant Supreme Court cases during the pre–Civil War period, *Prigg v. the Commonwealth of Pennsylvania* (1842), the court declared that the personal liberty laws of Pennsylvania were unconstitutional. The crossing of a state line to capture fugitive slaves, the court ruled, was the federal government's responsibility, as determined by the US Constitution and the Fugitive Slave Law of 1793, which permitted slaveholders or their agents to retrieve their human property in the North if they could show that the black people were fugitives. Not only did the actors in the drama, except for Margaret Morgan and her husband, argue their case before the highest court, but the lawyer who prosecuted the Pennsylvania kidnapping wrote a detailed tract about the events leading up to the decision.[1]

Most often the stories of slaves who brought their freedom suits before the courts in the southern states remain untold, while the important legal decisions following such suits, including the most famous case of *Dred Scott v. Sandford*, have spawned numerous books and articles. This book includes discussions of the laws and court decisions regarding freedom suits as well as consideration of the changing attitudes of white Americans toward freedom and free blacks; equally importantly, it seeks to illuminate the lives of unknown slaves and free persons of color (a total of 4,601 plaintiffs) who filed freedom suits, to trace how they fared in the course of their pursuit of justice, and to explore the significance of their suits to our understanding of the period between the American Revolution and the Civil War. A majority of the cases examined here were not appealed, nor did they create important judicial precedent, as the case of *Prigg v. Pennsylvania* did. Indeed, most of the cases ended at the county, circuit, or district court level of various southern states. Yet the narratives of both those who gained their freedom and those who failed to do so, and the issues their suits raised, shed new, bold, and timely light on race relations in America and on African American culture, on liberty and law, on the courts and their representatives, and on sectionalism and the coming of the Civil War.

Compared with the increasingly large number of slaves who remained in bondage throughout their lives, those who filed freedom suits represented only a tiny fraction of the whole. Still, the actions of this unique group reveal the hopes and dreams of the manifold others who likewise yearned to be free. Many whites recognized these desires on the part of their black charges. A pamphlet written anonymously in 1801 by Virginia's George Tucker, the young cousin of St. George Tucker, the author of *A Dissertation on Slavery*, articulated what many others believed and would believe in future years. "The love of freedom, sir, is an inborn sentiment, which the God of nature has planted deep in the heart: long may it be kept under by the arbitrary institutions of society; but, at the first favourable moment, it springs forth, and flourishes with a vigour that defies all check. This celestial spark, which fires in the breast of the savage, which glows in that of the philosopher, is not extinguished in the bosom of the slave." On his conviction that the fire of freedom borne in the breast of slaves could never be quelled by laws in the United States, Tucker recommended that Virginia transport its black population to unsettled "western lands" and there put them under the authority and control of the federal government. Tucker's pamphlet was published a few months after the conspiracy of the slave Gabriel was uncovered in Richmond, a plot that sent shockwaves through the southern states, but it nonetheless represented a truism even if his solution was neither practical nor feasible.[2]

During the decades following the American Revolution, state legislatures in the southern states passed numerous laws concerning race and slavery. Among them were statutes in many states that permitted slaves illegally held in bondage to file freedom suits in local courts. How, when, and why did black men, women, and children unjustly enslaved file petitions for their freedom? What were the backgrounds of the lawyers who assisted them in their pleas? How did judges and juries respond to their petitions? This book analyzes these questions. The fact that slaves and free blacks who believed they were illegally held in bondage could and did sue for their freedom in itself manifests the importance white southerners attached to the rule of law.

Of course, the vast majority of black people never had the opportunity to bring their cases to court, but the story of those who did charts the lives of pre–Civil War African Americans—their struggles, anxieties, frustrations, and desire for freedom. This study is informed by an analysis of 2,023 freedom suits brought by more than four thousand black people primarily in the Upper South

(Delaware, the District of Columbia, Maryland, Virginia, Kentucky, Tennessee, and Missouri) and Louisiana, as well as some cases in the Lower South (North Carolina, South Carolina, Georgia, Florida, Alabama, Mississippi, Arkansas, and Texas). In some measure, the "time and space" questions reveal how important and different state laws became reflections themselves of the differences in the economy and politics in the Upper and Lower South. Statutes in some states provided avenues toward freedom through the courts while in others such paths were virtually closed. This resulted in only a few cases over time in the Lower South. Yet decade by decade, the number of freedom suits in the South as a whole remained relatively constant.[3] (See tables 1 and 2.)

The suits cast new light on the laws and court systems, the legal process, and race relations in the decades between the Revolution and the Civil War. What emerges in the court proceedings, especially in the narratives and arguments presented by lawyers on behalf of their slave clients, is a stirring human drama of principle and perseverance in the face of adversity. Court records afford insight into how these suitors for freedom kept body and soul together; how they maintained histories of their families, friends, and loved ones; and how they found a way to gain entrance into courtrooms across the South. In fact, despite the legal framework of the suits, the disclosures of illegally held slaves and free persons of color provide the largest single collection of contemporary and real-time testimony of enslaved African Americans in the South. True, the narratives are fused with legalisms, and in most states, black people were barred from testifying against whites; still, at various times in a number of states, a few slaves and free blacks did testify in such a manner. Despite the limitations of the record, in the body of the petitions as well as in the evidence and testimony introduced in the court proceedings, the lives of these African Americans come sharply and poignantly into focus, as do many other aspects of southern society.

Freedom suits unveil a great deal about state laws, the workings of common law and chancery (or equity) courts, slaveholders' wills and deeds, term slavery, descendants of white and Indian women as well as free women of color, the question of residency, the journey toward freedom through self-hire and self-purchase, runaways, African American families, and lawyers and their slave clients.

This book brings to the fore a new, enlightening narrative about slavery and freedom in America. The history of freedom suits in the southern states from the founding of the nation to the clash between the North and South during the Civil War offers an unusual and perhaps unexpected view of interracial cooperation among blacks in bondage and their white legal representatives as well as the white members of their communities. Study of the freedom suits shows how the law worked in practice within both the local and appellate court systems. At the same time, it sheds light on other aspects of America's history between the

Revolution and Civil War: how the Mason-Dixon Line became a stark sectional divide, how southern society responded to slaves in its midst, how slavery expanded in the South even after the outlawing of the African slave trade, how the domestic slave trade grew and spurred the national political debates from the Missouri Compromise to the Dred Scott decision.

Frequently, freedom suits also evince the admirable character of those who presented their complaints to the courts: the gravity they attached to their families, their social and cultural values, their constructive relationships with certain whites, and, even when they were not conversant with the laws of the state, their understanding of justice and fairness and their determination to achieve free status. To be sure, only under special circumstances could such suits be filed, and in the Lower South except Louisiana various laws severely restricted such challenges, but the process and outcome of those cases disclose both the attitudes of whites and the values of African Americans.

It is very difficult to divorce an examination of freedom suits from the emotionally charged human drama that accompanied them. Families struggled heartrendingly to remain together; they braved the fear and anxiety of being sold and resold, often separately. Assiduously they recounted their life histories in the hope and prayer that they might succeed in acquiring their freedom. In fact, to disregard the potent emotions of the participants in these suits is to discount the enormity of the African American struggle for freedom as it was borne by the many thousands of others who did not file suits or by those who did but whose records have been destroyed or lost. In their suits, African Americans related to their lawyers and to the courts stories detailing their lives in bondage and presented their reasons for seeking free status. As to the authenticity of the stories, there are numerous ways to measure countervailing arguments, including testimony of witnesses, oaths signed by counsel, and especially the decisions of judges and juries. Even with these safeguards, however, it is apparent—but only extremely rarely—that occasionally plaintiffs fabricated some aspects of their lives to gain their freedom.[4] For the most part, the plaintiffs told their life histories as accurately as their memories allowed, duly recounting details about their owners, sales, trades, children, family members, and illegal enslavement.

The brief narratives presented in freedom suits were in some ways similar to fugitive slave accounts published in the North as part of the antislavery crusade. Both were presented by third parties—lawyers for illegally held slaves and ghostwriters for many fugitives—and both emphasized the evils of human bondage. But there were also marked differences. The fugitive slave narratives were unhindered by the rigors of a judicial proceeding. Indeed, many of the runaway slaves' stories could not be verified, and they could, at least in part, have been fabricated to gain a particularly dramatic desired effect. In contrast, it behooved slaves seeking their freedom in southern courts to be as forthright and accurate as possible. Most of the participants at trials were well acquainted with the owners as well as the slaves. Those judging the guilt or innocence of either party often knew the plaintiffs and defendants, and if they did not know them personally, they could rely on evidence about them from a broad spectrum of documents and corroborating testimony. Most plaintiffs in freedom suits spoke about their lives and their heritage. Their histories comprised events that had occurred years or even decades earlier, when they had been sold, and then perhaps resold or transferred; events that had taken them to neighboring counties or maybe different states, and had separated them from other members of their families. Their voices by necessity were recorded through the legal system by their lawyers and by court reporters, but nonetheless their thoughts and histories, their grit and determination to acquire freedom for themselves and their loved ones, ring strong and true.

Perhaps even more exceptional than the legal significance of these cases in the struggle of African Americans for freedom is the rendering they afford of voices rarely heard in historical documents. In these voices, in their sentiments and convictions, are social and legal history fused. They tell us how over several generations African American communities established themselves; they show us how hearsay and gossip among both whites and blacks contrived to create and recreate, to define and redefine, social roles. Their centuries-old voices expand our understanding of the cultural, social, genealogical, and economic relationships that shaped innumerable southern communities. These ties no less than the divide between diverse social groups point up the complexities of interracial relationships.

Despite the legal phraseology in the court records and, sometimes, the lawyers' arguments, the petitions and declarations made by the slave plaintiffs themselves speak plainly and with immediacy to their predicament. At times they could be eloquent. Amelia Green, a self-purchased North Carolina free woman of color who worked as a weaver, purchased her daughters out of bondage and then petitioned the Craven County Court for what were called licenses of emancipation. In 1796, writing on behalf of her daughter Princess, Green informed the court that she herself was "now far advanced in life" and felt "the infirmities of age growing upon her." So it was she feared that in "the awfull event of her Death," her "pious intentions" to free her daughter might be frustrated. She praised her daughter as "a good Girl, a Good daughter" who possessed a "mild and peacefull disposition and industrious habits."

Five years later, Green again stood before the court, this time petitioning for the freedom of another daughter, Nancy Handy: "Your Petitioner states that being aged & not long expecting to enjoy the pleasures of this world & to whom the womb of time is not open to inspect what may hereafter be brought forth or in what manner it may affect her daughter." She thus asked for a license to liberate her daughter Nancy, who had always conducted herself in a loving and faithful manner.[5] The abundance of personal history so immediately expressed by slaves and former slaves in their freedom pleas, coupled with other court documents and, on rare occasions, the testimony of black people themselves, presents us with perhaps the best source of real-time, firsthand information available to historians from the southern slaves' perspective. Freedom suits drew on legal precedent and colonial statutes stretching back to the seventeenth and eighteenth centuries, when a few African Americans, for a variety of reasons, presented petitions to local courts seeking their freedom. As early as 1667 an enslaved black man in Virginia named Fernando claimed in court that he should be freed because he was a Christian and had lived in England. Fernando's case was followed in 1691 by that of another Spanish-named slave, Don Francisco Condelarium, who complained that he was being unjustly held in bondage. The court ordered that he reappear at the next session and present evidence of this fact; returned to his owner during the interim, he failed to appear in court at the designated time. A Massachusetts slave named Adam was more successful in his bid for freedom. In 1694, his master, Boston merchant and jurist John Saffin, promised him his freedom once Adam had served him faithfully for seven years. When Saffin reneged on his promise, Adam sued. The case went before two sessions of the inferior court and four sessions of the superior court over a period of several years. In 1703, Adam secured his liberty. Such was not the case for a New York slave, Spanish-speaking Juan Miranda, who claimed his owner allowed him to purchase his freedom. During the 1750s, Miranda sought redress in the court on a number of occasions over nearly a decade, but his cases remained unresolved.[6]

Filing freedom suits during the colonial period was a difficult undertaking. Seeking out lawyers and convincing them to take the case was one problem; surviving the litigation was another. Litigation commonly proved to be an embarrassment for the families of slave owners, who often stood among the most well-established and prosperous members in their communities. In essence, slaves were accusing their masters, or their masters' kin and heirs, or the executors of their estates, of deceit, avarice, and duplicity. Such was the case in 1735 when James, the former slave of Samuel Burnell of Boston, accused Burnell's son of hiding or destroying four different wills that provided for his emancipation. During a trial, Burnell's son threatened to kill James for bringing suit. After two years of litigation, punctuated by hostility and threats, the legislature stepped in and passed a bill providing for James's freedom if he could post bond and not become a public charge. Problematic, too, was cost. Suits were expensive, and often protracted. Once an individual met all the legal burdens as a plaintiff and filed a suit, he or she could not count on the inclusion of his or her spouse and children in the suit. Some successful petitioners subsequently spent years in the courts in their attempt to extricate family members from bondage. Despite the problems and pitfalls, freedom suits kept the issue of slavery and freedom in the public eye and emboldened others to test the possibility of liberty. One black man ran a notice in the *New Jersey Gazette* warning prospective buyers that he expected "freedom, justice and protection" in the future through the laws of the state.[7]

During the era of the American Revolution, a number of slaves filed freedom suits in Virginia, Maryland, Delaware, Massachusetts, Rhode Island, and other New England colonies or states. Blacks asserted that they had been promised their freedom at the end of a specified term, or that they had been freed in a will or deed, or that they were children or grandchildren or kin of free female ancestors. In 1772, a jury in the Virginia General Court of Common Law ruled that Robin and ten other slaves were "free and not Slaves." The court offered no reason for its decision.[8] "Whole families," an opponent of slavery in the Chesapeake recalled, "were often liberated by a single verdict, the fate of one relative deciding the fate of many." In Massachusetts, juries became notorious for voting in favor of liberty. Elizabeth Freeman, a well-known black patriot of the revolutionary era, filed, and won, a freedom suit in 1781, a year after the new Massachusetts Constitution and its Bill of Rights proclaimed "all men free and equal." It took Massachusetts slave Quock Walker twelve years and three trials to achieve the same goal. The cases of Freeman and Walker resulted in a sweeping declaration in 1783 by the chief judge of the state's Supreme Judicial Court that the state's new constitution "effectively abolished" slavery within the commonwealth. Freedom suits in Pennsylvania and New York aided in advancing the abolition of the institution in those two states.[9]

By the time the Constitutional Convention met in Philadelphia in 1787 it was clear that the pronouncements regarding human liberty and equality as well as court decisions granting black plaintiffs their freedom prior to and during the Revolutionary War would not be codified in the US Constitution. Although the framers of the Constitution never used the words "slave," "Negro," or "slavery," they designated that the apportionment of members for the House of Representatives would be determined by counting the number of free persons in each state plus "three fifths of all other Persons" (meaning enslaved blacks). Further, the Founding Fathers specified that the importation of persons into the United States would not be prohibited for twenty years and that "No Person held to Service or Labour in one State, under the Laws thereof, escaping into another, shall, in Consequence of any Law or Regulation therein, be discharged from such Service or Labour, but shall be delivered up on Claim of the Party to whom such Service or labor may be due." In short, the African slave trade would be allowed to continue for at least two decades, and slave owners could retrieve their runaway slaves anywhere in the new union, including states where slavery was gradually coming to an end.[10]

Freedom suits persisted, however. In the southern states during the late eighteenth and the nineteenth centuries, thousands of slaves and their lawyers continued to file legal complaints, as they were called. Some observers and defendants believed that the suits posed a potential threat to the institution of slavery itself. As time passed, the laws regarding these suits became more restrictive, especially in the Lower South, and hearsay testimony was outlawed. Even so, a steady stream of African Americans appealing for liberty appeared in court, mostly in the Upper South and Louisiana but also in the Lower South. Indeed, despite the new legal codes and the changing nature of primary complaints, almost exactly the same number of cases, 646, occurred during the period 1779–1819 as during the 1840s and 1850s, 651, with a modestly higher number, 726, from 1820 to 1839. Throughout the period from the American Revolution to the Civil War, the suits demonstrated the power of local courts to free men, women, and children unjustly held in bondage.

Perhaps equally important to the evolving laws and the relatively constant number of suits over time are the unexpected insights freedom suits offer into the social, cultural, familial, racial, legal, and even political history of the period. They limn cultural interactions among slaves, free blacks, and whites; they define the role of African American women in maintaining family histories and sustaining oral traditions from generation to generation, traditions that, for a period at least, supported suits of the enslaved and won them freedom. The suits are revelatory as to the history of black families, the interaction of African Americans with whites, and the determination of free blacks in their attempts to free members of their families and fellow sufferers by seeking redress in local courts. The testimony in these cases adds invaluable detail and lends emotional resonance to the turbulent history of race relations in America.[11]

1

African American Women and the Genealogy of Slavery

At various times during 1792 and 1793, Anne Brown, a free person of color, gave four sworn depositions before the Annapolis alderman and mayor John Bellum concerning a large group of slaves who had filed freedom suits in the Maryland General Court of the Western Shore. The daughter of Mary Brown, commonly known as Mulatto Moll, Anne had grown up in the Swamp, an area located about twenty miles south of the city in Anne Arundel County. Her mother had been an indentured servant to Robert Lockwood, who owned four slaves and a small farm. As a child, Anne had lived on the Lockwood farm with her mother, her sister Mary Batson, and a young slave named Lenah. Lenah had arrived with her own mother, Maria, in Maryland about 1686 on a Guinea ship from the coast of West Africa. Anne's mother had declared many times that Maria "was to be free and was a Spanish woman." Anne had never heard any old person in the Swamp say that Lenah's mother was a slave.

Anne Brown's depositions served as evidence in sixteen freedom suits filed by members of the Boston family who traced their roots back to Maria. How and why the slaves took the surname Boston is not clear, but it was almost certainly used by Lenah and her ten children early in the eighteenth century. As the suits progressed, twenty-four other witnesses provided testimony, many of them on behalf of the slaveowning defendants, but none of them were deposed more than twice except for Anne Brown, who was called on to give testimony a total of six times, four in 1792–1793 and twice more in 1795 and 1797, the last when she was sixty-six. By then the suits had reached the Maryland High Court of Appeals.[1]

In these suits, black women played a significant role in the protection of family heritage. Unlike rulings in English common law, in which the condition of the child "dooth follow the state & condition of the father," state statutes and legal traditions in the United States mirrored Roman civil law: *partus sequitur ventrem* ("that which is brought forth follows the womb"). Thus, free women gave birth to free children, and consequently it was through female ancestry that slaves could test their freedom in the courts. In addition, while most slaveowners, including those of the Boston slaves, might be familiar with the work habits of their black charges, they took only a passing interest in their genealogies—and then usually only to locate an absentee slave who might be visiting a loved one. The suits of the Boston slaves show that most owners and members of white families had only vague notions, if any, as to how slaves were related to one another, and less sense of their ancestry in past generations.[2]

The American Revolution and its aftermath produced momentous changes in the United States—economic, political, social, cultural, intellectual, and legal—as the country struggled to come to grips with its status as a new nation. Perhaps no institution changed more distinctly than that of slavery, which came gradually to an end in New England and some mid-Atlantic states, while at the same time it became more firmly entrenched in the lower states of the South. Maryland stood at the crossroads between slavery and freedom, and for a brief period during the 1780s and 1790s, when the ideals of freedom were in the ascendancy, slaveowners manumitted thousands of blacks. The state's economy accounted in part for the manumissions: wheat and grain farmers in a northern tier of counties did not rely heavily on slave labor, and in urban centers such as Baltimore slaves could readily bargain for their freedom. In addition to the manumissions, slave families initiated large numbers of freedom suits, and beginning in the mid-1780s Maryland courts not only allowed hearsay evidence but also permitted free blacks and former slaves to testify.[3]

With a few exceptions, historians have failed to delve deeply into these suits or to focus on the families that filed them and the common law or chancery courts that processed them, or to uncover the full import of family histories among those held in bondage. They have for the most part ignored trial testimony, the backgrounds of lawyers and witnesses, as well as of plaintiffs and defendants, and the critical role played by African American women in presenting detailed genealogies of slave families.[4] Yet the struggle of the Boston slaves to obtain free status during this period of transformation indeed marked a high point in realizing the ideals espoused by an emergent nation. The legal system in that brief era of transformation was more egalitarian than it would be for generations to come.[5]

During the late eighteenth and early nineteenth centuries, a number of African Americans in Maryland filed suits similar to those brought by the Boston slaves; among them were the descendants of Eleanor Butler, or "Irish Nell," and they claimed their freedom on the grounds that their progenitor was a white woman. In 1681, Eleanor had married a slave, and at the time of the marriage a 1664 law that remanded the wife of such a union to perpetual slavery was still in effect (though it was soon to be repealed). One of her descendants' cases, in 1770, proved unsuccessful—the appeals court cited the 1664 law—but in 1783 a great-granddaughter of Irish Nell, Mary Butler, filed suit on the same grounds and eventually won her freedom as the descendent of a white woman.[6] Other plaintiffs—notably, members of the Shorter, Thomas, Queen, and Toogood families—similarly won suits based on complicated genealogical information about their ancestors stretching back many generations into the seventeenth century. In 1794, Basil Shorter was adjudged free because he was the great-grandson of Elizabeth Shorter, a white woman who had married a black man named Little Robin in 1681 "according to the then law." Once the details of her marriage had been established in the court records with the testimony of witnesses recalling what they had heard or been told or learned as common knowledge about the Shorters' ancestry, other members of the family were able to recover their freedom on the same grounds. In 1808, the great-great-granddaughter of Elizabeth Shorter was set free even after the Charles County Court ruled against her: the testimony of one white woman included such phrases as she "did not know of it of her own knowledge" but she "always understood" and heard it said. The appeals court, however, reversed the lower court's verdict, ruling that hearsay evidence was admissible.[7]

Not every plaintiff who called on kin and other African Americans to offer family history testimony on his or her behalf succeeded in the courts. Nathaniel Allen, aged about twenty-two, claimed he was "descended from a free Woman." The petitioner's mother, aged forty, testified in a deposition that she had had Nathaniel by a "Negro Man" and that, further, she was the daughter of Hannah Allen, a mulatto, who was generally considered in the community to be the daughter of a "White Scotch Woman" and a black slave. Also deposed was the petitioner's grandmother; she asserted that she always understood "from general Report and Believes a White Woman born in Scotland" was her mother, who died before she could remember. In this case the defendant produced laws passed in 1715 and 1728 that stated that mixed-race descendants of white women who had children by slaves were subject to the same punishments as white women who gave birth to "mulatto bastards." Women in these circumstances were to be sold as servants for seven years, and their children were to be bound in servitude until they reached the age of thirty-one. Nathaniel's case fell under these colonial laws; he would have to wait another nine years before he could be declared free. The evidence in this case, as in many others, derived from witnesses who were relating the rumors and tales and gossip and speculations their communities shared: evidence dependent on the credibility of persons other than, and as well as, the one who was testifying. On occasion witnesses were presenting double hearsay testimony, that is, a hearsay statement within a hearsay statement. Nonetheless, during this period in Maryland, such testimony was often accepted to be the only means to sort out the complex genealogies that determined a plaintiff's slavery or freedom.[8]

By 1792, the history of the Boston family of slaves already stretched back more than a century, to about 1686, when Maria and her young daughter, Lenah, arrived in Maryland on a slave ship. Although they were either of Spanish or Portuguese descent and free-born, they were sold as slaves to Robert Lockwood, a farmer in the area known as the Swamp. There is no extant description of Maria, but her daughter, as a young woman, was described variously as "yellow," "bright yellow," and "brown" of complexion, with long, straight black hair. It is likely that Maria, too, was a person of color, especially since she was sold as a slave.

The Swamp in Anne Arundel County was defined in an original patent from Lord Baltimore as six hundred acres of land located on the west side of Chesapeake Bay, about twenty miles south of Anne Arundel Town (later named Annapolis), and beyond the South River. It began "at a marked oak by a Cedar point near the mouth of a Creek running North East and by East by the Herry Creek bay... through the swamp." In the following years, the land defined by the grant and its surrounding area, with its brackish waters, cedar and cypress trees, and intermittent salt- and freshwater marshes and bogs, became known simply as the Swamp. Isolated and remote, it did not immediately attract settlers, but in time farmers and stock tenders began to move into the more habitable and elevated sections.[9]

A few among them also brought or acquired slaves, some imported from Africa or the West Indies, others purchased from neighbors in Virginia. The slaves who worked in the Swamp during its early settlement labored mostly on small farms. They cleared the land in marsh-free areas, they planted corn and vegetables, they raised cattle and swine, they cut cedar and cypress trees. With their owners they sometimes boated to nearby islands to cut oak and pine for lumber. Among the early slave arrivals were Maria and her daughter Lenah, as the property of Robert Lockwood. Ironically, much less is known about Lockwood than about his slaves and his one white indentured servant. In 1683, Lockwood served as a witness to a will probated in Anne Arundel County, and in 1709 his estate was inventoried following his death. At that time he possessed "1 Mallatto w^o that has 15 yrs. to serve - 15 pounds" and "2 Negroe women wth Children at their breasts - 60 pounds." By then, Maria had died and been buried on Lockwood's farm. The mulatto woman was Mulatto Moll, mother of Anne Brown and Mary Batson. One of the "2 Negroe women" was almost certainly Lenah, who, despite her straight hair and yellow complexion, subsisted as Lockwood's slave and was thus designated in the inventory as "Negroe."[10]

Following Lockwood's death, Lenah became the property first of Lockwood's widow, then of another family member, upon whose death she passed to a widow named Ann Jones and, on her demise, to the widow's son, Gassaway

Watkins. The circumstances of Lenah's bondage—the fact that she and her children and other kin lived in an isolated part of state during a period when most of the sales and transfers of slaves occurred among slaveholders within Anne Arundel County—created a relatively stable environment. Usually, when the Boston slaves changed hands, they became the property of their owners' family members or other residents of the Swamp. Despite the in-many-ways unhealthy climate and natural environs of the Swamp, that stability afforded the native-born populations in the area—both slave and free—longer, healthier lives, and they gave birth to a statistically impressive number of offspring who survived. The thirteen children of Mulatto Moll and the ten children of Lenah certainly exceeded the norm but all the more reflected the positive effects of their situation in this area of the state.[11]

Of course, no one who testified in court during the 1790s had ever seen or met Maria, and only a few among them could testify firsthand about her daughter Lenah. What witnesses could offer was information they had learned from their parents or other family members. By all accounts, the Spanish- or Portuguese-born Maria made an attractive, dignified impression. She wore good clothing and gold jewelry: a gold cross on a necklace, gold "bobs" on her ears, and gold rings on her fingers. The gold cross suggested that she may have been Catholic. Mary Batson, herself a free person of color, whose mother, Mulatto Moll, had been born on the eastern shore and brought to the Swamp in Anne Arundel County as a young girl by Robert Lockwood, recalled often hearing her mother tell how Maria had cared for her as a child. Moll believed that Maria should be free, Mary attested. The African American women who lived on the Lockwood farm and a few slaveholders who lived in the Swamp agreed: Maria should not have been held in captivity. Maria died at almost the same time as her owner; she was buried on the Lockwood farm with her gold cross on her chest.[12]

Maria's daughter Lenah likewise lived out her life in bondage. She had hair like that of an Indian, one witness said, and did not have "the looks of a negro or mulatto." Clearly, she, like her mother, was of Iberian descent (whether Portuguese or Spanish was a matter of disagreement); according to one deponent—the son of one of Lenah's owners—as well as the 1747 "certificate" of slaveowner William Foard, Lena and Maria arrived from Madagascar.[13] A few slaveholding farmers in the Swamp testified that the mother and daughter were likely free at the time of their arrival and were only later enslaved. Unfortunately, in all of the sworn testimony there is no reference to the work or duties Lenah performed on the farms of her several owners. In fact, the only reference to an occupation in regard to any member of either the Boston or the Brown families is a description of Mulatto Moll as an excellent seamstress; she evidently made clothing for William Foard's numerous slaves.[14] Lenah did, however, give birth to ten children who survived; on that point there was general consensus.

Lenah in her later years figured prominently in the memories of such witnesses as Dinah Watkins, who remembered Lenah vividly in images defined by her unusual complexion, her small stature, and her awkward gait—as Lena aged she apparently had considerable difficulty walking. The white children, Watkins noted, made fun of Lena because of her infirmities.[15] Like her mother, Lenah asserted to the end of her days that she and her children by all rights ought to be free. On one occasion a young boy overheard the son of her final owner curse "old Lenah, and tell her that she wanted to be free but that she never would."[16]

Over the years, however their family members might be dispersed by the death of an owner or by a transfer of ownership, Lenah's ten children maintained close ties with Mulatto Moll's thirteen. They communicated with each other often, in part because they lived in relatively close proximity to one another. Nearly all the Boston and Brown family members knew the story of Lenah's son Ned, who attempted to gain his freedom by running away. In all likelihood, Ned's belief that he should be free because of his heritage came from his mother, even though the incident occurred seven or eight years after her death. A "yellow fellow a bright mulatto," as one observer said, with "long hair like a mulatto's Hair, and as long as he ever saw mulatto's hair," Ned was determined to claim his heritage. In the mid-1740s, he demanded that his owner, Thomas Ratcliff, release him, and when his demand was rejected he set out on his own for Annapolis. He was captured before he reached the city in London Town, however, and severely whipped. Moreover, Ned lost his indenture document, which would have freed him on a designated date; after the incident Ned's owner burned the indenture and subjected him repeatedly to harsh punishments.[17] The incident resulted in the issuance of a "certificate," which was signed in 1747 by William Foard, a long-time resident of the Swamp. Asked about Ned's background, Foard correctly named Ned's grandmother as Maria (Foard was the only white witness to do so) and his mother as "Lenna"; he also stated that both women had always been slaves.[18]

Bacon Boston, Lena's grandson (the son of her daughter Violet), shared his uncle Ned's determination. He fled the slave labor on a farm owned by Gassaway Rawlings. Like the other owners of slaves from the Boston family, Rawlings would become a large land- and slaveholder in the latter years of the eighteenth century, with a 450-acre plantation called Larkin Hills that was worked by twenty-seven blacks. But in 1766, the year Bacon Boston ran away, Rawlings was just beginning his economic ascent.[19] In May of that year Rawlings advertised in the *Maryland Gazette,*

RAN away from the Subscriber, living near Mr. Jonathan Rawling's, about the Middle of last Month, a Negro Man named Bacon, he is about 6 Feet high; had on and carried away with him, a Fearnought [a heavy wool coat] and two Cotton Jackets, several Shirts, and other Cloaths; and is a bold impertinent Fellow.

Whoever will bring the said Negro to the Subscriber, or secure him in any Jail so as he may be had again, shall receive a Reward of Twenty Shillings Current Money. [20]

Like many other runaways, Bacon was young, still in his teens, and considered troublesome. He was quickly caught and returned. At the time, Rawlings also owned Bacon's brother, Anthony, who likely spread the word of Bacon's bold attempt at freedom among family members. There is little doubt that tales of such incidents and information about lineage and kinship were passed down by word of mouth from one generation to the next; they became the substance of the oral testimony by which the Boston slaves sought and fought for their liberty as a birthright.

The trial began on November 1, 1791, when eight slave plaintiffs and their lawyer filed suit in the General Court of the Western Shore in Annapolis. The general court served primarily as an appeals court; thus, there was no jury. Nevertheless, prior to 1796, the general court also accepted individual freedom cases. As the trial proceeded, another eight suits were added so that a total of sixteen slaves from the Boston family used legal means to seek their freedom. At the outset the plaintiffs were represented by George Jenings; the defendants' lawyer was William Cooke. The complaint was simple, only a few lines indicating that the Boston slaves were descendants of Lenah, a free "yellow" woman of Portuguese descent. As would be the case in future freedom suits across the Upper South and in Louisiana, the court then ordered the defendants not to punish the slaves for bringing their suits but, rather, to feed and clothe them well, keep them within the state, allow them to consult with their lawyer, and permit them to appear in court as necessary. Chief Judge Samuel Chase, who had signed the Declaration of Independence and would later become an associate justice of the US Supreme Court, ordered the defendants and their lawyer to appear at the next session. If they failed to do so, he said, it would be "at their own peril." A short time later, two other lawyers joined Jenings in representing the plaintiffs: Gabriel Duval, who later also became an associate justice of the US Supreme Court, and William Pinkney, who would soon be appointed by President George Washington as a commissioner to London under the Jay Treaty.[21]

Among the most telling aspects of the trial, at least with regard to the interconnections among Boston and Brown family members, was the fact that one to two years before the trial began five members of the owners' families— Anne Harwood, Elizabeth Rawlings, Richard Watkins, Richard Richardson, and Plummer Iiams—gave depositions in which they declared as one, in virtually the same phraseology, that they had never heard any member in their families aver that Lenah deserved to be free. On the contrary, she had always been considered to be a slave for life. Echoing these sentiments, Harwood, the daughter of Lenah's last owner, noted that Lenah had died as part of the estate of her father, Gassaway Watkins, and prior to that Lenah had been owned by Harwood's grandmother; never had Harwood heard her father, grandmother, or anyone else remark that Lenah, who had been brought to this country "in a Guinea Ship amongst other Slaves and sold as such," had any right to be free. Several of the witnesses added that, to their knowledge, none of Lenah's children or descendants had claim to free status.[22]

To counter these testimonies, the future plaintiffs called five witnesses of their own. Ann Watkins, who married into a family that owned several Boston slaves, offered testimony that confirmed the complainants' version of events. In one instance, when Thomas Sprigg came to her mother-in-law Margaret Watkins's home, Ann recalled, he asked her if she had heard anything about members of the Boston family seeking their freedom. Margaret Watkins told him she had and that "they ought to be free, and that it was their right." Thomas told her to remain silent, as he was among the owners named in the suits. Ann added that her mother-in-law had always maintained Lenah should never have been enslaved.[23]

The most important of the early witnesses who testified on behalf of the plaintiffs, however, was Mary Batson, Mulatto Moll's daughter and Anne Brown's older sister, who gave her age as between sixty and seventy. Having grown up in the Swamp on the same farm as Lenah, Mary knew both Lenah and her ten children well; Mary named each of them in her deposition (see Genealogy of the Boston Slave Family, ca. 1686–1798). She was also familiar with many of Lena's grandchildren and great-grandchildren. Mary had often heard her mother say that Lenah was very young when she was brought to America and that Lenah and her mother, Maria, were entitled to their freedom. Maria died in bondage— she was buried on the Lockwood farm, Mary's mother told her—and so did Lenah, when Mary was about fourteen. Mary recounted, too, the struggles of various Boston family members for their freedom, including those of Daniel, who was eventually set free, and Ned, who attempted to escape but failed and was afterward "used very ill."[24]

These pretrial depositions point up the interconnectedness among the Boston slaves and the children of Mulatto Moll, as the restrictions of bondage failed to inhibit communications among them. From generation to generation, whether they served different owners in far-flung areas of the Swamp or beyond, they managed to stay in contact with one another and thus shared not only news of recent events but also, continuingly, tales from the distant past. It was as if, to some measure, in family remembrances they were living in the past—where freedom might converge with possibility. For the slaves who filed freedom suits near the end of the eighteenth century, the possibility had become real. Very likely, in the circulation of news, the Bostons had learned of other suits by African Americans in courts where people of color were being permitted to testify against whites. It was probably Mary Batson who initially contacted the first counsel, George Jenings, to prosecute the Boston slaves' cause. She had maintained a lifelong, intimate relationship with the Boston slaves, and as a free person of color, she could move about the county and enter Annapolis unhindered. The timing suggests that the first counsel then contacted the two additional lawyers, Duval and Pinkney, to take depositions and prepare arguments. The pretrial depositions show not only a long history of the grievances that underlay the Boston slaves' suits but also a renewed hope in the possibility for a better future. The history and the hope both lie in the shared knowledge of the slave family's genealogy as it was preserved and perpetuated orally, from generation to generation, by African American women.

The defendants in the suits brought by the Boston slaves included some of the wealthiest landowners and best-known political leaders in the state. Virginia-born John Francis Mercer, who in 1790 maintained his large plantation with eighty-three slaves, five of them from the Boston family, later served as Maryland's governor.[25] Even before the American Revolution, Richard Sprigg Sr., who owned three members of the family, was renowned as a gentleman planter. After the war, in addition to his two-thousand-acre estate in Anne Arundel County called West River Farm, he held land and farms in three nearby counties; he owned a total of eighty-two slaves.[26] The Mercer and Sprigg families maintained close family ties through marriage, business arrangements, and the ownership of Boston slaves.[27] Benjamin Ogle, the son of a colonial proprietary governor, inherited the Belair Estate in Prince George's County. In 1790, he owned thirty slaves—among them Tamar Boston and her son George Boston—who worked as house servants in Annapolis, where he lived, and as field hands in Prince George's County.[28] Ogle, too, eventually became governor of Maryland. Richard Richardson, the defendant in four cases, was born in Anne Arundel County and listed in the 1776 Maryland colonial census as head of a household in St. James Parish, where he lived with his wife and seven children; he then owned seventeen slaves. By 1790, as a plantation owner, he had increased his slaveholdings to forty-three. The other defendants, while neither as wealthy nor as well known, nonetheless fit the profile of prosperous white Marylanders whose slaveholdings and land acquisitions placed them in the upper economic sphere.[29]

Whatever their background and property holdings, most of the defendants had no inkling that they had purchased or acquired slaves who might have legitimate claims to their freedom. The depositions indicated that most of the defendants had purchased or acquired the slaves in good faith, with little or no knowledge of their bondservants' family histories. It was therefore a shock to these esteemed landowners that they should be called before the General Court of the Western Shore to respond to questions posed by lawyers representing their human chattel. It was also time-consuming and costly. Most of the defendants could more easily afford to lose a few slaves than to meet the expenses of hiring lawyers, deposing witnesses, copying court records, and traveling to Annapolis.[30] Fines and court costs could run to hundreds of dollars, and in some cases several thousands. In fact, some owners complained that slaves were instituting suits of dubious merit because they knew it was less costly for their owners to free them than to pay for mounting a defense.

Edward Dorsey, an ironmaster who owned the son of Tamar, a great-great-grandson of Maria, complained in his deposition about the cost of defending himself against two non-Boston slaves. Their suits, he asserted, were "unjust and oppressive"; further, he had thus far expended more than £250 sterling, or $600—an amount more than the value of the slaves on the open market. Despite the costs, Dorsey went forward with the defense because he believed the suits were frivolous. Besides being forced to appear in court for action on a plaintiff's case, defendants and their lawyers sometimes felt it necessary to attend witnesses' depositions.[31]

Several of the defendants' witnesses, elderly members of slaveholding families, offered confused and contradictory recollections. Richard Watkins, for example, recalled that some fifty years earlier a slave woman named Leaner had belonged to his grandmother, Ann Jones, until her death, after which she belonged to his father, Gassaway Watkins. She had a dark brown complexion, he said, and as far as he knew, she never claimed her freedom. She was about sixty years old back then, and very gray. He heard that she had originally arrived "from beyond Sea" on a slave ship, but he never heard that she wore a necklace with a gold cross. His father's heirs did not object to enslaving Leaner's children, he said, as they had no fear that her children might claim their freedom. So it was that Richard Watkins called Lenah by the name Leaner and in his reference to her necklace (which, for good reason, he never saw her wear) he conflated information about her mother Maria, who wore a gold cross.[32]

Another defense witness, Quaker Richard Richardson (not to be confused with the defendant Richard Richardson), in his seventies, provided similarly puzzling testimony. He said Leaner was "imported from beyond Sea on a Negro Ship and was Sold as a Slave and up to the time of her death the said Leaner was always held as a Slave." She was owned by Samuel (not Robert) Lockwood and Anne Jones, he said, and she never claimed her freedom. Richardson also attested to knowing five of Leaner's children, including three owned by his grandfather, William Richardson. In his account, Richardson thus also conflated details from Maria's life with Lenah's. In regard to Leaner's five children, though, he was speaking of a person whose life experiences more closely matched Lenah's, as

Maria birthed only one. When asked whether he ever knew Lenah's mother, Richardson responded that Lenah did not have a mother in this country. Like Watkins, he had known Lenah fifty years before, as a very old woman, when she lived with Ann Jones. With the exception of Lenah's son Ned, he said, none of these slaves ever claimed free status.[33]

Of course, it might be expected that witnesses deposed so many years after events might contradict one another, garble their facts, and be confused about names. The defendants' testimonies also contained a number of other inaccuracies, especially when they were trying to remember information about Boston slaves who were owned by friends, neighbors, or distant relatives. Often the deponents recalled conversations of their parents or other family members that they had heard as children. Frequently, what they remembered from a time when they were eight-, ten-, or twelve-year-olds had inevitably grown vague or had been distorted by the passage of time.[34] Even when members of slave-holding families provided information about their own kin who owned Boston slaves they were sometimes unsure about how the slaves might be related to one another.[35] Two defense witnesses, at ages seventy-seven and eighty-seven the oldest to testify, recalled many people—black and white—who had lived in the Swamp during the early years of the eighteenth century, including Mulatto Moll and her children, but neither had ever heard anyone speak of a woman named Lenah, much less of her descendants' right to freedom.[36]

After the trial began, the plaintiffs called ten more witnesses to rebut the arguments offered by the defendants' counsel. Several were called to provide character references in defense of the whites who had spoken on behalf of the plaintiffs. Joseph Cowman, a Quaker, thus defended his neighbor Ann Watkins against the accusation that she had harmed her neighborhood by allowing slaves to gather at her home at night, "in numbers," to hear black preachers.[37] Of particular importance was the testimony of sixty-two-year-old Benjamin Carr, who had known Mary Batson for decades, including the ten years she had lived on his plantation. Everyone who knew her, Carr warranted, found her to be a woman of honesty, integrity, and veracity.[38] Other testimony by whites in support of the plaintiffs' freedom sometimes proved to be as vague as that of the witnesses for the defense. One witness recalled some old lady in the Swamp telling her many years before that she had heard rumors about people of color in the area being entitled to their freedom.[39] Mary Farro testified that her mother, who was a Ratcliff and until her death in 1790 had lived in the Swamp for years near Ann Jones, told her that Lenah was "as free as she was."[40]

The third of the African Americans to testify, Bacon Boston, was deposed in 1793, his age then about forty. Like Anne Brown and Mary Batson, Bacon traced the genealogy of various family members. He himself was the son of Violet, or Vi, who was, "as this deponent has always understood," the daughter of Lenah.

The affiant (as those who gave depositions were called) added that his nephew Richard Boston, who was petitioning the court against Joshua Warfield, was the son of his sister Dorcas, or Darkey, a daughter of Violet. He mentioned several other nephews as well as more distant relatives who by like rights should be freed. Though he did not remember that his mother had a sister Maria, named after her grandmother, Bacon Boston's testimony added several branches to the Boston slaves' family tree.[41]

By far the most compelling, factual, and accurate testimony came from Anne Brown. She filled in gaps in other witnesses' testimony and argued against the deponents who had spoken in support of the slaveholding families. Even more importantly, she cited a number of previous cases in which Boston slaves had won their freedom. More than any other witness, Brown drew on her own knowledge and her own experience in her testimony, and she made every effort to avoid hearsay evidence, although her description of the first Maria was based on information she had gotten from Lenah and a few whites during her childhood. Brown provided detailed kinship evidence about mothers, brothers, sisters, aunts, uncles, cousins, nephews, great uncles, great aunts, and second cousins. She spoke of Violet and Daniel, two of Lenah's ten children, and of Violet's daughter Nanny, whose daughter Betty Boston was Lenah's great-grandchild. Two other of Lena's great-grandchildren, John and Phillip Boston, were sons of Nelly, whose mother was Lenah's daughter Maria. Anne had been born on the same plantation as Nelly and had known her well, from the time she was a little girl until Nelly's death sometime between 1777 and 1781. Out of Anne Brown's remarkable memory and lifelong relationships with the Boston slaves emerged an extraordinary family history stretching back five generations.[42]

To permit both sides time to submit their evidence, Chief Judge Samuel Chase allowed the trial to extend for four years. During this period, Chase and the two associate judges of the general court admitted both the testimony of free blacks and hearsay evidence. In the midst of the trial, in 1793, Anthony Boston won his freedom in the general court: Anthony being "a descendant of Violet, the daughter of Linah, the daughter of Maria," a Spanish woman, and Maria being "not a slave, but free," it was therefore "considered by the court, that the said Anthony Boston be free and discharged from all further servitude." Anthony's suit, filed in 1790 in the Anne Arundel County Court, could well have been a test case for the other Boston slaves.[43] On October 13, 1795, the general court issued its decree in the sixteen cases under consideration: the arguments by both sides had been carefully and fully heard, the court said, and after "mature deliberation" it decided that the plaintiffs were entitled to their freedom due to their "being descended from a free yellow woman." A week later, the attorney for John Francis Mercer and Richard Sprigg Sr. took their case to the Maryland High Court of Appeals and forwarded copies of the depositions along with other evidence for its consideration. In 1797, the high court affirmed the lower court's decision without issuing a formal opinion. By this ruling of the high court, as well as by some manumissions on the part of slaveowners and a few other lower-court actions, a total of twenty-six Boston slaves acquired their freedom.[44]

Slaves in Maryland continued to sue slaveowners for their freedom in subsequent years, but even as the Boston slaves' trial was drawing to a close, the Maryland Assembly in 1796 passed a law altering the process of such suits. No longer, it stipulated, could such suits originate in the General Court of the Western Shore, considered by many to be "the most prestigious judicial body in the state." Rather, such future contests would be adjudicated in the county of the plaintiff's residency. In addition, both plaintiffs and defendants could request a jury trial, and appeals could be made only "as to matters of law." Further, if a freedom suit was dismissed and brought again by the same party, the court could order a stay until the court costs of the first case had been fully paid. Lastly, free blacks could not henceforth testify against whites.[45]

In presenting their cases in court, both the Boston slaves and the defendants had relied heavily on hearsay evidence. A few years later, the successes of the Boston and other slave families, based largely on hearsay evidence, outraged Maryland Attorney General Luther Martin. "Our courts have determined that general reputation, that such persons are descended from white women, or that they have exercised the right of freedom, is evidence to the jury," he asserted. "It is giving the power to ignorant persons to judge of rights." As examples, he cited the Butler, Toogood, and Queen families, noting that members of the Queen family had argued that they had ancestral connections with native Indians of South America. "In all these, and many other similar cases, hundreds of negroes have been let loose upon [the] community by the hearsay testimony of an obscure illiterate individual." For Martin and other proslavery advocates, freedom suits posed a grave risk to a slaveowner's right to possess human property. Although he did not mention the Boston slaves, the "obscure illiterate" slur might have been aimed directly at Anne Brown.[46]

In 1810, thirteen years after the Boston cases were decided in favor of the plaintiffs, twenty-two members of the Ogleton slave family filed freedom suits in Prince George's County, Maryland, under similar circumstances. Their claim, strikingly like that of the Boston slaves, stated they were unlawfully detained in bondage and "entitled to their freedom having lineally descended from a free woman" with, ironically, the same given name as the progenitor in the Boston trials: Maria. The plaintiffs, who were currently the property of eight different owners, argued that, as Maria was a free person, so were her children, grandchildren, and great-grandchildren. Since Maria had died probably during the 1730s, there was, as in the Boston case, conflicting testimony in regard to Maria's color and status.

One deponent, William King, age seventy-seven, said that his father had told him Maria "was an East Indian woman & had long black hair & that she ought to be free." Another deponent, Anthony Drane, age seventy-six, testified that his father, now dead sixty-five years, had once owned Maria, and judging from her language, wooly hair, and color—"as black as other negroes," according to Drane's father—he believed she was born in Africa. As with the Boston suits, the deponents had never seen the Maria they described, and King could not remember whether or not anyone other than his father had declared her to be an East Indian woman with long black hair. Despite conflicting details in the testimony, hearsay did not impede the Boston slaves' suits for freedom; they won their case.

The Ogleton slaves, with one exception, did not. In April 1812, the court ruled against the plaintiffs and dismissed seven of the eight suits, including those brought by Letty and her five children, Eliza and her three children, and eleven other members of the Ogleton extended family: a total of twenty-one slaves. In the eighth suit, the defendant, Bailey E. Clarke, failed to appear despite a summons. The court thus drafted a contempt citation and ordered that the petitioner, Sarah Ogleton, "be henceforth discharged from the service of the Defendant and all persons claiming under him in virtue of any contract." The courts' markedly dissimilar rulings in the otherwise similar Boston and Ogleton cases were indicative of Maryland's changing political atmosphere, the growing opposition to hearsay evidence, and the difficulty of reconstructing the genealogies of slave families without the testimony, disallowed since 1796, of African Americans.[47]

The following year, 1813, in a case taken on appeal from the District of Columbia Circuit Court, the US Supreme Court ruled on a suit brought by an enslaved woman, Mima Queen, and her daughter. Queen and her lawyer, Francis Scott Key, argued that Mima's ancestor, Mary Queen, had come to America as a free woman many decades before but had thereupon been sold into servitude for seven years; reportedly, she, like Maria Boston, wore fine clothes. At the trial in the circuit court, one witness confirmed the truth of the plaintiff's story, details of which he had been told by his mother and which she had been told by her father; two other witnesses testified to hearing similar, corroborative accounts from various people in the neighborhood, but they could not identify their sources. The defense objected to this testimony, and the court sustained the objections. When the court ruled in favor of the defendant, the plaintiffs filed a writ of error.

After the case had been argued in the Supreme Court, Chief Justice John
Marshall wrote the majority opinion. While he allowed that certain exceptions
to the hearsay rule might admit evidence about a progenitor's reputation in the
neighborhood so as to establish pedigree (family relationships), such evidence
could not be extended to determine an individual's status as an enslaved or free
person. He found the testimony in support of Queen's petition as a free person
to be intrinsically weak in that it failed to verify the asserted facts. It was thus "totally inadmissible." Marshall affirmed the lower court's ruling.[48]

One of the lawyers for the Boston plaintiffs, Gabriel Duvall, who by 1813
had become an associate justice of the Supreme Court, had fought for many
years against the counterrevolution following the American Revolution, as
white Marylanders sought to solidify the "peculiar institution" of slavery in the
Upper South. In his minority dissent to Marshall's opinion, Duval pointed out
that in Maryland many claims for freedom could be proved only with hearsay
evidence, because "no living evidence" existed. The admission of such testimony
in freedom suits had thus been affirmed by the unanimous opinion of the high
court of appeals after full and fair argument by the ablest counsel at the bar. "If
the ancestor neglected to claim her right, the issue could not be bound by length
of time, it [freedom] being a natural inherent right," Duval reasoned, and therefore found the argument for admitting hearsay evidence more compelling in
freedom suits than it was in cases concerning pedigree or land boundaries: "It
will be universally admitted that the right to freedom is more important than the
right of property."[49]

With regard to the rights of African Americans to freedom, many white
southerners would take exception to Duvall's contention. Even so, for a brief
period at the end of the eighteenth century, the courts of Maryland not only
permitted hearsay evidence but also allowed free blacks and former slaves to testify. There is little doubt that the legal system enabled African Americans like the
Bostons to file freedom suits, as did the judges who permitted the introduction
of hearsay evidence and ruled in the slaves' favor. But the struggles recorded in
the testimony of the Boston slaves and of families like them impart more about
race, slavery, and blacks' legal recourse, not to mention the complex genealogies
of African Americans, than does a study of the finer points of law. Freed blacks
and slaves themselves were instrumental in bringing their plight to light, and by
their efforts, the efforts of ordinary people, social, cultural, and legal structures
were shaped and reshaped. Without question, Anne Brown was a remarkable
woman with an extraordinary memory, but the import of her depositions, as
well as those of her sister Mary Batson and of former slave Bacon Boston, lies not
only in her recalling who survived whom but also, and more so, in recounting
how—and where and when and by the grace of whom—they survived in

a racially determined society. It appears, too, that Brown's, and Bacon's and Batson's, knowledge of white slave owning families was nearly as extensive as that of their own free or slave families.

On the contrary, slaveholders' knowledge of their slaves' personal history, let alone their familial history, was extremely limited, no doubt because most owners viewed their bondsmen and women as property. What is most surprising is how African American women built a culture out of family heritage, how they continued to maintain communication with family members despite their being separated, and how they kept alive hope in the quest for freedom among generations of descendants. The final decision of the Boston slaves' fate came more than a century after their progenitors arrived in Maryland; that their numerous suits, sixteen of them, were filed, and won, from different settings against different owners demonstrates the power and strength of their culture—it was not a separate "black culture" but rather an inclusive family culture comprised of slaves, free persons of color, and southern whites who sympathized with their plight. Within this culture, in spite of often adverse or woeful circumstance, African American women played a pivotal role as keepers, orally, of ancestral history that over an entire century bound together and strengthened the Boston and the Brown families.

Not all of the descendants of Maria and her daughter, Lenah, became free persons of color. By the early nineteenth century, many of the Boston family members remained in bondage—some of them down to the Civil War, probably. Records show that, in February 1859, the Baltimore City Criminal Court ordered Maria Boston, a woman of color, to be sold as a slave for a term of four years. A few weeks after her sale, for thirty-one dollars, Maria ran away. Soon captured, she was punished with an extension of her term of servitude. In 1862, a runaway slave named John Boston sent a letter to his wife, Elizabeth, who lived in Owensville, Maryland, very near the Swamp. John had found freedom not in the courts but in refuge with a New York regiment stationed in Upton Hill, Virginia, where he wrote:

> My Dear Wife it is with grate joy I take this time to let you know Whare I am i am now in Safety . . . this Day i can Adress you thank god as a free man I had a little truble in giting away But as the lord led the Children of Isrel to the land of Canon So he led me to a land Whare fredom Will rain in spite Of earth and hell Dear you must make your Self content i am free from al the Slavers Lash . . . I am With a very nice man and have All that hart Can Wish But My Dear I Cant express my grate desire that i Have to See you i trust the time Will Come When We Shal meet again And if We dont met on earth We Will Meet in heven Whare Jesas ranes.[50]

Genealogy of the Boston Slave Family, ca. 1686–1798[1]

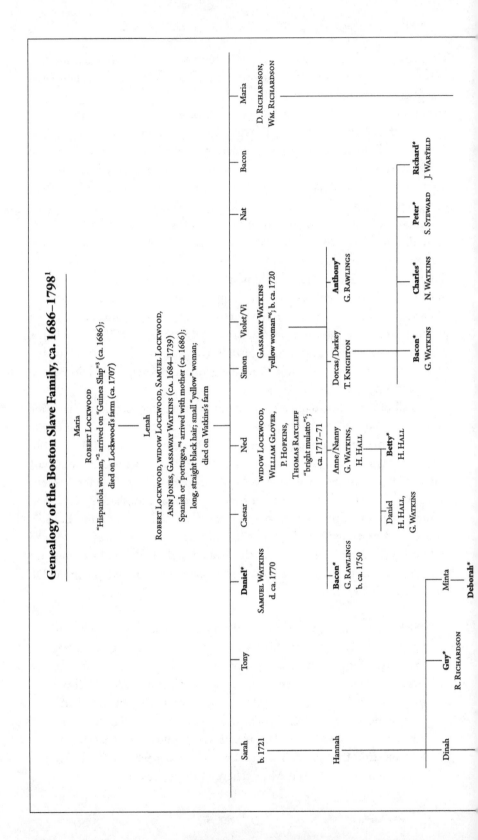

Peter*
R. RICHARDSON

John*
R. RICHARDSON

Nelly
THOMAS SPRIGG,
RICHARD SPRIGG SR.
d. ca. 1780

Tamar*
BENJAMIN OGLE

Benjamin*
R. SPRIGG

Philip*
R. SPRIGG

[illegible*]
E. DORSEY

Maria*
R. SPRIGG

Thomas*
B. OGLE

George*
J. MURRAY

John*
T. SPRIGG,
J.MERCER

Jenny*
T. SPRIGG
J.MERCER

George
R.SPRIGG
J.MURRAY

Nathan
R.SPRIGG

Daniel
R. SPRIGG

white woman + black slave

Henry*
J. MERCER

Anne*
J. MERCER

Bet*
R. SPRIGG

Daniel*
R. SPRIGG

Peter
R. WELLS

Charles*
"yellow"⁷
RICHARD SPRIGG SR.

"Mulatto Moll," "free Moll,"
or Mary Brown (ca. 1703–81),
indentured to Robert Lockwood,
Ann Jones, and William Richardson

Fanny*
J. MERCER

Ned   Mark   Isaac   Tom   (six other children)

Mary Batson
b. ca. 1725

Anne Brown
b. ca. 1731

Lucy

¹ Names in bold and marked with an asterisk are those who obtained their freedom. Names of owners are listed underneath names of slaves. Twenty-three Boston slaves won their freedom through the courts (although Guy Boston died during the final appeals process) and four were freed by their owners, including Lenah's son Daniel, who was set free by Samuel Watkins, and Jenny's children Bet and Daniel and her grandchild Charles, who were freed in 1798 by Richard Sprigg Sr.'s will. Not including Guy Boston, the total was thus twenty-six. Abstracts of some of the cases cited in this essay can be found in the Digital Library on American Slavery, created by the Race and Slavery Petitions Project and the Electronic Resources and Information Technology Department of University Libraries at the University of North Carolina, Greensboro, 2009, http://library.uncg.edu/slavery/. The names of the deposers for each case can be accessed from that website by entering the plaintiff's name and state in the search boxes. The original documents for the cases can be accessed through ProQuest's "Slavery and the Law Digital Archive."

² Deposition of Anne Brown, ca. 1792, found in *John Boston v. John Francis Mercer*, transcript of Records of the Court of the Western Shore, Md., 1791–1795, Court of Appeals (Judgments), November 1797, microfilm reel (M) 11015, case 15, Schweninger Collection (SC), Maryland State Archives (MSA).

³ Deposition of Anne Harwood, July 20, 1789, M 11015, SC, MSA.

⁴ Ibid.

⁵ Deposition of Richard Hopkins, May 21, 1793, M 11015, SC, MSA.

⁶ Deposition of John Tydings, October 25, 1791, M 11015, SC, MSA.

⁷ Copy of the last will and testament of Richard Sprigg Sr., 1797, MSS1M5345a108-109, Mercer Family Papers, Virginia Historical Society, Richmond.

Owners of Boston Slaves

Full names of slave owners, number of suits against those who became defendants in parentheses:

Edward Dorsey (1 illegible)

Henry Hall (1)

P. Hopkins

Thomas Knighton

Samuel Lockwood

John Francis Mercer (5)

James Murray (1)

Benjamin Ogle (2)

Thomas Ratclff

Gassaway Rawlings (2)

Daniel Richardson

Richard Richardson (4)

William Richardson

Richard Sprigg Sr. (3)

Thomas Sprigg

Stephen Steward (1)

Joshua Warfield (1)

Gassaway Watkins (1)

Nicholas Watkins

Samuel Watkins

Richard Wells (1)

2

Slave Plaintiffs and the Law

In 1835, a nineteen-year-old slave named Polly Anderson filed a suit in the Chesterfield County, Virginia, Chancery Court. Accompanied by her "next friend" and lawyer, James Burnett, a slaveholder, she traced her ancestry back two decades, to the date when her grandmother Amey and her mother, Letty, were freed by the 1805 will of Jordan Anderson Sr. Both Amey and Letty had then registered as free persons of color. Anderson explained that despite the fact that Amey and Letty had gained their freedom and registered at the county courthouse as free women of color, she had been turned over to Edward Elam as a slave when she was a young girl. Elam knew very well that she had been born free and was "not in law bound to serve him a day," but nevertheless he had sold her to William Watts, who had taken her to Hanover County and turned her over to his uncle, Robert White, a slave trader well known for "purchasing negroes in Virginia & transporting them to Louisiana & Mississippi for sale in those states, on speculation." Anderson stated further that she did not know if "she was sold as a slave absolutely, or only until she should attain her age of twenty-one years."

Fearing that it would be extremely difficult, if not impossible, for her to assert her right to freedom if she were sent to some distant part of the United States, Anderson was suing Edward Elam, William Watts, and Robert White, and requesting the court to restrain any one of them or any other party from transporting her out of the state. She asked, too, that the sheriff of Hanover County take her into custody and hire her out until "her right to freedom shall be finally decreed."[1]

The laws under which Polly Anderson brought her "bill of complaint," or "cause," as a matter of chancery, as equity suits were then called, stretched back to 1795, when the Virginia Assembly passed an act giving persons illegally detained in bondage the right to bring suit and be assigned counsel. The law was passed in response to the actions of out-of-state antislavery societies, which were attempting to divest Virginia slave owners of their property by burdening them with the heavy expense incurred in tedious and unfounded litigation. The Virginia statute created an "easy mode" for slaves and their counsel to recover

freedom "where it is unjustly and illegally denied." Slaves could thus file a complaint with a magistrate or court in their district, county, or corporation,[2] whereupon the magistrate was required to summon the owner or possessor of the slave
in order to answer the complaint in court and to post bond equal to the full value
of the black person. If the "master or holder" failed to provide such security, the
magistrate was then required to order the officer serving the complaint to take
the slave into custody until the next session of the court. The plaintiff would at
that point, upon petition, be assigned counsel *in forma pauperis* (in the character
of manner of a pauper) "for the recovery of his or her freedom."

It was incumbent on the attorney of record to investigate the circumstances of
the case and testify as to whether or not the evidence warranted a trial. If it did,
the judge would order the clerk to summon the slave owner or holder to appear
in court and answer charges. Any person who aided or abetted the prosecution
of a suit that failed would have to forfeit to the slaveholder one hundred dollars
for each slave, an amount that could be recovered by an action of debt. In 1798,
another act barred persons belonging to emancipation societies from serving
on juries in such cases and stipulated that the suits had to be tried immediately.
An "Act of January 17, 1818—January 1, 1820" republished the 1795 law and
added that slaves could now file their complaint in a superior court of law and
chancery.[3]

In the early years of the republic, the states in the South were left to their own
devices in dealing with the legal issues raised by slavery and freedom. In some
states, especially in the Lower South, for a slave to obtain free status generally
required either a special act of the legislature or proof of a heroic deed by the
petitioner, such as saving the life of a master or mistress or betraying a slave conspiracy, or the bond servant's performance of "meritorious service" on behalf
of the state or an owner's family. In 1796, the North Carolina Assembly passed
an act to "amend, strengthen and confirm the several acts of the Assembly of
this state, against the emancipation of slaves," by which no slave could be freed
except for meritorious service, as judged and decreed by the county courts
with the issuance of a license of emancipation, or by a special act passed by the
General Assembly.

Nonetheless, in practice slave owners did in fact manumit blacks who had not
performed meritorious services; for instance, they sometimes freed the children
of favored slaves as well as mulatto children they themselves had sired.[4] In 1801,
Georgia lawmakers declared that only the General Assembly could "manumit
or set free any negro slave or slaves, any mulatto mustizo, or any other person or
persons of color." It was therefore unlawful for the clerks of superior courts, or
any other officer of the state, to attempt to record any deed of manumission.[5] In
1818, Georgia lawmakers added that it was also illegal for any person to attempt
to free a slave by any will, deed, trust, agreement, contract, or stipulation, either

written or oral. An owner found guilty of breaking this law was subject to a fine not exceeding $1,000, while the slave in question was designated to be arrested and sold at public auction.[6] In South Carolina, the assembly in 1800 passed a law stipulating that it was not lawful for any owner to emancipate a slave except through a majority vote by a group of selected freeholders in the district upon hearing evidence as to the slave's character and ability to earn a livelihood. Two decades later, as in Georgia, only with passage of a special act by the General Assembly could a slave be freed in South Carolina. The early statutes in the Lower South made it extremely difficult not only for owners to manumit slaves but also, and to a greater extent, for blacks held illegally in bondage to petition the courts for their release from bondage. Still, in the early years following the revolution, a few African Americans with white sponsors did succeed in their pursuit of freedom.[7]

The great migration in the early nineteenth century took many slaveholders and yeoman farmers westward, and most of the new states in the Lower South likewise erected legal obstacles to manumission. In 1822, the Mississippi Assembly allowed that an owner could seek to free a slave in a will or "other instrument in writing, under his, her, or their hand and seal," as attested by two credible witnesses—but only, as in North Carolina, if the slave had performed a "meritorious act" or rendered some "distinguished service" to the state. Even then, the emancipation would not take effect until the General Assembly had enacted a private bill on the slave's behalf. Moreover, an emancipated slave could be used to satisfy an owner's debts or a widow's dower, prior to a final act granting emancipation (this was the case in most states).[8]

Similarly, the Alabama Constitution in 1819 declared that freedom could be achieved only if the enslaved person had rendered "some distinguished service" to be determined by a vote in the General Assembly. Again, the freed person could still be seized by creditors to pay the owner's debts or be returned to bondage for failure to earn a livelihood.[9] In 1807, the Louisiana territorial assembly denied free status to slaves who had run away, had committed a crime, or were under the age of thirty.[10] The age limit remained in effect until 1827, when the assembly allowed parish judges and police juries the authority to manumit younger Louisiana-born slaves under certain circumstances.[11] In 1830, Louisiana law required manumitted slaves who did not receive special exemptions because of a meritorious act to leave the state within thirty days; the law also mandated their owners to post a $1,000 bond to ensure their departure.[12]

Yet even in the Lower South, the avenue to freedom through the courts was not completely closed. In Louisiana, the Civil Code of 1825 noted that although slaves could not be a party to civil actions, either as plaintiffs or defendants, they could file freedom suits: this was the only indication in the code that those held in bondage could initiate a lawsuit.[13] In 1837, under an act titled "Freedom," the Arkansas Assembly passed a statute virtually the same as the Virginia law applied in the case of Polly Anderson. It allowed any person illegally detained in slavery to petition the circuit court and seek permission to sue *in forma pauperis*. If the petition had merit, the judge would assign counsel and direct the alleged owner to permit the plaintiff opportunities to confer with his or her attorney, to attend court sessions, and not to be subjected "to any severity on account of his application for freedom." Should the owner fail to meet these conditions, the petitioner could be taken into custody by the sheriff and hired out during the pretrial period, once a bond from the hirer, payable to the state of Arkansas, with the condition that the hirer would pay the sheriff the hiring wages, had been secured. The freedom suit would then be brought as "an action of trespass for false imprisonment."[14]

Similar laws, which designated the action as suits either for the courts of equity or the law courts, were passed in Mississippi in 1822 (the circuit equity courts), in the Florida Territory in 1824 (law courts), and in Georgia in 1835 and 1837 (the inferior courts, through a white guardian). These enactments were designed to protect both free blacks from being kidnapped and held "fraudulently and illegally in a state of slavery by wicked white men" and black slaves who should by rights have been freed but were still held in bondage. In each state, the presumed owner was required to post a security bond and answer charges. The plaintiff bore the burden of proof, the presumption of the court being that the black person was, until proven otherwise, a slave. If the court ruled in the plaintiff's favor—as, for instance, in the Florida law—a special entry in the record would declare the plaintiff free. In these and other new Lower South states, only a few people of color were able to bring their cases before the courts, but the laws remained on the books until the late antebellum era.[15]

Upper South states enacted laws similar to those employed by Polly Anderson and her counsel. In 1796, the year after Virginia passed its initial law, the Maryland Assembly enacted a detailed statute regarding freedom suits. It granted slave plaintiffs the right to file petitions in the county courts; it granted the courts the authority to summon defendants, issue summonses, secure witnesses, and impanel juries. Either side could seek a trial by jury, and either side could peremptorily challenge any of the twelve jurors to be impaneled. If there were not twelve jurors remaining after challenges, a *tales-juror*—a person selected from the bystanders—could be installed at the request of either party. If local sheriffs failed to administer the directives of the court in serving summonses, they could be fined. Each side had the right to appeal, but only concerning matters of law. Despite the fact that this 1796 Maryland enactment was designed to stem the surge of freedom suits during the 1780s and early 1790s, it provided a number of guarantees to people in bondage who believed they were being improperly or illegally detained. In subsequent years—notably 1819, 1829, and 1823—the assembly passed laws that permitted slave plaintiffs to continue their suits if deeds of manumission either lacked the proper signatures or failed to include the exact time and place of trial in the recording of individual cases.[16]

In colonial Delaware, a law passed in 1760 remained in effect long after the colony achieved statehood. It allowed black people to petition a court of common pleas for their freedom, whereupon the justices of the court would issue a summons for the presumed master to respond to the complaint. Subsequently, the court would also issue summonses for witnesses to be summoned by the sheriff, so that they might "give evidence in and upon the matters in such petition contained, under such pains and penalties, as by the rules and practice in the said court in others cases are usually appointing."[17] Every other state in the Upper South likewise passed statutes allowing slaves to sue for their freedom under defined circumstances. From its inception in 1801, under authority of the US Congress, the District of Columbia accepted the laws of both Virginia and Maryland, in sections ceded from those two states, including Alexandria County from Virginia and what became Washington County from Maryland. In 1816, the District's proposed code reiterated the right of slaves to sue for their freedom in the circuit court. They and their counsel were allowed a reasonable opportunity to secure depositions from witnesses, and slaveowning defendants were required to post a bond amounting to double the market value of any person filing a freedom suit.[18]

The Virginia laws were also adopted in Kentucky, where freedom suits appeared at an early date. In fact, they became so prevalent in 1808 that the Kentucky Assembly declared a two-year moratorium on suits prosecuted by persons of color who claimed their right to freedom on the grounds of Kentucky's failure to comply with the applicable 1780 gradual abolition act of Pennsylvania, or as a consequence of being transported into the state contrary to its laws, or as a result of the failure of owners to take an oath as prescribed by the laws of Virginia entitled "an act for preventing the further importation of slaves." The state later granted plaintiffs who won their suits the right to seek damages. In a few cases, African Americans did in fact receive compensation for the period of time they had been illegally held in bondage. In 1817, Tennessee passed a law permitting freedom suits in the county courts upon receipt of an affidavit by "some respectable person," either white or free black, to verify the charges against slaveholders. As in other states, should a trial be scheduled, the person claiming freedom could not be removed or taken out of the court's jurisdiction and the defendant would be obligated to post a "good and sufficient security" bond.[19]

In Missouri, during its territorial period, slaves could sue for their freedom under the 1807 statute that governed freedom suits in the Louisiana Territory. The object of the legislation, as the three judges of the Missouri Supreme Court explained in 1821, was to "afford plaintiffs of this description, all opportunity of having the question of freedom fairly put in issue between the parties." In the 1817 case of *Susan (a black woman) v. Hight*, which hinged upon the issue of residency in Illinois, the Missouri Supreme Court ruled that the circuit court's decision in favor of the master should be reversed and the cause remanded to the circuit court. Shortly after attaining statehood, in 1824, Missouri enacted a law titled "An act to enable persons held in slavery to sue for their freedom," by which any person unlawfully held in slavery could ask for permission to sue their alleged owner *in forma pauperis*. Plaintiffs had to present adequate grounds for their suits; if they were found to be sufficient, the court could permit the plaintiffs to file actions of trespass, thereby seeking monetary damages for false enslavement, similar to those noted in the code of South Carolina. Also an action of trespass was defined in common law as "trespass, assault & batter, false imprisonment," "trespass with force of arms," "trespass in the nature of ravishment of ward," or some combination of these actions. In reality, trespass declarations or narrations, as they were called, had little connection with actual circumstances surrounding false enslavement. Although this law in subsequent years underwent minor changes, its general features—allowing black men, women, and children to challenge wrongful enslavement and ultimately bring their cases to trial—remained in effect until the late antebellum era.[20]

Thus from Delaware to Missouri, and in Louisiana, laws permitted slaves to sue for their freedom in the local courts on claims that they were being illegally held in bondage. The laws were similar in many respects. Usually, they allowed slaves, in their own right and with counsel, to file petitions or declarations for their freedom. Once the legitimacy of the charges had been acknowledged, judges issued summonses for the defendants and witnesses to appear. Alleged owners were admonished to permit plaintiffs to have access to their attorneys, to travel unhindered to court, to call witnesses on their behalf, to attend depositions, and to be present at trial. As in Maryland in regard to the Boston slaves, the laws forbade presumed owners to mistreat or abuse their slaves in the event of a freedom suit. If additional time was needed to gather evidence or if judges believed untoward circumstances might arise, the court could order sheriffs to take the plaintiffs into custody and to hire them out for wages, which could be applied to the payment of court costs. Other states—among them, Georgia, Mississippi, Arkansas, and Florida—passed statutes with similar intent, but in areas heavily populated with slaves and where anti-black sentiment ran strong, few African Americans were able to take advantage of these laws. More often than not, what statutes established in principle was disregarded in practice. North Carolina and Texas both failed to enact legislation governing freedom suits, but in both states a few freedom suits came to trial. In fact, at one time or another African Americans successfully filed freedom suits in the local courts in every southern state, even in those where the final decision concerning a slave's freedom could be rendered only by general assemblies.

The laws governing freedom suits were closely allied with statutes concerning manumissions and term servitude. Unlike freedom-suit statutes, which remained on the books for many years after statehood, manumission laws changed more notably over time. Most Lower South states severely restricted the freeing of slaves in wills and deeds. In North Carolina (until 1831), South Carolina, Georgia, Mississippi, and Alabama (until 1833), only by legislative acts could freedom be granted; Florida prohibited manumissions altogether, as did Texas. Only in Arkansas did slaveholders have free reign to liberate slaves by wills and deeds.

In the Upper South and Louisiana, the laws governing emancipations were more lenient. Owners could manumit slaves without reference to heroic deeds, extraordinary acts, meritorious services, or legislative action. They could petition the county courts to validate a last will and testament, a deed of manumission, or some other "instrument" in writing, including a bill of sale, so long as the document was signed by the owner and attested to by one or two witnesses. Such transactions afforded no protection against creditors or the widow's dower, and owners were required to post security bonds with warranties that the emancipated slaves were not infirm, aged, mentally deficient, or unable to earn a livelihood.[21] The states had different definitions of old age, which ranged from thirty-five to fifty-five years; however, most of the states stipulated that if freed slaves became "chargeable," or a burden to the county, it was the former owner's responsibility to support the black person. A few states required owners or estate executors also to provide each freed person with a copy of a last will and testament or "the instrument in emancipation" that had been authenticated by witnesses or a clerk of court. Beginning with Virginia in 1806, a number of Upper South states at various times mandated that freed blacks leave the state. Nonetheless, the freed slaves, an early Virginia law read, would "thereupon be entirely and fully discharged from the performance of any contract entered into during servitude, and enjoy as full of freedom as if they had been particularly named and freed by this act."[22]

Manumission laws in Upper South states came with other provisions as well. In Maryland, it was not necessary to record the will or deed at the courthouse, but it did have to be executed, proved, or acknowledged. Further, a claim of dower would not prevent the emancipation if compensation to heirs could be affected by the sale of other property; if not, however, the slaves could be retained in bondage or sold to provide the dower. The Maryland law of 1790 repealed parts of two acts that had been passed during the colonial era and that "imposed a servitude to the age of thirty-one years on the issue of certain inordinate copulations," or the children of white women and black men. By inflicting penalties on the children for the "offenses of their parents," the 1790 law read, the colonial acts were contrary to humanity and the principles of Christianity.[23] In 1794, the Kentucky Assembly passed an act permitting owners to free their slaves by will, deed, or written declaration that had been proven by two witnesses in the county courts. It followed the Virginia law in requiring that the black persons be "fully discharged from the performance of any contract entered into during servitude, and enjoy as full freedom as if they had been born free." In recognition thereof, the clerk of court would then issue a certificate of freedom "on parchment" with "the county seal affixed thereto." Similar enactments were passed in Delaware, Virginia, Tennessee, and Missouri. Thus, the process in upper states was neither onerous nor subject to the often arbitrary decisions of general assemblies. How and when blacks, especially black women, were manumitted would become pivotal issues in a number of freedom suits.[24]

The legal systems in the Upper South continually made adjustments for the changes in methods of emancipation. In the first decade of the nineteenth century, the states passed statutes covering term slaves—that is, slaves promised their freedom at some date in the future, including the children of emancipated black women. The main concern for lawmakers was what to do with recalcitrant," "refractory," or "troublesome" slave men and women whose term of servitude was limited. In 1805, Maryland allowed the period of servitude to be extended for slaves who absconded, provided they had not done so because of "ill treatment" by owners. Under no conditions, though, could term slaves be sold or assigned to any person residing outside the state.[25] In 1810, the assembly stipulated that unless otherwise specified by the owner, the child of a term slave born during the mother's term of servitude would remain in bondage.[26]

That same year, the Delaware Assembly specified that the children of term slaves born during the mother's term of servitude would themselves be bound until they reached age twenty-five, if male, and twenty-one, if female, at which time they would become free and entitled to "all the immunities and privileges of free negroes or free mulattoes." Term slaves brought into the state by new residents would remain in bondage without limitations, except for those older than thirty-five. No term slaves could be sold out of the state without a special license granted by the courts of general quarter sessions or the Supreme Court. Owners who sold term slaves without a license were subject to indictment and a fine of $500, and the slaves themselves were declared to be free. Runaway term slaves, if captured, would have their servitude extended for a period of time determined by a court of equity.[27]

During the 1790s and early decades of the nineteenth century, the lofty ideals of the Revolution began to fade, and most owners who manumitted slaves freed only individual blacks who had loyally served the white families for many years, sometimes for generations. Some slaves, too, might be freed at some future date when a will was probated following an owner's death. A number of slave owners set specific conditions upon which black bondservants might acquire their freedom. They might, for instance, have to work diligently for a specified number of years, never attempt to run away, and prove not to be "troublesome" in order to secure their freedom at some future date or age. Some among the enslaved, especially in Delaware and Maryland, became indentured servants, with the indentures spelling out the requirements for their freedom. Other African Americans serving as term slaves themselves forwarded their pursuit of freedom by self-purchase or by purchase of their own family members. Some manumissions by deed, will, or indenture (in the case for term slaves) came about simply because it was more profitable for owners to free them in the near future than to retain them as slaves during an economic downturn when farmers and slave owners in the region might likely be struggling with increasing indebtedness, fluctuating crop prices, soil exhaustion, tight money, and inadequate roads. Some slaveholders and state leaders even felt that perhaps slavery was not economically the best labor system.[28]

Because the laws and patterns of manumission varied widely in the southern states, the free black population grew unevenly from region to region in the South. In the first decennial census in 1790, the Upper South boasted 30,158 free people of color, more than half the free blacks in the country. When compared to the 2,199 free blacks counted in the Lower South, the upper states claimed more than 97 percent of the South's free black population. Over the next twenty years, the number of free persons of color in the upper states more than tripled to 94,085, a figure that continued to mark a slight majority in the country, while free blacks in the Lower South numbered 14,180—a not insignificant rise, due largely to the Louisiana Purchase. Under Spanish rule (1769–1803), slaves in Louisiana acquired the right to own property and purchase their freedom under the law of *coartación,* which allowed slaves to hire out themselves in their extra time, eventually obtain a sum equal to their market value, and therewith purchase their freedom. The owner was obliged to accept the self-purchase petition if the slave was not disorderly or rebellious.

Under this system, found nowhere in Anglo- or Franco-America, the Spanish sought to protect the institution of slavery by creating a middle group of free blacks. By the end of the Spanish period, 1,490 blacks in New Orleans alone had acquired their freedom by cash payments: a remarkable achievement. This, coupled with the immigration in 1809 of three thousand French-speaking refugees who had been forced to leave Spanish Cuba because of hostilities between the mother countries, accounted for the fact that by 1810, the Louisiana Territory contained 7,585 free persons of color, most of them living in New Orleans and representing 44 percent of the city's free population. Thus, on the eve of statehood, Louisiana held more than half of the Lower South's free black population. These early population trends continued similarly, if more slowly, in later decades, as it became increasingly difficult, indeed virtually impossible, for blacks to acquire freedom in the Lower South, while the avenues to freedom in the upper states, although gradually tightening, maintained a range of options for owners and slaves, including the right of African Americans, accompanied by their attorneys, to file freedom suits.[29]

Some of the impetus behind the enactments regarding the freedom of blacks in bondage lay in the ideological and religious legacy of the American Revolution. In the two decades following the Peace of Paris, slaveholders who manumitted their slaves in the Upper South often construed their actions in antislavery and/ or religious terms. As if by moral imperative, they freed large numbers of slaves for the most part in their wills or in deeds registered in county courts. Because of the age limits set by state manumissions laws, however, the parties named in the documents would sometimes have to wait until they reached adulthood to realize their freedom, or they might, under the statutes, prove to be too old to be freed.[30]

In the 1780s, too, Quakers in Delaware, Maryland, North Carolina, Virginia, and the District of Columbia began working actively for the abolition of slavery. They were the first Christian sect in America to embrace the belief that slavery was an evil, for it belied the equality of all peoples in the eyes of God. They thus prohibited the ownership of human property. While some Quakers found their church's stance on slavery too radical, the great majority of Quaker slaveholders not only freed their slaves but also worked with antislavery and abolitionist groups to pass legislation that would bring to an end what they considered to be an evil institution.

Methodists and Baptists shared the same concerns, but they were more divided than the Quakers as to what action should be taken. Whereas some members of both denominations joined societies dedicated to the relief of persons illegally held in slavery as well as to the abolition of the institution itself, many of the slave owners among them defended the system on evidence that it dated back to biblical times. Members of both denominations were no less divided when they moved westward and set up congregations in the Upper South. Antislavery societies, often led by evangelicals who preached that the possession of persons as property was immoral and uncivilized, sprang up in Tennessee and Kentucky.

The new churches there brought together devout Christians who established rigid rules of conduct for the brothers and sisters, as they were wont to address each other, so that they might be worthy of celebrating the Eucharist. At the Mount Tabor Baptist Church in Kentucky members of the congregation washed each other's feet in keeping with early Christian practice. In that same church, in 1808, John Murphy, clerk of the church, rose from his seat and rescinded his fellowship with the Baptist congregation because members among it tolerated slaveholding. Others followed Murphy's example and withdrew their membership. Throughout the upper states other churches experienced similar divisions, which often pitted old friends against one another. Evangelicals based their opposition to slavery on their conviction that God alone ruled their consciences, and the laws enacted by governments could not supersede the will of God, who created all peoples equal. There is little doubt that in this early period of America's history, individuals of conscience in antislavery groups and related associations willingly assisted slaves in filing freedom suits.[31]

Prior to 1830, there were more antislavery societies in the Upper South than in the North. In 1827, according to the Ohio abolitionist Benjamin Lundy, 106 associations, with a total of more than 5,000 members, were working actively against slavery in the upper states, as opposed to only 24 similar societies with about 1,500 members in the North. In four Piedmont counties of North Carolina alone, 50 organizations, many of them led by Quakers, had been set up by the 1820s, as had similar abolitionist societies in the mountainous sections of eastern Tennessee and Kentucky. A number of delegates at Kentucky's first constitutional convention in 1792 spoke out against slavery, and in succeeding years a significant antislavery minority took seats in various general assemblies. After 1830, even though these groups continually came under attack by proslavery advocates, slaves filing freedom suits could readily find sympathetic whites to assist and support them in the legal process.[32]

Other laws in the upper states offered slaves and their lawyers further means to test the boundaries of slavery. In three states—Delaware, Maryland, and Virginia—and the District of Columbia, it was illegal to import slaves from other states in order to put them up for sale. The first law in the South to prohibit importation for this purpose was passed by Virginia in 1775, with the lawmakers arguing that the reproducing population of native-born slaves was sufficient not to warrant importing slaves from other states, the West Indies, or Africa, who, moreover, were likely to corrupt native-born blacks. The intent of such laws was not to dissuade out-of-state slaveholders from relocating in Virginia, or Delaware or Maryland or the District of Columbia; rather, it was to guarantee, by an oath on the part of the migrant slaveholders, that they would make no attempt to sell their slaves in the state before a prescribed number of years. These laws did not apply to slaveowning visitors, or sojourners as they were called, who were traveling through the states or the District of Columbia; nor did they pertain to persons claiming blacks by descent, devise, or marriage.

Maryland law required that migrants sign an oath before either a naval officer or tax collector, or provide testimony from a competent witness, to verify their avowal to become residents. Subsequent enactments in Virginia in 1785, Maryland in 1791 and 1796, and Delaware in 1787 and 1797 addressed how the state would honor the period of time, determined in the former state of residence, that term slaves were obliged to serve and whether to permit owners in adjacent states certain liberties to cross and recross borders with their slaves to work the land. Although many states in the South eventually passed anti-importation statutes, it was only in this portion of the Upper South and in Florida and briefly in Kentucky that blacks who were illegally imported by traders or owners intending to sell them "shall thereupon immediately cease to be the property of the person or persons so importing or bringing such slave within this state," as one law read, "and shall be free."[33]

The anti-importation laws in Delaware, Virginia, Maryland, and the District of Columbia, as well as in Florida, remained in effect with minor changes for many years and withstood numerous legal challenges. An act passed in 1827 by the Territorial Council of Florida, which granted freedom to slaves who were imported contrary to law, stood unchanged during the era of statehood.[34] In Maryland, in 1831, the importation of slaves was prohibited even when a slaveholder wished to establish residence, but this statute was reversed in 1849.[35] In addition to its anti-importation laws, Delaware in 1793 passed an act making it illegal to export slaves. Whereas "sundry Negroes and Mulattoes, as well freemen and slaves, have been exported, and sold into other states, contrary to the principles of humanity and justice, and derogatory to the honour of this state" (so the preface read), any person who would henceforth attempt to export, sell, or carry out of the state for sale any slaves to the Carolinas, Georgia, or the West Indies, without a license, would face a one-hundred-pound fine. Six years later, the state added that any slave exported without a permit would be "declared free." Whatever the motivation—religion, humanism, justice, or honor—states had the right to enact laws prohibiting importation or exportation of slaves if they so desired; by such laws slaves and their counsel had the right to sue for their freedom. In Delaware, so many slaves were filing freedom suits that slaveholders, in alarm, strove to hobble the process. In 1801, one Sussex County slave master introduced in the General Assembly a bill "compelling Negroes who petitioned for their freedom to give surety for the payment of the costs in the event that the complaint failed." The bill did not pass, but the slave owners continued to file complaints against those petitioning for their freedom. Such suits were "unjust and oppressive" for owners, they declared, because they were denied the service of the slave upon the filing of a freedom suit and no surety was required for payment to the owner for lost services. In practice implementation of the laws by counsel for slaves who were imported and sold, or who were sold and exported, often proved onerous. Nonetheless, a number of importees, especially in Delaware, did successfully file freedom suits under the importation/exportation statutes.[36]

The anti-importation laws assumed particular importance during the final decade of the eighteenth century. In 1791, news of the slave revolt led by Toussaint Louverture in the French colony of Saint-Domingue reached slave owners in America. Reports of pillage and conflagration—of slave rebels setting fire to buildings, homes, plantations; of rebel slaves massacring white as well as black inhabitants who attempted to escape—horrified southerners, as did the beheading of Marie Antoinette and King Louis XVI during the French Revolution. Struck by the excesses of the revolt and revolution, slave owners in the United States worried about the impact they might have on their own peace and security. It was in this atmosphere that discussions about gradual emancipation went silent and legislation markedly strengthened the peculiar institution. In 1796, for example, the Maryland Assembly prohibited considerably more than slave importations; it also denied free blacks the right to vote, to hold office, or to give evidence against whites. In addition, it placed age limits and health restrictions on slave manumissions. It put restrictions, too, on how and when freedom suits could be filed by blacks and their counsel. It did, however, afford protections to slave owners with regard to jury trials and payment of court costs.[37]

During the late eighteenth century and the early decades of the nineteenth, as the South strengthened its statutes concerning the peculiar institution, the states in the North gradually brought slavery to an end. In New England, this was accomplished either by judicial decree and court decisions (Massachusetts and New Hampshire) or by gradual abolition laws (Rhode Island and Connecticut). Contributing to the abolishment were the existence of relatively small black populations, the lack of economic vitality in a slave system (unlike the case in many areas of the South), and the legacy of the American Revolution, which was, in the words of William Cushing, associate justice of the US Supreme Court, "favorable to the natural rights of mankind."[38] In 1780, the Pennsylvania Assembly passed the first Gradual Emancipation Act, which stated that all "Negroes, and Mulattos" born in the state after its passage would no longer become "Servants for Life" but rather would become indentured servants until age twenty-eight, when they would be deemed free. Chattel slavery for life, the law read, was abolished. When members of the assembly considered an amendment that would extend the registration date to January 1, 1782, a group of African Americans petitioned the legislative body, explaining that "the great question of slavery or liberty, is too important for us to be silent. It is the momentous question of our lives." They beseeched the assembly to reject the amendment, which would in effect reenslave those released from bondage upon passage of the bill. The amendment was defeated. It was not until 1799 and 1804 that New York and New Jersey, respectively, enacted gradual abolition statutes.[39]

In the Old Northwest, where the Northwest Ordinance of 1787 had outlawed human bondage, the new states' constitutions abolished slavery. "That the general, great, and essential principles of liberty and free government may be recognized, and forever unalterably established, we declare," Article VIII of the 1802 Ohio Constitution began, "there shall be neither slavery nor involuntary servitude in this State otherwise than for the punishment of crimes, whereof the party shall have been duly convicted." The Indiana Constitution of 1816 employed the exact same wording, whereas the Illinois Constitution in 1818 declared that neither slavery nor involuntary servitude could "thereafter be introduced" into the state. Judicial decisions, gradual abolition laws, and state constitutions thus created the legal framework for freedom and in doing so, at least in the law, eliminated the principles by which human beings were held as property.[40]

With the gradual end of slavery in the North and the increasing vigor of the institution in many sections of the South, two different legal systems emerged in the United States. Among the resultant disputes that arose, none was more contentious than that over the implications of the Fugitive Slave Law of 1793. Under this statute, slaveholders or their agents could seize or arrest fugitives in the North, take them before either a federal judge or a county, city, or town magistrate, and present a case for ownership, either with oral testimony or cer- tified affidavits. If the case satisfied the officials, the owners could return to the South with their human property. In the North, however, by virtue of slavery's abolition, individual blacks could not be treated as property. Moreover, though African Americans were not citizens they were identified in the North as free persons, unlike in southern states, where their skin color defined them as slaves. They were, therefore, able to invoke certain rights, including those to pursue a trial by jury, to seek a writ of habeas corpus, and to obtain a writ *de homine replegiando* (to gain a release if held by a justice of the peace or a private person). By the second decade of the nineteenth century, states in the North, beginning with Ohio and New York, were also attaching new and more stringent penalties to the unlawful transport of a black person from their commonwealths. Various states passed laws to prevent kidnapping, to protect "Personal Liberty," or, as in New Jersey, "to prohibit the exportation of slaves or Servants of Colour out of this State."[41]

The Personal Liberty Laws, as they were called, did not prevent states in the North from discriminating against black people. Some passed laws that restricted the entry of free blacks into the state; others adopted enactments by which African Americans had to prove their free status or post bonds of between five hundred and $1,000 to guarantee good behavior. Violators of such measures could be forced to leave the state. In Illinois, "Negroes or mulattoes" who failed to produce freedom papers were considered to be, and treated as, runaway slaves. In addition, blacks held in bondage at the time a territory achieved statehood could, and often did, find themselves subject to long-term indentures. One Missouri woman who filed a freedom suit in that state claimed that she had been indentured to her master in the Illinois Territory in 1811 for a period of forty years.[42]

Free blacks hoping to establish residence in Ohio had to first submit certificates of manumission to the clerk of the county court and, after 1807, had to enter into bond with two or more property owners for $500 "to guarantee their good behavior and welfare." In Indiana, free blacks without a certificate of freedom from a court could be ordered to be removed from the state. Although some of these laws were not rigorously enforced, they did reflect an antiblack sentiment on the part of a large segment of the northern states' population. Also, in states with gradual abolition laws, freedom was no more than a word for former slaves who now found themselves indentured as servants for years upon years. In Pennsylvania, for example, if a slave mother gave birth in 1779 to a daughter who, at her maturity, then bore a child, the child would not be free from a labor obligation until the age of twenty-eight, probably during the 1820s or 1830s. Nevertheless, in law, chattel slavery was abolished in the North, and slaves who journeyed northward with their owners and established residency for a period of time could, and sometimes with success did, claim that they were free because they resided in a slave-free territory or state.[43]

Legal precedents permitting freedom suits stretched back to the colonial era. Slaves who could prove that their mother was white, even if their father was a slave, could sue for their freedom. As early as 1662, in Virginia, the first statutory provision on the subject stated that "all children borne in this country shall be held bond or free only according to the condition of the mother." This was a departure from English common law, by which children would follow the condition of the father, or, as one contemporary put it, the leprosy of the father's bondage. How and why the colonials chose to reject English common law and follow Roman civil law in this regard is not clear, but from the colonies' earliest years the principle of *partus sequitur ventrem* was the accepted doctrine. Ironically, the term itself never appeared in the law of the colonies or southern states.[44] Several of the colonies passed laws during the colonial era to protect parties illegally held in bondage. In South Carolina and Georgia, black people unlawfully bound in servitude were granted the right, once they had secured the aegis of white guardians, to file an action of trespass. In 1740, South Carolina passed an act stating that any Negro, mulatto, or mestizo born of a slave mother would absolutely and abidingly hold the status of slave, to be "held, taken, reputed and adjudged in law, to be chattels personal"; however, in cases where black or mixed-race persons were illegally being held in bondage, they, or any person or persons on their behalf, could by law file a petition or motion in the form of an action of trespass in a court of common pleas. In 1770, under the title "suits for Freedom," Georgia enacted a statute whereby a white person, serving as guardian, could apply by petition to his majesty's general court for an action of trespass, either during the sitting of the court or before any of the justices. During the same period, Delaware law specified that children born of white mothers and black fathers could bring suits of "trespass and false imprisonment, or any other action in the law."[45]

When, how, and if slave women acquired their freedom had a direct bearing on when, how, and if their children could also become free. If a mother gave birth to a child before the date or age of her future emancipation, the child would be deemed to have been born in bondage and would remain so, except in cases where a special provision had been made for the child in a will or deed or indenture. But if the mother gave birth after the date or age of her emancipation, the child would be considered to have been born free.

In instances where women scheduled to be freed on a particular date had, instead, been held in bondage beyond that date, it could be difficult to prove that their children should by law be free. So it was that such women's children and perhaps their grandchildren, and even their great-grandchildren, could find themselves hopelessly enslaved. As time and generations passed, for a slave child to prove that a grandmother or great-grandmother had been a free black became increasingly difficult, even with lawyers working assiduously to uncover legal documents establishing her emancipation and the birth dates of her children and grandchildren. In cases of term-slave women whose terms of servitude might have been extended, possibly several times, the difficulties for their children and descendants in freedom suits were compounded. So too were the problems when the maternal link was a black woman who had been sold and resold and resold again to various owners in different sections of the South.[46]

Another Virginia law also established precedent for freedom suits involving Native Americans. In 1705, the assembly authorized a "free and open trade for all persons, at all times, and at all places, with all Indians whatsoever." In 1787, the Virginia General Court ruled that Indians brought into the state after the passage of the 1705 bill could not be held as slaves. St. George Tucker, a professor of law at the college of William and Mary College and author of *A Dissertation on Slavery* (1796), later remarked that "all Indians" was probably a misprint and that it should read "all American Indians and their descendants in the maternal line, are free."[47] Thereafter it was discovered that the wording of the 1705 law was in fact exactly the same as that in an enactment of 1691. The principle established in the statutes was simple: trading with other nations, including Indian nations, disallowed the enslavement of any trading partners from those nations. Although arguments were subsequently advanced against this proposition, the precedent nevertheless stood the test of time, both in Virginia and other southern states.

If individuals could prove Indian heritage on the maternal side, they could, and often did, file freedom suits in either the common law or equity courts.[48]

Yet another avenue to freedom tested by slaves and their lawyers was that of residency or sojourn in a foreign country that had either outlawed slavery or declared it inoperable by virtue of a judicial decision. In the case of African-born slave James Somerset in England in 1772, Chief Justice Lord Mansfield of the Court of the King's Bench ruled slavery to be so odious that nothing could validly support it except "positive law." Since England bore no such law, the court declared Somerset, who was visiting England with his owner, to be free. Lord Mansfield later noted that the ruling did not emancipate slaves in England; rather, it provided them with legal redress against being removed from the country. In France, however, the assembly affirmed that any slave who trod on French soil thereby became free. This law was tested in the United States, especially in Louisiana, when a number of French Creoles and French-born immigrants returned to France with their servants during the 1830s and 1840s. In Mexico, the state of Coahuila y Tegas in 1827 adopted a constitution that proclaimed "no person shall be born a slave" hereafter—that is, after the publication and posting of the legislated document in each district—and after six months no slaves could be imported into the state. In general, only a few freedom suits based on foreign laws or judicial decisions were filed in the United States; in Missouri, for instance, several cases hinged on whether slavery had at any time been permitted by law in Canada.[49]

Numerous other arguments, most of them tangential or restricted in their applicability, were employed by slaves and their lawyers in freedom suits: the validity of master-slave contracts, for one. Most states had invalidated such contracts, but in a few—Delaware, Tennessee, and Louisiana—agreements between master and slave were found to be valid if they involved the subject of freedom. In isolated cases, too, in the District of Columbia, Virginia, and Kentucky, freedom contract suits—usually concerning African Americans who had purchased themselves or members of their families—were filed and found valid. And in 1842, a justice on the Tennessee Supreme Court, in a suit based on emancipation by will, ruled that slaves could not be deprived of certain rights: they could receive a bequest of freedom, they could receive an owner's personal or real property, and they could enter into a valid contract with their owner for their freedom.[50]

Most antebellum slaveholders would have taken exception to the Tennessee justice's declaration that slaves possessed certain rights. Slaves were property, after all; they were credited to be either real estate, literally, or chattel, tangible movable personal property. In matters of law they were referenced as things, except in criminal proceedings, where they were in fact recognized as persons. Slaves in the southern states possessed "few and humble rights," one

Kentucky judge lamented, while their owners were endowed with "all the rights, immunities and privileges which sovereignty can bestow." Among the rights that owners assumed regarding their property were those to will, deed, convey, trade, buy, sell, transfer, mortgage, and transport it. Indeed, the economy and wealth of the southern states was in large part built on and sustained by the appraised and market value of black people. Few doubted the hegemony of the slaveholding class over its human property. "By the laws of this state," a Maryland appeals court judge asserted, "a negro, so long as he is a slave, can have no rights adverse to his master; he can neither sue personally or by *prochain ami,* a 'next friend,' nor be sued, nor make a contract, nor acquire any rights under a deed, which either a court of law or equity can enforce." In short, black people were not only "proscribed by disabilities and disfranchisements" but were reduced in most circumstances to chattel.[51]

Still, slaves did possess some, narrowly defined rights. One key phrase in the Maryland judge's assertion qualifies the rights a slave does not have, as he "can have no rights adverse to his master." If an owner, in a will, deed, conveyance, bill of sale, surety bond, or other legal instrument, granted slaves their freedom, and if the slaves were not then duly released from bondage by heirs, executors, administrators, or others, they had the right—a right, plainly, not adverse to their master—in the Upper South and Louisiana to pursue a claim to freedom in a court of law or equity. In addition, the courts in every state refused to limit a slave's claim to freedom on the basis of laches (the doctrine that "stale" claims could not be litigated). Slave plaintiffs could thus bring their causes to court years or even decades after the date they believed they were supposed to have been freed.[52] If, therefore, term slaves had been held beyond the contracted period of service, or if children had been born of mothers who had remained thus enslaved, the mother and the children had the right to file freedom suits. Slaves also had other rights that might be adverse to the owner's wishes. Slaves brought into a state in violation of a nonimportation law had the right to lay claim to their freedom under statutes in several states and the District of Columbia. African Americans who resided in free territories or states or countries could, with their owner's consent, claim that they had a right to their freedom. "The property in slaves is not an absolute but a qualified property," another appeals judge commented on the issue of blacks who had been illegally imported into his state. Accordingly, the "coercive act" of an owner bringing slaves illegally into a state could not alter the rights of slaves in this regard.[53]

While certain rights did allow slaves to gain their freedom, free blacks in most southern states confronted a host of onerous laws restricting their movements and activities, including state laws denying them rights to enter a state, to gather with slaves, to own slaves except for family members, to establish churches and schools, to learn to read and write, to enter certain occupations, and to possess firearms, among others. In 1806, the Virginia Assembly enacted the first law stipulating that emancipated slaves could not remain in the commonwealth more than one year without obtaining permission from the legislature. "*And be it further enacted,*" the law stated, "That if any slave hereafter emancipated, shall remain within this commonwealth more than twelve months after his or her right to freedom shall have accrued, he or she shall forfeit all such right, and may be apprehended and sold by the overseers of the poor of any county or corporation, in which he or she shall be found, for the benefit of the poor of such county or corporation."

In subsequent years a number of other states—Alabama, Arkansas, Kentucky, North Carolina, Louisiana, Mississippi, Maryland, and Tennessee— enacted similar laws compelling freed African Americans to emigrate within specified time periods, ranging from immediately in Tennessee, to one month in Louisiana, to ninety days in North Carolina. These and other forced emigration laws underwent revision during the antebellum era. In 1850, for example, the Kentucky Constitution instructed the General Assembly to pass statutes that enacted as law the emigration of emancipated slaves from the state. Then, in 1851 and 1852, the assembly passed an act further requiring that freed blacks who failed or refused to leave be hired out for the benefit of the county until such time as they departed. The antiresidency laws usually allowed room for appeals, either through the courts or, more frequently, through state legislatures, but in either case the possibility of reenslavement clouded the lives of African Americans who had so recently acquired their freedom.[54]

In the minds of lawmakers, county judges, and appellate justices—most of whom were slaveholders—there was no contradiction between laws that forced freed blacks to leave a state and those that allowed illegally held slaves the right to sue for their freedom. Laws in the latter case were not so liberal as they might at first appear, in that the slaves' right to sue was in fact incidental to the rights of slaveholders to dispose of their human property as they wished. If executors refused to follow the emancipation dictates of a testator regarding slave property, laws in the Upper South and Louisiana as well as a few Lower South states permitted slaves in such cases to file freedom suits. If those currently in possession of the slaves refused to abide by a court order regarding a will, deed, or conveyance, they could be ordered to respond; if they attempted to remove the slaves from the courts' jurisdiction, they could be served with an injunction or an order to relinquish the slaves to the protective custody of the sheriff.

Slaves and their lawyers also had the right to appeal verdicts if they felt they had been denied their legal recourse. When lower courts ruled that slaves emancipated in a will could not contest the executor's decision in a probate court, slave plaintiffs were permitted to apply to chancery, or equity, courts. Although they were considered property, one Upper South appellate judge noted, the law recognized their personal existence, and, to a qualified extent, "their natural rights." "They may be emancipated by their owners; and must, of course, have a right to seek and enjoy the protection of the law in the establishment of all deeds, or wills, or other legal documents of emancipation; and, so far, they must be considered as natural persons, entitled to some legal rights, whenever their owners shall have declared, in a proper manner, that they shall, either *in presenti* or *in futuro*, be free."[55]

In 1846, a Maryland appeals court ruling mirrored decisions made across the Upper South and in Louisiana with regard to the rights of slaves when it came to the issue of freedom. While it was true that slaves possessed no civil rights and therefore could not institute a suit in a court of law or equity court except in cases concerning their freedom, they could, under certain circumstances, act as complainants and demand that the court order an executor, or some other party, to enforce the wishes of a master seeking to manumit his or her slaves after the payment of debts. The Maryland judge also noted that this principle was set forth by the US Supreme Court, in the 1835 case of *Fenwick v. Chapman*: slaves must be regarded as "capacitated for the purpose" of seeking their freedom as promised in a will or deed of manumission.[56] Of course, in many Lower South states, emancipation could be achieved only by obtaining a special act from the General Assembly; as a consequence, except in Louisiana, blacks filed only a few freedom suits.[57]

During the 1850s, among the most tumultuous decades in American history, new laws regarding people of color in various southern states reflected the fear and anxiety of many slaveholders toward free blacks. Six states passed statutes whereby free blacks could petition the courts and legislatures to become slaves. The first of these, passed in Virginia in 1856, provided a blueprint "for the voluntary enslavement of the free negroes." Any free persons of color—men, at least twenty-one years of age; women, eighteen—who were residents of the state could choose a master and enter slavery by submitting to the circuit court a petition that explained their wishes to be reduced to bondage. Two witnesses had to be present at the filing. The clerk of court then posted the request on the front door of the courthouse, where it served notice for one month prior to the proceedings. After thirty days the parties were called into court and examined in the presence of an attorney for the commonwealth to ensure that no injustice had been done to the petitioner. If no "fraud or collusion" was evident, the court then ordered that the free black person's value as a slave be appraised and that the prospective master post a bond "as the court shall prescribe" to prevent the black person from being a charge to the county. That done, the black person would become a slave, as if he or she had been born into that condition, and the proceedings would be entered into the court record. The children of free women of color who filed such petitions would "not be deemed to be reduced to slavery by such proceeding." Although few free blacks would file self-enslavement petitions, the fact of the statutes themselves was testament to the growing fear of free African Americans in the southern states and the mounting sectional conflict in the nation.[58]

In 1857, in the *Dred Scott* decision, Chief Justice Roger Taney of the US Supreme Court ruled that slaves had no rights that whites were bound by law to respect, including the right to sue for freedom, no matter what the circumstances. Nonetheless, even after this decision slaves continued to file freedom suits. In Kentucky, a large group of slaves who were to be freed under a will recorded in 1849 argued with their lawyer that the state's 1850 constitution and 1851 law requiring freed slaves to leave the state should not be applicable to their case. The chancery court judge agreed; he decreed that the slaves should be freed and that they could remain in Kentucky. "Indeed, although Africans are not parties to our political compact, we cannot suppose our [Constitutional] Convention could have been so unjust as to have disregarded any rights vested according to law or equity in a negro or a white man. The First section expressly preserved 'all rights' and 'claims, &c,' prior to its enactment as if the Constitution had not been adopted." This included the rights of slaves to seek their freedom.[59]

In 1853, an Arkansas slaveowner provided for the freedom of his nineteen slaves in Louisiana and Arkansas, or elsewhere, after seven years. He appointed his nephew to attend to the matter of the slaves' release from bondage. Following the owner's death, the slaves filed a petition for freedom, but the Arkansas Acts of 1859 prohibited further emancipations. However, Justice Hulbert Fairchild of the Arkansas Supreme Court, in a lengthy opinion, reasoned that the 1859 law should not affect instruments of emancipation made before the act, even if the emancipation was not to be completed until after its passage. The gift of freedom should be determined "solely upon its legal merits without partiality to an applicant because he or she may be defenseless and of an inferior race." Although the court ruled that the case was "prematurely brought," the opinion was issued without prejudice to "the rights of the plaintiffs to institute such further legal proceedings as they may be advised may be necessary to secure their rights."[60]

Louisiana had passed a law prohibiting emancipations in 1857, but Judge Henry Spofford stated in his opinion that a freedom suit initiated by a woman illegally held in bondage could "not destroy her vested rights."[61] Between 1857 and 1863, similar freedom suits were filed in ten southern states, including six in states of the Lower South, and the District of Columbia. Even near the onset of the Civil War, and during it, white southerners still attached relevance to the rule of law in matters of slavery and freedom.[62]

How did Polly Anderson and the other Anderson slaves freed in the will of Jordan Anderson Sr. fare in their quest for freedom? Like other blacks freed in wills, their experience extended over many years. In 1837, the year after Polly

Anderson presented her petition to the chancery court, four other slaves once owned by Jordan Anderson Sr.— Milly, Isbell, Esther, and Betty—also sued for their freedom. They charged that they were being illegally held in bondage by Anderson's son, Jordan Anderson Jr. Acknowledging that they were to remain Anderson Jr.'s property until Anderson Sr.'s widow died, provided they had reached age twenty-one, the four women pointed out that the widow had long been dead and not only were they all over twenty-one but so were their children. They requested the court for permission to sue Anderson Jr. *in forma pauperis;* they asked further to be provided with protection against possible "maltreatment and abuse" and afforded "a fair trial of their claim to freedom."[63] Two decades later, twenty-two descendants of "the Negro woman" Rachel, who had been freed under the same 1805 will, likewise sued for their freedom. They too asserted that they had been detained illegally in slavery by Jordan Anderson Jr. during his lifetime, and now, since his death, they were being detained illegally by Wilkins Hall, the executor of Anderson Jr.'s estate. The plaintiffs included slaves who claimed to be free either by the terms of the will itself or by virtue of their mothers' freedom at the time of their birth. Like the Anderson slave litigants and kin who preceded them, they asked the court to protect them from maltreatment and abuse and "to afford them a fair trial of their claim to freedom." It took many years, but in time Polly Anderson as well as the plaintiffs Milly, Isbell, Esther, and Betty, and ultimately all of Rachel's twenty-two descendants, won their freedom.[64]

3

Slave Plaintiffs and the Courts

In October 1851, Francis or Frank Jackson, "a coloured man," and his lawyer filed suit in the Superior Court of Law and Chancery, Campbell County, Virginia. They asserted that Jackson was born of free parents in Pennsylvania but had been "decoyed" into Virginia twelve or eighteen months earlier, when a horse dealer named Charles May had hired him as a drover. On their arrival in Virginia, May had sold Jackson as a slave to Samuel Scott. Five feet, eight or nine inches tall, stout, and "tolerably dark," Jackson "talked a great deal," according to one observer, "loud and fast." He had lost the end of one of his fingers down to the first joint.

In the months following his enslavement, Jackson had struggled to regain his freedom. On several occasions he had run away, only to be captured, jailed, and returned to his alleged owner. On one escape, into Botetourt County, with the assistance of some white residents there, he had filed a freedom suit, but Scott had posted bond and retrieved him from the county jail. After another escape, capture, and jailing, Jackson had been sold in August 1851 to a speculator, John W. Deshazer. He had taken Jackson to Richmond, where he advertised him for sale, but with no success. With no buyers forthcoming, he had then sent Jackson by boat to Lynchburg, there to be turned over to one Seth Woodroof. However, the captain of the boat had ordered Jackson himself to go find Woodroof when they moored in Lynchburg. Again Jackson had absconded. He was arrested near New London, only thirteen miles distant, and transported to the Campbell County jail.

In less than a year and a half, Francis Jackson had experienced firsthand the struggles facing free blacks illegally held as slaves in the Old South. Sold and resold, jailed and rejailed, Jackson strove repeatedly to tell his unfortunate story, twice in the form of freedom suits. With the case in Botetourt County still pending, and after several more failed escapes, Jackson and his lawyer again brought forward his claim, this time in the Campbell County Chancery Court. By then Jackson had learned how readily owners could post bond and retrieve their human property from jail; he knew how lawyers often swore an oath stating their belief that a suit had merit. He knew, too, how extremely difficult it was for them, however sincere their commitment, to garner evidence that would satisfactorily prove a black man's free status. During the time Jackson had been held at Jones's Negro Jail in Richmond, a white man, a resident of the city, took an interest in his case. He sympathized with Jackson in his plight, and he appeared to be disposed to providing assistance. Only now, months later, with Jackson in a county jailhouse more than a hundred miles away, it would be near impossible for the man to aid Jackson's counsel in gathering the necessary proof, were he still willing to invest the time and effort the task would require.[1]

In a prodigious two-volume study, *Commentaries on Equity Jurisprudence as Administered in England and America* (1836), Joseph Story, an associate justice of the US Supreme Court, wrote extensively about courts of law and courts of equity. In comparing the two court systems, he noted that both were "equally bound, and equally profess, to interpret statutes according to the true intent of the Legislature." Both courts, too, arrived at their decisions by reference to principles on which former cases had been decided, thus constantly adding to the "old jurisprudence" by enlarging, illustrating, and applying new doctrines and maxims.[2] Common law courts, however, operated under clearly defined restrictions. For one, they could not effect certain types of remedy, especially if mutual rights and the relative situations of a number of parties were involved. For another, law courts proceeded to trial with evidence that was generally drawn, not from the parties themselves, but from third persons—disinterested witnesses—and that was presented before juries. Law courts assigned limits to the exercise of their remedies, Story concluded, "far short of the principles deducible *ex aequo et bono* [equity and justice]."

Equity courts, by contrast, interpreted statutes broadly, and they could modify their opinions to meet exigencies. They could qualify, restrain, and model a remedy so that it appertained to different claimants; or they could adjust remedies so as to fit all the parties involved. To effect such remedies, equity judges, on whose decisions these cases rested, possessed authority not available in courts of law: They could issue temporary or permanent injunctions to prevent future wrongs (as opposed to granting redress only after the wrong had occurred). They could permit amended bills of complaint when new evidence surfaced. They could require defendants to answer complaints under oath, accept testimony from individuals primary to a case, and adapt their judgments to meet the rights of all the concerned parties. They prohibited laches (unreasonable delays), which were deemed acceptable only "in cases of where it is positively declared at law." In short, equity courts differed from law courts in "modes of proof, of trial, and of relief."[3]

One year following publication of Justice Story's *Commentaries*, Jacob D. Wheeler, a counselor at law, published *A Practical Treatise on the Law of Slavery*, which focused on state appellate decisions and opinions of the US Supreme Court. In a chapter titled "Of Suits for Freedom," Wheeler included discussions of actions, evidence, damages, and judgments in the execution of freedom suits. The cases could be brought in either equity or law courts, depending on the state, he wrote, and there was "no legal distinction between the assertion of a claim for freedom, and any other right." For plaintiffs who claimed they were illegally held as slaves, the evidence presented at trial should be treated the same as it would be in any other rights case. In Tennessee, where an action of trespass and false imprisonment could be brought, female slaves could file a joint action with their children, and evidence of reputation was admissible for plaintiffs claiming descent from Indian ancestors. In Virginia, plaintiffs could file suit as a pauper, and hearsay evidence was admissible to prove pedigree. In Louisiana, dark-colored plaintiffs who filed suit were presumed to be slaves, whereas light-colored persons were deemed to be free and the burden of proof to the contrary fell on the defendant. In other states, children of freed mothers could submit evidence that established their mothers' free status. In most states, damages for being held illegally in bondage would not be considered in cases where an owner believed the plaintiff was in fact his slave. Generally, the court could issue protective judgments for plaintiffs who feared being "carried out of the state."[4]

Although Story's theoretical *Commentaries* and Wheeler's *Treatise* captured important features of the court systems in the South during the antebellum era, they failed to reflect the bewildering complexity that attended the filing of freedom suits by slaves, or those deemed to be slaves. In fact, Story did not even mention such suits in his lengthy analysis of the equity, or chancery, courts, and Wheeler merely summarized a few dozen appellate cases. In both studies, what actually occurred in the law and equity courts was only scantily considered; how the courts functioned in freedom-suit cases, and how differently they functioned in different sections of the South, were ignored. Not all equity cases were heard without juries, as Story suggested, and not all common law cases were tried with juries, as one might infer from Wheeler's discussion of "actions" brought by African Americans. Neither Story nor Wheeler did more than scratch the surface of the court systems that confronted lawyers and their slave clients. Nor did either of them demonstrate how the systems functioned in practice, how they changed over time, and how the courts dealt with the fundamental human rights of slaves.

In some states, and especially in Virginia and Missouri, slave plaintiffs initiated their freedom suits with a request for permission to sue. As one appeals court judge noted, though, the leave to sue was a benefit intended for the plaintiff, and it could be waived.[5] For slave plaintiffs and their lawyers, then, the first order of business was to decide which court would offer an appropriate venue for their filing of the freedom suit. Should they choose a law court, as the common law courts were called, or a chancery, or equity, court? In the law courts judges based their decisions on custom and usage and on previous judicial decisions, while in chancery courts they relied primarily on statute law. In either court, plaintiffs and/or defendants could demand a jury trial, the inclusion of interrogatories (written questions) as well as depositions and/or testimony from witnesses, and the right to appeal.

Although in most states of the Upper South and Louisiana suits for freedom could be instituted without the leave of the court, lawyers often requested such leave, whereby either the lawyer or his client swore an oath stating that the facts presented in their opening petition were true.[6] In a few states, particularly in the Lower South, the law required that a white person, such as a guardian, file on behalf of a slave; Tennessee law prescribed that slave plaintiffs bring suit with what was called a "Near Friend," or "next friend"—usually a white person but on occasion, and permissibly, a free black. In both law and chancery courts, as the proceedings unfolded, judges could order owners to allow slave complainants to appear in court, to grant them "reasonable time" for consultation with their counsel, and to clothe, feed, and treat them well during the pendency of the suit. Owners were sometimes required to post bonds to this effect.[7] In both courts, the judge also had the authority to issue orders by which the sale of a plaintiff could be halted or the alleged slave could be placed in protective custody.[8] Many plaintiffs in both courts actively sought such protection because they feared, not unrealistically, that they might be transported out of the court's jurisdiction and separated from their families, friends, and loved ones.[9]

Chancery courts and common law courts bore other similarities as well. In a number of states, notably in Virginia, Kentucky, and Missouri, both courts permitted slave plaintiffs to sue *in forma pauperis*. Following the initial plea or petition by the plaintiff, the clerk of the court would issue a summons directing the sheriff to notify the defendant of the accusations, which required his appearance in court. After the sheriff had located the defendant and read the summons, he would return the document to the clerk with a notation that it had been served. In both courts, even prior to the beginning of the trial a judge could grant continuances from one session to the next if either party signed an affidavit explaining the need for more time to summon witnesses, obtain pertinent documents, or respond to charges and register countercharges. In both courts, too, before the trial began the defendant could file a *demurrer*, a claim that the plaintiff's arguments were insufficient at law. Both courts, with but a few exceptions, allowed slave plaintiffs and their lawyers as well as defendants to challenge potential jurors and request that they be excused.[10] Following the arguments, and sometimes after a number of continuances, juries delivered verdicts and judges issued decrees. Other authority common to both courts included the abilities to impanel a jury, and to instruct it; to set penalties for failure to appear; to declare nonsuits, mistrials, dismissals, and abatements; to rule on requests for a new trial; and to act on appeals.[11]

Judges in both common law and equity courts had the authority to declare a hung jury, as when the twelve jurors failed, after consideration of the evidence and due deliberation, to agree on a verdict. It took only one intransigent juror to effect a mistrial, which was the circumstance in a District of Columbia case brought by a slave plaintiff, Clara, against owner Dr. Thomas Ewell in 1820. Clara accused Ewell of seizing her and her five children while her freedom suit, in which he was also named the defendant, was being adjudicated in the circuit court. She worried that her children were "almost all small & helpless," and like many other slave plaintiffs, she feared that her master planned to "sell them away to distant places" before her freedom suit had been resolved. The case went to the jury several times, but to no avail. The panel was unable to reach a verdict, and the judge declared a mistrial.[12]

Other cases in both types of courts sometimes ended with a default judgment for one side or the other—when, for instance, the defendant submitted a successful demurrer, or if the defendant's failure to appear resulted in a case's dismissal. A default could also be ordered if either side failed to comply with the court's instructions or if the parties mutually reached an agreement. Defaults might be prompted, too, by such circumstances as misconduct on the part of a lawyer or a juror, suppression of evidence, errors in submission of evidence, the absence of witnesses, a request for a change of venue, a verdict against the law or evidence, the setting aside of a verdict, and acceptance of a motion for a new trial.

Most slave plaintiffs and their lawyers did understand the significant differences between the two court systems with regard to procedures, arguments, testimony, and judgments. Law courts required the submission of a declaration or narrative that included, in some combination, trespass, be it trespass with force of arms or trespass in the form of ravishment, assault and battery, and false imprisonment. An action of trespass was a personal tort, a civil wrong for which the plaintiff could seek a remedy. Since most plaintiffs who filed freedom suits in law courts sought damages from the defendant, the issue of an individual's freedom was superseded by that of the slave owner's alleged commission of a civil wrong against a free person. This emphasis of the common law process on charging the defendant for a civil wrong more often than not hindered groups of slaves or members of African American families from jointly filing a complaint.[13] Nor did law courts accommodate plaintiffs whose freedom suits relied heavily on the matters of wills, deeds, indentures, bills of sale, contracts of term servitude, and agreements made between master and slave, either in writing or orally.[14] In law courts, too, slave plaintiffs and their lawyers found it difficult to introduce as proof freedom at birth, manumission in the distant past, or descent from the free female ancestor.[15]

Thus, although slave plaintiffs might bring any number of different charges against the defendants, all of their cases alleged some form of trespass. Several states in the Lower South, including Georgia, Florida, Arkansas, and South Carolina, mandated that freedom suits be initiated in the common law courts. Some further required that the action be brought by white guardians.[16] In Delaware, following a successful freedom suit in a chancery, or equity, court, a black plaintiff could bring "trespass and false imprisonment, or any other action in the law," against a pretended master or mistress in common law court to cover the chancery court costs previously incurred.[17] In Missouri, a territorial statute, codified in 1824, dictated that freedom suits originate in the common law courts.[18]

A number of slave plaintiffs and their counsel filed complaints about the strict rules imposed on them by common law courts. In their arguments they employed the same language as that in the statute, saying that they were "remediless in the premises, by the Strict rules of common law,"[19] or "In as much as your oratrix is remediless in the premises at law and can only have redress in a Court of Equity."[20] One mother and her children who filed a freedom suit "on the common law side of this Court," as she said, lamented that she was "remediless and by the strict rules of the common law." She and her children found a remedy sometime later, after filing papers in the equity court where, as her lawyer noted, matters of freedom were "properly cognizable."[21]

A Kentucky court of appeals judge made much the same point in reference to another case: Judy and her children could not file "a joint action in a law court for personal and individual injuries, or for the assertion of personal and individual rights."[22] A few states attempted to mitigate these strict rules by allowing family members or their descendants or other groups of slaves to jointly file freedom suits. In 1820, a Virginia law stated that when freedom suits were brought in law courts by "one person for himself and others who are infants," the declaration of trespass should be considered informal and a single suit including many plaintiffs should satisfy the court. Such laws were rare, however, and even in Virginia, the letter of the 1820 law did not guarantee the enforcement of it.[23]

Often, blacks and their lawyers moved their cases to a chancery court when their attempts to acquire free status in a law court failed.[24] Even then, relying on the trespass writ alone by showing how slave plaintiffs had been illegally held in bondage, or unjustly confined in a county or private jail, or wrongly held by a justice of the peace, also frequently resulted in failure.[25] Still other plaintiffs and their lawyers took their cases to both the law and the equity courts to prove free status. Such efforts entailed often frustrating legal maneuvering over lengthy periods of time, and in the end success could prove to be elusive—due, in part, to the concerns and procedures of two distinctly different courts and, in no less part, to the determination of owners to retain control over their human property.

Perhaps no person understood the frustration better than the Maryland slave Isaac, who was imported into Virginia in the mid-1790s. In 1797, having resided in Virginia for more than twelve months, and therefore, by virtue of the state's anti-importation statute, being entitled to his freedom, he filed suit to that end in the Common Law Court of Campbell County, Virginia. Despite the strength of his argument—that he had been imported into the state in violation of the law— the suit ended with a hung jury. Two years later, Isaac and his lawyer again sued in the same court, and again they failed. The defendant argued that slaves had no right to sue their owners, and the jury evidently agreed—it found for the defendant. The owner then sold Isaac to Thomas Johnson. Again suffering enslavement, this time for more than a decade, Isaac again filed a suit, his third, in the Hustings Court of the Corporation of Lynchburg, from which it was later moved on certiorari ("to be more fully informed") to the chancery Superior Court of Campbell County for judicial review. The bill was dismissed. In 1812, Isaac filed his fourth suit, this one in the chancery court, but the court ordered a new trial at law. Finally, in 1815, in a fifth suit, a jury on the law side of the court found that "the pauper Isaac" was not a slave but a free man—except the defendant appealed to the superior court of chancery and the decree was reversed. The case was then appealed at the Supreme Court of Virginia, and the reversal was reversed. In 1816, nineteen years after filing his first plea, Isaac won his freedom.[26]

Cases like Isaac's demonstrate that law courts could and did at times rule in favor of slave plaintiffs. Usually, such cases rested on judicial precedent, but they also cited statute laws.[27] The mulatto slave Lucy and her lawyer sued on the law side of the Circuit Court of the District of Columbia in 1807, charging "trespass, for assault and battery and false imprisonment" as well as citing a violation of the Virginia anti-importation law (the District of Columbia accepted the laws of both Virginia and Maryland). The court ruled in favor of Lucy because the defendant had failed within sixty days of the importation, as was required by law, to sign an oath affirming that he had not brought slaves into the District of Columbia for the purpose of sale.[28] In South Carolina, a slave and her white guardian charged a slave owner with an action of trespass "in nature of ravishment of a ward." Phebe had been transported from Baltimore into South Carolina, and into slavery, at the age of twelve in 1806. In her suit, Phebe claimed she was the daughter of a free woman of color, and the evidence supported the claim. Ten years after her arrival, in 1816, a jury not only ruled in her favor but also awarded her $400 in damages for wrongful detention.[29]

After trespass in its various forms, the most common writ sought by persons allegedly being illegally held in captivity, especially free blacks claiming false enslavement, was the writ of habeas corpus, which had twelfth-century origins in English common law and had been codified in England since 1679. At first glance it might appear that bringing owners or slaves before the court to determine whether or not a slave was being illegally held could, in itself, provide access to free status, but in fact it was only a first step in the process. Free persons of color who had been arrested as runaways, jailed for not having proper freedom papers, or illegally retained in bondage by slaveholders took advantage of habeas corpus.[30] The writ afforded free persons of color their most important weapon against the whites holding them in captivity.

Thus, in the unlawful detainment case of Margaret Dorsey, was the marshal in the District of Columbia ordered to produce her in body in a City of Washington court, or otherwise face a court penalty: "To the Marshal of the District of Columbia—Greeting You are hereby Commanded to have the body of Margaret Dorsey [a free women of color], detained in your custody, as it is said, together with the cause of her Capture and detention before the Hon. William Cranch immediately, in his chambers in the City Hall in the City of Washington, to do, receive & submit to, what may be then and there considered of her in the premises."[31] Free black apprentices also availed themselves of the writ, sometimes with success.[32] In fact, habeas corpus could free a person only by the presentation of overwhelming evidence that established conclusively the person's free status, either by court decree or legislative act or by residence in a free foreign country. Two white witnesses, one from the island of Santiago and the other from the Cape de Verde islands, confirmed that four men enslaved in Virginia were in actuality free persons of color. On appeal, Henry St. George Tucker admitted that in the absence of legal documentation to the effect, a writ of habeas corpus was not the proper remedy for trying the right of the four men to freedom, but without it, he conceded, they were "altogether without protection from the grossest outrages" against their personal liberty. He upheld the writ and granted them their freedom.[33]

Most slave plaintiffs who sought a writ of habeas corpus did not fare as well. Law courts virtually invariably ruled that the writ in itself did not sufficiently support a slave's claim to freedom. In Georgia in 1831, an appellate court judge explained that although slaves were not without "many personal rights secured to them by law," they were "without the right of personal liberty"; therefore, as the writ of habeas corpus was designed to protect the personal liberty of an individual, it could not be applied to persons who did not enjoy personal liberty.[34] Other courts agreed that the writ was not applicable to freedom suits, although their rulings did not include assertions like the Georgia judge's about the "many personal rights" of slaves. An Alabama court ruled that slave owners were entitled to have their rights adjudicated according to statute—and not by a common law writ.[35] The Florida Supreme Court overruled a lower court decision granting freedom to the slave Dick, who had obtained a writ of habeas corpus on the claim that his mother was white. While the case for Dick's release from slavery afforded a "fair subject of controversy," the judge contended, the writ of habeas corpus was not the appropriate remedy.[36]

A Kentucky appellate judge concurred in principle: The writ of habeas corpus was not an appropriate proceeding for the trial of the right to freedom, because "the writ may be brought ex parte, intended for the benefit of a single person, and carried on without the knowledge of the persons directly interested in the decision."[37] In 1817, the three judges on the Tennessee Supreme Court ruled in a similar fashion. Although the plaintiff's olive complexion and straight black hair raised a presumption in her favor, the writ of habeas corpus could not, by the court's reasoning, be deemed to be a final decree for her freedom. Consequently, if she feared being sold or removed by her owner, a judge could issue an order for the sheriff to hold her in his custody. If she desired attestation on her behalf, she and her lawyer could obtain a security bond and "go in search of testimony." The correct remedy, said the court, was to file a bill of complaint in an equity court. The judge ordered Rebecca Renney, the complainant, to be held in custody "until a fair trial by a Jury could be had."[38] Every other southern state agreed with this argument and decision.[39]

On rare occasions, law courts issued other writs in connection with freedom suits, among them *de homine replegiando* (to replevy, or release, a man out of prison, or the custody of a private person); ejectment, whereby a number of persons could seek a joint right to land (or freedom); *capias ad audiendum judicium* (a writ issued by the court to the sheriff to force a defendant to appear); and fieri facias, which directed a sheriff to seize the goods or property—including slave property—of someone against whom a judgment had been rendered.[40] Even more infrequent, and in some ways more remarkable, was the effort of slaves and their lawyers to institute common law suits of trespass *vi et armis* ("with force and arms"), which charged owners with intentional injury to their person by violence; it was also called trespass on an individual by an illegal assault, battery, wounding, or imprisonment. As with habeas corpus, unless the petitioner was a free person of color, such cases were usually dismissed.[41]

In chancery or equity courts, a number of plaintiffs could jointly file a single complaint, as, for example, the recipients of freedom in a master's last will and testament, in a deed of manumission, or in a bill of sale granting emancipation at a future date. An article in the *American Jurist and Law Magazine* in 1829 asserted that equity courts provided "extraordinary" remedies for aggrieved parties by examining witnesses under oath, accepting petitions and responses from plaintiffs and defendants alike, and rendering decisions on such property matters as trusts, wills, deeds, distributions, partners in trade, ownership, and contracts. Equity courts could adjust their decrees to "all the varieties of circumstances," whereas common law courts, as Supreme Court justice Joseph

Story observed, were bound by fixed and absolute judgments, either for the plaintiff or for the defendant. So it was that over time, except in a few states, slave plaintiffs and their lawyers increasingly more often filed freedom suits in equity courts.[42]

A case in point involved Hannah and her son Robert, who, under terms stated in the will of Kentucky slave owner Lee White, were to be freed twelve months after his death, if they chose to go to Liberia. However, White had purchased Hannah and Robert from one John Jones only a short time before his death, and Jones's siblings, claiming title to the slaves under their mother Alice Jones's will, sued White's executors. In the end the White and Jones families reached an agreement, which did not free Hannah and her son. Thereupon Hannah, with the assistance of William S. Pilcher, sued for her freedom on charges that the White-Jones compromise defrauded her and Robert and her other children of their legally granted rights and that the damages to be paid to the defendants, White's executors, would deplete the funds designated by White's will for their transportation to Liberia. At that point, Hannah and her children were seized under a writ of habeas corpus. The court ordered a trial for Hannah, but her children were forced to sue separately in the common law court. In the midst of this ordeal Hannah died, and the case was taken up as a reviver plea in the chancery court. There Hannah's children won their freedom.[43]

Slaves and their counsel understood the benefits of filing papers in chancery when there were several charges to be adjudicated. Although witnesses could of course be deposed in both courts, the depositions later to be read at trial, testimony in the chancery courts could more readily bring into focus the numerous related issues and aggravating circumstances in the case. Also, equity courts relied primarily on state laws to determine outcomes, although legal precedent too was important. Not only could equity courts be more flexible than law courts in their procedures and application of rules, but also, unlike law courts, they could issue injunctions to compel persons to perform certain prescribed actions or to prevent them from doing so.[44]

In equity court, the initial bill of complaint—or bill of equity or bill in chancery, as such petitions were variously called—was likely to be considerably more comprehensive than a simple declaration of trespass, as it often included a broad range of issues to be addressed, rather than a strictly defined set of topics, as in courts of common law. Equity courts, too, allowed plaintiffs and their lawyers to submit cross-bills, amended bills, or supplementary petitions that might add new parties to the list of defendants or revise information in the original petition. Further, defendants, or respondents, as well as having the right to demur, could file cross-bills against any or all of the complainants, or against any or all of the co-respondents.

Cross-bills enabled defendants not only to answer a complaint but also to seek relief. Such procedures ensured that all parties to a suit would be fully heard and as much information as possible would be gathered for presentation to the court. Moreover, a chancery court judge could appoint a master in chancery, or commissioner, to deal with estate matters and emancipation. On the master's recommendation, for instance, the court might order an owner's sale of land instead of his selling slaves who were to be emancipated. Masters reported back to the court, sometimes over several terms or even years. In addition, the chancery court could rule on the validity of wills, which in some states required a trial by jury, or on the sanity or insanity of a testator. If one of the litigants or defendants in a chancery case died, the court could suspend the proceedings and restore the suit with "a bill of revivor."[45]

In Louisiana—a state exceptional in so many aspects of its history—the court system differed from the judiciary in every other southern state. Its civil law derived from Roman statute law as it evolved over centuries in continental Europe, especially in France, Spain, and Italy, as opposed to the common law of England, which based its judiciary process on custom and the decisions of judges. The civil law system in Louisiana differed from others in the South, too, with regard to division of property, elements of ownership, effects of mortgages, and the unlawful and intentional harm of others in the form of delicts (in French, *délits*), or torts. In that Louisiana's civil courts adhered to statute law in such matters, they did bear similarities to chancery courts in other states and, like them, strove to uncover equity in causes of slavery and freedom.[46]

Nothing points up the contrast between the law and chancery court systems in the southern states (excepting Louisiana) more emphatically than the "bill of complainant" in chancery suits and the declaration or narrative of trespass in common law. The petitions submitted by plaintiffs in common law freedom suits were brief, their focus usually a single issue. The pleas in equity, on the other hand, were often lengthy and complex, with pages of information about slave family backgrounds, and about when and where forebears, parents, siblings, cousins, and children had been bought and sold—all to show how, by their place of birth or status at birth, or by deeds of manumission or last will and testaments, or by violation of anti–slave importation laws, they, the African American petitioners, should be free.[47] They and their lawyers sometimes also showed how their particular situation, in the settlement of an estate, for instance, might be regarded under the laws in other states, as well as their own.

They might have found an example in William, a man of color in Tennessee, who sued for his freedom when the widow of his deceased owner refused to honor the emancipation granted him in the owner's last will and testament. William and his counsel cited the Tennessee Act of 1842, which allowed manumitted slaves "the right to future freedom" and the right to remain in the state following a request to the county court. William, like numerous others who found themselves in the same circumstance, secured white witnesses to testify on his behalf regarding the truthfulness of his complaint.[48] After an estate was probated, if it became clear that available funds were insufficient to satisfy creditors, the chancery courts could, and commonly did, order that manumitted slaves be hired out to balance the estate's finances or that other property be sold so that slaves could be set free in accord with the wishes of the deceased. Thus, the equity courts, relying on their state laws, had a much broader purview by which to grant slaves their freedom than the law courts did.[49]

One of the most effective tools available to slave plaintiffs in chancery courts was the injunction. Common law courts could issue orders, but injunctions were more far-reaching and potent. In essence, an injunction was a court order commanding or preventing an action, but it could be framed to accommodate the special circumstances of a case, thereby commanding "an act which the court regards as essential to justice, or restraining an act which it esteems contrary to equity and good conscience."[50] Requisite to the granting of an injunction was the court's confidence beforehand that the arguments presented in the bill of complaint had merit and that documentary evidence in their support could be produced at trial. In some states, slaves themselves signed their "X" on an affidavit, or oath, to confirm the facts presented in the case.[51]

As such, the oath served as a form of slave testimony. On other occasions lawyers and "next friends" verified the information. Injunctions were particularly valuable to slave plaintiffs who more often than not found it necessary to seek protection for their children or other family members before and during a trial. In their pleas for injunctions, plaintiffs in the Upper South frequently expressed fear that before their case reached the court they or their loved ones would be taken away to "the Carolinas and Georgia"—or even farther, to the Southwest— and be lost forever. Injunctions provided plaintiffs one sure means of preventing owners, buyers, traders, and any other opportunists from transporting them to distant locations before their case could be adjudicated. In their wording the injunctions threatened owners who failed to respond accordingly that they did so at their own peril.[52]

It is difficult to know how many injunctions in fact spared slave litigants a place in the coffles moving relentlessly across the South, but injunctions sought in freedom suits were for the most part granted. Complainants requested that defendants or their "agents or abettors" be forbidden from selling or removing them beyond the reach of the court and be "prohibited and strictly enjoined" from "anywise intermeddling with them or any of them," until the future order and decree of the court.[53] Injunctions not only prevented the sale of slaves; they also compelled slave owners to allow more time for a freedom suit to be adjudicated. For Clara and her two sons, however, any injunctive device came too late. The boys were taken from her in Alexandria, Virginia, and sold, while she herself ended up with her daughter in Louisville, Kentucky. It was there, in the Jefferson County Chancery Court, that she gained the necessary protection for her and her daughter. The court enjoined William Taylor, Charles Taylor, and Worden Pope "and all other persons be restrained from selling or sending away out of this County either of the Complainants until final hearing and decree."[54]

Injunctions, then, could effectively order a defendant or groups of defendants to desist in any effort to keep plaintiffs in bondage, sell them, or transport them out of the court's jurisdiction. They could also serve as a precursor to the issuance of a writ of fieri facias (also available in common law), which directed the sheriff to place slaves in the county jail in order to provide them with protective custody, until such time that the chancery court could hire them out for the duration of the period of litigation. A judge in Jefferson County, Kentucky, for example, ordered that a slave plaintiff be turned over to the marshal and then be hired out to some "fit and discreet person." The hirer, in turn, had to post a bond so as to ensure that he would treat the plaintiff humanely, would not send or employ him outside the district, would supply him comfortable and suitable clothing, would provide medical care if necessary, would allow him time to confer with his lawyer, and would guarantee his appearance in court for the trial.[55]

In response to the petition of a term slave who feared she would be sold into bondage for life, Judge William Cranch, a five-decade veteran of the Circuit Court of the District of Columbia, issued both an injunction prohibiting Henry Drain "from selling or transporting, or causing to be transported," a slave woman out of the District and a writ of fieri facias placing the petitioner under the protective custody of the sheriff. The court acted despite the fact that the black woman had not yet completed her term of servitude.[56] Judge Cranch believed

Construction of the Jefferson County courthouse in Louisville began in 1836 and was only partly finished five years later when the city and county government offices, including the county court, took up residency. A number of slaves entered this building with their lawyers to prosecute freedom suits. *Lewis Collins and Richard H. Collins, History of Kentucky, 2 vols. (Covington, Kentucky: Collins & Co, 1878), vol. 2*

that as freedom suits possessed "little or no analogy to an action at common law," they should not be subject to "the technical rules of pleading." Furthermore, an enslaved person seeking his or her freedom, he opined, was "a person prima facie incompetent to maintain an action at law." Freedom suits were essentially summary proceedings, in Cranch's estimation, and therefore should be framed in the simplest terms possible: that is, whether the complainant was a free person held in slavery by another person. The trial to determine this "simple fact" should, said Cranch, be decided by the equity court judge or jury or both; for, by so doing, it would not "suffer the merits of the case to be smothered in the technicalities of special pleading."[57]

Although Judge Cranch's criticism of the "technicalities of special pleading" on the law side of southern courts was not without merit, the cases that evolved in the equity courts did more than decide the "simple fact" of slavery or freedom. Indeed, as Judge Cranch readily knew, the chancery courts also dealt with cases involving contracts of term servitude and indenture, as well as wills and deeds, granting designated blacks their freedom at some future date. If the circumstances warranted, the injunction could be made perpetual. Injunctions could also be issued against estate executors, administrators, and the relatives of former slave owners when plaintiffs and their lawyers argued free status on the basis of a last will and testament.

Grace and her guardian requested an injunction from the equity court in Charleston, South Carolina, in 1817 to restrain the administrator of her late owner James Ryan's estate "from and against Selling and disposing of your Oratrix." For many years Grace had served as her former owner's nurse and "most Confidential Servant," and in his will he had set her free.[58] Not a few slave plaintiffs and their counsel found themselves "remediless" in common law court—as did husband and wife Lewis and Charity Gassaway and their lawyer, James Mandeville Carlisle, in the District of Columbia—and on that claim applied to the chancery court for a protective injunction. Not just husbands and wives, but entire families, including those whose members were being held by a various owners, could seek security by requesting injunctions. Overall, chancery courts had far greater latitude than law courts in issuing injunctions that addressed the varying circumstances in freedom suits, and could thus usually provide at least a measure of security during the pendency of a trial.[59]

A number of term slaves in the Upper South sought injunctions in chancery courts to prevent their sale, or the sale of their children, before and after their term expired.[60] In one such case, a group of Maryland term slaves, including a mother and her infant son, claimed that they were "entitled to their freedom at their respective ages of thirty one years"; however, they were currently in the possession of two white men who, they believed, had recently sold them. The buyer, they feared, was planning to take them out of the state, in violation of state laws regulating term slavery.[61] Unquestionably, the surest avenue to free status for many African Americans—if their claims lay in a will, or indenture, or deed of manumission; if their owners or they themselves were minors; if they had been sold to pay debts despite estate solvency; or if their freedom had come in the dying wish of their masters—was to file papers in chancery. It is doubtful that the slaves cited in the will of Virginia slaveholder John Williamson could have successfully brought their claim to a common law court. Williamson left instructions that upon his death, his slave labor force should become the property of his two sisters throughout their lifetimes. After their deaths, the slaves were to be delivered to a third party, a friend, with instructions that he liberate them "if the laws of the state permit it." In a single suit, the thirty-seven slaves petitioned for their freedom on the claim that the administrator of the estate had kept them enslaved contrary to the conditions stated in Williamson's will. They asked the chancery court to "declare your complainants entitled to their freedom and order that they be liberated."[62]

In general, the testimony in chancery dealt in more detail with more issues than did depositions in law courts. During the generation after the American Revolution, plaintiffs and defendants alike, primarily in the Upper South, commonly enlisted fellow residents to provide evidence in freedom suits. At the request of counsel, courts ordered persons who had knowledge of the case to appear before court-appointed officials and provide depositions. On this occasion lawyers sometimes submitted to the court interrogatories—written questions, agreed on by both parties, to be addressed by witnesses for the plaintiffs and/or defendants. The courts then issued notices as to when and where the evidence was to be taken. Although depositions were usually scheduled in the county seat or nearby communities, they might sometimes be set in more distant locations—adjacent counties or even neighboring states. The specific locations varied, from county clerks' offices and lawyers' workplaces to private homes and plantation houses and farm dwellings, to business establishments, saloons, and grocery stores. After a change of venue from St. Louis to Herculaneum, Jefferson County, Missouri, not only the testimony but also the trial in one freedom suit apparently transpired in a vacant storeroom.[63]

The witnesses were equally wide-ranging: farmers, planters, slave owners, overseers, townspeople, businessmen, local politicians, sheriffs, justices of the peace, estate heirs, and—during the early years—free blacks. Deponents began by stating their age, occupation, and residence. They then responded to questions: Did they know the plaintiff and/or defendant? How well, when, and in what circumstances did they know him or her? How familiar were they with the issues involved in the case? What circumstances made their observations pertinent? Did they ever believe that the plaintiff was a free person? Had they witnessed or observed a deed of manumission or last will and testament? The answers were recorded in writing and later read aloud during a trial. Usually counsel for both parties was present at depositions, and sometimes plaintiffs and/or defendants themselves attended.[64]

As might be expected, some of those who testified presented contradictory, uninformed, or ambiguous information; a few claimed to have no knowledge of the case; others appeared to have been coached, repeatedly using the same phrases and words in support of the plaintiff or the defendant. But most deponents responded with at least bits of factual information. And some effectively recited specific names, dates, and places in reference to events; or recounted details concerning bills of sale or slave importations; or recalled suspicious activities on the part of estate heirs and administrators; or confirmed the enslavement of free black children; or related particulars about cases of term servitude, the execution of slaveholders' wills, or deeds of manumission.[65] They also testified about free female ancestry, Indian heritage, and residency in a free territory or state.[66]

As surprising as the broad range of subject matter in the equity depositions was the significant number of white witnesses who were willing to be deposed. Many among them, especially the elderly, who comprised a significant portion of the deponents, did so despite considerable inconvenience. For witnesses, depositions usually took almost a full day, most of it spent waiting to testify. Added to that was travel time to and from the court-ordered location, often a day each way, although in some cases it entailed an entire week or more. For their expenses, the courts provided deponents only minimal compensation. Plus, in some communities, witnesses testifying on behalf of plaintiffs often suffered the displeasure or outright hostility of their neighbors. Nonetheless, most witnesses who were called to testify felt it was their duty to respond to questions that strove to establish the right of slaves allegedly held illegally in bondage to be free.

The depositions taken at the home of Jake Philpott in a small Kentucky town on September 1, 1846, "agreeable to the notice here annexed to be read in the Barren Circuit Court in a suit in Chancery on the part of the complainant Moses," were typical. All four of the deposed witnesses had attended the sale of Moses some fifteen years before, and all four confirmed that Moses's owner, who had died intestate, and his heirs had agreed that Moses should be able to purchase himself for $200, although he was valued at twice that amount. Because Moses had been promised his freedom on the condition of self-purchase, several of those deposed said they had not bid on him. Their testimony corroborated the facts of the case presented by the complainant, who had in time paid off the person who held the bond on Moses's self-purchase price. Moses thus acquired his freedom. Cases dealing with self-purchase agreements, slaves' purchases of loved ones, self-hires, unwritten promises by owners, and other equity matters could only be adjudicated by testimony in chancery courts.[67]

White women, many of them members of slaveholding families, were frequently deposed, as they often had knowledge of slave family histories, which was crucial in suits that hinged on black female ancestry or term servitude, or both. In many cases they also provided unique firsthand information about particular events and commonly drew on their memory of childhood experiences. In some instances, they recalled not only the names of slaves who had been owned by their families but also how and when they should have been released according to an indenture, a bill of sale, a mortgage, will, or deed. On occasion they offered testimony in support of children born to free or freed women. The testimony of white women was at times remarkably detailed, with specifics as to the circumstances under which certain slaves had been transported from one state to another after they were supposed to have been freed.

Jane Rankin testified twice, first in 1840 and again in 1842, in regard to the case of Phoebe Gillis, in bondage as a term slave despite the likelihood of her white ancestry. During her long life—Rankin did not know exactly when she was born but she remembered hearing, as a young girl, the muskets being fired at the Battle of Brandywine near Philadelphia in 1777—she had lived many years in Maryland with the family of Robert Wilson, who owned "the mulatto girl Dinah." Rankin recalled hearing Wilson tell his wife that Dinah's "time had been out long ago," and around 1802 there was much talk in the neighborhood about how Wilson was keeping Dinah in bondage, despite her having been born of a free white woman and therefore being free herself. The gossip irked Wilson, and he "ran Dinah off." Then he traded her young daughter, Phoebe, to John Blackburn for a horse and a barrel of whiskey. "I have seen Phoebe, in the past year," Rankin said, "and know her to be the daughter of said Dinah," thus to affirm Phoebe's white bloodline.[68] Other white women similarly testified in chancery cases concerning slave women and their children.[69]

In a scattering of equity court cases in Delaware, the District of Columbia, Maryland, Tennessee, North Carolina, and Louisiana, term slaves, former slaves, and free blacks were deposed to provide testimony against whites. Delaware, with its small African American population, stood alone among the southern states in its presumption that black people were free persons rather than slaves. As such, they could offer testimony.[70] In Maryland, a number of cases hinged on the depositions of former slaves and free people of color who could relate at some length hearsay evidence about females in a family's ancestry. Among the Maryland cases was that of the Boston slaves, whose successful suit rested on a female ancestor's "reputation in the neighborhood" as being free. In Louisiana, court testimony by free African Americans against whites was accepted throughout the antebellum era. In some parishes, a Louisiana judge observed, free persons of color were "respectable from their intelligence, industry and habits of good order." No incompetency to testify in reference to free people of color was indicated in any specific law; indeed, the Civil Code (article 2260) determined them to be competent witnesses: *"prima facie* worthy of credit" in both civil and criminal matters. Further, the testimony of manumitted slaves also constituted legal evidence under Spanish and Roman law, the judge concluded, and such was the "uniform practice of our courts, which are in the daily habit of permitting them to testify in prosecutions where the defendants are white persons."[71] By the second decade of the nineteenth century, however, most southern states prohibited such testimony, especially after the US Supreme Court in 1813 outlawed the introduction of hearsay evidence.[72]

A number of black people who enter courtrooms with their lawyers discovered that the common law courts were often inadequate to provide the redress they were seeking. Some judges went so far as to say that freedom suits possessed "little or no analogy to an action at common law." The equity, or chancery, courts (and civil courts in Louisiana) on the other hand, were designed to sort out different pleadings, permit a broad range of testimony, issue protective injunctions, require bonds from defendants, and issue complicated judgments dealing with groups of slaves as well as families seeking their freedom. The equity courts in the Upper South and the civil courts in Louisiana were governed by state laws favorable to allowing freedom suits; the anti-freedom statutes in most states of the Lower South made it extremely difficult to access courts, whether common law or equity.

Frank Jackson might well have ended up like so many other free blacks who had been lured away or kidnapped in the North and sold as slaves in the South, had a southern white man not paid him a visit in his cell at Jones's Negro Jail in Richmond and listened to his story. In August 1851, William John Clark, in a letter to Judge John Reynolds in Lawrence County, Pennsylvania, detailed the narrative that Jackson had related to him, and asked the judge if it was true that Jackson had been born of free parents. "I am a slaveholder," Clark confessed, but like most "holders and owners, we do not mean to see the liberty of any person entitled to it taken from them." He continued:

> I am one of the Old Committee of Virginia formed several years ago to look out for abolitionists/negro stealing villains/and intermeddlers with our slaves—at same time I am the friend of the oppressed and friendless, not regarding colour—I have been the means of restoring to their liberty in the last 15 years twelve negroes & mulattoes of both sexes, from four different states which has cost me time and money never refunded by any that I have relieved, but that I cared nothing for, being satisfied I did nothing but my duty. When I will go any lengths, as will most all persons in our state, to vindicate the freedom of those

entitled to it, I will go equally far and farther to arrest and punish the intermeddlers with our property and institutions.[73]

When the Jackson case finally went to trial in October 1853, Clarke's work was apparent. Included in the evidence were three depositions by Pennsylvania men: the honorable John Reynolds, Henry Pearson, and James S. Cossett, all of whom had known Jackson's mother, father, and siblings for many years. They testified that Frank's mother, Sarah Jackson, had obtained her freedom under Pennsylvania law at age twenty-eight in 1813 or 1814. About 1815, she had married Elijah Jackson, a free man of color, and the couple had had four or five children, the eldest being Frank, who was born free in 1819 or 1820. The parents still lived together as man and wife.

The defendant, John W. Deshazer, enlisted only one witness, Lewis E. Williams, who testified that he had been present at the Campbell County Court in Lynchburg when Charles May put some horses and "a Negro man" (Frank Jackson) up for sale. On Williams's recommendation, Samuel Scott had purchased the black man, who, over the next eight or ten months, had run away on several occasions. Each time he had been arrested and jailed, and each time Scott had posted a security bond to retrieve Jackson from jail. After yet another of Jackson's attempted escapes, Scott had asked Williams to remove Frank and sell him, which he did, to John W. Deshazer, after informing him of the circumstances prompting the sale. A short time later, Deshazer sent Jackson to Lynchburg, where he again fled and this time landed in Campbell County jail. Nonetheless, the evidence clearly favored the plaintiff. Still, it was not until 1855, some five and a half years after Jackson's arrival in Virginia, that the court issued its final decree. Francis or Frank Jackson was declared a free man. He quickly left the state and returned to Pennsylvania.[74]

4

Manumission by Wills and Deeds

In August 1810, John Stewart, the administrator of the estate of Alexander Stewart—planter, slaveholder, former Maryland assemblyman—who had died the month before, submitted three "papers" to the Somerset County Orphans' Court that purportedly comprised Stewart's last will and testament. One of them, which became Exhibit No. 1 in the case that ensued, declared that "each and every one of the negroes" Stewart owned at the time of his death should be freed "and serve no longer than the first day of January next." Those who were underage and therefore not yet eligible for freedom were to be turned over to benevolent masters who would—in addition to feeding, clothing, and treating them well—permit them to keep their wages as hirelings until they reached their majority. Stewart further made specific bequests to a number of his eighty-five slaves, especially those who had grown old in his service and conducted themselves always with loyalty and fidelity: to Dick, Saul, Emmy, Grace, Bess, and Sally, he bequeathed three hundred acres of land and a house; to Dick, he also gave a sorrel horse, two cows, a sow, pigs, corn, pork, furniture, and a bed. Others among his black servants received similar consideration, and three white relatives inherited bank stock and US Treasury notes. The other two "papers" made provisions for Stewart's burial arrangements and the distribution of his real estate.

The legal battle over the three "papers" began that summer and continued into the late fall, as the slaves and their lawyers, along with the three white relatives, filed a libel suit against John Stewart and others. That the alleged will, Exhibit No.1, had been written by Stewart a decade earlier, about 1800, was determined by the fact that several of the slaves mentioned in the document, including Dick, had died since that date. The surviving slaves and their lawyers contended that Exhibit No. 1 was Alexander Stewart's rightful will, whereas the other "papers" were invalid. The defendants claimed Exhibit No.1 to be of no force since it had been neither completed nor witnessed.

During the trial, a picture of Stewart as a benevolent slaveholder who hated his greedy relatives emerged. "I heard him say he always kept a will by him and was never without a will," attested Levin Collier, who lived a mile and a half away from Stewart's plantation and had worked for "Capt. Stewart" as a black-smith over a period of twelve years. Stewart's relations never came to visit him, according to Collier, and Stewart said that in any case he would rather have the devil appear on his plantation than any one of his kin. Moreover, Stewart had often told Collier that he planned to free his slaves.

Other witnesses for the libellants, as the plaintiffs were called, confirmed Collier's testimony: Stewart was a compassionate master who planned to free his slaves upon his death. George Atkinson, a close friend of Stewart, recalled the testator telling him that none of his slaves who remained loyal would ever serve any person following his death. Atkinson said Stewart "was as humane and indulgent a master to his negroes as any I ever knew in my life." On December 6, 1810, after nearly four months and a court record containing eighty-four pages of witness testimony, the orphan's court issued its final decree, declaring that the "paper" freeing the slaves, Exhibit No. 1, should be received and recorded as the authentic last will and testament of Alexander Stewart "so far as the same relates to the personal estate."[1]

Although the case brought by Stewart's slaves was unusual in that the slaves joined three white legatees in a libel suit against various members of the Stewart family, it did typify one common, and generally effective, way that slaves in the Upper South, and to a lesser extent elsewhere, acquired their freedom during the late eighteenth and early nineteenth centuries. Owners frequently provided that their slaves be freed following their deaths, and bondsmen and bondswomen who benefited by such provisions numbered in the thousands. Some owners stipulated in their wills that blacks whom they deemed loyal and trustworthy should be freed, if not upon the owner's death, at some time in the future. The children, or "issue," of female slaves were customarily emancipated at a date in the future, when they reached their majority or some designated age.

Owners commonly specified that if they should die before their wives, the slaves should be freed following the death of their widows, or, in some cases, during the widowhood, on the condition that the bondsmen and women treated the widow with respect and devotion. Other owners stated that their slaves should be hired out and that the proceeds for their labor should be used eventually to fund their transportation to another state or to West Africa, or simply to assist them in assuming their freedom. Often owners' wills were not registered at the courthouse until after the deaths of the testators, as was the case for Alexander Stewart. During this early period of emancipa-tion, a number of slaveowners would have agreed with Nathaniel Jones of North Carolina, who explained in his will in 1815 that he wished to free his slaves because it was the right of every human being to live in freedom and his conscience therefore would not allow him to destine his blacks to perpetual bondage. The Golden Rule, he noted, directed him to do unto "every human creature" as they would do unto him, and by so doing he hoped to die with a clear conscience and to appear without shame before his maker "in a future World."[2]

Such lofty ideals were likely not to be shared by the members of some slaveholding families, especially when slaves constituted a significant portion of a testator's wealth. Among the many ways that heirs, executors, and estate administrators denied testators' manumissions was to contest the validity of a last will and testament. Their aim being to prevent the freeing of slaves above all else, they usually argued that the will had been improperly published. The evidence in these cases was at best circumstantial, with witnesses, unable to recall salient information, providing only vague recollections or contradictory versions of the same incidents. In some states, heirs claimed a will to be improper because it had not been registered with the county, as required by law. Or, by filing for continuances and appeals, heirs could tactically drag out legal proceedings, sometimes over a period of years. Problematic, too, were instances of family members hiding or "suppressing" a will that granted family slaves freedom in the future.

A mistress who died in 1796 provided in her will that her executors should sell her slaves, but once the slaves reached age thirty, they "and their posterity after them" should be freed. She also specified that a particular female slave, Bazil, should be freed after eight years. The testator's husband kept the will hidden, however, and he sold the slave Bazil. When, nearly a decade later, the will was "found and proved," Bazil contacted a lawyer and filed a freedom suit. The legal question on which the freedom suit rested was when should the designated eight years commence: upon the date of the testator's death or when the will was legally proved? On appeal, the US Supreme Court held that the term began at the time of the testator's death. The plaintiff was therefore, the court asserted, entitled to her freedom. Many other slaves who had similarly been bequeathed their freedom in a last will and testament remained in bondage for extended periods of time beyond the designated date of their release because of a will's "suppression."[3]

Another course that a number of heirs and executors took to forestall action on testators' freedom clauses was to allege that the slaveowners were mentally incompetent at the time they composed their wills. Heirs argued their case for unsound minds on claims that the slaveowners had long lived alone with their slaves, or had become overly friendly with certain blacks in their service, or had appeared to be unduly influenced by their bondsmen and bondswomen. Or they testified to strange and aberrant behavior on the part of slaveowners who had became obsessed with religious doctrine, or had roamed about the countryside without purpose, or had lived with black women they referred to as their wives or, even more shockingly, had declared their intention to marry one of their slaves.

In his will, one Kentucky slaveowner freed "sundry negroes," including a slave named Grace, whom, he stated, he had wished to marry during his lifetime. Outraged, the executors asked that the will be set aside because anyone who professed such a "degrading" and "repugnant" union was surely bereft of mental capacity.[4] A slaveowner in Louisiana left instructions in his will that following his death, a particular slave, the mother of his son, be taken to Pennsylvania and freed there. The mother and son in this case were now actually owned by a third party, and the testator had set aside funds in his will for their purchase. The lower court granted both the mother and son their freedom, but on appeal the executor reported that the testator had committed suicide and was therefore insane. A jury agreed, and the lower court's decision was reversed.[5] In other cases, estate managers claimed testators had expressed opinions during their lives that plainly proved they were not only foolish and unwise but also irrational and incompetent. Contemporaries labeled such behavior "lunacy," "derangement," or "insanity." The judicial system referred to it as mental incompetence, that is, as being *non compos mentis*, "not master of one's mind."[6]

Some executors and heirs went to great lengths to prove a testator *non compos mentis*. A group of heirs in Kentucky claimed that prior to the composition of his will, the testator, whom they described as feeble-minded, had been declining in mind and body until finally he was struck by a palsy: a condition that "paralyzed his physical strength and greatly impaired, if it did not entirely destroy his mind." The heirs of South Carolina planter Elijah Willis charged that his will, dated 1854, was null and void under the 1841 act that forbade the freeing of slaves, despite the fact that Willis had transported the slaves to Ohio for the purpose of emancipating them. Just as they were landing on the Ohio side of the river border, in Cincinnati, Willis died. The heirs attempted to establish the testator's insanity on testimony that he often foundered "under gloomy depression of spirits—avoiding society on account of his connection with Amy." A "dark yellow woman," Amy had given birth to three of the master's children and had become the de facto mistress of the plantation, "us[ing] saucy and improper language" in the presence of whites and exercising undue influence over the slaveholder—notably, she had prevented his sale of the black man who had also fathered three of her children.

Contrary to the judge's instruction, a jury found the will invalid. The court of appeals reversed the lower court jury's finding and ordered a new trial. However disgusting the court might have found the circumstances of the case, it was clear that the testator's wishes in this instance were "perfectly consistent" with those of a sane person.[7] Other family members of slaveholders who had bequeathed freedom to blacks in bondage called on friends, neighbors, relatives, and physicians to establish the testators' bizarre behavior. One witness depicted an owner as being often confused and at times incoherent, "silly in the extreme and utterly impracticable," as well as completely irrational. Another professed that a testator was "in extreme mental agony, bordering on total despair and absorption on the subject of religion and his eternal destiny." How could such a person write a valid will? It was not possible, argued the heirs and executors, whereby they concluded the document should be deemed "palpably void."[8]

Executors, heirs, and estate managers, then, regularly employed duplicitous means to void the manumission instructions of testators, especially if a will granted freedom at some future date. The will written in 1801 by John Peyton of Virginia was typical in this regard. It provided that, upon his death, any slaves over age forty should serve one more year and then be freed; those in their thirties should be freed at age forty; those in their twenties, when they reached thirty-five; and those in their teens and younger, until twenty-one if male and eighteen if female. Slaves who were thus to be manumitted years in the future fell under the control of estate managers, who could, and often did, keep the bond servants in ignorance of the original owner's wishes. Alternatively, managers might turn very young slaves over to a legatee, who would then sell them before they reached the age of manumission. As responsibility for manumission lay with family members and executors, it could be very difficult for slaves to seek their freedom if, as was occasionally the case, they had not been informed of a master's beneficence in a will that had often been written and published a decade or more before.[9]

It does appear that most slaves were aware of their owners' intentions to set them free. Indeed, it behooved the master class to reveal such intent to their human chattel so as to ensure their loyalty and good behavior. Some owners, though, felt that the promise of freedom in the future might work in reverse, their slaves' future prospects diminishing the blinkered devotion and long labor of their present bondage. Even then, black people sensed the inclinations of the masters they daily served. A number of Alexander Stewart's slaves evidently asked him outright about his intentions in regard to their bondage after his death. What they were he never divulged; that they were benevolent his people suspected. However extensive the knowledge or sound the suspicions of the slaves, the executors and estate managers still strove to delay or circumvent the legal process of manumission. In time, new state laws aided them. Legislation made the freeing of slaves increasingly more difficult in the Upper South and virtually impossible in most states of the Lower South.

Far more common were executors, administrators, heirs, and trustees—most of them family members or close friends of the deceased—who simply chose not to honor the wishes of a testator, and rather than manumitting the African Americans in their custodianship, they retained them as a continuing source of profit. Again, this strategy could most readily be accomplished when emancipations were designated to take place in the future. Some executors who also acted as trustees compensated themselves by keeping the supposedly emancipated slaves in bondage. In Louisiana, one executor evaded compliance with an emancipation bequest by arguing that the female slave at issue, a native of Santo Domingo, should continue to work for him in order to reimburse him for his expenses in dealing with the estate. Eventually he created a bogus title of ownership.

Those estate managers and executors who failed to have titles of ownership transferred into their own names nonetheless kept the emancipated slaves in their service either as field workers on their farms and plantations or as labor-for-hire, at profitable rates, in nearby towns and cities. The express instructions of one testator that a particular female slave be freed within six months of his death worked to no effect on the executor who hired her out for many months beyond six—and pocketed all the proceeds.[10]

Even executors and heirs who wished to honor a master's intentions in regard to manumission confronted difficulties. The distribution of an estate after the death of a slaveholder was time consuming, costly, and frequently frustrating for the owner's surviving family members. Estate managers were required to appear in probate court and sometimes post sizable bonds, depending on the wealth of the deceased. They were responsible, too, for paying the estate's outstanding debts, collecting any amounts due, and then dividing the property among the heirs, after deducting the widow's dower, which usually comprised one-third of her deceased husband's real estate holdings. It was not uncommon for a family member or close friend who had been designated in a will to be an executor to refuse the duty, often for want of the wherewithal to post the necessary bond.

Executors also had to deal with heirs who contested the distributions in a will as it had been published and registered. Some owners either failed to publish their wills according to law—witnessed and certified—or published them in different, sometimes contradictory versions, so that a codicil in one version might free a slave who, in the codicil of another version, would be bequeathed to a member of the testator's family.[11] Or a legal technicality might nullify an executor's obligation. The appeals court in Virginia rejected the will of a slaveholder instructing his executors and trustees to free his favorite slave, James Gilbert, to whom he bequeathed three acres of land on his farm during his lifetime. "However much the testator desired that Gilbert should be free," the court ruled, "it was very clear that he was deterred by the difficulties which the law presented with respect to residence here."[12]

Some Georgia slaveowners directed that their slaves should be "manumitted and sent to a free state" rather than "sent to a free state and manumitted." This was a crucial mistake. The laws of 1801 and 1818 prohibited emancipation *within* the state of Georgia. Owners whose intentions were to free their slaves and ensure them livelihood on their plantations, or to bequeath land to slaves whom their wills had also emancipated, or to have their widows free their slaves within the state, erred in the same manner. Their wills were declared void. All such problems were compounded further when the owners set forth a list of instructions as to how and when to emancipate particular slaves.[13]

In Louisiana, executors who attempted to free slaves according to a master's will sometimes discovered that the masters had not complied with the laws governing estate distribution. This was especially true when owners had intended to provide for their slave concubines. In general, the heirs of white men who kept African American mistresses received the major share of the slaveholder's estate; according to statute, however, they were obligated to cede 10 percent of the estate's movable property (slaves were considered immovable property) to the owner's concubine. In 1828, Prudence, an elderly, "always well-behaved" slave and the master's concubine, sued for freedom on the basis of an 1828 will stating she should be freed upon her master's death. She lost her suit because 10 percent of the value of her master's estate was insufficient for Prudence to gain her freedom.[14]

Some states on occasion saw freedom suits filed by black women and/or children who had been not only considered, and treated, as family but also included and freed in a last will and testament or named in a deed of manumission. They contended that, as legatees, they had claim to their freedom and to any property that had been designated for their use. Legatees in this situation were in some cases transported by their owners to a free state in the North, most often Ohio or Pennsylvania, where they were granted a deed of emancipation. Once freed, they might stay north, though often they returned to the southern states and there petitioned the courts for status as a free person. Cases brought by the paramours of white slaveholders were sometimes contested by relatives of the deceased; heirs frequently fought bitterly to keep the black women in bondage. In other instances, the black women and their children were involved only tangentially in disputes over wills, while the white kin of the deceased battled over the wording of a trust estate or a property bequest that included the disposition of the owner's slaves. In such circumstances the black women had no recourse but to rely on the courts, juries, trials, and, often, appellate judges to uphold their late owners' desires as declared in a will or deed.

Suits brought by disputatious heirs of the owner—by widows, siblings, aunts, uncles, nieces, nephews, and cousins—challenged bequests that directly affected the destiny of other "family." The enslaved women "at the heart of these actions were not parties to the action," one student of the phenomenon recently wrote, despite their being named in the will or deed. Slaveholders' relationships with the black women who bore their mulatto children were unquestionably complex; while sexual exploitation could in many cases plausibly explain them, in many more, including those that contested the competence of a will's author, the testators clearly and compassionately—and despite community opprobrium—sought to guarantee and protect the well-being of their black families.[15]

Even when slaveholders' wills unambiguously made arrangements for the future freedom of slaves, and even if the blacks at issue had full knowledge of their promised destiny, the owners' heirs nonetheless had the right to sell some or all of the manumitted slaves in cases where the estate had been left heavily in debt. If property was insufficient to satisfy creditors, most states allowed heirs to put slaves up for sale or hired them out, even those who were supposed to be manumitted. Because prices for term slaves with only a limited number of years to serve ran much lower than those commanded by slaves who were bound for life, heirs and estate managers in some instances withheld from the prospective buyers the emancipatory intent of the original master. Or, if the buyer did know about the promise of future manumission, he and the seller in some such cases colluded in keeping it secret from the slaves, and in the passage of years it would be increasingly difficult, and more unlikely, for the enslaved person to discover the original master's intent.[16] By keeping males in bondage years after the date they were to be freed, those placed in charge of an estate were able to reap substantial profits from the black men's labor, and by holding female slaves similarly, they could continue for years to enslave and profit from black women's children, and even their grandchildren.[17]

Estate debts not only caused severe consequences for testators' slaves; they also posed knotty problems for estate managers and administrators. If creditors could be satisfied by profits from the sale of real property rather than of slaves, should the land be sold? If a testator had designated that certain property be sold in order to satisfy debts, should the testator's instructions be followed even if the sale might necessarily include slaves cited to be freed? Should creditors be allowed to present bills against the estate years after the probating of a will if it meant that manumitted slaves would have to be reenslaved and sold to meet the debt? Should or could slaves named for emancipation be hired out for long enough for their earnings to satisfy payments made by the estate? Although the courts in the various southern states responded differently to these questions, most of them took the matter of debts very seriously, and most of the time they sided with a chancery judge in Maryland who ruled that "the creditors are the first objects" to be considered when administering an estate where the testator had freed some or all of the human property. If it should be found that the residue of an estate was inadequate to pay outstanding debts, one court decision affirmed, slaves to be manumitted "may be decreed to be sold for that purpose, either for life, or for a term of years."[18] Some manumitted blacks not unreasonably feared that, after living at large for months or years, they might be returned to bondage in order to satisfy a testator's debts. One manumitted black man in Virginia related how he had been freed in his master's will and had enjoyed the "rights and privileges" of a free person of color for several years, until an advertisement placed him for sale to pay an old debt of his late master.[19]

A number of courts in the Upper South ruled that if the sale of real estate and other holdings would bring a sum sufficient to satisfy creditors, the land and personal property— rather than slaves who were to be manumitted—should be sold. A Kentucky judge, eloquent in his defense of this general rule, stated that slaves emancipated by a will occupied a "double character of property and legatees, or *quasi* legatees." As freedom was a legacy "above all price, humanity, justice and the spirit of our laws," slaves freed in a will should become a "most favored class of legatees." Yet in the very same case, the slave Nancy, who had been freed in the will of slaveholder Ann Burgess, was cast back into bondage so that the Burgess estate could settle its debts. In 1835, the US Supreme Court affirmed the Circuit Court of the District of Columbia's decision that slaves manumitted in a will should be freed and not be sold by executors to pay estate debts if the testator left other types of property, including real estate, of sufficient value to satisfy creditors. Clear as the decision was, it did not avert complications, especially in the cases of widows, who generally received life estates in realty rather than outright ownership, which usually went to the children.

When one slave owner devised his slaves to his wife "with express authority to dispose of them as she should choose at her death," the court intervened in favor of an emancipated slave named Caleb who had been sold by the executor of the husband's estate. Ruling that Caleb was "undoubtedly a freeman," the appeals court declared his sale to be "unauthorized and void." The lien reserved by statute in favor of the emancipator's creditors, the court explained, could not be "enforced by an execution against the assets which came, or could ever come, to the hands of the executor." Rather, it could be procured only "by a proceeding in which the person manumitted would be entitled to defend his rights, and [Caleb] should never be disfranchised for an instant, unless the debt of the pursuing creditor cannot be otherwise made, nor to a greater extent than the payment of it should render necessary."[20] A decree from an equity court in Albemarle County, Virginia, exemplifies the worst scenario for freed black slaves. After examining an inventory of estate assets the court was satisfied that the claims of creditors utterly prohibited the emancipation of the slave girl named Nancy, despite the humane intentions of the testator.[21]

One method to satisfy creditors that estate managers, trustees, and court-appointed commissioners often employed was to hire out pre-emancipated slaves, whose earnings were then applied against the debts of an estate. A short-term solution, such hires earned small amounts of money that the executor could not otherwise pay, but sometimes debts remained outstanding for a not-so-short period of several years. Some of the slaves who were arrested and jailed for purposes of hire came from estates that were either insolvent or absent any significant property other than human chattel. The earnings of African Americans on hire, either by auction or by private agreements, were rendered to the sheriff, commissioners, or executor responsible for payment of money owed. Some slaveholders included hiring provisions in their wills in order to insure the estate against insolvency. Hiring fees varied greatly over time and throughout the South, but in general the money earned resulted in a long and trying process for the black people involved.

A slave named Jane, who was emancipated by James Lanier in his will, encountered all of these problems. She was hired out to pay her owner's debts but when she could not earn enough to satisfy creditors she was arrested and jailed by the sergeant, or sheriff, of Petersburg, Virginia. Although Jane and her children labored on hire under the supervision of the sheriff for the next five years, the estate received a total of only eighteen dollars. For two years no fees whatever had been paid by her hirers. And in the previous year, the sheriff reported, Jane had become pregnant, so no one had bid on her services at a public auction.[22]

Hiring out proved to be an efficient means to an end for executors when a will emancipated slaves on the condition that they relocate to West Africa. Beginning in the 1820s, after the establishment of Monrovia, a settlement at Cape Mesurado, and continuing in subsequent decades, some slaveholders published wills in which they instructed the parties in charge of their estates to arrange for their slaves to be freed and settled in that West African colony. Many such slaveholders believed that emancipated slaves would never achieve social and economic equality in the United States, and thus they bequeathed freedom to their slaves only if they emigrated. Also, emigration to Africa indisputably complied with laws that required freed blacks to leave the state. Some owners directed their executors or heirs to place their freed slaves in the aegis of the American Colonization Society, a national organization instrumental in the founding of Liberia and active in promoting emigration to West Africa. Often owners set up trusts to help fund the resettlement of slaves, and in their wills enjoined their administrators to hire out the emancipated slaves so as to further generate funds that would assist not only in the payment of estate debt but also in covering the costs for the slaves' transportation, clothing, food, tools, and their day-to-day living during their first year abroad.

In Virginia, one civil suit for freedom was ultimately decided in the appeals court, which ruled that a group of slaves cited for emancipation should indeed be freed, but, before embarking for West Africa, they should be hired out until the debts of the estate had been met. The court appointed a commission to question each slave as to whether he or she wished to relocate in Liberia; mothers decided for their children. The court asserted that every such will or trust should "be construed liberally, in favor of liberty." Courts in Maryland, Kentucky, and Tennessee issued similar judgments.[23] Even in states of the Lower South—North Carolina, Georgia, Alabama, Mississippi, and Texas—the judiciary declared the validity of wills that specified arrangements for emigration and resettlement in West Africa. Of course, in some cases, granting slaves their freedom with permission for them to be hired out for the purpose of paying estate debts or collecting funds for their eventual emigration was not possible because of strict laws concerning emancipation; however, if slaveholders established trusts expressly for emigration that were simple and straightforward, the court sometimes declared them valid.[24]

Whether or not there were trusts, and despite the wishes of testators, a number of administrators—some of them acting independently, others in accordance with the demands of heirs—hired out freed slaves for unconscionably lengthy periods of time or simply sold them as slaves for life. Some of these administrators, in addition to setting up the sales at public auction, actively solicited buyers and vouched, falsely, for the titles of the slaves. Others swore out arrest warrants, and slaves recently released from bondage found themselves in jail, where they were held until they could be sold at private sales. The administrator of two estates in Maryland obtained court orders authorizing the hire or sale of two groups of slaves, whom the testators had freed, in order to pay the estates' debts. Only later did it come to light that the administrator had failed to prove the estates suffered an insufficiency of funds and had neglected to report wages that had already been received from hire as well as "certain other monies heretofore omitted in his accounts." Fraud was often obvious, but despite the likelihood that titles might be "tainted" and the bills of sale suspect, the selling of emancipated slaves went forward.[25]

The fact was that slaves were often the most liquid asset available to heirs and estate managers. An observation made in an 1830 court proceeding was applicable to most southern states: slaves could be converted to cash, a Kentucky judge noted, probably faster than any other type of property.[26] It was not uncommon for those managing the estates of deceased slaveowners who had freed some or all of their slaves to find themselves facing creditors with claims for payment. In some wills, testators set forth how any debts should be paid, either by the sale of perishable property, machinery, and livestock or by the sale of land. In others, such as the will published in 1789 by James Eppes of Virginia, testators stated that their bondsmen and bondswomen should be hired out until all the estate's just debts had been paid. After that, Eppes wrote, "it is my will & desire that they be set at liberty as free citizens with such goods & chattels as they shall then possess." Quite often, however, wills did not include specific instructions for payment of debt; so, it was the executors and heirs who had to determine how to deal with creditors demanding payment. They might become defendants in civil suits against the estate, or they might be respondents to writs of fieri facias, by which a marshal or sheriff was authorized to seize and sell certain property. The property seized was often the estate's slaves, who were jailed until such time that the local judge decided whether they should be sold rather than freed. In her 1831 will, Elizabeth Richmond of Maryland provided for the freedom of Ann Barnet along with her daughter, Ann Milly Gross, and her two grandchildren, Jacob and Jemmy Gross. The executor claimed that the estate was deeply in debt. As a consequence, the family of four was arrested, jailed, and advertised for sale.[27]

Though many slaveholders who wished to free their bondsmen and bondswomen did so in a last will and testament, many others in the Upper South and Louisiana sought to emancipate their slaves by filing deeds of manumission. In states where manumission by deed was permitted, the laws required that the deeds be properly witnessed, be certified under oath, and, on occasion, be recorded at the county courthouse.[28] In some instances, especially in the years following the American Revolution, the wording of deeds was similar to that in sections of last wills and testaments dealing with emancipation.[29] A Maryland slaveholder who signed a deed freeing his twenty-two slaves on Christmas Day 1784 declared that he had struggled with his conscience and found great relief in the act of emancipation. The deed, he said, was derived from "divine providence."[30] In 1790, a Virginia slaveowner wrote that he believed "all men by nature are equally free; and, from a clear conviction of the injustice and criminality of depriving my fellow-creatures of their natural right, do hereby emancipate or set free the following [twelve] men, women, and children."[31]

A Kentucky slaveowner evoked the struggle against Great Britain as a reason for his renunciation of any claim pertaining to the possession of human property: "I now freely and immediately, liberate and quit claim" five slaves.[32] Even decades after the American Revolution slaveholders were couching deeds of manumission in the rhetoric of the nascent republic: They affirmed their belief that all people were entitled to liberty and freedom; they expressed their desire to comply with Christian teaching by doing unto others as you would have them do unto you; they avowed that conscience denied them the right to hold other human beings in servitude. They wrote deeds contending that slavery was contrary to good public policy, inconsistent with republican principles, and incompatible with the spirit of the gospel. It also violated the Bill of Rights.[33]

The great majority of owners who fashioned manumission deeds, however, did not indulge in rhetorical flourishes, nor did they immediately liberate their slaves. Rather, they simply named the black men, women, and children who should be freed at some time in the future, providing that they deported themselves properly and demonstrated loyalty to their masters or mistresses. In an 1807 deed, one slaveholder stipulated that his slaves should be freed on the condition that they comported themselves well and served the owner's heirs and assignees "honestly, faithfully, industriously, and satisfactorily."[34] The wording in some deeds suggested that the slaves named for manumission at a future date should be allowed to hire out their own time, thus to be able to support their families and live as virtually free or quasi-free slaves. Slaveholders justified the granting of such privileges, while illegal, in light of laws that required of freed blacks the ability to earn a livelihood and maintain their families.[35] Some deeds, too, included provisos, or default clauses, that permitted the owner or a member of the owner's family to renege on a deed under certain conditions—if, for instance, the owner or a family member died without issue, or if the deed's designee failed to complete a specified amount of work in a specified period of time. In such cases, the slave or group of slaves would revert to the owner's estate as though the deed of manumission had never been penned. Some deeds were so vaguely worded that any infraction, however minor, might extend the term of servitude or cancel altogether the promise of freedom.[36]

There is little doubt that the ideology espoused during the American Revolution—not least, that all men were created equal—had an impact on slaveholders, as did the antislavery views embraced most notably by the Quakers, who forbade followers from owning slaves in 1788, as well as by various Baptist and Methodist congregations. Yet, the record of manumissions in eight Virginia counties between 1782 and 1806 shows how the early republic's ideals gave way in less than three decades to more practical considerations. Increasingly, slaves made arrangements with their owners to purchase themselves and their loved ones out of bondage; the owners were inclined to grant freedom as a reward for good behavior, along with a purchase price. Indeed, in half of the manumission deeds in the eight counties during the twelve years from 1794 to 1806, the owners freed their slaves in exchange for money or service. Only about one out of four deeds or wills evidenced antislavery sentiments, and in this way, "reinforced rather than challenged the South's peculiar institution." Most owners viewed slave ownership as their right and chattel as their property: as "my negro woman," "my negro man," "my several negroes"—the possessive case abounds in deeds and wills. Even after slaves were freed, owners often continued to refer to them in the possessive. During this period, too, delayed manumissions became increasingly more prevalent, so that bondsmen and bondswomen were required to work diligently, industriously, and loyally for a prescribed number of years before they would be freed. In short, manumissions did not undermine slavery but in many respects helped to reinforce the stability of the system.[37]

Owners who planned to manumit their slaves at some time in the future as expressed in a will or deed could, and frequently did, sell, trade, mortgage, or transfer their human property. Such transactions required that the bill of sale or the record of trade or mortgage include information relative to any deed of emancipation and future date of freedom. Some owners failed to heed, or simply ignored, this requirement; others complied, in which case buyers were likely to claim that they had not been thus apprised. Complications arose, too, when owners changed their minds as to the date of a future manumission and recorded the alteration not in the deed but in a will or codicil to a will. Meanwhile, the slave to be manumitted could be sold and resold. In the District of Columbia, the owner of a male slave named Fidelio sold him with the stipulation that he should be freed in six years. The new owner, however, designated in his will that Fidelio should be freed four years after his death, but then, in a codicil, stated that at his death all his slaves should be sold. Because the price commanded by slaves to be freed was in general lower than the market price for life-term slaves of the same age and ability, without a copy of a deed, a bill of sale, or a will promising future freedom, it was nearly impossible for a slave like Fidelio to file a freedom suit. A few owners kept the deeds in their possession; more than a few failed to register them at the courthouse. Although some states granted slaves their freedom if the courts found evidence other than manumission deeds—legal documents such as bills of sale, indentures, trusts, security bonds, and mortgage deeds—most states that allowed emancipations required deeds of manumission with proper witnesses to put them into effect.[38]

The same strictures regarding the children of slaves emancipated by a will applied to children whose mothers were to be freed at a future date by deeds of manumission. That is, if a slave mother still serving a designated period of time gave birth to a child, the child was born in bondage unless specific exclusions had been made concerning the black woman's "issue." This rule was binding even if the child was very young and left by the owner with the now freed mother as a practical convenience. Nor did it matter if the child grew up in the mother's care and both were considered by everyone in the community to be free persons of color. So it was that children and grandchildren of manumitted black women could at any time be claimed as slaves.

In 1805, in reference to the slave Polly, a Virginia slaveholder filed a deed of manumission that was to be executed in 1814. Prior to that date, however, Polly was taken to North Carolina, where she gave birth to a daughter. Years passed, and Polly and her daughter "acted in every respect as free persons," neighbors noted; nonetheless, according to the doctrine of *partus sequitur ventrem*, Polly's daughter was legally a slave. Therefore so was the daughter's son, who was born in the late 1820s. In 1838, Polly's grandson, probably under age ten, was sold into slavery. In a number of other cases in other southern states, children born to manumitted female slaves still in servitude were deemed to be slaves. By actions of detinue, the recovery of wrongfully held property, a member of a slaveholding family could claim such children as chattel at any time, in some instances when they had reached their teens or adulthood.[39]

When slaveholders changed their minds regarding deeds of manumission, they might destroy rather than register the document, or they might retain it but not file it in the county court. In other instances, owners who had filed their deeds with the court had then moved to a different county or another state, where they failed to refile the instruments of emancipation. It was not unusual for deeds of manumission to stagger the dates of the slaves' emancipation: some being designated to be freed in three years, others in five years, and still others in seven. In the interim the slaves could be sold, resold, mortgaged, or traded.

It seems doubtful that several among the slaves manumitted by Ann Key in the District of Columbia would not have been sold or traded during their lifetimes. Key stipulated that two of her slaves, Charles Henry and Frances Ross Wood, should be emancipated and set free after completing thirty years of service, beginning September 1, 1826, and ending on the same date in 1856. However, when the holder of the deed moved or sold the slaves with such a stipulation, the possibilities for owners to extend the period of servitude or simply to ignore the date of termination increased tremendously. Not a few owners contrived to keep manumitted blacks in bondage, with little concern about tampering with evidence to do so. While some chose simply not to file the deeds, others altered them in such a way as to prevent freedom. In Virginia, Joshua Miniard in 1797 "conveyed all his negroes and other estate" to his in-laws on the condition that they would provide both him and his wife with basic necessities during his lifetime and that, following his death, the slaves would be hired out to raise the amount of forty-five pounds per year in order to support his wife. Upon her death, the slaves were to be manumitted and set free. But once the slaves duly had fulfilled their obligation, it became clear that the bond serving as a deed of manumission had been altered: the words "set" and "free" and part of the word "emancipate" had been erased.[40]

Similarly, wills and deeds both provided for the immediate or future freedom of designated individuals, and possibly for their children as well; and both indicated how those named for emancipation should satisfy the laws of the state in regard to age, ability to work, good character, and means to emigrate within a given period. There were also significant differences between wills and deeds. Slaves freed in wills had to acquire the sanction of another court, as probate courts could not issue freedom papers, while those named in deeds of manumission were most often granted free status by the authority of the county courts. Nor was the freedom of those named for emancipation in deeds conditional, as in wills, upon a testator's death and the execution of the estate, in which problems concerning slaveholders' debts and legacies commonly arose. Neither did deeds, except in rare instances, transfer property to widows, nor did they factor a widow's dower into the costs of the emancipation process. Deeds were usually registered at the county court at or near the time of emancipation, whereas wills generally remained in private hands, often for many years, until the testator's death, when they were filed with probate courts. Also, deeds could be effectuated outside the South. Occasionally slaveholders transported their black mistresses and mulatto children to free states such as Pennsylvania, New York, Ohio, and Indiana, where they filed deeds to guarantee emancipation.[41]

White women who wished to free their slaves either by will or deed encountered difficulties not shared by their male counterparts. Married women—femes covert, by legal definition—essentially forfeited their right to any property either inherited or acquired prior to marriage, as by marriage it became part of their husbands' estates. During most of the antebellum period, then, married white women could not dispose of any property without their husbands' acquiescence. Even after the early enactments of married women's property laws—as in 1839, when Mississippi passed the first law in the country to protect married women's property as separate—they still needed their husbands' consent in the disposal of property. Married women were required, as they were in divorce and separation cases, to secure a "next friend," or *prochain ami*, in order to conduct any legal business pertaining to property during the early decades of the nineteenth century.[42] Single women, or femes sole, had the right to buy and sell land, slaves, and other property, but they sometimes found it problematic to bring cases into court. As for widows, if they headed slaveholding families, they were guaranteed a dower of a life estate in one-third of the husband's real holdings, unless otherwise specified in a husband's will. Land could be bequeathed by the husband to his widow, but only as part of a life estate, or ownership during the widow's lifetime then reverting to various heirs.

The actual division of the estate among its heirs depended on the ages of the deceased's children; if they were young, it could take years before a final distribution was rendered. During those years, if a widow wished to free some of the slaves, she could not do so unless she and her children, often represented by a guardian ad litem, agreed on a division of the personal estate. If some of the children were adults, they could contest any division proposed by their mother and thus delay any proposed manumissions. The estate's debts required consideration as well. If, for instance, the husband died with a number of creditors seeking payment of debt, the final probating of the estate could again be deferred, and in the meantime slaves who would have been manumitted by the widow might instead be sold to satisfy the master's debts. Such problems were compounded if the husband died intestate.[43]

Even when all went smoothly, with the property divided by agreement of the parties and the widow's deed of manumission filed in the county court, the children or the administrators of the estate could still contest the freeing of the slaves by citing (through legal counsel) laws that required slaves to be adults not over a specified age, to be able to earn a livelihood, and to be of good character. Sometimes, too, white widowed women did not want to comply with the instructions in the will of the deceased to free his slaves. To retain freed slaves as chattel, widows in this situation argued primarily that they could not secure their dower, once the debts were paid, if the slaves were emancipated. They thus renounced their husbands' wills despite written instructions that expressly forbade heirs, executors, or administrators to interfere with the wishes of the deceased.[44] Still other widows simply ignored the provisions concerning manumission.

When widows did want to free slaves in accord with their husbands' wishes, complications could doom their efforts. The twenty-two-year-old black man Tom was manumitted in a deed by his Virginia mistress, feme covert Anne Roberts, in 1782. Although the deed was signed shortly before the passage of the 1782 manumission law, which allowed owners to free slaves without the approval of the state legislature, Tom knew of many slaves who had been freed under the same circumstances as his and had gone at large with the support of the community. After several months of freedom, he discovered that his manumission was not valid under any circumstances because Anne's husband, a Loyalist during the American Revolution who had joined the British in 1775, had returned Virginia in 1783 and reclaimed his property, including Tom.[45]

African Americans thus faced numerous obstacles when filing freedom suits that cited wills and deeds. In some cases, they and their children had fallen into the possession of a person who did not legally own them but had nonetheless kept them in bondage. In other cases, despite owners having "freely and voluntarily" manumitted them, estate managers refused to honor the owners' plainly stated wishes. So it was indeed essential that slave plaintiffs and their counsel submit copies of last will and testaments or deeds of manumission, for when they failed to do so, the courts more often than not ruled in favor of the defendants.[46] The obstruction of freedom suits could hinge, too, on laws that had been enacted decades in the past. During his final illness, one Maryland planter called together several of his most loyal hands and disclosed to them that, in honor of their faithful service, he had signed a deed for all his slaves' emancipation, which was to take effect in two months, on Christmas day 1784. Word spread quickly in the slave quarters and prompted great excitement, even jubilation. When the owner died a few days later, however, the executor of his estate refused to honor the deed. After a trial and an appeal that together ran more than eight years, the owner's twenty-two slaves lost their suit for freedom on grounds of a law passed in 1752, and cited by the defendant, which prohibited owners in their final days "to give or grant Freedom to any Slave or Slaves."[47]

No doubt the twenty-two slave plaintiffs in the Maryland case had lost any hope of success years before the appeals court rendered its final decision. Like many others who similarly failed in their suits, the exultation they had experienced at the possibility of being freed was as intense as the despair on learning that their efforts had gone for naught. Freedom suits abound with plaintiffs' stories of promises broken, hopes forfeited, and dreams shattered—often on a legal technicality, as when owners failed to have their wills or deeds signed by at least two witnesses.[48] Nuncupative (oral) wills, of course, also posed problems. Two slaves filed a freedom suit in Ibberville Parish, Louisiana, in 1838, citing a will dictated by their owner on his deathbed. But because only four of the required five witnesses for a verbal will were present, the Fourth District Court rejected the plea. The appeals court ultimately ruled that the distance the fifth witness had to travel was a mitigating factor and thus reversed the verdict, but the two black plaintiffs had been retained in bondage throughout the four years of the appeals process.[49] Plaintiffs failed, too, because they exceeded the age limit applied to emancipation. Anna, slave of the late Leonard Boroughs, pled that her master not only provided for her manumission but also bequeathed her a portion of his estate. While admitting she was over the age limit of forty-five, she argued that the Maryland law was designed "to prevent persons held in slavery from being turned loose on the community when they become superannuated" and that she possessed "property more than sufficient for her maintenance." The local court ruled in her favor; the decision was overturned on appeal.[50]

To be sure, the great majority of wills and deeds cases never reached the courts, at least not as freedom suits, but among those that did, a significant number were successful in spite of the many difficulties. For many, the process included years of struggle, thwarted expectations, hiring auctions, and appeals. At each stage of the process, their voices resounded in statements written and spoken by their attorneys. They argued that they should not be sold to pay their masters' debts when estates held sufficient funds to meet such obligations without their sale. They contended that as the designated period of their enslavement had expired, they should be freed in accord with their masters' wishes. They and their lawyers produced documents to prove their right to freedom: copies of wills, bills of sale, mortgages, transfer deeds, manumission deeds, and other legal instruments. Community sentiment frequently sided with the plaintiffs; many white people, including slaveholders, believed that if owners chose to manumit their human chattel within the structure of the law, they should be permitted to do so. As a consequence, African Americans and their families found themselves being supported by whites who willingly testified on their behalf. During the process, plaintiffs remained vigilant, expectant, and hopeful; they were willing to take on these often contentious and challenging suits against their owners, members of their owners' families, or heirs to an estate. Sometimes even heirs and members of the slaveholding families sided with the plaintiffs so as to honor the wishes of a deceased slave owner.

In North Carolina, John Nelson, the brother of the slave Daniel's owner, stood up for the bondsman in a suit, that sought to verify his emancipation in his master's will. Nelson asked that his brother's wish be honored "within the bounds of the law" and in terms of the "certificate," or brief letter of recommendation, that his brother had given Daniel to allow him "Liberty to pass and re pass Where he pleases."[51] The suit was eventually successful. Other slaves likewise depended on the testimony of whites. In a suit brought by Hannah, who was described as the owner's "confidential house servant," she as claimant produced a copy of her master's last will and testament, which he had turned over to her for safekeeping. The will freed her and eight other slaves. Such trust was unusual, but slaves aware of their owners' wishes had reason to view the future with a measure of optimism—even though they had to wait, sometimes for years, until after the slaveholder's death to realize their freedom. Once realized, the erstwhile slaves in many southern states were required by law to leave the state, but the statute dissuaded few from staying. Most of those who won their suits either broke the law or sought dispensation to remain in their home communities.[52]

There is little doubt that some among those filing freedom suits, including those who eventually won, feared possible reprisals, mostly from their owners' white family members. The injunctions sought by a number of them, either in the bodies of their complaints or as separate requests, attest to their anxiety and, at times, torment. Their confidence in the validity of their complaints could not allay their fears, chief among them their sale to slave traders and the breakup of their families. Not a few cases were similar to the one brought by four Virginia slaves—Will, Burwell, Jane, and Lucy—who noted in their 1795 freedom suit that their owner, James Eppes, had instructed his executor to hire them out until his debts had been paid, after which they should be freed. At the time of their filing, the four had been hired out "from year to year," and they believed they had earned more than enough to discharge any demands against the estate. After their suit had been filed, their enslavement continued—as their apprehension and fear increased—for another two years, while the case wound its way to completion. In the end, the court decided in their favor.[53]

Plaintiffs fortunate enough to win their freedom did gain some protection from judges and juries in southern courts. In 1835, a judge in the District of Columbia ruled that manumission, once executed, "could not be recalled or revoked."[54] Judges in other southern states applied the same dictum. In a decision that might have been embraced by courts even in the Lower South, a Maryland judge wrote, in regard to a Baltimore man freed in a will and granted a "certificate of freedom," that "Once free and always free" was the maxim of law. The laws of manumission, he averred, were not passed to diminish or destroy slavery, or to promote slaves' comfort and happiness; indeed, the reverse was more likely to be the case, for slaves were "far better fed and clothed, more content and happy," and in point of "sobriety, virtue and moral character," they stood far above the free colored population. Rather, the laws regarding manumission were enacted to allow owners the right to dispose of their human property in any manner and to any end that they saw fit.[55]

Estate debt, resentful white family members, and rapacious slave traders were not the only problems slave plaintiffs encountered. Many of them also had to endure the appeals process. A significant portion—55 percent—of freedom suits dependent on wills and deeds went to appeals courts. Their reasons varied, but most estate managers expressed deep concern about financial losses, especially when groups of bondsmen and bondswomen, along with their children, filed a freedom suit.

Also, it appears that slaveholding defendants realized, correctly, that their chances of winning in an appellate court were far better than those of succeeding in the county courts, where nearly eight out of ten freedom suits involving wills and deeds were granted. Most appeals cases lasted at least a year or longer, and sometimes a number of years, during which the bond servants who were party to the case in appeal could be hired out by the authorities or held in the custody of their alleged owners. In either case, blacks facing appeals had cause for continued apprehension, especially after a county court had ruled in their favor. As hirelings, they faced possibly harsh treatment, no matter that hirers posted bonds promising to deal with them fairly. Worse, as returnees to their owners' estates, they would find themselves in the charge of white family members who often felt betrayed and angry at having been summonsed into court to defend their actions. Indeed, many of those in family custody were accused of fraud and dishonor.

What favored the slave plaintiffs in appeals cases was the fact that, with few exceptions, they based their complaints on written records, and if they could produce a certified copy of a will or deed in court, it went a long way toward establishing their credibility during an appeal, especially if whites testified as to the authenticity of the documents. This occurred in the freedom suit brought by Nancy, Benjamin, and Mary Green, who produced a deed of manumission signed in 1801 by Edward Strong of Queen Anne's County, Maryland, freeing Edward Green. The court record does not indicate the relationship between the owner and Edward Green, or the plaintiffs, who, in 1806, along with their lawyer William Scott, filed suit against Philip Crisfield at the Kent County courthouse in Chestertown, Maryland. In 1808, a jury found for the plaintiffs, but the defendant promptly appealed the case to the General Court of the Eastern Shore. In June 1813, more than seven years after the initial filing, the case was decided in the plaintiffs' favor. The deed proved to be a crucial piece of evidence. Spending seven years under the continued management and control of an alleged owner, however, tempered their enthusiasm.[56]

Suits like the Greens' occurred primarily in the Upper South and Louisiana, in states that allowed manumissions and emancipations until the late antebellum era. Appeals judges in these cases were frequently sympathetic to slave plaintiffs. Judge John Catron, for instance, ruled in a Tennessee case that a slave freed in a will, after securing a "next friend" and filing "a bill in equity," was "entitled, independent of his color or his civil condition, to have justice administered in the due course of law, without denial or delay."[57] From time to time, especially in cases concerning wills, slave plaintiffs, often with white next friends or guardians as well as counsel, filed freedom suits not only in the Upper South but in every southern state. If slavery brought monotony and despair to many of those held in its grasp, filing freedom suits, despite the problems and pitfalls, lent them hope and possibility.

In the 344 cases based on wills and deeds (17 percent of the total 2,006 freedom suits where primary causes could be determined), the plaintiffs and their lawyers won 64 percent of the suits, 55 percent on appeal and 78 percent in the county courts (results could be determined in 295 instances). In addition, as the southern population expanded, so too did these suits increase over time, 61 in the early period with a 61 percent success rate, 117 in the middle period with a 64 percent success rate, and 166 in the late period with 69 percent successful. Such a relatively high rate of success and the rise in the number of suits over time, including a few from every state in the South except Mississippi, would appear to contradict what was occurring in Southern politics as the nation moved toward the "irrepressible conflict." (See table 5.)

Following the decision in 1810 by the Orphans' Court in favor of Alexander Stewart's slaves and three heirs against eleven family members, the defendants appealed to the Maryland Court of Appeals. They argued, in error, that two valid wills focused on burial arrangements and the disposition of real estate but included no instruction as to the freeing of slaves. Apparently, the six judges on the court relied primarily on the testimonies of the physician Matthias Jones, who had attended Stewart at his bedside the night before he died, and the lawyer John Collman, who had been summoned that same night—July 21, 1810—to Longhill plantation to write Stewart's will from dictation. The doctor testified that Stewart had first asked him to write the will, and he had begun to do so, but then had admonished the dying man that it should be written by a lawyer. On the arrival of solicitor Collman, Jones had torn up the initial, incomplete version of the will. Over the next several hours, Collman had sat with Stewart as he dictated his last will and testament, and throughout, Collman testified, Stewart "appeared rational and gave very pertinent answers to any questions which I put to him."

The topic of freeing several slaves had arisen, Collman recalled, but Stewart had not dictated any instruction in that regard in a discrete section of the will. On its completion, Collman had read the will back to the testator, who had directed him to make one revision before telling him to set the document aside as he could "do no more that night." Once during this process Stewart had vomited and Jones had administered an opiate. Following the dictation, Stewart had begun to show "strong symptoms of delirium," as he had drifted in and out of consciousness. At one point he had asked if a "blood red" cat could be removed from a chair next to his bed and said that a man waiting to deliver a letter was standing outside his window, but of course no cat had claimed the chair and no one was standing at the window.

At the June 1813 term of the court of appeals, the judges ruled that the decree of the lower court "ought to be reversed." The eighty-odd slaves, who, alternately in apprehension and expectation, had borne their bondage during the two-and-a-half years of the appeal, would remain the property of various members of the Stewart family. The opinion contained only twenty-four words. It made no reference to the Maryland law designating age limits on manumission and requiring that manumitted slaves be able to earn a livelihood, thus excluding in any case the older slaves and the children. Neither did it rule on the requirement that wills be subscribed by at least two "good and sufficient witnesses." The appeals court judges determined that the wishes of the owner concerning his slaves and his substantial property holdings were plainly delivered as he lay verging on delirium on his deathbed. Even if the will cited as Exhibit No. 1 had been declared valid, the appeals court could still have ruled against the slaves' grant of freedom because the original suit was a libel suit, and as such, it could not stand in place of a freedom suit in a county court.[58]

5

Term Slaves

In February 1856, a Maryland slaveowner, Mary Duvall, had reached the end of her patience in attempting to control her term slave Delia Larkins, who was "in the habit of running away." It was not merely the expense and frustration of finding her on the run, including the cost of advertisements and dealing with slave catchers, but even without all of these problems Larkins remained obstinate, opinionated, assertive, independent, and aggressive. Duvall asked the judge of the Baltimore City Orphans' Court for permission to sell Larkins, either within the state or out of the state, as soon as possible. Such a sale was required by law once the judge declared that a slave's behavior was so egregious as to warrant removal, according the 1846 law permitting sales of recalcitrant term slaves. The judge listened to Duvall's testimony and issued a permit agreeing to the sale.[1]

Duvall then sold Larkins to slave trader Benjamin Campbell, who then sold her to speculator William Summerhill for $300. As a twenty-year-old mulatto woman in good health, she would have commanded a considerably higher price on the open market if she could have been sold as a slave for life. With that devious thought in mind, Summerhill transported her to Nashville, Tennessee, where he sold her for $1,000 to William A. Cheatham, the head physician at the Lunatic Asylum of Tennessee; Summerhill did not mention that she was a term slave.[2] When Larkins discovered the betrayal, she threatened to make the illegal sale public.

Disinclined to defending and exposing himself in a public scandal, Cheatham returned her to Summerhill, who, in turn, put her in the hands of another slave trader, Reese W. Porter, with instructions to sell her for what would be the third time in only a few months. Porter, widely known for his shady dealings in the buying and selling of human property, sold Larkins to a Davidson County farmer, Landon Harrison, for a life-term slave's price of $1,000.[3] Again defiant and outspoken, Larkins threatened to expose Harrison, and again the buyer returned her to the seller.[4] At this point, finally, she was able to contact a lawyer, slaveowner Rettson J. Meigs, who filed a suit on her behalf against Mary

B. Devough [Duvall], William Summerhill, and Benjamin Campbell. Larkins especially feared that she might fall back into the grip of Summerhill, who had beaten her, the suit alleged, "because he suspected her of communicating the above facts to the persons concerned" and planned to "carry her away, where it will be still more difficult than it is here, to make out her case." Delia Larkins and her lawyer requested that the court prohibit both any future sale without validating her term of service and any sale of her person outside Davidson County. In May 1857, the court granted both requests.[5]

For a variety of reasons—loyalty, intelligence, special skills, industry, meritorious service, sexual relationships, bearing an owner's child—slaves were often promised their freedom at some future date. Gaining the status of "term slave," which limited servitude to a specified number of years or until a designated age, was rare in the Lower South but fairly common in Delaware, Maryland, Virginia, the District of Columbia, and towns and cities across the Upper South. Both slave and master profited from such an arrangement: slaves, by securing the promise of liberty for themselves and possibly for their children; masters, by commanding a more substantial measure of loyalty on the basis of that promise. Most often these arrangements were put on paper—in wills, deeds, marital contracts, bills of sale, indentures, or mortgages—which stipulated that the person so named would gain his or her freedom after an owner's death or that of his widow, or when the bond servant attained a certain age. In some instances, owners expressed their desire that their slaves be freed at some future time both in deeds and in their last will and testaments. One Tennessee man arranged for the future manumission of his favorite female slave and provided that her children should likewise be freed, the females when they reached age twenty-seven, the males at age thirty.[6] Similar arrangements occurred regularly in other states. Some owners also provided terms for slave children, even when they were young. One Missouri owner, for example, stipulated in a bill of sale that his eleven-year-old slave Malinda as well as her brothers and sisters, who were being sold to Joseph Smith of Nashville, Tennessee, should be freed when they arrived "at the age of twenty-five or twenty-eight years."[7]

By definition, the benefits of such arrangements often lay in the distant future. Owners died, widows died, slaveowners' children died, and all the while slaves named to be one day freed remained legally in bondage. Years passed, and black families grew, the parents and their children often becoming not only an integral part of an owner's estate but also a gainful (and exploitable) one. Thus the legal documents were sometimes violated. Rather than surrender valuable property in accord with an owner's grant of term servitude, heirs and other family members often strove to keep term slaves permanently enslaved. Administrators of estates, executors of wills, widows, heirs, white children, creditors, business partners—they all employed ethically questionable if not outright illegal means to subvert the original intent of the owner. White family members sometimes "lost," hid, or destroyed the legal documents—last will and testaments, bills of sale, deeds, indentures—that supported any emancipation claims their slaves, usually fully aware of a deceased owner's wishes in their regard, might make. In some instances, years beyond the date of manumission prescribed by the deceased, owners in the same family simply refused to surrender the slaves. In 1803, a group of Virginia slaves won a judgment in the Virginia High Court of Appeals concerning the will of Andrew Dunscomb, who had stated that his slaves should be set free when they reached age twenty-six. The court ruled that two of the fourteen petitioners, Dick and Sylvia, should be freed immediately; that nine of them should be freed variously in 1805, 1813, 1818, and 1828; and that the three others should not be freed. Nearly forty years later, the descendants of the apparently successful petitioners in the 1803 case were still fighting for their freedom. Their two masters claimed them to be slaves for life and openly scoffed at the alleged age limit of twenty-six years.[8]

Economic risks could run high for white families who under false claim held term slaves in bondage. Slaveowners holding only a few term slaves in this manner stood to suffer significant financial losses if it were proved that the blacks were due their freedom. Even when freedom suits were filed many years after the slaves' dates of manumission, if the courts ruled in their favor the owners' property losses could be substantial. That was especially true if the black women in these suits had borne children after the date they should have been freed, as their children and, in some instances, grandchildren would also be covered in the manumission. In addition to bearing the possible loss of their human property, owners also suffered the burden of legal expenses, sometimes foregoing the benefit of slave labor throughout the legal process. When the process included appeals, it could extend over several years. In rare cases, too, depending on state laws, the court awarded the manumitted slaves damages for the time they were illegally held in bondage or hired out during the pendency of the trial.[9]

The bitter and protracted fight waged by members of the Hopewell family in St. Mary's County, Maryland, to retain ownership over seventeen slaves who filed suits for their freedom demonstrates how disastrous the outcome could be for white defendants. The seventeen slaves were children of Nan and Frances, who were daughters of Moll, a slave given by William Cole as a gift to his wife, Elizabeth, in a deed registered in November 1732. Nine months before the deed was signed, however, Cole, in his will, bequeathed Moll, along with several other slaves and their increase, to his wife during her lifetime; upon her death, he stipulated, the indicated slaves should be "free and for themselves."

It is probable that Cole told Moll about his will, but she nonetheless found herself—and her children and, eventually, grandchildren—bound in servitude to the Hopewell family long after the deaths of Cole and his widow. In 1779, on behalf of Moll's children and grandchildren, John Allen Thomas, an attorney and lieutenant colonel in the Continental army, filed four separate freedom suits in the St. Mary's Chancery Court. Producing a copy of the original will, Thomas argued that although it was written in June 1732, six months prior to the deed of gift, the last will and testament nonetheless superseded the November document. The county court rejected his interpretation, and Thomas appealed to the General Court of the Western Shore of Maryland. There he won a reversal: the general court decreed that the plaintiffs be released from bondage and that members of the Hopewell family not only pay the court costs but also compensate the blacks for their lost labor—an opinion that was upheld in 1784 by the high court of appeals. The decision delivered a devastating blow to the Hopewell family's wealth and property holdings.[10]

The actual number of African Americans who were promised freedom that they failed to attain at a specified future date will never be known. Some among them probably never knew that their bondage hinged on a belied promise. Others fell to the devices of slave traders who prowled towns and cities in search of term slaves to buy and then sell, at considerable profit, as slaves for life.[11] Most term slaves, though, were aware of their status, and they knew exactly the length of time that defined their period of servitude. In their petitions, they described their owners' deceit, avarice, and greed, as well as their own fears and panic when they discovered that slave traders or white family members planned to sell their loved ones or transport them out of the county or state.[12] One group of siblings, for example, related how their mother, only a servant for years, had given birth to them after her term of servitude had ended, and yet, contrary to law, they had been retained in bondage They recounted how wicked white men sought to profit from them and their children by conveying them outside the court's jurisdiction and peddling them to conscienceless slave traders.[13]

The horrific details in some of the plaintiffs' stories might have strained credibility had they not been substantiated by a number of witnesses. The nineteen-year-old Helen, a District of Columbia slave, was promised her freedom after twelve years of servitude, with the owner's added assurance that she would not be sold before that time. When she learned that her owner had made arrangements to sell her unexpired term for $140, she protested. After the buyer warranted that he would treat her well and would not sell her again, she acquiesced. Her new owner, Henry Drain, whom she later described as a near-penniless Irishman, then transported her aboard a steamboat to Fredericksburg, Virginia, where he promptly arranged to sell her to a woman for $300. In a turn with no want of dime-novel drama, Helen dove into the Rappahannock River and began swimming her way to freedom, only to be overtaken by Drain, who dragged her back onto the shore—not to prevent "the destruction of her life," she said, but to protect his investment. The sale fell through. On their eventual return to the

District of Columbia, Helen escaped again, this time successfully, and obtained a lawyer. She won a suit that forbade her owner from selling her for more years than she was required to serve.[14]

Helen's case was illustrative of numerous others filed by term slaves in the decades preceding the Civil War. Like Helen, many term slaves were sold at least once during their term of servitude; others were sold two, three, four, or more times. Such sales were sometimes conditioned on periods of servitude that ran longer than those originally granted to the term slaves or, in the worst possible scenario, on the bondage of supposedly term slaves for life. In either of these circumstances, term slaves could seek protection in the courts. Once they had secured the assistance of counsel, among the many challenges that term slaves faced was the uncovering of written evidence—be it a copy of a will, deed, indenture, bill of sale, or any other legal instrument—to substantiate their plight. If this evidence showed clearly that they had fulfilled their bond of servitude, they could petition for their freedom. If, however, their term of servitude had not yet expired, as in Helen's case, they could only seek an injunction or court order to ensure that their current owners, by the required posting of a bond, honored the original owners' wishes. Thus, the documents in which original owners promised their slaves' freedom at a future time served as contracts between the two parties. While such contracts were legally binding only in Delaware, Tennessee, and Louisiana, agreements to the same effect were on occasion upheld in courts elsewhere in the Upper South.[15]

Some term slaves were sold so many times and at so many sites that they found it difficult to remember, in consultation with their lawyers, exactly who bought them where and who sold them when. They were universally illiterate and possessed no bills of sale to prove who owned them at various times, relying on their own memory and the inquiries of their lawyers. Yet, they could often detail vividly incidents of hardship, disappointment, injustice, and ill use in their servitude. As their journeys took them from one location to another, sometimes one state to another, and frequently from one owner to another, term slaves found themselves especially vulnerable because they could not be differentiated from slaves for life except by an indenture or deed or some other legal document that lay in the hands of their original owners or had been registered by them in some county courthouse years before. Any evidence other than documents verifying term servitude was tangential in court proceedings. That being the case, term slaves able to petition the courts and file freedom papers probably represented only a small fraction of those who were illegally bought and sold. Once in the legal system, though, term slaves could glimpse a path to freedom—a path that at first barely glimmered with hope but that sometimes in time led them into the full light of freedom's possibility. Twenty-seven-year-old Simeon Clark found that path. Though born in New Jersey to a free woman of color, he was bound out at age twelve or fourteen for a term that was to end when he reached age twenty-one. His master, however, took him to Ohio and then Illinois, where he sold Clark to a slave trader as a slave for life. In 1832, after fleeing to Kentucky, Clark "secreted himself to avoid being taken off out of the State as a Slave" and two and a half years later won his freedom.[16]

In fact, term slaves fortunate enough to be able to file freedom suits could for the most part expect a fair and balanced hearing of the evidence in states where term slavery was relatively common during the decades leading up to the Civil War. At issue in these suits were equity and an owner's original intent, with owners being permitted to "dispose" of their human property in such manner—including time-limited bondage—as they saw fit. In most Lower South states, however, where emancipations were prohibited except by the legislatures, only a few such cases could be brought to the courts, and then only under unusual circumstances. "There is no statute bar to suits for freedom," Georgia Supreme Court associate justice C. J. McDonald wrote in an 1858 opinion concerning Maryland blacksmith Giles Price, a free black who had been enslaved for a term of fifteen years "for some crime." At the end of that period, a slave trader transported Price from Maryland to Georgia and there sold him to a resident for $1,800. Having served out his term, Price could not be sold as a slave, Justice McDonald explained, ruling that he was free man.[17]

In states of the Upper South and Louisiana, a number of term slaves filed freedom suits or sought the protection of the courts both during and after their terms of servitude. In a case typical of the early period, in 1793 Maryland slaveholder Nathan Harris resolved that his slave Cato should be freed after seven years. With this understanding, Harris sold Cato for £65, but in 1799 the new owner decided not to release Cato upon the expiration of his term. The original owner thereupon executed a deed of manumission. Although the county court ruled against Cato, the appeals court reversed the verdict. When a slave was sold for a said term of years, with agreement between the transacting parties that the slave should be freed at the end of the designated period, the judges ruled, the buyer, or vendee, was obliged to abide by the agreement.[18] Most judges in the Upper South and Louisiana ruled in term-slave suits that the masters' wishes should be honored, even when heirs and family members strenuously objected or went so far as to destroy the legal documents pertaining to the case. Complications commonly mired such cases, especially as testimony in the slaves' behalf often proved difficult to obtain, but a number of term slaves nevertheless gained their freedom while others of them received protective injunctions or court orders. In Kentucky, Chancellor George Bibb not only granted four men free status years after they should have been freed (a decision upheld on appeal) but also awarded each of them damages of $500.[19]

Term slaves who lived in towns and cities found it easier than those in rural areas to contact authorities, seek out sympathetic whites, and speak with lawyers, but even in rural counties, such as St. Mary's in Maryland, blacks could find whites sympathetic to their intent. In some cases, members of white, slaveowning families offered their support; in others, whites living in the same neighborhood as the term slaves were willing to testify in their behalf. Numerous depositions given at trial bore witness to such support.[20] It was from the stories of the slave clients themselves, however, that lawyers fashioned bills of complaint, as the petitions were called. In them, the plaintiffs asked for injunctions to prohibit owners and others from seizing or molesting them and their family members. Or they sought court orders prohibiting their sale, for once they were sold, they would find it virtually impossible to bring to light the facts of their original owners' intentions or to produce the necessary documentary evidence defining the number of years in their terms of servitude.

During the early decades of the nineteenth century, the ever-rising demand for slaves to labor in the cotton fields of the Lower South tempted traders and owners in various Upper South states to sell term slaves as slaves for life. Numbers of term slaves were, as one nineteen-year-old with eleven years yet to serve said, "illegally and unjustly" held by dealers in human flesh who planned "to remove [them] out of the District of Columbia for the purposes of trade &c."[21] In Maryland, four term slaves—Charity, Kitty, Mary, and Mary's infant—who were "entitled to their freedom at their respective ages of thirty one years" fell into the possession of two white men who, they believed, had recently sold them to a man with plans to take them out of the state. On the testimony of William Campbell, who himself owned four slaves, the court issued an injunction that addressed the concerns of the plaintiffs in their favor.[22]

Cases in which time-limited slaves were retained in bondage long past the prescribed end of their terms were not uncommon. Most often such disregard of slaves' interests was prompted by greed and avarice on the part of an owner or members of the owner's family, but on occasion it arose out of genuine confusion among whites as to the actual length of the slave's term of service. Sometimes owners wrote wills and deeds granting freedom to particular slaves at a date in the future, but then later added codicils to their wills or drafted new deeds that retracted or revised their original bequests. Family debts, too, sometimes resulted in creditors confiscating time-limited servants.[23] And some slaveholders simply ignored the wishes of an original owner. Stephen Smith, a Delaware term slave freed "by an instrument under seal" in 1816, remained in bondage until the late 1830s due to various claims brought on him by various white family and nonfamily members.[24] A slaveholding woman in Maryland designated that her slave Nancy should be freed when she reached age twenty-one, but before she did, Nancy's owner carried her off "under cover of darkness" to Kentucky.

Nancy's term of service would have expired the same year Smith received his "instrument of freedom," but, like him, she remained in bondage another twenty years, until the mid-1830s.[25]

In perhaps the strangest case of inordinate term servitude, a Virginia woman named Nan claimed that, according to a deed, she was bound to serve a term of twelve years, whereas her children's terms would end on their reaching age twenty-eight. In 1817, Nan was released and registered in Rockingham County as a free person of color, but long after Nan's death, her daughter Gracey and Gracey's nine children remained enslaved. Not until 1859 were they freed, when the Virginia Supreme Court of Appeals declared that there was nothing in the case to show that Nan was a slave, "except the fact of her color and African descent"—a presumption "repelled by the other facts proved in the case."[26] More than four decades after Nan had gained her freedom, her children and grandchildren won theirs.

Many of the slaves kept in bondage long after their terms had expired had in fact been sold as slaves for life. Often they were conveyed to states where the laws prohibited or inhibited the ability of African Americans to file freedom suits. In Louisiana, for example, slaves could not be freed prior to reaching age thirty unless special permissions were granted. When term slaves were permitted and able to bring suits in their home communities, the courts sometimes failed to provide assistance or relief, especially when time-limited servants had not yet served out their terms. Even under the most frightful circumstances, when blacks feared being taken out of county or state and enslaved for life, courts might decline to issue injunctions of protection. In such cases, the slaveholders retained ownership rights over their human property and the courts could offer that property no alternatives.[27]

Among the most vexing questions in the law of emancipation was whether children born to female slaves who had been promised their freedom in the future were entitled to the same benefit. The question arose almost entirely in the Upper South, where manumission continued during the nineteenth century. The laws covering emancipation differed from state to state, as did the precedents established by the courts. In 1799, in *Pleasants v. Pleasants*, the Virginia chancellor George Wythe and appeals judge Spencer Roane offered the opinion that as soon as the right of the mother to future freedom had been determined, she was free, as were any children born to her, and testators had no power to "impose any servitude on them." In short, they ruled that "the present right to future freedom is present freedom."

This view was repudiated in Virginia in 1824 in the case of *Maria v. Surbaugh*, wherein Virginia judge Spencer Green decided that the children born to female term slaves during the mother's term of servitude were born in, and remained in, bondage. The case was complicated, stretching back to 1790 when, in his will, a slaveholder instructed that Maria's mother should be freed at the age of thirty-one. Meanwhile, sold and resold, the mother gave birth to four children, including Maria, who was owned by the party Surbaugh. On reaching age thirty-one, the mother brought suit on behalf of herself and her children, but both the lower court and court of appeals ruled in favor only of the mother and did not free the children. Virginia appeals judge John Green explained that the 1799 decision of *Pleasants* contradicted the law of 1782 regarding emancipations. Unless the original owner had bound himself to support the children—children who could otherwise be sold, resold, and widely dispersed, according to the earlier law—the public would inevitably be burdened with their support. Maria and her siblings were therefore ruled to be "without any right to future liberty."[28]

Most states adopted Green's argument prohibiting the freedom of children born during a mother's term of servitude, unless owners specified that the children should also be freed. Yet there were countervailing arguments. In Tennessee, two cases hinged on the same question as that in Virginia's appeals court decision, but with quite different results. In *Crenshaw v. Matilda*, in 1827, Judge Jacob Peck affirmed a lower court's decision granting Matilda her freedom. Matilda, like Maria in Virginia, was born before her mother's term had expired. Matilda's mother, so her owner's deed had specified, was to be freed when she came of age, in 1806, but two years earlier, she bore her daughter Matilda, who was subsequently bound to a relative of the original owner. Years later, when Matilda sued for her freedom, Peck declared the "deed of emancipation was in *presenti*," as opposed to "*in futuro*," and thus the same deed that freed the mother also freed her future child. Matilda not only won her freedom but was also awarded ninety dollars in damages.[29] Similarly, in 1834, Tennessee chief justice John Catron wrote in his opinion regarding *Harris v. Clarissa* that if the effective date of emancipation was "doubtful," the court should "act in the spirit of the law of all civilized nations which favor liberty." Thus a grant of freedom at a future date conferred a "present right to freedom," and a child born to a person "bound to service for a term of years, who has a general right to freedom" was a child born free.[30]

Cases involving the children of term slaves defied consensus in the courts. They also raised a number of legal questions about term *slavery*: How and when should children of female term slaves be freed (if they should be freed at all)? Were wills and deeds the only means for such children to claim their freedom, or were agreements and "memorandums" and oral bargains also valid?[31] Could the children of time-limited slaves born during the "gap" before the date of their mother's freedom argue for their free status if their mother's owner had not included them in a deed or will? The legal questions arose mostly out of economic ones, slaves being property that their owners might wish to dispose of by granting them—and if female, perhaps their "issue"—free status at a future date. Still, even the most carefully worded last will and testament or deed could not anticipate what might happen to an estate or its owner's family and slaves years in the future, especially if a term of service ran several decades. It was impossible to know if those in term bondage would have completed obligations required by the estate before their documented release date, as in cases, for instance, in which care for a still-surviving elderly widow stood as a prerequisite for release.

The courts attempted to deal with any such contingencies, but with limited success. A few appellate courts, like the High Court of Appeals in Maryland, accepted as valid the various types of agreements for term slavery, but most states were reluctant to allow any oral arrangements in that regard or to permit damages claims for time spent in service after the prescribed term had expired.[32] Some high courts reversed lower court rulings that held children of term slaves in bondage if they were born during the mother's term of servitude, because, the higher court reasoned, the owner granted freedom to the mother and "her issue." A deed of emancipation "liberating a female and 'her increase' on a given day *in futuro,*" a Kentucky judge ruled, "emancipates all her issue born after the date of the deed."[33]

County courts decided on issues pertaining to term slaves' children as they arose in their jurisdictions. In a bill of sale, a District of Columbia owner stipulated that his female bondswoman should serve nine years and no longer. During that nine-year term she gave birth to Sarah, whom her mother's buyer retained in bondage long after the mother's term had ended. In her freedom suit, Sarah claimed her right to be likewise free, and the circuit court agreed: If a female slave should be sold to serve "the vendee" for a term of years, with an obligation by "the vendee" to manumit her at the expiration of the term, and if, during the term, the slave should give birth, the child was entitled to her freedom.[34]

Most children born during the servitude of term slaves did not share Sarah's good fortune. The laws applicable to their cases varied from state to state, and often they failed to address the issue. By the time some states finally did enact laws concerning the offspring of term slaves, numerous cases had already been adjudicated against the children. In 1849, Virginia passed a law providing that the "increase of any female" emancipated in a will or deed "hereafter made," who were born after the death of the testator, or the record of the deed, were to be freed at the time of their mother's release "unless the will or deed otherwise provides." The law overturned *Maria v. Surbaugh,* but it came too late in the antebellum era to make a difference for many of the children held in bondage after their mothers had been freed.[35] In some states, laws stipulated that children born during their mother's term were born in bondage and thus remained in bondage; in other states, laws designated that only adults capable of earning a livelihood could be manumitted.

In the 1833 case of Benjamin Jones, who was born during his mother's term of servitude, the Delaware Court of Errors and Appeals—despite the state's long history of support for its large, free black population—ruled that Jones was what he was born: a slave. In his dissent, Judge Samuel M. Harrington argued that the mother was not in a condition of absolute slavery when her son was born, but rather in a condition of "limited slavery, owing service for a limited period." Nor was it correct, Harrington contended, to assume in a country dedicated to the principles of liberty and personal rights that "property in slaves is precisely like every other species of property." Slavery was gradually ending in the North, he noted, citing as an example the state of Pennsylvania where, with fewer than one hundred slaves, the institution was virtually extinct. Some years later, the Delaware appeals court had apparently come to agree with Harrington; it granted Ann Elliott and her three siblings their freedom although their mother was a slave-to-be-freed when the children were born.[36]

A number of term slaves born during the mother's term of servitude, like Benjamin Jones, failed in their attempts to achieve free status.[37] As a result, young children often suffered the initially wrenching and then long pain of separation when their term-slave mothers were set free while they remained in bondage. In the many cases brought on behalf of children by their mothers and other concerned parties, at issue, for the purpose of the courts, was not the separation of mother and child but rather the original intent of the mother's owner in his or her arrangements for a time-limited term of slavery. If slaveholders failed to make provisions for "the slave and her issue" in the various deeds, wills, bills of sale, or other legal documents, the children by default became slaves for life. Often, when provisions were made, the children faced the prospects of decades-long bondage, until they reached the age of twenty-five or thirty-one or thirty-five. And until then, they almost always passed from one master to another and another, and were thus dependent on a current owner to honor a promise made by their original owner many years before.

When Joanna was purchased in 1797 as a term slave for twelve years, the bill of sale included no reference to any children she might bear during her period of servitude. The purchaser had transferred her to another family when, in 1801, she gave birth to Peter and, in 1803, to Lewis. Some time later the head of that family died, and a relative sold the two boys to a South Carolina trader as slaves for life. On learning of the sale, the original purchaser, who still owned the slaves, promptly executed a deed by which to manumit Joanna immediately—it was 1809, and her twelve-year term of service had ended—and obtained an injunction to prevent the removal of the children. The new deed, however, provided for the children's freedom on their attainment of age thirty-one, nearly a quarter century in the future.[38]

What complicated the claims of freedom by term slaves' children most was their sale and resale, and resale again and perhaps again, until it was difficult to determine if they, like their mothers, were term slaves or, as their owners were likely to maintain, slaves for life. The chances of their resale increased, too, as it was not uncommon for children, like Peter and Lewis, to be bound in service for terms years longer than their mothers'. In those years owners might move from one district, or county or state, to another, where they might sell their slaves with, or without, their term limits to new owners. Or they might seek court orders to extend the terms of time-limited slaves because they had become "troublesome property." Owners who fell into debt and mortgaged their estates might be forced to forfeit their human property.

Meanwhile, documents defining terms of servitude or dates of freedom could be lost or misplaced, and the daughters of the term-slave women cited in those agreements would themselves give birth to children who would similarly be bound in terms of servitude years beyond those of their mothers, or for life. Delia, a Maryland term slave who was sold to serve Jonathan Burch for ten years in 1819, fretted that her three children, all of them young at the time, were required to remain in servitude "till they should arrive to the age of thirty-five years." Under a purchase agreement, Burch had promised not to remove them from Maryland; so, when he did, Delia filed a suit in the circuit court of the District of Columbia stating that she and her children were being confined in a slave pen and were going to be transported to Alabama, where they would be held as slaves for life. Delia won an injunction, but it did not allay her anxiety about the future of her children, two girls and a boy.[39]

Some cases were complicated by conflicts in the laws of different states. When the "Negro Samuel" sued for his freedom in the District of Columbia Federal Circuit Court in December 1831, he encountered several problems. His mother's owner had been living in Maryland when he had freed her in a deed of manumission in 1796, but the deed had been subscribed by only one witness; as Maryland law (Acts 1796, c. 67, sect. 29) required two witnesses, the deed was deemed invalid. The owner had later moved to Virginia, and there, in his will, he had provided for the mother's freedom when she reached age twenty-five. Accordingly, the mother was freed, but her son had been born before she had reached the age of twenty-five, "that is before she was actually free," and therefore, by Virginia law, remained a slave.[40] In other term-slave suits complications arose because of the particular wording in a will or deed or other conveyance. If an owner stipulated that a female slave be freed after a given number of years, and willed further that any offspring born to her be freed upon reaching a designated age, the children were subject to the often extensive terms of their bondage, and their children were likewise forced into terms of slavery for many years.

In 1798, Virginia testator Joseph Pierce freed a number of slaves on the condition that they complete designated terms. Among them was Nancy, who was to be freed when she reached age thirty-one. Pierce also instructed that if any of his slaves bore children, they too should be freed at age thirty-one "and so on until they shall become free." Julianna, Nancy's daughter, was born before her mother reached age thirty-one, and so was Julianna's daughter, Frances Wood. In the 1850s Frances Wood sued for her freedom under the 1798 will. The appeals court ruled that the doctrine of perpetuities, which applied to personal chattel, did not apply to bequests of freedom for slaves. The plaintiff was born before her mother reached age thirty-one, and when Frances reached that age, under the will's construction, she could claim her freedom. This occurred nearly sixty years after her grandmother had gained her free status.[41]

The freedom suit won by Frances Wood six decades after the execution of Joseph Pierce's will pointed to the importance that the courts assigned to the intent of slaveholders in disposing of their human chattel. Even when the original owners' instructions as to how and when slaves should be manumitted were clear and specific, unforeseen circumstances could subvert a slaveholder's intent during a term of servitude. One legatee, though assigned in the will of Mary Brooke to take ownership of Kitty during the nine years of her future servitude, refused to accept the responsibility. Fearing that she might be sold out of the District of Columbia, Kitty filed a suit to require the legatee to abide by her former owner's instructions and post a bond to that effect. The jury found that Kitty was indeed entitled to her freedom in 1840, nine years in the future, and the court ordered "the original injunction to be continued, restraining the defendant from removing the petitioner from the jurisdiction" of the court and requiring the defendant to post a bond of $600 to that effect.[42]

The most critical period for many time-limited slaves was that when their terms began drawing to a close. The market value of slaves with only months or a year or two of bondage remaining plummeted precipitously, whereas huge profits could be realized by their masters if they were sold as slaves for life. In one such case, the Kentucky Supreme Court determined that the value of a group of term slaves increased twentyfold if they were marketed as slaves for life. The significant difference in worth provided a strong incentive to abrogate the promises made by an original owner regarding future freedom. Current owners could thus reap handsome profits from the sales, trades, and transfers of slaves.[43] Of course, some owners honored their commitments and signed deeds of manumission for the term slaves who had served them faithfully over a number of years. But others did not. The court records show numerous cases in which time-limited slaves nearing the end of their service had been betrayed by their owners, who were sometimes several owners distant from the original master whose signature had certified the indenture or legal document providing for a slave's future freedom.

In 1790, a Maryland slaveholding woman traded Will for another slave with the understanding that Will would serve the new owner for a term of seven years. The new owner signed a "memorandum," referred to as "his act and deed," promising to abide by the agreement. With the "prospect of freedom thus held out," Will went into the service of his new owner in Kentucky; at the end of the agreed-on seven years, however, the slaveholder refused to honor the memorandum. Soon afterward, Will filed a freedom suit in a law court, and lost. Years later, with the assistance of his former mistress, Will filed a suit in a chancery court and finally achieved his goal. It was then fully twelve years since his term of service had expired.[44] During the later stages of term bondage, too, time-limited slaves were most likely to be moved from one state to another, sold or resold to new owners or slave traders, and transported to the Deep South, where they were profitably marketed as slaves for life. At each stage of their journeys, term slaves recounted to anyone who would listen that they were "time-limited" slaves and could not be legally sold for terms beyond those of their servitude. Some nevertheless found themselves trapped in lives of perpetual bondage far from their homes and families, but others managed to make their pleas heard and to solicit assistance in obtaining their freedom.[45]

As might be imagined, it was extremely difficult for term slaves to bring their cases to court. They had to contact local authorities, confide in trustworthy (they hoped) whites about their situation, engage lawyers to file the necessary papers, and provide a roster of possible, usually white witnesses—witnesses willing, indeed, to testify against slaveowners who might be well known and respected members of the community. Term slaves always had reason to fear the reaction of owners cited in freedom suits. Proclaiming their innocence, owners often simply cast their word against that of the petitioners by maintaining that the slaves in question were in fact not time-limited servants.

If the suits drew the owners into protracted court battles over how or when or if the slaves should be granted free status, the owners might translate their resentment into maltreatment of the plaintiffs' fellow slaves and families. For many term slaves filing freedom suits, family lay worrisomely at the center of their concerns and considerations: Would a husband and wife be separated from each other or from their children, and if so, what could they do to protect loved ones? How would owners treat the children of term slaves if the children's terms were longer than those of their parents? What would happen to families when all its members were subject to different terms of servitude? Adding to the complexity were transactions of past owners that had been documented ambiguously or not at all: under what terms time-limited slaves had been transferred from one white family member to another, for example, or under what authority members of an owner's family had assumed the right to loan, hire, or sell particular slaves. And always difficult to verify were oral commitments made by owners to individual slave family members in regard to where and by what means each of them would live until the dates of their respective manumissions.

Concerns like these came into play in 1796 when a Delaware slave family—Comfort and Emanuel and their small children—found itself caught in the middle of a conflict between the executor of an estate and James Fisher, who had purchased the family as term slaves. The executor and the purchaser had agreed that the family should be kept together, and Fisher had willingly turned over a house and garden to the black family. The trouble arose when the executor informed Fisher that Comfort's term of servitude had expired. Charging fraud, Fisher in short order signed a contract by which a Georgia man gained purchase of the mother and her children. On learning of the sale, and the imminent separation in the family, Comfort, Emanuel, and the children fled. A short time later Comfort filed a freedom suit.[46]

Then, too, for long years or decades, term slaves every day faced the uncertainty of their future, and their children's, as it might be redetermined any day by some resolve on the part of the whites who possessed the legal right to their terms of servitude. In the passage of ten or fifteen years—a not uncommon term of servitude for young people—the legal owner could easily sell time-limited slaves with a number of years still due on their service, and their new owner could do the same. There were no prohibitions against sales and resales, except in states where laws prohibited sales out of the state—but not if the courts allowed the

Many term slaves in the Upper South feared being taken down the Mississippi River and sold as slaves for life in the New Orleans slave market. They experienced fear, anxiety, and often panic as they faced the unknown with a new master. They also felt great sadness at being torn away from family and friends, never to return. *William Henry Brooke, artist; courtesy, Historic New Orleans Collection, 1974.25.23.4*

sales because they found the slaves to be "recalcitrant" or "rebellious."[47] In many instances, time-limited slaves who had been sold and resold out of state had few opportunities to pursue freedom suits once they had completed their terms of servitude. Term slaves who lived in the fear of being exported had one slim alternative; they could apply for court orders that enjoined their owners to remain within the court's jurisdiction throughout the slaves' terms of servitude.[48]

Deeds and wills also posed problems for term slaves, as they not infrequently employed vague language as to the date a term of service should end, for instance, or as to the "good behavior" required of a slave during the time of service. The vagueness left interpretation open to the devices of the owner, who could, on grounds of what he or she purported to be bad behavior, have a term of servitude extended. Bills of sale also sometimes failed to cite the specific number of years that remained in the slave's term of servitude, or even that a term limited the tenure of the slave's bondage. The disclosure that a slave being sold was not a slave for life relied entirely on the discretion of the seller. If a seller withheld disclosure from a buyer, term slaves could seek out the aid of a party sympathetic to their story and quandary, although circumstances rarely enabled the possibility. "I will and bequeath to my niece Elizabeth Hamilton my negro boy Manuel Dodson, to serve for 27 years," stipulated Elizabeth Magruder of the District of Columbia in 1827, but halfway through his term Manuel Dodson was turned over to a slave trader, who transported him to Richmond, Virginia, and there put him up for sale. The trader told Dodson that his owner's will granting his eventual freedom had been declared null and void by an act of Congress. In 1843, Dodson did manage to secure a judgment in his favor, but he was required to serve any new master until 1854, when supposedly he would be freed.[49]

Seldom did term slaves who filed freedom suits with or on behalf of loved ones secure sound or lasting guarantees of protection for their families, even when court orders granted their pleas. When a grandmother in the District of Columbia pled on behalf of her daughter and her daughter's three children, whose recent buyer had acted contrary to an original contract and now intended, it was feared, to move them elsewhere, the court granted only that they would be held in the marshal's custody for a given period of time.[50] Also, term slaves who had been sold and resold often found their promise of freedom—despite the concrete evidence of a will or deed, and despite the supporting testimony of witnesses—either revoked or ignored by the court. Nor did rulings in favor of plaintiffs filing freedom suits ensure their future, as verdicts in the lower courts were not infrequently overturned on appeal.

In his 1823 will, a Maryland slaveholder freed his slave Caroline "and her increase" at age thirty-six. Caroline died in her early thirties, and when her daughter filed her freedom suit in 1851, she was in her early twenties. The Anne Arundel County Court ruled in the daughter's favor, but the appeals court reversed the verdict because the daughter, born about 1830, was only twenty-two or twenty-three years of age.[51] While legal precedent could account for the decision of the appeals court in Maryland, such was not the case in the ruling on Carmelite's freedom suit in Louisiana. Carmelite had been sold by her owner for a term of seven years, the time limit being a reward for her faithful services as a nurse for one of her mistress's children. The purchaser, Jean Lacaze, had acquired her to function as his concubine, and had eventually replaced her with another woman. But he did not free her. Alleging that Carmelite was "insubordinate and insolent"—that she had struck him and hit one of his white servants—he declared her unfit for freedom. Then he installed and put her to work in a brothel that he owned. The appeals court ruled in the defendant's favor.[52]

A few cases concerning term servitude reached the US Supreme Court. Could a slave validly argue, as petitioner Susan Vigel did, that she should be free on the basis of evidence that her mother, sister, and brother had been granted their future freedom under a last will and testament? Maryland slaveholder John B. Kirby died in 1828. In his will, by provisions allowed under Maryland law, he instructed that all of his slaves over age thirty-five should be emancipated, whereas those under that age should be freed when they reached thirty-five, if men, and thirty, if women. Kirby's executor, George Naylor, retained the petitioner's mother and sister—Sarah and Eliza, respectively—in bondage until Sarah, in 1838, and Eliza, in 1842, filed suits against Naylor, and obtained their freedom. Years later, when Sarah's other daughter, Susan Vigel, similarly brought suit, her lawyer requested that the records of the freedom suits brought by Susan's family members be presented to the jury as evidence, because only in the most unusual of circumstances would a six- or eight-year-old slave child—as Susan was in 1828—be separated from her mother in regard to the provisions in a slaveholder's will. The court denied the lawyer's request, and the jury was disallowed the evidence. The lawyer appealed the case in the US Supreme Court. Justice John Catron delivered the opinion of the court. The evidence in the case, Catron reasoned, was not inadmissible hearsay but, rather, direct testimony from actual court records. It was the jury's duty, therefore, to decide whether the evidence should be considered. The judgment of the circuit court was thus reversed and the cause remanded for another trial.[53]

The issues raised by time-limited slavery did not want for ironies, not least when term slaves attempted to sue for wages lost during their retention in bondage beyond their terms of servitude. Several states permitted such petitions, which were submitted either at the conclusion of a freedom suit or in a separate claim. Slaves who had not been duly freed on the expiration of their terms or who had been hired out during the course of their trial commonly felt frustration with their current owners. Frustration bred anger, hostility, vengefulness, and lawsuits. To sue for damages, though, the offended term slaves needed the support of whites whom they could trust to testify on their behalf. They also needed lawyers willing to take up their causes. Not all the southern states permitted hirelings to be paid wages that their labor had earned both after the failure of their owners to release them and during the process of their freedom suits.[54] The few states in which back wages cases could be filed included Maryland during the early years, Delaware, Kentucky, Tennessee, and Louisiana in its civil courts.

In Missouri, most wage suits were filed in common law courts, and while the judges and juries were supposed by law to allow payment for damages, in practice, especially after 1835 when a new law prohibited any further petitions in regard to earnings lost by term slaves, they were disposed to awarding one dollar or one penny as compensation to those who had won their freedom.[55] Prior to 1835, Missouri courts did on occasion award less farcical damages, but collecting the money due the plaintiff often proved to be difficult or impossible. The slave Jerry, who began his case in the Superior Court of St. Louis in 1819, eventually won his freedom and sued his owner for $170 in damages sustained by trespass and costs. Jerry never pocketed one dollar or one cent of the money, however, as the defendant could not be found anywhere in the county.[56] Other states denied the judiciary the right to award damages to hired term slaves, even when sympathetic judges favored slave plaintiffs. In 1809, Virginia chancellor Creed Taylor, a judge sympathetic to slave plaintiffs, ordered that the plaintiffs in a freedom suit could request a distribution of any surplus in a fund that had been raised from the profits of their hires after the estate debts were paid. The appeals court, however, reversed this section of the decree on the grounds that the profits could not be paid over to the freed men because they "were not free when the profits accrued." By the late antebellum era most southern states, including Maryland, had followed Virginia's lead.[57]

Still, in states where judges and juries were more sensitive to the plight of exploited term slaves, a few slave plaintiffs and their counsel did win damages. In Kentucky, term slaves were able to sue successfully for back wages as hirelings if they had been held beyond their term. In one instance, a former slave woman sued an estate executor by claiming that her owner had "devised to her her freedom" and directed his executors "to perfect it in six months." The executor had failed to do so, and the devisee won a judgment that compelled him to pay her the money she had earned as a hireling during that period.[58] Similarly, the Tennessee Supreme Court ruled that the term slaves Lavina and her son deserved compensation for the services they had rendered in bondage for six years after the date they should have been released. The clerk and master of the Giles County Chancery Court, the Supreme Court instructed, should itemize the hire or value of the hire for both plaintiffs during that period and pay them that sum, including interest. The court also ordered that the defendants pay the costs of the suit.[59] Several years after another Tennessee bondswoman achieved free status, she sued for damages and was awarded fifty dollars.[60]

As in Kentucky and Tennessee, the courts in Louisiana also ruled for the plaintiff in a number of cases in which term slaves sued for damages. Success for plaintiffs in these suits was usually linked to especially compelling arguments for their freedom and to reliable witnesses who substantiated their allegations. Some plaintiffs asked to be sequestered as hirelings so as to be secure from the reach of owners who might attempt to sell them during the court proceedings. In Louisiana, even children could file requests for sequestration with the assistance of a curator, as guardians were called in Louisiana. Because the state had become a center for the sale of kidnapped blacks, children were exceptionally vulnerable; it was not uncommon for them to be snatched off city streets in the North or Upper South and then transported to the Lower South, in particular to New Orleans, where they were sold into slavery. And although court decisions in freedom suits sometimes provided for damages, the amounts to be paid were likely to be small.

John Johnson, a sixteen-year-old man of color who was born of free parents in the state of New York, came to New Orleans as a waiter in service to the wife of Major General James Wilkinson of the US Army. In 1816, he was sold to a sugar planter as a slave for life and was taken to a plantation "where he has been held and treated as a slave in the most cruel manner." Johnson argued in court that even if his parents were slaves in the state of New York, by the laws of that state he was not liable to be held as a slave. He petitioned for his freedom and asked for wages from his labor. Though he was freed, he won only the court costs.[61] In subsequent years, slaves, primarily from New Orleans, who had spent time with their owners in France and thereby gained free status, generally succeeded in winning awards of monthly wages as well court costs.[62]

Term slaves, like other slave plaintiffs who filed freedom suits, introduced family histories to argue their status. They traced their lineage, especially on the maternal side; they related how and when their grandmothers and mothers should have gained or actually did gain free status; they identified the owners of their kin and where they had lived. They usually knew at least the approximate years of their parents' and grandparents' birth and knew the dates that promised them freedom in the original deeds of manumission. They included details of freedom suits in other states, where members of their families had been emancipated or by court order would be in the future; and they knew at what age and where other family members should have been freed. They recounted how white slaveholders had conveyed members of their families to different states; how owners had "knowingly, willfully, fraudulently" not only kept plaintiffs in slavery but also sold and sent them off to parts unknown, brothers and sisters who were all "entitled to freedom, all of which is contrary to equity and in direct violation of the laws of the land." The final decree in a Kentucky case that employed all of these evidentiary means did indeed grant the plaintiff Anthony his freedom; more significantly still, it further ordered that the sheriff of Cumberland County pay Anthony the money he had earned as a hireling during the long pendency of the suit, and it appointed a commissioner to oversee the payments. The defendant was required to pay court costs.[63]

Anthony's suit did not indicate the exact amount he was awarded in damages. Possibly, it was generous, as court records show that in some freedom suits term slaves received sizable damage awards. When one owner revoked his will "except the provisions thereof respecting his slaves," the disgruntled heirs kept Albert in bondage for an additional three years. He sued for his freedom and for the wages he had earned during the three years. The court ordered the appointment of a commissioner to collect $253.00 from the defendant for the plaintiff's hire in 1852 and 1853, and $110.00 from A. L. Childress, who had hired the plaintiff in 1854, and to pay that amount to the plaintiff, minus court costs and other expenses amounting to $49.62, including the $20.00 fee for his lawyer. The total amount Albert received was $315.38. Albert's award was extraordinarily large, but term slaves who sought lesser amounts were sometimes rewarded with at least the payment of court costs by the defendants and of hireling profits for a few months or a year.[64]

In some states, term slaves were successful in obtaining not only back wages but also any legacy that their owners might have bequeathed for them to receive upon the date of their freedom. Most of the court decisions in this regard were based on the presumed right of slaveholders to deal with their bond servants as they saw fit. Such legacies, especially when they involved real estate, were usually prohibited in states that denied residency to blacks once they were freed. But this was not always the case, particularly during the early period. In Prince George's County, Maryland, in 1817, the county court and court of appeals awarded a black girl her freedom; furthermore, noting that she had been purchased by her own father, who, as her master, had bequeathed her a plot of land, the court ruled that she should also be awarded the devised property.[65]

In 1815, Mitchell Kershaw of Sussex County, Delaware, published his will, in which he instructed that a number of slaves should be freed when they reached the age of twenty-one. He stipulated, too, that his executor should sell all his property, except for his widow's dower, and have the moneys received "put on interest by loan," eventually to be distributed equally among his slaves as they became free. Three years later, Kershaw died. His widow, Sarah Kershaw, averse to abiding by the provisions of the will, kept the slaves' trust funds for herself. On the farm she also cut and sold wood, for which she received "large sums" of money put "to her own proper uses and purposes." The term slaves and several freed blacks demanded that Sarah "and her confederates" pay them "such sum as shall be found due to them." The plaintiffs won their case, and several among them received $317.11, excluding payment of $21.52 for court costs and a one-third fee charged by their lawyers.[66]

In the District of Columbia, in 1828, Eleanor (Nelly) Gray produced the will of her owner, which declared that "from the day on which she shall attain the age of twenty five" she should be free "and manumitted from all claims of service." The executors, however, held her in bondage until she was twenty-eight. Despite questions as to her exact age, the court ruled in her favor that she should receive throughout her lifetime a forty-dollar annuity, as indicated in the owner's will, as well as the arrears of the annuity and the wages she had earned during the previous three years. Although such rulings in regard to wages and gifts were not commonplace, they do show that some courts responded sympathetically, yet by rule of law, to the plight of blacks in term slavery. On receiving proof that they had been kept in bondage illegally, the courts were capable often of judging matters of freedom and damages with due diligence and without aversion to ruling in favor of former slaves.[67]

The responses of term slaves to their situations varied considerably, depending on the integrity of the owners, the credibility of their promises pertaining to slave families, the nature of the labor they required, and the length of time they assigned to the terms of bondage. Term slaves with owners known for keeping their promises and abiding by the provisions in deeds, wills, bills of sale, and oral agreements were often disposed to forbearance as they focused on the possibility of future freedom. They also, and necessarily, sought to curry favor with whites who might speak for them should disagreements arise between them and their masters, who might employ them for wages when they gained their freedom. For the many term slaves living in Upper South communities, often under the ownership of masters with modest numbers of slaves, it was neither difficult nor uncommon to make acquaintance with a broad range of townspeople: black and white, young and old, men and women, slaveholders and small-business owners. With all of them it was to the advantage of time-limited slaves to maintain reputations for honesty and industry, on the basis of which they were able to cement important relationships that, in the event of complications with owners or executors, would help them to ensure free status at the end of their tenure. Term slaves who were hired out during the process of their freedom suits were afforded a further opportunity, that of working in employments outside their situations of servitude, although their wages went into the hands of the authorities.

Term slaves found it necessary to file freedom suits only when owners' promises were broken and they thus feared for their own and their families' welfare. In that eventuality, the responses of term slaves, at least of those with cases in the public record, ranged from hostility to denial. One owner noted that his

term slave George "refused to work honestly & faithfully," abandoned service
at various times, failed to display proper deference to the owner's family, and
threatened to run away. The owner had George arrested and jailed and sold
for $600 as a slave for life.[68] Equally and frequently more defiant were term
slaves who had passed through several owners since their early youth. They
not only threatened to run away, but actually did so. The owner of term slave
Jacob Blackiston—a free black purchased as a term slave after a manslaughter
conviction—described him as a person of "such a vicious and depraved disposition" that he posed a great risk to the community. Jacob, the owner said,
threatened to kill a justice of the peace, terrorized whites in the neighborhood,
and absconded from the owner's possession. In a petition to the county court,
the owner asked that Jacob be sold out of the state, as was allowed by state law in
cases relating to intransigent blacks.[69]

In 1821, another term-slave runaway, Louisa Marshall, a youngster of about
seven, had been taken out of Kentucky to Missouri, where she was then sold and
removed to Louisiana. Many years later, she ran away, and back to Kentucky.
In her Mercy County freedom suit, she produced witnesses who vouched for
the fact that her first owner, George Belcher, who had died in 1824, had provided for her future freedom at age thirty. Already past that age, Louisa won her
case. She then returned to Louisiana, probably to be near her family and friends,
and applied for freedom there as well. A lower court decided in her favor, but
that decision was reversed on appeal in 1858; decisions in the state of Kentucky
were not binding in the state of Louisiana, and in any event, an 1857 Louisiana
law prohibited all emancipations. The plaintiff found little solace in the court's
assertion that to sell Louisa as a slave for life would be a "wrongful act."[70]

Slaves sometimes made agreements with their owners to the effect that by
working hard and demonstrating they were faithful, obedient, and trustworthy
in their service, they could earn their freedom. In fact, many owners of time-
limited slaves described them in exactly those words, but in any case it was the
master who determined whether the black servant acquitted himself or herself
in such a manner as to be rewarded with freedom. Some slaves believed that they
had served their owners so faithfully, obediently, and trustworthily that they had
in essence become term slaves without any formal affirmation to that effect on the
part of their owners. In that belief, evidently, a North Carolina carpenter named
Jim had for years served his owner, Ebenezer Pettigrew, with "humility," "good
manners," and "faithful service." Following Pettigrew's death, when Jim learned
that he had received no mention at all, let alone future freedom, in his master's
will, his character changed dramatically. His new owner complained that Jim
manifested a "proud and wicked spirit" and that he had become consumed "with
a desire for freedom." This troublesome slave, the new owner averred, afforded
him no choice but to ship him to a slave market in New Orleans.[71]

Jim's plight aside, many term slaves who sued for their freedom, like those in suits regarding wills and deeds, fared well in the court systems. Among the 149 freedom suits involving term slaves (about 7 percent of the total freedom suits where primary causes could be ascertained), 65 percent were granted; in a modest 14 percent, the decision in the case is not known. The suits were filed primarily in the Upper South and Louisiana, but complaints were also brought forth in every state of the Lower South except Texas. Among the cases that were appealed, term slaves received a favorable ruling in 59 percent of the cases; among those that concluded in the county courts, 73 percent were granted. In all, it is clear that the courts considered these complaints with a solemn obligation to uncover the pertinent facts and, if they pointed to free status, assumed their responsibility to release the plaintiffs from bondage. A huge proportion, 87 percent, of the suits by term slaves came during the middle and late periods. The struggles of time-limited African Americans during these decades points to the wedge some of them were able to create—through individual effort and self-sacrifice—between themselves and their owners. It was, for them, a step toward freedom. (See table 6.)

Delia Larkins had struggled for more than a year to stay free from the grasp of owners who sought to sell her as a slave for life. In the process she had dealt or combated with numerous white people, including slaveowners and slave traders in Baltimore and Nashville, a physician in Nashville, a Davidson County farmer, and several lawyers as well as jailers, county court clerks, and judges. She had been jailed for her own protection as she had been severely beaten by the speculator who took her from Maryland to Tennessee. In May 1857, the Davidson County Chancery Court had prohibited her sale as a slave for life.

What happened in subsequent months, however, demonstrated how an astute, defiant term slave ably employed the legal system and various whites not only to provide her protection but also to ensure that her freedom date of February 1, 1861, would be honored. On November 29, 1857, Delia petitioned the Davidson County Court a second time, but this time with a new lawyer, Herman Cox, a slaveowner like her former counsel, but younger and more amenable to Delia's instructions.[72] In her second petition, Delia asked the court to ignore the affidavit that had been submitted two days before by her former lawyer, Rettson Meigs. In it, Meigs had called for the arrest of the two men who, he alleged, were attempting to take Delia out of the county.[73] Meigs had also demanded that Delia should be sold for the remainder of her term and that the proceeds of the sale should be remitted to him in order to cover his fees and court costs.[74] In addition, Delia requested that the court vacate and annul the previous, May 1857 decree, which had been issued in her favor. She explained that for more than a year she had feared further retribution from William Summerhill, but his recent death had removed that threat. Moreover, her new owner, Thomas

Smith, a wealthy planter with large property holdings, and his agent, H. H. Haynes—the two men Meigs had cited for arrest in his affidavit—had treated her well, she claimed, and she believed them to be honest and honorable men.[75] The record in Nashville does not show the outcome of Delia's second petition, but she was released to the custody of her new owner.

More remarkable still, sometime after these events unfolded but prior to the expiration of her term, she returned to Maryland and rejoined her family. Most likely, Smith had permitted her return. During her ordeal she had praised him for his loyalty and honesty. She believed that she "would not be run off & sold by him." In 1860, the US census listed one "Adelia" Larkins, mulatto, age twenty-four, as a resident in Baltimore with her father, Emele Larkins, a forty-eight-year-old mulatto barber; her mother, Eliza Larkins, a forty-seven-year-old cook; and her son, an eight-year-old mulatto boy, William, who was attending elementary school.[76]

6

Descendants of Free Women

In May 1822, eighteen-year-old Nicholas Tachaud and his lawyer, slaveowner Henry R. Denis, filed a freedom suit in the District Court of New Orleans Parish, Louisiana. Tachaud stated that he had been born of free parents on the island of Hispaniola in the city of Santo Domingo. Shortly before the French evacuation of the city in 1809, when he was four or five, his mother died and he was taken into the care of his mother's friend, a free woman of color. With her and the French soldier with whom she was living at the time, Tachaud traveled first to Charleston, South Carolina, and later to Augusta, Georgia, where he lived for a number of years. How he happened to arrive in New Orleans was not made clear, but at present, he claimed, he was being "unjustly & illegally detained" as a slave by Richard Richardson. Fearing that, without protection, he would be removed from the city, he requested to be placed in the custody of the sheriff until his case could be adjudicated. He pled, too, that Richardson be called on to answer the suit and pay "all such damages to this court as shall seem meet." Tachaud then took an oath by which he swore that every charge made in his petition was true; he signed the oath with his mark. In response, the court ordered the sheriff to take the plaintiff into custody and hire him out until further notice.

To uncover evidence in support of events that occurred thirteen years earlier, during a tumultuous period in Caribbean history and when Tachaud was a five-year-old child, presented many challenges for both the plaintiff and his lawyer. The fact that Nicholas remembered his journey out of Santo Domingo to Augusta did not sufficiently prove his status at birth. But who would know the facts of Nicholas's background, and how would any witness be able to counter the opposition of a slaveowner who denied his slave was indeed a free person of color?[1] Slaves who sought to establish their free status on their descent from free women, as Tachaud did, faced a daunting task. Proof that a mother or grand-mother or great-grandmother was free could require evidence going back thirty, forty, or even fifty and more years. In three or four decades, once-free ancestors could have been reenslaved, their contemporaries and a plaintiff's possible witnesses could have died or grown extremely old, and court records could have been lost or destroyed; even the most conscientious lawyers wearied of the long, often fruitless pursuit of genealogical data. Problematic, too, after a quarter or half a century, was the uncovering of extant, relevant legal documents such as wills, deeds, and court records. At the same time, lawyers for the defendants alleged to be illegally holding blacks in bondage were likely to be able to produce bills of sale, inventories, wills, titles, and deeds to prove ownership. Vigorously asserting their rights as slaveholders, defendants sought to prevent any loss of wealth in human property as well as any stigma that might be attached to the illegal retention of free persons of color in servitude.[2]

With few exceptions, however, the courts treated slavery and freedom as matters of fundamental importance. And remarkably, in the courts' examinations of various witnesses—in a few instances, including members of the slaveholding families—they managed to disentangle the intricate skein of genealogical relationships as vital strands of information randomly emerged.[3] Perhaps the most complex lineal cases involved several generations of one family whose members had been claimed as slaves at various times by different white owners. By the time these cases reached the courts, the families had significantly multiplied, their members now usually bearing different names, and not only had they been separated from each other when they had become the property of different slaveholders, but they had also been geographically removed from each other, sometimes by a distance of counties or states. Often they had been bought and sold, and resold, and traded and hired, and endured their bondage for many long years. No matter their lineage, their current owners, like their original owners, as well as any white slaveholding heirs in between, always considered the members of these plaintiffs' black families to be slaves. In unraveling confused genealogies, the lawyers for the plaintiffs faced a formidable, time-consuming task.[4]

Plaintiffs' knowledge of their genealogy was frequently likely to be sketchy, especially if they were young children—as not a few of them were—when they should have been freed. To fill in the gaps in their mothers' ancestral histories and thereby meet the courts' demands for specific evidence—names, dates, places, events—in freedom suits, a few African Americans fabricated parts of their family history, but this was extremely rare. In most states, plaintiffs or their lawyers were required to swear an oath, as Nicholas Tachaud was, avowing the truthfulness of the evidence they presented. In fact, in the great majority of freedom suits plaintiffs revealed a substantial knowledge of their heritage and past family relationships. Freedom suits based on plaintiffs' maternal ancestry fell into three categories: those that claimed descent from white female forbears, a relatively small group; those that asserted having Indian female forbears, also a small group; and by far the largest group, those that linked their heritage to free women of color.

In the period from the American Revolution to the Civil War, black men, women, and children joined their lawyers at courthouses throughout the South to realize their dreams of freedom. The great majority of freedom suits were filed by discernibly black African Americans; in fact, in only 10 percent of the cases on record were the plaintiffs described as being "mulatto," the term then preferred to define persons of mixed racial ancestry. In most of these suits, the issues of race and color remained secondary in importance to the substance of genealogical evidence and state laws and judicial precedents that awarded plaintiffs their free status. About 1806, the Virginia slave Nanny Pagee—who, according to the court record, appeared to be a white woman—and her children sued for their freedom. Nanny and her lawyer, however, did not argue on the basis of her color. Rather, they contended that when she had been brought from North Carolina to Virginia twenty-five years before, she had been sold at a sheriff's sale in violation of the state's 1778 nonimportation law. After five years of litigation that pivoted on the applicability of the 1778 law to Nanny's suit for freedom, the jury determined that the nonimportation statute had in fact been broken, and the appeals court upheld the verdict in favor of the complainant.[5] In the 1830s, another Virginia slave family argued that they were "in fact white persons, and therefore could never have been lawfully held in slavery." More convincing, though, was evidence that their owner, Barbara Wilson, had provided for their freedom in her will in 1819 and three years later had signed deeds for their emancipation.[6]

"Prescription [color] alone cannot be proof of slavery," the chief justice of the Kentucky Court of Appeals George Robertson wrote in his opinion concerning Pennsylvania-born Polly McMinnis in 1835. In Kentucky and Virginia, being a mulatto—a person of mixed white and black ancestry, with at least one-fourth African blood—was presumptive evidence of being a slave. "And, e converse, it has been as well settled, that being a white person or having less than a fourth African blood, is prima facie evidence of freedom." A lower court jury decided that enough African blood was flowing in Polly's veins to declare her a slave, but the court of the appeals chose to ignore the question of color. It determined that the plaintiff's birth subsequent to 1780, by Pennsylvania law, signified that she was "born free, though subject to apprenticeship till twenty-eight years old." The court ruled that Polly's right to freedom at age twenty-eight was not impaired by the fact that she had been brought to Kentucky before she had attained that age.[7] A similar case in Missouri involved "nearly white" sixteen- or seventeen-year-old Martha Drisilla, who argued that she was "so near white" she could not possibly have the legal specification of "one fourth of negro blood in her veins." She also related that, though freeborn, as a youngster she had been taken to Illinois by her owner and lived there in servitude for a lengthy period of time. The jury ruled in favor of the plaintiff not because of her color but because of her residency in

Illinois, where slavery was outlawed and where she had been illegally held in servitude for more than a year.[8]

Most judges and juries deemed black people to be prima facie slaves, although that presumption could be, as one judge said, "overcome by proof to the contrary."[9] While persons of mixed racial background might more likely be considered to be free persons of color, they too could be overcome by proof to the contrary. The case of *Gobu v. E. Gobu* in North Carolina early in the nineteenth century pointed up the kind of ambiguities that could challenge the discretion of the courts when freedom suits focused solely on color. Abandoned in a barn when he was about eight days old, Gobu had been found by a twelve-year-old white girl, who then kept him as a slave for a number of years. Thus Gobu's parentage and heritage were a blank, except for his olive-colored complexion—between "black and yellow"—and, as he began to mature, his long, straight hair and prominent nose. When Gobu sued for his freedom, for lack of any other evidence color became the focal issue. The state supreme court observed that blacks seeking their freedom were required to produce evidence that would "destroy the force of the presumption arising from his colour." However, the court was not aware of any stipulation "presuming against liberty" for persons of mixed race. "Such persons may have descended from Indians, in both lines, or at least in the maternal; they may have descended from a white parent in the maternal line or from mulatto parents originally free, in all which cases the offspring, following the condition of the mother, is entitled to freedom." Considering the many possibilities to rule in favor of liberty, such persons ought "not be deprived of it upon mere presumption: more especially as the right to hold them in slavery, if it exists, is in most instances, capable of being satisfactorily proved." The court ordered that Gobu be set free.[10]

Unlike the Gobu suit, the overwhelming majority of cases claiming freedom by virtue of white, Indian, or free-colored maternal ancestry required plaintiffs and their lawyers to provide proof of that ancestry, including the names of family members, as well as their owners, and the dates and locations of their servitude; of primary importance was the name of the female progenitor. Without such proof even fair-skinned plaintiffs found it difficult to acquire free status. One of the problems that arose in such cases after 1813—when the US Supreme Court ruled that hearsay evidence was not admissible to prove status—was that plaintiffs could no longer rely on white witnesses who recalled what their parents or grandparents or even great-grandparents had told them about mixed-race families. Another problem emerged with the changes in the political atmosphere; as the hostility of slaveowners toward the North grew more intense, with outbreaks of violence occurring along the Mason-Dixon line, the sympathy of whites toward slaves filing lineage-based (or otherwise-based) freedom suits diminished. In addition, by the time some slaves brought their suits to court, the ratio of African to white blood in their hereditary lines had often been so variable, and become so indeterminate, that a person with a white female ancestor might indeed be dark-hued or even black.[11]

Louisiana was unique among the southern states with regard to the import attached to the color of slave plaintiffs seeking their freedom. As early as 1810, in the case *Adelle v. Beauregard*, the Superior Court of the Territory of Orleans declared that mulattoes and other persons of color were presumed free. Persons of color did not include Negroes, or black persons. Judge Francois-Xavier Martin reasoned that persons of color might include descendants of Indians, whites, or free mulattoes. Louisiana thus became the only state where the burden of proof was on the defendant to show ownership, rather than the plaintiffs' requirement in other states to show how and when they became free.

By the end of the antebellum era, however, Louisiana had joined other states in ruling that color alone no longer sufficed as a reason for a court to presume on the basis of complexion that a person was not a slave. On the eve of the Civil War, after a parish court had ruled that a slave plaintiff was white and therefore free, the Supreme Court of Louisiana determined that she had not "made the faintest approach toward establishing these allegations" by presenting any evidence beyond the speculative opinions of physicians and the surmise of other witnesses that she was of Caucasian extraction. Self-evident though the plaintiff's fair complexion, blue eyes, and "flaxen hair" were, her owner submitted evidence and depositions to establish that he had purchased her in Arkansas. The judgment of the lower court was reversed and the case remanded. The presumption of freedom based on color was not *juris et de jure*, a presumption of law and right, the appeals court ruled, and must, therefore, yield to proof and evidence.[12]

However detailed and poignant slave plaintiffs' stories of their free ancestry might be, the courts could be swayed by slaveholders' attorneys who produced copies of legal documents to betoken permissible enslavement. They also commonly produced testimony from defense witnesses who declared that the plaintiffs, who claimed to be free, had in fact been "raised in a negro quarter and treated in every Respect as a slave." The legal battles of those who ended up in the "negro quarter" against slaveholders with the advantages of wealth, power, and position could take many years, and still end in defeat. The slave John traced his heritage back to his grandmother, an Irish indentured servant in Virginia during the 1780s, whose daughter—John's mother—had won her freedom from the Offutt family in a suit filed in Kentucky in 1818 or 1820. Her owners, however, had taken John and his siblings to Louisville in order to prevent them from filing a similar suit. The two older children did eventually succeed in gaining their freedom, but John, who had been born in 1813 or 1815, lost his suit in Logan County. He was subsequently taken by the Offutts to Missouri, where he lived as their slave for nearly twenty years. The Missouri Supreme Court ruled that the Logan County decision took precedence.[13]

Most of the few cases that focused exclusively on race and color were initiated during the late antebellum era. Although rare, they nonetheless afford an abundance of information about the workings of the legal system, cultural attitudes, racial mores, and the politics of the debate over slavery in the South on the eve of the Civil War. The outcome of the freedom suit filed by Abby Guy and her children, who claimed free status in Arkansas solely on the basis of their color, not only reflected the South's sociocultural perspectives but also highlighted the perceived biological differences between the races. After two trials and a venue change, the courts awarded Abby and her children their freedom: a verdict that the Arkansas Supreme Court upheld when the defendant appealed. In the local court, physicians were called to examine Abby; they testified that her color, hair, feet, nose, skull, and bones evidenced her to be white. In addition, all the plaintiffs were asked to remove their shoes and socks, so that the jury could inspect their bare feet. No one who was familiar "with the peculiar formation of the negro foot," the court noted, could doubt that the plaintiffs were of the white race.[14]

However, in most other cases based solely on the plaintiffs' color and physical attributes—even when their skin tone clearly denoted only a minuscule measure of "negro blood," or when the scrutiny of physicians, judges, and juries determined them to be "white"—the courts did not rule in the plaintiffs' favor. Without the admissibility of hearsay evidence by which to establish free female ancestry that might date back generations, plaintiffs were usually without proof of heritage. And it was far less difficult for slaveholders to produce documents when the burden of proof regarding ownership fell on the defendants. For proof, then, light-skinned plaintiffs filing freedom suits had to rely either on "living testimony" or documentation that confirmed the free status of their mothers or grandmothers. Testimony was limited strictly to that of witnesses with firsthand knowledge, who were often only the members of a slaveowner's family; and documentary proof, not often readily available, included court records, correspondence, journals, family papers, and depositions. The requirements did not facilitate the process for people of (lighter) color seeking free status.[15]

In the years following the US Supreme Court's decision outlawing hearsay evidence in 1813, the number of plaintiffs claiming white maternal ancestry declined. (See table 7.) Besides the difficulties of tracing genealogies in court records to prove white female heritage, plaintiffs in these cases faced another, constrictive problem: the stigma of miscegenation. Nearly all the witnesses who could be called on to testify on behalf of the plaintiffs in freedom suits based on ancestral claims were white, and thus reluctant to involve other family members or neighbors in what then constituted illicit interracial mixing. They were likely,

therefore, to fashion their testimony in a manner that more properly fit contemporary mores but did little to advance the case of the plaintiffs.[16] Stephen
Kindrall sued for his freedom in Alabama on a claim that his mother was white.
Born in North Carolina, he had been indentured in his infancy and bound in
service until he reached the age of twenty-one. Before attaining that age, however, he had been sold to a Georgia man, after whose death he had been sold
again, to Anthony Stoutenborough of Bibb County, Alabama, this time as a slave
for life. Kindrall was able to file a freedom suit on his claim in the local court, but
the suit was dismissed, probably because of the claim about his mother.[17] What
type of white woman gave birth to black children?

Courts grappled continually with the question of white ancestry. If persons
looked white, lived among whites, and acted white in their dealings with whites,
should they be considered white, and free?[18] Ironically, white was beside the
point in most white-ancestry cases. Neither race nor color was the issue. What
mattered was the line of descent, and proof that it connected the plaintiff to a
white woman. The legal irrelevance of race and color lay in the plainly evident
range in skin color, physical attributes, and facial features among any number of
plaintiffs—some of them children of white mothers and black fathers—involved
in freedom suits.[19] An apt example both of the irrelevance of color and the importance of ancestral evidence in such freedom suits involved the Kentucky
slave Gus, also known as Augustus, a fifteen-year-old minor described as "a
yellow boy." His mother was a widowed white woman named Thomasson, née
Miller, and his father a black man named Warren. Through testimony presented
by friends and relatives of Gus's mother—as well as one of the defendants who
spoke of the mother's love and unfailing, affectionate care for the little boy she
called Cub—the plaintiff's lawyer traced Gus's personal history from the time
of his birth to the date of his purchase as a slave after the death of his mother
in 1839. Although some of the testimony was hearsay, the facts pertinent to
the case raised no objections, and the court not only awarded Gus his freedom
but also granted him $397 in damages, the amount earned by his hire over the
five-year period of litigation. Although the plaintiff's color was mentioned—
the "yellow boy" Gus was also described by witnesses as a "dark mulatto" and
"darker than most mulattoes"—the issue central to the case was proof of free
female ancestry.[20]

Color among plaintiffs claiming white ancestry varied considerably. Some
looked "white" and some were dark-skinned, while others of mixed race stood
more ambiguously in between. In every southern state persons of dark complexion were presumed to be slaves and, as one court said in 1810, the burden of
proof was on the party claiming freedom. Only rarely could dark-complexioned
plaintiffs convince a judge or jury that their female ancestors, sometimes not
too distant, were white.[21] Problematic, too, for plaintiffs and their lawyers were

the laws that defined "negro" and "white," as they varied from state to state. In Virginia, "one-fourth or more Negro blood,"—or one black grandparent in a person's bloodline—determined whether a person was legally black and presumably a slave. Any person whose grandmother or grandfather was black shall be deemed a "negro," declared Missouri's 1825 statute law, which reenacted its territorial law; and any person with one-fourth or more negro blood shall be deemed a mulatto. The Missouri law did not, however, presume to assign the status of slave to either blacks or mulattoes.

In North Carolina, a man facing a charge of fornication and adultery because he had married a white woman claimed that he was neither African nor Indian but of Portuguese descent. The state supreme court, however, ruled that he was a person of color under the definition in the act of 1777 and the state constitution, which designated such persons to be "descended from negro ancestors to the fourth generation." In Texas and Tennessee, persons with "mixed blood to the third generation inclusive"—or one great-grandparent in the line of descent—were legally black. Most southern states in the antebellum era provided definitions in law as to what constituted a black and/or white person, but three states—Arkansas, Louisiana, and South Carolina—did not. South Carolina judge William Harper, acknowledging that there was no legal definition of "mulatto" or "person of color" in his state, advised the courts to instruct juries that when a "distinct and visible admixture" of Negro blood was discernible, the party should be designated a person of color. Despite the fine legal distinctions in the states' statutes, though, they were hardly ever cited in freedom suits, as the color of the plaintiffs was almost never the primary issue.

As a result, persons of color who filed freedom suits claiming white ancestry had but a single burden: to prove that a maternal progenitor in the family line was white. In 1791, the descendants of Maria, a free Spanish or Portuguese woman, won their freedom. By the time the trials were conducted, more than eighty years after her death, the plaintiffs were discernibly not Spanish or Portuguese but, as they were described in testimony, "negro" or "black," "brown," "yellow," and "bright yellow." Despite the evident mixture of race in Maria's descendants, the court deemed them free. Other early period cases yielded similar rulings. In 1794, for instance, Maryland slave Robert Thomas linked his suit for freedom to a free white woman named Elizabeth Thomas in his ancestry. When the defendant's lawyer attempted to impugn the character of Thomas's crucial witness, who, he said, "kept company with negroes," not only the plaintiff objected. Judge and jury declared in Thomas's favor, and the appeals court affirmed the lower court's ruling and verdict: "judgment for freedom."[22]

Like the Thomas family, the Butler, Shorter, Allen, Queen, and Booth families claimed to be kin to a free white woman, and to prove it, they and their lawyers collected and deposed numerous witnesses. Beginning in 1789, in support of

William Booth's freedom suit in Maryland, no fewer than twenty-six witnesses over a three-year period provided depositions that for the most part addressed his complex genealogical background. Among the deponents were John Balson, age eighty-six, and Eleanor King, age sixty-two, both of whom knew Booth's great-grandmother Kate or Catherine. Described by King as a mulatto with long, straight black hair and freckles, Catherine worked as a midwife and rode a horse on her rounds until she was old and gray. Catherine's mother, according to King, was "an English Woman." In one incident, King recalled, when Catherine was "in Liquor," she cursed King's father and asserted that she was "as white as he and her mother was a Gentlewoman." Another witness testified that Catherine was the mother of Jaffy, who was the mother of Ester, who was the mother of William Booth. Almost without exception, the plaintiff's witnesses noted that Catherine had always acted like a free woman. Nevertheless, Richard Harrison, a Calvert County planter, had listed "my servant Woman called Kate" in his 1713 will, with the instruction that she should be freed seven years after his death. The defense put the will into evidence as proof of Catherine's enslavement and produced witnesses in its behalf. The general court ruled against Booth, but the Maryland High Court of Errors reversed the decision. The weight of evidence, the high court said, indicated that William Booth's great-great-grandmother was white and that William was therefore entitled to his freedom.[23]

Slaves in Delaware, the District of Columbia, and Virginia filed similar lineage-related freedom suits in the early decades of the nation. They too relied on numerous witnesses to verify their genealogy either by hearsay or by firsthand knowledge of incidents in the lives of the plaintiffs' blood relatives. Although the court record does not indicate the outcomes in the 1782 suits brought by Justina and her probable brother Joshua in Delaware, it does show that thirteen witnesses provided information affirming the free white status of the plaintiffs' grandmother. Thomas Freeman, age seventy-nine, died before he could be deposed in support of Justina's case, but her petition for freedom included the testimony Freeman had rendered in Joshua's earlier suit. Freeman attested that Joshua and Justina's grandmother, Teresa, a white woman, had been left on the doorstep of Andrew Hamilton, Esquire, shortly after her birth. In 1735, when Freeman, then about thirty-two, was working with Archibald Craig on barn repairs at the farm of his uncle Charles Hillyard, he had overheard Craig arguing with Teresa, who had declared that she would "stay no longer. She would go away and leave them all." The next morning Mrs. Hillyard (Freeman's aunt) had told Craig not to quarrel with "the old woman" because she was freeborn and could leave any time she wished.[24]

Again, as in most of the early cases claiming white female ancestry, the color of the plaintiff was not the main issue for either the judge or the jury. The issue was, instead, proof of direct descent from a white woman. To that effect, in the decade following the establishment of the District of Columbia as the nation's capital in 1801, the members of several families—the Bentleys, Queens, and Davises—filed freedom suits in the District Circuit Court. The suits were interrelated to the extent that various members of the three families were related by marriage or blood. For instance, in the case of Mary Davis, her free mulatto aunt, Rosamund Bentley, testified on her behalf. In two of the cases, Mima Queen and her daughter Louisa sued John Hepburn, and Priscilla Queen sued Francis Neal, but the Queens in both cases traced their heritage back to the same white woman. In Virginia, three mulatto families—the Jacksons, Fletchers, and Coles—filed similar lineage-based freedom suits. In Maryland, families filing like suits put together genealogies revealed in part from listings in the first US census in 1790. In 1783, in North Carolina, Ruth Tillett of Pasquotank County, the daughter of a white woman and black man, alleged that she had been sold into slavery following the death of her mother. The man who had purchased her "was not ignorant of her Condition and Rights to Liberty," she claimed. Eventually she had escaped, but had been captured and sold again. Ruth Tillett won her freedom on a simple verdict: the court found that an examination of the witness testimony proved her allegations to be correct.[25]

The admissibility of hearsay evidence in the early period lent an advantage to plaintiffs filing lineage-based freedom suits. Indeed, during the early period just as many plaintiffs (twenty-eight) won their freedom claiming white female ancestry as during the next two periods combined. The total number, 104, during the three periods represented only 5 percent of the causes brought before the courts. During the period from the Revolution to the Civil War, among the white female ancestry cases, two-thirds of the plaintiffs gained their freedom—twenty-seven of thirty-seven, or 78 percent in the county courts, and twenty-nine of forty-seven, or 62 percent in appeals courts (excluding twenty cases without final results). Yet the number who achieved free status dropped from 90 percent during the early period to 52 percent during the latter two periods. This significant decline over time reveals the difficulty of proving ancestry without hearsay evidence. Some of the later cases did gain a measure of notoriety, but no matter the success or failure, the suits usually rested neither on the plaintiffs' physical attributes nor skin color but on documentary evidence proving white mothers or white female forebears or both. (See table 7.)

Plaintiffs who claimed Indian female heritage represented only about 4 percent of the court filings, and in those cases, as in white ancestry freedom suits, it was frequently difficult for plaintiffs to substantiate their claims with legally solid proof. Some failed, but the success rate among Indian claimants far exceeded that of plaintiffs with allegedly white mothers or grandmothers. Whereas white ancestry cases, after the prohibition of hearsay evidence in the courts, hinged problematically on the plaintiffs' ability to prove the status—slave or free—of a female progenitor, Indian claimants in ancestry suits had only to prove pedigree, because, by the early decades of the nineteenth century, most of the southern states had deemed Indian women to be free. For many years judges who dealt with "descent from Indian ancestress" voted *in favorem libertatis* from the purest of motives, a Virginia appeals court judge observed in 1831; in doing so, however, they failed to meet legal standards banning hearsay evidence and in error ruled that the onus probandi, or burden of proof, lay with the defendant, not the plaintiff. Thus, in their rulings, courts failed or refused to treat Indians as they would any other question of property.[26]

Legislation enacted during the seventeenth century in Virginia and Maryland, and during the eighteenth century in the territories that later became Louisiana and Missouri, clearly shows that some Indians were held as slaves. In 1670, Virginia passed an act by which all non-Christians imported by ship were to be enlisted as slaves, and in 1676 it enacted a law that committed Indians who were taken as captives in war to a lifetime of bondage. The latter law was repealed, then restored the next year, and in 1682, yet another act affirmed that "hostile" Indians could be enslaved, "any law usage or custom to the contrary" notwithstanding. In Maryland, early court records indicate that colonists regularly bought and sold Indian slaves for life.[27] In 1708–1709, an Anne Arundel County, Maryland, slaveholder petitioned the local court to hold a son of his Indian captive in bondage as his servant throughout the lifetime of the mother. The judge ruled that the Indian boy was a slave "during life."[28]

In Louisiana and Missouri during the French period (1673–1762) and Spanish period (1762–1803), in settlements all along the Mississippi River, including St. Louis, Indians were held as slaves. In 1756 and 1757, at Fort Chartres and elsewhere, one former resident observed, there were a great many Indian slaves, most of whom had been brought from different nations down the Missouri River by traders. The Indians were universally acknowledged as slaves, and frequently sold as such. After its establishment in 1764, St. Louis, too, quartered many "Indian slaves and only a few blacks." The early freedom suits in what later became the Missouri Territory accepted the fact that Indians could be bought and sold as slaves.[29]

The evidence demonstrating Indian freedom during the colonial period was equally as strong as the evidence substantiating Indian slavery. In Virginia, the 1705 law regarding Native Americans, in substance a reenactment of the 1691 law, essentially outlawed Indian slavery.[30] Some judges ruled that Indians who were imported as slaves were thereafter slaves, despite the statute's exemption of Indians from enslavement by virtue of their nations' participation in "free and open trade" with Virginia. Trade and slavery, they maintained, were separate issues, and the 1691 act citing "all Indians" as free probably meant "all American Indians." Nonetheless, Virginia courts ruled again and again that after 1691 all Indians and their descendants in the maternal line were free. In fact, George

Mason, a delegate to the Constitutional Convention and one of the authors of the Bill of Rights, counted hundreds of Indians who achieved free status during the late eighteenth century.

Among them was Hannah who, along with other Indian slaves, petitioned to be released from bondage by her owner. The case went eventually to the appeals court, which affirmed the lower court's decision granting her free status. In 1792, in Northumberland County, the Indian slave Tom and two others won their freedom when a jury trial in a law court produced a verdict that declared them free, although, according to the testimony of several witnesses, the plaintiffs' ancestors—Indians of "tawny complexion" with "long straight black hair"—had been brought to Virginia by sea. The following year, two other Indian slaves, Dick and Pat, also won their freedom in a jury trial that found them to be "lineally descended by the maternal line" from Judith, who was, or was descended from, an Indian woman.[31] In the early nineteenth century, the descendants of Butterfield Nan, an Indian woman in her sixties in the 1750s, won their freedom in Virginia. George Wythe, judge of the Henrico District Court of Chancery, on examining the skin color of the plaintiffs ("all of whom were before the Court"), noted that the grandmother, her daughter, and her granddaughter differed in their "shades," with the youngest being "perfectly white." As the defendants had failed to prove, under Virginia law, that the plaintiffs were slaves, and as he himself believed freedom to be "the birth-right of every human being," as enunciated in the Virginia Bill of Rights, Whyte ruled in favor of the plaintiffs. On appeal his decision was affirmed, but his "birth-right" phrase, the court noted, applied only to "white persons and Native American Indians" and not to "native Africans and their descendants who have been and are now held as slaves by the citizens of this state."[32]

Maryland courts took a similar stance. In 1803, Robert Moody cited several earlier freedom suits filed by members of his family, all of whom had been granted free status by claiming descent "in the female Line from an Indian Woman a Native of America." He, like the others, traced his lineage to Moll, or Mary, an Indian woman who had been held in slavery by Philemon Lloyd, a white planter.[33] Testimony in a Missouri suit likewise supported Indian freedom by citing a proclamation issued in 1769 by the Spanish governor of New Orleans; it forbade "the proprietors" of Indian slaves to "dispose of those whom they hold in any manner whatsoever unless it be to give them their freedom." Still, it was not until several court decisions in the early 1820s that Louisiana declared that Indians could not be enslaved, and not until the mid-1830s that Missouri decided similarly. In 1833, a St. Louis Circuit Court judge instructed the jury that "if they found the maternal ancestor of the plaintiff was an Indian woman, and that she was held as a slave in the province of Louisiana while it was held by the French, she and her descendants ought to be taken by the jury to have been lawfully slaves." The jury thus found for the defendant. The Missouri Supreme Court, however, overturned the verdict on the grounds that the judge had erred in his instructions to the jury. The defendant then appealed to the US Supreme Court, where the writ of error was dismissed for a lack of jurisdiction. In short, after 1834, Missouri accepted what other states had long acknowledged: matrilineal descendants of Indians were to be considered free.[34]

By then, in most southern states, Indian plaintiffs who could prove Indian female pedigree were granted their freedom. To establish proof, they still had to secure lawyers willing to try their cases, depose witnesses, and, if possible, search out court records. Hearsay evidence was often accepted—both in the early years and later, when hearsay, except in matters of pedigree, was deemed to be inadmissible—if it provided the only means by which to verify lineage. In Kent County, Delaware, in 1795, several witnesses gave testimony on behalf of Phillis, who, one said, was "rather darker than any of the nations of this Country, and still different from the common mulatto colour," and who, said another, had "straight black very much unlike the hair of Negroes imported from Africa." The witnesses in this case were deposed in Somerset County, Maryland; among them was seventy-year-old Sarah Ward, who knew both Phillis's mother and grandmother—and both of them, Sarah testified, were Indians.[35]

A few years later, in Maryland, a male slave claimed that he was descended "in the female Line from an Indian Woman a Native of America," and argued that he, bearing the same pedigree as other members of his family who had been set free, should be similarly favored by the court.[36] In 1827, fourteen years after the Supreme Court had ruled hearsay evidence in freedom suits to be inadmissible, the Tennessee Supreme Court affirmed a lower court decision in favor of Phebe, who, along with her mother, "was always said to be of Indian extraction." One witness testified to having often heard it reputed that Phebe's great-grandmother was an Indian. His testimony was admissible as proof of pedigree. Although the Tennessee Supreme Court disallowed some testimony, including that stating several of Phebe's kin "recovered their freedom by due course of law" in Virginia—without proof from county court this was inadmissible—it fully accepted testimony as to pedigree, and on that basis it granted Phebe her freedom.[37]

During the early period, perhaps the most remarkable freedom suit based on Indian heritage was filed by the descendants of Jane Gibson, a free Indian who died on Shirley Plantation in Charles City County in 1713 or 1714. As was the case among the Boston slaves in Maryland, Jane's descendants kept alive their kinship ties and their hopes of freedom over several generations. In 1805, the eminent counsel Edmund Randolph, a member of the Constitutional Convention and the first attorney general of the United States, filed papers on behalf of ten Gibson descendants in the Richmond City Superior Court. The plaintiffs, with the surname Evans, claimed they were blood relations to Gibson through the female line of their Indian heritage: their mother, Amy Evans; their grandmother, Sarah Coley; their great-grandmother, Frances Evans; and their great-great-grandmother, Jane Gibson.

As others of Jane's descendants had won their freedom in two separate Virginia suits, in 1792 and 1795, Randolph included in his papers depositions from the earlier trials, among them two given by eighty-one-year-old Robert Wills of Henrico County. As a young boy, at Shirley Plantation in Charles City County, Wills had attested, he had worked as an apprentice in the brewing of a diet drink for his master, Robert "King" Carter, who was afflicted with dropsy. So it was that Wills became "well acquainted with Jane Gibson and George Gibson her brother who were dark mulattoes" and free persons; he also knew Jane's two adult children, who bore the same names as the mother and brother and, like them, were free. At the time, Wills noted, Jane Gibson was extremely old, probably about eighty, and she died one or two years later. On the basis of testimony in the prior court cases and from his ten clients, Randolph drew up "A Genealogical of the Family of Slaves Claiming Freedom," the progenitor being "Jane Gibson an Indian Woman." The court accepted the depositions as well as the genealogical chart, and decreed that the ten plaintiffs be granted their freedom.[38]

Not atypically, the defendant in the Evanses' case took umbrage at being charged by his own human chattel with the illegal possession of slaves. In fact, Lewis B. Allen denied that he had ever heard of Indian slaves named Evans. As the trial date approached, he kidnapped the lead complainant, Charles Evans; tied him up; and carried him to an undisclosed location. It was rumored that Allen planned to flee and take with him some of the Evans slaves, so as to remove them from the court's jurisdiction. When Randolph discovered the intended abduction, he promptly wrote a letter to the judge requesting that the court prevent such a removal. The court took no action, however, and Charles Evans was indeed spirited away. Nine years later, in Lynchburg City, he and several other Evans family members filed a second suit against Allen; the case dragged on for years. In 1820, it slid into limbo when the court-appointed lawyer, Henderson Clark, a former Congressman, suffered a stroke and failed to appear in court with the plaintiffs. The case, long unresolved, was dismissed in 1821. The outcome was not uncommon, although the actual number of cases that failed because defendants managed to stay one step ahead of a subpoena by moving to another county or state is not known.[39]

Difficulty prevailed throughout the processing of Native Americans' lineage-based freedom suits. Like their African American counterparts suing for freedom, Indian plaintiffs had to endure long years in bondage while their cases crawled through the courts, and to pay court costs they often had to submit to being hired out. They had to deal with lawyers who were sometimes reluctant, if not timorous, in enlisting witnesses from the white community. On occasion, by court order, members of the same family had to file individual suits, and problematically, in the course of their various trials, discrepancies in their versions of events emerged. It took Mima, who claimed that she was the great-great-granddaughter of "a native American Indian named Judith," four years to extricate herself and her five children from slavery in Dinwiddie County, Virginia. Aside from the usual difficulties in obtaining witness testimony, Mima faced the problem of absentee ownership, as she and her children were actually the property of a young girl then residing in Tennessee. Mima filed suit in 1811, and the defendant failed to appear. Then in 1814, after the owner's marriage, her husband, James Hicks, claimed the Indian family as slaves. His attempt to seize Mima failed, but he did succeed in taking possession of the five children. Mima and her lawyer obtained a warrant against Hicks to prevent him from keeping the children and from leaving the state. A second warrant ordered the sheriff to place her and her children in protective custody so that they could appear before the superior court in Richmond and submit a supplemental suit. The family eventually won its freedom.[40]

A ploy popular with defendants in the trials of suits brought by Indian slaves was to contend that the plaintiffs were in fact black. Attributing to the Indian slaves features of the "negro race," defendants, with the aid of their witnesses, sought to prove that the plaintiffs were thus, by legal definition, human property. In a Missouri case that continued for more than thirty-three years, the descendants of Maria Jean Scypion—the daughter of a Natchez Indian woman and a black man named Scypion—claimed their Indian heritage ensured their freedom. In a suit brought by Maria's daughter Marguerite against Pierre Chouteau Sr., a quarter century after Maria's death, the defense called Auguste Chouteau, an elderly member of the owner's family, who testified that Maria was "brown in color with very wooly hair like that of a negress." Another defense witness confirmed Chouteau's description and added that Maria "was very black."[41]

In a few cases, even when substantial evidence pointed toward a successful conclusion for the plaintiff the suit for freedom failed. While most juries were sympathetic to pro-freedom arguments, some few apparently chose to ignore the weight of the evidence in favor of the plaintiff, especially when defendants produced witnesses whose testimony belied a plaintiff's more reliable assertions of Indian female ancestry. In the 1807 case of Nanny, for example, five witnesses confirmed the plaintiff's claim that she was the daughter of Joseph Dailey, a free man, and Sally Lawson, his wife and, more notably, the daughter of Sukey, "a Cherokee Indian woman who lived on the farm of Col. Byrd of Westover." The jury nonetheless found for the defendant.[42]

On occasion, too, the verdicts of juries who found for the plaintiff were overturned on appeal, usually because arguments citing colonial laws and decisions came into play. In fewer instances, suits that had been successful at the county level were, on appeal, declared nonsuits, as when due to "some misconduct on the jury." Some years after an appellate court's declaration of a nonsuit in an ancestry case, one lawyer argued on behalf of a client that his freedom was res judicata (a matter already judged) and that the entry of a nonsuit constituted laches (an unreasonable delay engendering prejudice against his client's cause). His client was free at birth, the lawyer asserted, being "the lineal descendant of an Indian woman." The appeals court rejected the argument.[43]

Such failures, however, were more the exception than the rule. The great majority of Indians who filed freedom suits on matrilineal claims were successful, although for some it took many years and changes in venue to escape the prejudice of judges and juries. Excluding a few cases in which no result could be determined or claims were only partially granted, 85 percent of Indian slaves' freedom suits ended in favor of the plaintiffs, the highest total percentage of any group in the South. More often than in Indian female ancestry cases, the courts accepted physical descriptions of plaintiffs and their ancestors, in large measure because all they had to prove was lineage, and not the status of ancestors; as a result, judges and juries in many of these suits accepted hearsay evidence long after such testimony was excluded in cases involving African Americans.

Again and again plaintiffs satisfactorily proved their descent from Indian women—for the most part in the Cherokee, Chickasaw, and Natchez Indian nations—and again and again, despite debates over hearsay evidence or over the incidence of Indian slavery during the colonial period, county court juries and appeals courts judges found for the Indian plaintiffs. Defendants had to show legal title to the Indian slaves they claimed to own, and they often failed to do so, clearly aiding the plaintiffs.[44] Of more ambiguous effect were courtroom requests that judges and juries examine the plaintiffs' physical lineaments: the tawny skin color and straight black hair, in some cases; the mulatto or African American features in others. Or they might look white and be able to allege descent from white as well as Indian women.

The Virginia slave Rose, born between 1778 and 1780 to a free Indian woman and a white slaveholder, had been sold at least four times before her twenty-first birthday and had ended up in Kentucky. In 1833, Rose and her children and grandchildren, thirteen in all, instituted actions of trespass against their owner. The trial produced much conflicting testimony, but there was unquestionably one point of consensus: that Rose was "very white—as white as most white children through the country"; so white that she was sometimes mistaken to be one of her original Virginia owner's children. Other testimony established that Rose had "more or less Indian blood," and some witnesses referred to her as an "as a bound or indented Indian girl." The lawyers for the plaintiffs secured three venue changes, from Whitley to Pulaski to Knox and finally to Estill County, where Rose and her kin won verdicts for their freedom. Although the verdicts were reversed and remanded on an appeal charging "an error on one instruction," Rose did later finally achieve her goal. The process took nearly nineteen years.[45]

Children born to free women of color, no less than those born in bondage, could easily be bought, sold, transferred, traded, or even kidnapped and taken away. Those who were transported from one state to another found it extremely difficult to file freedom suits, and in some cases they remained enslaved for years. Often they simply did not know that they had been born after their mothers had been granted freedom. Or if they did know specifically how and when a mother or grandmother had been freed, for a variety of reasons—inability to contact a lawyer, failure to secure documentation of status, fear of a slaveowner's retribution—they sometimes failed to file freedom suits. While sympathetic whites often willingly assisted the sons and daughters of free mothers in petitioning the courts and advancing their cases, they still found it difficult, as plaintiffs, to outmaneuver their owners. In 1824, Eliza Johnson stated in the District of Columbia Circuit Court that her mother had been manumitted at age twenty-five, before Eliza was born, but a member of the original owner's family had nevertheless sold Eliza to a "resident of Tennessee or Kentucky." She was about to be "carried off" after being confined to the local jail when her mother found a white friend to compose a letter on Eliza's behalf, stating: "All [her mother's] children were born free except the first Henry." At that, the court issued only a temporary restraining order against the alleged owner. Slaveowners or members of their families commonly took advantage of situations like Eliza's.[46]

Once a case entered the judicial system, among the most difficult tasks for plaintiffs was securing evidence to show that they were in fact descendants of "Free Parentage on the Female Side of their ancestry some few degrees remote being white & Free," as a group of nine Kentucky slaves asserted after members of their family had been sold and resold several times. If they did succeed in obtaining testimony to support their claims, owners were likely to rebut the evidence with documentation to establish a history of servitude in the plaintiffs' families. "Old Phillis Ann," originally from Maryland, was a free woman of color, she claimed, but she and her children had been taken to Kentucky as slaves. In Kentucky, members of her family had filed two freedom suits in Jefferson County, one in 1813 and one in 1822, both of them unsuccessful. They had later been sold to a man who lived in Mississippi, and they feared that he would take them to "the lower country and sell them" once again. Then, in 1833, yet another, new owner, and now the defendant in the freedom suit, contended that he had purchased Phillis and the others "for his own use and not for sale as merchandise," so that any fears of conveyance out of Kentucky were unfounded and Mississippi's anti-importation law obviously was not violated. The defendant also procured a witness who was prepared to testify that the allegedly free Phillis the Elder, and her mother and grandmother, in fact "were black negroes and slaves in Maryland." The court granted Phillis and her family an injunction, but their freedom suit was dismissed.[47]

To further counter black families' claims regarding the free status of mothers or grandmothers, slaveholders produced bills of sale, receipts, copies of inventories, transfer deeds, estate papers, and witness testimony to establish that the slave or slaves in question were not born by free women of color. However solid the plaintiffs' circumstantial evidence, they and their lawyers found it difficult to prove the status of a mother, especially if she had been taken to another state and had changed hands a number of times, unless they could—and often they could not—produce reliable, informed, white witnesses to support their claims. Nor did plaintiffs' tales recounting how they had been kidnapped as youngsters, or how their mothers had suffered an untimely death, or how they had been "clandestinely, forcibly and fraudulently" captured and taken away, sway the courts without white testimony corroborating the events. And even when their stories were proven to be in large measure true and their claims were substantiated by strong evidence, plaintiffs in lineage-based suits still sometimes failed to gain free status.

Born of a free mother in the District of Columbia, a man named Jackson found several witnesses to testify that he had served as a free seaman on the frigate *Constitution* during the 1820s, but the New Orleans District Court and the Supreme Court of Louisiana nevertheless accepted "several successive calls in warranty" by different vendors to prove that Jackson had been sold as a slave.[48] In other cases, whites testified that the plaintiffs' forbearers had been, and had even gone at large as, free persons of color, only to be countered by the defendants' witnesses with arguments that even so, the plaintiffs themselves could not be freed under the law because they were reportedly obstreperous, antagonistic, hostile toward white people, or under the age of thirty.[49]

Other court rulings against slaves were lodged in error on the part of plaintiffs: if, for instance, they had sought a writ of habeas corpus instead of filing a freedom suit, or had filed papers in the wrong county or court, or had failed to rebut critical pieces of a defendant's evidence.[50] The court clashes between slaves and slaveholders, some of whom were prosperous farmers, planters, and businesspeople, often pivoted on evidence from the sometimes distant past. Slaves who had in all probability been moved and removed, and sold and resold, had neither the resources to track down documents registered in distant counties or other states nor the access to potential witnesses from another time and place who might verify their narratives.[51] And when slave plaintiffs were able to gather creditable proof of a mother's free status at the time of their birth, their own freedom was not assured.

In 1821, the Virginia slave Lewis, a minor, appealed a decision denying him his right to freedom, despite documentary evidence that his mother had traveled with her owner to Ohio, where she had obtained a writ of habeas corpus and had subsequently been manumitted by her owner in a signed deed promising her freedom after two years of faithful service. The appeals court affirmed the lower court's decision against the plaintiff on several grounds: First, the owner's brief sojourn in Ohio did not constitute residency; second, a writ of habeas corpus in Ohio did not affirm the mother's right to freedom in Virginia; and third, the deed of manumission was composed and witnessed in Ohio, whereas it should have been submitted to a court in Virginia. If the documentary evidence presented to the court were to be accepted in favor of a black minor, the judge ruled, the "right of our citizens under the constitution to reclaim their fugitive slaves from other states, would be nearly a nullity."[52] Similar evidence of parental freedom in Connecticut and Massachusetts—with testimony that "common knowledge" avouched a woman was free, in one case, and that the plaintiffs, born free, had been abducted and transported to the South, in the other—failed to win the petitioners their freedom suits. In a suit filed twenty years after an alleged illegal importation from the North, the court ruled that in view of the two-decade lapse of time, it *could be assumed* that the "master had duly taken the [importation] oath required by law."[53]

What is striking, given all the obstacles in their legal paths, is that many slave plaintiffs did in fact win their freedom, even when the defendants opposite them were wealthy slaveholders and respected members of their communities. The judicial system was not unsympathetic to the arguments and evidence presented by plaintiffs and their lawyers in support of matrilineally based freedom suits. Lawyers strove diligently to establish for the court how and when plaintiffs' mothers acquired their freedom and how long after that significant event the plaintiffs were born. Assiduously they sought out witnesses to verify their accusations of illegal enslavement, tracked down documents to confirm manumissions they asserted, and in some cases produced illuminative—and evidentiary—family papers.

A Delaware suit included in its evidence a family Bible, in which a sheet of paper listed the names and birth dates of the children born to a manumitted mother, to prove that the plaintiffs had been born after their mother had been freed. The court of common pleas "ordered adjudged and decreed" that one of her children, Charles Smith, "is hereby declared to be free and entitled to all the benefits and privileges of free negroes and mulattoes within this state."[54] Unquestionably, as tools to prove plaintiffs' cases, family Bibles were exceptional; more commonly witness testimony or depositions provided children's birth dates to show that they succeeded the dates of their mothers' freedom. Wills and deeds, too, were produced to establish that particular owners had freed the female slaves who later gave birth to the children, now plaintiffs, filing suits to end their bondage by white family members.

In 1800, Maria Phillips and Richard Phillips, children of Phene, who had been freed by the court, won their freedom, too, in the Norfolk City Hustings Court. Phene's successful suit, having established a precedent, thus enabled and facilitated the freedom suit filed by children in the family's next generation. In this and other instances, the law, access to the courts, and a sense of identity created a feeling of optimism that crossed generations. A Missouri case built on precedence similarly favored the plaintiffs, if perhaps with less optimism and more complications in the process. In their suit, two young boys, Anson and Michael, represented by a next friend, William Clark, showed that their mother, Matilda, had been declared free more than thirteen years before in a decree "adjudged by the courts of Missouri under the territorial government." During the trial, however, the boys were kidnapped. Whisked out of St. Louis and across the countryside into Jefferson County, they landed in the custody of the sheriff who, having received word of the abduction, arrested their two kidnappers. On their return to St. Louis for the trial, with the assistance of Joseph Strother, a lawyer with wide experience in freedom suits, Anson and Michael won their freedom.[55] The kidnapping was not an isolated incident in the state; plaintiffs in freedom suits often faced recrimination and violence, usually engineered by the defendants.[56]

In 1833, the Missouri slave Sanford filed a suit on the basis of testimony from the widow of his mother's owner. She verified the fact that Sanford had been born after his mother had resided with her owner in the free state of Illinois for two years. The defendant and current owner (with the same surname as the widow), frustrated by the slave's suit and the widow's testimony, attacked Sanford "with great force and violence" and inflicted blows on his body. While most trespass writs employed similar language as a matter of law, the specifics offered in this case, including the exact day of the brutal assault, demonstrated this particular Boone County slaveholder's especially violent reaction to the inconvenience of a freedom suit. After the beating, the owner had Sanford jailed. The jury, however, awarded Sanford his freedom, and the court ordered the defendant to pay one hundred dollars in damages.[57]

Although most freedom suits were filed in the Upper South, the rule of *partus sequitur ventrem* ("that which is brought forth follows the womb") was recognized in every southern state. In North Carolina, South Carolina, Florida, Alabama, and Louisiana, slave plaintiffs, sometimes with white guardians, tutors, curators, or next friends, filed freedom suits and won their causes by proving that their mothers or grandmothers or more distant female progenitors were free. A number of these cases were appealed to higher state courts, as defendants in the Lower South tended to be avid defenders of the peculiar institution, especially during the two decades prior to the Civil War. Still, a few suits were filed with surprising results. In a suit filed in South Carolina in 1816, Phebe detailed how, as a youngster in Baltimore, she had been sent by her free black mother to work for a prosperous white family in the city, as was customary there among free blacks. When she was twelve, in 1806, the white family moved to Charleston, South Carolina, and took Phebe with them without notifying her mother. Nine years passed before Phebe brought a freedom suit, in which a Charleston jury rendered a verdict in her favor and awarded her $400 in damages for "wrongful detention in slavery" (her services, the court noted, were worth $40 or $50 per year). On appeal, the appellate court judge denied a motion for new trial, writing that the situation comprised "a base attempt to consign to slavery for life, this unfortunate being, whose very situation called loudly for the protection of every feeling and honest man."[58] Other states of the Lower South record similar, if few, rulings for children who were born to free women of color or were kin to more distant free female ancestors.[59]

Requisite to most kinship cases was, of course, proof of free heritage, and in the majority of the suits the matrilineal evidence was overwhelmingly in the plaintiffs' favor. Only rarely was color an issue, in large measure because the complexion of plaintiffs ranged so widely—from black to dark or pale mulatto ("griff" or "brown" or "yellow") to "light skinned" and "nearly white"—as to be insignificant. Even in Louisiana, where persons of mixed race were deemed to be free, the fundamental issue was not skin color but ancestry: how and when a plaintiff's mother or female progenitor did in fact, and according to reliable testimony, gain her freedom. In 1816, when Almira, a "minor of color" in New Orleans, sued under the aegis of a next friend, several witnesses who had lived in St. Domingo testified that Almira's mother had been the concubine of her master there and that he had freed her in his will before Almira was born.[60]

When seaman Daniel Hancock, a man of color, filed a suit claiming that he was being unlawfully detained as a slave, he provided his lawyer in St. Landry Parish with a list of people in the North who could testify that he had been born of a free mother in Connecticut. Among them was Mary, a free woman of color in New York City, who supplied a deposition stating that she had known Hancock from the time he was a little boy and "always knew the plaintiff to be free." Her mother ran a boardinghouse in the city, she said, and Hancock had frequently stayed there when his ship was in port. Local slaveowners, including one Alexander Robb, also testified in Hancock's behalf.[61] Plaintiffs and their lawyers seeking to establish kinship ties not only strove to secure depositions but also searched out copies of wills and deeds; researched statutes germane to kinship in other, pertinent states; and collected testimony both in and outside the town, county or parish, and state of a plaintiff's current residence. In reviewing a case in which the claim of free ancestry was linked to a will registered in Virginia, the North Carolina Supreme Court acknowledged that slaves were commonly referred to as "stock"; however, in its opinion, the court stated, the intention of the testator in his will was clear: some of his stock should be held in captivity to help raise "his children and his young negroes," but all of his "negroes" should eventually be freed. The Virginia law of 1782, the court pointed out, allowed emancipation by will. It thus affirmed the verdict of freedom for the plaintiff.[62]

Despite the exclusion of hearsay evidence, testimony about a mother who "acted as a free-woman" or about an enslaved minor or thrice-sold adult whose mother had been freed before his or her birth resonated with judges and juries, even in states where freedom suits were rare. Of all the suits, including appeals cases, claiming the free status of a mother or grandmother or sometimes a great-grandmother, those that succeeded outnumbered those that failed by a margin of nearly three to one. The decisions favored the plaintiffs less often in the appeals courts than in the county courts. Still, in the former, blacks throughout the decades from the American Revolution to the Civil War won more than half of the appeals, whereas, in the latter, with notable consistency during the middle and late periods, they won in nearly four out of five suits.

In all, descendant-issue freedom suits represented almost exactly 1 out of 5 court battles (401 of 2,006 total where the cause was indicated); individual men and individual women, as well as women with children, constituted 3 out of 4 among them, but there was also a significant number of children (forty-six boys and thirty-six girls), who, with a parent or next friend as what were essentially guardians, filed freedom suits. Besides positive outcomes in a large proportion of the cases what is striking about these ancestry suits is the remarkable memories of the plaintiffs, whether telling about their own journey or about the journeys of their parents, grandparents, great grandparents, and even further back in time, personal histories passed down by word of mouth from generation to generation. With the exception of Indian plaintiffs, neither race nor color was the primary issue in these cases; rather the question was who became free, how, and when. There is little doubt that plaintiffs had retained a great deal of family

The Genealogy of the family of slaves claiming

Frank or Frances purchased from a Wm Lightfoot by Colo. William

Tom	Sarah-Coley	Thompson,
Given to Nicholas Merewather by, Colo Wm Merewather and afterwards became the property of Doctor Walker and ran away.	lived with her master till his death	died a young man in Colo. William Merewather's family,

Kate,	Beck,	Hannah,	One deformed the
Allotted to William Hudson at the division of William Merewather's Estate.	allotted to Wm Hudson at the Division of the estate	allotted to Rich. Merewather at the division of the Estate.	

Milley	Mingo	Salley	Harry	Nancy	Isney	Hel.

Archy   Jim   Robert   Meluh.

During his arguments regarding freedom for eleven slaves with the surname Evans, Virginia lawyer Edmund Randolph referred to a genealogical chart that he created to prove that the plaintiffs were distant descendants of the Jane Gibson, an Indian woman, and therefore free. *Library of Virginia, Records of the Circuit Superior Court of Chancery, no. 236, Box 4; Slavery and the Law Digital Archive, PAR 21680501*

of slaves claiming their freedom

foot by Colo. William Merewether

omson

& a young man in Colo.
iam Merewether's family

One deformed Child — one Ditto.   Amey

the   A ouching child allotted to Richd Merewether
late   with Sarah Coley and after Richardsdeath,
                                   to Thomas Merewether by the Cast will of Richa.

        Amey   Nelly   Rachel   Ben
                            troubled with
                            the Epeliptic
                            fits & dead in
                            June 1793.

information, information that once it was related to counsel could be verified with documentary evidence. They told of past owners, sales, hires, and the birth of children. The narratives were filled with anxiety, fears, betrayals, at times loss of hope, not unlike what the great majority of slaves probably experienced over the years. Yet, members of this small group were the fortunate ones who could recount family histories and struggle for a new life in freedom.

After Nicholas Tachaud filed his freedom suit in the Orleans District Court, the judge ordered the sheriff to take him into custody for his own protection and hire him out during the pendency of the court proceedings. The plaintiff shared with his lawyer, Henry R. Denis, what little he knew about his heritage, and cited who in his personal history might be able to verify it. During the next eleven months Denis tracked down enough witnesses to be able to reconstruct his client's history and heritage. One witness, Hermine Boiredan, a free woman of color, recalled Nicholas as an eight-year-old boy in Augusta, Georgia. She had not known Nicholas's mother, who had died three years before, but she did know the mother's friend who had taken responsibility for him and treated him as if he were her own child "in the enjoyment of his freedom." At that time the mother's friend was living with a white man, one Mr. Pelletier, as his housekeeper or mistress. Denis also located several free women of color and one free man who had migrated to New Orleans during the French evacuation of Santo Domingo in 1809, when the Spanish recaptured the country. In fact, there were hundreds of such émigrés in the city, and some had been acquainted with Nicholas's mother, Françoise Dupuy, a free woman of color, as well as his father, a white French army officer. One witness had lived on the same street as Nicholas's family in the city of Santo Domingo before the evacuation; another had sailed on the same evacuation ship with the boy and his mother's friend to Charleston.

During the trial the witnesses testified in open court, and were cross-examined by the defendant's counsel as to how they knew the plaintiff's mother was free and how they were able to recognize him if they had had not seen him since he was a boy of four or five. Several witnesses testified that because Nicholas still bore such a striking resemblance to his mother, he was easily recognizable, even after thirteen years. As for his mother's status as a free woman, one witness pointed out that she was "reputed and always considered as free and would not have been permitted to live in Santo Domingo in the manner she did had she been a slave." Another witness recalled that Nicholas's mother had received a monthly ration of lard, for which she would have to have been free. And another noted that she had possessed a passport, and passports were issued only to free persons. On April 24, 1823, the jury reached a verdict granting Nicholas his freedom. "The Court being satisfied with the verdict of the Jury order that the plaintiff be forever released from the power and control of the defendant, and that the defendant pay costs."[63]

Genealogy of an Indian Family

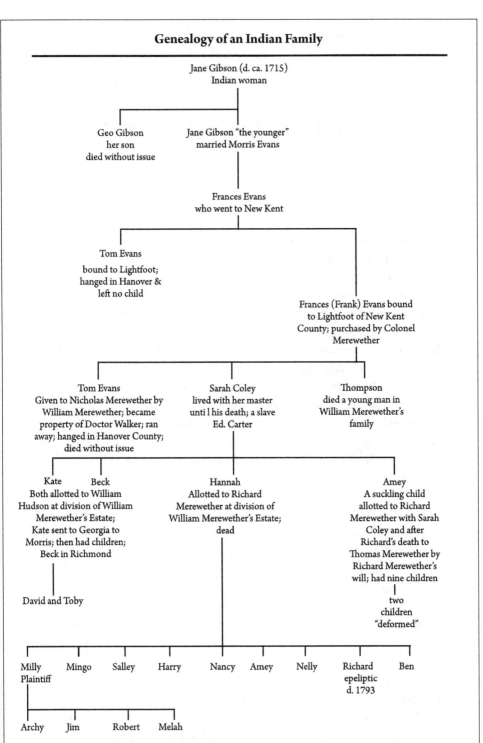

*format altered from original; two partial genealogies combined; some phraseology was revised for clarity; "The Genealogy of the family of slaves claiming their freedom," ca. 1795, with PAR #21680501 http://hv.proquest.com.libproxy.uncg.edu/

7

The Question of Residency

In 1826, thirty-five-year-old John Merry explained to the judge of the circuit court in St. Louis that he was born in the village of Kaskaskia, Illinois, four years after the passage of the Northwest Ordinance. His mother was a black woman in bondage. Despite his mother's status, according to his lawyer and Illinois law he had been born free. Nevertheless, he had been held as a slave, first by a white man and then, through a deed of sale or a deed of gift, by the white man's son. In addition to birth and residency supporting Merry's freedom suit, he and his lawyer noted, a "verbal agreement and contract" between Merry and the white man's son allowed that Merry would be able to attain his "natural liberty" once he paid the son $450. At that time a number of African Americans were working in the lead mines in the area, and it is likely that Merry was permitted to do so and to keep a portion of his earnings for his own purposes. The son, however, reneged on the bargain. In a not uncommon occurrence, he also had Merry arrested and jailed, and subsequently put him on a steamboat to New Orleans. There, at the slave market, he was sold to a Louisiana man in 1825. In time, outraged at the "injustice & oppressive fraud," Merry ran away, and eventually, despite many hardships, he made his way back to Kaskaskia. Not long after, he was seized by two men and, as a slave for life, was again jailed in St. Louis.[1]

The question of residency can be traced back to the Somerset case in England in 1772, in which the Court of the King's Bench declared that slavery could exist only if it was supported by "positive law."[2] In 1791, French law held that "tout individu est libre aussitot qu'il est en France," or that, roughly translated, any person who sets foot on French soil becomes free.[3] In the United States, the North initiated the process to end slavery during and after the American Revolution with the passage of various laws, ordinances, and state constitutions that restricted or abolished the institution.[4] The Missouri Compromise, which resolved the political controversy over the admission of Missouri to the Union in 1821, also restricted the expansion of slavery, but not in the proposed state itself. The debate in Congress focused on the need to maintain a balance between the free and slave states in the US Senate.

The compromise thus allowed Missouri to enter the Union as a slave state and Maine as a free state; however, the final bill also declared that, except for Missouri, slavery would not be permitted anywhere else in the territory acquired by the Louisiana Purchase north of the 36°30' parallel north, which marked the southern border of the state. Many politicians feared the conflict that underlay the compromise might, in the future, split the nation apart. The controversy over slavery was "like a fire bell in the night," Thomas Jefferson wrote, and he "considered it at once as the knell of the Union." In 1854, the Missouri Compromise was repealed by the Kansas-Nebraska Act, and three years later it was declared unconstitutional by the Supreme Court in the *Dred Scott* decision; still, for most of the antebellum era, the geographical boundaries of slavery in the western territories were defined by the compromise.[5]

What effect did these various laws, ordinances, and constitutional requirements have on southern slaveholders who traveled to the North with their human property, either for extended stays or permanent residency? Or on slave buyers whose purchases had lived in the Lower North or in free territories in the West? Or on slaveowners who sought to hire their slaves out across state lines or territorial boundaries? In the North, most of the questions raised by the laws concerned definitions of residency, and what constituted residency was yoked to slaveholders' intents. Did they purpose to live in the North? Did the fact that their slaves accompanied them constitute an intention to establish residency? Did the owners and their slaves then remain in the northern state long enough to permissibly establish residency? In law, the primary question was whether or not owners, in the relocation of their property, had introduced slavery into a free state.

During most of the antebellum era it was not illegal for owners to travel with their slaves in the northern states and territories. New York even passed a law in 1817 that allowed slaveholders to visit the state for up to nine months with their human property.[6] The law was rescinded in 1841, but the resultant possibility that any slave entering the state (except fugitives) could be freed did not dissuade many thousands of southerners from traveling to northern "watering places" during the summer months and bringing with them their black maids, nurses, butlers, cooks, and men in waiting. They fully trusted that the inviolability of property espoused by the Founding Fathers would protect them from any supposedly legal seizure of their slaves during their travels. Nonetheless, if slaves could show that their owners had transported them to a northern state and had remained there for more than a visit, or had acted as a resident, or had hired them out for lengthy periods in a "free state," they could, and sometimes did, file suits for their freedom according various enactments and constitutional requirements in northern states.[7]

In most of the freedom suits charging illegal residency, slave plaintiffs claimed either that they had been born in a southern state but had been taken by their owners to a free state or territory, where they had remained for an extended period, or that they, or their mothers or earlier female ancestors, had been born in free territory and had been brought to the southern states as slaves for life. In addition to the difficulty, common to so many freedom suits, of gathering evidence to prove what had occurred in the sometimes remote past, residency cases held another burden for the plaintiffs, as they had to prove the intention of their owners without the benefit of wills or deeds or like documents indicating such intent. Depositions posed a problem, too, as key deponents in these cases were likely to be resident in other, perhaps distant states; the depositional process could, and often did, take months, or even years. In the face of such obstacles, plaintiffs, with their counsel, had to show that their owners had exercised "ordinary acts of ownership and dominion" over them in the North—acts, as one black woman said, commonly associated with the authority of a master over a slave.

The Kentucky slave Julia won her suit for freedom by showing that her owner had hired her out, first in Pike County, Illinois, and then in Missouri. When she was taken ill, her owner had her returned to Illinois, where she stayed until she recovered her health. The Missouri Supreme Court ruled that the owner's actions did not constitute those of a person who was passing through Illinois as a visitor or traveler. Travelers might be delayed by illness, swollen streams, broken wagons, or the like, but Julia's owner had not been delayed in Illinois. Rather, he had remained there with the express purpose of making the state his home.[8]

Other slave plaintiffs, through their counsel, offered similar evidence. Some asserted they had resided with their owners in states where slavery had been outlawed or was gradually coming to an end; some claimed their mothers had been relocated in a free territory with their owners for extended periods of time. While producing documentation of the sales and resales of slaves complicated residency cases, most plaintiffs had adequate mental records of when they had been bought and sold and when and where they and their children were born. They also usually had history—the names of relatives and their owners, the dates and places of their servitude, the family's grounds for freedom—that they had garnered from their parents. In one case, a slaveowner had taken a two-year-old slave girl and her mother from Kentucky to the Indiana Territory in 1807, and seven years later had sold his rights to the child. With her, the new owner had returned to Kentucky. An appeals court judge ruled that the slave girl had acquired her freedom when the original owner had taken up residence in the Indiana Territory. The judge added that he was not aware of any Kentucky law that could reinstate slavery once it had been nullified. Judges and juries in every southern state would have agreed with this precept; as the Louisiana Civil

Code of 1825 declared, "emancipation, once perfected, is irrevocable, on the part of the master or his heirs." Moreover, the appeals court judge affirmed that Kentucky, as part of a "confederated government" (meaning the United States), should make every effort to respect the laws and institutions of neighboring states. Such comity eventually waned, but until the uneasy 1840s and 1850s it generally characterized the attitude of courts in the South.[9]

Owners were similarly thwarted by the courts when they connived with prospective buyers to circumvent the Northwest Ordinance and state laws prohibiting slavery by selling slaves to a vendee in Ohio or Indiana but keeping the bill of sale in the vendor's southern slaveholding hands. A jury in Virginia ruled that the slave Fanny was free by virtue of her residence in Ohio, which, by the consent and connivance of the Virginia owner-seller who retained the bill of sale, "dissolved the connection of master and slave."[10] The courts sided, too, with plaintiffs whose lawyers could prove that they had been born in a free state or in a state where slavery was gradually ending. If they had been born after the passage of the gradual emancipation law in Pennsylvania, for instance, they had thereby become indentured servants, and if they had been taken out of the state and sold as slaves for life, they could claim their freedom.[11] Most slaves claiming residency in free territory filed their freedom suits in border states and Louisiana, but in a few cases, the claimants had been sold and resold, moved and removed, and ended up in the Lower South. Indeed, they had spent the greater part of their lives in bondage before they had discovered that because they had once resided in free territory, they could rightfully demand their freedom.

Shortly after Mississippi achieved statehood, Harry and two other slaves won a freedom suit on appeal by showing that in 1784, thirty years before they had been transported to Mississippi, they had been taken from Virginia to Vincennes, Indiana, where they had lived until 1816. The counsel for the plaintiffs argued that the 1816 Indiana Constitution outlawed human bondage.[12] The ruling of the Mississippi Supreme Court in favor of three enslaved black men who had resided in the North was not the exception. Freedom suits filed on behalf of African Americans who, for a significant period of time, had resided with their owners in states like Illinois, Indiana, Michigan, Ohio, and Pennsylvania, and had then returned to the South, more often than not succeeded in the courts.[13]

Nearly half of all the freedom suits filed in Missouri—a proportion far exceeding that in any other state—involved the question of residency, in part because of its location across the Mississippi River from Illinois and the trafficking of African Americans between those two states to meet demands for labor. Yet other states—notably Maryland, Virginia, and Kentucky—also shared miles upon miles of borders with northern states, but residency-based freedom suits in those southern states numbered far fewer than they did in Missouri. Mostly, what accounted for the high occurrence of freedom suits in Missouri was the receptivity of its courts to residency-based cases, in which judges and juries tended to rule favorably on behalf of the plaintiffs, especially in St. Louis. The cases on record began as early as 1810, more than a decade before Missouri's statehood, and continued until the *Dred Scott* decision, nearly five decades later. The freedom suit that established judicial precedent was decided in 1824 by the Missouri Supreme Court.

The slave Winny had been taken by her master and mistress from Kentucky, first, to the Indiana Territory in 1795, then, several years later, to St. Louis; after her arrival in the Gate City, she had borne nine children. On appeal, the Missouri Supreme Court proclaimed that Winny's residency in the free territory that later became the free state of Illinois entitled her and all her children to their freedom.[14] In 1834, in the St. Louis Circuit Court, a suit brought by Rachel and her lawyer presented arguments against William Walker, her owner—arguments almost exactly the same as those put forth by *Dred Scott* twelve years later— in which they claimed that because she had lived in areas where slavery was outlawed by the 1787 Ordinance as well as the 1820 Missouri Compromise, she should be freed. In reversing a lower court's verdict, Justice Mathias McGirk asserted that "no authority of law or the government" compelled Rachel's owner to keep her as a slave either at Fort Snelling or in the Michigan Territory. Rather, the master did so "without any other reason than that of convenience" and there-fore had now to face the consequences of introducing slavery into the Michigan Territory "contrary to law."[15]

As blacks held in bondage learned of slaves who had gained their freedom on residency claims or as they themselves became aware of legal possibilities open to them if they, or their mothers or grandmothers, had been born in or had traveled to and lived in free territories, the numbers of cases increased. So did the successes. Apparently, then, despite the difficulty of enlisting whites at distant locations to act as witnesses, most plaintiffs did manage to produce depositions in support of their cases. Usually, when suits failed, the plaintiffs had been unable to secure corroboration for their claims from witnesses or from court documents in the North. In some cases, too, the lawyers for the plaintiffs lacked familiarity with relevant laws and statutes in northern states. On occasion, following their lawyers' advice, plaintiffs filed their papers in the wrong courts, while others lost due to the complexity of their cases or misinterpretations on points of law.

When the court decided against Amy in 1822, she was in her mid-fifties. Born of an African mother in Pennsylvania twelve years before the gradual abolition act, she had been taken by her owner to Maryland, then to Virginia, and in 1790, after sale to the defendant in her suit, to Kentucky. The defendant rebutted the claim of her, and her mother's, residency in abolitionist Pennsylvania by arguing that the gradual abolition act applied only to those born after its passage; there-fore, the plaintiff's African-born mother was in fact and always a slave, as was

Amy.[16] In other cases, owners successfully argued that although they had dwelt in a free state or territory with their slaves for many months, they had had no intention of establishing residency in a locale where slavery was outlawed or being gradually abolished. They had simply been detained by circumstances beyond their control.[17]

Until the late antebellum era, slaveholders, accompanied by their human property, could travel in the North without threat of law. However, as the definition of sojourning varied from state to state, some slaveowners who had stayed in the North for only a few weeks sometimes found themselves summoned as defendants in southern freedom suits. On occasion, so did owners who sent their slaves across the Ohio River, either to run errands or to assist a family member. In 1844, at the request of her master, the female slave America journeyed from Greenup County, Kentucky, to Hillsborough, Ohio, there to assist his ailing daughter. America stayed in Ohio for two weeks. Upon her return to Kentucky she filed a residency-based freedom suit and won a verdict in the Greenup County Court. The appeals court, however, reversed the decision. It reasoned that America had been sent to Ohio "for a merely temporary purpose," and that if, in principle, a slave's setting foot on Ohio soil could deprive owners of their human property, then owners who sent slaves across the Ohio River on the most trivial errand, or the most pressing emergency, would be placed at great risk.[18] If those in bondage remained longer in northern states or territories, they would better their chances of gaining free status.

Witnesses' observations of slaves' behavior during their sojourns in the North also affected their chances for freedom. Henry traveled with his owner from Kentucky to Indiana, then back to Kentucky. After a second visit to Indiana, where, according to one witness, he acted "as a free man," Henry again crossed the Ohio River back to Kentucky, but this time in the employment of a man herding horses—the man who then jailed and sold him as a slave for life. The Chancery Court of Jefferson County, ruling in Henry's favor, stated that his alleged master (the horse herder) as well as the person who purchased him acted "wickedly & fraudulently."[19]

Also dependent on the issue of residency were freedom suits in which slave plaintiffs claimed that, at the time of their birth, their mothers were living or had lived in a state where slavery was gradually ending or had been abolished. Although their mothers were still slaves, the children were by law deemed to be indentured servants and could not be held as slaves for life, even if they were now resident in a slave state. As one Virginia slave named Susannah and her lawyer contended, she had been born in Pennsylvania after the passage of the 1780 law and had subsequently been taken with her slave mother to Virginia. According to Pennsylvania law, by virtue of her birthplace she was born not into slavery but into indentured service until she reached the age of twenty-eight years. At the time of her suit, she was already forty-two years old, and thus entitled to her freedom. A jury found in her favor.[20]

Residency was cited, too, by southern slaves who had traveled north and remained with their owners in a northern state for an extended period of time, even though they had later returned with their masters to the South. Two Virginia slaves, Betty and Pleasant, gained free status on the claim that as small children they had traveled with their owner and his family to Massachusetts, where they had stayed for one year before returning to Southampton County in Virginia. Their freedom suit, which included their children, was rejected by the circuit court, but the verdict was reversed on appeal. When a slaveowner and his family assumed residency in Massachusetts, Judge Dabney Carr wrote, their slaves were thereafter presumed to be free.[21] Rationalization by slave owners about why they had stayed in the North with their slaves for an extended length of time—usually for reasons of health, their own or family members', or to attend to the care of ailing loved ones resident in the North—apparently had little impact of the outcome of the suits. At least until the 1840s, courts in the South were inclined to favor the plaintiffs in residency cases, as many southern judges were disposed to respect the laws and judicial decisions in northern states like Massachusetts. As one Louisiana appeals judge summarily stated in regard to a suit concerning the extended stays of white families and their slaves in the North, the slaves became ipso facto free.[22]

When southern slaves who had been hired out in the North filed freedom suits, they encountered problems particular to their sometimes ambiguous situation. In Delaware, Maryland, Virginia, Kentucky, and Missouri, slaves who had been hired out in the North for any period of time could, on their return, assert their right to freedom, both by freedom statutes in the North and nonimportation laws in the South. In Kentucky, Missouri, and Louisiana, slaves hired out in Ohio, Indiana, and Illinois won a number of cases because they had remained in free territory long enough to be subject to, and benefit from, the laws of those states. Some hirelings and their lawyers argued that the extended length of their stays in northern states in essence established their residency there. However dubiously most southerners might view the right, or presumption, of a person in bondage to declare residency status, southern courts frequently accepted slaves' arguments on this point.

Hirelings worked at many tasks, mostly as laborers on farms, where they tended livestock, harvested crops, cleaned stables, hewed timber, and built fences. Among the hirelings in the antebellum years were, now and then, skilled artisans—carpenters, masons, blacksmiths—some steamboat hands, and even a few touring musicians and entertainers. Missouri slave hirelings worked in the lead mines, coal mines, and salt works of Illinois. In fact, the 1818 constitution of Illinois explicitly permitted hired slaves to work in the Massac County salt mines, and in later years, despite prohibitions, slaves took on a variety of jobs in the state's river towns.[23] Whatever their employment, once they had crossed state lines and worked for a year and more in a free state or territory, some hired slaves were prompted to file freedom suits based on their residency in a nonslaveholding locality.

The slave David, who was hired out by his Maryland owner to a man in Pennsylvania, claimed his freedom as a resident of a state where slavery was gradually ending. The Maryland General Court declared him free.[24] The St. Louis slave Vincent was hired out for a number of years during the 1820s as a laborer at the Saline, Illinois, salt lick. He had gone to Saline periodically, first from Kentucky and, after his original owner's death, from Missouri, where hired slaves were permitted to work out of state for one year. In 1829, when his current owner decided to sell him, Vincent filed a freedom suit. The lower court's ruling in favor of the owner was overturned by the Missouri Supreme Court, which concluded it a fraud to return a hireling to the state for a few days each year in order to evade the one-year restriction on out-of-state hires. The remanded suit, however, ended with the jury finding in favor of the defendant: "We the Jury find the Plaintiff a slave."[25] Other Missouri slaves who worked as hirelings elsewhere in Illinois also filed freedom suits, in some cases, after working out of state for only a few weeks;[26] or, as one plaintiff said, "at various times between the years 1839 & 1841."[27]

In a practice called self-hire, slaves on occasion were allowed by their masters to go to northern states and hire out their own time, on the condition that they turn over a portion of their earnings to their masters. The fact that self-hire was illegal in most southern states did not prevent its practice, especially since both parties profited from the arrangement. Of course, nothing prevented these hirelings from absconding, either to some northern state or, in later years, to Canada. Usually, though, they returned to the South, in large part out of concern that their families were in bondage to their owners there. The personal histories of the self-hired slaves who sued for their freedom, like those of slaves hired out by their masters, also evinced a new measure of self-confidence and a fresh sense of autonomy as they had been able to move about without hindrance and to realize more fully the value of their labor.

In deciding if a slave with his master's permission could hire himself or herself out for an extended period, the Missouri Supreme Court found that a self-hire was in essence no different than a slave being moved to another state and being hired out there by his or her owner acting as a resident.[28] The same court invalidated the 1807 Illinois territorial law and the section of the 1818 Illinois Constitution that permitted whites to hold persons in servitude under any prior contact or indenture. Such contracts and indentures, the Missouri court averred, amounted to "qualified slavery" and were thus a violation of the Northwest Ordinance.[29] Courts in Kentucky and Louisiana made similar decisions. A Pennsylvania-born slave who was hired out to an innkeeper in Cincinnati, then later transported to Louisiana, where he was sold as a slave for life, filed for and won his freedom in a Louisiana district court. The judge ruled that he became free by virtue of having resided in Ohio with his owner's consent; the ruling was upheld on appeal.[30]

If a hireling had been sent to a free territory by a hiring agent without the owner's knowledge or consent, the slaveholder then had grounds for retaining his human property in the event of a freedom suit. "I never gave the plaintiff permission or order to go to the state of Illinois, whilst he was in my possession," a former slaveholder in Missouri testified on behalf of his daughter, the wife of a defendant in a freedom suit. It was true, he admitted, that six or seven years before, his white employee, a German man, had taken the plaintiff across the Mississippi River for a few days to help harvest a crop of hay, but he had done so without authorization. At that time the plaintiff had been ten or twelve years old. The court ruled in favor of the defendant in this case, which also serves to illustrate the license that plaintiffs and lawyers were willing to assume in their definitions of residency.[31]

Prosperous slaveholders whose business or pleasure frequently took them away from their homes and farms sometimes left slaves for hire in the hands of agents. Thomas Jefferson, a black man who was "lame" in one leg, spent eight months as a hireling working on a farm in Illinois. Upon his return, he sued for his freedom on the grounds of his residency in a free state. The owner countered that at the time of Jefferson's hire, he was completely unaware that his bondsman had been hired out by his agent for labor in a free state. One set of instructions to the jury read: "If the jury find from the evidence that the plaintiff, while in the state of Illinois, was the slave of Charles W. Dreshsler and do not find that he was in the State with the knowledge and consent of the said Dreshsler, they will find for the defendant." The evidence so indicated, and the suit was denied.[32]

Likewise, slaves who absconded to the North and hired themselves out without their owners' permission had no grounds to sue for their freedom, although a few attempted unsuccessfully to plead residency claims in southern courts.[33] Some slaves were hired out as sailors, boat hands, or mates on seagoing vessels, and some as bargemen on the Ohio and Mississippi Rivers. A few among them attempted to gain free status in the courts, but, as one judge noted, their work as hirelings did "nothing towards engrafting slavery upon the social system" of the states through which they passed.[34] Slave women who were hired out to work on steamboats as chambermaids or washerwomen sometimes tested their status when the steamboats traveled up the Illinois or Mississippi Rivers into free territory, but most of them failed.

There was no single definition of residency for hirelings. Some cases rested not so much on the length of time spent in free territory or on the intent of the owner but rather on what appeared to be a measure of sympathy for the plaintiff. Following her owner's death in Loudoun County, Virginia, Sarah became a life-estate slave, or the property of his widow, Margaret Prosser, during her lifetime. When Margaret decided to move to Morgan County, Illinois, she hired Sarah out to her son-in-law in Catlettsburg, Kentucky. Her term of hire expired in late November 1840, and the son-in-law then transported Sarah to her owner's residence in Illinois, from which she was to be taken to St. Louis and again hired out as soon as possible. That winter, however, a bitter cold spell that froze over the Mississippi River delayed travel, as did the illness of Sarah's daughter, who became so dehydrated by dysentery that she died. Not until late February was Sarah finally sent to St. Louis and hired out. When she filed her freedom suit a few years later, the court ruled that her residency of three months in Illinois, whatever the owner's circumstance, made her a free woman.

In other suits during 1780s and '90s and up through the 1840s, slaves who had lived or visited for a period of time in nonslaveholding countries also tested the courts by filing freedom suits. In 1791, Charles Mahoney of Prince George's County, Maryland, filed a freedom suit in which he claimed that his maternal ancestor, Ann Joice, had been conveyed by her owner from Barbados to England, and then by Charles Calvert Baltimore, Third Baron Baltimore, to Maryland, where she served as his slave between 1678 and 1691. The primary argument put forth by Mahoney's lawyer, Gabriel Duvall, maintained that Ann's stay in England had guaranteed her freedom in keeping with the Somerset decision. Over the course of eleven years and three trials, lawyers for the plaintiff and defendant argued numerous issues, including whether setting foot on English soil was the same as setting foot on French soil, and disputed points of law. They discredited hearsay evidence. Ultimately the lower court and general court both ruled in Mahoney's favor, but in 1797 the court of appeals reversed and remanded the case because the lower court had refused to direct the jury that Joice was a slave under Maryland law. When the defendant uncovered evidence that Ann was probably a "guinea negro" who had never set foot on English soil, the high court decided in 1802 in favor of the defendant. At the time of Ann's arrival, the judges noted, Maryland law required that imported blacks and their children be deemed slaves for life.[35]

Residency issues were also raised in freedom suits filed against slaveowners who had immigrated to the United States from the Caribbean. The 1791 slave revolt in Saint-Domingue, eventually led by Toussaint l'Ouverture, prompted thousands of French-Creole families, including many slaveowners with their human chattel, to flee the country. In 1793, the slaves in Saint-Domingue were emancipated, and the next year, those in all the other French-held territories in the Caribbean, by an edict from the French National Convention.[36] Most of the French-Creole slaveholders and their families first migrated to Cuba, but when the Spanish assumed control of the island, they moved on to Louisiana. A few settled in other southern states, where they faced laws prohibiting the importation of slaves.

The freedom suits against slaveholding émigrés, like those against owners who had traveled with slaves to free territories, focused on the definition of residency: the question being whether foreign-born arrivals now dwelling with their human property in southern states were residents or sojourners. As sojourners, they could retain possession of their slaves. As residents, in certain states, including Maryland, they could not, and their slaves would by law be declared free.[37] Responding to the upheavals in the Caribbean islands, in 1792 the Maryland legislature passed a law allowing émigrés asylum and the right to retain their domestic or house slaves, five for each family and three for each individual.[38] Although the law was repealed five years later, a few slave plaintiffs used it as the basis to sue their owners. When the slave Lewis and his lawyer sued for his freedom in Frederick County, Maryland, they argued that prior to his arrival in Maryland Lewis had never been a domestic servant, as he would have to have been according to the law. Lewis won a jury verdict, which was upheld on appeal.[39]

The definition of "sojourner" was general enough to lend an advantage to the defendants in several freedom suits. When Caribbean slaveholders fled for their lives, their families, and those of their slaves, were often, and sometimes permanently, split up, with spouses and children, white and black, perhaps ending up at great geographical distances from each other. During the early nineteenth century in Santo Domingo, in the midst of a slave uprising, the slaveholding De Fontaine family managed to escape, but to two different locations: the husband to St. Jago, Cuba, and the wife and their son to Baltimore, Maryland. In 1805, with hopes of recovering his former estate, the husband returned to Santo Domingo and joined the French army. He recovered only two slaves, whom he sent to his wife, and later that year, when Santo Domingo was in the midst of a slave revolt, he was killed in battle. In 1808, when his widow, seeking to regain at least some small portion of her late husband's fortune, went back to Santo Domingo, she left her son and two slaves in the care of a guardian in Maryland. Some years later, when Madam De Fontaine instructed an agent to ship her son and the two slaves back to Santo Domingo, the blacks, Marine De Fontaine and Betsy De Fontaine, filed a freedom suit. The courts ruled against them on the grounds that, despite their having lived more than ten years in Maryland, their owner, Madam De Fontaine, was defined as a sojourner who therefore had the right to hold her human property.[40]

For other slaves from the Caribbean, the matter of an alleged owner's residency was less important in freedom suits than the slave's status prior to arrival in the United States. In such cases, it was virtually impossible for plaintiffs to produce documentary evidence supporting assertions in regard to their status on some Caribbean island, or establishing how and when they had traveled to the United States, as official records had been mostly destroyed in the upheavals of their homeland. Occasionally, even minimal circumstantial evidence of heritage proved to be sufficient for the courts. The French-speaking Tennessee slave Clarissa won her freedom on the claim that as a free woman of color, she had been taken from a French colony in the West Indies to Virginia, where she had been sold as a slave. The only evidence offered by Clarissa's counsel in support of her claim was that she spoke French and had always told people that she was a free person in her native land. The documents did not even reveal the specific island of her residency (Guadeloupe was mentioned in the suit involving her son). The state supreme court nonetheless overturned the verdict of the Rutherford County Court and ruled in Clarissa's favor.[41]

Other persons of color who were being held as slaves in the United States claimed that they had lived as free persons of color in Saint Domingue, or that they had been freed in Saint Domingue at the time of the general emancipation, or that they had acquired their freedom during their stay in Cuba.[42] In 1818, Metayer, a New Orleans woman of color, failed in a suit claiming that her master in Hispaniola had freed her in 1803 and that she had lived as a free person ever since. Spanish law permitted slaves who had acted as free persons either for ten years in the presence of their masters or for twenty years in their absence to go free. Metayer failed to meet the twenty-year standard. She did prove, however, that she had lived in Haiti at the time of the general emancipation, on which grounds she was granted her freedom. This was the first formal recognition in Louisiana courts of Haiti's sovereignty.[43]

Residency in other foreign countries provided the basis for a few of the freedom suits on record. In 1840, Pierre, a Missouri slave, claimed to be free because his mother, Rose, had been born in Montreal, Lower Canada, in 1768, and had then been taken to Prairie du Chien in the Northwest Territory, which was at that time under British control. His sister and brother, Charlotte and Louis, filed similar suits, in which they too argued that because slavery did not exist in Canada, their mother had been born free. The documentary evidence was not easy to obtain, and the freedom suits, which went into appeals, went unresolved for many years. Not until the second year of the Civil War was Charlotte's suit decided in her favor. Two years later, Louis's achieved the same result, but in the meantime he had spent nearly four years in jail.[44]

Another unusual plea came from Isabella, a slave in St. Mary's Parish, Louisiana, who filed a freedom suit claiming that years earlier she had been taken by her then owner from Mexico to Sabine, Texas. Saliently, during the time of her residence in Mexico, President Vincente Guerrero had issued a decree, published and circulated in 1829, abolishing slavery in the republic. The plaintiff's lawyer called a witness who confirmed the decree and quoted from it, but the Louisiana Supreme Court ruled that without proper proof, specifically, a copy of the decree itself, the written slave laws of Spain took precedent.[45] Other plaintiffs failed to acquire freedom when they cited residency in Madagascar, a slave-trading kingdom.[46]

Residence in the North, Canada, Mexico, or the Caribbean islands was not the only requisite that enabled blacks in bondage to apply for status as freemen and freewomen; so did travel to free countries. Small in number though the petitioners were, slaves with proof of temporary residency in free countries abroad tested the interpretation of the southern laws invoked in freedom suits. In the years following the Louisiana Purchase and then Louisiana's statehood in 1812, many French Creoles resident there returned to France for extended visits, often with maids, waiters, housekeepers, wet nurses, au pairs, or other trusted servants. Upon their return to Louisiana, some among those bond servants filed freedom suits arguing that they had resided in a country where slavery was prohibited and were therefore free.

Priscilla Smith, for one, claimed that in 1835, by which time she had been in servitude to the widow of her original owner, Michael Smith, for some years, she had accompanied the widow to Paris, where she and her mistress had lived for several months. On their arrival back in New Orleans, though, the widow's agent "took domination over her"; he ordered her to hire herself out and give up her wages to him on behalf of the widow. In 1837, Priscilla filed suit on grounds that she was free by virtue of her extended stay in Paris and therefore no person had "a right to exercise ownership over her." The parish court denied the application, but the Louisiana Supreme Court reversed the decision and granted Priscilla her freedom.[47]

Other of the petitioners with similar claims—girls and young women but for the rare exception—had been resident in France anywhere from a few days or weeks to five years. In some cases, their owners had told the plaintiffs about the prohibition of slavery in France and thus deigned to treat them as free persons during their trip and residency abroad; then, upon their return, the owners had either had the slave girls sold or hired out under their authority. Some plaintiffs, too, averred that aboard ship to and from the Continent they had traveled as if they were free passengers; one plaintiff claimed even to hold a valid passport. With the slaves' discovery on their return that their owners had no intention of releasing them from bondage, in spite of the French law granting them freedom, came the filing of freedom suits. Some plaintiffs sought damages for wages forfeited when they had worked abroad as well as on their return to the United

States. Arséne, a woman of color also known as Cora, claimed that payment for the work she had done during her "extended residence" in a country where slavery was not tolerated and for the services she had provided upon her return to New Orleans amounted to $1,200.[48]

Plaintiffs in some instances had given birth to children after they had returned to the United States; in their freedom suits, therefore, they requested that their offspring be included in their plea. As such pleas were often filed years after the plaintiffs' return stateside, the children named in their petitions were likely to be near or in adulthood. In other cases, slave children who had actually traveled abroad with their mothers filed freedom suits when they became adults, and included their children in their petitions. In 1822, Plany had journeyed with her mother and her mother's owner to France, where they had resided for several years. She filed her suit in 1847, a quarter-century after her residency, and requested that her three living children also be freed.[49] The New Orleans slave Tabé claimed that because she had lived in France for three years, she as well as the three children she had borne subsequent to her return to Louisiana should be released from bondage. The slave Aurore had lived in France so long, between 1818 and 1823, and spoke the language so well that she was called the "Parisienne." After her sojourn abroad, she gave birth to the five children she included as plaintiffs in her freedom suit. The First District Court judge in this and most other similarly argued foreign-residency cases ruled that the women had acquired their freedom upon their arrival in France and that their children had therefore been born of free mothers, and thus were likewise free. Some plaintiffs cited the Louisiana Civil Code, Article 196: "The children born of a woman after she has acquired the right of being free at a future time, follow the condition of its mother, and becomes free at the time of her enfranchisement, even if the mother should die before that time."[50]

Almost without exception residency-in-France arguments successfully established the right to freedom for both the slave plaintiffs and their children. They owed that success primarily to one lawyer, Jean Charles David, who argued a large percentage of the French-residency cases before the district courts. Untiringly, for weeks or even months per case, he pursued evidence and unfailingly produced reliable witnesses to attest that his clients had indeed resided with their owners in France. He queried the defendants as well as persons who knew them to ascertain facts in support of a case. In the district courts, and on a few occasions before the Louisiana Supreme Court, he argued persuasively that French law not only prohibited slavery in France but also allowed his clients to secure their freedom there. Further, he contended in most cases, slaveowners were fully aware of French law in regard to servitude but chose to travel and sojourn with their bond servants in defiance of it.

In 1848, David traveled to West Baton Rouge Parish to speak with a slave, Marie, who, he learned, had accompanied her owners, Dr. and Mrs. Doussan, to France in 1831 and had resided there for about a year. David then informed the Doussans in a letter, which was delivered to them via Marie, that he planned to name them as defendants in Marie's freedom suit. Her petition requested that the Doussans be subpoenaed to appear in court, answer the charges, and forfeit payment to her for the value of lost wages. The district court "adjudged, ordered & decreed that the plaintiff is free."[51]

Jean Charles David's proficiency at winning residency-based cases gained him a reputation that prompted a few owners who journeyed to France with their servants to make a "confession of judgment," by which they renounced all claims of ownership.[52] Unintentionally, David was also largely responsible for the revisions of the statues addressing the issue of residency in Louisiana law. In 1846, the General Assembly passed an act outlawing both French-residency and free-state-residency claims for freedom. With this act the many years of judiciary comity came to an end. Still, as the new law was not retroactive, French-residency suits, at least, continued.[53]

Or they did until 1852, when, in the case of *Liza (c. w.) v. Dr. Puissant et al.,* the Supreme Court ruled that the 1846 statute should be rendered retroactive. In 1821, the twelve-year-old Liza traveled with her owner to Bordeaux, France, where they resided for a few months. In 1830, Liza's owner transferred his deed on her to his daughter as a wedding present. In subsequent years Liza gave birth to seven children, and on their behalf as well as her own she sued for freedom in 1850. On appeal, the judges asserted that Liza had dwelt in France only as a sojourner, not as a permanent resident, and therefore, by the 1846 statute, did not qualify for freedom. Chief Justice George Eustis, who had previously ruled in favor of black plaintiffs on numerous occasions, concurred.[54] Such decisions in residency-based freedom suits coincided with the intense political struggles that erupted in the nation during the late 1840s and 1850s and were concomitant with the passage of increasingly more repressive antiblack laws in southern states. Until then, though, foreign-residency claims proved to be an effective means to a slave plaintiff's end. While such claims represent only a small fraction of the freedom suits, they do demonstrate the importance that courts, judges, and juries in the southern states attached to the status of black people in the country of their origin as well as to statutes that outlawed human bondage in foreign countries.

From the early years of statehood through the antebellum era, southern states passed numerous laws and constitutional restrictions concerning the importation of slaves. These laws did not prohibit slaveowners from leaving their home state either to establish residency elsewhere or to purchase slaves out of state for their plantations. Rather, the laws were designed to regulate slave traders,

factors, and slaveholders who brought slaves into a state for the purpose of selling them. Anti-importation statutes were often repealed or amended, but nearly
every state prohibited the introduction of slaves for sale at one time or another.
Between 1789, when Georgia and Virginia passed their initial anti-importation
statutes, and 1855, when Louisiana and Virginia passed their final such acts,
lawmakers enacted approximately 235 measures dealing with the importation
of slaves. Only four states—Missouri, Arkansas, Florida, and Texas—failed to
enact anti-importation laws. "The introduction of slaves into this State as merchandise, or for sale," a typical restriction read, "shall be prohibited from and
after the first day of May, eighteen hundred and thirty-three."[55]

Most slaveholders who supported these enactments believed that slaves
imported from out of state would have a toxic effect on the native black
populations, and thus constituted a danger to the stability of the social structure.
In 1840, Robert J. Walker, a Louisiana lawyer arguing a case against slave trader
Robert Slaughter in Mississippi, articulated the sentiments of many owners in
the Lower South. The transportation of blacks in chains from one state to another rendered nearly all of them dangerous, Walker argued; migrants would not
only seek vengeance on their masters but also endeavor to inflame the passions
of other slaves in the state. The notion that blacks native to a state remained
loyal, contented, and industrious while imported slaves posed the threat of rebellion was of course not borne out by events such as the Louisiana slave revolt of 1811, the Gabriel conspiracy and Nat Turner revolt in Virginia, and the
Denmark Vesey plot in South Carolina; nonetheless, state legislatures, especially
in the states of the Lower South, continued to enact anti-importation laws by
which to control the states' slave trade and to punish those who violated their
regulations.[56]

The constitutional question as to whether the buying and selling of slaves
who had been transported from one state to another should come under federal
jurisdiction and the interstate commerce clause of the US Constitution was decided in favor of the states; for although slaves were considered to be both chattel
and real property (and thus subject of federal regulation), they were also human
beings and consequently not merchandise by the same definition as other property. Even so, constitutional questions concerning importation persisted for
many years. In 1819, Maryland slaveholder Robert Wright requested permission to import slaves into Delaware. He argued cogently that he possessed a land
patent from the state of Delaware; that he feared the loss of his holdings if the
land was not cleared and cultivated in the near future; that he needed slaves in
order to clear the land; and that, as the Constitution of the United States promised, "the Citizens of each State Shall be entitled to all privileges and Immunities
of Citizens in the Several States." Wright's case proved to be no exception; the
courts ruled, as they had again and again, that individual states maintained

the right to control, and restrict or prohibit, the importation of slaves.[57] As an appeals court judge noted in a criminal case against a trader who had entered Kentucky with intent to sell a slave, commerce in slaves was a matter of a peculiar character to be determined by the internal regulation of each state, over which Congress held no authority.[58]

As a consequence, each state formulated its own laws and imposed its own penalties regarding importation. The laws in most states stipulated that the slave or slaves be confiscated and the trafficker be fined an amount of several hundred dollars, a portion of which was allotted to the informant.[59] Meanwhile, the appeals process in the various states further refined and interpreted importation statutes. Although the penalties differed from state to state, throughout the South the illegal importation of slaves constituted a serious criminal matter.[60] At least it did in principle; in practice, only a small fraction of the offenders were apprehended and prosecuted, while the domestic slave trade flourished throughout the decades preceding the Civil War.

Several states—Delaware in 1787 and 1797, Maryland in 1783 and 1796, and Virginia in 1778 and 1785—passed statutes proclaiming that any "negro, mulatto or other slave" brought illegally into their state, by land or water, for sale or to reside, should immediately cease to be the property of the owner and thereby become free.[61] Florida later passed a similar statute.[62] But Kentucky during its early years inherited the Virginia law and subsequently legislated its own act, which did not include the grant of freedom to the slave.[63] When the District of Columbia was created in 1801, it inherited the importation laws of Maryland for Washington County and those of Virginia for Alexandria County. The District later submitted to Congress its own code, defining the consequence of illegal importation as not "a mere penalty upon the person so importing or bringing in any slave" but a "right and privilege, and for the benefit of the person so imported." Although this code and its successor in 1855 were not enacted into law, the proposed codes served as a guide in importation cases.[64] In 1787 and 1793, Delaware passed anti-slave-export laws, which required that owners apply for permits to export their slaves and declared that "every slave otherwise exported" would thereby become free.[65] No other state followed Delaware's example. Laws granting freedom to illegally imported slaves remained in effect throughout the antebellum era; the existence of those laws did not, however, guarantee their enforcement.

All of the importation-exportation statutes granting freedom involved the question of residency, in regard to both the slaveholders and their human chattel. Each of the states—Maryland, Virginia, Delaware, and Florida—and the District of Columbia stipulated that slaveholders planning to assume permanent residency in the state had to comply with certain requirements, including the signing of an oath to the effect that their slaves had been resident in their home state for a designated period of years prior to their relocation and that their slaves, as well as they themselves, would remain in their new state for the length of time necessary to be deemed permanent residents. The oath had to be signed within a given number of days. Slaveholders who were merely traveling through a state, or stopping to visit friends, family, or business associates, were defined as "sojourners" and thus exempted from laws pertaining to residency.[66]

In the years following the various states' enactments granting freedom to imported slaves, a number of African Americans filed freedom suits in the county or circuit courts. Some who had been transported across state lines learned about the legal possibilities available to them from other slaves, often slaves who themselves had previously brought suits. Others learned of the statutes from lawyers prepared to assist blacks in unlawful bondage. Some discovered the opportunity that importation laws afforded them only after many years, or even decades; their claims speak of owners who brought them illegally into a state and masters who hired them out across state lines in contravention of the law. In light of the huge number of black people who were moved in and out of the states in the Upper South, it is clear that only a tiny fraction of the slaves who were imported (or exported) in defiance of the laws were able to file freedom suits. Unlike the criminal prosecutions in other residency-based freedom suits, cases charging unlawful importation were filed as civil contests that pitted slaves against their masters.

Not surprisingly, then, only a modest number of plaintiffs filed claims citing anti-importation statutes, some out of fear that their masters might sell them before they could bring an action. Others were reluctant to file because, if they did win, they would be forced to leave the state according to the free black expulsion statutes (as in Virginia after 1806 and Maryland after 1831) and to abandon families, friends, and loved ones. What is surprising is that a significant majority of the slaves who did file suits won their freedom.[67]

In general, slaveowners moved their slaves from one location to another without scrutiny. Only if local residents, other slaveholders, or blacks themselves raised questions about an illegal importation did such cases reach the courts. In the four areas of the South where most of the cases occurred—Delaware, Maryland, Virginia, and the District of Columbia—black people discussed the laws that permitted them to file illegal residency freedom suits. If a black person had knowledge of the importation statutes and contacted a lawyer, testimony then posed a trying, time-consuming problem, as the witnesses, by the very definition of the claim, lived in a different state. Often depositions in Maryland cases would have to be taken in Virginia or Delaware, and Delaware testimony in Maryland or Pennsylvania. No matter how carefully the courts might try to ensure that the process move forward in a timely fashion, it could take at least a year and sometimes longer for a claimant's lawyer to gather the necessary evidence.

Meanwhile, enslaved plaintiffs remained in limbo.[68] After filing freedom suits, a few among them, despite court restrictions on alleged owners, were not heard from again. In 1803, for example, David, who lived in Kent County, Delaware, filed a freedom suit claiming that Nathan Baynard of Queen Anne's County, Maryland, had illegally held him as a slave, but when his case came before the court, David failed to appear.[69]

Most plaintiffs in illegal importation suits, though, did appear. Standing before a judge, justices, jury members, lawyers, and court observers, they bore mixed emotions: unease, anxiety, sometimes fear, and almost always buoyancy at the prospect of their lives finally—perhaps years after the illegal act against them— being changed for the better. In 1807, a Maryland slave filed a suit twenty-one years after his former owner, a lifelong resident of Somerset County, Maryland, apprenticed him to a blacksmith in Delaware. When the owner died, his widow hired out the plaintiff in Delaware and then, after the period of hire, brought him back to Maryland. At trial, by virtue of the Maryland nonimportation act, which was read to the jury, the plaintiff was granted his freedom.[70] So were the plaintiffs in a suit filed in regard to the documentation of their relocation in Virginia. In their argument, they and their lawyer pointed to the fact that the owner's wife, not the owner himself, had signed the importation oath required by the 1792 law. The jury voted for the plaintiffs' freedom, and the appeals court affirmed the verdict: the signature of the actual owner on the oath was mandatory.[71]

The Maryland slave Rebecca Ringgold, along with her two children, Araminta and William, filed a freedom suit twenty-eight years after Rebecca had been taken by her owner to Missouri for a period of about a year. The three plaintiffs claimed that Rebecca's subsequent return to Maryland with her master violated the state's 1831 nonimportation act. According to that act Rebecca should have been freed upon her return, and thus so should the two children born to her after her return. The appeals court overturned a lower court ruling against the plaintiffs and granted the Ringgold family its freedom.[72] In the northeast quadrant of the Upper South, where illegal importation provided grounds for blacks to sue for their freedom if they had been hired out in another state, or had been taken to an adjacent state and sold, or if their owners had failed to meet the letter of the law in regard to importation requirements, a number of slaves not only brought suits but also gained free status.[73]

The case of Maryland plaintiff Robert Oakes answered the question as to whether the time spent by a slave hired out in an adjacent state exceeded the statutory limit in that state even when periods of hire had occurred intermittently over several years. On various occasions Oakes had traveled from Maryland to Virginia for a month or more in order to assist his owner "raising Stones" from a quarry, stones which they had then transported to a "manufactory at Baltimore." In July 1806, the parties and their lawyers appeared in court and after "all and singular the premises being by the Court here seen, heard, and fully understood, and mature deliberation thereupon had," Robert Oakes was granted his freedom and his owner was ordered to pay him $1,099 for his "costs and charges." The Maryland Court of Appeals upheld the verdict on the grounds that when added together, the total number of months spent by the petitioner at various times in Virginia exceeded the one-year limit stipulated by Virginia law.[74]

Delaware boasted a large number of importation cases. The antislavery views of some Christian denominations, most notably Quakers and Methodists, which sympathized with the plight of black people, as well as the willingness of prominent lawyers in the state to argue their cases, created a favorable environment for slave plaintiffs. The petitions they filed were in most cases so brief that the issue of importation, which was unstated, had to be inferred from the states in which the depositions had been taken (Maryland, Virginia, and Pennsylvania) and from the phrase that the plaintiff should be freed "by the laws of this state." Delaware law declared it to be illegal to import slaves into the state for any reason, including their being hired out. By dint of the Delaware law, slave hirelings from Maryland discovered they could bring suit against their owners, even when the owners' land abutted the state line and the slaves' hires took them only a mile or two into Delaware.

The protestations of owners who would thus lose their human property hardly affected the county courts in Delaware; almost invariably they ruled in favor of the hirelings. In one case the appeals court determined that although the Maryland slave had crossed the border to work on a farm in Delaware for only a few days, the nonimportation law applied and entitled the hireling to his freedom.[75] Indeed, in Delaware anti-importation laws could trump all other arguments. The debate over Beck's petition for freedom in Delaware's Kent County Court and later the court of appeals focused on whether she was a slave for life or a term slave (whose term had been served out), until testimony established that Beck, now resident in Delaware, had been purchased from an owner in Maryland. The appeals court thereupon ruled that she had been illegally imported and "adjudged negro Beck free."[76] In 1827, the state did make one concession to slaveholders: If it happened that their farms straddled a state line, it was permissible for them to "lawfully employ" their slaves on any portion of their property.[77]

Delaware, too, was the only southern state to pass a law granting freedom to slaves who had been illegally exported—that is, without a court-issued license.[78] The law was passed amid growing concern about the kidnapping of free blacks and theft of slaves who were then quickly transported out of the state and sold to buyers headed for "southern markets." In 1801, more than three hundred Delaware residents petitioned the General Assembly to halt the "most detestable of all crimes, so common among us, the crime of man-stealing." Another, separate complaint later addressed the "iniquitous traffic" in kidnapping free blacks.[79] The kidnappings and thefts, however, continued decade after decade as the price of slaves rose precipitously, along with the demand for them nearly everywhere in the South. Only rarely did exported slaves and abducted free blacks manage to extricate themselves from profit-driven traders; even more rarely were the traders arrested and prosecuted.[80] When Minus Brown was kidnapped, his wife hastily sought out a white friend, John Noble, who later testified that he had seen Brown twice: The first time Brown had been "sitting tied in a gig" in Sussex County, Delaware; the second time, eight days after, he had been handcuffed and was being held in a garret at the house of slave trader George MacGee in New Market, Maryland. Brown won his freedom. Most of the other abducted blacks were less fortunate, as they were exported from the state by slave traders.[81]

The antiexportation law continued for many years to provide a means to freedom for slaves illegally transported out of Delaware, in some cases long after the exportation itself had occurred. In an 1834 appeals case, the three children—Sarah, Grace, and Bayard—and seven grandchildren of the deceased slave Amelia won their case upon the discovery of events that took place three decades before. Early in the 1800s a slave trader had illegally transported Amelia into the state of Maryland, where he planned straightaway to sell her. Amelia,

Chained or yoked together, slaves moving across the countryside in coffles from the Upper to the Lower South and from various states to the west were a common sight. Black men, women, and children were forced to march along well-worn trading roads, sometimes to the sound of fiddle music, as traders on horseback kept a watchful eye. Very few among them were able to escape, and after arriving in distant locations they were either sold to individual farmers and planters at auction or in private sales. *New York Public Library, b11672871*

however, had escaped and made her way back to Delaware. She had died many years before the appeals court in 1834 declared itself "unanimous in the opinion, that the petitioners are entitled to their freedom"; that the exportation of Amelia had, ipso facto, established the grandmother's freedom; and that the "right and title to freedom . . . attaches the moment the offence is committed, which is prohibited by statute." In reference to the same case, Chief Justice John Layton asserted that without question slaves had rights that were protected under the law, and that those very rights, duly lodged in the principles of humanity, had led the state's lawmakers in 1793 to pass an anti-exportation law.[82] Further, those "principles of humanity" applied not only to slaves exported from the state for the purpose of sale but also to hirelings sent out to labor in neighboring states. They, too, could—and did—apply for their freedom.[83]

Although the majority of anti-importation suits brought by slaves were successful—about 59 percent of all cases, with 69 percent in the lower courts and 49 percent in appeals courts—slaveholders were not without responses that sometimes swayed judges and juries. Perhaps no civil suit better illustrates the persuasive effect of a defendant's response than the case brought by the slave family of David Cross against William Black, a slaveowning cooper in Anne Arundel County, Maryland. In 1835, Black decided to move to Missouri with his family and his slaves: David Cross; his wife, Airy; and their six children. On the way to Missouri, Black ventured into Ohio to meet up with his brother, who was also planning to move west. Shortly after their arrival, however, Black was confronted by two members of an antislavery society and was forced to sign manumission deeds for David Cross's family, but not for David himself, as he was thought to be a free man. (He might well have also looked like a free man; testimony described him and his family as being nearly white.)

Now fearing the loss of "the greater and more valuable" portion of his property, Black decided to return with the Cross family to Anne Arundel County. Once back in Maryland, Black quickly sold David and his son Charles—both of them coopers like their master—as slaves for life. The Cross family sued. By then, the importation laws of Maryland had been revised several times, most recently in 1831, with the provision that slaves who obtained their freedom through violations of statutes prohibiting the sale of imported slaves had two choices, either to be sent to Liberia or to "leave the state forthwith." Black argued that he should not be deprived of his slave property because of his absence from the state of Maryland. Whatever might have been the intentions of his departure, the time away, in fact, constituted only a temporary sojourn, and thus his return with his slaves should not be construed as "importation within the meaning of the acts of assembly." The jury and court of appeals agreed. Throughout the period of the owner's absence, the appeals court reasoned, his slaves were "attached to his person; dependent on his movements; and their will merged in his."[84]

Other slaveowners made arguments similar to Black's. They asserted that although they had departed their home state with their slaves, sometimes for lengthy absences, and then returned, they had not meanwhile relinquished their residency. The definition of residency was key to many importation cases, as owners contended—whether they had traveled with their slaves for a time, whatever its length, to other southern states or the North or foreign countries— that their absence abroad had been, by any account, temporary: a sojourn, not a new residency. Consequently, their return with their slaves to their established home state residence did not constitute an illegal importation of their slaves.

In 1790, a woman moved with her slave Sam from Virginia to North Carolina, where they lived for three years. They then returned to Virginia, and nearly three decades later, in 1819, the woman sold Sam. He filed a freedom suit claiming that he had been illegally imported into Virginia twenty-six years before. Sam and his lawyer convinced both the county and the superior court judges that he should be freed. The court of appeals, however, overturned the two verdicts on the grounds that the owner had never renounced her citizenship in Virginia nor had she ever acquired citizenship in North Carolina. Although it was true, Judge Roane wrote, that slaves who were purchased in North Carolina and brought into Virginia could claim their right to freedom under the importation statute, Sam could not, in fact, because he had not been purchased out of state. Rather, he had been the property of his owner both before and after the importation. Thus was Sam's right to freedom "barred under that circumstance."[85] Most courts would have agreed with the instructions given to the jury in the District of Columbia Circuit Court in 1820s: if an owner and his slave departed the state, or the country, without intention to settle elsewhere, or if the owner was unsure as to whether he might or might not take up a new residence, his return to the state with his slave did "not constitute importation against the act of assembly."[86]

One can only imagine the anger of owners who lost their slave property because of their knowing, or not, violation of the importation laws. Some owners indeed claimed not to have been aware of the laws that they had been charged of violating. On exactly that claim, Maryland resident Henry Ward Pearce in 1788 asked the Delaware General Assembly for an exemption from the law because he had not been cognizant of that state's statute when he had sent two male slaves to work land he owned in Delaware.[87] Other owners, though mindful of the enactments, did not realize or believe that their actions were subject to the statutes; this was especially true of owners who took slaves with them on jobs in another state for months at a time, but under the one-year limitation. Owners who in fact had moved permanently to another state with their slaves were sometimes able to convince a court that they had complied with the importation laws in that they had signed in the required timely manner the oath attesting to their residency of at least three years in their state of origin, and they had professed their resolve not to place their slaves on the auction block.[88]

In some instances, owners successfully argued that if a slave had indeed been taken to another state to be sold, but the sale had not been consummated and the slave had been brought back to the state of origin, the anti-importation law had not been broken.[89] Other owners won victories in the courts because they were verifiably not the "absolute owners" of the blacks. They either shared the ownership of the slave with other parties or possessed only a life estate in the slave, whereas the law designated unqualified ownership. In 1817, in a case brought by a group of slaves who had been imported into Virginia from North Carolina, the appeals court ruled in favor of the master. Because the slaves were possessed as a woman's "life estate only," and thus would revert to kin following her death, they could not claim freedom under the nonimportation laws.[90]

At trial, arguments about absolute ownership, shared ownership, and life estates often clouded the fact that a slave was illegally imported. Verdicts in cases in which the relation of issue to statute was not so clear-cut almost inevitably went into appeal, and appeals courts made every effort to judge them in terms of the intended meaning of the words that shaped the statutes. As it turned out, though, among all the freedom suits that were filed in the courts, importation cases represented the lowest proportion of decisions that favored the slave plaintiffs.

In one instance, in July 1802, the father of a slaveowner transported his son's slave, London, from Maryland to Alexandria, Virginia, without his son's knowledge or consent, and hired him out. The father died around Christmas 1802. In March 1803, the son, a resident of Maryland, again took possession of London, and in April, as he himself was planning to move to Alexandria, the son also hired London out in Alexandria. In June the son completed the move to Alexandria and in July took the oath in regard to importation as prescribed by Virginia law. London filed a freedom suit charging that he had been illegally imported before his owner had taken the mandatory oath. The jury ruled in his favor, but the US Supreme Court overturned the jury verdict, because, wrote Chief Justice John Marshall, the "acts of bringing the negro into the state, and of removing into it" by the owner, did not need to occur concurrently.[91]

In the few other cases that went on appeal to the US Supreme Court, the decisions, whether they upheld or overturned lower court verdicts, sided with the slaveholding class. One importation opinion addressed a lower court's ruling that a Virginia slave family should be freed because the owner's family failed to provide proof that it had met the 1792 registration requirement for slaves entering the state. The fact that the suit had been brought to court some thirty years after the importation prompted the Supreme Court to reverse the lower court's verdict. If all the participants, including magistrates and other county officials, were

dead, the opinion read, it could be assumed that the owners had signed the necessary oath and had complied with other sections of the importation law.[92] Time in
this instance proved to be on the side of the defendant. Such cases were appealed
to the nation's highest court not necessarily because of their juridical significance
but rather because it provided the only avenue for appeal from the District of
Columbia Circuit Court. As might be expected, given the inviolability of property espoused by the founding fathers, the appeals were generally decided in favor
of slaveholders, and thus established precedent, albeit on narrow grounds.[93]

Despite such rulings, slaves and their lawyers continued to file importation-
based freedom suits, and they sometimes succeeded in uncovering crucial evidence that, had they not done so, would have committed them to a lifetime
in bondage. Slaveholders who brought their human chattel into the states of
Delaware, Maryland, and Virginia and the District of Columbia but failed to sign
the required oath or sold their slaves before the designated waiting period had
expired were likely to find themselves defendants in court battles over ownership.
In some cases, the slaveholders had no knowledge of the importation statutes; in
others, they did but failed to comply fully or properly with the requirements of
the law. In almost no cases were slave traders named in freedom suits, so they did
not share the outrage of owners who discovered not only that they could be sued
by slaves but also that they could be divested of their property, should the courts
declare the imported blacks free. Of course, some slaveowners did comply with
the laws; they signed the requisite oaths, submitted proof of ownership, and provided testimony necessary to show ownership for the time period required by
their new states of residence. Even so, they were not immune to litigation.[94]

The changing political atmosphere for slaves who challenged the system of
bondage by filing freedom suits was manifest in the most widely known Supreme

> INFORMATION WANTED—Being informed from
> a respectable source, that a suit is pending in Virginia for
> the freedom of several colored persons who claim they are
> the children of FLORA, once the slave of Benjamin Scott,
> formerly a resident in this county, but liberated by him, and
> afterwards, about the year 1782, carried into the State of New
> York and sold, as is claimed by Oliver Hanchett and Davis
> Brunson, and thence transported to Virginia—Any informa-
> tion on this subject *speedily* given to Dr. HAWES or A. M.
> COLLINS, will greatly subserve the cause of humanity.
>   Hartford, Aug. 4.   d&w46

In freedom suits, plaintiffs and lawyers often needed information
about events in the distant past. Published in the town of Hartford,
Virginia, this notice (ca. 1850s), endorsed by Dr. Hawes and
A. M. Collins, requested facts from any "reliable source" about a
free woman of color named Flora, freed before 1782. *Connecticut
Courant, August 4, 1842*

Court case of the antebellum era, *Dred Scott v. John F. A. Sandford*. Purchased in St. Louis by John Emerson, a military surgeon, Dred accompanied Emerson, between 1833 and 1837, to posts in Illinois and the Wisconsin Territory, where slavery had been prohibited by the Northwest Ordinance, the Constitution of Illinois, and the Missouri Compromise. When Dr. Emerson died unexpectedly in 1843, Dred, along with his wife, Harriet, and their two children, became the property of Irene Emerson. In 1846, with the assistance of abolitionists, both Dred and Harriet Scott presented actions of trespass and false imprisonment to the St. Louis Circuit Court against Irene Emerson. The *Dred Scott* case went to trial and retrial, and after a decade of appeals and reversals in state courts and a federal court, it arrived, in 1856, at the US Supreme Court.

The following year Chief Justice Roger B. Taney, in a lengthy majority opinion, wrote that Scott was not a citizen of Missouri as he claimed. African Americans were "not included, and were not intended to be included, under the word citizens in the Constitution, and can therefore claim none of the rights and privileges which that instrument provides for and secures to citizens of the United States." Further, blacks were "regarded as beings of an inferior order and altogether unfit to associate with the white race, either in social or political relations; and so far inferior that they had no rights which the white man was bound to respect." The holding that people of African descent were not citizens

The *Dred Scott* case was front-page news for *Frank Leslie's Illustrated Newspaper*, which portrayed the husband and wife in the most important freedom suit in the nation's history. It took eleven years to be resolved and ended in 1857 with Chief Justice Roger B. Taney's statement that black people had "no rights which the white man was bound to respect." *Frank Leslie's Illustrated Newspaper*, June 27, 1857; New York Public Library, b16468401

for purposes of federal jurisdiction, however, did not directly affect their ability to file freedom suits in county courts. These cases continued following the decision, including during the early years of the Civil War.[95]

Throughout the trials of this famous case, the southern states closed ranks against the permission of freedom suits brought by slaves who lived in free territories in the North and the Northwest. And after the Taney opinion, the law forbade the acceptance of such suits in the federal court system. Although numerous cases in Missouri and elsewhere before the mid-1840s had employed the very same arguments as Dred and Harriet Scott, but to very different results,[96] from the mid-1840s onward most of the freedom suits citing residency in free territory as the primary complaint came to the same end as *Silvia v. Joel Kirby*. In 1853, the lower court rejected Silvia's complaint, despite the fact that she had lived as a slave with her owner in a territory where slavery was outlawed; nor had she ever been guilty or convicted of any crime, which provided the only lawful reason for involuntary servitude.[97]

The unassailable definition of slaves as property was fundamental to the southern laws regulating slavery, and whenever possible the local courts strove to uphold the rights of slaveholders to buy, sell, transfer, deed, bequeath, mortgage, and punish slaves as they saw fit. When they did not, when they denied an owner the right to his or her property on the basis of laws enacted in another state or country, they did so out respect for the sanctity of the law if it was applicable to the claims of a particular case. Only by upholding the laws that governed slavery could slavery be protected, and perpetuated, even if, ironically, those laws also sometimes freed slaves by virtue of questionable or plainly illegal acts on the part of their owners, as in many of the cases involving residency.[98]

In the American South, positive law was as essential to the preservation of the peculiar institution as it was in the North to the abolition of human bondage. The shades of difference, and sometimes stark contrasts, in the interpretation and implementation of slavery statutes that themselves varied from state to southern state, and that in the 1850s diverged irreconcilably from the North, were symptomatic of the conflicts that would eventually divide the nation. Indeed, the claims made by southern blacks for their freedom because they had lived with their owners or worked as hirelings in the North, or had resided in free countries such as France, or had been brought into states in violation of anti-importation statutes, exposed but scarcely abated the tensions growing between the North and South. Yet, even in the face of the evolving national crisis in the 1840s and 1850s, southern courts continued to defend the rights of bondsmen and bondswomen to sue for their freedom; for that matter, even after *Dred Scott*, local courts still, if less frequently, tried freedom suits and state appeals courts still ruled on their verdicts. The slaveholding states thus continued to uphold a legal structure that acknowledged the legislation of northern states as well as foreign countries in regard to human bondage and that, at the same time, ensured the northern states' recognition of the southern states' own laws governing, and protecting, the institution of slavery. As strange as it was ironic, freedom suits in fact reinforced the legal foundation of the "peculiar institution" that they continually challenged.

In 1826, John Merry filed a residency-based freedom suit after he had been seized by two men in the Illinois village of Kaskaskia—how they learned of Merry's whereabouts remains unclear—and had been taken back to St. Louis, where he was again jailed as a runaway slave. Through access to the St. Louis Circuit Court system, Merry gained permission to file his suit *in forma pauperis* with the assistance of a court-appointed lawyer Joseph Charles Jr., the attorney of record, and Merry filed a claim declaring trespass, assault with force of arms, and false imprisonment contrary to the laws of the state. They requested a jury trial and sought damages of $600.

The primary argument in their case hinged on residency: Merry had been born in what later became Illinois, and was therefore free. Within a relatively short period, the court subpoenaed the two defendants (the two men who had jailed Merry), empaneled a jury, and called a number of witnesses. The judge instructed the jury that if the plaintiff was "a negro," he should be presumed to be a slave unless there was evidence to the contrary; further, if the jury found that the plaintiff was born a slave in Illinois of "a negro mother held in slavery there before the year 1787" and there was no evidence of his emancipation, the jury should find for the defendants, which it did. Merry and his attorney filed exceptions to the verdict and appealed to the Missouri Supreme Court. Merry signed an oath with his mark stating that his appeal was being made not to prolong the litigation but as a matter of law. Seven months later, the Missouri Supreme Court ruled that John Merry was a free person. The Northwest Ordinance, the high court asserted, was a positive law, and it had established that slavery could not exist in the Territory. As a result, it was clear that any person born in what later became Illinois after the passage of the Ordinance could not be held in bondage. The high court therefore declared: "John is free."[99]

8

A Journey toward Freedom

I am "a free man and entitled to exemption from servitude," Baltimore slave Beverly Dowling pled in the freedom suit he filed in 1835 against Sophia Bland and Austin Woolfolk. Except, his assertion of "these rights" aside, he was now deemed a criminal, having been jailed as a fugitive slave, and was currently being detained as a bondsman. Like many other slaves in the city, Dowling had been permitted to hire his own time and, with his earnings, to purchase his freedom. In 1833, he negotiated with his owner, Sophia Bland, a self-purchase agreement whereby he would procure his freedom for the amount of $200, $100 less than his owner proposed. During the next nearly two and a half years, Dowling kept a "boot black Cellar" in Gay Street, ran an oyster house in the same neighborhood, and served as a waiter on a steamboat running between Baltimore and French Town.

In all these endeavors, he "went at large and acted as a free man," as he did toward the end of his self-hire period when he traveled to New York City as a personal servant to Jerome Bonaparte, a young non-slaveholder. In New York, Dowling worked as a waiter on a steamboat that plied the North River (the southernmost stretch of the Hudson). He returned to Baltimore in October 1835 to make the final payment of twenty-seven dollars, by which he would acquire his freedom. He duly contacted the owner's agent, James O. Law, and instructed him to deliver the final installment to the owner. Law, however, refused to accept the money. Instead, he had Dowling arrested as a fugitive slave and then arranged to sell him to Austin Woolfolk, who owned one of the largest slave-trading firms in the country. Its advertisements in newspapers and broadsides blared: "CASH and the HIGEST PRICES for . . . NEGROES."[1]

Aside from the time he suffered a serious unspecified illness, Beverly Dowling had functioned successfully throughout the period of his self-hire as an independent, self-sustaining individual. He had pursued a number of economic ventures, moved freely from place to place, and traveled from Baltimore to the District of Columbia and then to the North; he had also avoided dealing with his owner's agent. The problem was that during most of this time Dowling's owner was living in Annapolis, and she had tried to manage his self-hire through the agent James Law. Sophia Bland also owned five other nearly free and equally independent Baltimore slaves, among them Dowling's ailing ("far gone with consumption") sister, Harriet, who on one occasion scraped together seven dollars on his behalf, and her husband, Savoy, with whom she lived in a small frame house opposite Beverly's cellar business on Gay Street. The other three were Eliza, a hireling so well liked by her employers that one said he would rather hire her than own slaves; Rachel, a member of the Baptist Church, and also a hireling, who lived at the corner of Howard Street and Cherry Alley; and Rachel's son, John, who could read and write and "fancied himself as a dandy," albeit his feet were "deformed" and he walked "leaning on a stick."

About Dowling and her other five slaves, Bland wrote to her agent: "I have been always much attached to the whole family"—she did not specify their relationships—"The mother was my maid from my childhood. I have indulged them too much[.] My feelings have even been rather tender." Without doubt, in the agent's estimation, Dowling hardly deserved tender feelings. "As to Beverly," Law wrote to Bland in the manner of an apology, "I hardly know what to say." What he did say, snidely, was that for quite some time he had tried "to see his lordship but without success." Neither his owner's feelings nor her agreement to his self-purchase were counting for much when Dowling filed his suit, and he was now caught up in the tortuous legal system. His ability to extricate himself would depend on how effectively he, with his counsel and the testimony of his white friends, could argue the case of an honest, hard-working, diligent, self-purchased slave.[2]

Neither the situation nor the legal case of Beverly Dowling and his kin was uncommon in the southern states. In towns and cities and, less frequently, rural areas, in both the Upper and Lower South, thousands upon thousands of enslaved men and women were able to negotiate with their owners for self-hire and self-purchase, as they could offer prospective employers a wide range of skills. They could work as blacksmiths, brick masons, carpenters, coopers, mechanics, barbers, laundresses, seamstresses, tobacco twisters, servants, laborers, farm hands, porters, hucksters, draymen, and ship caulkers—the list is far from complete. Often a sizable portion of hirelings' earnings went to their owners, especially if they were working toward the purchase of themselves or loved ones, but most slaves on hire were allowed at least a small share of their wages for themselves.

History's most famous self-hired bondsman, Fredrick Douglass, articulated the views of many who strove toward freedom through self-hire when he recalled: "I was to be allowed all my time; to make all bargains for work; to find my own employment, and to collect my own wages; and, in return for this liberty, I was required, or obliged, to pay him [Douglass's master] three dollars at the end of each week, and to board and clothe myself, and buy my own calking

[sic] tools." Hard though the bargain was, being quasi-free "armed my love of liberty with a lash and driver, far more efficient than any I had before known," and it proved to be a privilege, "another step in my career toward freedom." In most states, self-hire, which allowed a slave autonomy to a significant degree, was illegal, but enforcement of the laws against it was nearly impossible, especially when owners like Sophia Bland were so willing to grant it. The statutes against self-hire, according to one historian, "languished as dead letters on the statute books of the South." Or as a lawyer in Savannah, Georgia, lamented in 1856: "There are you may say, Hundreds of Negroes in this city who go about from house to house—some carpenters, some house servants, etc.—who never see their masters except at pay day, live out of their yards, hire themselves without written permit, etc." Though he found the practice of self-hire "very wrong," he also owned that "the less said and done in cases of this kind the better."[3]

Most self-hired slaves shared the sentiment: the less said the better. For they knew they were breaking the law by moving from place to place, wherever their employment might take them, or by working at jobs out of the state, as Beverly Dowling did. However, if they maintained a low profile, established a reputation for industry and good behavior at the workplace, cultivated a network of associates—employers, owners, sympathetic whites, free persons of color, other hired or self-hired slaves—to vouch for them in times of crisis, they could usually manage to support themselves and their families. Men worked at jobs in everything from iron manufacture to tobacco shops, and took advantage of any opportunity for "overwork"—exceeding the daily quota—and extra pay; women operated informal cook shops or worked as laundresses and domestics.[4] They all cherished their independence and autonomy, the more so because they realized how fragile their liberty might prove to be under their uncertain, and illegal, circumstances. Sometimes even liberty could not compensate them for economic hardships. Many owners permitted self-hire only after their bondsmen and women's most productive years had long since passed, and with them so had their chances for ready employment. Five southern states enacted laws to prevent "illegal emancipations" for elderly or infirm slaves, which added to the woes not only of virtually free but of aging slaves.[5]

The possibilities open to self-hired and nearly free blacks intent on obtaining their legal freedom being next to nil, the most determined among them sometimes turned to their owners for help in the form of self-purchase. Owners frequently found such proposals to be to their advantage, as by permitting slaves to hire themselves out in their effort to buy their freedom, the slaveholders netted a not inconsequential income often over years of time without relinquishing ownership of their human property during that time. Once self-hired slaves gained their owners' written or oral approval, they pursued their goal—papers declaring them free—usually with exceptional diligence and long-borne hope.

Freedom in most instances of self-purchase did not come through suits filed in the courts. Only when an agreement had been breached by either the slave or the owner did litigation occur.

The agreements varied. Some were oral, with their promises entrusted to the slaveholder's family. Others included bills of sale, whereby manumission was guaranteed once the slaves had satisfactorily met the conditions of their hire and, from the earnings for their labor, had completed a designated number of payments at a designated amount to their owner. In a few instances, the agreements were recorded in deeds and registered at the courthouse. Others were written on a certificate, or pass, allowing bondsmen and women to pass and re-pass from one town to another to find employment. Still others were drafted as what would be considered "contracts," which included the amount of money, including interest, to be paid to the owner over a given period of time. The agreements often employed the phrase "good behavior" as a requisite for slaves during the period of their self-hire. For example, in 1800, slaveholder Ninian Willett of Maryland agreed to free his self-hired slave, John, if he were paid "three pounds eighteen shillings and nine pence per month at the end of every month," and if John "behave[d] himself well until the first day of January Eighteen hundred and two, and if at any time before that day the said Negro John or any person on his behalf shall pay the said Ninian T. Willett the Sum of three hundred dollars." However the agreements varied in type, most of them stipulated that freedom for self-hired slaves came at a clearly defined purchase price.[6]

Some owners wrote special permission passes stating that the slaves carrying them had the right to conduct business on their own with the consent of their masters. Others provided permissions to self-hire slaves, particularly those with readily employable talents, to cross and re-cross the Ohio River.[7] As a result, self-hires sometimes "went at large" for months, or even years, in their efforts to earn the sums required both to sustain themselves and to pay their "freedom dues," as payments to their owners were called.

A few owners signed deeds detailing the conditions that would have to be met by slaves seeking freedom through self-purchase before their actual achievement of legal manumission.[8] Most of these agreements by deed were negotiated in the Upper South and Louisiana, especially when the doors to legal freedom began closing in the Lower South during the nineteenth century. George Clark of the District of Columbia signed a deed in regard to Adam Johnson, his self-hired slave, after Johnson filed a freedom suit against him in 1822. The owner promised "to liberate & set free my negro slave Adam Johnson, for the sum of three hundred and fifty Dollars to be paid to me by the Said Adam in three equal annual payments from the date of this Instrument—& the said Adam is at liberty to work for himself & to dispose of his time labour & the proceeds thereof from this day till the End of three years—And I do hereby declare that I make this bargain with the said Adam freely & with the bona fide intent of discharging him from Slavery as soon as the said sum of three hundred and fifty Dollars are paid." Such deeds thus served as contracts between master and slave. They were also void in all but three states—Delaware, Tennessee, and Louisiana. Still, they attest to the ability of self-hired slaves to effectively negotiate bargains with their owners, if necessary, by threatening them with the filing of a freedom suit.[9]

The bargains, though, were difficult for self-hired blacks like Adam Johnson to fulfill. They sometimes had to work for years in order to pay for their freedom. Between three and five years was perhaps the average, but self-hires of seven or ten years, or longer, were not unheard of. For out of their earnings self-hired slaves not only had to pay their freedom dues but also had to support themselves as well as, in some cases, their families. Even in good times, that was difficult. In bad times, it was next to impossible. Problems in the southern economy, including the fiscal woes of the 1790s and depressions in 1819–1822, 1837–1842, and 1857–1858, struck self-hired slaves especially hard. Often, too, the families of virtually free slaves were dependent on them for assistance, even if not for subsistence—their masters could be expected to provide food and shelter.

In addition, as the value of slaves in the Upper South gradually rose during the antebellum era, so did the cost of freedom by self-purchase, from about $300 during the early period to between two and three times that amount during the late antebellum period. In Louisiana, self-purchase agreements could run as high as $1,000 or more. During the early 1820s, in New Orleans, one enterprising self-hired slave who owned a coastal trading vessel, by his own industry and some financial assistance of white friends paid his owner the remarkable sum of $1,700 of the agreed-on $1,800 for his freedom (about $31,000 in today's dollars).[10] Moreover, the terms of self-hire often began after slaves had labored for many years in bondage as hirelings. The Kentucky slave Sam had been hired out for twelve years before his owner wrote him a pass: "Sam is permitted to labour for him Self, and also, has the privilege to work on board steam boats Either up or down the [Ohio] River." Having already, as a hireling, earned three or four times his purchase price, Sam agreed to pay $450 for his freedom. In 1835, at the age of forty-three, he set out to accumulate the self-purchase money; he worked first as a laborer on the Louisville and Bardstown Turnpike and then found work in the growing Ohio River city of New Albany, Indiana. When his owner died, the estate administrator claimed Sam as a slave, whereupon Sam filed a freedom suit. The court ruled in Sam's favor neither because of his hard work and good behavior nor because he made regular payments to his owner. Rather, it determined that the owner's pass issued to Sam was tantamount to a deed of manumission.[11]

Not all self-hired blacks whose owners had issued and then rescinded certificates allowing them to pass freely between states were able to claim their legal freedom when, like Sam, they brought their cases to court; but some among them found judges and juries who were sympathetic to their cause. After all, the complainants were usually the most industrious and productive slaves in their communities, and they had capably negotiated with their owners for self-purchase. Typical of them was Reuben, who, according to witness testimony during an interrogatory, had proved himself to be "a better hand, and a laborer on whom much greater reliance could be placed, than any other of the Negroes" engaged in the construction of a gristmill.[12] Other self-hires were similarly described as being reliable, hard-working, skilled, intelligent, honest, and ambitious.[13]

Among the freedom suits involving self-purchase or the purchase of loved ones, slightly more than half were successful. Some judges and juries held that freedom could be claimed on a contractual basis, even when one of the parties to the agreement was a slave. While only the states of Delaware, Tennessee, and Louisiana by law allowed slaves the right to purchase their freedom through contractual arrangements, Kentucky, North Carolina, South Carolina, Maryland, and Virginia recorded judicial decisions that ruled in favor of the complainants in bondage. In South Carolina during the 1790s, a female slave hireling whose earnings exceeded her monthly wages used the funds for her extra labor to purchase a slave girl named Sally, and then freed her. When the hireling's owner himself laid claim to Sally, she filed a freedom suit. As the defendant, he argued against his hireling's right to free Sally because whatever she possessed in fact belonged to her master. In the 1790s South Carolina still allowed emancipations, and Chief Justice John Rutledge charged the jury with the following: "If the wench chose to appropriate the savings of her extra labour to the purchase of this girl, in order afterwards to set her free, would a jury of the country say no?" He trusted not. They were too humane and upright, he hoped, to do such "manifest violence to so singular and extraordinary act of benevolence." The jury returned a verdict in favor of Sally.[14]

Some self-hired African Americans were able in fact, if not by law, to extricate themselves from bondage and live as free blacks. They also lived in fear, however, that the legality of their status might be called into question. The passage of time gained them some sense of security as they found jobs, earned wages, made contracts, rented houses, and hired out their children. Some professed that they had been freed by a benevolent owner, or that their mothers had been free at the time of their birth; others claimed they had purchased themselves as well as members of their families from their masters. Yet, however fully they might live and act like free persons of color, according to the law, they were still slaves, and they sometimes found themselves caught in legal disputes that cast their alleged free status into doubt.

In 1849, Baltimore slave Rebecca Garrett and her six children were arrested as fugitive slaves. They filed a suit on the grounds that Rebecca's husband of eighteen years was a free black man and that her mother, Beck, had been freed in the 1805 will of an Anne Arundel County woman. At trial, witnesses testified that Rebecca and her children had always been deemed to be free. The Baltimore County Court deemed likewise and ruled in the complainants' favor. The appeals court, however, overturned the decision: There was no evidence that a deed of manumission had been executed for Rebecca and no provision in the will for Beck's "issue." In addition, there was no indication that the early estate was properly administered and allowing any slave quasi-freedom was not "a legitimate mode of manumission."[15]

The issue critical to self-hire and self-purchase agreements was whether slaves had the legal right to enter into contractual arrangements with their owners. Many slaveholders, including those who allowed their slaves to self-hire, were persuaded that black people were not able to negotiate contracts with their owners because, as slaves, they by definition lacked "will." As one judge asserted, a slave could not "bind himself, at law, to pay money to his master, even for his freedom."[16] Slaveholders often took advantage of such arguments, especially after they had reneged on a self-hire agreement and sold the hireling as a slave for life, despite the contractual promise of freedom. As a consequence, self-hired blacks who had labored diligently for their freedom would discover that they had spent years in what proved to be a fruitless effort.

While lower courts might rule on the slaves' behalf, the appeals courts would invariably reverse the rulings by declaring the agreements invalid. No declaration or promise made to an enslaved person for his or her benefit, one court ruled, could be enforced in either law or equity.[17] "This is to certify that Richard, my negro, wishes to purchase himself, and it is my wish that he should do so; therefore, he is at liberty to work for himself, so as he may be able to accomplish his object," one owner promised. "Upon his finally paying one hundred dollars he then is to be free." Within a year, however, the owner had sold Richard as a slave for life, and the court ruled in the owner's favor: "A contract between a master and his slave cannot be enforced."[18] The status of the slave, an Alabama Supreme Court justice noted, was the "entire abnegation of civil capacity." Slaves had no right to engage in a contract and had "no authority to own anything of value."[19]

Although some judges adhered to a strict dictum that slaves could not be party to a contract because they were not persons according to the law, other judges and juries sought to secure equity for the parties involved, including freedom for self-hired and self-purchased slaves. Because the law courts could not adjudicate complex cases that involved agreements, estates, creditors, payments, surety bonds, and deeds, virtually all of the contract-based freedom suits were submitted to chancery, or equity, courts, where the documentary details of the journey toward freedom could be examined, argued, and verified. The equity courts could rule more readily than the law courts on the two fundamental questions in these cases: Did the original owner promise to free his human chattel if certain conditions were met, and did he have the means to do so, considering his creditors and/or other obligations? Equity courts, too, could aptly sort out the competing claims of white family members when an owner had extended an oral agreement to allow self-purchase. In one of the more unusual cases brought to the equity courts, a self-hired black man had purchased himself at auction.[20]

More typical was the case of the Tennessee slave Adam, who had secured an agreement with his owner stating that if he were sold, he could obtain his freedom by repaying the new owner his purchase price. In 1841, Adam was sold, whereupon he turned over "notes bonds and evidences of debt upon good and Solvent persons" for $550 to his new owner, more than half of his $901 purchase price. The new owner wrote a deed of manumission, and Adam soon "engaged in business [and] acquired property in his own name, and in all respects, acted as a free man." After some months, however, Adam was seized for payment of his owner's debts, jailed, and then sold again. He escaped his third owner, and with the aid of white friends he filed a freedom suit. After an eighteen-month investigation by the master of chancery, and with the financial assistance of his next friend, William Garrett, Adam gained his freedom.[21]

Even in states of the Upper South, where legal contracts between slaves and their owners were commonly declared void, plaintiffs could argue that justice would be served if an owner had promised freedom to slaves who thereupon had hired themselves out and in due time had paid the agreed-on amount for their release from bondage. To succeed in such cases, plaintiffs could not rely on testimony regarding an oral agreement and nearly always had to produce a copy of the written contract between the slave and owner. In some cases of self-purchase, self-hired slaves had paid a substantial portion of the agreed-on purchase price but had failed to make the final payment or payments. However sympathetic the courts might be toward slaves who had demonstrated initiative and industry, judges and juries found it incumbent on them to rule in favor of the masters.

Yet in Kentucky, where court opinion was markedly mixed when contracts between owners and their human property were at issue, some freedom suits did go in favor of slaves whose payments for self-purchase fell short, as they were permitted to continue "to go at large" for their own benefit in order to raise an agreed-on purchase price.[22] In a freedom suit filed in Jefferson County, Kentucky, Mary King, wife to a free black husband, produced a written contract in which her owner, Henry Pope, promised to free her upon receipt of $600.

As she was able to raise only $350, Pope had her arrested and jailed. In court, Pope admitted to the agreement but contended that no tribunal had "the right or the power, under the constitution and laws of the land, to deprive him of the possession and services of his slave." The court disagreed; it enjoined Pope from selling Mary and ordered that she be allowed to seek employment and wages under the supervision of the marshal. Her husband posted a $250 bond to ensure the balance of her purchase price. Two years later, "in consideration of the Sum of Six Hundred dollars to me in hand paid by James King and Mary his wife," Pope "emancipated manumitted and set free" Mary King.[23]

While Mary King had the apparent benefit of a free black husband with a network of white friends to act on her behalf, plaintiffs in most self-hire cases had to rely on the testimony of whites either in depositions or in open court. Indeed, testimony by whites, slaveholders and non-slaveholders alike, was crucial in establishing the structure of the self-purchase agreements, the amounts of and time limits on payments, and the wording of bills of sale, as well as the personal values and attitudes of the plaintiffs. Testimony came from members of the families being sued, their neighbors and friends, and townspeople familiar with the plaintiffs. Witnesses came forward even for self-hired slaves who had moved to another county or state or who were filing suits years after they should have been rightfully freed.

In 1808, Daphne Lawson paid her owner, John Taylor of Hanover County, Virginia, seventy-five pounds, whereupon he executed a bill of sale to Robert McCracken who, in turn, promised to emancipate Daphne upon her payment of ten dollars to him. She in due time paid him the ten dollars; he broke his promise. McCracken moved away with her in his possession as a slave for life. Twelve years later, in Daphne's successful Henrico County freedom suit, the witness Peyton Drew testified on her behalf that Daphne had paid the "whole amt due him [McCracken]."[24] In 1809, a District of Columbia self-hired slave, Joseph Cooke, negotiated an arrangement similar to Daphne's with his mistress: upon his sale by her, the new owner would promise to allow him the liberty to go at large so that with his earning he could purchase himself. The bill of sale, which was witnessed by the mistress, her husband, and the buyer, stated the conditions of the sale. The buyer, however, failed to fulfill them. Some eighteen years later, after Cooke was seized for the debts of his owner, the husband of his former mistress testified that he had been present when the bill of sale was signed and that it included the promise of freedom.[25]

Still, the testimony of whites did not guarantee that self-hired slaves would be able to bring their cases before the court or that, if they did, they would secure their freedom, no matter how strong their arguments. Some among them, even after they paid the final installment, did not succeed in their suits. Estate settlements, too, could block the path to freedom for self-hired slaves, as when an owner who had promised to manumit a slave on self-purchase died before the agreed-on purchase price had been fully paid. Upon the owner's death, the slave would be included in the property of the deceased's estate—a decidedly precarious position, unless provisions had been made to ensure that the self-purchase agreement would be honored by the heirs and relatives of the deceased owner. In the absence of such provisions and of good will on the part of the owner's survivors, quasi-free slaves who had gone "at large" and labored for their "own use" could, as some did, find themselves reined back into bondage. In some cases, the self-hired slaves had paid their owners hundreds of dollars over a number of years, but even if they could produce receipts as proof of these transactions, they could still be, and sometimes were, denied free status because they had not paid the full amount of their agreed-on purchase price.

In a District of Columbia case, lawyer Francis Scott Key argued that because the virtually free slave Joseph Brown had paid his owner $850 of the agreed-on $900, equity would be served if the slave were freed after his payment of the $50 balance. No contract or agreement between a master and slave could be enforced either at law or in equity, Judge William Cranch of the circuit court ruled, "and therefore a verbal agreement to give a slave his freedom on the payment of a certain amount cannot be enforced, though the master had already accepted most of the consideration."[26] Although Judge Cranch ruled favorably in a number of freedom and habeas corpus suits, he was disposed to ruling against self-purchase agreements, oral or otherwise.[27]

The greed and duplicity of slaveholders are apparent in varying degrees in the cases brought against them, but to no degree more poignant than when owners, having granted slaves semi-free status and promised them self-purchase, went back on their word and retracted the bargain. The injury to the self-esteem and hope that had been engendered in the quasi-free slaves by the opportunity and privilege of self-hire made the pain of betrayal all the more keen. Most self-purchase agreements permitted blacks to transact their own business and negotiate their own hiring agreements, so long as they paid the installments on their purchase price in a timely manner, and customarily they collected receipts from their owners to document the payments. One self-hired black man in Kentucky entrusted the receipts he accumulated to a white gentleman who had hired him for many years. When the slave's owner asked to examine the documents, the gentleman obliged. Snatching the receipts from him, the owner then "tore them to pieces," and declared that he had decided to hold the black man "in perpetual slavery."[28]

In the 1840s and 1850s, as the sectional crisis deepened, slaves seeking their freedom by citing self-purchase agreements found the courts increasingly less receptive to their stories of struggle, hardship, and sacrifice. Even in Louisiana, where the acceptance of contracts for freedom submitted by self-hired persons of color had a history that stretched back to the French and Spanish colonial periods, the courts began to disavow their validity. In response to a freedom suit filed in 1854, the Pointe Coupee Parish District Court judge Thomas Colley determined that an 1849 self-purchase agreement was no longer valid because acts of the assembly in 1852 and "at the last session" had changed "entirely the manner of proceeding to obtain the emancipation of a slave."

Among other requirements, the suits now had to be filed by the master against the state, whose interests would be defended by the district attorney arguing against the suit; and the owner was also now required to produce a bond with good and sufficient security, conditional on the emancipated slave's good behavior. Since the law in effect at the time of the contract had been thus repealed, the judge wrote, the master had now to comply with the new statutes. As for the plaintiff, Colley was "of the opinion that the judgment of the court cannot give him [the plaintiff] the status of a free man" because the case, though rightfully founded in equity, must be governed by "the present state of our legislation." The laws were passed, he noted, because "as a general rule it is a dangerous thing to emancipate a slave and that it adds to an intermediate class, the very condition of which has a tendency to excite discontent among those who are left in the inferior state."[29]

Yet even in a political atmosphere continually more averse to emancipation, a few quasi-slave blacks who had earned enough in wages for their self-purchase were able to win their freedom—most notably in Tennessee, due to an inclination of its courts toward what one scholar termed "judicial liberality." Although Tennessee was one of the three states that allowed and acknowledged self-hire and self-purchase contracts (often under different guises) between masters and slaves, its judges and juries, no less than those in other, more conservative states, were subject to external pressures, including the economic interests of slaveowners. In addition, between 1831 and 1854, the state legislature passed different laws to curtail the freedom of blacks by requiring freed slaves either to leave the state or be transported to the west coast of Africa.

Still, the state had a long history of dealing with freedom suits in a positive manner; the term *quasi-slave*—for blacks who were freed by their master but not yet freed by the state—originated in Tennessee. And in 1846, Judge Nathan Green of the state's supreme court wrote his oft-quoted opinion that a slave was not in the "condition of a horse" but made in the "image of the Creator": "He has mental capacities, and an immortal principle in his nature, that constitute him equal to his owner, but for the accidental position in which fortune has placed him." Few were the judges in other states who would have agreed with such sentiments, but, by reason of them, in Tennessee freedom suits by virtually free slaves continued to be adjudicated up to the eve of the Civil War. In 1859, Isaac, an industrious slave who purchased himself after eight years of labor, won his freedom. Upholding a lower court decision, the state supreme court ruled that "an agreement between master and slave by which the master, for valuable consideration, conveys the slave by bill of sale to a third person, with the oral agreement between the slave and the such third party, that the slave is to serve him, in consideration of the amount advanced to his master, for a specified time and then be entitled to his freedom, creates a trust in favor of such slave, which the Court of Chancery will enforce."[30]

Self-acquisition was an integral—and for many blacks, crucial—component of the slave system, although it was more likely to be realized in towns and cities, where hirelings could readily find employment, than in rural areas. Whether in urban or rural circumstances, though, slaves in pursuit of self-purchase had to labor for years to accomplish their goal, and even then, after making monthly payments for two or three or five years. Situations became still more difficult when purchase included not just the slave's self but also a spouse and children, or when self-purchased men and women sought subsequently to acquire their spouses and children under similar agreements with owners. Complications arose when, for instance, family members had been dispersed to different masters, or when self-purchased men's wives, still in bondage, bore children whose purchase would likewise have to be negotiated, because they had been born into their mothers' status. Once they had set up time-payment plans with the owners, free blacks worked at any jobs available in order to meet the payments, often of a significant amount, and sometimes with assistance from white as well as black friends, that would in time buy freedom for their loved ones. Perhaps.

Elizabeth Tripplet, a free black in the District of Columbia, arranged to purchase her husband, Austin Tripplet, for the amount of $160, to be paid to the owner in monthly installments of $5. Elizabeth did not miss a single payment, and when the amount due had been met after thirty-two months she executed a deed of manumission for her husband. The owner, however, decided not to abide by their agreement. For his part, Austin then filed two freedom suits: one on the law side of the court, where he and his counsel discovered that his case was "wholly remediless"; the other in the court of equity, where such matters were "properly cognizable & relievable" and where he won his freedom.[31]

To the blacks who traveled it, the road toward freedom afforded little comfort or rest. Anxiety, fear, hardship, stress, and prayer were more common. Worry was a constant: worry about working and earning and saving enough to satisfy the terms of contracts, which might include interest clauses adding 6 to 8 percent onto the purchase price; worry about owners who might, like Austin Tripplet's master, in the end disregard the agreement. A Tennessee free black, Robert Brooks, negotiated an agreement to purchase his wife, who was valued at $500, from her owner for a price of $175. The owner indicated that, eager though he was to emancipate her, he was unable to bear the whole expense, so

Brooks signed "a note, bond, mortgage, bill of sale or other instrument" with a third party. When the note became due, however, Brooks was not financially able to redeem it, and his wife, and now two daughters, were sold to another owner. They filed a freedom suit arguing that "in a civilized and Christian State like Tennessee, the laws will not tolerate a contract so monstrous as that of a husband selling his wife or a parent his child." They were granted their freedom.[32]

When free black husbands, fathers, wives, and mothers were unable, usually for legal reasons, to emancipate their slave spouses and children, they often chose, for their families' protection, to retain them in bondage. This was in response to laws in a number of states requiring freed slaves to leave the state. Protection became problematic, however, when creditors filed liens on their property, which included their family members in bondage. Kentucky free black Levi Jones had purchased his two daughters, Emily and Betsy, from their owner, but a creditor, Robert Adams, asserted in March 1846 that the "negroes were born in slavery—when their mother was a slave & had never been set free by Jones," and further, that not only could Jones not set them free until he paid his debts but also, meanwhile, "the negroes are liable for the debts." Adams therefore demanded proof of "any contract, agreement, writing or deed or of any mode or manner whatever by which said Jones has emancipated" his daughters as well as his two grandchildren, because the Jones family members were "Africans in blood and if free must be shown to be so." Nonetheless, after lengthy litigation, Emily and her two children, as well as Spicy, probably Emily's granddaughter, succeeded in their suit for freedom.[33]

Levi Jones was not alone among free blacks who held and protected their family members as slaves either because of insufficient funds to pay for them outright as agreed on with their owners or because of restrictive state laws. Throughout the Lower South, except in Louisiana, emancipations were all but prohibited except by acts of state legislatures, and even in the Upper South the laws concerning manumission were becoming less liberal. Unless a free black husband who had purchased his wife and children also secured their legal freedom from the state, they would be considered to be slaves. Families could be sundered when some of their members were born prior to the passage of an act restricting the freedom of slaves and others were born after. In Tennessee, the specific date of purchase could determine whether or not a family could continue living together if they were purchased before and after the 1831 statute requiring freed blacks to leave the state.

Susannah Williams, too, filed a freedom suit for herself and her six children, all of whom, in this case, had been born after she had been purchased by her husband. She brought her case in 1806 to the Anne Arundel County Court in Maryland because her husband, who had recently been declared mentally incompetent, had failed to take the proper legal steps necessary to acquire their freedom papers. She was more successful: by a special act of the legislature on her behalf, the court was instructed to execute for her and her children a deed of emancipation according to law.[34] Other suits claimed that owners had promised the plaintiffs and their children free status if, after the owners' deaths, they paid the estates designated amounts. It could take many years to effect self-purchase in this manner, and during that time not only was the price of blacks steadily rising but also the slave families were growing, as some plaintiffs had given birth to additional children. In either event, heirs to the estates were frequently reluctant to abide by self-purchase agreements that plainly worked to their economic disadvantage.[35] In such situations blacks who had been promised freedom might instead be held in bondage for many years, or permanently; if they were released, they might later be reclaimed as slaves by members of their former owners' families.

In 1822, Benjamin Jarman, a slave in North Carolina, purchased his son David from his owner, Edward Williams, at a reduced price. Subsequently, based on Williams's testimony praising his former slave as "distinguished for his honesty, industry and fidelity to his master," David was freed by a judgment of the superior court. More than three decades later David was claimed by a white man on the grounds that his father, Benjamin Jarman, had been a slave at the time of the purchase and therefore could neither own nor emancipate his son. In 1858, the appeals court ruled that the former owner's title to David was "undoubtedly divested in favor of the plaintiff, either by his [Williams's] acts in connection with the proceedings of the Court, or by his long acquiescence afterward." Thus, every "presumption ought to be made in favor of his [David's] actual emancipation according to all the requirements of law."[36]

The southern state most demonstrably sympathetic toward free blacks who sought to purchase family members still in bondage was Delaware. Unique among the slaveholding states in a number of ways, Delaware alone granted free status to slaves who could show that they were about to be illegally exported, and as early as 1787 the state outlawed the domestic slave trade. Prior to 1830, Delaware boasted a manumission rate even higher than that of either New York or New Jersey, where gradual abolition statutes were in effect. The drop in the state's slave population easily exceeded a decline in any other southern state; more than nine out of ten African Americans in Delaware claimed free status by 1860. In Kent County, where many of the early freedom suits were filed, the 1860 census listed only 203 black people in bondage, whereas free blacks numbered 7,271. Also, the children of term slaves, if they were born during the period of what was called half-freedom—before the date of the mother's manumission— assumed the status not of slave but of indentured servant until age twenty-five, as opposed to age twenty-eight in Pennsylvania. Delaware, too, was one of only three states that acknowledged the validity of contracts for freedom. In no other state was the influence of Quaker abolitionists in support of freedom suits more strongly felt. And in Delaware law there was no distinction anywhere drawn to set apart blacks from whites.[37]

In Delaware, with slave prices declining and slavery on the wane, the opportunity for free blacks to purchase members of their families rose. In one instance, an owner simply gave a free black father his infant son as a gift on the condition that he later pay a designated amount. The father met the condition and the owner manumitted the child "in due Form of Law."[38] In another instance, a free black father, described as being "legally married" to his slave wife, purchased his son from her owner and then, because free blacks could not own slaves in Delaware, bequeathed him to a white man until he reached age twenty-five. Upon the white man's death, however, the son was sold as a slave for life. In 1838, the court offered a remarkable justification for its actions in favor of the son's freedom. The court "ought not to recognize the right of a father to hold his own children in slavery. Humanity forbids it. The natural rights and obligations of a father are paramount to the acquired rights of the master; and the moment the father purchases his child and these rights become blended in the same person, the lesser rights and obligations are merged in the greater, and the child is free."[39]

In most purchase cases, in Delaware and elsewhere, it was free black husbands and fathers, rather than wives and mothers, who worked to rescue their spouses and children from bondage. The liberation of enslaved wives was indeed the more pressing concern, for it lessened the number of children who would be born into slavery. The husbands and fathers in these cases were often not part of the formal court proceedings; instead, they worked behind the scenes to negotiate terms and accumulate funds for the acquisition of their loved ones. In a statistical study of five northern Maryland counties (Carroll, Cecil, Frederick, Harford, and Washington), among the 114 slaves purchased by free blacks, 41 of them were wives who had been bought by their husbands, while only 3 husbands had been purchased by their free black wives. Most of the slave children, too, had been purchased by free black men.[40]

Testimony by whites, slaveholders and non-slaveholders alike, was vital in cases that involved self-hire, self-purchase, and purchase of loved ones. Whites familiar with both the plaintiffs and the defendants were called on to vouch for the hard work, industry, and honesty of the free, quasi-free, indentured, or enslaved blacks bringing suit. They provided depositions detailing what they knew of payments due or made to owners, what jobs the plaintiffs had pursued to accumulate their funds, and what their cases might presume with regard to state laws. They also confirmed particulars in the backstories of the plaintiffs: where they had lived previously, when they came to reside in the community, what they had done since their arrival, how they had established their usually admirable reputations. They cited the names of owners; they verified the terms of agreements and contracts promising free status. By their testimony they were, in effect, defining the very nature of slavery itself, as well as the conditions on which the enslaved might be freed. Some among the deponents actually purchased the slaves involved in a case, simply in order to free them, as the slaves themselves had already paid their owners significant sums on the purchase price.

Described as an Old School Presbyterian clergyman, John H. Gray of Memphis, owner of ten slaves, paid $700 for Billy, whom he was encouraged to assist, he said, because Billy himself had by then paid his former owner most of the purchase price. Gray found Billy to be a person "of good behavior and very orderly, and unexceptionable character." Further, Gray noted, Billy had lived in the state prior to January 1, 1836, as required by Tennessee law, and he planned to move to Liberia once he had purchased his two slave sons. By virtue of the testimony provided by this prominent, respected white clergyman, Billy Armour (who took the surname of his former owner) was emancipated and set free.[41]

White citizens were also called on to testify against owners who had gone back on their promises in matters of self-purchase. In their testimony, they recounted the efforts, and struggles, of enslaved blacks who hired out their time and out of their earnings managed, over many years, to save enough, finally, for their self-purchase, only to be sold as slaves for life by unscrupulous owners. They testified, as well, to the pain and torment suffered by black families who had been split apart by their owners' unwarranted actions, and they asserted that, in fairness and equity, owners should be held accountable to honor agreements they had made with their self-hired slaves. Some witnesses related how, after the deaths of owners who had promised their slaves free status, heirs and relatives, ignoring the last wishes of the deceased, assumed possession of the blacks and ensured their bondage. Absent documentation, cases against defendants were very difficult to prove; they demanded commitment on the part of white witnesses to garner evidence that would expose the slaveholder to the satisfaction of the court. Lawyers fashioned the complaints and plaintiffs provided the pertinent facts, but without the testimony of white witnesses they would have little chance of winning a favorable verdict. Witnesses who also had knowledge of the state's manumission laws, as many did, often served as guardians of slaves seeking their freedom in the Lower South.[42]

In February 1820, nine months before the passage of the South Carolina law stating that "no slave shall hereafter be emancipated, but by act of the legislature," Charleston resident J. E. Holmes, acting as guardian of "a Negroe wench named Catherine," filed suit in the Charleston Equity Court against the heirs of Dr. Plumeau, Catherine's deceased owner. Plumeau had a reputation for buying self-hired slaves below market value, promising them their eventual freedom, and then breaching his agreement with them; his heirs shared his want of scruples. Holmes produced two witnesses who testified that when Catherine's original owner sold her to Plumeau, he had included a promise of self-purchase in the bill of sale. Clearly, as Holmes declared, Plumeau was a duplicitous and despicable man who had "defrauded the negroe of her rights." In 1822, the equity court declared Catherine's freedom contract to be valid but not operative, because the 1820 law now barred such manumissions. Undeterred, Holmes petitioned the General Assembly, which ruled that a slave could contract for her freedom "by leave & with permission" of the master.[43]

Holmes's efforts on behalf of Catherine went beyond ordinary, to be sure, but in a number of other cases, too, whites willingly invested time and effort to assist blacks in their freedom suits, especially self-hired blacks who had maintained reputations for good behavior and honored their contractual obligations over a period of years. As witnesses, they recapitulated the terms of the agreements masters had made with their slaves on self-hire to affect their freedom. They supplied information about the hirelings' employments. They testified as to how, as hirelings, the plaintiffs had dutifully, out of their monthly earnings, set aside the dollars necessary to meet the payments for their self-purchase. Some whites also provided funds to the plaintiffs for the execution of security bonds, if necessary, or aided them in the filing of requests for injunctions to prevent owners from leaving the court's jurisdiction, or contacted lawyers for them and assisted them in filing freedom suits.[44] Sometimes, like Holmes, they sought out witnesses to verify claims regarding deeds of manumission or bills of sale that promised freedom.[45] In cases with claims naming multiple defendants, they helped to uncover the whereabouts of the named parties so that they could be served with summonses.[46] In some instances, they served as what were called a "next friend," in law the plaintiff's advocate, or in Louisiana as a "curator," fulfilling the same function.

In one such instance, a curator guided a family of Louisiana slaves through the legal process upon their submission of a freedom suit claiming that both their grandmother and mother had been manumitted in St. Jago de Cuba in 1806 after self-purchasing their freedom. During the trial, the mother died, and the curator readily facilitated the continuation of the suit for her children and one grandchild. Working with the plaintiffs' lawyer, the curator produced a Spanish transcript of a judicial proceeding that occurred before a tribunal in St. Jago de Cuba and that proved the mother's free status. They also obtained expert oral testimony on points of Spanish law pertinent to emancipation. When the court rendered a verdict in favor of the defendant—the judge refused to permit "parole [oral] evidence to prove the law of Spain"—the curator helped the plaintiffs in their appeal to the Louisiana Supreme Court, which ruled that the district court judge had erred by excluding parole testimony and that he should have admitted into evidence the transcript establishing the free status of the now deceased self-purchased mother.[47]

In the late eighteenth century and intermittently throughout the nineteenth, in Delaware, Maryland, Virginia, and later in the District of Columbia and Kentucky, various white antislavery groups, usually with a religious affiliation, assisted in the financing and prosecuting of freedom suits. Most of these groups were short-lived, and as antiabolitionist sentiment grew increasingly stronger throughout the South, the groups either died out or remained silent and resisted involvement. Some churches disowned members whose views sympathized with the attempts of enslaved blacks to gain their freedom. Still, from time to time even in the antebellum years, an antislavery organization would emerge for a brief period in the Upper South.

The sale of fifty-two-year-old Sarah Carter, a slave cook and "maid of all work" in the District of Columbia—she also did business on the side as a laundress and had practiced as a midwife for many years—along with her fourteen children and grandchildren, prompted a number of antislavery whites in the District to form a "bureau of humanity." William Chaplin, a Harvard graduate and lawyer, led their effort in 1845 to assist Sarah's free black husband, Luke Carter, about seventy years old, in the purchase of his wife and family in Richmond, Virginia. They succeeded in the matter of Sarah—Luke raised $114 and accepted $68 from northern abolitionists; Chaplin paid the remainder—but the children and grandchildren, including a number of adults were sold to a new owner. The notoriety of the case spurred Chaplin to establish a fund for "the redemption of meritorious captives" in their self-purchase and prosecution of freedom suits. About the same time, Chaplin and several like-minded associates aided Lucy Crawford in her successful freedom suit against slave trader Hope H. Slater. All in all, though, antislavery activists assisted blacks suing for their freedom in only a few, isolated cases.[48]

Far more significant than the sporadic efforts by antislavery advocates to affect the legal process attendant to freedom suits was, again, the testimony of white southerners: local residents and businesspersons, slaveholders and yeoman farmers, who could present evidence to the courts either to substantiate or disprove the contentions of plaintiffs or defendants or both. Cases of self-hire, self-purchase, and the purchase of family members were especially problematic because they usually involved agreements between slaves and their owners, and sometimes other parties as well. Key to the agreements were financial terms, so evidence of financial transactions was crucial, and witnesses had to be relied on to provide essential documentation like receipts, promissory notes, bonds, bills of sale, written agreements, and payment schedules. Even with substantial evidence, however, cases often ended, like that of Letty Brown in the District of Columbia, with the decree asserting slaves were "incapable of contracting."[49]

The complexity of purchase cases and the vital importance of white testimony is more manifest in *Nancy Ann v. Peter Talbott and William Shephard*, filed in 1844 in Jefferson County, Kentucky. As the judge indicated in his decision, a number of witnesses had stepped forward to testify in regard to various issues that complicated the case: a slave husband, Lewis, having won a lottery, arranged for Peter D. Talbott to purchase his wife, Nancy Ann, from her owner, William Shephard, for $500. In 1840, Talbott paid the owner $450, and Nancy Ann was permitted "to go free" until Talbott could comply fully with the terms of the contract and then free Nancy Ann in accord with the laws of the state. In 1844, however, as witnesses had testified, Talbott was making arrangements with slave traders to have them kidnap Nancy Ann and "run her out of the state."

Having considered the testimony of the witnesses as well as the arguments put forth by the lawyer for the defendants, the judge determined in a three-page verdict that the defendants were correct in maintaining that a slave could not argue a suit based on a contract he was not, and by law could not be, party to, but that Talbott was "altogether wrong in supposing the statute was made or can be permitted for the benefit of a trafficker." It was also correct, the judge noted, that the money won in a lottery, in strict fact, belonged not to the slave but to his mistress; however, the judge allowed, the law "will indulge the presumption" that the original owner took the money and made the agreement with the husband under the belief that Lewis's mistress "would ratify the transaction." Indeed, both the mistress and the second defendant, William Shepherd, who had sold Nancy Ann to Talbott, testified to that effect in court. To avoid possible criminal prosecution that Talbott was planning to "perpetuate a vile fraud," the judge ordered him to sign a deed of manumission for Nancy Ann within ten days, with the admonition that if he failed to do so, the chancery court would "empower & direct to execute such a deed for him and report the same for confirmation."[50]

Even in states where self-purchase contracts were valid according to law, the testimony of white witnesses weighed heavily in a court's final decision. In a Louisiana freedom suit, testimony by whites established that a slave mother had, with a bidder at an auction, fashioned an oral agreement by which she would pay the man half of her purchase price if, in return, he would emancipate her and not resell her two children. The mother paid the buyer $220. Another child, Gaudet, who was, as witnesses confirmed, born after the sale and after her mother's emancipation, sued for her own freedom in 1848. However necessary it would appear that the act of emancipation pertaining to Gaudet's mother should be in writing, the Louisiana judge wrote, Spanish law (*Las Siete Partidas*), which authorized the right of slaves to contract for their freedom, had become part of the Civil Code of Louisiana in 1825, and neither Spanish law nor the Civil Code subjected these contracts to any "particular formality." The plaintiff therefore should enjoy her liberty, the judge ruled, and the defendant should be quieted forever in making his claim.[51]

When whites testified against black plaintiffs seeking to purchase themselves—the words "insolvent," "deceptive," "vicious," "idle," "troublesome," and "refractory" were commonly used to describe their bad behavior (as they were in testimony regarding runaway slaves)—more often than not the courts ruled also against the plaintiffs, especially if they were struggling to raise the money for their self-purchase.[52] There were cases, too, when the testimony of several credible white witnesses clearly affirmed a plaintiff's free status by virtue of self-purchase but failed to sway the court in the plaintiff's favor. Billy Kelley of Tennessee bought himself in 1829 and for six years lived as a free black. Then, in 1835, he was forcibly reenslaved and his free papers were destroyed. Without documentation, he could rely only on witnesses in his freedom suit, and freedom proved to be elusive.[53]

Prior to Beverly Dowling's Baltimore freedom suit, agent James O. Law had written the slave mistress Sophia Bland three letters in regard to his supervision of her virtually free slaves. About Dowling, he complained, he had not seen him "for some time," and he had not had the time to search Dowling out as he had been busy attending to the loading of a ship's cargo of flour. Law reported, too, that he had collected several hundred dollars from hiring out Bland's slaves, including one hundred dollars from Dowling and thirty-six dollars from the hireling Eliza. Law fretted over Rachel and her son, who were apparently beyond his powers to supervise. He had no idea what she or her son looked like, or where they lived. Even if he were able to track them down, he would have difficulties selling them, as he would have to place them in confinement until such time that he could ship them off on a slave-trading vessel: all of which would prompt, he feared, "a hue and cry [to] be raised by the blacks that they were going to be sold to Georgia." Furthermore, there were people in Baltimore who would believe them, even though those people were "ignorant of the true state of the thing." Consequently, Law declined to sell Rachel and her son despite his promise to do so because he feared charges would be brought against such actions.

At trial, the petitioner's attorneys, Alexander Cheves and Thomas Yates Walsh, objected to the inclusion of Law's letters in evidence on grounds that they were prejudicial. The court agreed, and it refused to allow the letters, or any part of them, to be read to the jury. The defendant objected and "prayed leave to except," or appeal, to no avail. The attorneys Cheves and Walsh successfully argued Dowling's case. Beverly promised to pay interest on his delayed payments and to undertake jobs so that with his earnings he could cover the outstanding installments on his self-purchase; more importantly, his mistress permitted him to contact employers, earn his own wages, and enjoy a separate and autonomous existence as a self-sustaining virtually free slave.

However, the key issue in the case was not the self-purchase agreement or Dowling's ability to seek employment, as slaves in Maryland could not enforce any "alleged contract" with their owners. Rather, it was Dowling's trip to New York City and subsequent return to Baltimore. Despite the fact that neither the agent nor the mistress had knowledge of his out-of-state travel and residence, the judge ruled that upon Dowling's return, by reason of the 1796 slave nonimportation law any claim on him assumed by Sophia Bland constituted importation "within the meaning of the act." The appeals court affirmed the verdict for freedom; if such actions were allowed, the court averred, the law's provisions "would be liable to great evasion." Thus, the nearly free slave Beverly Dowling acquired his legal freedom. By 1840, he and his wife and their three daughters under the age of ten had relocated to New York City.[54]

9

Runaways

Confined in a jail cell in New Bern, North Carolina, for six "long and weary months," Connecticut-born free black Abraham Carpenter repeatedly tried to explain: In April 1829 he had shipped out of New York City on the schooner *Fox*, which was carrying a cargo of lime to a fort being built at Beaufort, North Carolina. Upon arrival, he had left the crew and traveled up the Neuse River to Craven County, where, in August, he was arrested and jailed as a fugitive slave. Because, like many runaway slaves in jails across the South, he had no freedom papers to prove his status, the jailer made an effort to locate his owner by placing advertisements in the local newspaper. Abraham was tall, thin, about twenty-one, and light-complexioned, the ad noted, and it urged any person with claim to him as a slave to come forward, produce the legal title, and pay the jail fees, whereupon Abraham would be released into the owner's custody.

The authorities in New Bern also followed up on Abraham's story that he had been born of free parents near Stamford, Connecticut, by sending a request to a leading citizen in that community for a deposition concerning Abraham's possible free status. The communication was so poorly written, however, that the recipient, Ard Reynolds, thought it was an inquiry about a runaway who had fled from North Carolina to Connecticut, and thus, as Reynolds lamented several months later, he had disregarded it. Abraham admitted to the authorities that he had gotten into trouble in Connecticut, where he had been convicted of theft and sentenced to ten stripes at the public whipping post, and that he had run away from home to go to sea. But whatever his faults in the past, he pleaded, he was a free man born of free parents in a free state. His father lived in a place called Horseneck, between Sawpits and Stamford, in Fairfield County, and Abraham, in a jail cell far from home, feared he might never again see him or "the face of any friend" who could vouch for him as a free person. Abraham told his story to anyone who would listen, over and over, until someone did.[1]

Abraham Carpenter's predicament was by no means exceptional. Free persons of color were continually being mistakenly identified—or willfully challenged—as slaves in the southern states. Local authorities, and even private citizens, commonly confronted free blacks traveling from county to county in their home states or venturing into neighboring states or visiting from the North, and demanded of them proof of their free status. If they could not produce acceptable freedom papers—deeds, certificates, copies of wills, court records, proofs of residency, or similar documents—they could be held, like Carpenter, until their legal status could be determined. Consequently most free colored people stayed close to home, though not necessarily by choice, as some states prohibited the entry of free blacks on penalty of being sold and other states forbade their departure. In many places, if they could not be vouched for by anyone in the community, they could be arrested, detained, and jailed as runaways. Even free blacks who had acquired property or had established themselves respectably in their communities, including free persons of color in Louisiana who had become planters and slaveholders, or who boasted a number of white friends and "protectors," were sometimes taken for slaves.[2]

Free blacks arrested and jailed as runaway slaves often found it difficult to extricate themselves from bondage. In 1831 the "Address to the Free People of the United States," published in the *Liberator*, stated that free blacks moving through the slave states "are liable to be taken up, in every town and district, on suspicion as runaway slaves, thrust into prison, confined six days or more, and sometimes sold into bondage for their jail fees." Although "six days or more" was certainly an underestimate, the chances of free blacks being jailed as runaways were painfully real.[3] Newspapers in the southern states covered the jailings of blacks who could not document claims that they were free and related the outcomes for the suspect runaways at auction sales, sheriffs' sales, and private sales. (The laws varied from state to state, but in most, if blacks jailed as runaways had not been claimed by an owner within a given number of months or a year—the time period depended on the jurisdiction—they could be sold at auction.)

The *Richmond Enquirer* in Virginia reported the detention of a well-dressed, dignified North Carolina black man as a runaway slave. He pleaded with the jailer to write to anyone in Weldon, North Carolina, to confirm his status, but the jailer refused to comply.[4] The *Nashville Whig* carried an article about two members of the Delany family who insisted they were free even as a slaveowner who lived thirty miles below Natchez, Mississippi, claimed them as his property.[5] "DETAINED—at the Jail of the Parish of St. John Baptiste, a MULATTO," read a typical newspaper notice, this one in the *New Orleans Bee*, "who pretends that he is free."[6]

In circumstances already unfortunate, then, free blacks could furthermore be legally enslaved or reenslaved, or be otherwise reduced to virtual slavery. In some instances, free persons of color convicted of a crime were sentenced to lengthy terms of indentured servitude, and often their indentures were then sold and resold so that they became, in effect, slaves for life. In other cases, they

A number of cities in the South maintained special jails, or pens, for slaves awaiting shipment to a new location. Slave pens in Alexandria, Virginia, did a brisk business, especially after the city was returned from the District of Columbia to the state of Virginia in 1846, and the slave trade was outlawed in the District in 1850. The latter development drove much of the trafficking in human property across the Potomac River. *Library of Congress, LC-DIG-cwpb-01468*

were charged with crimes and held in jail so long that they sometimes actually requested to be sold.

In 1795, Ceasar Colick was arrested in Kent County, Delaware, and jailed on suspicion of murder, a charge that he denied. Without a formal indictment, Colick had spent seven months in prison when he asked the sheriff to sell him at public auction.[7] Similarly, Samuel Legg, a Delaware free person of color, was held on suspicion of a felony for so long that he too requested to be sold by the sheriff at a public sale in order to pay the jail fees. Others in similar situations requested to be sold into servitude "agreeable to the Laws of this State."[8] In 1826, Maryland free black Peter Sweeper was convicted of conveying slaves to freedom in Pennsylvania. Sentenced to banishment and seven years of servitude,

Sweeper was purchased and taken by his buyer to Tennessee, where he remained enslaved for a number of years beyond the term of his servitude. In 1835, he filed a freedom suit; the lower court ruled in his favor, as did the appeals court when, in 1838, it decreed his freedom.[9] Sweeper was among the fortunate few once-free blacks who were able to bring a case to court, but most of them simply melted into the slave population.

Freedom for free blacks in the South was always precarious. In Prince Edward County, Virginia, in 1847, twenty-seven black men were listed on the county's inventory of "free Negroes to be Sold for taxes," including seven members of the Bartlett family.[10] Heirs to a slaveowner's estate often took up blacks freed by the testator to satisfy his debts, a practice that was legal only if the free persons of color had not yet been granted formal emancipations. It was not legal when a Virginia sheriff proceeded to levy an "execution on the bodies" of Louisa and Eliza Alexander, mother and daughter, who had enjoyed "all the rights of free persons" until they were advertised to be sold to pay their emancipator's debts.[11]

Free persons of color who were arrested and jailed as runaway slaves faced a slippery situation. With literally thousands of runaways being reported in the South each year, law enforcement officers, from county sheriffs to local police to state marshals, kept a sharp lookout for blacks who were unfamiliar or seemed suspicious to them. Public notices detailed the height, weight, gender, and color of runaways and also described any scars or other distinguishing characteristics that might identify them. Codes in each state dictated how and when rewards for their capture could be offered and how they would be sold at sheriffs' auctions if no owners stepped forward to claim them. The bitter sectional conflict that eventually erupted in civil war evolved in part out of this very issue, as the treatment of runaways not only denied freedom to slaves but also rescinded it for blacks already free. Many southerners believed firmly that the capture and incarceration of runaways were fundamental to the peace and stability of a slave society, but at the same time they were also bound by tenets of law and custom that prohibited the arrest and sale of free blacks as slaves—not that such laws prevented free African Americans from being kidnapped and sold into bondage.

The law also provided free blacks who had been wrongly jailed as runaways with a viable option: they could seek a writ of habeas corpus (literally, "you have the body"), or, as it was sometimes called, *habeas corpus ad subjiciendum* ("you have the person to be subjected to examination"). A judicial mandate, the writ required that a detained person be brought before a judge in order to determine whether the state or any individual had the right to continue holding him or her in detention, and it could therefore be served on jailers, marshals, constables, sheriffs, policemen, justices of the peace, and other officials. Either the detainee or the lawyer representing him or her could petition for the writ, a right that was accorded to all free persons, whether white or black, by the US Constitution,

which declared that "the privilege of the *Writ of Habeas Corpus* shall not be sus-
pended, unless when in Cases of Rebellion or Invasion the public Safety may
require it."[12]

The writ did not require that the *corpus* be released from confinement; rather,
it initiated a process to determine whether or not the evidence warranted continued imprisonment, or, in the case of free blacks jailed as runaways, to prove that
they were not slaves. Historically, in England and the United States, the common
law writ of habeas corpus had been established to permit a person who stood
accused of an offense to call into question the charges. As a constitutional right, the
writs were acknowledged in all the states, northern and southern, from the post-
Revolutionary era through the antebellum period, and the courts duly recognized
the right of free blacks to seek the writ. Proof of status in these instances differed
from the petitions, or narratives, in freedom suits, because the writs were more a
remedy than a cure. They protected the black petitioner only from unlawful detention and did not guarantee any other rights. Occasionally, black plaintiffs and their
lawyers requested the courts to consider the writ in lieu of, and to the effect of, a
freedom suit, but such cases were invariably dismissed. The writ, then, served primarily as a means to prove that free blacks were not runaway slaves.[13]

It was not unusual for free blacks who were traveling within a home county or
from one county to another in their home state, perhaps to visit friends or maybe
to seek employment, to find themselves, instead, in a law officer's custody—and
for more than a few hours or days if no one could vouch for them. Particularly
during periods of slave unrest or after a rash of runaways, free blacks who were
unknown in a community could be, and often were, arrested. Freedom papers
sometimes offered protection, but frequently free persons of color were arrested
despite the fact that they were carrying documents to prove their status, such
as emancipation decrees, deeds of manumission, and letters or certificates from
their former owners. The suspicions of local authorities were likely to count for
more; declaring the documents forgeries, they would confiscate the papers and
refuse to return them to the black person now in their custody.

When a North Carolina free black man, Edward Hammons, was confronted
by a law officer in Craven County, he produced a certificate of freedom signed
by the clerk of court in Chatham County, nearly 150 miles away. Hammons
was arrested and jailed on December 10, 1840. He remained incarcerated until
June 8, 1841, when Judge Mathias E. Manly ruled on a writ of habeas corpus
that there was "no sufficient ground for the allegation of the warrant." The judge
added that, as Hammons was insolvent, the state would pay the jail fees: not a
small concession, since Hammons could have been hired out by the sheriff until
he had earned enough from his wages to reimburse the jailer.[14] Hammons's predicament was not uncommon. Even after producing what were called "free papers," numerous other free blacks were arrested and jailed.[15]

In 1835, Jones H. Jenkins claimed that he was a free person of color and thus illegally confined in the District of Columbia jail as a runaway slave—this was the second time he had been arrested on this charge. In the first instance he produced his freedom papers and was released. In the second, he explained that his freedom papers were taken from him and not returned. After he requested a writ of habeas corpus, his freedom papers were delivered and he was released. *Copy of freedom certificate, 23 July 1835, Slavery and the Law Digital Archive, PAR #20483501*

The signature at the bottom of Jones H. Jenkins's freedom papers, releasing him from jail, was that of William Cranch, who served on the District of Columbia Circuit Court bench for fifty-four years. Appointed in 1801, he became chief judge in 1806. Cranch ruled on many freedom suits during his tenure and was generally empathetic to the plight of blacks seeking to be released from bondage. *Library of Congress, LC-USZ62-109848*

Most of the arrests of free black persons as runaway slaves occurred in cities and towns. During the late eighteenth and early nineteenth centuries, the African American populations, both free and slave, grew significantly—often doubling in number and, as regards free blacks, quadrupling—in the District of Columbia, Baltimore, Alexandria, Richmond, Petersburg, Norfolk, and Charleston. In Baltimore, the number of free persons of color increased by a remarkable 1,656 percent in just twenty years, between 1790 and 1810. In subsequent decades, urban areas along the eastern seaboard and on the western periphery of the South as well as in the Gulf states continued to attract free blacks. In Louisville, Nashville, St. Louis, and New Orleans, they settled, and among them mingled fugitive slaves who had migrated to cities to avoid detection.[16] The intermingling of runaway slaves and resident free blacks—indeed, they were often members of the same family—of course complicated the pursuit of fugitives for the authorities; so did the demographic profile, which made it difficult to distinguish runaways from their free black counterparts.

As a result, the authorities not infrequently arrested and incarcerated free blacks as fugitive slaves, especially those who could not immediately produce freedom papers. Once they were jailed pending a determination of their status, they had few options except to protest their freedom and find a lawyer willing to petition the courts for a writ of habeas corpus. Their lawyers required them to provide a biography: who their former owners were, how and when they had acquired their freedom, where they had lived in their youth, what families, black and white, they had grown up with, where they had worked on hire, who had otherwise employed them and at what occupations. Relevant too, of course, was any information regarding their freedom papers: if they had been stolen, or how they had been seized by the authorities at the time of their arrest.[17]

Although it was a painstaking and often lengthy process, at the end of it free blacks who secured writs of habeas corpus were in a large measure successful in regaining their liberty. Often, after examining the evidence submitted to support the court's issuance of writs, judges released the petitioners from confinement. In the Lower South, the wait time between arrest and issuance of the writ was usually several months, sometimes longer, and it could indeed take months to procure evidence of free status when the wrongfully detained blacks, prior to their arrests as runaway slaves, had journeyed from the Upper South or the North. By mail, they or their lawyers contacted whites in their distant hometowns who could vouch for their good character, former owners who could provide copies of manumission deeds, or clerks of courts where their manumission had been recorded. Then they waited for the responses, for copies of important documents, or for depositions and affidavits from trusted white friends.

The case of free black Richard Coleman, who was arrested and jailed as a fugitive in Warren County, Mississippi, was unexceptional in this regard. Both of his parents were free persons of color in Virginia, and after their deaths Coleman had worked for William Morgan under an indenture before journeying to Vicksburg, where had found employment working on the railroad—and had been incarcerated in the summer of 1836. Some weeks after his arrest he and the court received an affidavit signed by David Atway, a farmer in Henderson County, Tennessee, and dated August 24, 1836; it confirmed that Coleman was a free person of color. Yet Coleman's request for a writ of habeas corpus was not submitted to criminal court until January 30, 1837. Within a few days he was discharged. The process, however, took more than six months, time that Coleman had spent confined in the Vicksburg jail.[18]

In habeas corpus cases, as in freedom suits, the color of the plaintiffs was rarely a factor. Evidence might include descriptions of detainees' skin color, but only for purposes of identification, not for determination of status, which, as in freedom suits, relied on documentary proof of the petitioner's freedom. The salient question was not whether the person was free because of his or her color but, rather, whether the person was free according to the laws of the state.[19] Even in Louisiana, where the law *presumed* that light-skinned persons of African descent were free and dark-skinned "Negroes" were slaves, in both freedom and habeas corpus suits the outcomes depended not on assumptions but on state statutes and documentary evidence. Only in the very rare case when proof of free status could not be established by any other evidentiary means were judges compelled to follow Louisiana law and release a person by virtue of his or her skin color or physical features.

Jailed as a runaway slave in East Baton Rouge Parish, in 1851, Adaline (also spelled Adeline) insisted that she was "a free woman of *Indian Blood*" who had been illegally detained as a slave; her "color, complexion, and hair," she said, proved her status. Nonetheless, she remained in jail for three months while the sheriff placed an advertisement in a local newspaper for her owner to come forward (without result) and the court contacted a white woman in New Orleans who was suspected of being her owner (without response). In the end, the judge discharged her from captivity on a writ of habeas corpus that was issued on the basis of her color and physical appearance.[20]

By the 1830s court sessions in towns and cities of the Upper South commonly included requests for writs of habeas corpus by free people of color jailed as runaways. The writs were almost always granted, and most of the petitioners were released from custody. The wait time—usually a few days and, at most, a few weeks—was considerably more tolerable than the months of incarceration in the Lower South. But then, in the Upper South cases, it did not usually take months to summon witnesses because in general they lived in proximity to the scenes of the arrests. When they could not appear in person, they mailed or delivered to the court letters, copies of legal documents, and affidavits avowing

that the detainees were not runaway slaves. One respondent, John Adams, a resident of Queen Anne's County, on the Eastern Shore of Maryland, apologized for
his inability to make the journey to the District of Columbia in order to testify
on behalf of a free black jailed as a runaway, but he did send a letter to the court,
and sometime later he visited the jail to help the black man work for his release.[21]

The arrests of free blacks as runaways often occurred during sweeps of towns
and cities by law enforcement officers seeking fugitives. During a sweep in the
District of Columbia, Jones H. Jenkins was arrested and jailed. "I have no doubt
but that he is a free man, his mother Avey is at present in my employment,"
Robert Leslie of Petersburg, Virginia, wrote in response to Jenkins's request for
assistance. Leslie stated that he had employed Jenkins's mother at various times
over many years, and knew for a fact that she was born free, "so of course her
son Jones must also be free." Leslie also arranged for certified copies of Jenkins's
yearly registration as a free black to be sent from the Petersburg Corporation
Court, which described him as being about five feet eight inches tall, with brown
skin and a small scar above his left eyebrow. Shortly before Jenkins's release,
the authorities discovered that this was the second time he had been wrongly
arrested on the same charge.[22]

The arrest and adjudication of runaway slave cases often scored low on effi-
ciency. To reduce "the great annual expense" of arresting and jailing blacks on
suspicion of being runaways, the Maryland General Assembly passed a law in
1824 that required justices of the peace and sheriffs to provide the clerk of the
Baltimore City Court, within forty-eight hours of an arrest, detailed information relative to potential owners and arrested runaways in their "commitment
papers." The failure of local authorities to comply with this prescript could result in a fine of fifty dollars "for each and every offence." While the new law was
enacted to streamline the arrest and adjudication process, it overwhelmed local
authorities responsible for processing the numerous, and often wrongful, arrests
of suspected runaway slaves.[23]

The fear, and danger, shared by wrongly arrested free blacks was of enslavement. Even after a sheriff's advertisement of their arrests had run its course and
no potential owners had claimed them, they still needed to prove their free
status to prevent their sale at a public auction. Some free blacks failed to, usually because they could not provide testimony from whites on their behalf or
because emphatically negative testimony disposed the courts to order that they
be sold as slaves or forced to sign long-term indentures. John Henry Doman, a
free orphan of color, age sixteen, was arrested in Baltimore County, in 1856, as
a fugitive slave. Although he ostensibly had a free aunt living nearby, she did not
testify. A local white man, however, attested to the orphans, court that Doman
drank to excess, idled away his time, had not secured a guardian, and was likely
to become a "charge upon the county." As a result, the court apprenticed him to

a free black man for five years, during which time he would labor as a farm hand and gardener; at age twenty-one, if he had given up his "bad habits," Doman would be entitled to a suit of clothes or the "customary freedom dues." If not, his prospects for becoming a free black remained bleak.[24]

The tenuous position of free blacks in the South forced them to maintain constant vigilance. Many practiced caution in their dealings with whites, and some were even wary of relationships with slaves and other free persons of color. To protect themselves, they rarely strayed outside the community where they lived and maintained cordial relations with a few sympathetic whites who, they trusted, would vouch for them in times of crisis. Despite their efforts to safeguard themselves and their families against injustices, however, some among them were still wrongly arrested, jailed, advertised, and sold as runaway slaves. Nor was it out of the ordinary for free people of color to be kidnapped in the North and transported to a southern state—or seized in one southern state and removed to another—there to be sold as slaves. Relocated on remote farms and plantations, alone and isolated from white sympathizers to vouch for their status, they had little hope and less chance to extricate themselves from bondage as they toiled, sometimes for years, in cotton or sugarcane fields—Solomon Northrup's *Twelve Years a Slave* offers a case in point. A few attempted, mostly without success, to escape their kidnappers; others ran away after they had been installed at a new location, but almost always they were captured by the authorities and in due time returned to their owners. Not infrequently, jails in the southern states could barely contain the numbers of captured runaways and free blacks charged as runaways, who, like Abraham Carpenter, were listed in the authorities' advertisements.

The actual number of free blacks who were kidnapped and/or falsely arrested is unknowable, but abductions were not uncommon, and in total, over time, they certainly ran to a count of many thousands. Slave traders profited especially substantially in the sale of abducted blacks, as the only cost they incurred was that of transport. Slaveholders, many of whom benefited from deals with the traders, nonetheless, in large part, lamented the practice of kidnapping, and five states—Delaware, Virginia, Tennessee, Georgia, and Mississippi—and the District of Columbia passed laws with harsh penalties against the kidnapping of free blacks.[25] In Delaware, the assembly legislated in 1787 and 1793 to make kidnapping a felony. In 1826, punishment included a fine between $1,000 and $2,000, sixty lashes, and imprisonment in solitary confinement for up to seven years; a second offense warranted the death penalty. In 1841, the number of lashes and years of imprisonment were reduced while the fines were increased.[26]

Like many other slavery statutes enacted in the southern states, the laws against kidnapping were rarely implemented, and if they were, indictments and convictions were few. Indeed, because the kidnapped free blacks were frequently children, many cases against the perpetrators were never even made. Then, too, most often the witnesses to the abductions were other free blacks or slaves, neither of whom could testify against whites, with the exception of free blacks in Louisiana (and intermittently in several other states). In the years following the American Revolution the kidnapping of free blacks in Delaware and Maryland came to be so widespread that complaints reached the halls of Congress. The rise in prices for slaves in more southerly states spurred unscrupulous traders all the more to engage in the sale of kidnapped free blacks. Organized gangs, too, were turning huge profits from human trafficking, to the consternation of southerners; one opined that the gangs acted "in defiance of every principle of moral and legal obligation." And sometimes law enforcement officials participated in the trafficking as well.[27] During the antebellum era, when slave prices soared in the Lower South, the trafficking in kidnapped blacks expanded even more. "The pecuniary advantages to be derived from this iniquitous traffic," as a grand jury in Delaware found, in 1817, allowed many kidnappers "to evade the vigilance of existing laws, or set them at open defiance."[28]

Kidnapped free blacks were more likely to flee their captors than to bring their cases to court, or to flee them in order to bring their cases to court, if in a nearby town or city they could find support from a white person sympathetic to their stories of abduction and enslavement. The stories, related in a few pages of testimony, were far more brief in their telling than Solomon Northrup's meticulously detailed slave narrative and memoir but they were no less riveting in their accounts of violence and brutality, their recollections of incarceration and dark journeys in ships' dungeons, their painful images of heavy chains, wooden yokes, and twenty stripes across the back from a lash. Their tales retold their personal histories: how they had come to be free, where they had spent their youth, what occupations they had pursued, when and where they had been abducted, and how after years of grim servitude they had finally been able to garner the attention of the legal system.

Some of the abductees had been born of free parents in the North; others had been freed in southern states. Most had been snatched off city streets in Philadelphia, Baltimore, the District of Columbia, Pittsburgh, or Cincinnati. All had been wrenched away from friends and family, and had been borne south in pens and shackles to be sold as slaves. Their words harbored the pain of their separation from parents and children and spouses, and afterward the anguish, despair, longing, and anxiety in their passage with unknown captors to distant, unfamiliar places. Redemption then was barely a faint hope, and fainter as they endured for days and months and years the indignities and cruelties inherent in the "peculiar institution." Free blacks who had been in their teens at the time of their abductions recalled their lives with their parents and siblings before they had been taken away, and recounted how difficult it had been to defy their captors and alter their destinies as they were sold and resold, removed from one state to another, and attached to farms and plantations far from the reach of their former homes, often, like Northrup, in Louisiana.[29]

Only a few kidnapped free blacks succeeded, with the aid of sympathetic whites, in bringing their cases to court, but most of them also were released from bondage once they had provided the southern justices with proof of their freedom: an often protracted process, if only because of the geographical distances, that added months to the petitioners' jail time. Their alleged owners, meanwhile, produced proof of their purchases at auctions or private sales. The case of Harriett Scott affords an example. Born of free parents in Rhode Island, Harriet eventually moved with her family to Marietta, Ohio. For years, she commonly journeyed back and forth between Ohio and Kentucky, where, on one of her excursions, she was kidnapped and forced into slavery. Probably with the help of her parents, she initiated a freedom suit in Kentucky, but, while awaiting its outcome, she was abducted by two white men who transported her to New Orleans. She somehow managed to escape and stowed away aboard a steamboat, only to be discovered by the captain. He turned her over to the jailer in St. Landry Parish, in whose custody she remained more than twenty months: from May 20, 1829, when, with her lawyer, Benjamin Linton, she filed a freedom suit seeking a writ of habeas corpus, which was dismissed; to September 18, 1831, when she again sought a writ. It was issued on the same day and set Harriet Scott free.[30]

John Roach fared no better upon his abduction; yet, for all his difficulties and the odds against him, by sheer chance, or a happy accident, he too regained his freedom. As a youngster, John had assisted his free black mother, Elizabeth, with her clothes-cleaning business in Philadelphia by collecting laundry from mates and officers aboard the ships docked in the harbor. He was in his teens when he was abducted and conveyed to Louisiana, where he was sold as a slave to a planter in St. James Parish. About a year thereafter, in late 1816 or early 1817, he escaped to New Orleans and was soon jailed as a fugitive. He petitioned the court *in forma pauperis* for his freedom, but he could provide no proof of his freedom prior to his arrival in Louisiana. It was when his alleged owner appeared at the jail to reclaim his property that fortuitous circumstances brought to the same jail a white seaman "on suspicion of debt." He recognized the young man as the same free black boy who used to pick up his laundry years before. At the trial, despite a rigorous cross-examination, the seaman maintained he had become "acquainted with Elizabeth Roach about seven years before—that she resided at that time on Second Street in Philadelphia—that she was a free woman of color, in the enjoyment of her liberty—that said Elizabeth Roach is the mother of the plaintiff John Roach." In the end, the court agreed; the twenty-one-year-old Roach was set free.[31]

Apparent in the freedom suits filed by free blacks who claimed they were abducted and/or arrested as runaways is the commitment of the Louisiana and other southern courts to the pursuit of truth and proof, no matter the extended periods of time it might take to set in place depositions from Indiana, Ohio, Pennsylvania, or New York. In some cases, too, the abductions had occurred in a southern state, and in those cases, as well, the courts usually released the free black petitioners from their wrongful bondage. While the suits filed represent only a tiny fraction of the probably thousands of free blacks who were carried off into slavery or held as runaway slaves or became fugitives fleeing from their alleged owners, they do illuminate the principles that guided the judiciary process in cases involving the peculiar institution: the acceptance of enslaved person's narratives, the pursuance and admission of testimony by witnesses in the North or some distant state, and the judgment of cases on their merit rather than the emotion of the day. Some cases continued for more than a year and included twenty or thirty pages of sworn testimony. A few cases entailed so few particulars that the requests for habeas corpus could not be issued, or, if they were issued, they were overridden by the judge. Most cases, though, ended with judgments favorable to the plaintiffs.[32]

It was unusual for African Americans filing freedom suits to run away. While they portrayed themselves as victims of avaricious slave traders or ruthless slave owners in their suits, they also realized that without the assistance of white witnesses, the support of white lawyers, and the sympathy of white judges and juries, they would never gain or regain their freedom. For them to run away, then, would not only most likely end in their capture but would also jeopardize any accord they might have established with the court. They therefore exerted every effort to maintain cordial relations with whites in the community, slaveholders among them, who might provide testimony on their behalf, just as they likewise strove, for the benefit of the legal system, to sustain reputations of honesty and integrity.

Along with clauses referent to age and the ability to earn a livelihood, the manumission acts of a number of the states in which emancipations were permitted also included moral turpitude phrases. In 1800, South Carolina required that freed slaves be persons "of good character." In 1808, Louisiana stipulated that freed blacks demonstrate "honest conduct," meaning that they had not run away or committed any criminal act in the previous four years.[33] In 1816, Virginia passed an emancipation law that included the phrase "general good character and conduct." In 1842, Tennessee followed South Carolina's phraseology and added that the court should inquire into "the character and conduct of the freed slave."[34] Other states allowed freedom only for "meritorious services."[35] That plaintiffs and their lawyers recognized the importance attached by the courts to character is evident in their petitions as well as witness testimony, which often commented, either directly or indirectly, on the plaintiffs' personal qualities, such as honesty, loyalty, diligence, and industriousness—qualities that would be cast deeply into doubt should a petitioner run away.

Still, desperation could drive blacks in bondage to abscond, even during the process of their freedom suits. Term slaves, especially, were prone to anxiety when they were held in bondage beyond the date that they were scheduled to be freed, and the further that date receded into the past, the bleaker grew their prospects for the future. The decision to take flight did not come lightly, for it affected not only the term slaves themselves but also their families. Children and spouses, however beloved by the prospective absconder, were more a hindrance than help, even if the wife or husband was a free person of color.[36] The pressure to flee intensified, though, when it was paired with the term slaves' fear of their imminent sale and, thus, separation from their loved ones by their removal, as a Delaware woman rued, to "the Carolinas or Georgia."[37] It was a fear that often preceded the expiration of the term slaves' periods of servitude if, for instance, by their assertions of independence and autonomy, they had failed to maintain amicable, and suitably deferential, relations with their owners or members of their owners' families.

Unlike the vast majority of runaway slaves, many term bondspeople fled primarily not to escape their masters but to initiate legal actions against them. They sought out sympathetic whites in nearby communities who could assist them in bringing their cases to court. They contacted lawyers to file their suits. They pled for legal recognition of their status. They solicited the courts for injunctions to prevent their sale or the sale of their family members by vindictive masters. The injunctions were often granted, but they were hardly ever perpetual, and thus unable in many cases to guarantee protection for the full term of servitude.[38] Term-slave runaways who fled far from their home communities, especially if they absconded to a different state, found it almost impossible to acquire their freedom.

A few term-slave runaways did gain free status after filing complaints in the local courts, but only under the most unusual circumstances. In the District of Columbia, Fidelio learned in April 1800 that a bill of sale from Lund Washington to James R. McDermott promised him his freedom in six years. Apparently dissatisfied with his new owner, he ran away, the owner promising a reward for anyone who would flog him and have him arrested. Fidelio was well known about the city, the owner wrote, and might be hiding around "Mrs. Young's," where he had a wife. Captured and returned, he remained with his new master until the owner's death when he discovered his term had been shortened to four years. When this did not come to pass, he ran away again, and while on the run he found a lawyer and brought a freedom suit in the circuit court. In the court's deliberations it was shown that in his will McDermott said Fidelio should be freed after four years, but in a codicil he ordered that all of his slaves should be sold. In 1807, the widow, Alice McDermott, placed an ad in the *National Intelligencer* promising a reward to anyone who lodged him in jail or brought him to her "securely tied." Despite these events, Fidelio won his freedom suit. The court ruled that the codicil did not revoke the will's bequest of freedom.[39]

Other term-slave runaways who filed freedom suits were similarly successful when they and their lawyers produced documents proving that their terms had expired.[40] In the District of Columbia case of George, who absconded after being detained for an extra year—his owner complained that he had "expended two hundred dollars to get him back again"—the court issued a verdict for the petitioner.[41] Like George, many fugitive term slaves sought determinedly to obtain a legal affirmation of free status. They realized that if they wished to remain close to their families and communities, their chances of doing so were better by legal means than by running the risk of being swept up by slave catches or by relying on a masters' probity. Instead of defying the legal system, as did most runaways, they ran away in order to embrace it and thus achieve legal confirmation of their free status.

In addition to disputes over terms of servitude, distance from loved ones, inflictions of harsh punishments, or the want of a lawyer could also prompt some slaves to run away. They moved swiftly but secretly from place to place. Hiding from the authorities, though, sometimes proved to be difficult.[42] In 1818, when the Delaware slave Hannah absconded from a new owner to escape his harsh treatment, she took refuge in a cave. What happened next to Hannah—at this juncture she appears not to have yet connected with her daughter, Sarah, whom she would include in her eventual freedom suit—is unclear, but at some point thereafter she fell into the hands of a slave trader. The authorities were informed, and the sheriff along with another man gained entrance to the trader's house, where they found Hannah in "Irons," crying and "very much in distress." Armed with a writ—it was against the law to export slaves for sale from the state of Delaware—the sheriff took Hannah into protective custody. Subsequently she and her daughter won a freedom suit. Nine white residents testified that the defendant was "a Negro Trader and deals in Negroes" and acquired "negroes for exportation."[43]

In other runaway cases, acts of duplicity by owners or their family members with regard to self-purchase agreements occasioned the slaves' flight. These cases arose mainly in the Upper South and Louisiana, where manumissions were legal through most of the antebellum era, but self-purchase agreements in themselves were not legally binding in most states. Consequently, slaves in pursuit of self-purchase were at the mercy of owners and their families. Self-purchase entailed extraordinary effort and forbearance. During the 1820s, in Virginia, a young male slave could buy himself for about $350; in Louisiana, for about

$700. A generation later the prices had nearly doubled. Still, for many slaves freedom was worth the price, and to meet it, most of those who had garnered self-purchase "contracts" were permitted to hire out their own time. In the cities of the Upper South, the portion of slaves who hired out ranged from 62 percent in Richmond, 52 percent in Lynchburg, 50 percent in Norfolk, to 24 percent in Louisville; there were also substantial numbers of self-hired slaves in the District of Columbia, Baltimore, Nashville, St. Louis, and New Orleans. They worked in a wide range of occupations, both skilled and unskilled, including some of the most dangerous jobs in mining or in clearing swamplands.[44] And they worked diligently, industriously, and patiently to stay in good favor with their owners. To be deceived and to have the promise of freedom withdrawn, then, constituted more than betrayal; it was cause to abandon the owners' city residences or farms or plantations. It was cause to abscond.[45]

Absconding in most such cases proved to be as hopeless as the situations from which slaves with inconsequential self-purchase agreements fled. They were usually captured and incarcerated.[46] Those that brought their cases to court fared poorly, even in Louisiana, a state that permitted self-purchase contracts, due to a clause in the manumission law that conditioned freedom on a slave's good behavior (which absconding was not) in the four years prior to the suit. In a number of instances it didn't matter that self-hired slaves had paid their full purchase price and the owners reneged on the bargain, if, out of frustration, resentment, or outrage, the slaves ran away. In such cases, the courts invariably ruled in favor of the slaveholder. Then, too, with the ever-rising prices for skilled blacks in the Lower South, especially in New Orleans, concomitantly raising the prices of self-purchase, payments sometimes fell short. By 1835, François, a thirty-eight-year-old experienced hatter in Louisiana, had paid his owner $740 of his $1,170 agreed-on self-purchase price. When he was sold, the new owner agreed that once François had paid the outstanding balance of his full purchase price, he would be freed. By 1843, François had been again sold and resold, and he had paid his owners a total of about $1,040 (approximately $26,000 in today's dollars) over a period of fifteen years. Angry and frustrated, he became what was called a "perpetual runaway," but he was eventually captured, jailed, and consigned to the chain gang. When he finally managed to bring his case to court, he lost, as the defendant was able to prove that François was guilty not only of running away for weeks at a time but also of "the still worse habit of drinking."[47] Other runaways, despite some remarkable efforts to purchase themselves, suffered the same fate, especially in states where laws forbade slaves to enter into contracts with their masters. Runaways chanced to lose more than their court cases; the possibility of freedom, with or without a contract, dwindled with every recapture. As one angry Arkansas owner told a runaway, after he had been apprehended, returned, and severely whipped: "I will not set you free, and will show those legs that they shall not run away from me."[48]

Runaway quasi-free slaves—also referred to as "nominal slaves," "virtually free slaves," or nearly free bondsmen and women—were vulnerable as well. Independent and autonomous, ambitious and hard-working as they were, their very strengths could place them in a precarious situation with owners who sought to maintain control over their quasi-free property. To do so, owners would restrict the blacks' relatively free movement, would demand a larger portion of their earnings, would refuse them permission to travel to visit loved ones, and would disregard any supposedly contracted promises of future freedom. Quasi-free blacks maneuvered as best they could within the system. Some of them, like Frederick Douglass, dreamed of a new life in the North, but most of them considered the South their home and their communities a haven ensured by families and friends and, not least, white "protectors."

Only as a last resort, then, did virtually free blacks choose to be fugitives. The nearly free Virginia slave Emanuel was routinely permitted to visit his wife in the District of Columbia, but on the occasion of one such visit he failed to return by the stipulated date. He had been absent several months when the owner dispatched an agent to apprehend him. Emanuel, however, "escaped and eloped"; the owner, in his turn, sold Emanuel while he was "running." With little in the way of evidence to support his claim for freedom, Emanuel nevertheless filed a freedom suit in the District's Circuit Court. It was rejected.[49] The Mississippi slave Pelagie Brown absconded because her owner refused to sell her with the "Special Condition" that she should be emancipated. She went undetected for twelve years in New Orleans, where, according to an article in the New Orleans Picayune, she "had a house well furnished, and was in the habit of letting out in rooms." Upon her discovery, she was arrested as a fugitive. She, too, lost the court battle against her owner.[50] A few slaves with the privileges of a quasi-free status or with the earnings to effect self-purchase fared better in their suits, albeit they had been arrested as runaways.[51] The great majority of virtually free slaves, however, recognized the power and authority of the master class and strove to achieve their freedom by appeasement rather than the risky alternative of abscondence.

More prone to abscond than term, self-purchased, and quasi-free slaves were blacks in bondage who had been promised but denied their freedom or who had lived in a free state or territory. On occasion they fled even after filing freedom suits; the slave Samuel, for instance, anticipating an adverse decision by a local court, broke out of jail and "escaped to places unknown" in the Mississippi Territory.[52] Slaves who had run away because they had been kept in bondage in spite of an owner's bequest of freedom in a will filed freedom suits by the same reason. Claims based on an owner's will, though, could be problematic, for however explicit the bequest and unambiguous the testator's intent, the slave's freedom was also likely to be conditional on the satisfaction of estate debt. "As it is my wish and desire that all my female negroes may be free at my decease," Maryland slave owner Elizabeth Richmond, who died in 1831, wrote, "unless my debts should require the sale of them, in which case I desire, that as many of them that is under the age of twenty-five, may be sold until they arrive at that age." It was stipulated that children under age six or seven should remain with their mothers. At the time of Richmond's death, one of her female slaves, Ann Barnett, over age thirty, was living in Baltimore and acting as a free woman. Five years later, she was arrested and jailed as a runaway slave. Ann sued the executor for her freedom and argued that the jury should be allowed to examine the record of the estate's income from hirelings so as to be able to determine whether that amount was sufficient to pay the testatrix's debts. The lower court ruled in favor of the plaintiff, and the appeals court concurred: the funds to pay debts were sufficient and the "right of the petitioner to her freedom could not be resisted."[53]

Not all cases ended as favorably for runaway slaves who had not been freed according to terms spelled out in a will or deed. Often the runaways had maintained good relations with their owners, but after the owner's death they had fallen under the control of heirs who had refused to abide by the testator's wishes or had indeed destroyed the will. To sort out the contending interests of the slaves, either as individuals or as family groups, and the heirs challenged the courts, the courts strove to ascertain the facts pertinent to the case and arrive at a just decision. On occasion, though, the courts extended less tolerance to slave plaintiffs who had absconded, even when documents clearly established their right to freedom. A plaintiff in New Orleans claimed that her deceased mistress had left a will instructing her son-in-law and executor to free her and her two children. Instead, the son-in-law had had her arrested and jailed—for two years. Witnesses for the defendant testified to the plaintiff's "bad reputation," her "thievish and insolent" character, and her habit of running away. The court ruled against her, as it did in the case of another New Orleans woman with a record as a runaway, on one occasion having remained at large for eight months.[54] In Louisiana law, as in the minds of many slaveholders, running away precluded any claim to freedom.[55] Runaways fared much the same in other states, though not by law. Usually they had been arrested and detained when they filed freedom suits, but their pleas fell on unsympathetic ears.[56] When an eight-member family in St. George's County, Maryland, discovered that their deceased owner's executor had no intention of freeing them in accordance with the owner's will, they absconded as a group to the District of Columbia. The executor offered a $300 reward for their apprehension, an offer published in the *National Intelligencer*. Shortly thereafter, the family was captured and jailed as runaways.[57]

Some blacks in bondage ran away for the express purpose of filing suits—in particular slaves who had been removed from Virginia to the District of Columbia and then sold to a party outside the District—because they had learned that Maryland state law in 1796 required an owner to be three years resident in the District prior to any such sale. An owner's violation of that law granted the slave freedom.[58] Some slaves likewise absconded to file suits when they learned that law and the courts in some states granted freedom to slaves if they had lived in the North with their owners, or with their owner's permission, for a length of time before returning to the South.[59] Notably in Delaware, the District of Columbia, and Kentucky, the fact that the plaintiffs in these cases were also runaways had little effect on the outcomes. More pertinent were the laws concerning slavery and freedom. Judge William Cranch of the District of Columbia, who ruled on many of these cases, made clear his priorities in an 1831 decision on the suit of a perpetual runaway, Mary, whose disgruntled owner had "sold her running." The judge refused to instruct the jury that the characterization of Mary as a run-away denied her the benefit of the anti-importation law. The jury found for the plaintiff.[60]

Kentucky courts often ruled similarly, but lodged their judgments primarily in the documentary evidence of wills and deeds. Among the more remarkable local decisions in the state were four favorable rulings on four suits brought by four men claiming their freedom by reason of their owner's will, in which William White of Jefferson County included a clause stating that the four men should work a farm on Goose Creek for eight years (1826–1834) and then be freed. White's heirs, however, had destroyed the will and created a "bogus bond," by which they held the four men in bondage several years past 1834. During that period, denied their freedom, "they all absconded, and did all abscond at one and the same time," one witness explained. "Willis also absconded once previously to that time, and Turner on several occasions previous to the general absconding." Upon their capture and return, they each filed a freedom suit against White's heirs. In 1840, Chancellor George M. Bibb not only decreed the four plaintiffs their freedom but also awarded each of them $500 in damages (each of three of them, as one of the plaintiffs, Charles, died prior to Bibb's final decree).[61]

Rarely did slave plaintiffs, having filed freedom suits, flee, because if they were captured, as runaways almost inevitably were, they would then be incarcerated for the months-long duration of the court's action on their suits. So, the cases of Jane Millis and Milly were exceptional. No one doubted that the Delaware slave Jane Millis hated being held in human bondage. In the 1822 case, one former owner testified that she had probably poisoned his horses, and he had heard her say that if he were "out of the way," she would quickly put her mistress "out of the way," too. Another witness related what happened the day she absconded: Her owner had taken her to Dixon's Tavern in Queen Ann's County, Maryland, where he planned to sell her to a slave trader in defiance of Delaware exportation law. As the transaction was being completed that mid-morning, Jane had escaped through a second-story window, jumped on top of a milk house, dropped down to the ground, and fled across the countryside. Eventually she had returned to Smyrna, Delaware, where she won her long-pursued freedom on the grounds of illegal exportation.[62]

The twenty-nine-year-old Missouri servant Milly claimed her freedom not on grounds of exportation law but by reason of residency statutes. In April 1819, she and her two young children, ages two and four, filed suit on the claim that Milly had lived with her owner in Illinois for two years. The owner replied that he had indeed taken Milly from Kentucky to Knox County in the (free) Indiana Territory, in 1805, but that they had agreed to an indenture by which she would be required to serve him for seventy years. On August 14, 1819, the court issued a writ of habeas corpus ordering the owner to appear in court with Milly, who had been released on her own recognizance. Three days later, the owner reported that Milly had run off and he had neither seen nor heard from her since. Nor would he or the court, ever. Anomalous as it was for black women to abandon family with whom they had filed a freedom suit, it is likely that Milly fled without her children.[63]

After passing more than six months in a North Carolina jail as a fugitive slave, Abraham Carpenter finally convinced the postmaster of New Bern, Thomas Watson, to try again to contact his father and other persons familiar with his family in Connecticut. Once he learned of his son's predicament, Isaac Carpenter, a loyal father despite Abraham's rebellious and delinquent behavior, immediately came to his aid. Then sixty, Isaac Carpenter had struggled for a life-time to raise and care for his family; an honest, hard-working, long-time resi-dent of Greenwich, Connecticut, he had also gained the respect of many white residents. He first went to see Ard Reynolds, whom he had known for many years, and asked him to write a letter on his son's behalf. Abraham was "a free man and a bad man," Reynolds wrote, "but notwithstanding his bad conduct I feel it my duty as an act of humanity to give this information to you that he may not be sold as a Slave." At the end of the letter, he referred the authorities to his brother, Hunter Reynolds, Esquire, a lawyer in Windsor, Bertie County, North Carolina, who, he said, would vouch for his truthfulness. Isaac meanwhile solicited other residents to verify that Abraham was freeborn, and seventeen cit-izens of the town of Greenwich signed a certificate to that effect. On March 9,

1830, Judge Robert Strange of the Craven County Court issued a writ of habeas corpus for the "Keeper of the Common Jail" to bring before him Abraham Carpenter and to state the cause of his detention. On the same day in the late afternoon the parties met at Bill's Tavern in New Bern. Upon hearing the evidence the judge ruled that Carpenter was indeed a free person and ordered his immediate release.[64]

10

Husbands and Wives

Arising some miles west of Dover, Delaware, the Choptank River, named for an Indian tribe, meanders southwest across the Delmarva Peninsula bay. It was on the banks of the Choptank—then heavily forested with oak, hickory, and chestnut trees—about three miles north of its head of navigation, at Edenton (later Denton), Maryland, that the first Hardcastles settled in 1748. In what was then Queen Anne's County—it was later incorporated into Caroline County—on the west bank of the Choptank, Robert Hardcastle established Hardcastle Landing, where he erected a gristmill and a comfortable home. Robert and, in time, his son Thomas prospered as millers, landowners, farmers, and businessmen.[1] During the American Revolution, they and their families supported the Continental forces, with Robert ranking as a first lieutenant and his grandson, John, as a second lieutenant in the local militia. Thomas served as a Caroline County justice of the peace.[2] In 1781, Thomas built an imposing brick mansion north of Goldsborough; it was called Castle Hall and was described as the most significant structure in northern Caroline County. The family's 1,268 acres of land[3] also accommodated Hardcastle's Mill, a large brick building that stood at the turning point for boats on the Choptank and functioned as a shipping center.[4] By the early nineteenth century, the Hardcastles were among the most well-known and well-to-do families along the Choptank. Together they owned large tracts of farmland, a splendid mill, and seventy-one slaves.[5]

Around 1802, John Hawkins, a twenty-year-old term slave, was hired as the "tenant" at Hardcastle's Mill by an arrangement with William Hughlett. Born and raised in Caroline County, Hawkins had been owned first by Joseph Dixon, a small slaveholding farmer, who had sold him, when he was in his teens, to Hughlett. How Hawkins acquired term-slave status is not known, but it is likely that he paid his owner for the privilege, by which he was in effect purchasing his future freedom. He was, however, unquestionably a slave when he began his tenancy, although he was responsible for managing the millworkers who ground wheat into flour for allotments to local families and shipments to Philadelphia and abroad. In due time his term of servitude expired and Hawkins became a free man.[6]

In the meantime, he had started a family with a slave named Lydia, owned by John Cooper, a farmer who lived near the mill, and during the first decade of the nineteenth century the couple had four children: Benjamin, born about 1802; Anna, about 1804; and Nancy and William, born in 1808 and 1809 respectively. Lydia had at first been living on her owner's farm, but after the birth of Benjamin she moved to the mill to live with her husband and raise their family. Lydia had in fact been permitted by her owner to go "at liberty" as a quasi-free slave. A neighbor who had known the family when they lived together at the mill recalled that the father and mother "always acted as free persons." He noted, too, that Lydia's owner had provided them with grain and meat "to assist them in supporting themselves while they were there."[7] In 1807, when Cooper moved to Kent County, Delaware, he allowed Lydia to remain behind with her family, and on January 1, 1810, she was formally freed when Cooper signed a deed of manumission.[8]

Lydia's four children, however, remained in bondage and according to the deed of manumission would not receive their freedom until they reached the age of twenty-five. Until then, they remained the property of John Cooper, although they were allowed to reside with their parents until such time that they became "serviceable." The children had not yet entered their teens when they were taken from their parents and placed in the service of Cooper's two sons. About 1813, Samuel B. Cooper took possession of the older two children—Benjamin, then about eleven, and Anna about nine—whom he removed first to Delaware, then to Tuckahoe Neck in Maryland's Caroline County, and—in 1816 or 1817— back to Delaware.[9] In 1819, when Nancy and William were eleven and twelve, John Cooper's other son, Richard D. Cooper, turned up at Hardcastle's Mill and laid claim to the younger two children, whom he took to his rented farm in Whiteleysburgh, Delaware. They remained there for a year and a half,[10] during which time Cooper rented William to a local farmer with property straddling the Maryland-Delaware line. William proved to be of little help at "thinning" the corn crop, and after a few months the dissatisfied farmer returned him to Cooper, complaining that William was too young and too small to do a decent day's work and not even worth his "victuals and clothing." About 1821, Cooper moved back to Nine Bridges, Maryland, along with the two youngsters.[11]

The history of the Hawkins family is unusual only in that the documentary evidence detailing the lives of a single African-American family is so complete. How many families were similarly sundered is incalculable, but the grim statistics tracking the vigorous domestic slave trade in the counties on Maryland's Eastern Shore, and indeed throughout the Upper South, during the antebellum era suggest that many families experienced anguish like the Hawkinses. By the 1820s, the interregional slave trade accounted for a huge portion—about 70 percent—of the slaves migrating annually from the Upper South to the lower states. Of them, about one in ten was a teen and one in eleven was in his or her twenties. After 1815, a slave residing in the Upper South had about a one-in-three chance of being traded out of state. Of all the interstate sales— approximately two-thirds of one million—that were made by traders, one out of four ruptured a nuclear family, either by forcibly separating one spouse from another or by taking a child from one or both parents. About half of the African Americans traded were of marriageable age, yet only 2 percent of the slave trade comprised spouses with their children. Thus, nuclear families complete with husband, wife, and children were almost totally absent from the domestic slave trade. Even discounting marriages that were broken voluntarily or because of a husband's death, three out of four mother-offspring sales still effected the painful separation of husbands from wives and fathers from their children. Anguish is immeasurable, all the more so in that these statistics do not include the in-state or in-county buying and selling that also rent apart so many slave families.[12]

Only a tiny fraction of the African Americans who found themselves ensnared in the domestic slave trade were able to extricate themselves from their situations through the courts. However, the freedom suits they filed are revelatory in their depictions of the plight suffered by slave plaintiffs generally and, more particularly, of their own personal struggles to maintain family unity in the face of imminent disruption. Manifest, too, are the emotions attendant to their efforts—the anguish, fear, trepidation, sorrow, pain, torment, and anger— as, driven by the immediacy of their possible separation, mothers and fathers, husbands and wives, strove to protect the cocoon of family. The principle of *partus sequitur ventrem* (slaves followed the condition of their mothers) accounts for the disproportionately large number of women who filed suits on their own and their children's behalf, usually on claims of manumission by a deed or will, even though the male-female ratio among those who filed suits remained about equal. Free black fathers, however, often assumed an active role in the prosecution of suits filed by their slave wives and children, as John Hawkins did so tirelessly. Fathers thus acquired visibility in the judiciary process pursuant to their families' freedom suits, whereas they were usually notably absent in the records of slaveholders, who defined the African American family in terms only of the mother and child or children.

The anxiety among black family members that they might be separated and sold or have members of their families sold before they had filed a freedom suit, or that they might be removed by their owners outside the court's jurisdiction during the course of a trial, sometimes escalated into panic. To allay their fears, some families, even before suits were filed, requested protective injunctions against owners, traders, estate managers, and heirs, who, they said, planned either to sell them or to take them out of the court's jurisdiction. Clara, a woman of color in the District of Columbia, echoed the sentiments of many other plaintiffs when she said she had "just grounds to fear & believe" that she and her children "will not be safe in his [the defendant's] possession," as she believed that he planned to "sell them away to distant places."[13]

The urgency in these requests was not unwarranted, nor was the dread that families might be fractured before the court could render a decision about their status. Children were in fact taken from their parents and either conveyed to "distant places" or retained by whites who refused to surrender them, as injunctions ordering that parties involved in such actions to cease and desist indicate. Some injunctions sought to protect a family member who might have been, or in the event that he or she might be, sold; others, to protect a wife, husband, or child who had without question changed owners. In the latter cases, the persons involved in the sale and/or purchase were often cited. Indeed, some injunctions listed by name two or three owners or traders who possessed various family members, not only husbands, wives, and children but also brothers, sisters, aunts, uncles, nieces, and nephews. In 1807, District of Columbia slave Andrew Ross petitioned for freedom for himself as well as for his sister and her two children, and at the same time requested an injunction to prevent his owners, specified by name, from taking away or selling any one or all of them.[14] Ross was thus spared the anguish of the free black father in Maryland who had made arrangements to purchase his wife and child from their owner only to discover in 1818 that they had been transferred by the owner to his sister, the owner claiming that the father had given up "all rights" to his slave wife and child.[15] He was also spared the terror of a mother in Kentucky who related to the court how she and her two sons "were taken off in the night . . . by force" and how the abductor who held them planned to take them to "distant parts where she will not be able to procure testimony of her freedom."[16]

When the chancery, or equity, courts issued injunctions (they could not be issued by law courts), the wording was clear and unambiguous. "Whereas Negress Sally Baker for herself and her two children Jeffery and Mary Baker has filed her Bill of Complaint in the Circuit for the County," one read, "for certain reasons and considerations therein set forth," the owner or owners or the agents of the owner or owners "[are] strictly prohibited from moving or selling out of this Washington County in [the] District the said Negroes or any one of them until their petition for freedom which they have filed in his Court shall be determined or until the further order of this Court in the premises."[17] The chancery court could put the family members in protective custody, if it was deemed necessary, or could require a bond equal, or nearly equal, to the value of the family members held in bondage. It could also afford the protection granted by an injunction to families who feared they had already been sold and within hours would be transported, probably separately, out of state. Such was the case in Maryland for Charity, Kitty, Mary, and Mary's infant son, who claimed that they were entitled to their freedom "at their respective ages of thirty-one years," but they had now come into the possession of three different white men who planned to remove them out of the state and make them slaves for life.[18] Likewise, a North Carolina woman who sought an injunction to protect her and her three children asserted that they had been sold to a man who would either try "to run her, & her children off & sell them" or return them to the owner, whom she "verily believes would send her to the South & sell her, as he is engaged in the Traffic of Slaves."[19]

A common, not unreasonable fear shared by many plaintiffs in the Upper South was the possibility that their families would be sold to slave traders who would transport them to the Lower South and sell them separately to planters and farmers. Their requests for injunctions pointed to "traffickers" in human flesh, unprincipled "negro traders," and factors willing to break up slave families for a profit. Many traders, too, refused to deal in small children, so they would buy the parent and leave the children behind. The fear of sale to traders especially prompted slaves who had been granted manumission at a future date, or who would be freed upon the probating of a will, to seek injunctions. Some suits related harrowing stories of family members who had already been taken off by force in the middle of the night and were now being readied for transport to "distant parts" where they would not be able to procure testimony of their freedom.[20] When the free black mother of nine children agreed to move to Kentucky to be with her slave husband, his owner, she explained, had acted "in bad faith": he had invited a slave trader to inspect her children for possible sale. The request for an injunction to prevent the husband's owner from selling her and her children was granted.[21]

Others were less fortunate. Often plaintiffs were racing against time to obtain court action in a freedom suit against owners and traders who were seeking to arrange a sale of slave families. Sometimes they had only just learned from newspaper advertisements for their sale that they were in jeopardy, even if they were free or about to be freed.[22] Or they had by chance heard rumors that a former master had "designs upon their freedom" and was planning, as two free black children in Virginia said, to move away and sell them "as slaves in foreign servitude."[23] A Kentucky woman in her forties who had lived in the Michigan Territory as an indentured servant for a number of years and then returned to the South managed to save one of her daughters and herself from a sale, but she was unable to gain protection for her slave husband and their five other children, who were "carried off" by a man named Robert Turner despite, she said, being entitled to their freedom: a heart-rending, soul-piercing outcome for a mother named Sally.[24]

At best, injunctions that were issued and served on defendants could often offer only limited protection, especially for term slaves who sought to safeguard their families from future sales with court orders that they not be exported from the state during the time—in many cases, years—remaining in their term. The problem was that between the issuance of an injunction and the expiration of a term a decade or more later, events could have altered the complexion of a case; parents bearing the term might have died and the children, now growing into adolescence, would have increased in value to their owners and in the eyes of speculators. The court could require that an "ample and sufficient" bond be posted by the owner of a term slave, but which conditions for either party might apply at the expiration of "said term of service" in twenty years, as one injunction stated, were not at all certain.[25]

In one such case, despite an injunction against their removal, the fate of three generations of an Alabama slave family that had been freed in a will was drastically altered when the executor of the estate "clandestinely" conveyed them to Tennessee for the purpose of "selling or disposing of them as slaves."[26] Still, many slave families' fears of "imminent peril of being deprived of all benefit" of their freedom were abated when those who obtained injunctions—which included the great majority of those who sought them—were able to secure some measure of protection, at least for a period of time, against being sold or being taken out of the courts' jurisdiction.[27]

Because slaveholders for the most part defined slave families in terms of the mother and her offspring—the status of the father being inconsequential by law to that of a child at birth—slave husbands and fathers only rarely filed freedom suits that also included their wives and children or other close family members. Even more rarely did they and their counsel file what might be called "family suits" in common law courts. So the filing of a family suit in a Kentucky county court by the slave Ralph, "an old man of color," along with his wife and daughter, both named Jenny, was in every way unusual. The suit alleged that the family's former owner, Thomas Hogan, "did freely and voluntarily" manumit them after they "had served him faithfully for many years and borne with humble submission the galling yoke of Slavery." After the master's death, however, they had been seized and sold by Thomas Jones, the administrator of Hogan's estate, who, opined Ralph and his lawyer, did not have "the fear of God before his eyes, but [was] moved and seduced by the mammon of avarice and unrighteousness." Ralph and his lawyer asked that the new owner be prevented from removing them from the jurisdiction of the court, and that Ralph and his family be permitted to attend when the court heard the suit they had filed to establish their freedom. The suit was denied.[28]

Far more common was the intervention by free black fathers seeking to extricate loved ones from bondage. Most courts of the Upper South and Louisiana allowed free blacks to file suits on behalf of family members, either as plaintiffs, co-plaintiffs, or next friends, whereby they acted in the capacity of a guardian although they were not referred to as such in the court proceedings. In cases brought on behalf of slave children, free black fathers contacted lawyers, arranged for the drafting of complaints (in a few instances, the fathers themselves wrote the complaints), and accompanied their children in court. In Delaware, free black fathers filed a number of suits in the court of common pleas to effect the release of their sons and daughters either from oppressive indentures or from slavery. Abraham Emory, for one, in the capacity of co-plaintiff, accompanied his son Toney and his daughter Phobe in the Kent County Court in 1804. He pled for their release from bondage on the grounds that they were being illegally detained. Other free black fathers went to court as next friends rather than co-complainants, but their purpose was the same: to secure free status for their children.[29]

Whereas the Delaware freedom suits brought by free black fathers tended to be simple and straightforward, with little detail in regard to the background of a case, the suits filed in other states usually included a considerable measure of specific information in their charges against owners, traders, estate administrators, and heirs. Bacchus Beall, a free person of color in Maryland, served as the next friend for his two sons in their case against the administrator of an estate who had claimed the boys as estate property when they should have been freed. The father traced the history of his family, and noted particularly that his wife, Rachel, a term slave, had in fact been freed before the boys' birth. The defendant argued that the mother had been freed only because her behavior had been "so bad" that the owner's widow "would not agree for her to come home." The county court ruled in favor of the children, but the court of appeals overturned the verdict and ruled in favor of the defendant.[30] In the District of Columbia, free black Lewis Butler, as a next friend suing on behalf of his son John, asked the law court to issue a writ of habeas corpus in order to free him from the possession of a Georgetown slaveholder who was holding him illegally as a slave. The defendant, Sampson Simms, then produced a deed of indenture, in which the boy, at age fifteen, had indentured himself until he reached age twenty-one and promised to "demean himself honestly, faithfully and obediently as a good servant should do." The court, however, granted the writ ordering the boy out of Simms's custody.[31]

Free black fathers also intervened on behalf of wives, mothers, fathers, and other slave kin, not uncommonly by seeking to purchase the loved ones.[32] Permission to purchase was gained by agreement, sometimes in the form of a contract, with the slave relative's master. If an owner died, however, free black husbands and fathers were likely to discover that any such agreements had been voided by estate heirs and estate administrators who cited the need to divide up the property and sell slaves in order to meet the estate's debt. As one administrator put it, even though a free black husband had paid the purchase price for his wife, he did not have the right to demand her freedom.[33]

In some cases, free men of color bargained with masters to reduce the asking price for a wife or daughter or son, and succeeded; but often the slaveholders took advantage of the husbands' or fathers' desperation. Self-purchased Kentucky free black Jacob Sampson, "exercising the rights & privileges of a free man," paid the owner of his wife Elizabeth and their four children $250 as part of a purchase price, as per an agreement. Following the owner's death, Sampson continued to pay the heirs "several sums of money" in his mistaken belief that they were "authorized to receive it." The heirs did not inform Sampson otherwise, and Sampson lost the suit he filed against them. The heirs not only kept the money but also retained the wife and children.[34]

Free blacks in other states encountered similar difficulties in dealing with owners, heirs, estate administrators, and sometimes even fellow free blacks. In 1840, a Charleston, South Carolina, free black husband and father, Peter Dewees, secured the assistance of a fellow free person of color, John Francis, in purchasing his wife and children. Indeed, Francis agreed to buy Dewees's family from their owner and to pass the title to them on to Dewees once he had been fully reimbursed. After some years, though, Francis demanded payment in full of the balance outstanding on the agreed-on price of $1,000. When Dewees failed to raise the full amount, his "friend" sold the wife and children. And when, in 1854, fourteen years after the agreement with Francis, Dewees had finally saved the money to pay the amount in full, the new owner refused to accept the original terms of purchase. He complained that Dewees's wife was "unsound," that the eldest daughter was "completely deaf," and that the second daughter had "a large and ugly mark upon the face which greatly deteriorates from her value"; but he would not sell.[35]

A Tennessee slave wife found herself in much the same predicament as Dewees's wife. Her husband, too, had borrowed part of the money to pay for her and their two daughters, but the "note, bond, mortgage, bill or sale or other instrument" had been transferred to a third party who was demanding payment in full. The slave wife, Eliza Brooks, and her lawyer argued that the purpose of the sale was to procure the emancipations of Eliza and her daughters and that the note holder should not be permitted to force her husband into the gruesome act of selling his own wife and children. The court agreed with the plaintiff and released the family to her husband, Robert Brooks.[36]

Many free black men succeeded in purchasing loved ones, not solely by reason of their persistence. As more and more free persons of color entered skilled occupations with earnings that enabled them to acquire land and personal property, especially in the Upper South and Louisiana, slaveholders became increasingly more willing to assist the most exemplary among them in achieving the unity and freedom of their families by purchase. Certainly the successful efforts of free men of color in that purpose accounted in part for the growth of the free black populations in Delaware, Maryland, Virginia, North Carolina, and Louisiana during the early period of the republic.

By and large, private purchase transactions did not require the sanction of the courts; however, if husbands and fathers wished to gain legally acknowledged free status for their families, they had no recourse but the courts, or, in some states, the state legislatures—and then, if freedom was granted, by law in most states, they would have to leave the state. As a consequence, either to avoid exit laws or to forgo what could be a fruitless petition for freedom in the state assembly, free black men frequently chose to keep in bondage the wives and children they had duly purchased, duly having been by a long, often grueling process. For purchase could take years, even when the men passed the greater part of their earnings—often more than one hundred dollars a year—on to the slaveholders who owned members of their families. During the late antebellum era the earning power of free blacks rose significantly, but purchase payments still commanded a substantial percentage of the blacks' new wealth. The $1,000 that Peter Dewees paid over a period of fourteen years would be the equivalent of about $26,000 in today's economy.[37]

Whatever the advantages of maintaining slave status for families freed by purchase, the security of their situation remained a cause for their free husbands' and fathers' concern: What would happen, for instance, if the head of the household sheltering them fell ill? Or went into debt? Or died? Such contingencies prompted free black men, in states where it was possible, to pursue the acquisition of free papers for their family members through the courts. In some cases, they contacted lawyers for assistance in filing the freedom suits on behalf of their slave kin, rather than acting as next friends or co-plaintiffs. In others, they joined with their slave relatives in a suit. The narratives in the suits were often predicated on the wording of state manumission laws, which required descriptions of the parties to be freed along with commentary on their character. The free blacks appealed to judges, and sometimes to juries as well, with evidence as to the age of their wives (some states had enacted age limits for emancipations), the length of their unions, the children they had borne together, and the character of their spouses—their industry, honesty, reliability, and trustworthiness; or, as one Tennessee husband put it, his wife and children possessed "industrious habits & have uniformly conducted & demeaned themselves as peaceable persons & have always manifested a proper respect & submission, to the white population of this community."[38]

North Carolina free black Job Hazell said in 1821 that he wished to free his wife "in consequence of and as a reward for meritorious services by her performed" during their thirty years together. Among those services was her assistance to him in saving enough money to purchase their thirteen-year-old daughter, whom he also sought to emancipate, from her owner. Furthermore, she had instilled in their family members "habits of sobriety and industry"; their other children, still in bondage, were "valuable servants to their respective owners." Hazell's appeal followed almost exactly the wording of the state's man-umission law concerning industrious habits and "meritorious service."[39] Similar arguments were employed by free black men in suits to gain legal freedom for their slave mothers, fathers, sisters, brothers, aunts, uncles, nephews, and some-times grandparents.[40]

Manumission law in Louisiana required evidence of "good and faithful serv-ices" and "good conduct," and free men of color, in suits filed to free the wives and children and other relatives they owned, provided testimony to that effect, often using the language of the statute. In accordance with the law, they also sometimes requested an exemption from the state's requirement that only slaves over age thirty could be manumitted. When François Larche, a free man of color, petitioned for the freedom of his "natural children & slaves," a boy named Zalsin and a girl named Charlotte, both of them "under the age of thirty years," he requested that the parish court authorize him to file a "deed of emancipation" and order the sheriff to make "the usual publications" in a local newspaper con-cerning the impending emancipation so that he could "legally manumit" his two "natural children and slaves."[41]

Like many freedom suits filed in Louisiana, and unlike those in other states, the case brought by Eugène Alexisto, a free black father and husband, to the po-lice jury in St. John the Baptist Parish made a point of skin color. As the owner of a twenty-three-year-old mulatto woman named Azurine and her two "griff" children (i.e., offspring of a black and a mulatto), eight-year-old Eugène and six-year-old Agathe, Alexisto wished to free his family "from the bonds of slavery" and, at the same time, to reward Azurine for her good and faithful service. He attested that he was the "natural" father of the children and that his wife had always exemplified "good conduct," in that, and as required by state law, she had never run away or committed any crime or misdemeanor.[42] In Louisiana freedom suits, complexion, griff or otherwise, and the "natural" relation of a fa-ther to a child were as relevant as proper conduct.[43] To further their "natural" offsprings' cases, some free colored fathers had their slave children baptized; as one New Orleans father explained, since his son had been baptized "as free," he was "so considered" by everyone ever since. On being advised that his son's freedom was "not valid," the father asked the court then to make him "really free" so as to ensure that he would not be treated as a slave after the father's death.[44]

The struggle of free black John Hawkins to liberate his family did not end with the abduction of his two youngest children. In 1820, at the November Term of the Kent County Court of Common Pleas in Delaware, acting as what was essentially a guardian, Hawkins filed two suits on behalf of his four children against Samuel Cooper and Richard Cooper, the two sons of his wife's former owner, John Cooper. Over the next two years, Hawkins obtained depositions from a dozen Delaware and Maryland residents who verified the ages of the children and the names of the owner's sons, and confirmed the fact that the children had been taken by the sons from Maryland into Delaware and then back to Maryland: Benjamin and Anna by Samuel Cooper, Nancy and William by Richard Cooper. In May 1822, six witnesses were deposed. Fifty-five-year-old John Bennett stated that he had known the plaintiffs from the time they were born; that they had lived at Hardcastle's Mill with their parents, John and Lydia Hawkins; and that at a young age they had been taken from their parents by Cooper's sons and transported into Delaware, where they had remained for varying periods of time. Betsey Faulkner confirmed Bennett's testimony, as did sixty-year-old John Connor, who noted that he had known the parents as well as the children "since they were small." Perhaps the most damning evidence against the two defendants came from their own father, John Cooper, who testified that when he had discovered Richard had taken Nancy and William from Maryland into Delaware in defiance of the state's nonimportation law, he had chastised his son and told him to return them to Maryland. In response, Richard had told him that if he did they would be "apprehended & sent off in some other direction," referring to the anti-importation statute in that state.[45]

Despite the evidence, transcribed and submitted to the court, the suits never went to trial. At every biannual session over the next two and a half years the defendants requested and received continuances. At the November 1824 term, Hawkins discontinued the suits by placing his mark on the court order.[46] It is highly probable that the Hawkins children were finally freed, especially since John Cooper and his son Samuel, despite being a defendant, both favored the manumissions.

John Hawkins and Lydia, meanwhile, had been living in Caroline County, Maryland, and had had three additional children—Charity, Sally, and John—all of them freeborn after their mother's manumission. But the father's difficulties were not over. In 1826, John Cooper's son-in-law, John Willoughby, who lived near the Hawkins family in Caroline County, convinced Cooper that the manumissions he had executed in Delaware were not valid in Maryland and that Cooper thus faced possible prosecution for allowing his former slaves to move there. Willoughby, who owned no slaves, then "seduced" Cooper into signing a deed that conveyed Lydia and her three freeborn children to Willoughby and to Cooper's sons, Richard and Samuel, as well as to other white relatives. Soon afterward, Willoughby and Richard Cooper had Lydia and her three children incarcerated at the Sussex County jail with "the intention of selling them to southern traders."

When they learned of the jailing, John Cooper and Samuel Cooper demanded, and obtained, the release of the black family. Lydia and her children were not bothered again during John Cooper's lifetime, but in 1836, following his death, Willoughby again took unwarranted action against them. With a gang of armed men he kidnapped the Hawkinses' three children, along with the children of other women who had been manumitted by John Cooper, and bore them to the jail in Queen Anne's County, Maryland. Willoughby's objective to sell them to "foreign traders, or carry them to the south himself" was thwarted by Samuel Cooper who, in an oath he cosigned with two of his siblings, declared that his father had "never pretended" that Lydia and her three children were slaves; that he had never signed a deed for their sale a decade earlier; and that he had wished to "protect them in their Just rights." The case for their freedom was still pending in Queen Anne's County, Maryland, when John Hawkins petitioned the Delaware General Assembly to pass an act that would affirm the legality of his wife's manumission and the free status of his three children. In 1840, John Hawkins, age about fifty-eight, headed a household in Caroline County that included two free black women between ages twenty-four and thirty-five, and a girl under age ten. He had apparently rescued several of his children and perhaps a grandchild, but he had almost certainly lost his wife Lydia, who probably died during the late 1830s. John Hawkins's struggles over a period of nearly seventeen years delineate but one case among many that constantly manifested the pressures on free blacks in their perseverant efforts to secure and maintain the freedom of their families.[47]

11

Mothers and Children

On Friday, August 17, 1838, Anne Edinbro, a twenty-year-old term slave, filed a suit in the Circuit Court of the District of Columbia for the county of Washington sitting as a court of chancery. Although not mentioned in the proceedings, Anne was not present in the courtroom; the suit was filed by her mother, former term slave and quasi-free black Jane Edinbro, acting as what was called a "next friend," or guardian. The panic-stricken mother explained through her counsel and in a sworn deposition on the same day that two nights before Robert Earle had entered her home and forcefully taken her daughter off into the night. Earle told the mother that he was the rightful owner of Anne and his "avowed purpose" was to sell the young woman to "a negro buyer" who would take her to "Georgia or anywhere else that he chose." In fact, Jane soon discovered that Earle had already sold Anne to David Waters, described as a "buyer of slaves." Late in the afternoon, Jane went to Waters's home, but his wife told her that he was probably on his way to Georgia.

The day after the abduction, Jane not only obtained the services of the well-known lawyer, Clement Cox, but notified her former mistress, Mary Heugh, who owned Jane's five other term-slave children. Heugh also confronted Earle seeking the whereabouts of Anne, but he refused to say where she was, telling her that "he had her safe" in close and secret custody. Unlike Earl's response to Jane, however, he told the mistress that he did not intend to sell Anne out of the District as required in the deed of Anne's future manumission, which was to be on December 31, 1846. In response to the complaint, the court granted the injunction and ordered the two defendants to appear and answer the charges.[1]

As suggested by the case of Jenny Edinboro, it was far more common for slave mothers to bring freedom suits with their children than it was for slave fathers. Although black men were regularly listed in estate inventories and frequently cited in journals, correspondence, diaries, and even magazine articles and religious tracts, slave fathers rarely figured in the definition of family either by slaveholders or in law. Although no state other than Louisiana (in 1806) enacted a law prohibiting the sale of children under ten without their mothers, owners in every state linked slave children only to the mother. Hardly ever did the sale of a slave family include the slave father.

Pregnant mothers were all the more prized, as buyers—especially large plantation owners and wealthy urban slaveholders with cash to place in a long-term investment—were always on the lookout for what were called "good breeders." The value placed on slave women who had borne or potentially could bear children is apparent in the advertisement of a plantation owner wanting to purchase "a negro woman about twenty four or five years of age of good qualities that would breed." So, too, a planter in St. James Santee Parish, South Carolina, instructed one of his heirs to be sure "to buy young Breeding wenches." Another planter specified in his will that a slave named Leah should be hired out until the owner's youngest daughter reached age eight, and if the "said negro woman should not breed or increase" by that time, she should be sold.[2] Similarly, the guardian of a young heir to an estate in Maryland, petitioned an orphans court to sell a female slave who had failed to "increase": She had already lost four babies who had died shortly after birth and, the petitioner reasoned, she was thus unlikely to produce any healthy babies in the future.[3] Then there was the Virginia slaveowner Fleming Saunders who complained bitterly about having been placed in charge of his deranged sister-in-law's slaves, among them a number of "breeding women with their families." Since they could not be hired out without great difficulty, he had been "put to great trouble, inconvenience, and expense" in raising "a large number of young negroes & their mothers."[4] Though Saunders, atypically, saw no gain in the fertility of the slave women in his charge, he did, like all slaveowners, overseers, plantation managers, factors, traders, and planters, define the slave family as mothers with their children.

Slave mothers who filed suits for their freedom with their children were exceeded by those who filed without them by a ratio of about 2.5 to 1. The women who sued alone often did so without choice, because they had already suffered the loss of their children to the slave trade, which had taken them to distant areas of the southern states. Suits that were filed by women with their children in common law courts were almost invariably rejected, and the children were required, with guardians, to file their own individual claims for freedom.[5] Chancery, or equity, courts, however, allowed mothers filing suits with their children more latitude, and they could petition for freedom on grounds that they had previously been manumitted, or had lived in a free territory, or were descended from a free woman of color, a white woman, or a woman of Indian ancestry.[6]

In 1797, in Maryland, Rachel Baker, her three children, five grandchildren, and two great-grandchildren, along with Henny Baker and her five children and two grandchildren, claimed that they were "descended from an Indian woman named Moll or Mary that the Said Moll or Mary was a free native of America."

As a consequence, they argued, they were entitled to their freedom "from their birth" and were thus being unlawfully held as slaves by John Paca of Queen Anne's County. The court granted the two women and their three generations of children free status.[7] In those early years in Maryland, female slave plaintiffs had another advantage: free mothers, without being co-petitioners or next friends, could testify in court on behalf of their children.[8]

In Delaware, a number of black women sought to free themselves and their children. It is sometimes difficult to determine the slave or free status of the mothers, as they are cited in the court records simply as "a Negro," "Negro woman," "woman of color," or "mulatto women," or are otherwise listed in a group as "people of color." In addition, the plaintiffs often did not include in their claims specific details as to why they and their children should be freed; nor did they document particulars regarding their search for a lawyer, their drafting of arguments and contacting of witnesses, or their appearance in court. What is clear, however, is that many black women exerted extraordinary efforts to protect their offspring.[9] One mother of a large family told the court that it should take action quickly, since she had already lost several of her children, who had been sold and transported to the most distant "Parts of this Continent." She was petitioning for herself and her remaining children. Other plaintiffs simply stated that they and their offspring were being illegally detained in bondage and therefore, according to law, should be declared free.[10]

In suits filed in the early decades of the nineteenth century, female slave plaintiffs and their children, primarily in the Upper South and Louisiana, charged that they were term slaves who had been denied their right to freedom upon the expiration of their servitude.[11] Further, if they were pleading together with their children and, in some cases, their grandchildren, they argued, validly, that the offspring born after the mother's term had ended were equally free. Many of these petitions evince a sense of urgency, because if the courts failed to act promptly, family members included in the suit feared they might be transported to another state and sold as slaves for life.[12] Other plaintiffs claimed that they and their children were being held in bondage despite the fact that they had been freed in a deed of manumission.[13] Still others asserted that free black relatives had purchased them and their children but the purchases had not been recorded, or that they had been emancipated by the courts years earlier. Such was the case of a Louisiana woman who claimed in 1817 that a judgment rendered in a Spanish court many years before had freed her and her six children.[14]

Many suits filed by slave women and their children in the states of the Upper South and Louisiana claimed that they had been granted freedom by their owners in wills and deeds but had not been permitted to assume it. In some estate cases, as they were called, relatives of the testator refused to honor the conditions of the will upon his or her death, and often the slaves that suffered the effects of the heirs' bad faith were women and their children.[15] The Tennessee slave Nancy recounted in the suit she filed with her lawyer how her late mistress, Sally Mahan, had become so attached to her and her children that "she never intended that they should be held in slavery after her death but would emancipate and set them free." Mahan's brother had been present when she prepared her will, and he had told her that the best way to ensure her slaves' emancipation was to bequeath them to him on the condition that he would arrange for their freedom. Not only had he then chosen to disregard his deceased sister's last wishes; he had also put up Nancy and her family as collateral for a mortgage— and, during the progress of Nancy's freedom suit, he sold one of her children, Mahala, age eight, to Richmond Tyree.[16]

The Virginia slave Barbara and her two children made a similar claim against her owner's adult children when they failed to abide by the terms of a last will and testament promising the slave family their freedom upon the owner's death. Like many other plaintiffs, Barbara feared that their owner's heirs were planning to send her and her children "to distant parts" and force them "to be detained forever in Slavery."[17] Some estate cases occurred in states where it was highly unusual for slaves to file freedom suits, such as Florida. There, in 1836, the slave Belinda asked the court to require the executors of her former owner's estate to provide funds for the emancipations of herself and her children, as per stipulations in the owner's will. The executors argued that Belinda and her children were being retained to serve as security for the owner's unsettled debts, but the court ruled in favor of the slaves nonetheless.[18] Estates that remained unsettled for lengthy periods often caused women and their children undue suffering. During a long-extended case in Missouri, the slave mother Malinda witnessed the death of one of her children; another slave, Sena, became critically ill during her pregnancy and lost her child. The administrator lamented a pattern of infant mortality and approved payments for doctors, funerals, and coffins.[19]

Among the most wrenching personal narratives in family-filed freedom suits are those related by free mothers of color.[20] Fear and anxiety prevail in grim accounts of former owners or their agents who had taken children from their free mothers and retained them in servitude, or were planning to place them on the auction block.[21] Or of children and loved ones who had already been sold to slave traders now preparing to convey them outside the court's jurisdiction.[22] Or of strangers, appearing as if out of nowhere, who had seized the children of long-freed black women and sold them as slaves.[23] In panic, a Pennsylvania-born free black woman in Kentucky pleaded that the sheriff take her and her daughter Emily, who were about to be forcibly removed from the state and sold into slavery, into custody until her suit for freedom was decided, or else that the defendants post bond sufficient to ensure they would not remove the petitioners from the court's jurisdiction.[24]

In Virginia, a free woman of color and her daughter were confiscated by one of her deceased husband's creditors, who then advertised them for sale; in desperation, the mother sought an injunction to prevent herself and her daughter from being cast into bondage.[25] Other free women and their children were jailed or put in what were called "work houses" after an owner's creditors had seized them and arranged for them to be sent to New Orleans, the slave trading capital of the South.[26] No matter how long a woman of color had been free or how long after she had gained her free status her children had been born, there were no guarantees that free mothers and their children would not be apprehended and detained in custody, "depriving them of their liberty," as one Missouri free woman of color said of herself and her infant child, "without any charge of a criminal or supposed criminal nature . . . without any just cause whatever."[27] Another Missouri free woman recounted what could happen when authorities did not respond to a mother's plea: She had been transferred to and from five different men, "all negro and slave traders and dealers"; after her sons were born they too had been confined in "negro yards or Jails."[28]

An auctioneer extols the value of the human property to an audience of men who purchase slaves. On the auction block, the downcast mother and the frightened child await their fate. Such scenes occurred regularly in locations across the South. *Edmund Ollier, Cassell's History of the United States, 3 vols. (London, New York: Cassell, Petter & Galpin, 1874), vol. 3, p. 199*

Free women of color, then, had to be constantly vigilant of anyone who might pose a threat to themselves and their children. As protective measures, they sometimes sought out whites with whom they could establish amicable relationships, and in a few instances, they asked slaveholders to act as next friends in court actions to extricate their children from bondage.[29] In the towns and cities of the Upper South, they engaged lawyers who had reputations for assisting black people in precarious or dangerous situations. They initiated court actions to secure injunctions and writs of habeas corpus so as to be able to pro-tect themselves and their children from unscrupulous slave traders and illegal removals as well as unwarranted detentions. In the slave-trading center of the District of Columbia, in numerous instances, free black women and their chil-dren, as well as abducted boys and girls in their teens, who were being held in jails and readied for removal to South Carolina or Georgia, filed complaints against owners or traders who, they alleged, planned to ship them south.[30] In the 1847 case brought by Winny Cryer, she attested that she and her child, Turner, had been living as free people in the District of Columbia for more than twelve years but were now being claimed by a white woman as her property. Either the white woman or her agent, Winny believed, intended to sell them out of the District, in which event they would have no recourse to prove their free status. Winny's freedom suit also included her other son, Joshua, who was in jeopardy as well. In her petition to sue, as in her request for an injunction, Winny's fears for herself and her sons are palpable. Both petitions were granted.[31]

Instances in which free black women were able to purchase their children were few, as they rarely had the wherewithal to meet the price that owners set on freedom. For the most part, free black women worked at menial tasks or labored in the fields, so their earning power hardly compared to that of skilled free black men; and since many free women of color were the sole support of their families, what little money they did earn could barely feed their children let alone buy them their freedom at costs reaching hundreds of dollars. Equally rare were purchases of slave husbands by their free black wives. Almost without excep-tion, free women of color who wished to "ransom their enslaved kin and dis-entangle their families from white masters," as one historian wrote, confronted challenging economic conditions.[32] Not only was their earning power usually low, but also the white masters were not, by and large, favorably disposed to long-term installment plans when they could sell the slave children to traders for immediate and more money, in the face of and in spite of of legal restrictions.

The few women who did manage to purchase husbands or children or both lived mostly in towns and cities, where they worked as seamstresses, laundresses, cooks, nurses, and midwives. After the purchase, they, like many of their male counterparts, often chose to keep their family members in bondage because of the difficulties in obtaining legal emancipation through the state legislatures,

especially in the Lower South (excepting Louisiana). Among the more remarkable cases of kin-purchase was that of Amelia Green, who, in Craven County,
North Carolina, first purchased her own freedom with her earnings as a weaver
and then bought her three daughters from their owners, after which she assisted
in freeing several of her grandchildren.[33]

The state most open to cases like Amelia Green's was Louisiana, where a
number of free women of color not only bought their slave children and loved
ones out of bondage but also submitted freedom petitions to parish judges and
police juries for their legal emancipation. In some instances the women were
persons of property—a few were even prosperous slaveholders—whose economic independence and interconnections with other free colored families, or
clans, often of French Creole heritage, enabled them to manage and even ma-
nipulate the requisites of the legal process for the benefit of their slave offspring.
They tendered petitions that reflected the terms and conditions of the state's
manumission statutes, and as terms were revised and conditions were added
they adjusted their pleas to meet the new requirements. After 1827 the state
assembly permitted parish judges and police juries to decide on the manumission of slaves under age thirty, but only if the slave plaintiffs were resident and
had been born in Louisiana and if it was agreed that they had cause sufficient
to allow emancipation.[34] Added to the laws in 1830–1831 was the requirement
that manumitted slaves leave the state within thirty days of their emancipation,
although exceptions could be granted if the slaves could prove that they had provided "long, faithful or important services" to a master or mistress "in the preservation of their lives" or had performed meritorious services to the state. On such
grounds free women of color obtained exemptions for their family members,
and some among them posted the required $1,000 bond.

In 1834, when a middle-aged free grandmother in New Orleans sought to
free her two children and three grandchildren, including seven-year-old Patrice,
she won their freedom by asserting that they had all had performed "meritorious
service."[35] In their pleas to the parish courts, free black mothers also praised
the abilities of their adult slave children to earn livelihoods as shoemakers,
blacksmiths, bricklayers, carpenters, and other skilled workers. The adult children were, as a French-speaking free woman of color who had purchased her
two sons said, "capable in every respect" of earning a living; and she extolled
both boys as being industrious, sober, and well regarded in their community.
Exception was granted. As in other states with "meritorious service" statues,
Louisiana made exception by additional criteria as well. To a remarkable degree,
at least until the mid-1840s, Louisiana free women of color succeeded in their
court pleadings to legally free their loved ones from bondage.[36]

On rare occasions, entire families—husband, wife, children, and other kin—
filed freedom suits: rare because the economic forces working against family

unity were so enormous. Less rare but hardly common were suits filed by children, as minors, usually with a free parent acting as their next friend. In 1805, five Delaware slaves with the surname White, all minors, filed freedom suits in the court of common pleas with a free black, Job White, serving as their next friend. The five plaintiffs—the children or perhaps grandchildren of Job—claimed that they were being illegally held in bondage by George Dehorty, who had brought them into the state as slaves from neighboring Maryland in violation of Delaware's slave importation law. The defendant was subpoenaed to answer the allegations, and eventually, after depositions were taken in Maryland and introduced into the court proceedings, all five acquired their freedom. The final decree was issued almost exactly five years after they had filed their original suits.[37] In Kentucky, slave mother Siller sued for her freedom with her eight children. Subsequently, however, as the court record indicates, eight individual suits were filed, one by each child with Siller as their next friend. The minors claimed that their great-grandmother was an Indian woman in Virginia who had attained her freedom through the courts in that state, but at age five their mother had been brought to Kentucky as a slave. The matrilineal argument won Siller and her eight children their freedom.[38]

Urgency and poignancy typify many of these suits as the children with their lawyers were suing to prevent their possible or actual sale and transportation out of the state, and consequently their separation from their parents and siblings. Nowhere in the southern states were people of color truly safe from slave traders, and sometimes unscrupulous slaveowners. They dealt in human property without compunction, and the buying and selling of children, especially young blacks in their teens, was no exception. With a parent as a de facto guardian, slave children thus sought injunctions to forestall being torn away from their families. If, as it often happened, they had been taken up by the authorities, or locked in a jail cell or a slave pen, they then had to rely on their lawyers to convey the urgency of their situation.[39]

In some cases, minors, with a parent as next friend, contended that they had been freed in a will or deed and had been living with their families as free children of color; so for them too, fears of separation prompted them to depend on lawyers reputed to be able to provide them protection. Eliza Chapman and Robert Chapman, minors and siblings, with their mother Kitty Chapman as next friend, for example, enlisted Francis S. Key and Robert P. Dunlop of Georgetown to file their freedom suit. The lawyers informed the court that the siblings had been manumitted in the will of a slaveholder in Prince George's County, Maryland, and for a number of years they had lived in freedom, until recently when two men had claimed them as slaves for life and sold them to slave trader Robert Fenwick, who planned to take them to Louisiana. They asked that the siblings be removed from Fenwick's illegal possession.[40]

It is not known how many freed teenage slaves were later reenslaved and separated from their parents, but there is little doubt that only a few were as fortunate as Eliza and Robert Chapman, who regained free status. Many more ended up on rice, cotton, or sugar plantations in the Lower South, despite the desperate efforts their parents made to protect them. Yet the few who, with the assistance of a parent and a lawyer, filed freedom suits fared well in the courts, as judges issued orders and subpoenas to prevent their sale or transportation or both out of the court's jurisdiction until the question of their slavery or freedom could be determined. Brunetta Barnes, "an infant within the age of twenty-one years, to wit the age of fifteen years," and Archibald Barnes, "infant of colour, under the age of twenty-one years to wit of the age of Sixteen years," engaged Peter Charleville of St. Louis to serve as their next friend in a suit against John Berry Meachum, a free black who was holding them as slaves. The young plaintiffs charged Meachum with ill treatment—he had beaten and assaulted them on a number of occasions—and with illegal bondage, as they were born of a free mother. It is possible that their next friend was also their father, in that Archibald's middle name was Charleville.[41]

Louisiana law required that minors filing a freedom suit be attended by an adult acting as a next friend or by a curator (the civil law term for guardian). In some cases, in addition to the minors' requests that they be sequestered for protection by the sheriff while their suits were pending and that they be granted damages for illegal enslavement in the court's decision, underage plaintiffs asked that the court appoint a curator on their behalf.[42] Some curators were free family members, although the names and details regarding curators in the court records often fail to clarify their relation to the plaintiffs, who were sometimes—and to their advantage—of mixed origin. For unlike the courts in the other southern states, the courts in Louisiana considered persons of mixed origin to be free until they were proved to be otherwise.[43] In a few of the suits, the minors not only claimed white ancestry but asserted that they themselves were in fact white by birth. On that very claim a New Orleans woman won her freedom in 1824, despite a witness's testimony that the plaintiff had told him she was born in Virginia the daughter of a slave "mulattress."[44] White ancestry, however, was not an essential for minors seeking their freedom in Louisiana, where young plaintiffs generally fared well, especially in the New Orleans District Court. In a complicated case that entailed the gradual emancipation law in the state of New York, the New Orleans court ruled in 1816 in favor of John Johnson, a sixteen-year-old person of color, who was deemed to be entitled to his freedom "the moment he was removed beyond the limits of said State."[45]

One case involving minors reached the US Supreme Court. In an 1835 suit, a District of Columbia slave, Sarah Ann Allen, claimed that she and her two daughters had been freed nine years before in the will of Rachel Wallingford for diverse considerations, including a payment of $150. At that time, Sarah had been only nineteen; her older daughter had been three and the younger just five months. The defendant argued that Maryland law did not permit the manumission of children at such young ages, but the district court disagreed and ruled in favor the plaintiffs. The defendant then appealed to the US Supreme Court, which was the appellate court for the District of Columbia Circuit Court. In his opinion, Georgia-born Associate Justice James M. Wayne determined that the Maryland law of 1796 did not prevent the manumission of children in general, only of those who from "infancy, age or decrepitude" would become a burden to the community. "It would be an unreasonable restraint upon the privileges of manumission, as it is granted in this act, if it were interpreted to exclude the manumission of mother and her infant child, the former being of healthy constitution and able to maintain it, as of other children who, in the natural progress of human life, would be able, in a few years, to maintain themselves by labor, and who would find in their adolescence persons who would gladly maintain them for the services they could render." The Maryland law, Wayne reasoned, fixed only an older age limit on manumission, and if the lawmakers had wished to include a younger age limit, they would have specified it.[46]

The possibility of separation—of parents from their children, of spouses from each other—haunted slave families, especially when one spouse or a parent had been manumitted while the husband or wife or children remained in bondage.[47] Freedom suits, if they succeeded, as two cases in Maryland did, could ensure the family's unity. When Sophia Tydings, a forty-three-year-old married woman of color and mother of ten, was manumitted by Ann Franklin, she faced the woeful possibility of separation not from her husband, who had always been free, but from "her children [who] are now Slaves," since they had been born during their mother's bondage. Because her children were also "of very tender age," the youngest of them still "an Infant at the breast," Tydings asserted that "it would be impossible for her to remove from the State at this time," as Maryland law required of manumitted slaves. Tydings was thus petitioning the court to grant her a permit to remain in the state with her children. She proffered, too, "evidence of her good character and conduct."[48]

Another former slave, Peter Rollins, who had been recently "liberated and set free by his late Master Thomas Oliver," informed the court that he was the father of a number of slave children currently in the ownership of Major Charles Hammond. So was their mother, Rachel, a servant woman, with whom Rollins had lived for nearly twenty years. "Prepared to Exhibit satisfactory proof of his conduct & character," Rollins asked that the court grant "unto him a Permit, to remain as free in the District aforesaid for this year to come." Rollins's lawyer cited the 1832 act of the assembly (chapter 281) granting people of color who had demonstrated good behavior the right to obtain a permit and remain in the state for one year. The court duly noted the plaintiff's "Extraordinary good Conduct."[49] In the cases brought by both Rollins and Tydings the Maryland courts allowed their part-slave and part-free families to remain intact at least for one more year.

Other suits for freedom were brought to the court by fathers, mothers, and children together, as families. Their claims were usually based either on free ancestry dating back several generations or on manumissions of their families by a will or deed. Often facing the imminent possibility of being split apart, the litigant black families waited in abeyance as wills were contested, deeds challenged, and family heritage disputed.[50] Trials and appeals sometimes went on for several years. During the early years of the republic, nuclear families or groups of nuclear families frequently won their freedom, but in the nineteenth century it became increasingly difficult for slave families to bring their suits to court, much less achieve free status. Economics of course and again came into play, with alleged owners arguing that the loss of whole families of slaves effected a significant financial loss, but as a rule the courts weighed the evidence discerningly. Even when they did decide in favor of the plaintiffs, however, the African Americans who gained their freedom still suffered the pain and anguish of losing other family members by sale, transfer, or transportation out of the courts' jurisdiction. About 1802, the Kentucky slave Sally was taken to the Michigan Territory. After some years, and after the indenture she had signed had expired, she and her son Armistead were brought back to Kentucky. Shortly before she filed her freedom suit Sally learned that that her owner, Robert Turner, had "carried off her husband & five of her children who were entitled to their Freedom and threatens to do the like with her & her child." Sally won freedom for herself and Armistead, but in light of her losses it was almost certainly a heartbreaking victory.[51]

In Montgomery County, Maryland, Martha Toogood no doubt experienced similar despair when the county court ordered two of her four daughters—Rachel Ann, age five, and Sally, age three—"to be sold by Henry Gaither until the children arrive at age twenty-five" following the execution of a debt incurred by Henry Toogood, Martha's husband and the father of her children, for seventy dollars.[52] Court records document equally poignant cases in which verdicts granted some members of a family their freedom but determined that others be retained in bondage.[53]

Nine southern states required newly emancipated men and women to leave the state within a given period of time, ranging from one year in Maryland, Virginia, and Alabama, to "immediately" or thirty or ninety days in Tennessee, Louisiana, North Carolina, and Mississippi.[54] In Missouri, a statute mandated that slaves freed during the 1840s and 1850s would be forced to leave the state, and in Kentucky an 1850 law (as instructed by a revised state constitution) stipulated that all slaves freed by a will or deed were henceforth forced to "depart from the state" or have their freedom revoked—in fact, the Kentucky law read, their freedom could not be attained until after they had departed.[55] A statute enacted by the Texas Republic, and which was later adopted by the state as well, ordered that free blacks who had arrived in Texas after Independence Day on May 2, 1836, would be forced to emigrate.

Most states permitted exemptions from these enactments, either by an appeal to a county court or a petition to the state legislature.[56] Free black husband and father Clem McClary Sr. purchased his wife and two children a few days before the enactment of the 1831 Tennessee law requiring freed blacks to leave the state. Eleven years later he petitioned the Williamson County Court for the freedom of his wife, Rachel, and his now six children, the latter four having been born after the passage of the 1831 law. Witnesses described the family as persons of good character, and McClary posted a $5,000 good behavior bond, cosigned by five white men, to protect his family. Rachel and her children were granted their freedom with an exemption that allowed them to remain with McClary in the state.[57] Although the forced emigration laws in most states were not strictly enforced, and in some states were even ignored, penalties for residence without exemption could be severe. "*And be it further enacted,*" read the 1806 Virginia law, which remained on the books for the next five decades, "That if any slave hereafter emancipated, shall remain within this commonwealth more than twelve months after his or her right to freedom shall have accrued, he or she shall forfeit all such right, and may be apprehended and sold by the overseers of the poor of any county or corporation, in which he or she shall be found, for the benefit of the poor of such county or corporation." Forced emigration laws and exemption statutes were enacted at various times in the southern states, and in most states, as in Virginia, they were updated and revised.[58] Whether or not they were strictly enforced, they cast a shadow of fear and anxiety over the households of many black families.

Exemption petitions required proof, often with white testimony, that the newly emancipated blacks were honest, forthright, industrious, and skilled enough to earn a living. They required, too, sound reasons for the petitioners' exception to the emigration statute. Newly won freedom was a mixed blessing for many blacks if they had family and kin still in bondage, for the emancipation laws were forcing them not only to leave the state but also to abandon wives, husbands, children, siblings, aunts, uncles, grandparents—any relatives—and friends. They would indeed be leaving home in every sense, both the people and the place—their native state and the particular area where they had dwelt and labored, and belonged, most of their lives. Their petitions often traced the history of their families and expressed the love they bore for their spouses and children; they also indicated their acceptance by whites in the community. A Mississippi man declared that any separation from his slave wife would destroy his future happiness.[59] A Virginia man, who was "considerably advanced in years," in 1810 stated that every night he prayed he would be able to stay near to his loved ones in bondage; indeed, he avowed, to abandon them within twelve months as the law required would be far worse than remaining in slavery.[60]

Some petitioners related how they had been able to purchase the freedom of some family members but not others, and how they could not bear the prospect of leaving behind them a child or children, a wife or a husband, or other kin as they set forth to some "land of Strangers." Because some southern states prohibited the immigration of free blacks, that land of strangers in some cases was the North, where the newly emancipated would be forever lost to their "kindred and friends."[61] As the daughter of a recently deceased free black barber in Virginia who had provided for her freedom in his will articulated it, leaving Virginia would force her to abandon every friend and family connection she had on earth, "to sunder every habit and association which years have fostered and matured." Under such conditions freedom would become a "cruel mockery."[62]

In these petitions newly freed blacks, as well as their white supporters, spoke, too, of the emotions roused at the contemplation of their forced emigration: the agony of being exiled, the torment of abandoning parents and siblings, the "sorrows and vicissitudes" of never again seeing a wife or child, the misery of severing all ties of "flesh and blood."[63] Many of the petitioners would have shared the sentiments of Aaron Griffith, a black minister who purchased his own freedom. "Aaron does not wish to be emancipated & sent off," a group of Monroe County, Virginia, whites said in a petition to the General Assembly, "on account of his wife and children who are slaves & reside here." Griffith had told them that he would choose slavery over freedom if he were forced to abandon his loved ones.[64] The laws did not require freed slaves seeking exemptions to base their pleas in family relationships, but many more did. "Your petitioner Milly Brown, a free colored woman, respectfully represents to your Worships that she wishes to remain in the state of Tennessee under the provisions of the several acts of the General Assembly in relation to free persons of color," because, having been born and brought up in a state that she had never left, with all of her relatives, friends, and associates living nearby, she was "unwilling to be separated from them." Furthermore, relocation in a free state was not a satisfactory alternative; despite the "pretended philanthropy for our race" in the North, she argued through her lawyer, the situation facing backs there was, in fact, deplorable. In the conclusion to Milly Brown's petition, the lawyer pled that "her life is as dear to her, her liberty as sweet, her love of home as pure and unsullied as that of the most favored in the land, and submits to your worships whether all these endearing ties are to be broken, and her life rendered worthless and burdensome for no other crime than that of being a [freed] mulatto."[65]

Even petitioners who would not be separated from their families by emigration found it difficult to consider leaving their home state. Freed by their owner but kept in bondage, a family of seven Tennessee slaves—Lizy and her children Bob, Susan, Violet, Reynolds, Jacob, and Ellie—triumphed in a chancery freedom suit. They then petitioned the General Assembly not to be forced to go to West Africa as required by law.[66] Lizy pled that she was about sixty-five years old and so "very infirm" that she needed her sons Reynolds and Jacob's constant care "in the decrepitude of age," as did her son Bob, age about forty-five, who suffered very bad health. Her daughter Susan, too, had depended on the assistance of her brothers "for many years." To alter their situation so drastically by forcing them to emigrate to West Africa, Lizy argued, would endanger her well-being, and Bob's, and the family's means of livelihood.[67]

What happened to Anne Edinbro following the 1838 suit in the District of Columbia Chancery Court? In the weeks and months that followed, Anne's mother Jane remained distressed, fearful, and apprehensive, as she hunted for her daughter. Most of the leads ended as did the possibility of the defendant Waters hiring Anne to a Mr. Davis "near the Potomac Bridge." When she found the family they told her "that no such girl had ever been there." Her anxiety grew when Waters refused to accept an offer made lawyer Clement Cox to purchase Anne for the same price (of $150) he had paid for her. Finally in April 1839, after the two defendants appeared in court and denied the allegations, saying Robert Earle legally purchased Anne's term in 1836, Jane learned that Anne might be held in the private jail known as the Georgia Pen, owned by slave trader William Williams.

The slave pen fronted on a residential street in Washington with the dome of the Capitol clearly visible from its location. The three-story brick dwelling, covered with plaster and painted yellow, housed slaves in damp and moldy cells in the basement dungeon as they awaited shipment to distant locations in the South. Jane dispatched her daughter and Anne's sister Harriet, a term slave age about twenty-five, to uncover if this were true. In three subsequent depositions, two by the mother and one by Harriet, it became clear that Anne was held in the private jail. Harriet Edinbro testified in April 1839 before a justice of the peace that she had, with of group of whites, gained access to the jail, and saw Anne in her cell. Since then, she had not heard anything of her release. In the end, the injunction failed to protect Jane's daughter Anne and she was shipped off to parts unknown.[68]

12

Lawyers and Their Slave Clients

On August 3, 1841, forty-six-year-old Pierce Butler, a successful lawyer in Louisville, Kentucky, stood with his client Wesley Brown, alias Wesley Jackson, a slave, before a judge in the Jefferson County Chancery Court. A slaveholder himself, Butler owned eight slaves—three children, three adult men, and two adult women—and had real estate holdings estimated in 1850 at a value of $48,000, which set him among the city's most prosperous residents. His household included his wife Elizabeth, age thirty-five, and their one-year-old daughter, Ann Elizabeth (Nannie), as well as two older boys surnamed Butler, who were probably Pierce's sons by a previous marriage. No doubt, given his wealth and social position, Butler primarily represented clients who were similarly well situated, as the income from his law practice was unquestionably substantial. Now and then, though, he took on the cause of a slave who claimed to be illegally held in bondage, if he found the case worthy. He apparently did so when, on one of his occasional visits to the county jail, Butler met a twenty-six-year-old black man named Wesley Brown.[1]

Although Brown knew relatively little about his early life, he did know, or had been told, that as a young child, he had been taken from Maryland and transported to Kentucky, where he had been sold as a slave for life, despite the fact that his original owner had provided for his future freedom in a will. Brown believed that his current owner was a slave trader named T. L. Huff, who was planning to remove him out of the state and sell him, either in a private sale or at public auction. Brown's story prompted Butler to pursue the case. He located a witness able to testify, in a deposition sworn before a justice of the peace, as to some of the circumstances germane to Brown's cause, and the next day Butler appeared in chancery court to make a plea on his client's behalf. He informed the court that a Maryland man named Sluper had stated in his will that Brown was to be manumitted when he reached age twenty-one. Upon Sluper's death, however, one of his sons had claimed Brown and sold him as a term slave (the bill of sale stated so specifically) to Thomas J. Godwin, who, in turn, had removed Brown to Kentucky and resold him as a slave for life to Francis Bumaker, although both parties were fully aware of Brown's term-slave status. Butler explained that at that point he had not yet been able to secure a copy of the will but planned to file it as an exhibit as soon as possible. He asked that Brown, meanwhile, be released from jail and be hired out by the sheriff during the pendency of the suit. He also requested that the judge issue an injunction to restrain the slave trader Huff from removing his client out of the court's jurisdiction. He cited three defendants: Godwin, Bumaker, and Huff.

Butler obtained the injunction and the case was continued pending further discovery. During the next six weeks he gathered additional evidence—and discovered that he had made several significant, factual errors in his original plea. In an amended petition, on September 17, 1841, Butler apologized for his mistakes, noting that his client "only knew by report that he had such a claim." Butler then disclosed that Wesley Brown had belonged originally to the estate of Stephen Donaldson of Frederick County, Maryland, not to a man named Sluper, and that it was Donaldson who had provided for Brown's future freedom in his will. Also, it was Donaldson's son who had assumed possession of Brown, in disregard of the terms of the will, and had then sold him as a term slave to Jonathan Sluper, who in turn had sold him to Thomas J. Godwin, who had removed him to Kentucky and sold him as a slave for life to two parties, who had afterward sold him to Francis Bumaker, who had since sold him to Stephen G. Chenowith, the jailer of Jefferson County. Although Butler's new evidence totally revised his earlier plea, which had been drafted in haste to protect his client, it also reflected what many slaves in their mid-twenties had commonly experienced as they were passed often a half-dozen times from owner to owner.

With the revised plea, Butler entered into the court record the copy of a mortgage in Frederick County that indicated Brown's term of servitude would expire in 1849. Nonetheless, Butler argued that Brown should be released immediately from bondage on the grounds of an 1817 Maryland law stating "that all negroes who shall be slaves for a term of years & who shall be taken out of the state of Maryland, or who shall be sold for a longer period than they are bound to serve shall thereafter become free." Despite the amended petition, however, the case remained on the docket, as a final verdict could not be rendered until Butler had received a copy of the Maryland owner Stephen Donaldson's will and presented it to the court.[2]

The suit filed by Pierce Butler on behalf of Wesley Brown points up the obstacles that lawyers—variously termed solicitors, counsel, and attorneys— encountered in their efforts to uncover and document the history of their clients' often multiple ownership in order to build a case for their freedom. Because Brown had been only a child when he was transported to Kentucky, his lack of knowledge about his early years was understandable, but it hampered Butler's efficacy in his first plea to the court. Also, because the document vital to

Brown's case was a slaveholder's will that had been registered more than twenty-five years earlier in the state of Maryland, and Brown had been sold numerous times since, Butler faced, and met, a challenging commitment to extensive detective work. Then, once Brown's original owner had been identified and the terms in his will ascertained, there was the inevitable waiting time for a certified copy of the will, which, upon delivery, Butler would present as evidence to a judge and jury. Lawyers like Butler realized that success in such cases hinged on proof of the original owner's intent with regard to his or her slaves, either in a will or in another legal document such as an indenture, a deed of manumission, or a marriage contract. A ruling for freedom under the law almost without exception required documentary evidence as well as corroborative testimony from witnesses.

Like Butler, lawyers who chose to represent African Americans who claimed to be wrongly enslaved often first encountered or learned of their clients in county jails, where stories of illegal detentions frequently circulated, or in local courthouses where the probate of a will freeing slaves, or an owner's grant of term servitude, or a person of color's freedom claim, might capture an attorney's attention. In some instances, lawyers received complaints from white family members about executors or estate administrators detaining blacks who were supposed to have been freed; in others, they were contacted directly by free blacks or African American family members about terms of indentures that had expired or promises of freedom in wills or deeds that had gone unhonored. They sometimes learned about denials of freedom to blacks from magistrates, justices of the peace, sheriffs, and deputies; or they were appointed as counsel by the court when wronged slaves took their cases to the authorities or to white friends willing to offer assistance. Rumor, too, was a source of clients, especially in rural communities where reports spread quickly about widows who were holding their deceased husband's slaves in bondage despite his wishes, or about slave traders who were offering to buy or sell blacks who had been or should have been freed, or about slaveholders who refused to abide by their own deeds of manumission. In towns and cities of the Upper South—notably, Dover, Baltimore and Annapolis, the District of Columbia, Richmond, Louisville, Nashville, and St. Louis—lawyers received potential freedom-suit clients in their offices.[3]

Although lawyers in the Upper South and Louisiana were heedful of opportunities to represent black litigants in freedom suits, their motive was not pecuniary, as their fees, which were often provided by the court, were for the most part very small. They did not use the phrase *pro bono publico*, but most of the attorneys did indeed file petitions in the interest of justice and, at least in their minds, for the public good. A few among them held antislavery views or in some measure had misgivings about the peculiar institution, but the majority of them, like Pierce Butler, were themselves slaveholders who nevertheless felt it was their duty, as both slaveholders and lawyers, to ensure that the laws concerning the institution were fairly and equitably enforced. They sought to maintain the integrity of the statutes enacted by state legislatures, to safeguard the sanctity of the legal process, and to defend the rights of slaves or free persons of color who, they deemed, had been unfairly treated. In short, they argued, promises of freedom that had been made to slaves should be honored. As property, slaves had no legal rights or grounds to sue for freedom except in strictly limited circumstances—if, for instance, they had been assured their freedom by their owners in a deed or will, or were the children of female slaves who had been freed, or had cause to be emancipated on conditions defined in state laws. The lawyers representing them in freedom suits believed that by enforcing the laws regulating slavery they were protecting, not undermining, the institution, and the courts, by granting freedom to slaves who were being unlawfully detained, were enabling the southern states to preserve their slave-based economy and class-structured society.

The few members of the bar who did file freedom suits with the hope of monetary gain were sorely disappointed. Most courts refused to grant damages in freedom suits, and in the rare cases that damages were awarded the payments went not to counsel but to the plaintiff. In Missouri, after 1835, damages in common law suits were prohibited, although plaintiffs in tort cases often received, merely as a gesture, a payment of one penny.[4] Even lawyers with a record of successes in freedom suits saw only minimal compensation.

Between 1843 and 1850, New Orleans lawyer Jean Charles David, the owner of a few slaves, prosecuted at least fifteen cases based on a single argument: his clients had been taken by their owners to France, where slavery was outlawed. He succeeded in most of these complaints, and continued to file them after the state prohibited "free soil" suits in 1846. In one instance, in which the defendant had not even contested the suit, David filed a supplementary petition for damages alleging that the owner had treated his slave client Charlotte cruelly by forcing her to wear ankle chains while she labored in the fields and by having her flogged by the sheriff for an unnamed offense and, on another occasion, by a field slave on the plantation. When a defense witness asked Charlotte if she "was not ashamed to give trouble to her master," who had acquiesced in her freedom suit, she replied that "it was not her, it was her lawyer," to whom she herself had already paid sixty dollars. In hopes of being well compensated, David similarly sought out and represented slave women in Orleans, West Baton Rouge, and Iberville Parish who had traveled to France.[5]

A surprising number of the lawyers who assumed freedom suits on behalf of black complainants stood at the top of their profession. In Delaware, antislavery Methodist leader Richard Bassett, who introduced legislation to facilitate manumission and to ban the sale of slaves to parties in the Carolinas, Georgia, and the West Indies, filed at least twenty-seven freedom suits over a period of thirty-one years (1781–1812).[6] In Maryland, John Boucher Morris, Gabriel Duval, and William Pickney represented numerous black clients, including the Boston slaves and Mary Queen of Charles County in her suit against Reverend Charles Neal of the Roman Catholic church. When the latter case was dismissed in 1808, Queen's lawyers requested a change of venue and a new trial on the grounds that justice could not be fairly served in the heavily Catholic Charles County.[7] Also in Maryland, slaveholder and attorney Nicholas Brewer Jr. presented five freedom suits in the four years between 1830 and 1834, when, like his father before him, he ascended to the bench as a judge.[8] In the District of Columbia, Francis Scott Key argued more than one hundred cases on behalf of slave plaintiffs and free blacks illegally held in bondage over a thirty-three-year period, from 1807 to 1840. Highly successful though he was in winning his causes, Key was by no means an abolitionist, or even antislavery. He himself owned slaves, and later in his legal career, as US attorney for the District of Columbia, he prosecuted several high-profile cases against abolitionists on charges of "seditious libel." Like many solicitors who represented slave clients, Key was primarily concerned that state statutes be correctly implemented.[9]

So, too, were James Breckenridge, Edmund Randolph, George Wythe, George Keith Taylor, Philip Norborne Nicholas, and William Wirt, all of them distinguished lawyers who argued freedom suits before the law and chancery courts in Virginia between 1794 and 1811; three of them—Randolph, Nicholas, and Wirt—later served as attorney general of the United States. In Kentucky, slaveholder Ben Mills Crenshaw prosecuted ten freedom cases on behalf of slaves in the four years between 1840 and 1844, when he rose to the state's court of appeals, of which he later became chief justice.[10] From 1818 until his death in 1854, Tennessee lawyer, politician, and planter Ephraim H. Foster represented black clients in noteworthy cases. In 1818, before the Davidson County Court, he sought the manumission of the African-born slave Simon, who was "sober, industrious, hard-working and a firm believer in the Christian religion." In another case, he himself posted a $1,000 security bond for Anna, a slave who was honest and "strictly obedient to heredity." In 1851, he petitioned the court to free the son of a slave woman whom he had known for many years. The young man, he told a nine-judge panel, was "industrious, honest, moral, & humble & polite & in fact has so conducted himself as to gain the confidence & the respect, the good wishes and constant patronage of all who know him."[11]

In Louisiana, German immigrant Christian Roselius, who became one of the state's most distinguished lawyers and later served as the state attorney general, acted as counsel for Ann Maria Barclay in the late 1850s. He averred that two decades earlier Ann Maria had been taken to Ohio by her owner, George Botts, a slave trader, and had there been freed. Upon their return to Louisiana she had acted as a free person, but when Botts died, his executor had seized her as estate property. Roselius, himself a slaveowner, argued in the Second District Court that Ann Maria's freedom papers were valid because they had been obtained before Louisiana's 1842 statute that prohibited owners from manumitting slaves by moving them to a free state. The executor appealed the verdict in favor of the plaintiff, but the Louisiana Supreme Court affirmed the district court's decision: the state had always stood against indiscriminate manumission, it said, but now "it has become altogether prohibitive, probably in consequence of injudicious and impertinent assaults from without upon an institution thoroughly interwoven with our interior lives." Nonetheless, in this case the law was clear: Ann Maria Barclay was a free woman.[12]

In 1816, five years before Missouri's statehood, St. Louis lawyer and slaveowner Mathias McGirk represented two slave clients and their children in freedom suits, and in 1818, he personally posted a hundred-dollar bond for Susan in her action against Henry Height and guaranteed the costs of appeal.[13] Noted for his "strong vigorous intellect, and fine retentive memory," McGirk became a justice on the Missouri Supreme Court in 1820, and in 1824, along with George Tompkins, he wrote a Missouri Supreme Court opinion vital to freedom suits, since it paved the way for courts in the state to rule that slaves who had been carried into Illinois with the express purpose of remaining there long enough to acquire the character of residents did, by virtue of such residence, become free.[14] Two other prominent attorneys, both of them owning a few slaves, who represented plaintiffs in Missouri freedom suits were Hamilton Gamble, a future governor of the state, and Edward Bates, subsequently a judge and the US attorney general in President Abraham Lincoln's cabinet. Clearly, their willingness to defend slaves did not adversely affect their professional standing or impede their rise in politics.[15] Before his death in 1830, Isaac McGirk, Mathias's brother, prosecuted seventeen freedom suits on behalf of slave clients.[16]

Another Missouri attorney, Montgomery Blair, who represented the plaintiff in surely the most widely known antebellum freedom suit, *Dred Scott v. Sandford*, declared firmly his belief that in his home state, as well as throughout the South, "almost every lawyer feels bound to give his services when asked in such a case arising in the community to which he belongs" (and he personally financed his own travel and covered any expenses he incurred in defending Scott to prove it). Blair may have been overstating the facts, but, still, in the Upper South and Louisiana at least a thousand lawyers did indeed take up the cause of slaves seeking their freedom through the courts.[17] A majority of them were slaveowners, maintained a practice, sometimes with a partner, in a town or city, and welcomed a wide range of clients: businesspeople, small farmers, laborers, craftsmen, women, and large plantation owners. With rare exceptions, primarily in Delaware, solicitors neither fostered antislavery sentiments nor supported abolitionist organizations. Like Montgomery Blair, many of them believed it was simply their duty to represent those who had no legal voice, but most of them did not attach any high-minded or altruistic motives to their professional responsibility. Rather they took freedom cases largely for personal and legal reasons: personal, because they had met the wronged parties face to face and had heard their painful stories; legal, because in their minds it was clear that laws had been broken and legal precedent ignored. Only lawyers and the courts could provide a remedy.[18]

Inevitably, lawyers who committed themselves to righting the wrongs suffered by their clients drew the ire of slaveholding defendants, who denied any wrongdoing and produced valid bills of sale and other legal documents to prove ownership of the complainants. Although the defendants were sometimes slave traders seeking to convey human property out of the court's jurisdiction for sale and profit, they were as often small farmers, planters, and townspeople who accused counsel of meddling in their personal affairs, acting in a fraudulent manner, and, in one case in the District of Columbia, "treacherously" urging a black client to run away until his freedom case could be resolved.[19] The changing public attitudes toward race and slavery during the early national period as well as the decade prior to the Civil War with new antiblack restrictions and laws probably dissuaded some lawyers from taking on freedom suits. One early-period Maryland lawyer, acknowledged, for instance, that his slave clients had a solid case but he was "not yet Abolition-mad enough to run the hazard of the expense." By and large, though, lawyers called on to represent blacks suing rightfully for their freedom were willing to run the hazard, and only rarely did they experience any overt hostility from either the defendants or other whites, despite the fact that they lived in a world where acts of violence were commonplace.[20]

To ensure their clients' protection, among the first actions taken by lawyers engaged in freedom suits was to secure court orders from law courts and injunctions from chancery courts to constrain alleged owners from removing, exporting, selling, or otherwise stifling slave plaintiffs. Especially in the District of Columbia, Baltimore, Richmond, Nashville, Louisville, St. Louis, and New Orleans, slave traders ready to purchase or sell any "likely" men, women, or children roamed the streets.[21] A slave trader's acquisition of a slave plaintiff, in particular, required immediate action and extraordinary effort on the part of counsel to prevent the imminent exportation or resale of his client.

The petitioners Eliza and Robert Chapman, minors of color, with their mother Kitty Chapman as next friend and with Francis Scott Key and Robert P. Dunlop as their counsel, established in their plea to the circuit court in the District of Columbia that the siblings had been manumitted in a will by a Prince George's County slaveowner. Key and Dunlop then sought an injunction and "further security" from the court to protect the petitioners by forbidding the slave trader Robert Fenwick or his "agents or abettors" to remove the children from the District. Judge James Morsell issued the injunction but did not grant "further security," stating he did not have authority to do so, whereupon Dunlop promptly wrote a letter to enlist the aid of another judge, William Cranch. Dunlop indicated to Cranch that he had conversed with other members of the bar, all of whom agreed that additional security could be required in freedom suits, and he stressed that in the Chapman case it was essential, as his clients were about to be removed to Louisiana.[22]

In fashioning a suit to present to the court, lawyers necessarily relied in large measure on their clients' accounts not only of events and owner-slave relationships pertinent to the cause for their freedom suits but also of their own and their families' histories. They listened to their clients' recollections and allegations, and they learned. They discovered who owned their clients when, and how they had come to know that they were cited in a will or deed of manumission; how they had been told that they would be freed upon their owner's death, and whether their children would be freed with them or at some future time, perhaps upon the death of the owner's widow, if they served her faithfully; where, when, and why they had been sold and resold after their term of slavery had expired; how with their masters they had traveled outside their home state in the South, or sojourned in the North, or visited foreign countries for months at a time; what they knew of their genealogy, and how their mothers or grandmothers were free women of color, or white or native Indian women, according to family history, or lore. In only a few cases did the clients possess copies of wills, deeds, mortgages, bills of sale, or other legal documents provided to them by their owners to ensure their future freedom. The lawyers listened, and generally they found truth in their clients' stories. In Virginia, at the outset of freedom suits, lawyers often swore an oath affirming their belief that the plaintiff's allegations were true.

With substantial assistance from their clients, then, lawyers were able to wed slave accounts to legal strategy. By gathering facts and gleaning details as to the slaves' original ownership, changes in ownership, family relationships, and travel, lawyers were able to formulate the arguments for their clients' freedom suits.[23] Although the pleas were filtered through the voices of the lawyers, most of the essential facts and often key phrases in them came from the accounts of the black plaintiffs. Some slaves were themselves already familiar with state laws that might be applicable to their cases, particularly statutes that prohibited importation of slaves into a state by non-residents unless the owners had followed specified procedures. Certainly by the 1830s many blacks in Missouri were aware that if they spent a lengthy period of time, with or without their owners, in a free territory or a free state, they could file suits to extricate themselves and their children from bondage.[24]

Without doubt, slaves needed the assistance of lawyers to work their way
through the legal morass of technical terms, court requirements, filings, and
appeals. Still, though most lawyers' clients probably had never heard of an injunction or a writ of habeas corpus, they did know enough of the law, through
word of mouth and family lore, to ask their counsel for immediate protection
for themselves and their children from owners, slave traders, heirs of an estate,
and other "evil disposed persons who wished to do them grievous bodily harm."
They knew, too, that if they had been promised their freedom at a particular age
or at some specified date in the future, or if they or a spouse had paid their owner
an agreed-on amount for its cost, they were being wronged if they were being
held in bondage without regard to those arrangements. They recognized the importance of such "contracts" to themselves and to their families; in fact, some
slave plaintiffs, especially in reenslavement cases, referred to agreements with
their owners as valid "contracts." They also knew that if their mother or grandmother, or any direct female ancestor, had been born free, they too were born
free, as were their children and grandchildren. A few clients had evidently heard
as well about the possibility of filing a petition *in forma pauperis* to seek their
"rights and immunities."[25]

The occasional slave clients came to counsel with creditable knowledge of the
provisions in state statutes relating to their particular circumstances. In 1845,
Caroline Bascom, a twenty-one-year-old mulatto woman living in Missouri,
recounted to her attorney how her mother had been taken as a slave from
Delaware into Maryland several years before Caroline was born. Aware, probably through her mother, that "all slaves imported therein for sale or to reside"
would be freed, Caroline reasoned that since her mother should have been freed
upon entering Maryland, and as she had been born subsequent to her mother's
residence there, she should now be freed. Instead, she was being held in bondage
by John H. Ferguson, the administrator of the estate of Hiram Bascom, and confined to the county jail.[26] Likewise, a Tennessee woman who had been held in
bondage with her children for many years claimed their right to be freed because
she was "the immediate offspring of Lucinda and Thomas Lee, free Citizens of
the Town of Boston in the State of Massachusetts" and her parents "altho' of a
black hue, had the Happiness to be born free people, and as such, enjoyed all the
benefits of freedom."[27]

More valuable to attorneys than their clients' knowledge of law was their recall of personal history: the people who had shaped it, the places that had staged
it, the events that had shattered it. Most of the slave plaintiffs could recite the
names, and often the ages, of their children, mothers and fathers, grandparents
and great-grandparents, who frequently figured significantly in family anecdotes
that had been passed on orally from generation to generation. Most of them,
too, could name the owners, renters, leasers, and hirers who had for a time

determined their destiny. They remembered, too, how, when, and where they or
their children had been bought or sold by their owners or, worse, had fallen into
the hands of slave traders. Etched in their memories was the distress when loved
ones were sold and shipped to distant locations or when they were subjected
to severe corporal punishments by their owners. Equally painfully remembered
were the losses or deaths of spouses, children, siblings, parents, and more distant
kin. The agony of separation—of that moment they were torn away from their
families, never to be seen again, and were caged for transport to another state or
territory—stabbed again in recollection. In this reservoir of personal information rendered orally to counsel lay the foundations for the plaintiffs' petitions
and, as importantly, a history of slavery and heritage of freedom vital to their
families' next and future generations.

From their clients' accounts lawyers constructed often moving and powerful
biographies to show how plaintiffs had been brought into bondage but had ultimately been unjustly retained as slaves, and to argue why they should be freed.
Only rarely did arguments make issue of a plaintiff's skin color, but age frequently
figured as a significant factor, especially when plaintiffs were minors according
to the law. Significant too were any changes in ownership, as were purchases and
sales, especially of black children, and wills and deeds and "contracts," not only as
aspects to the plight of the plaintiffs but also as reflections of the attitudes, values,
habits, and pecuniary interests of the slaveholding class. Because owners and,
perhaps to a lesser degree, their slaves were in general familiar to many people in
the community, it behooved lawyers to be as precise, truthful, and forthright as
possible in their charges. They thus framed their arguments against defendants
in terms of state law, sometimes by citing specific statutes that bore on the situation in the case: if, for instance, slave plaintiffs or their children were supposed
to have been freed, or had been born free, but remained mired in perpetual
bondage to their owners; or if slaveholders or slave traders had disregarded or
circumvented laws designed to protect the process of manumission and term
servitude. They described how defendants had subjected their clients to abusive
punishments and incarcerations, had subverted their rights with illegal sales and
purposeful misreadings of legal documents, and had devastated them by taking
children away from their mothers or fathers from their families. They wove their
pleas for redress into narratives of the human injustices and illegal coercion that
their African American clients had suffered at the will of their owners.[28]

To effectively formulate arguments for the court required a lawyer to be familiar with state laws concerning slave manumission, importation, term servitude, and other acts or processes that, if violated, might be applicable to the
prosecution of a client's case. Violation of the law required proof, and proof required documentation. It was incumbent on lawyers, then, to search out copies
of documents like deeds of manumission, wills, legislative decrees granting

freedom, and term-slave indentures to establish how and when owners had granted freedom to the slaves now in suit. Documentary evidence was often available at the local courthouse, but searches sometimes took lawyers to other counties and, on occasion, other states. Not unusually, and common in importation and free-state-residence cases, laws in a client's current home state conflicted with those in another state germane to the plea; so counsel's knowledge of the law had to cross state lines too. Since all the states of the Upper South and Louisiana permitted owners to free their slaves in a will or deed, lawyers for clients currently in one of those states could use a document of manumission received in another of the states to substantiate a cause for freedom.

Among the most difficult charges to prove was illegal importation into the states of Delaware, Maryland, and Virginia, as well as the District of Columbia, where freedom was awarded to imported slaves in certain circumstances, but resourceful attorneys produced records of purchases, sales, mortgages, indentures, and court cases to successfully prosecute importation-based suits. To provide evidence that clients presently being held in bondage in the South had at one time resided in a free territory or a free state, lawyers usually sought out depositions from white parties familiar with and sympathetic to the black families involved. In many cases, residence-based and otherwise, attorneys had to study state laws and judicial precedents to determine if their tenets had in fact been in effect at a time that their clients could have been legally freed. Sometimes, too, attorneys had to research the genealogies of their clients' families in order to trace their ancestral roots in freedom.[29] Occasionally, attorneys sought out persons to provide character references for their clients, although such certificates, as they were called, rarely appeared in the court record, and when they did, they had little sway on judges and juries. "This is to certify that I have known the Bearer Rachel Steel for thirteen years and know her to be an honest upright woman one that can be trusted," read one such certificate. More significant to Rachel's case was the testimony of the witness Charlotte Grimes of St. Louis, who stated that the plaintiff's master and mistress, whom she knew, had permitted Rachel to hire herself out either on a steamboat or in the city. However, Rachel's counsel, R. M. Field, argued for her freedom not because she had hired out her own time but because she had been hired out by a previous owner for nine months in Keokuk, Missouri Territory, "North of the line of 36° 30' north latitude," where slavery was outlawed. The plaintiff noted that such "hiring and employment" made her a free woman, "as she is advised."[30]

Some cases demanded substantial amounts of the lawyers' time, inevitably when potential witnesses were resident in different counties or distant states. Gathering evidence could take up to a year or more, during which time plaintiffs either continued in servitude to their alleged owner or were hired out by the sheriff. Lawyers' attempts to obtain depositions or subpoena

Rachael Steel and her lawyer A. M. Field presented their successful freedom suit in 1845 to the circuit court of St. Louis, the location of many other Missouri suits, including those brought one year later by Dred and Harriet Scott. *Missouri History Museum*

witnesses, meanwhile, might produce no more than a note from the local sheriff stating that the person could not currently be located in the county, and often when subpoenas were served, the witnesses failed to appear on the court date. Some lawyers submitted requests for summonses to be served to a wide range of people who might or might not be able to provide testimony relevant to a case, and who, if they had to travel a considerable distance to attest that they knew little or nothing about the plaintiffs or the defendants named in the suit, were likely not to appear. For out-of-county (or state) witnesses essential to the prosecution of the case, travel to court could take days, and they received little compensation for their time. In 1836, attorney and slave owner Edward M. Holden of Perry County, Missouri, certainly made a genuine attempt to muster witnesses for a suit brought by a black woman who had been manumitted more than a year before by her Maryland owner but was still being held as a slave. Over a period of twenty-five months, Holden requested and obtained subpoenas for eleven potential witnesses in Perry, Madison, and Scott Counties, and also contacted potential deponents in Carlisle, Pennsylvania, and Anne Arundel County, Maryland—and failed to acquire any testimony on his client's behalf. Holden lamented that he could not "Safely go to Trial without the Testimony."[31]

Lawyers for slave plaintiffs generally had more success than Holden in obtaining testimony on their clients' behalf. The lawyer for Daniel Hancock, a man of color in St. Landry Parish, Louisiana, spent three years gathering evidence to prove his client's free status. In court, the plaintiff's testimony and documents from other states, including a deposition by Mary, a free woman of color in New York City, outweighed by far the defendant's failures to prove Hancock was born a slave and to produce a bill of sale. The judge ruled in Hancock's favor.[32] In 1845, James Mandeville Carlisle, a District of Columbia attorney, filed a suit in behalf of James Becket, a self-hired slave who was seeking to prevent his sale out of the court's jurisdiction. Carlisle contacted a fellow lawyer in Prince George's County, Maryland, from whom he obtained a copy of his client's former owner's will. Duly "proved & recorded," it promised twenty-six-year-old Becket his freedom when he reached age thirty. The court granted Carlisle's client an injunction to ensure that he would not be removed out of its jurisdiction, and some five years later Carlisle produced "a Credible Witness" who validated the will. Becket's freedom was at last secured.[33] Indeed, five years was an unusually long time for a freedom suit to continue, but one year was not. For lawyers to secure copies of documents, to locate and depose witnesses, and to present findings to the court often took a year or more. Court-granted continuances allowed attorneys the time necessary to research and construct their cases for plaintiffs as well as their responses to allegations brought by defendants. Typical was the twenty months it took John Q. A. King, a twenty-six-year-old lawyer in Cumberland County, Kentucky, to secure the copy of a 1793 deed of emancipation from Albemarle County, Virginia, then to research the emancipator's heirs, who had sold his client, and fashion an amended complaint that included them as defendants. In response to the defendants' claim that the emancipation deed was a forgery, King produced three witnesses who affirmed that the deed was valid.[34]

The length of time that cases like Becket's and King's required to resolve did not diminish counsel's sense of urgency when filing freedom suits. In the body of their initial petitions they sometimes sought not only free status for their clients but also a protective injunction to safeguard them from being sold to "Foreign negro buyers," or, if they had already been sold, to prevent them from being conveyed out of the court's jurisdiction; otherwise, counsel argued, their fate would be sealed. Lawyers in the firm of Brent and Brent in the District of Columbia pled that their client was about to be sold to "Foreign negro buyers": a transaction that would "deprive him of his rights." Their client was "remediless at Law and cannot have relief but from your Honors," counsel noted ("Law" here referring to the common law courts, which posed difficulties to the prosecution of such cases and did not issue injunctions), and argued that he should be granted an injunction in order to be able to "prosecute his said rights and that he may have every benefit he is entitled to from a fair and full trial in his case."[35] Baltimore attorney John McCulloch, too, had cause for anxiety, as his client, Lucy Crawford, had been sold to the slave trader Hope Slatter, who regularly advertised in the *Baltimore Republican and Commercial Advertiser* that he would provide "CASH FOR NEGROES" and could always be found at the Owing's Globe Inn, corner of Howard and Market Streets. McCulloch asked for an order to protect his client against her possible sale by Slatter outside the District of Columbia, where Crawford had been living for many years as a self-hired slave with a promise of future freedom. If Slatter were to transport her to Baltimore and sell her, McCulloch argued, he would be violating the Maryland anti-importation law.[36]

The legal process attendant to freedom suits was complex, and lawyers initiated it only when they were satisfied that the information supplied to them by slave clients would reasonably support arguments for their freedom. In some jurisdictions, they began by requesting that their clients be permitted to sue *in forma pauperis* and that the court appoint them as the plaintiff's legal counsel. They then confirmed that the evidence they had uncovered warranted that the plaintiff's case be brought to trial. In Southampton County, Virginia, in 1807, for an example, the attorney Richard W. Byrd asked the court that he be permitted to represent a group of slaves whose claim that they had been manumitted in a deed was substantiated by a bond. Byrd affirmed that he was a practicing attorney in the county, that he had examined the evidence in support of the allegations, and that he had concluded the plaintiffs were entitled to their freedom. As lawyers often did in Virginia and other states in the Upper South, he was bringing the complaint "without fee or reward." Unlike other lawyers, he also informed the court that because he was representing black plaintiffs in a freedom suit it was possible that he would be losing the custom of local slaveowners. He noted, too, that, by law, he faced a possible fine of one hundred dollars if he were purposely aiding or abetting a false prosecution. The court, apparently considerate, assigned Byrd as counsel, and the judge ordered the defendant not to remove the plaintiffs from the court's jurisdiction.[37]

Subsequent to their initial actions, counsel consulted further with their clients on plantations and farms, at city residences, in county court offices, in law offices, and sometimes—like Pierce Butler—in jail cells. If they learned of any special animosities between their clients and the slaveowners, lawyers customarily requested either that the owner post bond on his or her promise not to remove or mistreat their clients or that the sheriff place them in protective custody and hire them out for the duration of their suit. Prior to trial, lawyers asked the court for summonses, subpoenas, orders, and writs so as to secure witnesses for testimony in court or in depositions. Occasionally, during the late eighteenth and early nineteenth centuries, African Americans served as deponents for the plaintiffs, but by the 1830s and '40s all the southern states, except for Delaware and Louisiana, had passed laws preventing free blacks from testifying against whites; the laws were not always strictly observed. To enlist neighbors, townspeople, farmers, planters, friends, and acquaintances as witnesses often posed problems for attorneys because among the defendants named in freedom suits were likely to be locally prominent and influential slaveholders against whom many whites were reluctant to testify. Other whites simply did not care to be involved with freedom suits. When necessary, lawyers also presented amended petitions to the court even as they continued to research county court records for pertinent documents and to process the cases for their clients, usually for months, and sometimes longer, as cases were commonly carried over from one court session to the next. Solicitors also attended jury selections, abided by court orders, and filed writs of error, or appeals, against unfavorable verdicts and decrees.[38]

With rare exception, slave clients were illiterate, so their attorneys strove to ensure that their rights were properly represented in court. They submitted amended and supplementary petitions. They drafted interrogatories (queries) for witnesses and produced replications (the plaintiff's responses to answers made by defendants). They questioned witnesses, often extensively, as when they were trying to establish the terms of nuncupative (oral) agreements and wills. They presented copies of estate inventories, administrators' accounts, probate records, commissioners' reports, testimonials, acts of emancipation, trustees' reports, newspaper notices, indentures, and deeds of emancipation. They also stood ready to object to any aspect of a case that might be detrimental to their client's interest; they closely followed the progression of orders, subpoenas, notices, injunctions, summonses, sheriff returns, demurrers (objections on grounds of legal insufficiency), interlocutory (temporary) decrees, writs, and continuances. And they accompanied their black clients into court during each stage of the proceedings.[39]

The two most difficult tasks for lawyers representing plaintiffs in freedom suits were securing documentary evidence in support of their clients' claims and prevailing on whites to testify in their clients' behalf. Many last will and testaments providing for emancipations indicated the slaves to be freed by only their first names, and included no descriptive details that might further identify them as an individual to be freed; likewise, mortgages deeds. Bills of sale and manumission deeds offered more information, but it was still the lawyer's charge to prove that the slave cited in a will, deed, mortgage, or other legal instrument was in fact the plaintiff or verifiably the descendant of a free woman.

Merely acquiring the documents could prove to be an onerous task, especially if they had been filed many years, or decades, earlier, or if they were located in distant county courthouses, or both. One alternative was to send to the county

A rare drawing of a black man and his lawyer discussing a case appeared in print after the
Civil War, but the chains on the man's wrists and ankles and the jail bars in the background
symbolize the struggle from slavery to freedom. *William Wells Brown,* My Southern Home:
The South and Its People *(Boston: A. G. Brown, 1880), p. 88; State Historical Society of
Missouri*

court a written request for copies of pertinent documents, but responses to such
requests usually came slowly and often without the documentation. The more
expeditious alternative was to contact a fellow lawyer who had ready access to the
local court housing the documents and might have some acquaintance with the

slaves in the case as well. As it happened, the Kentucky lawyer and slaveowner Thomas Smith did. James L. Murray contacted Smith for information in regard to a freedom suit he was prosecuting in St. Louis in 1831 for Jane and Charlotte, two descendants of a female slave who had been manumitted in 1787 in Maryland by Richard Dallam in his will. In response, Smith wrote that the slaves freed in the will and their descendants were now scattered over several states, but he had "taken some pains to investigate the title of these unfortunate people to their freedom & entertain no doubt of their right." Indeed, Smith had acquired a certified copy of the deed of emancipation, copies of the records pertaining to several freedom suits brought by other family members, and a certified copy of the Maryland law regulating manumission. For further information, he advised Murray to write to attorneys J. D. Maulsby and James Boyle in Harford and Anne Arundel Counties, Maryland. If there was anything more he himself could do, Smith added in closing, "I should be perfectly willing to contribute & charge no unreasonable fees." Cooperation between lawyers—sometimes in the same firm, often in different counties or even states, as was the case with Murray and Smith—was vital in the discovery of evidence and acquisition of documents crucial to the successful prosecution of freedom suits in which manumitted slaves had been transported to various states across the South. Without Smiths, Murrays would be at a loss in their pursuit of justice for their clients.[40]

As essential as documentary evidence to the prosecution of freedom suits were depositions, which likewise consumed a considerable amount of lawyers' time and effort. In some cases, it was necessary for the lawyers to seek out witnesses close enough to the slaveholding families to have knowledge of the emancipations in a will or manumissions in a deed, or of the freed parties' descendants, in order to clarify facts and verify details in often conflicting claims made by plaintiffs and defendants in their interpretations of the documents. Such witnesses were all the more important when the records failed to offer conclusive proof or were no longer extant. At the depositions—which took place most commonly in court clerk's offices, but also, in some instances, at law offices, private residences, farmhouses, and taverns—a county official, either a magistrate or a court-appointed commissioner, first administered the court oath (that evidence shall be "the truth, the whole truth, and nothing but the truth") to the deponent, who then responded to a set of questions presented by lawyers for both the plaintiffs and defendants. The responses would be recorded and read eventually in court at the trial; in freedom suits, depositions were far more common than in-court testimony.

Lawyers for both the plaintiffs and the defendants were customarily present at depositions, unless the witnesses and essential evidence were located in a distant county or another state. Under such circumstances, counsel for both sides made arrangements to have the depositions conducted in absentia. In 1782, a Delaware lawyer filing a suit in behalf of his slave client Justina arranged to have two depositions taken from a sixty-seven-year-old woman in Philadelphia, one before the chief justice of the Pennsylvania Supreme Court and the second, some months later, before a justice on the same court.[41] In another instance, in regard to his slave client, Maryland lawyer James Brice asked the Anne Arundel County Court to authorize depositions before commissioners in Washington County, Pennsylvania, who, he requested, should swear an oath that they would "faithfully and without partiality to any or either of the parties take the examination and depositions."[42] A Missouri counsel seeking to prove that his client Vincent worked as a hireling in the free state of Illinois for a lengthy period of time arranged for eight depositions in Kentucky, where Vincent had been resident prior to Missouri, and Illinois.[43]

During the early period of the republic in Maryland, throughout most of the antebellum era in Louisiana, and intermittently in Delaware, the District of Columbia, Kentucky, North Carolina, Tennessee, and Missouri, blacks could, and did, testify against whites.[44] Notable in Maryland were the depositions filed in the cases of the Boston slaves, but free persons of color also testified in other of the state's freedom suits.[45] In Delaware, a plaintiff who could not secure testimony essential to his 1801 freedom suit from a white witness was permitted to testify on his own behalf in open court that he had been hired out in Maryland in contravention of the Delaware exportation law.[46] Among the most remarkable examples of this type of testimony occurred in Randolph County, North Carolina, in 1830, despite laws forbidding it. Guided by her counsel—slaveholder John Motley Morehead, later to become governor of North Carolina—Jane Dawson, held in slavery in Randolph County by William Hogan and Joshua Swain, not only petitioned the court for her freedom (claiming she was the granddaughter of Polly Jones, a white women who had lived in Pasquotank County) but she testified for more than an hour in her own behalf. Her testimony, detailed, poignant, and powerful, was countered by a number of depositions by elderly slaveholders in Pasquotank County (236 miles to the east) who claimed there was no truth to the slave's assertions; they testified in unison, using the same words and phraseology. In the end the case went unresolved in the court records.[47]

Two Kentucky lawyers, Elisha Smith and John A. Morris, produced an affidavit signed by the slave Rose in support of her objection to being hired out in Whitley County. Under oath she attested that she had a freedom suit pending in another county, and if she were hired out in Whitley, she believed, she would be unable to procure testimony necessary for her suit or to otherwise attend to its prosecution. In addition, because she had brought her suit, she said, she was hated by many of the county's residents who, she feared, might run her out of the county or see her murdered before the next court session.[48] The lawyer for another Kentucky slave arranged for the plaintiff's brother, free black Seaman Thomas, to provide a similar affidavit in his sister's behalf.[49] In Bedford County,

Tennessee, when the lawyer for his slave client Mary Vance called her free black mother, Rosana Porter, to testify, the defendant objected on grounds that it was contrary to law. The court, however, allowed the mother's deposition.[50]

In Missouri, lawyers in several cases presented sworn affidavits by black plaintiffs that were accepted as testimony by the courts. Peter, a man of color held in bondage, being sworn, stated that a number of witnesses had been summoned on behalf of the defendant, whereas his key witness, Henry Walton, had proved to be "ineffectual, he falling Short of expectations of this deponent," albeit other members of the slaveholding family had informed him that Henry's disclosures would be "sufficient to prove him entitled to his freedom." The jury nonetheless brought in a verdict against the plaintiff.[51] Gustavus Bird filed two suits on behalf of Cary Ewton who worked as a slave in the lead mines of Galena, Illinois, one in August 1829 and the other in March 1831. In both suits, his client testified before a justice of the peace and signed an affidavit concerning his circumstances, the second one to explain that he had missed his court dates because he had been working on a steamboat to New Orleans and was therefore often out of the city. Also, at the time of his second trial, he had fallen so ill that he was under the care of a physician, although his ailment had not exempted him from his owner's harsh treatment and the "want of food & clothing & being forced to work." He would, however, be ready to present his case at the next term, he said.[52]

With the exceptions of early Maryland and antebellum Louisiana, testimony by free blacks in freedom suits occurred only infrequently, but that it occurred at all evinces the determination of counsel (and the courts) to introduce all the facts relevant to a case. The vast majority of testimony in the suits came from white witnesses: neighbors, friends, townspeople, estate managers, heirs, physicians, sheriffs, deputies, slave traders, slaveowners and members of their families. As most of the witnesses had some association or acquaintance with the slaveholding families, they were usually testifying on behalf of the slaveowning defendants, but they could also often provide information and insight into the circumstances of the African Americans seeking their freedom.[53]

Lawyers representing the plaintiffs called on their former owners for testimony regarding their sale and purchase of slaves, their removal of slaves from one state to another, and their residence with slaves in states where gradual abolition laws were in effect. They sought testimony from witnesses familiar with owners who had kept term slaves in bondage after their term had expired.[54] They explored the family backgrounds of their black clients with members of the white families who had owned them. From white family members and neighbors they elicited testimony about executors who had refused to honor self-purchase agreements between slaves and their owners and about widows who had chosen not to abide by the wishes of their deceased husbands concerning future emancipations.[55] Kentucky lawyer Thomas Marshall commissioned several witnesses to show that the widow of a large slaveowner in Woodford County had not only refused to comply with her late husband's instruction that his adult slaves be freed but also received the proceeds from their labor and "appropriated the same to her own use."[56]

Witnesses were especially important to legal counsel in cases where documentation was likely to be scant or wanting, as in suits based on the illegal import or export of slaves and on the kidnapping and enslavement of free blacks. In 1792, Delaware lawyer John Fisher, who filed a suit on behalf of George Pinkston, deposed four white witnesses who testified that Pinkston's owner, David Maxwell, had hired him out as a mill hand across the state line in Caroline County, Maryland. At that point, Fisher was arguing his case on the charge that Maxwell had failed to obtain a proper export license as required by law, but at the very time the case went to trial the Delaware Assembly passed a law granting freedom to any slaves who had been exported by their owners, whether by license or not.[57] A Tennessee lawyer representing Billy Kelley deposed two white witnesses who traced his client's history over a period of nearly fifteen years. Kelley had lived as a free person of color until 1835, when he had been enslaved by Henry Trott, who had then destroyed Kelley's freedom papers and sold him to Samuel Laughlin. Upon Laughlin's death in about 1850, one of his heirs had claimed Kelley as a slave for life, and later sold him to Thomas Smartt. Depositions in cases like Kelley's could mean the difference between slavery and freedom, as they provided factual data—the names of the various owners, the dates of ownership—and added salient detail to the backgrounds of the plaintiffs.[58]

Lawyers usually worked closely with their clients in determining whom they should call as witnesses and in formulating the questions they would ask in the depositions. It was much less common for the clients to attend the deposition itself, but when they did, court records show, they engaged in discussions with their attorneys about the testimony in the course of the hearing. Even more rarely were clients allowed by their attorneys to address a question to the deponent, but on occasion it did happen, as in the case of *Siller et al. v. Anderson R. Bowles et al.* To establish Siller's free status, the Kentucky lawyer Mills Crenshaw, a slaveowner, had secured a copy of the ten-page court transcript from Richmond, Virginia, in which it was determined that Siller's mother, Mima, was a free Indian woman. Thus did the court "adjudge order and decree that the complainant is a free person." In the suit Siller was also suing for damages in the amount of the wages that she and her children, being free persons of color, would have earned as hirelings. Her lawyers argued that, by Kentucky law, the plaintiffs were due a "reasonable reward" and that the defendants should therefore be required to pay the demanded amount. During a deposition at the law office of Crenshaw & Ritter in Glasgow, Kentucky, on August 23, 1842, Siller was allowed to question James Cummins, a longtime resident of the area and the owner of one slave, regarding the amount in dollars that the plaintiffs would have earned.

Question by Compl[ainan]t
Are you or not well acquainted with me, and if so state how long you have
Known me Since I came to the possession of John F. Bowles dec[ease]d
Answer I am well acquainted with you. I have Known you to be in the
possession of said Bowles since the year of about 1819.
By same State if you please what my service would be worth for the time you
mention [with] interest 1819 until now, by the year
I would not suppose taking the fact of you having children into account,
your services would be worth more than from $20 to $25 per year, and
I think they were worth the same.

Siller continued with further questions: How long had he known her children? Had her children ever performed services for him? What was the work
they performed and how much was it worth annually? The drama of the moment
aside, the fact of it—a former slave directing questions to a white slaveholder in
a formal deposition—points to the regard and trust that were sometimes shared
by lawyers and their slave clients. In the end, though, Siller failed to obtain monetary damages.[59]

Given the relevance of issues such as importation and export, removal
and residency, abolition, abduction, and a robust and rogue slave trade, the
representation of clients in freedom suits necessitated counsel's familiarity
with relevant "laws, usages & customs" not only in their own state but in
other states, both southern and northern, as well. They became conversant
with statutes that prohibited the transportation of slaves from one state to
another, state codes that prevented the importation of slaves, legislation that
outlawed slavery in New England and the Northwest and that instituted its
gradual abolition in New York, New Jersey, and Pennsylvania. They were
cognizant of the Pennsylvania statute stipulating that any "indentured
person of color" who was moved outside the state was thereby entitled to
his or her freedom; the Maryland law prohibiting the manumission of slaves
over forty-five years of age "to prevent persons held in slavery from being
turned loose upon the community when they become superannuated"; and
the Congressional compromise of 1819–1821 prohibiting slavery north of
the southern boundary of Missouri. Thus a Missouri lawyer could argue that
his client Dolly should be declared free because her owner had resided at the
"French River mines in the North Western Territory & kept and detained her
there six months contrary to the laws, usages & customs of that Country."[60]
They also researched, and in their arguments drew on, legal precedents, including the right to liberty for *villeins*—the class of feudal serfs who held
the legal status of freemen in dealing with all persons except their lords—
established by English common law.

When points of law proved to be elusive, they consulted with fellow attorneys to determine how to proceed. So it happened that John Ennis, an attorney in the District of Columbia, enlisted the aid of his friend and fellow lawyer James Carlisle when the court seemed to have blocked his one sure path to a verdict in favor of his slave client, Betsey Burk. She was suing for her freedom on grounds that she had been transported from Virginia into the District of Columbia "contrary to an Act of [the Maryland] Assembly." Ennis had obtained an injunction to prevent Burk's owner from removing her from the court's jurisdiction, and he was in the process of interviewing potential witnesses when he met a white shoemaker named Singleton, whose testimony, Ennis was certain, would set his client free. Singleton, however, refused to testify; and because Burk had not signed an affidavit verifying the truthfulness of the statements she had made to her lawyer and subsequently to the court in her original petition, the court could not issue a subpoena requiring the witness to testify. To demonstrate to the court the unfairness of its own rule, Ennis called on James Carlisle, who had argued more than a dozen freedom suits in the circuit court between 1837 and 1856. In his testimony, Carlisle asserted that to require the affidavit "would be a denial of justice in the vast number of cases," and in the case of the petitioner Burk, the oath "would be merely nugatory—she being black." In Carlisle's opinion, because the testimony of Singleton, a credible white witness, would clearly show that the plaintiff was entitled to her freedom, he should be subpoenaed and compelled to testify. The judge granted the request and issued a subpoena. Ennis brought forth his witness and secured an order declaring his client to be a free person of color.[61]

The general assemblies and the courts in a number of southern states recognized that slave plaintiffs did not have the means to pay lawyers for the prosecution of their freedom suits. A Maryland judge observed that from the early years of statehood, legislatures in Maryland had acknowledged the inability of enslaved African Americans to pay for litigation in their behalf, nor could they expect other parties to cover their legal fees; it was therefore, the judge averred, the responsibility of the courts to "secure to negroes the rights designed for them by law."[62] The courts did sometimes order that small fees be paid to lawyers as part of "court costs," but the payments barely covered a small fraction of what would be the normal costs for counsel.

In Delaware, during the early decades of the nineteenth century, court costs included $2.67 for plaintiffs' attorneys,[63] and in Maryland the allowances for lawyers' fees ranged from $3.33 to $6.66.[64] Although lawyers' fees varied from state to state and over time, lawyers could expect between one hundred and several hundred dollars for suits that took an equivalent amount of time. Most lawyers, then, took on freedom cases without the promise, or hope, of just compensation. The cost for the actual filing of a freedom suit was not burdensome: from about ten or fifteen dollars in the early period to twenty-five dollars in the middle period, and somewhat larger sums in the 1840s and 1850s, plus charges for preparing an original narration in a law court or petition to a chancery court. Further costs, however, could become substantial, what with expenditures for travel to obtain documents and depositions, for the issuance of summonses and subpoenas, for time and attendance at multiple court sessions, for the provision of plaintiffs' responses to the answers and responses of defendants, and for the preparation of briefs when cases were appealed. Even in the 1790s, as evident in a number of early freedom suits filed in Maryland, these suits could run into the hundreds of dollars.

Solicitors who claimed payment from an estate on the basis of receipts for expenditures incurred during a long and tedious litigation were not much more assured of compensation than those who, in a few, mostly unsuccessful cases, sued their former clients or their former clients' free black relatives for payment due on services rendered.[65] Nor could attorneys who filed damages suits on behalf of their freed clients, and themselves, be confident of reimbursement. By 1839, O. B. Hubbard, a Kentucky attorney and slaveowner, had spent four years seeking to prove the free status of Peter Sweeper, a Baltimore free black who had been sentenced to seven years in servitude in 1826 for assisting runaway slaves. In 1835, Hubbard posted a $500 bond to gain custody of his client, and at a cost of $30 hired an agent to travel to Baltimore to locate witnesses able to identify Sweeper. Hubbard himself spent four days, and between $68 and $100, in Baltimore to gather evidence, and then paid a key witness $150 to cover the costs of his travel from Baltimore to Jackson County and forty-four days of lodging. After winning Sweeper his freedom, Hubbard sued for damages for himself and for his client's lost labor (Sweeper had been held in servitude two years past the expiration of his indenture). A jury awarded them $743.30, but the appeals court reversed the verdict on grounds that the labor of a free man wrongfully held in slavery was "not the subject matter of account."[66]

Lawyers were sometimes able to secure funds for their services when their clients were hired out during during the course of a suit or after being released from jail in order to pay the debts of a former owner. More likely than not, though, they would receive only a portion of the hirelings' wages, which would hardly compensate them for the months of time invested in building a case for the client and keeping watch over her or him. Virginia lawyer David May found himself in that very situation in 1841. After dealing for years with the troubles of Jane and her children, who were held in bondage pending the payment of her owner's debts—albeit Jane's pregnancy at one point discouraged any potential employers from bidding on her at a public hire—May sued for damages in the circuit court. He was awarded $160 for his services, an amount considerably less than he would have earned in other cases demanding so much commitment and time.[67]

In Tennessee, when the defendants in a suit conceded that the twelve slave plaintiffs were entitled to their freedom and, to avoid further litigation, waived all claim to ownership, the court included a payment of $200—deemed to be "reasonable compensation"—for each of the lawyers in the costs of the suit. To cover those costs, the twelve freed slaves were hired out from 1858 to the end of the Civil War. The arrangement thus permitted them to remain in the state as hirelings rather than to be shipped to Liberia, as required by an 1854 law. It also allowed for their lawyers' compensation, although $200, which would be received years after the court's decision, amounted to a mere fraction of the legal fees that their services commanded in cases other than freedom suits.[68]

The services of Felix Grundy, a prominent Nashville attorney who would later serve as a US senator and attorney general of the United States, might have commanded considerably more than a court's token payment. An article in the *National Anti-Slavery Standard,* perhaps with bias, related the disheartening circumstances of Mary Davis, an "unmixed Cherokee Indian" who was sold into bondage as a child, a destiny she no doubt shared with many others. As an adult in Nashville, the industrious Mary was permitted to hire herself out, and over a period of years she was able to purchase herself for $500 and her daughter Ellen for $800: a remarkable total of $1,300, equivalent to roughly $26,000 in today's money. Upon learning that several Indian slaves who had been brought with her to Tennessee had filed a freedom suit and won their liberty, she consulted Felix Grundy about filing a similar suit on behalf of her other daughter, Elizabeth, and her son James. Grundy advised Davis that the costs she would bear in litigating a freedom suit would exceed the costs of a negotiated purchase. "This discouraged her," her son explained, "and she gave up."[69]

The great majority of solicitors who agreed to prosecute freedom suits were industrious, effective, dedicated, and, in large measure, successful. A few, however, made procedural errors, failed to produce proper evidence, filed petitions in the wrong court, or sought improper relief for their clients. When a Missouri lawyer failed to file the declaration of trespass required by state law, the court ruled that the plaintiff's petition therefore contained no fact "which would amount to trespass either by the statute or common law."[70] Another attorney erred in using a petitioner's "leave to sue" as his common law "declaration" of trespass and false imprisonment. As Justice Edward Bates pointed out, the permission to sue was "wholly ex parte and preliminary to the suit," whereas the declaration was requisite to the suit itself, which "must show upon what ground the plaintiff claims a right to freedom."[71] A few solicitors proved to be uncertain as to the exact wording of the laws regarding freedom suits in their home state, and a few others failed to appeal an adverse verdict despite their promises to do so.[72] Several neglected their performance of due diligence in researching the backgrounds of their clients. Of one young lawyer's presentation in Virginia, the judge commented that it "was too imperfect for this Court to determine the question of law arising from it."[73]

Among the most common "imperfect" filings were those submitted to common law courts, or what was called the "law side" of the court system. In these cases lawyers charged slave owners with trespass, assault and battery, and false imprisonment, and sometimes sought a writ of habeas corpus as well, in order to provide their clients with an avenue to freedom. Originating in England, habeas corpus was a legal instrument by which to safeguard individual freedom against an arbitrary state action; of course, in the South slavery was not an arbitrary action but an institution—one with precedent stretching back to the seventeenth century—that was recognized by each state in its constitution and legal codes. Still, in cases requiring immediate action to protect the plaintiff, the courts were inclined to issue writs to that purpose.[74]

Lawyers who argued "false imprisonment" without an additional claim—residency in a free state, descent from a free woman, manumission by a will or deed, violation of importation laws or the like—often failed, even when juries agreed that the plaintiffs should be released from bondage. Because of the laws in South Carolina, Delaware, Missouri, and Florida, where plaintiffs in freedom suits were directed to the common law courts, plaintiffs were not permitted to file joint actions of assault to sue "for personal and individual injuries" or to collectively assert "personal and individual rights."[75] Even when slave plaintiffs separately filed individual suits claiming "trespass and assault," or separately sought a writ of habeas corpus, their lawyers sometimes failed to gain freedom, or protection, for them, because the common law court was not the proper venue for such suits and, as the lawyer for one defendant argued, the actions "were not sufficient in law." To succeed, freedom suits filed by groups of slaves had to be tried in equity, or chancery, courts, where lawyers could offer arguments and present witnesses' depositions on behalf of the plaintiffs and defendants before judges and juries.[76]

At times legal counsel presented specious arguments on behalf of their clients. An argument that several lawyers apparently favored was that a monetary legacy or special gift bequeathed to a slave in an owner's last will and testament constituted "an implied emancipation," or, as one lawyer put it, permitted the slave to be "constructively emancipated."[77] Such suits were almost always dismissed. Likewise, lawyers who filed cases based on owner-slave agreements invariably faced defeat, except in a few cases in Delaware, Tennessee, and Louisiana. In general, no matter how sincere the owners' wishes and how clear their intentions in contracts releasing their slaves from bondage, the agreements, or contractual arrangements, written or oral, were invalid. The Kentucky lawyer on behalf of what he termed "substantially free" slaves argued that they should be legally freed by virtue of the alleged written or oral agreement, but he failed to convince either the lower court or the appeals court. "Slaves cannot maintain a suit in their own names, to have a contract for their emancipation specifically executed, because not being free when the suit is brought as is apparent from the contract itself, and the object of the suit, they cannot assert any right," the judges in the appeals court reasoned; in their condition as slaves they "cannot be parties to a contract, although it was for their benefit."[78]

More common than lawyers' miscalculated arguments were their mistaken filings. Because counsel relied primarily on the testimony of their clients in regard to ownership—clients who had frequently been bought and sold more than once, and whose family members had often been dispersed in different states—solicitors occasionally filed suits against the wrong parties, as Pierce Butler did on the basis of incorrect information. In their haste to file papers so that they could protect their clients from being sold or traded, they at times named not only previous owners in their initial suits but also estate executors, heirs, relatives, associates, and sometimes individuals who bore no relation to the case. Errors occurred, too, when slaves had been placed in the hands of estate administrators or probate authorities but were actually owned by other parties. It was especially difficult to determine ownership when slaves had been passed as gifts from one white family member to another without a written bill of transfer or receipt in acknowledgement. Nor did strong circumstantial evidence or convincing testimony in support of a client's free status preclude inaccuracies in the listing of defendants.[79]

Despite the intricacies of court procedure and the mistakes of legal counsel in some cases, lawyers won a majority of the cases for their slave clients between the American Revolution and the Civil War. Of the 663 cases that were appealed, excluding the few that remained unresolved, about 57 percent were decided in favor of the plaintiffs, as were about three out of four of the county court freedom suits (678 of 871). Requests for injunctions and writs of habeas corpus were invariably granted, although they had no effect on the final disposition of a freedom suit. Habeas corpus could, however, result in the release of free persons of color from unlawful bondage. In each period, there was a steady stream of favorable verdicts: during the early period of slavery (1779–1819) 56 percent of the appeals cases and 71 percent of the county cases succeeded; during the middle period (1820–1839), 64 percent of the appeals and 79 percent of the county court cases were granted; and during the late period (1840–1863), 55 percent of the appeals and 79 percent of the county court cases were granted. Although fewer county court cases were brought during the late period, lawyers won favorable verdicts for their black clients in the great majority of county court suits and more than half of the appeals cases despite the turmoil and conflicts leading up to the Civil War. What is remarkable is that from one generation to the next, lawyers and their slave clients were mostly successful in the appellate courts as well as the various county court jurisdictions. In all, at least two out of three freedom suits ended in freedom for complainants. (See appendix and tables 3 and 4.) Such figures stand as a tribute to the lawyers who, for scarcely nominal fees, worked diligently on behalf of their clients in freedom suits, to the slave plaintiffs who afforded their counsel not only substantive information but also illuminative personal histories, and to the judges and juries who attached importance to the rule of law in a slave society.[80]

Pierce Butler was one of those diligent attorneys. Thirteen months after submitting his first amended bill of complaint, Butler filed a second amended bill in which he presented evidence that Wesley Brown's Maryland owner Thomas Godwin had taken him from Baltimore, to Madison County, Indiana, where, contrary to the laws and constitution of that state, he forced Brown into "menial labor & involuntary service" for a lengthy period of time. Correcting previous information, Butler showed that Godwin had then moved to Kentucky and sold Brown to two individuals who in turn sold him to Francis Bumaker who sold him to Stephen G. Chenowith, the jailer of Jefferson County. Butler also produced an authenticated copy of Stephen Donaldson's will, which resolved Brown's much disputed status. In it, Donaldson, Brown's original owner, stated in effect that following the death of his wife, Brown should serve as a term slave.

As he had in September the year before, Butler again argued that his client should be immediately released and compensated for his services during his illegal enslavement at an estimated amount of $150 per year. Brown signed an oath with his mark to affirm that he believed the details set forth in the amended bill were accurate. In his response, Godwin claimed to have known nothing about Brown's Maryland owner or the man's will until its recent presentation to the court. In Butler's third and final amended bill, dated October 1, 1844, he and his new law partner, slaveowner Andrew Jackson Ballard, summarized the facts in the case: how Brown had been sold successively to six different owners by the time he was twenty-six years old, how long he had been retained in bondage as a term slave since the death of his original owner, and how his subsequent owners had broken the law by not indicating in the bill of sale that he was in fact a term slave and by transporting him out of the state of Maryland. Butler asserted that Brown should be free "by virtue of the act [of Maryland] and the aforesaid fraudulent omissions."[81]

In the final decree, on October 14, 1845, the court determined that Wesley Brown was "entitled to his freedom & he is hereby declared to be a free man." Brown waived all claims against the defendants, and the court ordered David B. Allen, who apparently had signed the bond for Brown's release, to receive "the money now in Court and may hereafter be paid into court [as] proceeds of the hire of the complainant since the institution of this suit." Each party was ordered to pay his own costs.[82]

Pierce Butler's motive in taking on Brown's case was not pecuniary. Nor did he entertain antislavery sentiments. Certainly he was not wanting legal work, as his calendar was busy with cases for his white clients. Butler simply felt compelled to defend a black man who was being held illegally in bondage. That he did so with such remarkable energy and perseverance attests to his professional integrity and his dogged determination to right what he perceived to be a grievous wrong. The actual facts of the case emerged, or were uncovered by Butler, over three years of service, and as the amended bills reflect, on several key issues in regard to Brown's owners he was forced to admit his own mistakes about Brown's owners and their movements. Yet, in the end, he won freedom for his client,[83] because he was willing to invest the time necessary to sort out the points of law appertaining to wills, deeds, and mortgages referent to his client in three states.

Butler was not alone among southern lawyers in the recognition of injustices suffered by blacks illegally held in bondage. From their clients' histories counsel fashioned often eloquent and always illuminative court pleas that provided just cause for the grant of freedom. It was not unusual for some of the most distinguished solicitors in their communities and states to defend African Americans and even those who were less well-known provided their black clients with advice, counsel, and a way to navigate the complicated legal processes and laws in the various states.

13

The Vass Slaves of Virginia, 1831–1861

"In the name of God Amen," Philip E. Vass of Halifax County, Virginia, wrote on August 8, 1831, "[I,] being of sound mind and disposing Memory, Calling to reflection the Mortality of my body & being desirous to dispose of My Earthly possessions; do ordain this to be my Last Will and Testament." Unmarried and without children, Vass left both his land and his interest in a farm owned by his late father, Philip E. Vass Sr., in Rockingham County, North Carolina, as well as specified personal items, to his nieces, nephews, sisters, and brother. In addition, he expressed his "Wish and desire . . . that my two Servants, Mary and Jacob, and all my Interest in the undivided Servants belonging to my fathers Estate, be Emancipated and that the Sum of Two thousand dollars, be appropriated out of any Moneys, belonging to my Estate to purchase in the State of North Carolina a tract of land," which, he instructed, should be of good quality, its worth at least four or five dollars per acre and its size not less than 250 acres or more than 300 acres.

Again by his "wish and desire," Vass indicated that on the land the emancipated slaves should "build out of Good Oak logs, three logs above joist, with Cabbin Rough well covered with Good Slabs," a dwelling house; he noted, too, that if a second dwelling was required, it should be situated not less than two or more than three hundred yards from the original building. Further, Vass stated, "My Wish & desire is that my Negroes be furnished with Two Good Work horses and the Necessary plantation tools to Make a Crop with, & two good Milk Cows, Meat & corn for the first year." In the event that any of his slaves became "Roguish," or a nuisance to the community, Vass prescribed that he or she or they should escheat to the commonwealth of Virginia and be transported out of the country to Liberia. He also made known his wish that the freed slaves should never have the right to sell or dispose of the land which would escheat to the state.[1]

Vass's sympathies with the small group of slaves who had loyally served him and his father for a number of years are apparent in his bequests. To ensure their fulfillment, he appointed his father's longtime friend, Halifax tobacco planter Isaac Medley Sr., as executor of his estate, and he asked Medley to have thirty-nine-year-old James Young, a close friend, supervise the relocation of the freed slaves to North Carolina. He left further instructions that, upon his death, Young should hire a "White Man Workman" to accompany the freed male slaves to North Carolina and to oversee their construction of the dwelling according to the specifications in the will. The women and children, meanwhile, were to be hired out, with all the proceeds from their hire going to the estate. Vass expected that within the year following his death Young should have settled all of the manumitted slaves in North Carolina.[2]

On August 21, 1831, two weeks after Philip Vass wrote his will and less than one hundred miles to the east of Halifax County, the largest slave revolt in US history erupted. Nat Turner, leading a small band of slaves in a bloody march across the countryside in Southampton County, Virginia, left in his wake about sixty dead white men, women, and children. The revolt was quickly suppressed, and Turner and most of his followers were hanged, but the South would never again be the same. When Vass died the next year, fear, anxiety, and suspicion charged the political atmosphere of the South, and the destiny of the Vass slaves over the next nearly three decades needs to be read in a context of what might be called the post-Turner era.[3]

Historians have for many years considered the Nat Turner revolt to be a watershed event in southern and, indeed, American history. Following the revolt, whites in Virginia and elsewhere viewed their slaves differently, as if even the most seemingly loyal blacks might in fact be plotting an insurrection against them. Slaveholders tightened plantation rules, increased patrols, strengthened surveillance in towns and cities, and enacted a series of laws to secure stricter control of their black charges. If they had regarded "outsiders" from the North with suspicion prior to the revolt, after it they began to eye Yankees as conspirators in a cause against them. As sectional hostility intensified during the 1840s and 1850s, so did the compulsion among southern whites to exert increasingly more control over the slave population. While white Virginians were divided on numerous economic, political, religious, and cultural issues, they were of one mind in the matter of the "peculiar institution" and the status it assigned to blacks in southern society. They opposed the growth of a free black population and supported the southern position in defense of slavery on such political issues as the Wilmot Proviso in 1846, the Kansas-Nebraska Act of 1854, and John Brown's raid at Harpers Ferry in 1859.[4]

Certainly what happened to a small group of slaves in one Virginia county during the post-Turner era affords us a riveting narrative that places its subjects

HORRID MASSACRE IN VIRGINIA·

An 1831 woodcut depicts scenes from the Nat Turner rebellion: a white mother and her three children beg for mercy at the feet of a slave raising a hatchet as a company of dragoons pursues the rebels to quell the revolt. *Library of Congress, LC-USZ62-38902*

in a unique set of circumstances,[5] but that narrative also offers insights into the values, attitudes, yearnings, and desires that drove and shaped not just the Vass slaves but also the larger population of blacks at that same historical moment. They are, like the Boston slaves in an earlier era, representative. Like the Boston slaves, too, the Vass slaves maintained family ties in a hostile and sometimes menacing environment, developed friendships with a number of white protectors, and with vigilance and determination stood up against the prevailing anti-black attitudes. The times—the turbulent early years of the republic for the Boston slaves and the divisive decades preceding the Civil War for the Vass group—framed their plights differently, but both groups filed freedom suits, both found lawyers to defend their actions, both appeared in court to protest their enslavement, and both ultimately, after many years, won freedom for some of their members. In both cases, too, the defendants named in the suits included the largest and wealthiest slaveholders in their communities.

The Boston slaves did, however, have two distinct advantages, in that the courts admitted hearsay testimony into evidence and allowed free African

Americans to testify, whereas the Vass slaves had to rely solely on white testimony and could not tap the memories of black witnesses to construct family histories and build cases for freedom. Even so, in their pursuits of freedom, both the Boston and Vass slaves encountered a judicial system that proved to be committed to fairness in the examination of evidence and that valued lawyers and judges who were determined to seek a remedy according to the law.

The slaves freed by Philip Vass's will included his two personal servants, Jacob, age about twenty-one, and his quite older sister Mary, age about forty-five, as well as four others cited as servants in his father's estate: Patsey or Patty, also about forty-five; Meriweather, described as a "Negro Boy" worth $300, age about eleven; Sam and Matilda, whose ages can only be estimated from their appraised values in an 1832 inventory. It lists Sam as a "Negro Man" worth $525, so he was probably in his late twenties or early thirties, and Matilda as a "Negro Girl" worth $175, so in all likelihood a youngster about five or six. All six slaves had previously been owned by Vass's father.[6]

Though relatively young, about forty, when he died in 1832, Philip E. Vass had accumulated a considerable estate. According to the 1830 census, he then possessed sixteen slaves, all of whom were under the age of twenty-four. In addition to his own land and slaves, he had inherited substantial property from his father, who died in 1825, and upon his mother's death in 1830 he received $3,000 due her from a civil suit, and more: "I give and bequeath all the balance of my Estate of whatever nature or kind it be both real and personal," Elizabeth Vass wrote in her will in 1828, "unto my well beloved Son Philip E. Vass and unto his heirs and assigns forever." As his mother's executor, Vass posted a $12,000 bond, which would indicate that the six slaves Vass named in his will constituted a relatively small portion of his total holdings at the time of his death.[7]

Vass, however, did not die in the comfort of his own or his family's financial and social circumstances. In 1830 he became embroiled in a bitter dispute with Henry Polly, a longtime resident of Halifax County, probably over payments or charges for work Polly had done on the Vass farm. A landless and aging laborer, Polly possessed little in the way of property: a horse, a saddle, a rifle, a shotgun, a feather bed, and 1,700 pounds of tobacco—the value in total not in excess of $120. The dispute went unresolved, but it did end—bloodily. The record does not indicate why Vass did what he did, only that on October 21, 1830, in a physical altercation, Vass stabbed Polly repeatedly with a knife. Later that day, Polly died as a result of his multiple wounds. Shortly thereafter, Vass was indicted for murder and convicted of "maliciously, feloniously and willfully" killing Polly. He was sentenced to a lengthy term in the state penitentiary in Richmond, where he signed and dated his last will and testament. He died the following year in his prison cell.[8] It was an ignominious end for a scion of wealth and prestige, and it presaged the future decline of the Vass family fortunes.

Shortly after Vass died, the other heirs of Philip E. Vass Sr. filed suit against the younger Philip's executor for a division of his slaves, including the "servants" he had designated in his will to be freed. In 1832, the court ordered that four-teen of the elder Vass's slaves be divided into four lots worth $1,181 each. Two of the lots went to the elder Vass's two daughters—Affiah Ewing and her hus-band George B. Ewing, Sarah Womack and her husband Edward Womack—and a third went into the estate of his late son James Vass, who had died unexpect-edly. The estate of Philip E. Vass, deceased—with Isaac Medley now the exec-utor of both the younger and elder Philip E. Vass estates—received the fourth lot, which included Sam, Meriweather, Patty (whose appraised valued stood at only $200), and Matilda.⁹ Thus, within months after Vass's death, the four slaves cited in his will, according to the wishes in his father's will were placed in Philip E. Vass's estate.¹⁰

Complicating matters further, the executor of the estate of James Vass filed suit against the executor of the estate of Philip E. Vass to have the latter's will declared null and void. In such an event, the slaves that were to be freed would instead be included in the residuary property of the estate and thus apportioned among the various heirs, one of them notably being the estate of James Vass. At a session of the Halifax Circuit Superior Court of Law and Chancery, the exec-utor of James's estate declared Philip's will to be a fake and a fraud, and he urged that it not be accepted by the probate court. "This day came the parties by their attorneys," the court record read, arguing back and forth, questioning and cross-examining "Sundry Witnesses," seeking to advance their particular cause. The court ruled that the will was authentic and ordered that James Vass's executor pay the court costs.¹¹

Although Philip Vass had strived to ensure that the slaves he named in his will would, upon their emancipation, lead independent lives in a new setting, his endeavor was thwarted by the state of North Carolina. When James Young, as he had been instructed, attempted to free Vass's trusted servants and set them up as independent farmers on a tract of land in North Carolina, he discovered that the Old North State, like other southern states, prohibited the entry of free blacks. On their entry into the state as freed persons, they would each face a fine of $500 and, if that sum were not paid, would be "held in servitude not more than 10 years." Until the question of migration could be settled, the $2,000 allocated for purchase of the land would remain in limbo, as would the status of the servants freed in Vass's will.¹²

Vass's slaves, including his personal servants Mary and Jacob, meanwhile fell under the control of one of the wealthiest and most successful tobacco planters in Virginia. Isaac Medley owned thousands of acres of land in Halifax County; his property ran along five creeks—Difficult, Terrible, Birch, Miry, and Polecat—and lay on both sides of the Dan River.¹³ In 1830, he owned about seventy-five slaves, but nearly half of them—44 percent—were either too young, under age ten, or too old, over age fifty-five, to labor as full field hands.[14] During the 1830s, Medley increased his acreage under cultivation and added to his slave labor force. Still, among the 106 slaves he owned in 1840, nearly 52 percent of them were either too young or too old for arduous field labor. The percentages—large and, a decade later, larger—suggest that Medley was more committed to maintaining a stable work force and keeping black families together than he was to "stocking" his plantation with "prime field hands" in order to produce maximum profits.[15]

With all of the legal wrangling among various Vass heirs for a portion of property attached to two Vass estates it was difficult for Medley to stay out of court. Not only did he have to answer to the heirs of Philip E. Vass Sr., but he had to come up with some plan concerning the slaves that the younger Philip E. Vass had designated for emancipation. In regard to Mary, Jacob, Patsey, Sam, Meriweather, and Matilda, he decided to monitor their activities and hold them in bondage until the matter of their relocation could be resolved, at which point, if the court determined favorably, he would release to them the $2,000 currently in abeyance. Despite his substantial wealth, Medley fretted about losing the money in security bonds that, as executor, he had put up for Vass's slaves and about the liability for their market value, which he might face if he had acted on a decision that was later rescinded by the courts.

Some years later, Medley noted that he had been a neighbor and friend of the elder Vass for nearly thirty years, and had been well acquainted with the slaves freed by his son. In that time, he said, he had "never heard any charge against them of dishonesty or bad behavior," and Jacob, who had lived on Medley's plantation for some eight years, as had Mary, was an extremely "honest Man orderly and well behaved."[16] Others of the younger Vass's slaves were periodically hired out to various farmers and planters in the area. In 1832, Samuel, for instance, worked on hire to Robert Hurt for part of the year, and Medley himself paid the Vass estate $114 that same year for his own hire of Jacob and Mary. The record does not show exactly where the slaves other than Jacob and Mary lived after Philip E. Vass's death, but it is clear that they remained in Halifax County.[17] It is also clear that more than a few years passed before they were able to assert their rights to freedom under Virginia law.

Finally, in 1840, eight years after the death of Philip E. Vass, the six slaves formerly in his charge, with the assistance of Richard Logan, a wealthy, slaveowning lawyer who had administered the will of Elizabeth Vass, petitioned the superior court of law and chancery in Halifax County for permission to sue for their freedom. The slaves stated they were entitled to their freedom under Philip E. Vass's last will and testament, which identified two of them by name and specified the other four as "Slaves belonging to the estate of Philip Vass the Elder dec[ease]d (the father of the said Philip E. Vass)." They argued that Isaac Medley had illegally held them in bondage and had refused to permit them to register as free persons. "Your petitioners being poor and unable to pay the Costs of prosecuting a suit for the recovery of their freedom," the slaves concluded, "pray that your honor will permit them to sue in *forma pauperis* [and] will assign them counsel and do whatever may be necessary to enable them to initiate and Carry on their suit against the said Isaac Medley for the recovery of their freedom."

The slaves' attorney attested to William Leigh, the superior court judge hearing the case, "I have examined the facts and Circumstances on which the petitioners claim the right to freedom which are Correctly Stated in the foregoing petition, and I am clearly of the opinion from these facts that the Said petitioners are of right free persons and not slaves."[18] Judge Leigh granted the slaves permission to sue *in forma pauperis* and assigned Logan as their permanent counsel. The judge then outlined how the slaves, with the benefit of their lawyer, would proceed: they would first travel unhindered to the court clerk's office, there to file papers for the issuance of subpoenas; subsequently, they would call witnesses to offer testimony in their behalf and attend the depositions of those called before the court; and finally, they would appear at the trial which would determine their fate. In addition, Leigh "ordered that their said Master [Medley] do not presume to beat or misuse them upon this account."[19] Leigh's instructions in essence matched those delivered to the Boston slaves by Maryland Judge Samuel Chase nearly a half-century before as well as, in between, many other judges' instructions at the outset of freedom suits across the southern states.

Leigh's final order was for the clerk of the court to issue a subpoena: "The Commonwealth of Virginia to the Sheriff of Halifax County Greeting: You are hereby commanded to summon Isaac Medley ex[ecut]or of Philip E. Vass dec[ease]d to appear before the Judge of our Circuit Superior Court of Law and Chancery."[20] A week later, with Medley in the courtroom, the slaves brought their case before Judge Leigh, claiming that by virtue of Vass's will they were entitled to their freedom and to the $2,000 set aside for their resettlement in North Carolina. They noted that several cases in regard to the estates of Philip E. Vass Sr. and Philip E. Vass Jr. had already proceeded through the court, which, in 1839, had found both estates to be debt-free; therefore, with no creditors wanting payment, it would not be necessary for any of the slaves cited for freedom to be put up for hire or sale. They thus asked to be immediately released from bondage.[21]

Isaac Medley took more than six weeks to respond. In June 1840, now in his late sixties, in yet another appearance before the Halifax County Superior Court, Medley attested that he was the executor named in the wills of both of the Philip E. Vasses; that the elder Vass had, in his will, indeed assigned some of the slaves currently in question to his son; and that neither of the two Vass estates were encumbered by any debts. Further, he declared, he was more than willing to liberate the six plaintiffs "under a fair construction of the will and all the specifications and provisional Conditions thereof." Members of the Vass family, however, were not so willing, Medley reported, so that if he were to free the plaintiffs, he would then be liable to the Vass heirs for payment of the slaves' market value by virtue of their inclusion in a residuary legacy. He pointed out, too, that the four "undivided" slaves were not mentioned by name in either will and argued that Philip E. Vass had died before a division could be made of his father's estate, so it was not clear who should benefit from the provisions in the wills. He also noted that North Carolina law prohibited the entry of free blacks into that state. Consequently, Medley was refusing to release the plaintiffs from servitude without "the sanction of some tribunal Competent to decide upon their right to freedom."[22]

The Vass slaves brought their cause under several laws that had been enacted many years before. In 1795, the Virginia Assembly legislated a statute that allowed persons illegally detained as slaves the right to bring suit and be assigned counsel; the law was updated in 1798 and again in 1818–20.[23] Slaves alleging illegal detainment could thus file complaints against the person who had wrongfully assumed their ownership.[24] Although the intent of such statutes was to insure the inviolability of property and to protect the rights of slaveowners, even in death, to dispose of their property as they saw fit, the laws in this case favored the Vass slaves. Despite Medley's arguments and the testimony of various Vass heirs, the slaves won a resounding victory. "This cause came on this day to be heard on the bill answer & exhibits and was argued by Counsel on consideration whereof the Court is of opinion that the plaintiffs were emancipated by the will of Philip E. Vass dec[ease]d," Judge Leigh ruled on April 12, 1841, after having considered the case for more than a year, "and doth adjudge order and decree that the defendant do forthwith deliver to each of them a copy of the will of the said Philip E. Vass dec[ease]d, the instrument by which they are emancipated certified by the Clerk of the Court of the County of Halifax and that he do cease any act of ownership or authority over them."[25]

Seven and a half months later, in November 1841, three of the former slaves— Jacob, Mary, and Patsey—petitioned the Virginia General Assembly for the right to become free black residents of the state. They had been informed, they said, that emancipated slaves could not remain in Virginia more than one year without permission to do so by a special act of the legislature.[26] Jacob, now about thirty-three, pled that his wife and three children, all slaves, were so endeared to him by "the most tender ties of affection" that he could not bear the thought of leaving them; he would remain with them, he said, even if it meant returning to bondage. Mary, now fifty-five, said that she had "many near relations" in slavery and was "verry desirous to remain with them the balance of the time she has to live." Patsey, also in her mid-fifties, with slave relatives and slave children, stated

that she was "verry unwilling" to leave her husband "who was tender and kind
to her."

The three newly freed blacks even asked Isaac Medley to write a recommendation in their behalf. Despite their suit against him, he apparently empathized with
them in their plight, as he responded positively to their request. (Notably, in his
answer to their bill of complaint he had made it clear that he had no interest in the
matter of controversy except as an executor.) With Medley's commendation—
he deemed them to be persons of integrity and good behavior—attached to the
petition, Jacob, Mary, and Patsey asked that the General Assembly pass a private
act to exempt them from the 1806 law requiring emancipated blacks to leave the
state or else face seizure by the sheriff and sale at public auction.[27]

Not even the recommendation of a well-known slaveowner swayed members
of the General Assembly, however. Five days after its referral to the Committee
on the Judiciary by Thomas Watkins, the representative from Halifax County,
the petition was rejected.[28] To enjoy the fruits of their freedom, it now appeared,
the Vass slaves had but one option: to leave the land of their birth and journey
to the North. Patsey, however, could not imagine a life without her husband of
many years, an accomplished shoemaker and a free black man of good reputation named Terry Daniel, or without her slave children, now adults, who lived in
the same neighborhood.[29] She submitted her own petition:

> To the General Assembly of Virginia: Respectfully sheweth your
> Petitioner, Patty Daniel, residing at Halifax Court-House, Virginia;
> That she is a woman of color and was formerly a slave, the property
> of Philip E. Vass of the said County, who died some twelve years ago,
> having emancipated her, with several other slaves, in his will; that the
> validity of the will was contested in a suit brought in the Superior Court
> of Chancery for the said county, which suit remained undecided until
> last October twelve months, when a decree was made, pronouncing the
> will valid & the slaves free; that all the slaves included in such decree
> have since obtained their free-papers & removed out of the state, except
> your petitioner, who has continued to reside where she did when the
> decree was made.

Patsey had always lived in Halifax County, she concluded, and wished to remain
"where she has lived so long and where she enjoys the society of her husband
and her children."[30]

All but one of the facts that Patsey included in her petition were true. The
"several other slaves" manumitted by Philip E. Vass's will had not, in truth,
"removed out of the state." Indeed, like Patsey, they too had remained in Halifax
County, where they were subject to possible arrest and reenslavement. To her

petition Patsey also attached an endorsement, signed not by one slaveowner but by fourteen whites, among them James Young and several other Halifax County slaveholders: "We the undersigned do certify that we are well acquainted with the petitioner and her husband and that all the facts stated in the above petition are true to the best of our knowledge and belief; and consequently, we do heartily unite in petitioning your honorable body, in her behalf, to grant her the liberty desired." It is doubtful that most of the signatories did not know that the other former Vass slaves were still resident in the area in defiance of the law—or that they felt any compunction about signing an official document that contained this particular falsehood. But neither Patsey Daniel's heartfelt plea nor the support of fourteen local whites made a difference. Her petition, too, was promptly referred to the Committee on the Judiciary, and within a few days it, too, was rejected. Almost exactly one year earlier the petition filed by Patsey with Jacob and Mary had met the same fate.[31]

Meanwhile, several heirs to the estate of Philip E. Vass—three of his sisters (Apphia Ewing, Mary Boyd, and Elizabeth Shepard [also spelled Sheperd and Sheppard]), along with two husbands, sued Isaac Medley for his failure as executor to pay them interest on the funds belonging to the estate. They contended their brother had stipulated that after the final settlement of his debts, all such funds should be disbursed at lawful interest for the benefit of the legatees; and included in those funds, they argued further, was the $2,000 that had been designated for the resettlement of the freed slaves: As it was now clear that the blacks could not move to North Carolina, "the appropriations before referred to, for the settlement of said emancipated slaves are nugatory & void & cannot be carried into effect and the said appropriations must fall into the residuum of the said estate." In short, they were demanding the $2,000 as well as "past and accruing interest on the same."

Judge William Leigh listened attentively to the arguments, and he found little to doubt in the sisters' contention that they should receive the interest on funds of the estate being held by Vass's executor. Leigh therefore ordered that Medley pay the Ewings nearly $140, including an additional sum of $36, "being one fourth of the amount of interest which has accrued upon the funds" during a one-year period. Leigh, however, was not convinced by their argument in regard to the $2,000 principal. It was clear to him that the money should go to the emancipated slaves, for whose benefit it had been designated, even though they could not move to North Carolina. To more mindfully arrive at a decision in the matter, Leigh appointed a commissioner to investigate issues related to the Vass slaves in the case: How much money did Medley receive from the hire of the slaves between the date of the testator's death and that of the slaves' emancipation? How did Medley utilize the slaves who were not hired out during this period? Did he permit some of the slaves to live with whites without requesting hiring contracts? Did he allow some of them "to have the benefit of their own labor"? Only when he had the answers to these questions, Leigh advised, would he be able to determine if Medley had submitted an accurate account of the estate's cash on hand.[32]

The former slaves were in a quandary. If they remained in Halifax County, they would face the possibility of reenslavement, despite their white allies; if they removed to North Carolina, they would most likely be captured and cast back into bondage; if they migrated to the North, they would be forced to leave their loved ones, probably forever. If, on the other hand, they were granted special permission to enter the state of North Carolina, they could avail themselves of the $2,000 to purchase farmland and build a farmhouse; and if they did it in Rockingham County, just across the state line and about fifty miles to the southwest of Halifax Court House—only a few miles east-to-west separated the two counties—they would be but one county away from family and friends, dangerous and illegal though it would be to be crossing the state line for visits with them. The freed Vass slaves had hit on a solution.

So, in December 1844, with the assistance of lawyer Richard Logan and their longtime friend James Young, the five of them—Jacob, Mary, Patsey, Meriweather, and Matilda (Sam, the sixth, had died)—petitioned the North Carolina General Assembly for permission to enter the state and claim their inheritance. "They therefore cast themselves on the indulgence of your Honourable body," they explained, "and humbly entreat that the benevolent intentions of their former master towards them may be suffered to be carried into execution by removing the restrictions which now prevent their availing themselves of all the benefits of the provision made for them by his will."[33] Their petition was referred to the Committee on Propositions and Grievances, and along with it came a thick packet of documents: copies of trial transcripts, court orders, the judge's decrees, and Philip E. Vass's last will and testament. The committee members quickly determined that they had neither the time nor inclination to evaluate this "strange and unprecedented" request, and the chairman asked that they be released from considering the matter. The ears of the North Carolina assemblymen, like those of their Virginia counterparts, were deaf to the freed Vass slaves' entreaty.[34]

Since the outset of the Vass slaves' freedom suit the fortunes of various Vass family members had begun to decline. The property from the two estates, although substantial in the whole, had been distributed among many relatives, each of them receiving modest amounts of cash from the sale of land and a few personal items. Vass's three sisters were heir to only a few slaves each, some of them children. The suit that the three sisters filed against Isaac Medley to secure the interest payments from estate funds indeed evinced a measure of their desperation, due in part to the outcome of the freedom suit, which deprived the estate of a potentially handsome sum of money. Even after Samuel's death, the appraised value of the five remaining slaves, considering the appreciation in prices during the 1830s, would have been considerable. Moreover, the heirs were forced to pay court costs and lawyers' fees.[35]

Perhaps no one suffered more harshly than Sarah L. Womack, another of Philip E. Vass's sisters, who lost most of her land and slaves, and self-regard, to her husband. At the time of her marriage in 1827, Sarah was living "in easy and Comfortable Circumstances having property real and personal of considerable value." She owned fourteen "likely and Valuable slaves," a tract of land in Halifax County, and some lots in the town of Danville. Upon taking her marriage vows, however, all but her personal property went to her husband, Samuel Womack, who, within a few years, began selling off her land and slaves.[36] "Mr Womack Sold my little yellow girl [Elvira] Friday Morning" to New Orleans slave trader Thomas McCargo for $800, Sarah wrote in 1836, "which Almost broke my poor heart."[37] Mr. Womack almost broke her heart again when he "Commenced a System of harsh Cruel & abusive treatment." He whipped and beat her on a number of occasions, and at least once he threatened to take her life. He brought into their home another woman, with whom he lived "in open adultery," and about 1836, he drove Sarah out of the house with orders never to return. For the next several years, she wandered from place to place; she lived now and again with neighbors and friends, and led a hand-to-mouth existence. When she arrived at the Medley plantation in 1840 for an extended stay, Medley found her to be "in a delicate state of health and destitute of almost every comfort." In 1841, she filed for divorce.[38]

The five former Vass slaves continued to risk the possibility of their reenslavement by remaining in Halifax County with their slave families. It was common knowledge among whites that they had been denied special permission from the legislature to stay in Halifax County, yet they were able to go about their business with little interference from local residents. In the 1850 US census their names did not appear among the few hundred free persons of color in the county (compared with more than fourteen thousand slaves and nearly twenty thousand whites).[39] Nor were they listed, as required by law, in the county's register of free blacks.[40]

It would have been extremely difficult for the freed Vass slaves to have continued living in Halifax County as illegal residents without the acquiescence and protection of white residents. In James Young, who with dedication and loyalty took on the responsibilities that Philip E. Vass had asked of him, they found their staunchest advocate and supporter. By 1850, the fifty-eight-year-old Young was a prosperous merchant who owned real estate valued at $6,000 as well as a 610-acre farm that produced two thousand pounds of tobacco. He also owned twenty-eight slaves, half of whom were children under twelve, a fact that lessened their value. Whereas he had lived alone with his slaves in earlier decades, he now shared his residence with four other whites, among them the fourteen-year-old John Young, who was attending school, and a twenty-one-year-old overseer.[41]

In 1850, with James Young as a court-appointed trustee to look after their interests, Jacob, Patsey, Meriweather, Mary, and Matilda resumed their suit to obtain their legacy of $2,000. The Halifax County Superior Court ruled against them. Again with Young and lawyer Richard Logan offering assistance, they took their case to "a special court of Appeals in the State Courthouse in Richmond," where they argued that the legacy should not revert to the residuary estate, and thus to the white Vass heirs, because the money had been earmarked specifically for the relocation of the freed slaves. On January 16, 1855, Judge Lucas Powell Thompson, known for his erudition and "purity as a judge," agreed. Having carefully read the transcript and reviewed the arguments of counsel for both sides, he concluded that the superior court judge had erred in his decision and that the ruling should be reversed and annulled. Thompson thus ordered the appellee, Medley, to pay the appellants' court costs and remanded the case back to the superior court in Halifax County with an order to make sure the inheritance went to the former slaves.[42]

By the early 1850s, the seventy-eight-year-old Medley had become one of the wealthiest slaveowners in the entire state of Virginia. His 120 blacks and plantation lands plus other real estate were valued at $42,000, a huge sum at the time. Among the 55,063 slaveholders in Virginia, only 116 owned more than 100 black people, thus putting Medley in the top fifth of 1 percent among Virginia's owners. He would in fact have had more than 120 slaves had he not already begun to pass on some of them as gifts to his future heirs. Like other members of the planter aristocracy, Medley hired his own private physician who lived with him on his plantation. So did his forty-year-old son, Isaac Medley Jr., who owned fifteen slaves in his own right and acted as overseer of his father's plantation.[43]

When Judge Thompson of the court of appeals in Richmond reversed the decision of the Halifax County Superior Court regarding the $2,000 legacy and ruled in favor of the former Vass slaves, nearly a quarter-century had passed since Philip E. Vass's death and more than a decade since the five Vass slaves had won their freedom and petitioned two state legislatures for exception to residency statutes. Impressively, with the assistance of the ever-loyal James Young and the lawyer Richard Logan—who by 1850 had holdings in real estate and slaves (113 of them) worth $35,000—they had succeeded in suits brought to the courts against one of the richest slaveowners in the state. There is no evidence that suggests either Logan or Young had any special grievance against Isaac Medley Sr., or that Medley harbored any ill will toward them or the Vass slaves, whom he in fact assisted during the eight years he held them in slavery.[44] Indeed, the sympathy that Medley—and Young, as well as other whites in the community—afforded the five freed blacks in their plight to remain in Halifax County without residency status enabled them to continue living, as they had most of their lifetimes, among their families and friends. Two of them, Mary and Patty, were now approaching seventy; Jacob was in his mid-forties, while Meriweather and Matilda were in their thirties. The years had only deepened the bonds of kinship and friendship among slaves and free blacks alike who had made a county in south central Virginia home.

Ironically, the victory of the former Vass slaves in the Richmond appeals court effected their unalterable defeat. In providing a blueprint for the circuit court to follow in disposing of the case, Judge Thompson ordered that the lower court appoint a group of commissioners to decide whether the blacks should "be removed to and settled in some of the states of the Union or emigrate from the United States and settle in the Colony or Commonwealth of Liberia." In either case, the sum of $2,000, with interest, should be turned over to James Young, or a newly appointed trustee, for the "use and benefit of the legatees or such of them as may elect to leave the state in defraying all necessary expenses including extra costs of suits in county and circuit courts or court of appeals and the expenses of their removal to the place of their election." The five freed blacks thus faced the fruition of their worst fears: to be uprooted from their Halifax County homes and to be separated forever from their slave families and friends. Should they elect to remain in Virginia, they would be put up for sale on the auction block. While they might end up in the hands of area residents, they would unquestion-ably bring more profit in the purchase of slave traders who would then trans-port them to cotton or sugar plantations in the Lower Mississippi River Valley.[45] Nevertheless, they would not leave the county for another four years.

In 1855, James Medley, who, following his father's death, became the ad-ministrator of the Estate of Philip E. Vass, reported that on October 1, 1855, he had $4,783.52 cash on hand: $2,000 "willed for Emancipation of Slaves"; $2,700 "Interest to date on $2000"; $47 interest to be paid on $4,700 be-tween October 1855 and December 1855; and $36.52 interest to be paid on the $2,747 between December 5, 1855, and February 27, 1856, for a total of $4,783.52. In December 1856, as directed by the court, Medley turned over $4,739.17 ($44.35 was due the estate) to trustee James Young for the benefit of the emancipated slaves.[46] In 1858, the court issued an order for the Vass slaves to register as free persons of color as required by law; and four of the original six slaves—Jacob, Mary, Meriweather, and Matilda—along with two others, Harriet Matilda and Peter, probably children of Matilda, did in fact register as directed, with five whites acting as their "protectors."[47] Not until the following year, when outbreaks of violence were increasingly fueling the sectional crisis and the fears of free blacks, did the former Vass slaves still in Halifax County reluctantly gather together their meager belongings and depart for the North.

They also collected the $2,000 promised to them nearly three decades before; the trustee retained the substantial interest for their future benefit.[48]

By 1859, then, the long struggles of the Vass slaves not only to gain their freedom but also to exercise it in their home state and county had, it appeared, come to an end. The freedom case, however, was not closed. In 1860, on the eve of the Civil War, Philip P. Vass and Emiley B. Haden, a nephew and niece of the long-deceased Philip E. Vass, petitioned the state legislature in regard to the matter of "a large number of Slaves" whom their uncle had emancipated many years earlier in his will, with directions that his real estate should be sold and the proceeds vested in land in another state for the use and benefit of the emancipated slaves. The nephew and niece traced the history of the legal dispute that had ensued over Vass's will and that concluded with the final judgment of the appeals court, whereby, they noted, "the Negroes were carried to the state of Ohio." However, they alleged, one of the "said Negroes," Meriweather, had returned to Halifax County and, by so doing, had forfeited his claims to freedom. As they were in indigent circumstances, and lawful heirs of Philip E. Vass, they pled that Meriweather be turned over to them as their slave.[49] As it happened, Meriweather Vass had indeed returned to Halifax County to visit his slave wife, Nicey, and their eleven-year-old daughter, Sophia. He escaped his reenslavement with the assistance of James Young and Richard Logan, who both loaned him small sums of money and helped him avoid arrest.[50]

Within a few years, cases like that brought to the Virginia state legislature by Philip Vass's nephew and niece would become moot, as the Civil War would bring to an end the system of slavery in the South. Still, this coda to the history of the slaves that Vass had freed is instructive. It points up the tenuous hold on personal liberty that "free persons of color" actually possessed. Even under the best of circumstances freed slaves daily faced the very real possibility of being cast back into bondage. The case shows, too, the significant role that white friends and protectors and lawyers played in the destiny of freed slaves, not to mention the threat posed to that destiny by slaveholders' families eager to recover slave property that had been lost by dint of emancipation. Heirs were frequently prepared to wage lengthy legal battles in order to regain possession of manumitted slaves and restore title to what would have been a substantial portion of their inheritance. And affectively, the case confirms what historians have observed and asserted for many years: family ties among African Americans were so strong that blacks like Meriweather were often willing to risk, and sacrifice, their hard-won freedom to be with loved ones.[51]

The Vass slaves' long pursuit of freedom, and then for rights attendant to that freedom, took them from the county to the state appellate courts, where they met mostly, and remarkably, with successes. In the legal arena, then, the experience of the Vass slaves was not unlike that of many other manumitted slaves who, both before and after the Turner revolt, brought their cases to local courts in Virginia and elsewhere in the South. Indeed, by the eve of the Civil War about one out of four free blacks in the state of Virginia had either been manumitted after the 1806 law denying freed blacks residency in the state or was the child or grandchild of a post-1806 manumitted slave; thus, 25 percent of the free blacks in Virginia were, like the Vass slaves, illegal residents.[52] Like the freed Vass slaves, too, they relied on the goodwill of sympathetic whites and the assistance of white "protectors" so as to be able to remain in their communities despite the law. The continued existence, and growth, of this white contingent attests to the personal loyalty and sincere concern that men like Richard Logan and James Young extended to "privileged" slaves even in the midst of the prevailing political and sectional ferment.

Perhaps more importantly, the experience of the Vass slaves in the suits for their freedom and rightful legacy makes manifest the fact that the equity afforded the black plaintiffs at the appellate level in the southern court system was also rendered at the local level in the county courts. Circuit superior court judge William Leigh, for one, demonstrated a determination in the Vass case to adhere to the principles of justice and equity without regard to the prevailing social attitudes and the political climate—what might be termed "legal formalism"— to a degree that was striking. Elected by the people of the Third Judicial District to the circuit court on which he served more than a quarter century, Leigh nonetheless sought to protect the rights under the law of the Vass slaves against the property grievances of various white Vass heirs. The position he assumed, by the dictates of the law, was hardly a popular one; nor did his decrees accord in any way with the decisions of either the Virginia or the North Carolina General Assemblies, as both bodies rejected petitions presented by the former Vass slaves as free persons of color. Indeed, Leigh's decrees were more favorable to the black plaintiffs than they were to the members of a once-prosperous white family.

Whether Leigh might have been guided in his judicial decisions by any political motive or social cause is unknown. Nor is it entirely clear why lawyer Richard Logan and trustee James Young remained firm for decades in their commitment to aiding the Vass slaves as they struggled to gain their freedom and right to residence in Halifax County. Nor, for that matter, do we know why Philip E. Vass singled out Jacob and Mary and the four "undivided Servants" for manumission in the first place. It seems to be apparent that at the time Vass composed his will, the four adult slaves—Jacob, Mary, Patsey, and Sam—were valued not only for their industriousness, hard work, and loyalty but also as favorites of both Philip and his deceased father. It would seem, then, that they were manumitted because of their exemplary character. While Logan and Young no doubt felt obliged to follow the instructions in Vass's will upon his death, it seems unlikely they would have proceeded along the paths they did, sometimes at personal risk, without a measure of admiration for the slaves themselves. However, as slaveowners, Logan and Young did not adhere to any antislavery rhetoric or abolitionist principles, although they might have found the noise of anti-free-black pronouncements being publicly aired by white residents and slaveholders only slightly less abhorrent.

No less assiduous than Logan and Young in his acknowledgment—and execution—of the terms of Philip Vass's will was Isaac Medley, who rarely faltered in his management of the Vass estate or in his protection of the Vass slaves, even if he was cast as a defendant in their freedom suit. Still, the primary concern for Medley as well as for Young and Logan was the disposition of the Vass property according to the wishes of the testator, not the property—including six slaves—itself.

The disposition of property, as documented in a will or deed, is what mattered, too, under the law. But the freedom of that property came with conditions, with statutes that limited residence or forced migration to Liberia. Still, in the suits of the Vass slaves over the course of a racially conflicted quarter century in post-Turner Virginia, the law ruled in favor of the plaintiffs—ironically, not to their ultimate benefit—and against a white family greedy and acquisitive in its decline. The Vass case indeed epitomizes the triumph not of the plaintiffs but of the law. The local judicial process, while fraught with pitfalls and often tortuous in its procedures, proved to be on the whole balanced and equitable. Nor did its rule of law in general harm the interests of slavery or slaveholders. In fact, it abetted them, for by upholding the legal dictates with regard to slaves the court enabled proslavery southerners to defend righteously the morality of their peculiar institution against the onslaught of abolitionist rhetoric from the North.

Conclusion

Other slave societies in the Americas allowed bond servants to pursue their freedom through use of the law and tradition, but only in the slave society of the US South during the late eighteenth and nineteenth centuries could blacks in bondage become plaintiffs with their lawyers against slaveowners in freedom suits.[1] The laws in the southern states sometimes required slaves and their lawyers either to present preliminary requests for permission to sue or to submit pretrial summaries of the arguments that they would employ to challenge the legitimacy of their enslavement. Some states, particularly in the Lower South, also obliged the plaintiffs to engage a responsible white person as a next friend, or guardian, or tutor to accompany them into court and file suit on their behalf, especially if they were minors. Such cases amounted to only a small fraction of the total number of freedom suits, and even in these cases the slaves were referred to as plaintiffs and appeals went to the appellate courts under the names of those in bondage. This did not mean that more people in bondage in the United States gained free status than did those in colonies or other countries in the Americas, as such was certainly not the case; but it did demonstrate that the laws permitting a small number of black people to test their status in the courts were uniquely designed to honor the bequests of slaveholders who wished to free their slaves in wills and deeds.

The development of chancery, or equity, courts, which expanded substantially during this period in the United States, further facilitated the legal process in such suits, on occasion even in the Lower South. In some instances free blacks and, more rarely, slaves were allowed to provide testimony for the court, usually in the form of depositions. The laws, too, covered causes for suit other than the benevolence of slaveowners who wished to manumit designated slaves. They accorded the right to file freedom suits to the descendants of free women of color, free white women, and Native American women as well as slaves who had lived in free states or territory, or visited a free country, or been illegally imported into a slave state. Term slaves who had fully served the time specified by their master and illegally held free blacks could also sue for their freedom. As a consequence, African Americans found themselves subject to a legal system that could be as harsh as it could be just and equitable. That black plaintiffs, even though their numbers were small, achieved their freedom through due process in the courts attests to the distinctive legal system that evolved in the US South in the decades between the Revolution and the Civil War.[2]

Most other slave societies in the Americas were colonies of European nations, and in general they followed the statutes and precedents of their mother countries in regard to bond servitude. Even after colonies gained their nationhood, though, the manner in which slaves attained free status in South America, Central America, and the Caribbean differed widely. In Brazil, long-standing customs allowed slaves to amass a *peculio*—savings—large enough to indemnify their price and obtain a "letter of liberty." In addition, although they could not sue in their own right, a *curador*—a legal guardian or trustee—could petition on their behalf, provided that they had been promised free status by their owners or had paid their purchase price. Unlike in the United States, however, an owner in Brazil could revoke a slave's liberty after it had been granted, and slaves could not speak for themselves by submitting their own petition.[3]

In Cuba, and probably in other Spanish colonies as well, slaves possessed the customary right of *coartación* (that is, they could purchase their own or their children's freedom by agreeing to pay an owner, first, an initial fixed sum and, thereafter, the balance in installments, their amount determined by prevailing market values). In 1842, these customary rights were codified into law and accepted by many justices and jurists as true legal rights, to be respected even against the will of owners.[4]

Remarkable though they were, such laws and customs did not allow slaves to control the process; rather, local officials called syndics, mostly slaveowners and planters, initiated the procedures and oversaw their execution. In Spanish Peru, notaries and secretaries submitted complaints to the *Audiencia*, a tribunal in which "the sovereign of Spain gave personal attention to matters of justice" and to an ecclesiastical, or secular, court, representing the sovereign of Spain. Some of these complaints involved free status.[5] In Martinique, Guadeloupe, and French Guiana, three French colonies of the Caribbean, slave men and women could take advantage of *rachet*—redemption—a policy whereby they could purchase their freedom from their owners for a fixed sum, so long as they and their owners could agree on an acceptable price.[6] Under such customs and laws in the Caribbean and South and Central America, large numbers of bondsmen and bondswomen acquired their freedom, and the free colored populations in the colonies and countries grew rapidly. Certainly, the courts aided the slaves seeking freedom in these South and Central American societies, but they did not allow slaves themselves to file freedom suits against their owners as they could in a number of states in the US South.

Self-purchase was not as common in the United States as it was elsewhere in the Americas. In fact, it was uncommon. In the Lower South, most states restricted, and later prohibited, manumissions except by the state legislatures, whereas in the Upper South it became increasingly more difficult in the decades before the Civil War to move from slavery to freedom through the courts. Nowhere in the US South, either by custom or law, were slaveowners obliged to accept the purchase price offered by a slave in exchange for his or her freedom, or to let a slave's savings indemnify a purchase price, or to enter an agreement whereby bond servants might pay for their freedom or their children's in a series of installments. If self-purchase did occur, it was by private agreement, possible only with the acquiescence of the owner and enforceable by law in only three states—Delaware, Tennessee, and Louisiana—where contracts for freedom were upheld in the courts. Owners could, and sometimes did, renege on such agreements. The owner of Virginia slave Fanny Smith promised to free her and her two children if she paid him her extra earnings over a period of ten years. Shortly before the final payment, he sold her.[7]

In stark contrast to other slave societies, too, was the multitude of state and federal laws in the United States, among them the laws regulating the export and import of slaves, the privilege of filing suits and obtaining counsel, and the claims of freedom based on residency in free territory. Such "local" laws contrasted with the national enactments governing slavery in South America and the Caribbean. In the United States, the arguments in freedom suits retraced and attempted to establish family histories by which the past would justify legal action in the present, since cases were based on the premise of slaves as property; in other slave societies, however, custom and law focused not on past circumstances but on future prospects, as through self-purchase, whereby slaves could realize themselves as persons. It is ironic that as the doors to freedom opened in many slave societies in the Americas, including the one to total abolition, they appeared to be closing in the US South. Even then, though, and down to the outbreak of the Civil War, slaves in parts of the South continued to have access to the courts of law and of chancery, and as plaintiffs they succeeded in winning a number of favorable rulings. As one justice in early Maryland declared, slave suits were nothing more than an "application to get the benefit of a right which the party was entitled to before, but which was denied him."[8]

In his study *Topics of Jurisprudence Connected with Conditions of Freedom and Bondage*, written in 1856, John Codman Hurd reasoned that freedom suits made slaves "legal persons," so that in states where the suits were allowed, a successful plea changed the fundamental relationship between the master and slave.[9] Although their numbers were very few and their rights to petition were restricted to allegations of being illegally held in bondage, slaves could file suits, call witnesses, obtain subpoenas, request juries, and on occasion seek damages.

Such complaints, unusual as they were, could be brought only with the assistance of counsel under exceptional circumstances, but the laws that permitted freedom suits remained on the books in a number of states until the late 1850s. On the eve of the Civil War, Thomas Cobb of Georgia published a treatise on the law of slavery. In the chapter "Suits for Freedom," he pointed out that in every southern state "the Negro" could institute legal action to recover his freedom when he was unlawfully detained in bondage. Most often, the case hinged on the desire of the master, either in a will or deed, to grant his slaves their freedom, and consequently, slaves had the right either to sue executors who failed to abide by the wishes of the owner or to sue a legatee who refused to file manumission papers as instructed.

Still, other laws also permitted, as they had for decades, illegally held blacks to seek free status. In these instances, statutes of limitations did not apply, and prospective plaintiffs could not be denied access to the courts for reasons of poverty, general ignorance, color, or enslavement.[10] In 1851, three justices of the peace in Fairfax County, Virginia, voiced their complaints about the black people filing these suits, which were "unsupported by any evidence whatsoever" and divested owners of their valuable property for months or longer while the case proceeded through the courts. It appears that slaves, like the Boston kinship group in eighteenth-century Anne Arundel County, kept alive the vision of freedom, and when an opportunity arose, they seized it. They filed freedom suits.[11]

Freedom suits came to an end during the Civil War as the nation underwent a catastrophic struggle of four years, duration and unimaginable death and destruction, a war that began as a fight to preserve states' rights and ended as a battle against human bondage. The history of a tiny group of four thousand black people who instituted 2,023 freedom suites over nearly a century pales in comparison. Yet, these suits permit an inside view of slavery that is unique. The voices of African Americans can be heard as they sought to defend their families and discover the possibility of gaining free status by bringing to the fore a number of arguments about their owners' deeds and wills and their owners' desire that they should serve a term of years. They also posed questions about their heritage, being children or grandchildren of free women of color, free Indian women, or white women. They learned about residency laws and residing for any length of time in a free territory or state or being imported into a state despite anti-importation laws. They even considered that agreements with their masters concerning self-purchase and purchase of loved ones as viable "contracts" and though winning only of a few of these cases they challenged the system as unfair and inequitable.

The freedom suits, primarily in the Upper South and Louisiana, offer a profile not unlike a profile of the great majority of black people who struggled under the yoke of human bondage. They included those on large plantations, small farms, and in towns and cities. The petitioners were mostly black but some were persons of mixed racial heritage, percentage-wise about the same as the 10 percent listed in the pre–Civil War slave census returns as "mulattoes." They included a number of privileged blacks who attained quasi-free or virtually free status. Their pleas represented the attitudes and values of many with regard to the sanctity of their families as well as their determination to protect their children and other loved ones at almost any cost. Also, like many others, they at times experienced violent retributions, sales and resales, and exportation, and they found themselves in jails, slave pens, and taken by slave traders who were moving relentlessly toward the Lower South. Their desire for freedom, articulated by their legal counsel and at times in their own words, probably pulsated through the hearts and minds of many others held in bondage. They brought their suits even though many realized that if they were successful they would be forced to abandon friends, family, and the communities where they had many attachments. Many who remained at home in defiance of anti-residency laws lived in constant fear of returning to slavery.

At the same time the suits reveal how many white people came to their aid and support, including lawyers, members of slaveholding families, townspeople, and many others who testified in their behalf. In fact, the plaintiffs who won their freedom would not have done so without the assistances of those who served as "protectors" in times of crisis. Viewed from the perspective of race relations, the suits show white empathy and compassion for those held illegally in bondage. White "friends" and acquaintances gave depositions against slaveholders who were well known and prosperous members of their communities. Nor were courts, juries, and judges unsympathetic to their plight, often admiring plaintiffs' determination and resolve for freedom and ruling in their favor.

It is clear that the courts in states where such cases could be brought were concerned about justice and equity. Perhaps the words of a Kentucky judge expressed it best when, in 1833, he lamented the complexity of the legal system when it came to slaves. They were considered both people and property; they were tried under special rules and laws; they faced unique problems in both criminal and civil courts. Slaves possessed "few and humble rights—proscribed by disabilities and disfranchisements" whereas their owners were "endowed with all the rights, immunities and privileges which sovereignty can bestow." The system was wrought with "great complexity and perplexity," and the "code of jurisprudence" in this regard was "a confused compound of contrarieties." But "the law must prevail," he declared. "Equity follows the law."[12]

The cases not only illustrate how African Americans struggled to acquire their freedom within the system but also suggest the unique role of black women in the slave regime: how they fought to keep kin together and prevent the sale of loved ones; how they recalled and recited the names of ancestors dating back many years, sometimes generations; and how some among them had to deal with being the children of their white owners. The struggles of black women to extricate themselves from bondage took on added significance. If they were successful their future offspring would also be free. They fought against owners, heirs, creditors, traders, and others to obtain their freedom, opposed in these efforts because they were not only valuable property themselves but they and their children often constituted a substantial portion of a slaveowner's estate.

But most of all freedom suits open up a new body of evidence that exposes the attitudes, values, and determination of those held in bondage to acquire their freedom. The voices of enslaved people are rarely heard and the immediacy of their pleas for protection and freedom offers a perspective that is both dramatic and exceptional, as they tell us about their fears, anxieties, anticipations, and dreams. There is little doubt that the cases go beyond the trials and court battles, revealing cultural, social, genealogical, and economic relationships among the various participants.

Perhaps no suit better illustrates this than the one brought by Jinny Dawson in Randolph County, North Carolina. Not only did she file a freedom suit through her lawyer, future governor and slaveholder John M. Morehead, relating, as did so many others, her life's history, but despite being held as a slave she was permitted to testify on her own behalf. This was rare for free blacks as well as slaves, yet it probes the depths of others illegally detained as captives. On August 5, 1830, in a five-page, 1,340-word deposition, she told the court about her mother and grandmother, a white woman, and her seven children, three of whom lived with her and four others who lived with three different owners in nearby counties of Guilford and Montgomery and distant county of Camden. She and her deceased mother had always protested their enslavement, had run away on various occasions, and had demanded to be released, but to no avail. She anxiously noted that her current owner, a man named Swain, "sometimes threatens to sell her & her children & she fears that he will do so." If he does, they will all be "run off" forever to some distant land. In addition, Jane's husband, free black Robert Dawson, took an oath saying that he had listened to the "affiant" Jinny Dawson give her deposition and to his knowledge all the facts presented were true "& those not of his Knowledge" he believed to be true. Jinny Dawson was granted an injunction preventing her owner from taking her and her three children away, but after three years the freedom suit remained unresolved.[13] Although very few free blacks and slaves provided such testimony, most freedom suit plaintiffs presented the same type of evidence about their families and loved ones through their lawyers, who in many instances used slaves' words and arguments in their presentations to the courts. In this way, the thoughts, feelings, and attitudes of those in bondage became part of the legacy of southern slavery.

Over time, suits for freedom, like the numerous state laws controlling their lives, changed and evolved. The changes could be seen in the primary causes for filing suits, from heritage-based white and Indian ancestry filings during the early period to a large portion of illegally held free blacks and residency cases in the middle and late periods. The cases involving term slaves during the early period represented only a small fraction compared with those during the middle and late periods, while the cases involving illegal importation represented nearly twice as many during the early period as the other two periods combined. Yet the proportion of freedom suits in each time period remained relatively constant over time, with 32 percent of the total in the early period, 36 percent in the middle period, and 32 percent in the late period, revealing a steady flow of litigation over the years, all the more surprising when considering the changes occurring in virtually every aspect of southern society. The small number of suits in the Lower South, excluding Louisiana before the mid-1840s, was a reflection of the stringent antifreedom statutes in most of the Lower South states, culminating a few years before the Civil War with harsh antiblack laws. The large rice, cotton, and sugar plantations, working huge gangs of slaves, and the growing sentiments of slaveowners toward secession, created an economic and political environment hostile to freedom. Yet even in the Lower South, following the *Dred Scott* decision, a few freedom suits found their way on to court dockets.

Appendix

A BRIEF PROFILE OF FREEDOM SUITS
AND RESULTS

An Explanation of the Data

The following tables contain information on 2,023 freedom suits, beginning in 1779 with the suit of Jude Fisher in Delaware and ending in 1863 with the plea of Pleasant Lee in North Carolina. Each suit contains twenty-seven variables, including, among others, an identification number, date, state, county, name of plaintiff(s), color of plaintiff (when mentioned), court jurisdiction, principal argument, different actions (trespass, sue *in forma pauperis*, habeas corpus, injunction, etc.), "next friend" or guardian in some cases, number of petitioners, whether or not a jury trial and/or appellate case, name of defendant(s), name of lawyer(s) when available, and the result. The collection does not include all of the freedom suits presented in the southern courts during the period but is probably representative of others, coming as they do from two hundred counties and Louisiana parishes as well as the fifteen slave states and the District of Columbia. Finding a result was not possible for about 15 percent of these cases. It was especially difficult to uncover county court results when the court minutes were not extant and/or the verdict was not included with the original court proceedings. As with all statistical evidence, the various percentages cited in the chapters should be viewed as rough approximations. Nevertheless, it is highly probable that the cases are representative of the larger picture. Broken down by states, the database includes the following number of freedom suits:

Alabama	13
Arkansas	10
Delaware	318
District of Columbia	427
Florida	7

Georgia	9
Kentucky	245
Louisiana	210
Maryland	181
Mississippi	13
Missouri	304
North Carolina	34
South Carolina	18
Tennessee	55
Texas	5
Virginia	<u>174</u>
	2,023

Table Abbreviations

CV	Change of Venue
CVD	Change of Venue, Denied
D	Denied
DAA	Denied, Appealed, Affirmed
D DAA	Denied: Denied, Appealed, Affirmed
D DARR	Denied: Denied, Appealed, Reversed, Remanded
D DiAA	Denied: Dismissed, Appealed, Affirmed
D GARev	Denied: Granted, Appealed, Reversed
D GARR	Denied: Granted, Appealed, Reversed, Remanded
D GDR	Denied: Granted, Denied, Reversed
DefNF	Defendant Not Found
DeniedA	Denied, Appealed
DisA	Dismissed, Appealed
DisAg	Dismissed, Agreement
DisARev	Dismissed, Appealed, Reversed
DisByPlff	Dismissed by Plaintiff
DisAA	Dismissed, Appealed, Affirmed
Discon	Discontinued
DisWP	Dismissed Without Prejudice
G	Granted
GAA	Granted, Appealed, Affirmed
G DACV	Granted: Denied, Appealed, Change of Venue
G DARev	Granted: Denied, Appealed, Reversed
G DARR	Granted: Denied, Appealed, Reversed, Remanded
G DisARev	Granted: Dismissed, Appealed, Reversed
G DisARR	Granted: Dismissed, Appealed, Reversed, Remanded

G GAA	Granted: Granted, Appealed, Affirmed
G GACV	Granted: Granted, Appealed, Change of Venue
G GARR	Granted: Granted, Appealed, Reversed, Remanded

Table 1 **Results of Appeals Cases by Time Period**

Early Period, 1779–1819

Appeals Case	Number
Denied	
D DAA	32
D DARR	1
D GARR	6
D GARev	30
D DisAA	6
Total	75
Granted	
G GAA	70
G GARR	2
G DARev	16
G DARR	9
Total	97
Undecided	2
Total	99
Total	**174**
	56 percent granted

Middle Period, 1820–1839

Appeals Case	Number
Denied	
D DAA	57
D DARR	4
D GARR	13
D GARev	18
D DisAA	1
Total	93

Middle Period, 1820–1839

Granted

G GAA	96
G GACV	3
G GARev	2
G GARR	13
G DARev	22
G DARR	12
G DisARR	2
Total	150

Court Action

Abated	2

Undecided

	3

Total	**248**
	62 percent granted

Late Period, 1840–1863

Appeals Case	Number

Denied

D DAA	45
D DARR	2
D GARR	16
D GARev	32
D DisAA	12
Total	107

Granted

G GAA	83
G GARR	2
G DARev	21
G DARR	14
G DisARR	10
Total	130

Undecided

	4

Total	**241**
	55 percent granted

Table 2 **Results of County Court Cases by Time Period**

Early Period, 1779–1819

Case	Number	Details
Denied		
Denied	24	Includes 1 not prosecuted
DeniedA	8	
Dismissed	39	Includes 2 DisA and 1 DisAg
DisWP	3	
Discontinued/Not Brought Forward	14	
Total	88	
Granted		
G	191	
Granted Agreement	14	
Granted/Appeal	7	
DefNF	5	
Total	217	**71 percent granted**
Court Actions		
Abated	2	
CV	2	
Total	4	
Unknown Results		
Partially Granted	78	
DisByPlff	6	
No Result	63	
Total	147	
Total Freedom Suits	**456**	
Injunctions		
Granted	6	
Total	6	

Early Period, 1779–1819

Habeas Corpus

Granted and Released	2
Denied	1
Granted and No Decision on Release	6
No Result	1
	10

Total Injunctions/Habeas Corpus	**16**
Total Suits	**472**

Middle Period, 1820–1839

Case	Number	
Denied		
Denied	34	Includes 3 defaults; 1 CV
Denied/Appeal	1	
Dismissed	9	Includes 2 DisA and 1 DisAg
DisWP	2	
Discontinued/Not Brought Forward	4	
Nonsuit	13	
Total	63	
Granted		
Granted	198	Includes 3 DisWP by defendant lawyer
Granted Agreement	4	
Granted/Appeal	1	
DefNF	30	
Total	233	**79 percent granted**
Court Actions		
Abated	9	
CV	3	
Total	12	

Middle Period, 1820–1839

Unknown Results

Partially Granted	34	
DisByPlff	15	
No Result	27	Includes 1 granted, no result
Total	76	

Total Freedom Suits 384

Injunctions

Granted	32	
Granted/Dismissed	6	Includes 2 DisByPlff
Denied/Dismissed	7	
Agreement	1	
Total	46	

Habeas Corpus

Granted and Released	18	
Granted	8	
Denied	5	Includes 1 dismissed
Granted and No Decision on Release	16	
No Result	1	
Total	48	

Total Injunctions/Habeas Corpus	94

Total Suits 478

Late Period, 1840–1863

Case	Number	
Denied		
Denied	33	Includes 1 default; 1 granted, 1 denied
Dismissed	19	
Nonsuit	7	
Total	59	

Late Period, 1840–1863

Granted

Granted	182	Includes 3 DisWP by defendant's lawyer
Granted Agreement	14	Includes 6 DisByPlff; 3 nonsuits
DefNF	27	
Granted/Appeal	1	
Total	224	**79 percent granted**

Court Actions

Abated	1
CV	2
Total	3

Unknown Results

Partially Granted	8	
DisByPlff	29	
No Result	24	Includes 1 granted but no result
Total	61	

Total Freedom Suits   347

Injunctions

Granted and Freedom	8	Includes 2 by agreement; 2 DefNF
Granted, No Result on Freedom	14	Includes 1 granted, dismissed
Denied/Dismissed	1	
No Result	1	
Total	24	

Habeas Corpus

Granted and Released	10
Granted	14
Granted and No Decision on Release	10
Denied	3
No Result	2
Total	39

Total Injunctions/Habeas Corpus   63

Total Court Actions   **410**

Table 3   **Results, Primary Complaint: Wills and Deeds**

Wills & Deeds: Appeals Cases

Denied	Granted	Percentages and Totals
3 D DARR	21 G DARev	
27 D GARev	10 G DARR	
9 D GARR	2 G DisARev	
35 D DAA	65 G GAA	
6 D DissAA		
1 Nonsuit		
81	98	**55 percent granted**

Unknown Results

1 No Result

Total Wills & Deeds Appeals		180

Wills and Deeds: County Court Cases

Denied	Granted	Percentages and Totals
13 Denied	83 Granted	
7 Dismissed	1 G Agreement	
2 Default	1 Granted/Appeal	
2 Nonsuit/non pros	6 G DefNF	
1 Denied/Appeal		
25	91	**78 percent granted**

Unknown Results

14 DisByPlff

13 Granted No Result; primarily habeas corpus or injunction

11 No Result

10 Partially Granted

48

Total Wills and Deeds County Court		164

Wills & Deeds: Appeals and County Court Cases

Denied	Granted	Percentages and Totals
13 Denied	83 Granted	
7 Dismissed	1 Granted/Appeal	
3 D DARR	21 G DARev	
27 D GARev	10 G DARR	
9 D GARR	2 G DisARev	
35 DAA	65 GAA	
6 DissAA	1 G agreement	
2 Default	6 G DefNF	
3 Non suit/non pros		
1 Denied/Appeal		
106	189	**64 percent granted**

Total Unknown Results

14 DisByPlff

13 Granted No Result; primarily habeas corpus or injunction

12 No Result

10 Partially Granted

49		**14 percent unknown**
Total Wills and Deeds Appeals and County Court		295
Total Wills and Deeds Cases		344

Table 4 **Results, Primary Complaint: Term Slaves**

Term Slaves: Appeals Cases		
Denied	*Granted*	*Percentages and Totals*
5 D GARev	1 G DARR	
5 D GARR	11 G DARev	
16 DAA	4 G DisARev	
5 DissAA	29 GAA	
31	45	**59 percent granted**

Unknown Results
1 PG

Court Action

1 Abated

Total Term Slaves Appeals   78

Term Slaves: County Court Cases		
Denied	*Granted*	*Percentages and Totals*
6 Denied	38 Granted	
4 Dismissed		
1 Discontinued		
1 D GDR		
1 CVD		
1 Nonsuit		
14	38	**73 percent granted**

Unknown Results

1 DisByPlff

11 Granted No Result; primarily habeas corpus or injunction

5 No Result

2 Partially Granted

19

Total Term Slaves County Court   71

Term Slaves: Appeals and County Court Cases

Denied	Granted	Percentages and Totals
6 Denied	38 Granted	
4 Dismissed	11 G DARev	
5 D GARev	1 G DARR	
5 D GARR	4 G DisARev	
16 DAA	29 GAA	
1 D GDR		
5 D DissAA		
1 Discontinued		
1 CVD		
1 Nonsuit		
45	83	**65 percent granted**

Unknown Results
1 DisByPlff
11 Granted No Result; primarily habeas corpus or injunction
5 No Result
3 Partially Granted
1 Abated

21		**14 percent unknown**
Total Term Slaves Appeals and County Court		149

Table 5 **Results, Primary Complaint: White Ancestry**

White Ancestry: Appeals Cases

Denied	Granted	Percentages and Totals
5 D GARev	2 G DARev	
3 D GARR	27 GAA	
7 D DAA		
3 DisAA		
18	29	**62 percent granted**

Unknown Results
None

Total White Ancestry Appeals		47

White Ancestry: County Court Cases

Denied	Granted	Percentages and Totals
7 Denied	22 Granted	
3 Dismissed	3 G DefNF	
	2 G Granted/Dismissed	
10	27	**72 percent granted**

Unknown Results

14 No Result

4 Partially Granted

18

Total White Ancestry County Courts	55

White Ancestry: Appeals and County Court Cases

Denied	Granted	Percentages and Totals
7 Denied	22 Granted	
3 Dismissed	27 GAA	
5 D GARev	2 G DARev	
3 D GARR	3 G DefNF	
7 DAA	2 G Granted/Dismissed	
3 DisAA		
28	56	**67 percent granted**

Total Unknown Results

14 No Result

4 Partially Granted

18	**18 percent unknown**
Total White Ancestry Appeals and County Court	102

Table 6   **Results, Primary Complaint: Indian Ancestry**

Indian Ancestry: Appeals Cases

Denied	Granted	Percentages and Totals
2 D GARev	6 G DARR	
2 D GARR	1 G DARev	
2 DAA	12 G GARR	
	8 GAA	
	2 G GARev	
	3 G DACV	
6	32	**80 percent granted**

Court Action
1 Abated

Unknown Results
1 Partially Granted

Total Indian Ancestry Appeals		40

Indian Ancestry: County Court Cases

Denied	Granted	Percentages and Totals
2 Denied	38 Granted	Includes 1 G Released
3 Dismissed		
1 Default		
6	38	**86 percent granted**

Unknown Results
1 DisByPlff

1 No Result

3 Partially Granted

5

Total Indian Ancestry County Court Total Indian Ancestry County Court	49

Indian Ancestry: Appeals and County Court Cases

Denied	Granted	Percentages and Totals
2 Denied	38 Granted	Includes 1 G Released
3 Dismissed	8 GAA	
2 D GARev	1 G DARev	
2 D GARR	3 G DACV	
2 DAA	12 G DARR	
1 Default	2 G GARev	
	6 G DARR	
12	70	**85 percent granted**

Court Action
1 Abated

Total Unknown Results

1 No Result

4 Partially Granted

1 DissByPlff

6		**7 percent unknown**
Total Indian Ancestry Appeals and County Court	89	

Table 7 **Results, Primary Complaint: Free Black Ancestry**

Free Black Ancestry: Appeals Cases

Denied	Granted	Percentages and Totals
7 D GARev	6 G DARR	
4 D GARR	3 G DARev	
13 D DAA	18 G GAA	
24	27	**55 percent granted**

Unknown Results
1 Partially Granted

Total Free Black Ancestry Appeals   52

Free Black Ancestry: County Court Cases

Denied	Granted	Percentages and Totals
13 Denied	57 G Granted	
7 Dismissed	7 G Agreement	
2 Discontinued	2 G Released	
2 Nonsuit	6 G DefNF	
	1 G/Appeal	
	5 G DissByPlff	
24	78	**76 percent granted**

Court Action
3 Abated

Unknown Results
5 DisByPlff
19 21 No Result
6 Granted No Result
21 Partially Granted
53

Total Free Black Ancestry County Court   155

Free Black Ancestry: Appeals and County Court Cases

Denied	Granted	Percentages and Totals
7 Denied	57 Granted	
13 Dismissed	18 GAA	
4 D DARR	3 G DARev	
7 D GARev	6 G DARR	
1 D Discont	7 G Agreement	
13 DAA	2 G Released	
3 Nonsuit	6 G DefNF	
	1 G/Appeal	
	5 G DissByPlff	
48	105	**69 percent granted**

Court Action
3 Abated

Total Unknown Results

5 DisByPlff

19 21 No Result

6 Granted No Result; habeas corpus and injunctions

22 Partially Granted

54		**25 percent unknown**
Total Free Black Ancestry Appeals and County Court	210	

NOTES

Abbreviations

AAETSU	Archives of Appalachia, East Tennessee State University, Johnson City
ADAH	Alabama Department of Archives and History, Montgomery
CAHUT	Center for American History, the University of Texas, Austin
CCBSL	Civil Courts Building, St. Louis, Missouri
CCH	County Courthouse
DSA	Delaware State Archives, Dover
JCCASN	*Judicial Cases Concerning American Slavery and the Negro*
KCCCP-CJD	Kent County Court of Common Pleas—Continuance/Judgment Docket
KDLA	Kentucky Division of Libraries and Archives, Frankfort
LV	Library of Virginia, Richmond
MDAH	Mississippi Department of Archives and History, Jackson
MNDCA	Metropolitan Nashville-Davidson County Archives
MSA	Maryland State Archives, Annapolis
MoSA	Missouri State Archives, Jefferson City
NA	National Archives, Washington, DC
NCDAH	North Carolina Division of Archives and History, Raleigh
NOPL	New Orleans Public Library
PAR	Petition Analysis Record
RUSCC-CDRCF	Records of the United States Circuit Court, Chancery Dockets and Rules Case Files
RUSDC-SHCP	Records of the United States District Court, Segregated *Habeas Corpus* Papers
SC	Schweninger Collection
SCDAH	South Carolina Department of Archives and History, Columbia
TSLA	Tennessee State Library and Archives, Nashville
UArLRSL	University of Arkansas at Little Rock, School of Law
UNO	University of New Orleans
USMSPC	United States Manuscript Population Census
USMSSC	United States Manuscript Slave Census

Note on Sources

Most cases in this study have been drawn from a digital library on American slavery (https://library.uncg.edu/slavery/), an eighteen-year project at the University of North Carolina at Greensboro, underwritten by the National Endowment for the Humanities, the National Historical Publications and Records Commission, the Charles Stewart Mott Foundation, and the University's Jackson Library. The website includes abstracts of the suits and other information including the names of each African American mentioned, whether slave or free. In 2012, ProQuest put the entire manuscript collection, roughly 140,000 pages of documentary evidence, online in its "Slavery and the Law Digital Archive," subscribed to by many libraries and archives.

In the notes that follow, many cases are cited with a PAR, or Petition Analysis Record number, an eight-digit code in the digital library that identifies the document by series (1 = legislative, 2 = county court), state, year, and number within the year. The fifteen states and the District of Columbia are assigned two-digit codes: Alabama = 01 through Virginia = 16. The year denotes the last three digits of the year in which the petition was filed, e.g., 804 = 1804. The final two digits represent the order in which a specific petition was entered within the given year. Thus, the freedom suit of the slave John in Sussex County, Virginia, in 1804 is cited as PAR 21680402.

Summaries of many of the appellate cases are found in the Helen Catterall, ed., *Judicial Cases Concerning American Slavery and the Negro*, 5 vols. (Washington, DC: Carnegie Institution, 1926–1937; reprint, New York: Octagon Books, 1968 [citations are to the reprint edition]) and in the state reports of appellate courts or in both. Some of these state reports were put online but are cited here by their original titles as the lengthy "http" addresses have sometimes become obsolete.

Every attempt has been made to uncover the final disposition of each freedom suit, including perusing census records, private collections, court minutes, and various other sources. At times it was not possible to discover the petition's final resolution, especially when court minutes are not extant or docket pages are missing. In some instances, therefore, the phrase "No decree with petition" has been used. Otherwise, "Granted" or "Denied" is indicated following the PAR number or at the end of a citation. For appellate cases, the outcome follows the ruling of the appeals courts (i.e., "GAA" granted: appealed, affirmed [meaning the original grant of freedom was affirmed]; "D GARev" denied: granted, appealed, reversed; or "D GARR" denied: granted, appealed, reversed or reversed and remanded [meaning the case was reversed or returned to the lower court for further consideration]). For cases denied and appealed, the following abbreviations have been employed: "DAA," "G DARev," and "G DARR." The first letter in each acronym indicates whether the suit was either granted or denied. All results, including cases where the names of appellants (defendants appealing the verdict) appear first, concern the fate of the slave plaintiffs.

Introduction

1. *Argument of Mr. Hambly, of York, (Penn) In the Case of Edward Prigg, Plaintiff In Error, v. The Commonwealth of Pennsylvania, Defendant In Error: In the Supreme Court of the United States* (Baltimore: Lucas and Deaver, 1842), in Fugitive Slaves and the American Courts: The Pamphlet Literature, 4 vols., ed. Paul Finkelman (New York: Garland, 1988), 1:121–156; Kermit L. Hall, Paul Finkelman, and James W. Ely Jr., eds., *American Legal History: Cases and Materials*, 3rd ed. (New York: Oxford University Press, 2005), 229–234; Paul Finkelman, *An Imperfect Union: Slavery, Federalism, and Comity* (Chapel Hill: University of North Carolina Press, 1981), 132, 134; Paul Finkelman, "*Prigg v. Pennsylvania*: Understanding Justice Story's Pro-Slavery Nationalism," *Journal of Supreme Court History* 2 (1997): 51–64; Joseph Nogee, "The Prigg Case and Fugitive Slavery, 1842–1850: Part I," *Journal of Negro History* 39, no. 3 (July 1954): 185–205; Joseph C. Burke, "What Did the Prigg Decision Really Decide?," *Pennsylvania Magazine of History and Biography* 93, no. 1 (January 1969): 73–85; Thomas D. Morris, *Free Men All: The Personal Liberty Laws of the North, 1780–1861* (Baltimore: Johns Hopkins University Press, 1974), chap. 6; Melvin Urofsky and Paul Finkelman, *A March of Liberty: A Constitutional History of the United States*, vol. 1: *From the Founding to 1890* (New York: Oxford University Press, 2002), 352–354.

2. George Tucker, "Letter to a Member of the General Assembly of Virginia, on the Subject of the Late Conspiracy of the Slaves; With a Proposal for Their Colonization" (Baltimore, 1801), quoted in Winthrop Jordan, *White over Black: American Attitudes toward the Negro, 1550–1812* (Chapel Hill: University of North Carolina Press, 1967), 561–562.

3. Freedom suits: filings by decade

Year	Appeals	County	Total
1770s and 1780s	10	42	52
1790s	40	132	172
1800s	56	163	219
1810s	68	135	203
1820s	104	204	308
1830s	144	274	418
1840s	114	245	359
1850s and 1860s	127	165	292
Totals	663	1,360	2,023

4. *Malotte, f.w.c., v. Hackett and Newby*, No. 2712, First District Court of New Orleans, 5 March 1849, in Judith Kelleher Schafer, *Becoming Free, Remaining Free: Manumission and Enslavement in New Orleans, 1846–1862* (Baton Rouge: Louisiana State University Press, 2003), 24–25.

5. Petition of Amelia Green to the Court of Common Pleas of Craven County, North Carolina, September 1796, in Records of the County Court, Slaves and Free Negroes 1788–1860, NCDAH. PAR 21279602. Granted. Petition of Amelia Green to the Court of Pleas and Quarter Sessions of Craven County, North Carolina, December 1801, in Records of the County Court, Slaves and Free Negroes 1775–1861, NCDAH. PAR 21280108. Granted. See Catherine W. Bishir, *Crafting Lives: African American Artisans in New Bern, North Carolina, 1770–1900* (Chapel Hill: University of North Carolina Press, 2013), 12, 75, 76, 79.

6. Warren M. Billings, "The Cases of Fernando and Elizabeth Key: A Note on the Status of Blacks in Seventeenth-Century Virginia," *William and Mary Quarterly* 30, no. 3 (July 1973): 467–474; Lorenzo Johnston Greene, *The Negro in Colonial New England, 1620–1776* (New York: Columbia University Press, 1942), 296–297 [*Adam v. Saffin*]; Graham Russell Hodges, *Root and Branch: African Americans in New York and East Jersey, 1613–1863* (Chapel Hill: University of North Carolina Press, 1999), 130; Thelma Wills Foote, *Black and White Manhattan: The History of Racial Formation in Colonial New York City* (New York: Oxford University Press, 2004), 149; Kathleen M. Brown, *Good Wives, Nasty Wenches, Anxious Patriarchs: Gender, Race and Power in Colonial Virginia* (Chapel Hill: University of North Carolina Press, 1996), 223–225, 227–236.

7. Lorenzo Johnston Greene, *The Negro in Colonial New England, 1620–1776* (New York: Columbia University Press, 1942), 295–296; Catherine Adams and Elizabeth H. Pleck, *Love of Freedom: Black Women in Colonial and Revolutionary New England* (New York: Oxford University Press, 2010), 131; Edgar J. McManus, *Black Bondage in the North* (Syracuse, NY: Syracuse University Press, 1973), 149–50, 153 [New Jersey *Gazette*]; Edward Raymond Turner, *The Negro in Pennsylvania: Slavery, Servitude, Freedom, 1839–1861* (Washington, DC: American Historical Association, 1911; reprint, New York: Negro Universities Press, 1969), 63n38. Citations are to the reprint edition.

8. *Robyn, Hannah, Daniel, Cuffie, Isham, Moses, Peter, Judy, Archy, Sylvia, Davy and Ned v. John Hardaway*, 2 May 1772, Williamsburg, Virginia, General Court (Colonial), Judgment 1772, Acc. 33700, Case 04-1470-02, State Government Records Collection, LV. Granted.

9. George William Van Cleve, *A Slaveholders' Union: Slavery, Politics, and the Constitution in the Early American Republic* (Chicago: University of Chicago Press, 2010), 26–28 [case of Peter Lee in 1764 in New Castle County, Delaware]; Van Cleve also noted freedom suits in Massachusetts, Rhode Island, New Jersey, and Pennsylvania; in Massachusetts, see *Caesar v. Greenleaf* in *A Slaveholders' Union*, 303n76; Robert Cover, *Justice Accused: Antislavery and the Judicial Process* (New Haven, CT: Yale University Press, 1975), 46 ["juries became notorious"]; Ira Berlin, *Many Thousands Gone: The First Two Centuries of Slavery in North America* (Cambridge, MA: Harvard University Press, 1998) 91–92, 281 ["whole families"]; Benjamin Quarles, *The Negro in the American Revolution* (Chapel Hill: University of North Carolina Press, 1961), 38–39 [mulatto woman]; Adams and Pleck, *Love of Freedom*, 138–139 [Massachusetts Constitution of 1780]; Elaine Foreman Crane, *Ebb Tide in New England: Women, Seaports, and Social Change, 1630–1800* (Boston: Northeastern University Press, 1998), 146; Arthur Zilversmit, *The First Emancipation: The Abolition of Slavery in the*

North (Chicago: University of Chicago Press, 1967), 104n35; Arthur Zilversmit, "Quok Walker, Mumbet, and the Abolition of Slavery in Massachusetts," *William and Mary Quarterly* 25 (October 1968): 619–622; Harry Down, "Unlikely Abolitionist: William Cushing and the Struggle against Slavery," *Journal of Supreme Court History* 29, no. 2 (June 2004): 128–129; Woody Holton, *Black Americans in the Revolutionary Era: A Brief History with Documents* (New York: Bedford/St. Martin's, 2009), 78–79; John Wood Sweet, *Bodies Politic: Negotiating Race in the American North, 1730–1830* (Baltimore: Johns Hopkins University Press, 2003), 235–388 [suit of Mary Wamsley]; Leon A. Higginbotham Jr., *In the Matter of Color: Race and the American Legal Process; the Colonial Period* (New York: Oxford University Press, 1978), 206–207.

10. US House of Representatives, *The Federal and State Constitutions, Colonial Charters, and Other Organic Laws of the States Territories, and Colonies*, 59th Cong., 2nd sess., 1909, 7 vols. (Washington, DC: Government Printing Office, 1909–), 1:19, 22, 26 [US Constitution].

11. A few of the suits in this study have been drawn from secondary sources, including, most prominently, William E. Foley, "Slave Freedom Suits before Dred Scott: The Case of Marie Jean Scypion's Descendants," *Missouri Historical Review* 79 (1984–1985): 1–23; Michael L. Nicholls, "'The squint of freedom': African-American Freedom Suits in Post-Revolutionary Virginia," *Slavery and Abolition* 20, no. 2 (August 1999): 47–62; Kelly Marie Kennington, "Law, Geography, and Mobility: Suing for Freedom in Antebellum St. Louis," *Journal of Southern History* 80 (August 2014): 575–604; Lea VanderVelde, *Redemption Songs: Suing for Freedom before Dred Scott* (New York: Oxford University Press, 2014); Arnold Taylor, *Rose, a Woman of Colour: A Slave's Struggle for Freedom in the Courts of Kentucky* (New York: iUniverse, 2008); James H. Kettner, "Persons or Property? The Pleasants Slaves in the Virginia Courts, 1792–1799," in *Launching the "Extended Republic": The Federalist Era*, ed. Ronald Hoffman and Peter J. Albert (Charlottesville: University Press of Virginia, 1996), 136–155; Christopher Doyle, "Judge St. George Tucker and the Case of *Tom v. Roberts*: Blunting the Revolution's Radicalism from Virginia's District Courts," *Virginia Magazine of History and Biography* 106 (Autumn 1998): 419–442; Eric Gardner, "'You Have No Business to Whip Me': The Freedom Suits of Polly Walsh and Lucy Ann Delaney," *African American Review* 41, no. 1 (Spring 2007): 33–50; Thomas F. Brown and Leah C. Sims, "'To Swear Him Free': Ethnic Memory as Social Capital in Eighteenth-Century Freedom Petitions," in *Colonial Chesapeake: New Perspectives*, ed. Debra Myers and Melanie Perrault (Lanham, MD: Lexington, 2006), 81–106. Other suits have been taken from the website titled "O Say Can You See: Early Washington, D.C, Law & Family," http://earlywashingtondc.org/.

Chapter 1

1. Depositions, Anne Brown, ca. 1792 (twice), 1793 (twice), October 17, 1795, June 3, 1797, in Records of the General Court of the Western Shore, Maryland, 1 November 1791, in SC, *John Boston v. John Francis Mercer, Fanny Boston v. John Francis Mercer, Fanny Boston v. John Francis Mercer, Anne Boston v. John Francis Mercer, Jenny Boston v. John Francis Mercer, Maria Boston v. Richard Sprigg, Philip Boston v. Richard Sprigg, Benjamin Boston v. Richard Sprigg*, Microfilm M 11015, Volume 4239-2, Documents 12–19, SC, MSA; Related Documents: Court Record, 1791–1793 with *Boston, et al. v. Mercer, et al.*; Depositions, Anne Harwood, July 20, 1789; Elizabeth Rawlings, 20 July 1789; Richard Watkins, 10 March 1790; Richard Richardson, 10 March 1790; Plummer Ijiams, 4 August 1790; Mary Batson, 7 August 1790; Depositions, John Welch, 3 February 1791, 24 February 1791; Robert John Smith, ca. 1791; Ann Watkins, 4 June 1791; John Tydings, 25 October 1791; Thomas Gibbs, 3 November 1791; Mary Cruchly, 4 November 1791; testimony of Benjamin Carr, 16 October 1792; Depositions of Benjamin Atwell, 21 May 1792; Alice Taylor, 23 June 1792; Certificate, William Foard, 10 August 1747; Depositions, John Norris, 8 and 13 October, 1792; Margaret Gassaway Watkins, 21 May 1793; Richard Hopkins, 21 May 1793; Dinah Watkins, 21 May 1793; Mary Farro, 21 May 1793; Joseph Cowman, 25 May 1793; Bacon Boston, 15 June 1793; William Harwood, 25 May 1795; Court Record, 1793–1795, Order and Appeals, 1795, with Order of Appeals 1795, Records of the Court of Appeals, June Term 1797, which includes the following cases: *Bacon Boston v. Gassaway Wakins, Richard Boston v Joshua Warfield, George*

Boston v. James Murray, Guy Boston v. Richard Richardson, Peter Boston v. Richard Richardson, John Boston v. Richardson, Deborah Boston v. Richard Richardson. The record from the General Court of the Western Shore, including the depositions of Ann Brown and others, was forwarded to the court of appeals. Anne Brown's 1797 deposition along with a deposition from one of the previously freed Boston slaves, Bacon Boston, was included at the end of the other depositions in the case of *Philip Boston v. Richard Sprigg.* Other cases mentioned by Anne Brown included *Nelly Boston v. Richard Sprigg Sr., Peter Boston v. Stephen Steward, Anthony Boston v. Gassaway Rawlings, George Boston v. James Murray, Tamar Boston v. Benjamin Ogle, Thomas Boston v. Benjamin Ogle,* and an unidentified family member v. Edward Dorsey, Microfilm M 11015, Volume 4239-2, SC, MSA. GAA.

2. Henry Swinburne, *A Briefe Treatise of Testaments and Last Willes ...* (London, 1590 [1591]), 44, quoted in Thomas D. Morris, *Southern Slavery and the Law, 1619–1860* (Chapel Hill: University of North Carolina Press, 1996), 43 ["dooth follow"]; Christopher Tomlins, *Freedom Bound: Law, Labor, and Civic Identity in Colonizing English America, 1580–1865* (Cambridge: Cambridge University Press, 2010), 457 ["offspring"]. The first law to state "all children borne in this country shall be held bond or free only according to the condition of the mother" was passed in Virginia in 1662. This became the guiding principle in subsequent years. See William Waller Hening, *The Statutes at Large: Being a Collection of All the Laws of Virginia ...* (Richmond, VA, 1810), 2:170, quoted in Morris, *Southern Slavery and the Law,* 43–48, quotation, 43.

3. T. Stephen Whitman, *Challenging Slavery in the Chesapeake: Black and White Resistance to Human Bondage, 1775–1865* (Baltimore: Maryland Historical Society, 2007), 80–83 [hearsay evidence]; Christopher Phillips, *Freedom's Port: The African American Community of Baltimore, 1790–1860* (Urbana: University of Illinois Press, 1997), 35–36 [testimony in freedom suits]; James Wright, *The Free Negro in Maryland, 1634–1860* (New York: Columbia University Press, 1921; reprint, New York: Octagon Books, 1971), 79 [manumissions by free blacks].

4. Jessica Millward, "'That All Her Increase Shall Be Free': Enslaved Women's Bodies and the Maryland 1809 Law of Manumission," *Women's History Review* 21, no. 3 (June 2012): 363–378; Eric Robert Papenfuse, "From Recompense to Revolution: *Mahoney v. Ashton* and the Transfiguration of Maryland Culture, 1791–1802," *Slavery and Abolition* 15 (December 1994): 38–62; Thomas F. Brown and Leah C. Sims, "'To Swear Him Free': Ethnic Memory as Social Capital in Eighteenth-Century Freedom Petitions," in *Colonial Chesapeake: New Perspectives,* ed. Debra Myers and Melanie Perrault (Lanham, MD: Lexington, 2006), 81–105; Kathleen Fawver, "The Black Family in the Chesapeake: New Evidence, New Perspectives," in Myers and Perrault, *Colonial Chesapeake,* 51–80; Sean Condon, "The Significance of Group Manumissions in Post-Revolutionary Rural Maryland," *Slavery & Abolition* 32 (2011): 75–89; Sue Peabody, "'Free upon Higher Ground': Saint Domingue Slaves' Suits for Freedom in U.S. Courts," in *The World of the Haitian Revolution,* ed. David Geggus and Norman Fiering (Bloomington: Indiana University Press, 2009), 261–283.

5. For the secondary literature on Maryland, see William L. Calderhead, "Slavery in Maryland in the Age of the Revolution, 1775–1790," *Maryland Historical Magazine* 98 (Fall 2003): 306–307, 314–318; Ira Berlin, *Slaves without Masters: The Free Negro in the Antebellum South* (New York: Pantheon, 1974), 33; T. Stephen Whitman, *The Price of Freedom: Slavery and Manumission in Baltimore and Early National Maryland* (Frankfort: University of Kentucky Press, 1997), 63–67; Jeffrey R. Brackett, *The Negro in Maryland: A Study of the Institution of Slavery* (Baltimore: Johns Hopkins University Press, 1889; reprint, New York: Negro University Press, 1969), 152–153; Max Grivno, *Gleanings of Freedom: Free and Slave Labor along the Mason-Dixon Line, 1790–1860* (Urbana: University of Illinois Press, 2011), 38–39, 45; Eva Sheppard Wolf, *Race and Liberty in the New Nation: Emancipation in Virginia from the Revolution to Nat Turner's Rebellion* (Baton Rouge: Louisiana State University Press, 2006), 74; Matthew Mason, *Slavery and Politics in the Early American Republic* (Chapel Hill: University of North Carolina Press, 2006), 16–19; Seth Rockman, *Scraping By: Wage Labor, Slavery, and Survival in Early Baltimore* (Baltimore: Johns Hopkins University Press, 2009); Lorena Walsh, "Rural African Americans in the Constitutional Era in Maryland, 1776–1810," *Maryland Historical Magazine* 84 (1989): 327–341.

6. Petition of Mary Butler to the General Court of the Western Shore, Maryland, October 1783, in SC, *Mary Butler v. Adam Craig,* Microfilm M 11015, Frame 6, Volume 4239-2, Document/

Case 3, MSA; Related Documents: Transcript of Court Records, 1767–1770, ca.1784–1789; Deposition, Ann Hedskin, 27 May 1786; Depositions, John Hooper Broom and Joseph Thompson, 29 May 1786; Deposition, Jane Howard, 21 September 1767; Depositions, Ann Whitehorn, Samuel Abell Jr., Nathaniel Suit, William McPherson, Edward Edelen, Benjamin Jameson, Thomas Bowling, William Simpson, Joseph Jameson, and Mary Crosen, 27 May 1767; Deposition, Elizabeth Warren, 17 September 1765; Deposition, Samuel Love Sr., 18 September 1765; Deposition, John Barneson, 10 September 1765; Court Record, 16 October 1770; Court of Appeals Record, October Term 1787, with *Butler v. Craig.* GAA.

7. *The Maryland Reports: Being a Series of the Most Important Law Cases Argued and Determined in the General Court and Court of Appeals of the State of Maryland, from October, 1790, to May, 1797,* 3 vols., comp. Thomas Harris Jr. and John M'Henry (New York: I Riley, 1813), *Basil Shorter v. Henry Rozier,* October 1794, 3:238–240. GAA. *Maryland Reports, Robert Thomas v. the Reverend Henry Pile,* October 1794, 3:241. GAA. *Reports of Cases Argued and Determined in the Court of Appeals of Maryland in 1806, 1807, 1808, 1809,* comp. Thomas Harris and Reverdy Johnson (Annapolis, MD: Jonas Green, 1826), *Shorter v. Boswell,* December 1808, 2:359–362. G DARev.

8. Petition of Nathaniel Allen, Anne Arundel County, Maryland, to the General Court of the Western Shore, September 1794, in SC, *Nathaniel Allen v. Richard Higgins,* Microfilm M 11015, Volume 4239-2, Document/Case 28, MSA; Related Documents: Court Record, September 1794–November 1796; Depositions, Jane Allen, Hannah Allen, and Nace Allen, 18 September 1794, with *Allen v. Higgins. Maryland Reports, Richard Huggins v. Nathaniel Allen,* October 1796, 3:504–510; Appellate Court Ruling, June Term 1798, with *Huggins v Allen.* D GARev. The white Scottish woman was also named Hannah Allen. See Carter G. Woodson, "The Beginnings of the Miscegenation of the Whites and Blacks," *Journal of Negro History* 3 (October 1918): 342; Wright, *The Free Negro in Maryland,* 27–28; JCCASN, *Higgins v. Allen,* Md., 3 Har. and McH. 504, June 1798, 4:55; *Proceedings and Acts of the General Assembly of Maryland, April 26, 1715–August 10, 1716* (Baltimore: Maryland Historical Society, 1883–), 133–138.

9. For descriptions of Lenah, see depositions of Anne Harwood, Elizabeth Rawlings, Richard Watkins, Mary Batson, John Welsh, and John Tidings in note 1, this chapter. For land patent see MPL 4/288-289, 4/519-520, MSA.

10. Inventory of Robert Lockwood, 13 June 1709, *Maryland Prerogative Court (Inventories and Accounts) 1674–1773,* Vol. 29, Roll 68-4, CD no. 1, 1708-9, pp. 270–273 (CD pp. 147–149), MSA, in http://www.freeafricanamericans.com/prerogative.htm. Apparently Mulatto Moll, whose mother was white and father was a black slave, was indentured to Lockwood until she reached age twenty-one. This would have been an unusually long indenture but perhaps her mother wished to provide some sort of protection for her young daughter. For early settlers in the Swamp, see Virginia White Fitz, *Spirit of Shady Side Peninsula Life 1664–1984* (Shady Side, MD: Shady Side Peninsula Association, 1984), 2, 5, 40, 49; for the farming and stock raising in the Swamp, see Karen Mauer Green, *Maryland Gazette Genealogical and Historical Abstracts 1727–1761* (Galveston, TX: Frontier Press, 1989), 114; Chancery Court Record, 11 March 1767, October 1769, Maryland Hall of Records, 17,724 1-35-1-3, pp. 280–281; Maryland State Papers (Red Book) 20, item 86 (82); Maryland State Papers (Series A) Box 11, item 36C; Will of Sele Tucker, 21 January 1782, Anne Arundel County, Record of Wills, MSA. At this time, the use of the Portuguese word "Negroe" was probably synonymous with "slave." John Thornton and Linda Heywood, *Central Africans, Atlantic Creoles and the Making of the Anglo-Dutch Americas, 1580–1660* (Cambridge: Cambridge University Press, 2007), 244–245.

11. Russell Menard, "The Maryland Slave Population, 1658–1730: A Demographic Profile of Blacks in Four Counties," *William and Mary Quarterly* 32 (January 1975): 48.

12. Depositions of Mary Batson, 7 August 1790, Anne Brown, ca. 1792, and Richard Richardson, 10 March 1790, in SC, *John Boston v. John Francis Mercer* and *Fanny Boston v. John Francis Mercer,* Microfilm M 11015, Volume 4239-2, Cases 15 and 16, SC, MSA; Copy of Certificate, or affidavit, William Foard, 10 August 1747, in note 1, this chapter. Mary Batson noted that Maria was buried wearing her necklace with a gold cross.

13. Depositions of Richard Richardson, 10 March 1790, Anne Brown, ca. 1792, and certificate, William Foard, 10 August 1747, in note 1, this chapter.

14. Deposition of Anne Brown, ca. 1792, as shown in note 1, this chapter.

15. Depositions of Dinah Watkins, 1 May 1792, Thomas Gibbs, 3 November 1791, and Margaret Gassaway Watkins, 21 May 1793, as shown in note 1, this chapter.

16. Depositions of John Welch, 3 February 1791 and 24 February 1791, as shown in note 1, this chapter; USMSPC, Anne Arundel County, Maryland, 1790, image 24, ancestry.com; Will of John Welsh, 6 January 1783, Anne Arundel County, Maryland, will in http://www.mosesrawlings.freeservers.com/welshfamilyhistory.html.

17. Depositions of Mary Batson, 7 August 1790, and John Norris, 13 October 1792, as shown in note 1, this chapter.

18. Certificate, William Foard, 10 August 1747, and Depositions of John Norris, 8 and 13 October 1792, in note 1, this chapter.

19. For Rawlings's landholdings, see Patent 1297, Gassaway Rawlings, 6 December 1770, MSA S1189-3366; Maryland Indexes (Assessment of 1783) Index, 1783, MSA S1437; Anne Arundel, Road River Hundred, p. 5, MSA S1161-1-12 1/4/5/44 [Larkin Hills]; for slaveholdings, see USMSPC, Anne Arundel County, Maryland, 1800, image 25; Anne Arundel County, 1810, image 14, ancestry.com; *Jonathan Waters et al. v. Gassaway Rawlings, et al.*, 6 August 1803, Chancery Court Papers, 5593, MSA, S512-5705 [list of mortgaged slaves]; also see Edward C. Papenfuse et al., eds., *A Biographical Dictionary of the Maryland Legislature 1635–1789*, vol. 426 (Baltimore: Johns Hopkins University Press, 2008), 230–231, 346.

20. Maryland *Gazette*, May 1, 1766, supplement, Anne Arundel County, May 1, 1766, found in Lathan A. Windley, ed., *Runaway Slave Advertisements: A Documentary History from the 1730s to 1790*, vol. 2: *Maryland* (Westport, CT: Greenwood, 1983).

21. Petitions of John Boston et al., to the General Court of the Western Shore, Maryland, 1 November 1791, in SC, *John Boston et al. v. John Francis Mercer; Maria Boston et al. v. Richard Sprigg Sr.*, 1 November 1791, Microfilm M 11015, Volume 4239-2, Documents 12-19, MSA; Related Documents: Court Record, 1791–1793 with *Boston v. Mercer*, et al. The name Lenah was spelled "Lenar" and "Lener" in two of the petitions.

22. Depositions of Anne Harwood, 20 July 1789, Elizabeth Rawlings, 20 July 1789, Richard Watkins, 10 March 1790, Richard Richardson, 10 March 1790, and Plummer Ijiams, 4 August 1790, in note 1, this chapter. Only one of their ages was specified (Ijiams was seventy-two), but judging from their recollections they were all in their sixties and seventies.

23. Deposition of Ann Watkins, 4 June 1791, in note 1, this chapter.

24. Deposition of Mary Batson, 7 August 1790, in note 1, this chapter.

25. Frank F. White Jr., *The Governors of Maryland 1777–1970* (Annapolis, MD: Hall of Records Commission, 1970), 47–49; USMSPC, Anne Arundel County, Maryland, 1810, images 19, 21, ancestry.com; Anne Arundel County, 1820, image 10, ancestry.com.

26. Provincial Court Land Records, 1763–1765, Vol. 703, p. 586, MSA; aomol.net/000001/000703/html/am703--586.html; USMSPC, Anne Arundel County, Maryland, 1790, image 25, ancestry.com ; copy of the Last Will and Testament, Richard Sprigg Sr., 1797, Mercer Family Papers, MSS1M5345a108-109, Virginia State Historical Society, Richmond; Receipt, Richard Sprigg Sr., executor of Elizabeth Sprigg, 3 August 1791, MSS1M545a89-95, with Sprigg's Will; Request, Elizabeth Sprigg to Richard Sprigg Sr., 20 January 1796, MSS1M5345a112, and Disposition of Slaves, in part for "Mrs. Mercer and Miss Sprigg," n.d., MSS1M5345a17, with Sprigg's Will.

27. Richard Sprigg Sr., for instance, gave a copy of his will to Mercer, providing his friend with instructions about how to emancipate a few loyal slaves, including members of the Boston family. Last Will and Testament, Richard Sprigg Sr., 1797, Mercer Family Papers; USMSPC, Anne Arundel County, Maryland, 1790, ancestry.com, image 25; USMSPC, Prince George's County, Maryland, 1790, image 15, 1800, image 17, ancestry.com; http://bioguide.congress.gov/scripts/biodisplay.pl?index=S000752, LC.

28. Frank F. White Jr., *The Governors of Maryland 1777–1970* (Annapolis, MD: Hall of Records Commission, 1970), 43–44; USMSPC, Prince Georges County, Maryland, 1790, image 20 [country estate with twenty-six slaves]; USMSPC, Annapolis, Anne Arundel County,

Maryland, 1790, image 45 [residence with four slaves]; USMSPC, Annapolis, Anne Arundel County, Maryland, 1800, image 6 [residence; he possessed eleven slaves], ancestry.com.

29. Maryland Colonial Census 1776, ancestry.com; USMSPC, Anne Arundel County, Maryland, 1790 and 1800, images 15 and 25, ancestry.com.

30. Unfortunately only the court costs for the appeal to the high court of appeals were included in the court transcript, and these are undecipherable. The lawyers for the plaintiffs worked pro bono.

31. Whitman, *Challenging Slavery in the Chesapeake*, 55; *Laws of Maryland, Session Laws*, 1793, chap. 36, MSA [Edward Dorsey]; Deposition of Alice Taylor, 3 June 1792, in the case of *Daniel Boston v. Henry Hall*, in note 1, this chapter 1.

32. Deposition of Richard Watkins, 10 March 1790, in note 1, this chapter.

33. Deposition of Richard Richardson, 10 March 1790, in note 1, this chapter.

34. Depositions of Dinah Watkins, 1 May 1792, Thomas Gibbs, 3 November 1791, Margaret Gassaway Watkins, 21 May 1793, in note 1, this chapter.

35. Deposition of Richard Hopkins, 21 May 1793, in note 1, this chapter.

36. Depositions of Alice Taylor, 23 June 1792, and Benjamin Atwell, 21 May 1792, note 1, this chapter; Benjamin Atwell was listed in the 1776 Maryland census as living in St. James Parish; in 1778 he took the oath of fidelity; in 1790 he was cited in the census with no slaves and with five whites in the household. He was illiterate. USMSPC, Anne Arundel County, Maryland, 1790, image 11, ancestry.com.

37. Deposition of Thomas Gibbs, 3 November 1791, in note 1, this chapter [criticism of Ann Watkins]; Deposition of Joseph Cowman, 25 May 1793 [defense of Ann Watkins], in note 1, this chapter. According to the 1790 census, Joseph Cowman, despite being a Quaker, was listed as possessing eleven slaves; even before the American Revolution, he lived in close proximity to Ann Watkins, who possessed four slaves. USMSPC, Anne Arundel County, Maryland, 1790, image 14, ancestry.com.

38. Testimony of Benjamin Carr, 16 October 1792, in note 1, this chapter.

39. Deposition of William Harwood, 25 May 1795, in note 1, this chapter.

40. Deposition of Mary Farro, 21 May 1793, in note 1, this chapter.

41. Deposition of Bacon Boston, 15 June 1793, in note 1, this chapter.

42. Depositions of Anne Brown, ca. 1792 (twice), 1793 (twice), 17 October 1795, 3 June 1797, in note 1, this chapter.

43. *Maryland Reports*, 3:139-140; JCCASN, "Maryland: Introduction," and *Rawlings v. Boston*, Md., 3 Har. and McH. 139, May 1793, 4:3, 51. GAA.

44. The additional suits included *Bacon Boston v. Gassaway Watkins, Peter Boston v. Stephen Steward, Richard Boston v. Joshua Warfield, George Boston v. James Murray, Guy Boston v. Richard Richardson, Peter Boston v. Richard Richardson, John Boston v. Richard Richardson*, and *Deborah Boston v. Richard Richardson*. Before the high court's decision, Guy Boston, one of plaintiffs, had died. In addition, Richard Sprigg Sr., who died in 1798, bequeathed three Boston slaves their freedom at the request of his wife, including Bet Boston, Bet's son Charles, and her brother Daniel. The total, then, of Boston slaves freed over the years was twenty-six (copy of the Last Will and Testament, Richard Sprigg Sr., 1797, Mercer Family Papers).

45. *Laws of Maryland, Made and Passed at a Session of Assembly, Begun and Held in the City of Annapolis on Monday the Seventh of November, in the Year of our Lord One Thousand Seven Hundred and Ninety-Six* (Annapolis, MD: Frederick Green, 1796), chap. 67; three Supreme Court justices—Samuel Chase, Gabriel Duvall, and Thomas Johnson—were drawn from the General Court of Maryland. Robert Ireland, *The Legal Career of William Pinkney, 1764-1822* (New York: Garland, 1986), 3; http://bioguide.congress.gov/scripts/biodisplay.pl?index=D000578 [Duvall]; http://bioguide.congress.gov/scripts/biodisplay.pl?index=c000334 [Chase].

46. JCCASN, *Mahoney v. Ashton*, Md., 4 Har. and McH. 63, October 1797, 295 and June 1802, 4:4, 53–55, D GARev; Whitman, *Challenging Slavery in the Chesapeake*, 82.

47. Prince George's County Court Docket and Minutes, "Imparlances," or Continuances, 10 September 1810; "Trials," April Term 1812; the depositions were taken in September 1811. Petition of Letty Ogleton, Henry Ogleton, Michael Ogleton, Lucy Ogleton, Suckey Ogleton, and Charles Ogleton to the District Court of Prince George's County, Maryland, 10

September 1810, in SC, *Letty Ogleton, et al. v. Philip Soper*, Microfilm M 11024, Frame/Pages 3, Volume 4239-26, MSA; Related Documents: PARs 20981010, 20981012, 20981013, 20981014, 20981015, 20981016; Summons, 10 September 1810, with *Ogleton, et al. v Soper*. Denied. PARs 20981011–20981015; Millward, "'That All Her Increase Shall Be Free,'" 369, 377; Martha Hodes, *White Women, Black Men: Illicit Sex in the Nineteenth-Century South* (New Haven, CT: Yale University Press, 1997), 256–257. See Petition of Milly Ogleton to the District Court of Prince George's County, Maryland, 10 September 1810, in SC, *Milly Ogleton v. Osburn Boone*, Microfilm M 11024, Frame/Pages 2; 9, Volume 4239-26, MSA; Summons, 10 September 1810; Answer, Oswald Boone, ca. 1810; Deposition, Anthony Drane, 4 September 1811; the surname is illegible, but it appears Drane (or Drain in 1800) is the person deposed; USMSPC, Prince George's County, Maryland, Rockcreek and Eastern Branch Hundreds, 1810, image 4, ancestry.com; Deposition, William King, 5 September 1811, with *Ogleton v. Boone*. PAR 20981010. See also "Pet for Freedom" by *Sarah Ogleton v. Bailey E. Clarke*, 10 September 1810, Prince George's County Court Docket and Minutes, "Imparlances," or continuances, which contained the final judgment in her favor.

48. *Mima Queen and Child, Petitioners for Freedom, v. Hepburn*, 1813, in *Reports of Decisions of the Supreme Court of the United States, with Notes and a Digest*, comp. B. R. Curtis (Boston: Little, Brown, 1870), 2:535–539. DAA.

49. *Mima Queen and child, Petitioners for Freedom, v. Hepburn*, 5 February 1813, Supreme Court of the United States, http://supreme.justia.com/us/11/290/case.html [includes full text of case]; JCCASN, *Mima Queen and child v. Hepburn*, 11 U.S. (D.C.) (7 Cranch C. C. 290), February 1813, 4:4, 165–66 [includes synopsis]. DAA.

50. William E. Beale to the Orphans Court of Baltimore City, Maryland, 21 March 1859, Microfilm M 11026, Frame/Pages 294, Volume 4239-14, SC, MSA; [Maria Boston] John Boston to his wife, 12 January 1862, National Archives, Records of the Adjutant General's Office, 1780s–1917, *Eyewitness*, http://www.archives.gov/exhibits/eyewitness/html.php?section=9. There is no evidence that Elizabeth Boston received the letter. It was intercepted and eventually forwarded to Secretary of War Edwin Stanton. The probability is great that Maria Boston and John Boston were members of the Boston kinship group: the surname was very unusual if not unique. John Boston lived near the Swamp, and his given name, although common, was also in the Boston family tree. For the struggle of other possible family members during the 1850s, see Petition of Daniel Boston to the Orphans Court of Anne Arundel County, Maryland, August 1853, in Register of Wills, 1851–1874 (Petitions and Orders), *Daniel Boston v. Henry Owens and Robert Gale*, Microfilm CR 63,128, Frame/Pages 35–37, SC, MSA.

Chapter 2

1. Petition of Polly Anderson and James Burnett to the Circuit Superior Court of Chesterfield County, Virginia, 22 October 1835, in Ended Chancery Court Causes, *Polly Anderson and James Burnett v. Edward B. Elam, William Watts, and Robert White*, Box/Drawer 446, Entry Folder A 1842, LV; Related Documents: Oath, James Burnett, 22 October 1835; Court Record, February 1836–18 January 1842; Injunction, 24 October 1835; Notice, James Burnett, 18 October 1836; Depositions, Jordan Martin, Elizabeth Johnson, Elizabeth J. Elam, 21 October 1836; Answer, Edward B. Elam, 21 October 1836; Order of Execution and Sheriff's Return, 20 April 1836; Subpoena, 5 April 1836, with *Anderson v. Burnett et al*. PAR 21683503. Injunction granted. Burnett owned two adult slaves. Although cited as a "next friend," he wrote the petition and appeared before a justice of the peace under oath to affirm the accuracy of the facts presented as was required by law for lawyers in some states who presented petitions for freedom. USMSPC, Chesterfield County, Virginia, 1830, p. 455.

2. The state of Virginia, unlike other states in the South, created "corporations" for every large city in the state. The corporations assumed the same legal structure and many of the responsibilities (registering deeds and wills, court actions) as county courts, in Richmond, Petersburg, Lynchburg, Norfolk, and other cities.

3. For how the laws worked in practice, see Christopher Doyle, "Judge St. George Tucker and the Case of *Tom v. Roberts*: Blunting the Revolution's Radicalism from Virginia's District Courts," *Virginia Magazine of History and Biography* 106 (Autumn 1998): 428;

Michael L. Nicholls, "Strangers Setting among Us: The Sources and Challenge of the Urban Free Black Population of Early Virginia," *The Virginia Magazine of History and Biography* 108 (Spring 2000): 160–161. The statutes included *Acts Passed at a General Assembly of the Commonwealth of Virginia, Begun and Held at the Capitol, in the City of Richmond, on Tuesday, the Tenth Day of November, One Thousand Seven Hundred and Ninety-Five* (Richmond, VA: Augustine Davis, 1796), 16–17; John Codman Hurd, *The Law of Freedom and Bondage in the United States*, 2 vols. (Boston: Little, Brown, 1862; reprint, New York: Negro Universities Press, 1968), 2:6; *Acts Passed at a General Assembly of the Commonwealth of Virginia, Begun and Held at the Capitol, in the City of Richmond, on Monday the Fourth Day of December One Thousand Seven Hundred and Ninety-Seven* (Richmond, VA: Augustine Davis, 1798), 5; Joseph Tate and George Mumford, *Digest of the Laws of Virginia, Which Are of a Permanent Character and General Operation; Illustrated by Judicial Decisions* (Richmond: Smith and Palmer, 1841), 869–871.

4. Henry W. Farnam, *Chapters in the History of Social Legislation in the United States to 1860* (Washington, DC: Carnegie Institution, 1938), 381; Guion Griffis Johnson, *Ante-Bellum North Carolina: A Social History* (Chapel Hill: University of North Carolina Press, 1937), 594; John Hope Franklin, *The Free Negro in North Carolina, 1790–1860* (Chapel Hill: University of North Carolina Press, 1943), 20–21.

5. *Acts of the General Assembly of the State of Georgia, Passed at Louisville, in November and December, 1801* (Louisville: Ambrose Day and James Hely, 1802), 71–72; *Digest of the Laws of the state of Georgia: Containing All Statutes and the Substance of All Resolutions of a General and Public Nature and Now in Force, Which Have Been Passed in This State Previous to the Session of the General Assembly of Dec. 1837* (Athens, GA: Oliver H. Prince, 1837), 787.

6. *Acts of the General Assembly of the State of Georgia, Passed at Milledgeville, at an Annual Session, in November & December 1818* (Milledgeville, GA: S. & F. Grantland, 1818), 128–129; *A Codification of the Statue Law of Georgia, Including the English Statutes of Force: In Four Parts, to Which Is Prefixed a Collection of State Papers, English, American, and State Origin* (Augusta, GA: Charles E. Grenville, 1848), 806–807.

7. Andrew Fede, *People without Rights: An Interpretation of the Fundamentals of the Law of Slavery in the U.S. South* (New York: Garland, 1992), 144–145; Laura Edwards, "Status without Rights: African Americans and the Tangled History of Law and Governance in the Nineteenth-Century U.S. South," *The American Historical Review*, 112, no. 2 (April 2007): 365–393; *Acts and Resolutions of the General Assembly, of the State of South-Carolina, Passed in December, 1800* (Columbia, SC: Daniel & J. J. Faust, 1801), 39–41; *Acts and Resolutions of the General Assembly of the State of South-Carolina, Passed in December, 1820* (Columbia, SC: D. Faust, 1821), 22; for the difficulties in later years, see: JCCASN, *Morton v. Thompson*, S.C., 6 Rich. Eq. 370, May 1854, 2:441–42. DAA.

8. *Laws of the State of Mississippi* (Jackson, Mississippi: P. Isler, State Printer [ca. 1823]), 198–199; William Goodell, *The American Slave Code in Theory and Practice: The Distinctive Features Shown by Its Statutes, Judicial Decisions, and Illustrative Facts* (New York: American and Foreign Anti-Slavery Society, 1853), 341.

9. US House of Representatives, *The Federal and State Constitutions, Colonial Charters, and Other Organic Laws of the States Territories, and Colonies,* 59th Cong., 2nd sess., 1909, 7 vols. (Washington, DC: Government Printing Office, 1909), 1:111–112 [Alabama]; 4:2045 [Mississippi].

10. *A Digest of the Civil Laws Now in Force in the Territory of Orleans, with Alterations and Amendments Adapted to Its Present System of Government* (New Orleans: Bradford & Anderson, 1808), Title VI, "Of Master and Servant," chap. 3 "Of Slaves," article 25, https://books.google.com/books?id=HW1GAQAAIAAJ&printsec=frontcover&source=gbs_ViewAPI#v=onepage&q&f=false; Thomas Gibbes Morgan, comp. and ed., *Civil Code of the State of Louisiana: With Statutory Amendments, from 1825 to 1853, Inclusive; and References to the Decisions of the Supreme Court of Louisiana to the Sixth Volume of Annual Reports* (New Orleans: J. B. Steel, 1853), 30–31.

11. Judith Kelleher Schafer, *Becoming Free, Remaining Free: Manumission and Enslavement in New Orleans, 1846–1862* (Baton Rouge: Louisiana State University Press, 2003), 4–5; *Acts Passed at the First Session of the Ninth Legislature of the State of Louisiana, Begun and Held in Donaldsonville, on the Third Day of January, One Thousand Eight Hundred and Thirty-One, and*

of the Independence of the United States of America the Fifty-Fourth (New Orleans: John Gibson, 1831), 98, 100.

12. *Acts Passed at the Second Session of the Ninth Legislature of the State of Louisiana, Begun and Held in Donaldsonville, on Monday, the 4th day of January, A. D. 1830, and of the Independence of the United States of America, the Fifty-Fourth* (Donaldsonville, LA: C. W. Duhy, 1830), 92, 94.

13. Morgan, *Civil Code of the State of Louisiana*, 1825, p. 28; Judith Kelleher Schafer, *Slavery, the Civil Law, and the Supreme Court of Louisiana* (Baton Rouge: Louisiana State University Press, 1994), 220.

14. *Revised Statutes of the State of Arkansas, Adopted at the October Session of the General Assembly of Said State, A. D. 1837, in the Year of Our Independence the Sixty[-]second, and of the State the Second Year* (Boston: Weeks, Jordan, 1838), 416–418. The law was approved December 18, 1837, and was put in force by proclamation of the governor on March 20, 1839; it remained in force through 1856. See *A Digest of the Statutes of Arkansas: Embracing All Laws of a General and Permanent Character, in Force at the Close of the General Assembly of 1846* (Little Rock, AR: Rearson & Garritt, 1848), 543–545; *A Digest of the Statutes of Arkansas; Embracing All Laws of a General and Permanent Character, in Force at the Close of the Session of the General Assembly of 1856* (Little Rock, AR: Johnson & Yerkes, 1858), 550–552.

15. *Laws of the State of Mississippi [June 1822]*, 198–199; Goodell, *The American Slave Code in Theory and Practice*, 341; *Acts of the General Assembly of the State of Georgia, Passed in Milledgeville at an Annual Session in November and December, 1835* (Milledgeville, GA: John A. Cuthbert, 1836), 101–103; Hurd, *The Law of Freedom and Bondage*, 2:191; *Acts of the General Assembly of the State of Georgia, Passed in Milledgeville at an Annual Session in November and December, 1837* (Milledgeville, GA: F. L. Robinson, 1838), 248–250; *A Codification of the Statute Law of Georgia,* , 802–805; *A Compilation of the General and Public Statutes of the State of Georgia; with the Forms and Precedents Necessary to Their Practical Use* (New York: Edward O. Jenkins, 1859), 595–596, 625–630.

16. *Laws of Maryland, Made and Passed at a Session of Assembly, Begun and Held in the City of Annapolis on Monday the Seventh of November, in the Year of Our Lord One Thousand Seven Hundred and Ninety-Six* (Annapolis, MD: Frederick Green, 1796), chap. 48; James Wright, *The Free Negro in Maryland, 1634–1860* (New York: Columbia University Press, 1921; reprint, New York: Octagon Books, 1971), 60; David Skillen Bogen, "The Maryland Context of Dred Scott: The Decline in the Legal Status of Maryland Free Blacks, 1776–1810," *The American Journal of Legal History* 34 (October 1990), 393–395.

17. The act of 1760 was reprinted in *Laws of the State of Delaware Passed at a Session of the General Assembly, Which Was Begun and Held at Dover, on Tuesday, the Third Day of January, and Ended on Tuesday, the Twenty-fourth Day of the Same Month, in the Year of Our Lord One Thousand Seven Hundred and Ninety-seven, and of the Independence of the United States of America the Twenty-First*, 2 vols. (New-Castle, DE: Samuel and John Adams, 1797), 1:380–384.

18. Philip J. Schwarz, *Slave Laws in Virginia* (Athens: University of Georgia Press, 1996), 126; *Laws of Maryland, Made and Passed at a Session of Assembly* [in 1796], chap. 68; *Code of Laws of the District of Columbia: Prepared under the Authority of the Act of Congress of the 29th of April 1816* (Washington, DC: Davis and Force, 1819), 275–276; Mary Tremain, *Slavery in the District of Columbia: The Policy of Congress and the Struggle for Abolition* (New York: J. P. Putnam Sons, 1892), 22. http://www.unz.org/Pub/TremainMary-1892. The Code, written by Chief Judge William Cranch of the circuit court, was not accepted by Congress, but the processes outlined were accepted in the District.

19. *Acts Passed at the First Session of the Sixteenth General Assembly for the Commonwealth of Kentucky, Begun and Held at the Capitol in the Town of Frankfort, on Monday the Twenty-eighth Day of December, in the Year of Our Lord One Thousand Eight Hundred and Seven, and of the Commonwealth the Sixteenth* (Frankfort, KY: William Hunter, 1808), 28–29; *Digest of the Statute Laws of Kentucky, of a Public and Permanent Nature, from the Commencement of the Government to the Session of the Legislature, Ending on the 24th February, 1834, with References to Judicial Decisions*, 2 vols. (Frankfort, KY: Albert G. Hodges, 1834), 2:1140–1141 [prologue of 1808 statute]; *Acts of the General Assembly of the Commonwealth of Kentucky, December Session, 1839* (Frankfort, KY: A. G. Hodges, 1840), 172–173 [damages]; *Acts Passed at the First Session of the Twelfth General Assembly of the State of Tennessee, Begun and Held at Knoxville, on*

Monday the Fifteenth Day of September, One Thousand Eight Hundred and Seventeen (Knoxville, TN: George Wilson, 1817), 107.

20. Kelly Marie Kennington, "River of Injustice: St. Louis Freedom Suits and the Changing Nature of Legal Slavery in Antebellum America" (PhD diss., Duke University, 2009), 30–31 [1807 Territorial law]; Petition of Susan to the Circuit Court of St. Charles County, Missouri, 2 May 1817, in Records of the Circuit Court, *Susan v. Henry Hight*, Document/Case 127, CCBSL; Related Documents: Supreme Court Record, 25 September 1821; Supreme Court Opinion [incomplete], 27 September 1821; Supreme Court Records, 24 September 1821, 13 October 1821; Plea of Trespass, Susan, ca. May 1817; Summons, Henry Hight, 9 June 1817; Sheriff's Return, 24 July 1817; Summons, William Thompson, 16 January 1818; Action of Assault and Battery, Susan, ca. May 1817; Jury Verdict, ca. May 1817, with *Susan v. Hight*. G DisARR. PAR 21181701. For quote of the three judges, see JCCASN, *Susan (a blackwoman) v. Hight*, 1 Mo. 18, September 1821, 5:124; Hurd, *The Law of Freedom and Bondage*, 2:169 [Missouri law of 1824]; *The Revised Statutes of the State of Missouri, Revised and Digested by the Eighth General Assembly during the Year One Thousand Eight Hundred and Thirty-four, and one Thousand Eight Hundred and Thirty-Five* (St Louis: The Argus Office [ca. 1836]), 284– 286, 587–588; *Laws of the State of Missouri, Passed at the First Session of the Eleventh General Assembly, Begun and Held at the City of Jefferson, on Monday, the Sixteenth Day of November, in the Year of Our Lord, One Thousand Eight Hundred and Forty* (Jefferson City, MO: Calvin Gunn, 1841), 146; *The Revised Statutes of the State of Missouri, Revised and Digested by the Eighteenth General Assembly, During the Session of One Thousand Eight Hundred and Fifty-four and One Thousand Eight Hundred and Fifty-Five* (Jefferson City, MO: James Lusk, 1855), 809–812.

21. Ira Berlin, *Slaves without Masters: The Free Negro in the Antebellum South* (New York Pantheon, 1974), 138–139; *Laws of the State of Delaware* [in 1797], 2:884–885; *Laws of Maryland, Made and Passed at a Session of Assembly, Begun and Held in the City of Annapolis on Monday the First of November, in the Year of Our Lord One Thousand Seven Hundred and Ninety* (Annapolis, MD: Frederick Green, 1790), chap. 9; William Waller Hening, *The Statutes at Large; Being a Collection of All the Laws of Virginia, from the First Session of the Legislature in the Year 1619*, 13 vols. (Richmond, VA, 1823), 11:39–40; Hurd, *The Law of Freedom and Bondage*, 2:3–4 [Virginia 1782]; James H. Kettner, "Persons or Property? The Pleasants Slaves in the Virginia Courts, 1792–1799," in *Launching the "Extended Republic": The Federalist Era*, ed. Ronald Hoffman and Peter J. Albert (Charlottesville: University Press of Virginia, 1996), 142; *The Statute Law of Kentucky; with Notes, Praelections, and Observations on the Public Acts, Comprehending Also, the Laws of Virginia and Acts of Parliament in Force in this Commonwealth; the Charter of Virginia, the Federal and State Constitutions*, 3 vols. (Frankfort, KY: William Hunter, 1809), 1:241–246; *Acts Passed at the First Session of the Fourth General Assembly of the State of Tennessee, Begun and Held at Knoxville, on Monday the Twenty First Day of September, One Thousand Eight Hundred and One* (Knoxville, TN: George Roulstone, 1801), 84–86.

22. Hening, *The Statutes at Large*, 11:39–40; Hurd, *The Law of Freedom and Bondage*, 2:109; *The Statute Law of Kentucky*, 1:241–246 [contains Virginia laws regarding slavery and emancipation between 1753 and 1790]; *Laws of the State of Delaware* [1797], 2:885–887 [creditors could sue for damages]; *Revised Statutes of the State of Delaware, to the Year of our Lord One Thousand Eight Hundred and Fifty-two, Inclusive* (Dover, DE: Samuel Kimmey, 1852), 252–256; Timothy S. Huebner, *The Southern Judicial Tradition: State Judges and Sectional Distinctiveness, 1790–1890* (Athens: University of Georgia Press, 1999), 26.

23. The "inordinate copulations" phrase was included in colonial laws passed in 1715 and 1728. *Laws of Maryland* [1790]; Hurd, *The Law of Freedom and Bondage*, 2:20. In Maryland, the 1790 manumission law was not rescinded until the eve of the Civil War. Wright, *The Free Negro in Maryland*, 59; *The Revised Code of the District of Columbia, Prepared under the Authority of the Act of Congress, Entitled An Act to Improve the Laws of the District of Columbia, and to Codify the Same, Approved March 5, 1855* (Washington, DC: A. O. P. Nicholson, 1857), 168–169. Congress failed to authorize this code, and it too (as in 1816) served only as a guide.

24. *Acts Passed at the First Session of the Third General Assembly for the Commonwealth of Kentucky, Begun and Held at the Capitol, in the Town of Frankford, on Monday the Third Day of November, in the Year of Our Lord, One Thousand Seven Hundred and Ninety-four, and in the Third Year*

of the Commonwealth (Lexington: John Bradford, 1795), 34–35; Hurd, *The Law of Freedom and Bondage*, 2:14. The Kentucky act repealed every law heretofore in force concerning the emancipation of slaves (i.e., the Virginia statutes of 1753, 1778, 1782, 1785, 1786, 1787, 1788, 1789, and 1790). J. Blaine Hudson, "In Pursuit of Freedom: Slave Law and Emancipation in Louisville and Jefferson County, Kentucky," *Filson History Quarterly* 76 (Summer 2002): 287–326; *Laws of the State of Delaware Passed at a Session of the General Assembly, Which Was Begun and Held at Dover, on Tuesday, the Third Day of January, and Ended on Tuesday, the Twenty-fourth Day of the Same Month, in the Year of Our Lord One Thousand Seven Hundred and Ninety-seven, and of the Independence of the United States of America the Twenty-First*, 2 vols. (New-Castle, DE: Samuel and John Adams, 1797) 1:4–8; John W. Patton, "The Progress of Emancipation in Tennessee," *Journal of Negro History* 17 (January 1932): 67–102; *The Revised Statutes of the State of Missouri* [1834–1835], 587–588.

25. *Laws of Maryland, Made and Passed at a Session of Assembly, Begun and Held in the City of Annapolis on Monday the Fifth of November, in the Year of Our Lord One Thousand Eight Hundred and Four* (Annapolis, MD: Frederick Green, 1805), chap. 90.

26. *Laws of Maryland, Made and Passed at a Session of Assembly, Begun and Held in the City of Annapolis on Monday the Sixth of November, in the Year of our Lord One Thousand Eight Hundred and Nine* (Annapolis, MD: Frederick Green [1809]), chap. 146. In 1810, the Assembly again prohibited the sale of term slaves out of the state. Hurd, *The Law of Freedom and Bondage*, 2:21.

27. *Laws of the State of Delaware, Passed at a Session of the General Assembly, Begun and Holden at Dover, on Tuesday, the Second Day of January, and Ended on Friday, the Second Day of February, in the Year of Our Lord, One Thousand Eight Hundred and Ten, and of the Independence of the United States of America, the Thirty-Fourth* (Dover, DE: Printed by John B. Wooten, 1810), 337–340. The law required children of term slaves to be registered at court within one year after their birth and receive a certificate showing their name, age, and sex; *Code of Laws of the District of Columbia* [1816], 199, 247; JCCASN, *Hudgens v. Spencer*, Ky., November 1836, 1:335–336; *Digest of the Statute Laws of Kentucky, of a Public and Permanent Nature Passed Since 1834, with References to Judicial Decisions* (Frankfort, KY: Albert G. Hodges, 1842), 227.

28. Eva Sheppard Wolf, *Race and Liberty in the New Nation: Emancipation in Virginia from the Revolution to Nat Turner's Rebellion* (Baton Rouge: Louisiana State University Press, 2006), 53, 63–64; St. George Tucker, *A Dissertation on Slavery: With a Proposal for the Gradual Abolition of It, in the State of Virginia* (Philadelphia: Mathew Cary, 1796), 91, 95.

29. Berlin, *Slaves without Masters*, 46; Thomas N. Ingersoll, "Free Blacks in a Slave Society: New Orleans, 1718–1812," in *The Louisiana Purchase Bicentennial Series in Louisiana History*, vol. 11: *The African American Experience in Louisiana, Part A: From Africa to the Civil War*, ed. Charles Vincent (Lafayette: Center for Louisiana Studies, 1999), 159, 161; Paul F. Lachance, "The Limits of Privilege: Where Free Persons of Colour Stood in the Hierarchy of Wealth in Antebellum New Orleans," in Vincent, *African American Experience*, 428–446; Herbert E. Sterkx, *The Free Negro in Antebellum Louisiana* (Rutherford, NJ: Fairleigh Dickinson University Press, 1972), chap. 4; Schafer, *Slavery, the Civil Law*, 180–185.

30. Hening, *The Statutes at Large*, 2:109; *The Statute Law of Kentucky; with Notes, Praelections, and Observations*, 1:241–246.

31. Donald G. Matthews, *Slavery and Methodism: A Chapter in American Morality, 1780–1845* (Princeton, NJ: Princeton University Press, 1965), chap. 1; James Essig, *The Bonds of Wickedness: American Evangelicals against Slavery, 1770–1808* (Philadelphia: Temple University Press, 1982); Douglas Ambrose, "Of Stations and Relations: Proslavery Debates in Early National Virginia," in *Religion and the Antebellum Debate over Slavery*, ed. John R. McKivigan and Michael Snay (Athens: University of Georgia Press, 1998), 38–40; Monica Najar, "'Meddling with Emancipation': Baptist, Authority, and the Rift over Slavery in the Upper South," *Journal of the Early Republic* 25, no. 2 (Summer 2005): 157–159; Stanley Harrold, *Subversives: Antislavery Community in Washington, D.C., 1828–1865* (Baton Rouge: Louisiana State University Press, 2003), 24–25; Molly Oshatz, *Slavery and Sin: The Fight against Slavery and the Rise Liberal Protestantism* (New York: Oxford University Press, 2012); Alice Dana Adams, *The Neglected Period of Anti-Slavery in America (1808–1831)* (Boston: Ginn, 1908), chap. 12.

32. Elizabeth Fox-Genovese and Eugene Genovese, *The Mind of the Master Class: History and Faith in the Southern Slaveholders' Worldview* (Cambridge: Cambridge University Press, 2005), 231 [membership], 235 [Kentucky]; Gordon E. Finnie, "The Antislavery Movement in the Upper South before 1840," *Journal of Southern History* 35, no. 3 (November 1969): 319–342; Caleb Patterson, *The Negro in Tennessee, 1790–1865: A Study in Southern Politics* (Austin: University of Texas Press, 1922), chap. 4.

33. Hening, *The Statutes at Large*, 12:182 [1785 Virginia law]; *Laws of Maryland Made and Passed at a Session of Assembly, Begun and Held at the City of Annapolis on Monday the Seventh of November in the Year of Our Lord One Thousand Seven Hundred and Ninety-One* (Annapolis, MD: Frederick Green [1792]), 249–250, chap. 57, 583–584; *Laws of Maryland Made and Passed at a Session of Assembly* [1796], 249–250, chap. 67; Hurd, *The Law of Freedom and Bondage*, 2:74–75; *Laws of the State of Delaware Passed* [1797], 1:4–8; Patience Essah, *A House Divided: Slavery and Emancipation in Delaware, 1638–1865* (Charlottesville: University of Virginia Press, 1996), 51.

34. Farnam, *Chapters in the History of Social Legislation*, 335.

35. Wright, *The Free Negro in Maryland*, 38.

36. Hurd, *The Law of Freedom and Bondage*, 2:74–76, 76n1; *Laws of the State of Delaware Passed* [1797], 2:884–885, 885 [1793 supplementary act]; JCCASN, "Delaware Introduction," 4:212–213; *Allen v. Negro Sarah*, Del., 2 Harrington 434, June 1838, 4:224–225; *Laws of Maryland, Made and Passed at a Session of Assembly Begun and Held in the City of Annapolis, on Monday the Twenty-First of April, in the Year of Our Lord One Thousand Seven Hundred and Eighty-Three* (Annapolis, MD: Frederick Green [1784]), chap. 23. Most of the southern slaveholding states passed laws or constitutional restrictions concerning slave importations: Kentucky in 1794; Virginia in 1778, 1785, 1788, 1789, 1790, 1792, etc.; Tennessee in 1812; Georgia in 1798; Delaware in 1789; Maryland in 1796; North Carolina in 1794; South Carolina in 1800, 1801, 1802; Missouri 1835; Arkansas in 1838; Mississippi in 1837; and Louisiana in 1826. Ten of the twelve states that framed constitutions passed laws prohibiting the introduction of slaves for sale from other states. At least six of the new states affirmed in their constitutions the power of assemblies to pass these laws and Congress acknowledged the rights of states to pass such statutes and conceded that these constitutions were "not repugnant to the Constitution of the United States." In 1841, the US Supreme Court, in the case of *Groves v. Slaughter*, said that cases arising from the domestic slave trade were state issues. At this late date, Delaware, Maryland, Virginia, Florida, and the District of Columbia permitted illegally imported slaves to claim their freedom.

37. David Geggus, *Slavery, War, and Revolution: The British Occupation of Saint Domingue, 1793–1798* (New York: Oxford University Press, 1982), 305; Papenfuse, "From Recompense to Revolution," 17, 48–49, 60–61 [quote]; Christopher Phillips, "The Roots of Quasi-Freedom: Manumission and Term Slavery in Early National Baltimore," *Southern Studies*, new series 4 (Spring 1993): 43; T. Stephen Whitman, *Challenging Slavery in the Chesapeake: Black and White Resistance to Human Bondage, 1775–1865* (Baltimore: Maryland Historical Society, 2007), 68; *Laws of Maryland Made and Passed at a Session of Assembly* [1796], chap. 67.

38. Junius P. Rodriguez, ed., *Slavery in the United States: A Social, Political, and Historical Encyclopedia*, vol. 1 (Oxford: ABC-CLIO, 2007), 558.

39. Arthur Zilversmit, *The First Emancipation: The Abolition of Slavery in the North* (Chicago: University of Chicago Press, 1967), 113–115, 123–124, 128–129; Thomas D. Morris, *Free Men All: The Personal Liberty Laws of the North, 1780–1861* (Baltimore: Johns Hopkins University Press, 1974), 7; Essah, *A House Divided*, 63; David Nathaniel Gellman, *Emancipating New York: The Politics of Slavery and Freedom, 1777–1827* (Baton Rouge: Louisiana State University Press, 2006), 176–178; Eric Foner, *Gateway to Freedom: The Hidden History of the Underground Railroad* (New York: W. W. Norton, 2015), 43–44; Matthew Mason, "Necessary but Not Sufficient: Revolutionary Ideology and Anti-Slavery Action in the Early Republic," in *Contesting Slavery: The Politics of Bondage and Freedom in the New American Nation*, ed. John Craig Hammond and Matthew Mason (Charlottesville: University Press of Virginia, 2011), 14–15.

40. Leon Litwack, *North of Slavery: The Negro in the Free States, 1790–1860* (Chicago: University of Chicago Press, 1961), 3; Zilversmit, *The First Emancipation*, 192–194; Edgar McManus, *Black*

Bondage in the North (Syracuse, NY: Syracuse University Press, 1973), 174–175; Gary B. Nash, *Forging Freedom: The Formation of Philadelphia's Black Community, 1720–1840* (Cambridge, MA: Harvard University Press, 1988), 63–65; Gary B. Nash and Jean R. Soderlund, *Freedom by Degrees: Emancipation in Pennsylvania and Its Aftermath* (New York: Oxford University Press, 1991), 177; US House of Representatives, *The Federal and State Constitutions*, 5:2909 [Ohio 1802]; 2:1070 [Indiana 1816]; 2:980–981 [Illinois 1818].

41. Morris, *Free Men All*, 7–12, 21, 219–222; "Fugitive Slave Act of 1793," http://www.ushistory.org/presidentshouse/history/slaveact1793.php.

42. Petition of Dunky to the Circuit Court of St. Louis County, Missouri, 6 April 1831, in Records of the Supreme Court, Case Files, *Dunky v. Andrew Hay*, Box/Drawer 536, Document/Case 29, MoSA; Transcript of Court Record, 6 April 1831–10 May 1834; Clerk's Certification, 22 May 1834; Assignment of Errors, Andrew Hay, Supreme Court, 3 June 1834; Opinion, Supreme Court, 21 October 1834, with *Dunky v. Hay*. PAR 21183206 and PAR 21183110. GAA.

43. Farnam, *Chapters in the History of Social Legislation*, 220; Litwack, *North of Slavery*, 70; Stephen Middleton, *The Black Laws: Race and the Legal Process in Early Ohio* (Athens: Ohio University Press, 2005), 49–51.

44. Thomas Morris, *Southern Slavery and the Law, 1619–1860* (Chapel Hill: University of North Carolina Press, 1996), 43–44.

45. *Acts of the South Carolina General Assembly [1740]*, transcription from David J. McCord, ed., *The Statutes at Large of South Carolina, Vol. 7, Containing the Acts Relating to Charleston, Courts, Slaves, and Rivers* (Columbia, South Carolina: A. S. Johnston, 1840), 397; *A Codification of the Statue Law of Georgia*, 802–803; *A Compilation of the General and Public Statutes of the State of Georgia*, 595–596; Goodell, *The American Slave Code in Theory and Practice*, 297–298; *Laws of the State of Delaware Passed [in 1797]*, 1:380–384 [act of 1760 republished]; William H. Williams, *Slavery and Freedom in Delaware, 1639–1865* (Wilmington, DE: Scholarly Resources, 1996), 111. The Delaware act of 1760, which allowed persons of color to sue on their own behalf, set precedent for suits brought by African Americans during statehood.

46. JCCASN, *Free Jack v. Woodruff*, N.C., 3 Hawks 106, June 1824, 2:46–7. GAA. Petition of Phillis Thomas, Mary Thomas, Sarah Thomas, Harry Thomas, Charles Thomas, Ann Thomas, Moses Thomas, William Thomas, George Thomas, John Thomas, Elizabeth Thomas, Ester Thomas, and Rachael Thomas to the Circuit Court of Jefferson County, Kentucky, 27 March 1822, in Records of the Circuit Court, Case Files, *Phillis Thomas, Mary Thomas, Sarah Thomas, et al., v. James Burks*, Box/Drawer 1-25, Document/Case 1842, KDLA; Related Documents: Affidavit, Seaman Thomas, 27 March 1822; Answer, James Burks, 24 January 1823, with *Thomas, et al. v. Burks*. PAR 20782204. Dismissed. Conway Robinson, *The Practice in the Courts of Law and Equity of Virginia, Volume 1: Containing Practice in the Courts of Law in Civil Cases* (Richmond, VA: Samuel Shepherd, 1832), 429.

47. *A Dissertation on Slavery: With a Proposal for the Gradual Abolition of It, in the State of Virginia* (Philadelphia: Printed for Mathew Carey, 1796)

48. JCCASN, "Virginia: Introduction," 1:161–169.

49. James Oldham, *English Common Law in the Age of Mansfield* (Chapel Hill: University of North Carolina Press, 2004), chap. 17; "The Somerset Case," http://www.nationalarchives.gov.uk/pathways/blackhistory/rights/docs/state_trials.htm; "French Slavery," http://slavenorth.com/columns/frenchslavery.htm; Hurd, *The Law of Freedom and Bondage*, 2:195 [state of Coahuila y Tejas]; JCCASN, "Missouri: Introduction," 5:112–113 [slavery in Canada].

50. Essah, *A House Divided*, 41; *Acts Passed at the First Session of the Twentieth General Assembly of the State of Tennessee, 1833* (Nashville: Allen A. Hall & Frederick S. Heiskell, 1833), 99–100; Schaffer, *Slavery, the Civil Law*, 226–227; JCCASN, *Greenlow v. Rawlings*, 3 Humphreys 90, April 1842, 2:514–515.

51. Petition of Philis Thomas Sr. et al., 11 September 1833, in Records of the Circuit Court, Case Files, *Philis Thomas Sr., et al. v. William Hunt*, Box/Drawer 1-44, Document/Case 3181 ["confused compound of contrarieties"], KDLA. 20783316. Injunction granted, dismissed. JCCASN, *Susan (a colored woman) v. Ladd*, Ky., 6 Dana 30, October 1837, 1:338. G DARev; and *Nancy (a colored woman) v. Snell*, Ky., 6 Dana 148, April 1838, 1:333. GAA. Arnold Taylor, *Suing for Freedom in Kentucky* (BookLocker.com, 2010), 100–114; Petition of Dennis to the Chancery Court of Jefferson County, Kentucky, 29 March 1842, in Records of the Circuit

Court, Case Files, *Dennis v. Evans C. Beard,* Box/Drawer 2–62, Document/Case 3522, KDLA; Related Documents: Answer, Evans Beard, 20 May 1842; Replication, Dennis, 20 September 1842; Depositions, Spilman Hord and Christopher Graham, 28 June 1843; Correspondence, James Taylor to Dennis Isom, 7 April 1841; Decree, 18 July 1843, with *Denns v. Beard.* PAR 20784206. Granted. JCCASN, *Wicks v. Chew,* Md., 4 Har. and John. December 1819, 4:67; *Digest of Maryland Reports,* 2 vols. (Baltimore: Cushing and Brother, 1847), 2:726, 731.

52. Geggus, *Slavery, War, and Revolution;* Bernie D. Jones, *Fathers of Conscience: Mixed-Race Inheritance in the Antebellum South* (Athens: University of Georgia Press, 2009), 87.

53. Hurd, *The Law of Freedom and Bondage,* 2:74–76, 76(n.1); *Laws of the State of Delaware Passed [in 1797],* 2: 884–885, 885(n.a) [1793 supplementary act]; JCCASN, "Delaware: Introduction," 4:212–13 and *Allen v. Negro Sarah,* Del., 2 Harrington 434, June 1838, 4:224–225; Petition of Sarah, Phebe, George, Polly, Amy, Grace, Michael, Milley, Levin, John, Bayard, and Jonathan Turner to the Superior Court of Kent County, Delaware, 24 May 1834, in Records of the Superior Court, *Sarah, et al. v. Andrew Allen,* Microfilm Reel R79.3, DSA. PAR 20383402. GAA. *Laws of Maryland [in 1783],* chap. 23.

54. June Purcell Guild, ed., *Black Laws of Virginia: A Summary of the Legislative Acts of Virginia Concerning Negroes from Earliest Times to the Present* (Richmond: Whittet & Shepperson, 1936; reprint, New York: Negro Universities Press, 1969), 72, 106; *Acts Passed by the General Assembly of the Commonwealth of Virginia, Begun and Held at the Capitol, in the City of Richmond, on Monday the Second Day of December, One Thousand Eight Hundred and Five* (Richmond: Samuel Pleasants, 1806), 36; Morris, *Southern Slavery and the Law,* 372; Berlin, *Slaves without Masters,* 138–139; Schaffer, *Becoming Free,* 6, 12; Whitman, *The Price of Freedom,* 98; Farnam, *Chapters in the History of Social Legislation,* 354–355, 374; *Laws Made and Passed by the General Assembly of the State of Maryland [in 1831] at a Session of the Said Assembly, Which Was Begun and Held in the State House, at the City of Annapolis, in the County of Anne Arundel, on the last Monday of December . . . and Concluded on Thursday the Twenty-fourth Day of February, A. D. 1831, in the 55th year of the Independence* (Annapolis, MD: J. Green, 1831), 1068–1070; For Kentucky, see US House of Representatives, *The Federal and State Constitutions,* 3:1310; Alexander J. Chenault, "*Jones v. Bennet:* The Bifurcated Legal Status of Early Nineteenth Century Free Blacks in Kentucky," *The Modern American* 5 (Spring 2009): 29n, 33, 36; JCCASN, "Kentucky: Introduction," 1:276; *The Revised Statutes of Kentucky, Approved and Adopted by the General Assembly, 1851 and 1852* (Frankfort, KY: A. G. Hodges, 1852), 645.

55. JCCASN, *Catherine Bodine's Will,* Ky., 4 Dana 476, October 1836, 1:334–335 ["considered as natural persons"]; JCCASN, *Aleck v. Travis,* Ky., 4 Dana 242, June 1836, 1:333–334 ["recover damages"]. G DARev. *Digest of the Statute Laws of Kentucky,* 227–228; JCCASN, *Richard v. Van Meter,* D.C., 20 Fed. Cas. 682 (2 Cranch C. C. 214), December 1827, 4:180. DAA. The judge noted, "An attachment for contempt will lie against a master who attempts to remove his slave out of the jurisdiction of the court after he has notice or knowledge of the slave's petition for freedom; the court will also order the plaintiff to be brought into court under the protective custody of the marshal."

56. JCCASN, *Peters v. Van Lear,* Md., 4 Gil 249, December 1846, 4:102–103. G DARR; *Reports of Cases Argued and Determined in the Court of Appeals of Maryland by Richard W. Gill, Clerk of the Court of Appeals,* vol. 4: *Containing Cases in 1846* (Annapolis, MD: Robert F. Bonsall, 1850), 249–265.

57. For Louisiana, see: JCCASN, *Marie v. Avart,* 6 Mart. La. 731, June 1819, 3:461–462; and *Berard (f.w.c.) v. Berard et al. (f.p.c.),* 9 La. 156, December 1835, 3:506; *Angelina v. Whitehead et al.,* 3 La. An. 556, August 1848, 3:592; *Julia Arbuckle (f. w. c.) v. Bonny et al.,* 5 La. An. 699, November 1850, 3:608; Petition of Julia Arbuckle to the District Court of Orleans Parish, Louisiana, 11 October 1848, in Records of the Fifth Judicial District Court, Case Records, *Julia Arbuckle v. Victorine Thérèse Nancy Verries Bonny,* Microfilm, Reel 11, Louisiana Collection, Document/Case 2,523, NOPL; Related Documents: Judgment, 1 March 1849; Depositions, John H. Morehead, et al., 23 December 1848, with *Arbuckle v. Bonny.* PAR 20884847. GAA. JCCASN, *Vail v. Bird,* 6 La. An. 223, March 1851, 3:613. In Alabama, after 1833, the county courts adjudicated freedom suits, and in Arkansas the law permitted slaves to be freed in wills and deeds until 1858. Berlin, *Slaves without Masters,* 138–139.

58. *Acts of the General Assembly of Virginia, Passed in 1855-6, in the Eightieth Year of the Commonwealth* (Richmond, VA: William F. Ritchie, 1856), 37–38; Ted Maris-Wolf, *Family Bonds: Free Blacks and Re-enslavement Law in Antebellum Virginia* (Chapel Hill: University of North Carolina Press, 2015), 103–106; Emily West, *Family or Freedom: People of Color in the Antebellum South* (Lexington: University Press of Kentucky, 2012); West, "'She Is Dissatisfied with Her Present Condition': Requests for Voluntary Enslavement in the Antebellum American South," *Slavery and Abolition* 28, no. 3 (December 2007): 329–50.

59. Petition of Alfred, Hannah, Ellen, Charles, John, Charlotte, Stephen, Charlotte, Thomas, Louisa, David, Gibson, Jesse, Jesse, Gabriel, Peter, Humphrey, Sylvia, Maria, Cynthia, Mary, Rachel, Hannah, Sarah, Malinda, Susan, and Samuel B. Smith, next friend, to the Chancery Court of Jefferson County, Kentucky, 30 January 1856, in Records of the Circuit Court, Case Files, *Alfred, et al. v. Joseph R. Underwood and William F. Bullock*, Box/Drawer 2-163, Document/Case 11587, KDLA; Related Documents: Answers, Joseph R. Underwood and William F. Bullock, 30 January 1856; Decree, 1 February 1856, with *Alfred, et al. v. Bullock*. PAR 20785604. Granted.

60. JCCASN, *Phebe v. Quinlin*, Ar. 21 Ark. 490, July 1860, 5:259. DAA.

61. JCCASN, *Louisa Marshall v. Mrs. Charles Watrigant et al.*, 13 La. An. 619, June 1848, 3:663. D GARev; Schafer, *Slavery, the Civil Law*, 259–260.

62. JCCASN, *Pauline (f. w. c.) v. Hubert*, 14 La. An. 161, March 1859, 3:670. D GARev; and *Price, Guardian, v. Executor*, 14 La. An. 697, July 1859, 3:674; *Deshotels et al. v. Soileau*, 14 La. An. 745, August 1859, 3:675–676; *Stephenson v. Harrison*, Tenn., 3 Head 728, December 1859, 2: 576–577; *Milton (of color) v. McKarney*, Mo. 175, October 1860, 5:214–15. DAA; *State, ex rel. Tucker, v. Lavinia (a person of color) [and] State v. Wilkes (a slave)*, 25 Ga. 311, May 1858, 3:62. GAA. Petition of Joseph Johnson and Henry Johnson to the Circuit Court of Talbot County, Maryland, 11 January 1858, in SC, *Joseph Johnson and Henry Johnson v. William S. Ridgaway and Joseph B. Lowe*, Microfilm M 11026, Frame/Pages 3, Volume 4239-30, MSA; Related Documents: Affidavit, 18 August 1858, with *Johnson v. Ridgaway*, et al. PAR 20985847. Granted. Petition of Elias and Quarles T. Mayfield to the Chancery Court of Giles County, Tennessee, 9 March 1859, in Chancery Court Cases, *Elias and Quarles T. Mayfield v. Joseph C. Inman*, Microfilm Reel 145, Frames 2686-2892, Document/Case 1632, TSLA; Related Documents: Order, 9 March 1859; Injunction Bond, 2 March 1859; Decree and Appeal, ca. March 1861, with *Mayfield v. Inman*. PAR 21485909. Granted, appealed. Petition of Isaac Franklin to the County Court of Frederick County, Virginia, March 1858, in Ended County Court Causes, *Isaac Franklin v. Thomas Miller*, Record Group Packet 159, Box/Drawer 159, LV; Related Documents: Attorney's Opinion and Jury Verdict, March 1859; Last Will and Testament, Henry Coe, 2 April 1829; Order, 1 June 1829; Affidavit, Jane Scrivener, 26 April 1858; Certification of Affidavit and Agreement, 28 April 1858, with *Franklin v. Miller*. PAR 21685809. Granted.

63. Petition of Milly, Isbell, Esther, and Betty to the Circuit Superior Court of Chesterfield County, Virginia, 28 March 1836, in Ended Chancery Court Causes, *Milly, Isbell, Esther, and Betty v. Jordan Anderson Jr.*, Box/Drawer 460, Entry Folder 1855, LV; Related Documents: Court Opinion, ca. March 1836; Deposition, Anna Anderson, 21 September 1836; Notice to Take Deposition, Jordan Anderson Jr., 3 September 1836, with *Milly et al. v. Anderson*. PAR 21683601. Granted.

64. Petition of Betty, Rebecca, Nelson, Peter, Aggy, Caroline, Edmund, Sylvia, Dolly, Winny, Vina, Joe, Orange, Isham, Isbell, Rachel, Sarah, Louisa, Maria, Mary, Sophia, and Lydia to the Circuit Court of Chesterfield County, Virginia, 5 May 1856, in Ended Chancery Court Causes, *Betty, Rebecca, Nelson, Peter, Aggy, Caroline, Edmund, Sylvia, Dolly, Winny, Vina, Joe, Orange, Isham, Isbell, Rachel, Sarah, Louisa, Maria, Mary, Sophia, and Lydia v. Wilkins Hall*, Box/Drawer 460, Entry Folder 1855, LV; Related Documents: Jury Verdict, ca. 5 May 1856; Attorneys' Opinions, 5 May 1856; Answer, Wilkins Hall, ca. 5 May 1856; Bill of Exceptions, Wilkins Hall, 8 May 1856; Deed of Emancipation, Jordan Anderson Sr., 7 April 1790; Last Will and Testament and Codicil, Jordan Anderson Sr., 1 January 1805; Recording of Will, Jordan Anderson Sr., 9 December 1805; Order, 2 November 1850; Bond, Wilkins Hall, 8 December 1850; Deposition and Cross Examination, Rhoda Coats, 15 April 1856, with *Betty, et al. v. Hall*. PAR 21685601. Granted.

Chapter 3

1. Petition of Francis Jackson to the Circuit Superior Court of Campbell County, Virginia, 14 October 1851, in Records of the Circuit Superior Court of Chancery, *Francis Jackson v. John W. Deshazor*, Box/Drawer 1855, Circuit Court Building, Rustburg, Virginia.

2. Joseph Story, *Commentaries on Equity Jurisprudence, as Administered in England and America*, 2 vols. (Boston: Gray, 1836; reprint, Washington, DC: Beard Books, 2000), 1:13, 17.

3. Story, *Commentaries*, 21–25, 61–62, 219.

4. *A Practical Treatise on the Law of Slavery Being a Compilation of All the Decisions Made on That Subject, in the Several Courts of the United States, and State Courts*, comp. Jacob D. Wheeler (New York: Allan Pollock Jr., 1837), 388–415.

5. JCCASN, *Tramell v. Adam (a Black man)*, 2 Mo. 155, May 1829, 5:136. GAA.

6. In Virginia, regarding leave of the court, see JCCASN, *Coleman v. Dick and Pat*, 1 Wash. Va. 233, Fall 1793, 1:101–102, n2. GAA.

7. JCCASN, *Evans v. Kennedy*, N.C., 1 Haywood N. C. 422, October 1796, 2:13–14; and *Abram Bryan v. Wadsworth*, N.C., 1 Dev. and Bat. 384, December 1835, 2:73. DAA. Petition of Henrietta Bell to the Circuit Court of Jefferson County, Kentucky, 19 December 1827, in Records of the Circuit Court, Case Files, *Henrietta Bell v. James Cummins*, Box/Drawer 1-12, Document/Case 900, KDLA; Related Documents: Order, ca. 1827; Final Decree, 14 November 1829, with *Bell v Cummins*. Subpoena issued; case dismissed by complainant; settled in 1829; discontinued. PAR 20782721. Petition of Milly, Hannah, Washington, Henry, Joseph, Susan, Betty, Fanny, Hannah, and Susan to the County Court of Harford County, Maryland, 3 March 1819, in SC, *Milly, Hannah, Washington, et al. v. William Hughes*, Microfilm M 11014, Volume 4239-3, Document/Case 34, MSA; Related Documents: Court Record, 18 May 1819; Last Will and Testament, Margaret Coale, 23 July 1776; Deed of Manumission, 3 March 1819, with *Milly et al. v. Hughes*. GAA.

8. Petition of James H. Peck to the Circuit Court of St. Louis County, Missouri, 23 February 1822, in Records of the Circuit Court, *James H. Peck v. Francois Vallois and John P. Cabanna*, CCBSL; Related Documents: PARs 21182101, 21182702; Summons, Gregoire Sarpy, Pierre Provonchere, 23 February 1822; Sheriff's Return, 23 February 1822; Plea of Trespass, Pelagie, 26 February 1822; Sheriff's Return, 1 March 1822; Summons, John P. Cabanne, 26 February 1822; Pleas, John P. Cabanne, 19 June 1822; Summons, Gregory Sarpy, Peter Provonchere, 23 December 1822; Sheriff's Return, 27 January 1823; Summons, G. Sarpy, Peter Provonchere, 18 March 1823; Sheriff's Returns, 29 April 1823, 2 May 1823, with *Peck v. Vallois, et al.* PAR 21182205. Abated. Petition of George to the Circuit Court of Cape Girardeau County, Missouri, 25 September 1838, in Records of the Circuit Court, *George v. Jacob H. Neely*, CCBSL; Related Documents: PARs 21183801, 21185502; Copy of Affidavit, Thomas B. English, 18 September 1838; Copy of Order, 18 September 1838; Copy of Sheriff's Return, 25 September 1838; Copy of Order, 25 September 1838, with *George v Neely*. PAR 21183808. Granted.

9. Petition of Philip to the Circuit Court of Fayette County, Kentucky, 14 July 1836, in Records of the Circuit Court, Case Files, *Philip v. John L. McDowell and Thomas Noble*, Box/Drawer 113, KDLA; Related Documents: Declaration, Philip, 6 October 1837; Answer, John L. McDowell, 22 September 1838, with *McDowell and Noble*. Dismissed, McDowell said he "would not defend" [law court]. PAR 20783619. No decree with petition.

10. JCCASN, *Mason v. Matilda*, D.C., 12 Wheaton 590, March 1827, 4:179; *Reports of Cases Civil and Criminal in the United States Circuit Court of the District of Columbia, 1801-1841*, 6 vols., comp. William Cranch (Boston: Little, Brown, 1852). 2:343–346. G GARR.

11. Although this website deals with Illinois, the court systems in other states were similar. The most important courts in each jurisdiction, North or South, included the common law, chancery or equity, criminal, probate, and appellate courts. http://www.lawpracticeofabrahamlincoln.org/reference/reference%20html%20files/pleading%20and%20practice.htmlCommon.

12. Petition of Clara, Frank, Maria, Sophia, Eliza, and Lewis to the Circuit Court of the District of Columbia, 12 April 1820, in RUSCC-CDRCF, *Clara, Frank, Maria, Sophia, Elizia, and Lewis v. Thomas Ewell*, Record Group 21, Box/Drawer 11, Document/Case 251, NA; Related

Documents: Copy of Note, John P Margert, 9 June 1815; Summons and Court Order, Thomas Ewell, 12 April 1820, with *Clara, et al. v Ewell*. PAR 20482001. Granted.

13. Petition of Mary, Samuel, and Edward to the Circuit Court of St. Louis County, Missouri, 5 November 1850, in Records of the Circuit Court, *Mary, Samuel, and Edward v. Louncelot H. Calvert*, CCBSL; Related Documents: Order, 5 November 1850; Supplemental Petition, 5 November 1850; Copy of Order, 5 November 1850; Subpoena, Louncelot Calvert, 5 November 1850; Sheriff's Return, 5 November 1850; Depositions, James Hendrickson, Henry Hendrickson, William Maxwell, Henry Wise, 25 September 1851, with *Mary, et al. v. Calvert*. PAR 21185012. Petition granted; supplemental petition filed, dismissed by plaintiff. The defendant argued for judgment by default because there was no separate declaration of trespass submitted for the children as the statute required and "no other declaration could be filed than one in trespass" and that the petition did not contain "any fact which would amount to trespass either by the statute or common law." St. Louis Circuit Court Historical Records Project, 1851, no. 29, pp. 9–10, no. 287, http://www.stlcourtrecords.wustl.edu/

14. Petition of Jane McCray to the Circuit Court of St. Louis County, Missouri, 12 September 1845, in Records of the Circuit Court, *Jane McCray v. William R. Hopkins, Eliza O. Miller, William B. Miller, et al.*, CCBSL; Related Documents: Order, 12 September 1845; Plea of Trespass, Jane McCray vs. William R. Hopkins, Eliza O. Miller, William B. Miller, et al., November Term 1845; Bond, Ferdinand Risque, John W. Hanson, n.d.; Summons, William Hopkins, Eliza O. Miller, William B. Miller, et al., 23 October 1845; Copy of Order, ca. 23 October 1845; Sheriff's Return, 25 October 1845; Agreement to Reinstate Case, William Hopkins, Eliza O. Miller, William B. Miller, et al., ca. November 1848, with *McCray v. Hopkins, et al*. PAR 21184506. Plea of trespass filed, dismissed, reinstated. She was permitted by the heirs to go free.

15. John Codman Hurd, *The Law of Freedom and Bondage in the United States*, 2 vols. (Boston: Little, Brown, 1862; reprint, New York: Negro University Press, 1968), 2:269; Kelly Marie Kennington, "River of Injustice: St. Louis's Freedom Suits and the Changing Nature of Legal Slavery in Antebellum America" (PhD diss., Duke University, 2009), 30–31, 33, 35, 58, 252.

16. *A Digest of the Statutes of Arkansas: Embracing All Laws of a General and Permanent Character, in Force at the Close of the General Assembly of 1846* (Little Rock, AR: Rearson & Garritt, 1848), 543–545; *A Digest of the Statutes of Arkansas; Embracing All Laws of a General and Permanent Character, in Force at the Close of the Session of the General Assembly of 1856* (Little Rock, AR: Johnson & Yerkes, 1858), 550–552; Hurd, *The Law of Freedom and Bondage*, 2:192; *A Codification of the Statue Law of Georgia, Including the English Statutes of Force: in Four Parts, to Which Is Prefixed a Collection of State Papers, English, American, and State Origin* (Augusta, GA: Charles E. Grenville, 1848), 802–803; *A Compilation of the General and Public Statutes of the State of Georgia; with the Forms and Precedents Necessary to Their Practical Use* (New York: Edward O. Jenkins, 1859), 595–596; *Acts and Resolutions of the General Assembly of the State of South-Carolina, Passed in December, 1820* (Columbia, SC: D. Faust, 1821), 22.

17. The act of 1760 was reprinted in *Laws of the State of Delaware Passed at a Session of the General Assembly, Which Was Begun and Held at Dover, on Tuesday, the Third Day of January, and Ended on Tuesday, the Twenty-fourth Day of the Same Month, in the Year of Our Lord One Thousand Seven Hundred and Ninety-seven, and of the Independence of the United States of America the Twenty-First*, 2 vols. (New-Castle, DE: Samuel and John Adams, 1797), 1:380–384.

18. Kennington, "River of Injustice," 58, 103.

19. Petition of Robert Trunnel to the Circuit Court of the District of Columbia, 3 January 1842, in RUSCC-CDRCF, *Robert Trunnel v. Hope H. Slatter and Alexander Hunter*, Record Group 21, Rules 4, Box/Drawer 53, Entry Folder 20, Document/Case 202, NA. PAR 20484205. Dismissed.

20. Petition of Martha Ann Smith to the Circuit Court of the District of Columbia, 6 September 1843, in RUSCC-CDRCF, *Martha Ann Smith v. Thomas Burch*, Record Group 21, Rules 4, Box/Drawer 56, Entry Folder 20, Document/Case 287, NA. PAR 20484301. Granted.

21. Petition of Evaline Blue, Fanny Blue, Wallace Blue, Charly Blue, Ann Blue, Emily Blue, and Laura VietchTacon, to the Circuit Court of the District of Columbia, March 1843, 1820, in RUSCC-CDRCF, *Evaline Blue, Fanny Blue, Wallace Blue, et al. v. John W. Williams, Mary*

S. Williams, and William S. Colquhoun, Record Group 21, Rules 4, Box/Drawer 55, Entry Folder 20, Document/Case 258, NA; Related Documents: Injunction, John W. Willliams, Mary S. Williams, and Alexander Hunter, 20 March 1843, with *Blue, et al., v Colquhoun, et al.* PAR 20484305. Granted.

22. JCCASN, *Beaty v. Judy and her children (persons of color),* Ky., 1 Dana 101, April 1833, 1:323–324. Granted, appealed, reversed, and remanded "with instructions to set aside the verdict, and dismiss the suit without prejudice."

23. The Virginia law read: "Where such action is brought by one person for himself and others who are infants, the declaration, trespass, assault, &c., by the informal, is substantially good." *Virginia Act of January 17, 1818–January 1, 1820,* in *Digest of the Laws of Virginia, Which Are of a Permanent Character and General Operation; Illustrated by Judicial Decisions* (Richmond, VA: Smith and Palmer, 1841), 869 n(e).

24. JCCASN, *Will (a negro) v. Thompson,* Ky., Hardin 52 n., May 1805, 1:280. G DARev. and *Thompson v. Wilmot,* Ky., 1 Bibb 422, June 1809, 282–283. GAA. Petition of Mary to the Circuit Court of Jefferson County, Kentucky, 15 June 1827, in Records of the Circuit Court, Case Files, *Mary v. Henry Dougherty,* Box/Drawer 1–21, Document/Case 1564, KDAH; Related Documents: PAR 20782706; Depositions, Alexander Wallace, Robert Dougherty, Polly Doak, Peter Mahin, Sarah Dougherty, and John Johnson, 15 September 1827; Order, 15 June 1827, with *Mary v. Dougherty.* PAR 20782707. Granted.

25. Petition of Frank to the Hustings Court of Richmond City, Virginia, 14 March 1796, in Hustings Court Suit Papers, *Frank v. Elizabeth Eng,* Box/Drawer 1796–1797, Entry Folder 1, LV; Related Documents: Court Record, November 1796–March 1797; Attorney's Statement, 14 March 1796; Bill of Sale, Nicholas Scherer to Jacob Ege, 29 November 1782; Summonses: Elizabeth Ege, 3 May, 20 June 1796; John Tucker and Royal Short, 16 November 1796; Alexander McRobert, et al., 15 November 1796; Daniel Powcase, 12 October 1796, with *Frank v. Eng.* PAR 21679602. Dismissed.

26. JCCASN, *Isaac v. Johnson,* Va., 5 Munford 95, February 1816, 1:126–127. G DARR.

27. In 1846, in *Caesar Peters, et al., v. John, Matthew S., and Joseph Van Lear,* the Maryland High Court of Appeals decided that a claim to freedom could only be established by a judgment in a court of law, and the petition must originate in the county where the petitioners resided, "under the direction of his owner." Chancery courts could not pronounce freedom for complainants but could direct executors of estates to execute deeds of manumission. The slaves would then be able to claim their freedom in a court of law. Slaves possessed no civil rights and were incapable of instituting a suit, either in a court of law or equity, but they could according to the 1796 law, chap. 67, sec. 21, assert their freedom under a deed or a will, although pending the outcome they would be "treated as a slave." Slaves claiming a right to freedom under the same will could bring a single claim against an executor. "Equity has no power to determine, by decree, the right to freedom, nor to order an account of the value of the services of the complainants while detained as slaves." Only the executor at law, John Van Lear Jr., not the others who withdrew, should become a defendant. *Reports of Cases Argued and Determined in the Court of Appeals of Maryland by Richard W. Gill, Clerk of the Court of Appeals,* vol. 4: *Containing Cases in 1846* (Annapolis, MD: Robert F. Bonsall, 1850), 249–265.

28. JCCASN, *Mulatto Lucy v. Charles Slade,* D.C., 15 Fed. Cas. 1091 (1 Cranch C. C. 422), July 1807, 4:160. GAA.

29. JCCASN, *Pepoon, Guardian of Phebe (a woman of Color) v. Clarke,* S.C., 1 Mill 137, May 1817, 2:301–302; *Reports of the Judicial Decisions in the Constitutional Court of South Carolina, Held in Charleston and Columbia, 1817 and 1818,* 2 vols. (Charleston, SC: John Mill, 1819), 1:137–142. GAA. The appeals court denied a motion for a new trial.

30. Petition of Jones H. Jenkins to the Circuit Court of the District of Columbia, 27 July 1835, in RUSDC-SHCP, Record Group 21, Box/Drawer 1, Entry Folder 28, NA; Related Documents: Correspondence, Robert Leslie to William Brent, 24 July 1835; Copy of Freedom Certificate, Jones H. Jenkins, 23 July 1835; Confinement Note, Samuel Stettinius, 20 June 1835; Writ of *Habeas Corpus,* 28 July 1835; Marshal's Report, 29 July 1835; Decree, 29 July 1835, with Jenkins's suit. PAR 20483501. Granted. For similar testimony, see Petition of Sally Boothe to the Circuit Court of the District of Columbia, 9 November 1835, in RUSDC-SHCP, Record Group 21, Box/Drawer 1, Entry Folder 28, NA; Related Documents: Writ of

Habeas Corpus, Sally Boothe, 9 November 1835; Order, 11 August 1835; Affidavit, Theodore Mead, 22 October 1835; Affidavit, Robert Ball, 9 November 1835, with Sally Boothe's petition. PAR 20483503 [arrested as a runaway].Granted. Petition of Matilda Smith to the Circuit Court of the District of Columbia, 26 October 1857, in RUSDC-SHCP, Record Group 21, Box/Drawer 2, Entry Folder 28, NA; Related Documents: Writ of *Habeas Corpus*, Matilda Smith, 26 October 1857; Warrant, Matilda Smith, 17 October 1857, with Matilda Smith's petition. PAR 20485702 [free person of color]. Granted. Chris Naylor, "'You Have the Body': Habeas Corpus Case Records of the U.S. Circuit Court for the District of Columbia, 1820–1863," *Prologue Magazine* 37, no. 3 (Fall 2005): no page numbers given.

31. Petition of Margaret Dorsey to the District Court of the District of Columbia, 27 July 1836, in RUSDC-SHCP, Record Group 21, Box/Drawer 28, Entry Folder 28, NA; Related Documents: Affidavit, William P. Palmer, 25 July 1836; Writ of *Habeas Corpus*, Margaret Dorsey, 27 August 1836; Marshal's Return, ca. 1836; Order, 27 July 1836, with Dorsey's petition. PAR 20483601. Granted.

32. Petition of Robert Nelson and Edward Woodland to the Circuit Court of the District of Columbia, 26 November 1856, RUSDC-SHCP, *Robert Nelson and Edward Woodland v. Alfred Jones*, Record Group 21, Box/Drawer 2, Entry Folder 28, NA; Related Documents: Order, 26 July 1856, with *Nelson, et al. v. Jones*. PAR 20485601. Granted.

33. JCCASN, *De Lacy v. Antoine*, Va., 7 Leigh 438, April 1836, 1:182–183; *Reports of Cases Argued and Determined in the Court of Appeals and in the General Court of Virginia*, vol. 7, 2nd ed., comp. Benjamin Watkins Leigh (Richmond, VA: Gary & Clemmitt, 1867), 438–451, *De Lacy, Vice Counsul v. Antoine and others*, April 1836. GAA.

34. Mark Tushnet, *The American Law of Slavery, 1810–1860: Considerations of Humanity and Interest* (Princeton, NJ: Princeton University Press, 1981), 41–43; JCCASN, *State v. John N. Philpot*, Dudl. Ga. 46, July 1831, 3:13–14.

35. JCCASN, *Field v. Milly Walker*, 17 Ala. 80, June 1849, 172. GAA.

36. JCCASN, *Clark v. Gautheir, in behalf of Dick (a person of color)*, 8 Fla. 150, 1859, 3:120. D GARev.

37. JCCASN, *Weddington v. Samuel Sloan (of Color)*, Ky., 15 B. Mon. 147, December 1854, 1:412–413. GAA.

38. JCCASN, *Renney v. Field*, 4 Hay Tenn., 165, August 1817, 2:488–489. DAA.

39. Minutes of the US Circuit Court for the District of Columbia, *Habeas Corpus*, 10 July 1807, 13 April 1808, Microfilm M-1021, Reel 1, pp. 618–619, NA; Minutes of the US Circuit Court for the District of Columbia, *Habeas Corpus*, Henry Darnal, 9 January 1832, in Microfilm M-1021, Reel 3, n.p., NA; Petition of Patience, Juliet, Levin, George, Rhoda, Arthur, Nathan, Peggy, and David to the County Court of Somerset County, Maryland, 23 April 1825, in SC, *Patience, Juliet, Levin, et al. v. Isaac Morris, Joshua Morris, John Morris, et al.*, Microfilm M 11014, Volume 4239-1, Document/Case 8, MSA; Related Documents: Transcript of Court Record, Somerset County Court, 23 April 1825-31 May 1827, with *Patience, et al. v. Morris*. PAR 20982503. GAA. Petitions of Dick, Bartlett, and Harry to the Circuit Court of Fayette County, Kentucky, 17 September 1813, in Records of the Circuit Court, Case Files, *Dick, Bartlett, and Harry v. Benjamin Clarke*, Box/Drawer 32, KDLA; Related Documents: Orders, ca. 1813; Jury Verdicts, ca. 1813; Pleas of Trespass, 1813; Last Will and Testament, Mildred Clark, 7 November 1807; Instrument of Emancipation, 3 March 1811, with *Bartlett et al. v. Clarke*. PARs 20781304, 20781306, 20781308. Granted.

40. Judith Kelleher Schafer, *Becoming Free, Remaining Free: Manumission and Enslavement in New Orleans, 1846–1862* (Baton Rouge: Louisiana State University Press, 2003), 3; Kennington, "River of Injustice," 31–33; Petition of George Winters to the Circuit Court of Jefferson County, Kentucky, 21 October 1833, in Records of the Circuit Court, Case Files, *George Winters v. Joseph Dough*, Box/Drawer 1-45, Document/Case 3249, KDLA; Related Documents: Oath, William Elliott, 21 October 1833; Order, 21 October 1833; Court Record, 1834, with *Winters v. Dough*. PAR 20783312 [trespass, assault and battery, and false imprisonment]. Dismissed. See note 9, this chapter. *Philip v. John L. McDowell and Thomas Noble*. PAR 20783619 [*trespass vi et armis*]. No decree with petition. JCCASN, *Venus Huger and Sarah, her child (free persons of color), suing per prochienami v. Barnwell (a free person of color)*, S.C., 5 Richardson 273, January 1852, 2:429–430. DAA. *Thorne v. Fordham*, S.C., 4

Rich. Eq. 222, January 1852, 2:430–431 [*de homine replegiando*]. Granted. Petition of John to the County Court of Sussex County, Virginia, 1804, in Loose Court Papers, Deed of Emancipation, Deed Book H (1 October 1795), 375, *John v. John Collier*, Box/Drawer 157, Sussex County Courthouse, Sussex, Virginia; Related Documents: Court Opinion, 5 July 1804; Deed of Emancipation, 1 October 1795; Summonses, John Collier, 23 June 1804, 5 July 1804, 20 September 1804; Sheriffs' Returns, ca. September 1804, with *John v. Collier* [*capias ad audiendum judicium*]. Granted. JCCASN, *Clifton v. Phillips*, S.C., 1 McCord 469, November 1821, 2:319–320. GAA. *Reports of the Judicial Decisions in the Constitutional Court of South Carolina*, comp. D. J. McCord (Columbia, SC: Daniel Faust, 1822), 469 [ravishment of a ward]. Granted.

41. Petition of Philip to the Circuit Court of Fayette County, Kentucky, 14 July 1836, in Records of the Circuit Court, Case Files, *Philip v. John L. McDowell and Thomas Noble*, Box/Drawer 113, KDAH; Related Documents: Declaration, Philip, 6 October 1837; Answer, John L. McDowell, 22 September 1838, with *Philip v. McDowell*. Dismissed on law side. PAR 20783619. No decree with petition.

42. No author, "Chancery Jurisdiction," *American Jurist and Law Magazine* 2, nos. 3–4 (October 1829): 315, drawn from tracts by Jeremy Jones, Joseph Park, and C. P. Cooper, https://books.google.com/books/about/The_American_Jurist_and_Law_Magazine_Ame.html?id=WKhLAAAAYAAJ; Story, *Commentaries on Equity Jurisprudence*, 1:27–28. Today, common-law pleadings have been abolished in the United States; modern rules, based in federal civil codes, allow complainants to accomplish the same purpose as trespass declarations in former times.

43. Petition of Robert, Henry, Milton, Emeline, Harriet, and Fanny to the Chancery Court of Jefferson County, Kentucky, 19 October 1839, in Records of the Circuit Court, Case Files, *Robert, Henry, Milton, Emeline, Harriet, and Fanny v. Laurence Young, Robert W. Glass, Wilkins Tannehill, et al.*, Box/Drawer 2-36, Document/Case 2058, KDLA; Related Documents: Copy of Last Will and Testament, Lee White, 9 August 1833; Copy of Last Will and Testament, Alice Jones, 8 July 1812; Opinion and Decree, 31 July 1840; Decree, 5 January 1841, with *Robert et al. v. Young, et al.* PAR 20783916. Granted.

44. Robert J. Johnson Jr., "Trial by Fire: Abraham Lincoln and the Law" (PhD diss., City University of New York, 2007), 62; Petition of Edward Chase to the Circuit Court of the District of Columbia, Washington County, 28 June 1849, in RUSCC-CDRCF, *Edward Chase v. Thomas Greenfield*, Record Group 21, Rules 5, Box/Drawer 66, Entry Folder 20, Document/Case 607, NA; Related Documents: Injunction, Thomas Greenfield, 28 June 1849, with *Chase v. Greenfield*. PAR 20484902.Granted.

45. Petition of Charles [the elder], Mary, Adam, Amy, Lydia, John, Moses, Charles [the younger], George, Mariah, Tony, Caroline, Mary Ellen, John, William Henry, and Georgeanne to the Circuit Court of Princess Anne County, Virginia, November 1857, in Chancery Court Papers, *Charles [the elder], Mary, Adam, et al. v. John J. Burroughs*, Box/Drawer 9, Document/Case 4-1860, LV; Related Documents: Audit of Executor's Accounts, 25 May 1857; Petition to Sue *in forma pauperis*, ca. November 1857; Attorney's Statement, ca. November 1857; Order, ca. November 1857; Answer, John Burroughs, 27 May 1858; Depositions, Tully B. Stone, James P. Wright, and James E. Bell, 24 July 1858; Depositions, Walter Land, Walter S. Way, 13 July 1858; Correspondence, William Starr to John J. Burroughs, 22 July 1858; Commissioner's Report, 20 May 1859; Decree, ca. 22 September 1859; Executor's Report, ca. 15 May 1860, with *Charles et al. v. Burroughs*. PAR 21685728. Granted.

46. Warren Billings, ed., *The Historic Rules of the Supreme Court of Louisiana, 1813–1879* (Lafayette: University of Southwestern Louisiana, 1985), 2–3, 9–11; Mark F. Fernandez, *From Chaos to Continuity: The Evolution of Louisiana's Judicial System, 1712–1862* (Baton Rouge: Louisiana State University Press, 2001), 53.

47. Petition of Mary to the Circuit Court of Jefferson County, Kentucky, 26 November 1807, in Records of the Circuit Court, Case Files, *Mary v. Jacob Fenton and William Trigg*, Box/Drawer 1-1, Document/Case 181, KDAH; Related Documents: Summons, Jacob Fenton, 26 November 1807; Sheriff's Returns, ca. 1807; Amended Bill, ca. 1810; Answer, William Trigg, 18 May 1810, with *Mary v. Fenton et al.* PAR 20780707. Granted *pro confesso*; dismissed against Trigg who had sold her to the codefendant.

48. Petition of William and L. Pepper to the County Court of Robertson County, Tennessee, 5 February 1855, in Supreme Court Cases, Middle Tennessee, Box/Drawer 112, TSLA; Related Documents: Bill of Exceptions, ca. February 1855; Decree, 5 February 1855; Court Record, 5 February 1855; Bond, J. S. M. Johnson, et al., 5 February 1855; Court Record, 6 December 1855; Supreme Court Opinion, ca. December 1855, with William and Pepper suit. PAR 21485508. GAA.

49. Petition of Amanda to the Chancery Court of Jefferson County, Kentucky, 18 September 1843, in Records of the Circuit Court, Case Files, *Amanda v. James Heisle and Shipley Owen*, Box/Drawer 2-73, Document/Case 4156, KDLA; Related Documents: PAR 20784313; Order, 18 September 1843; Receipts, Charles Clarke, 6 February 1846, 19 February 1847, and 23 May 1848; Amended Bill, 7 November 1845; Testimony, Thornton Smith, 11 February 1847; Copy of Deed of Gift, Samuel Heisle, 26 August 1841; Certificate, 4 October 1841; Commissioner's Report, 19 September 1845; Order, 23 December 1845; Commissioner's Report, 23 July 1846; Marshal's Report, 12 February 1847; Hiring Report, 3 February 1846; Decree, 4 June 1847, with *Amanda v. Heisle et al.* PAR 20784312. Granted. Petition of Nancy Ann to the Chancery Court of Jefferson County, Kentucky, 22 November 1844, in Records of the Circuit Court, Case Files, *Nancy Ann v. Peter Talbott and William Shephard*, Box/Drawer 2-78, Document/Case 4491, KDLA; Related Documents: Amended Bill, 28 January 1845; Receipt, Peter Talbot to Lewis Thomas, 20 April 1840; Amended Bill, 8 April 1845; Decree, 23 March 1845, with *Nancy v. Talbott et al.* PAR 20784416. Granted.

50. Bryan A. Garner, ed., *Black's Law Dictionary*, 7th ed. (St. Paul, MN: West Group, 1999), 788.

51. In one case in Maryland, the appeals court reversed and remanded a lower court decision rejecting an injunction because it had no affidavit. In 1846, Maryland passed a law making slaves "incompetent to give testimony in any case in which a white person is interested." JCCASN, *Negroes Charles and others v. Sheriff*, 12 Md. 274, July 1858, 4:135.

52. Johnson, "Trial by Fire," 62; Petition of Edward Chase to the Circuit Court of the District of Columbia, 28 June 1849, in RUSCC-CDRCF, *Edward Chase v. Thomas Greenfield*, Record Group 21, Rules 5, Box/Drawer 66, Entry Folder 20, Document/Case 607, NA; Related Documents: Injunction, Thomas Greenfield, 28 June 1849, with *Chase v. Greenfield*. PAR 20484902. Granted.

53. Petition of Eliza Johnson, Elizabeth Theresa Johnson, Josephine Johnson, Frances Johnson, and Jane Saunders to the Circuit Court of the District of Columbia, 16 March 1857, in RUSCC-CDRCF, *Eliza Johnson, Elizabeth Theresa Johnson, Josephine Johnson, et al. v. John F. Sharretts*, Record Group 21, Rules 5, Box/Drawer 92, Entry Folder 20, Document/Case 1249, NA; Related Documents: PAR 20485501; Injunction, John F. Sharretts, 16 March 1857, with *Johnson et al. v. Sharretts*. PAR 20485703. Granted.

54. Petition of Clara Thomas and Ann Thomas to the Circuit Court of Jefferson County, Kentucky, 28 March 1822, in Records of the Circuit Court, Case Files, *Clara Thomas and Ann Thomas v. William Taylor, Charles Taylor, and Worden Pope*, Box/Drawer 1-26, Document/Case 1934, KDLA; Related Documents: Order, 28 March 1822, with *Thomas et al. v. Taylor et al.* PAR 20782205. Discontinued by complainants' counsel.

55. Petition of Claiborne to the Chancery Court of Jefferson County, Kentucky, 14 August 1844, in Records of the Circuit Court, Case Files, *Claiborne v. James H. Overstreet, John W. Taylor, Mr. Talbert, and Stephen R. Chenowith*, Box/Drawer 2-77, Document/Case 4405, KDLA; Related Documents: PARs 20782511, 20784019; Subpoena, 20 January 1845; Depositions, Joseph Stratton, Samuel Shannon, and Isaac Newman, 21 January 1845; Deposition, David Harris, 22 January 1845; Questions for Witnesses, ca. 1845; Marshal's Report, 13 September 1844; Decree, 31 January 1845, with *Claiborne v. Overstreet et al.* PAR 20784411. Granted.

56. Petition of Helen to the Circuit Court of the District of Columbia, 24 September 1825, in RUSCC-CDRCF, *Helen v. Henry Drain*, Record Group 21, Rules 2, Box/Drawer 31, Entry Folder 20, Document/Case 130, NA; Related Documents: Decree, 24 September 1825; Opinion, Buckner Thurston, 25 October 1825; Bond, Fleet Smith, 12 November 1825, with *Helen v. Drain*. PAR 20482501. Granted. A writ of *fieri facias* is a writ of execution directing a sheriff to take goods or property of someone against whom a judgment has been rendered.

57. JCCASN, *Thornton v. Davis*, D.C., 23 Fed. Cas. 1147 (4 Cranch C. C. 500), March 1835, 4:192. Injunction granted.

58. Petition of Grace and E. Ferguson, Guardian, to the Equity Court of Charleston District, South Carolina, 9 July 1817, in Records of the Equity Court, Bills, *Grace and E. Ferguson v. Lawrence Ryan*, Microfilm Reel CH192, Document/Case 1818-32, SCDAH. PAR 21381708. No decree with petition.

59. Petition of Lewis Gassaway and Charity Gassaway to the Circuit Court of the District of Columbia, 14 October 1856, in RUSCC-CDRCF, *Lewis Gassaway and Charity Gassaway v. Adam Rose*, Record Group 21, Rules 5, Box/Drawer 91, Entry Folder 20, Document/Case 1206, NA; Related Documents: PAR 20485605; Order, 14 October 1856, with *Gassaway, et al. v. Rose*. PAR 20485606. Granted.

60. Petition of Catherine Henderson and Benjamin Henderson to the Circuit Court of the District of Columbia, 9 December 1833, in RUSCC-CDRCF, *Catherine Henderson and Benjamin Henderson v. Harriet Loyed and Mr. Freeman*, Record Group 21, Rules 3, Box/Drawer 41, Entry Folder 20, Document/Case 274, NA; Related Documents: Deposition, Hugh Smith, 9 December 1833, with *Henderson et al. v. Loyed et al.* PAR 20483302. Granted.

61. Petition of Charity, Mary, and Kitty to the Equity Court of Montgomery County, Maryland, 10 October 1818, in SC, *Charity, Mary, and Kitty v. Adam Robb, Henry Lansdale, and Alexander Robb*, Microfilm M 11024, Frame/Pages 1, Volume 4239-25, MSA; Related Documents: Answer, Adam Robb, 19 May 1819; Affidavit, William Campbell, 10 October 1818; Attorneys' Agreement, July Term 1820, with *Charity et al. v. Robb et al.* PAR 20981813. Injunction granted.

62. Petition of Simon, Lewis, Willis, Dick, Addison, Joe, Anthony, Peter, Cargill, Martha, Judith, Charlotte, Maria, Harriett, Sophia Ann, Nancy, Desdemona, Caroline, Alabama, Dinah, Margarett, Obidard, Jim, Ellick, Mary, Eliza, L. R. Edwards, Diadama, Zobiara [?], Elizabeth, Thadeus, Sarah, Euphemia, Morgana, Quebeck, Lucy, Julia, Martha, and Louisiana to the Circuit Court of Southampton County, Virginia, March 1851, in Chancery Court Papers, *Simon, Lewis, Willis, et al. v. Polly Williamson Branch, Edwards Butts, and Joseph T. W. Summerell*, Box/Drawer 65, Document/Case 16-1856, LV; Related Documents: PAR 21685428; Court Record; Order, November Term 1847; Commissioner's Report, 29 December 1847; Answer, Polly Branch, 1 August 1851; Answer, Joseph T. W. Summerrill, 15 September 1851; Depositions, Sally Womble, Calvin Stephenson, John P. Boykin and Thomas Boykin, 23 October 1852; Court Record and Decree, 10 November 1854; Decree, November Term 1855; Administrator's Report, 8 November 1856; Inventory of Slaves, Estate of John Williamson, n.d., with *Simon et al. v. Branch et al.* PAR 21685127. Granted.

63. William E. Foley, "Slave Freedom Suits before Dred Scott: The Case of Marie Jean Scypion's Descendants," *Missouri Historical Review* 79 (1984–1985): 20.

64. Petition of Richard Booth, Ann Arundel County, Maryland, to the General Court, 12 May 1789, in SC, *Richard Booth v. David Weems*, Microfilm M 11015, Frame/Pages 4, Volume 4239-2, MSA; Related Documents: PARs 20979902, 20981109, 20981825; Court Record, 9 October 1789; Order, 29 July 1789; Deposition, John Batson, 26 September 1789; Court Records, 1789–1792; Depositions, Eleanor King, Joseph Mumford, and Edward Booth [alias Brown], 3 June 1791, Alice Taylor, 14 October 1791, John Wood, 3 May 1792, Mary McKinsey, 20 May 1792, Elaskington Gardner, 9 May 1792, Mary McKinsey, 20 May 1792, Henry Wilson, 27 May 1790, John Welch, 25 May 1792; Interrogatories, ca. 1792; Depositions, John Carr, John King, James Gibson Sr., William Armager, Mary Brown, Philemon Lloyd Chew, Thomas Lane, Joseph Crandele, 3 May 1792, William Wood, ca. May 1792, Nehemiah Birckhead, Morgan Wood, Robert Ward, 18 May 1792, Elizabeth Batson, 24 May 1792; Copy of Last Will and Testament, Richard Harrison, 10 July 1713; Inventory, Estate of Richard Harrison, 9 April 1717; Depositions, Mary McKenzie, 31 May 1792, Richard Harrison, 2 June 1792; Court Record, Order, and Appeal, 9 October 1792; Request for Records, 12 November 1793; Certification of Copy, 10 May 1794; Plaintiff's Costs, ca. June 1794; Copy of Petition, Depositions, Orders, Court Records, with *Booth v Weems*. PAR 20978908. G DARev. Petitions of Reubin, Antigua, Patience, and Isaac to the Court of Common Pleas, Kent County, Delaware, 1795, in Records of the Court of Common Pleas, *Reubin, Antigua, Patience, and Isaac v. Peggy Handy*, DSA; Related Documents: Deposition, Levin King, 14 April 1795; Commission, John Done, May Term 1795, with *Reubin et al. v. Isaac et al.* PAR 20379510; filed May 1791, KCCCP-CJD, May 1791 thru May 1792, p. 82, Reel 3, Frame 423, continued;

rule depositions be taken on both sides, December 1794, continued thru May 1797, cited May Term 1791, p. 32, Reel 4, Frame 238, *Reuben et al. v. Isaac et al.*, p. 2, Reel 3, Frame 446, 3 August 1798 "not to be brought forward." PARs 20379510, 20379511, 20379512, 20379513. Petition of Reuben to the Court of Common Pleas, Kent County, Delaware, 10 December 1795, in Records of the Court of Common Pleas, *Reuben v. Daniel James*, DSA; Related Documents: Interrogatories, George Ferguson, May 1796; Interrogatories, George Ferguson, 1797; Affirmation, George Ferguson, 3 May 1797; Commission, Caleb Boyer and Matthew Driver, May 1797, with *Reuben v. James* KCCCP-CJD, May 1796, p. 158, Reel 3, Frame 304, (filed December 1795) order for commission to issue calls for Maryland residents to give depositions, continued to November 1797; court judgment, December 1795, Reel 4, Frame 454, included 4 August 1798 "opinion that the petition of the petitioner aforesaid be dismissed," with *Reubin et al. v. Handy and James*. Appealed.

65. Petition of Thomas Simmons to the District Court of Orleans Parish, Louisiana, 13 October 1821, in Supreme Court of Louisana Collection, *Thomas Simmons v. Robert H. McNair*, Book 1,145, UNO; Related Documents: Court Records, 5 October 1820–1830 January 1826, including: Deposition, Sarah Kennedy, 12 October 1821; Orders, 13 October 1821, 20 February 1822; Supplemental Petition, ca. 22 February 1822; Answer, William Wyer, 13 March 1822; Notarial Act of Sale, John Hewlett to William and Nathaniel Myer, 5 October 1820; Answer, R. H. McNair, 18 March 1822; Answer, John Hewlett, 20 April 1822; Supplemental Petition, 6 October 1823; Deposition, Rachel Moss, 2 October 1823; Deed of Emancipation, 29 March 1804, certified 31 July 1823 and 1 September 1823; Answer, Edward E. Parker, 9 October 1823; Copy of a Bill of Sale, John Hewlett to William and Nathaniel Myer, 5 October 1820, certified 9 October 1823; Bill of Sale, William and Nathaniel Wyer to Edward E. Parker, 21 August 1822; and Supreme Court Opinion and Decree, 30 January 1826, with *Simmons v. McNair*. PAR 20882173. GAA.

66. Petition of Betsy to the Parish Court of Natchitoches Parish, Louisiana, March 1812, in Records of the District Court, *Betsy v. Lewis Latham*, Document/Case 70, Natchitoches Parish Courthouse, Natchitoches, Louisiana; Related Documents: Order of Summons, 2 March 1812; Order of Guardianship, n.d.; Record of Case Dismissal Affidavit, ca. 1814; Affidavit, John L. Pettit, 25 March 1812; Petition, Lewis Latham, 19 May 1812; Order of Dedimus Potestatem ("we have given the power"; it refers to a commission directed to a judicial officer or an individual by name, authorizing him to take the deposition of the witness), 18 May 1812; Questions for Interrogatories, 27 January 1814; Depositions, Daniel McNiel and Mary McNiel, March Term 1814; Court Record of Dismissal, ca. 1814, with *Betsy v. Latham*. PAR 20881205. Dismissed.

67. Petition of Moses to the Circuit Court of Barren County, Kentucky, 12 June 1844, in Records of the Circuit Court, Equity Judgments, *Moses v. George Wilcoxen, Catharine Wilcoxen, Daniel Wilcoxen, et al*, Microfilm Reel 218714, Document/Case 1505, KDLA; Related Documents: PARs 20782904, 20783822, 20783922; Amended Bill, 18 September 1845; Depositions, James Hardy, Elias Smith, William Harlow, and Drewery Roberts, 1 September 1846; Decree, ca. June 1847, with *Moses v. Wilcoxen, et al*. PAR 20784408. Granted.

68. Petition of Phoebe Gillis to the Circuit Court of Fayette County, Kentucky, 2 June 1840, in Records of the Circuit Court, Case Files, *Phoebe Gillis v. Esther Morrison and Henry Clay*, Box/Drawer 119, KDLA; Related Documents: PARs 20784008, 20784009; Depositions, Jane Rankin, 24 November 1840, 26 April 1842; Answers, Henry Clay and Esther Morrison, 20 July 1842; Agreement, 5 December 1843; Sheriff's Report, 18 October 1845, with *Gillis v. Morrison, et al*. PAR 20784010. No decree with petition.

69. Petition of Winny Cryer and Turner Cryer to the Circuit Court of the District of Columbia, 22 January 1847, in RUSCC-CDRCF, *Winny Cryer and Turner Cryer v. Elizabeth Cocke and Peter E. Hoffman*, Record Group 21, Rules 4, Box/Drawer 60, Entry Folder 20, Document/Case 454, NA; Related Documents: PAR 20484703; Affidavit, Mary McDonald, 22 January 1847; Injunction, Elizabeth Cocke and Peter Hoffman, 22 January 1847, with *Cryer et al. v. Cocke et al*. PAR 20484702. Granted.

70. JCCASN, "Delaware: Introduction," 4:211. Free women of color were competent to serve as witnesses on two grounds: at common law there was a strong presumption of freedom, and reputation of status was proof of freedom.

71. JCCASN, *State v. Levy and Dreyfous*, 5 La. An. 64, January 1850, 3:601. As indicated else-where, "credit" referred to the importance accorded character, reputation, and personality in determining the fate of those caught up in the legal system. Laura F. Edwards, "Law, Domestic Violence, and the Limits of Patriarchal Authority in the Antebellum South," *Journal of Southern History* 65, no. 4 (November 1999): 733–770; Laura F. Edwards, *The People and Their Peace: Legal Culture and the Transformation of Inequality in the Post-Revolutionary South* (Chapel Hill: University of North Carolina Press, 2009), 3.

72. *United States v. Mima Queen and child*, 11 U.S. 290, 7 Cranch, (1813), http://supreme.justia.com/us/11/290/case.html. DAA. JCCASN, *Jenkins v. Tom*, 1 Wash, Va. 123, Fall 1792, JCCASN, 1:99. DAA. *Pegram v. Isabell*, Va., 1 Hen and M. 374, June 1807, JCCASN, 1:114, 117; *Reports of Cases Argued and Determined in the Supreme Court of Appeals in Virginia: With Selected Cases, Relating Chiefly to Points of Practice, Decided by the Superior Court of Chancery for the Richmond District*, 2 vols., comp. William W. Hening and William Munford (Philadelphia: n.p., 1808), 1:387–390. D GARR. *Gregory v. Baugh*, 4 Randolph 611, February 1827, JCCASN, 1:64n, 65n, 66, 68n, 147, 163. *Reports of Cases Argued and Determined in the Supreme Court of Virginia* (n.p.: Michie Co., 1900), 752 ["belief in the neighborhood"]. D GARev.

73. William John Clarke to John Reynolds, 28 August 1851, in Records of the Circuit Superior Court of Chancery, *Francis Jackson v. John W. Deshazor*, Box/Drawer 1855, Circuit Court Building, Rustburg, Virginia.

74. Petition of Francis Jackson to the Circuit Superior Court of Campbell County, Virginia, 14 October 1851, in Records of the Circuit Superior Court of Chancery, *Francis Jackson v. John W. Deshazor*, Box/Drawer 1855, Circuit Court Building, Rustburg, Virginia; Related Documents: Answer, John W. Deshazer, 22 November 1851; Deposition, Lewis E. Williams, 10 October 1853; Depositions, John Reynolds, Henry Pearson, James S. Cossett, 12 October 1853; Decree, October 1855; Correspondence, Benjamin Ferris to William H. Shaw, 12 August 1851, with *Jackson v. Deshazor*; injunction granted; discontinued; freedom granted. PAR 21685105. In 1850, Virginia-born Elijah Jackson, age sixty-five, black, and without property, lived in Lawrence County, Pennsylvania, with his wife, Pennsylvania-born free black Sarah Jackson, age fifty-six. In 1860, free black Francis Jackson, age forty-five, an illit-erate Pennsylvania-born laborer, and his wife, Susan Jackson, age forty, lived in Alleghany City, Pennsylvania. He possessed personal property worth $25. USMSPC, Lawrence County, Pennsylvania, Neshannock Township, 1850, p. 197; USMSPC, Alleghany County, Pennsylvania, Alleghany City, 3rd Ward, 1860, p. 952. In 1850, Irish-born William J. Clarke, age forty-nine, headed a household with his wife, Jane, and his six children, ages eighteen to one. His realty was valued at $20,000, and he owned three slaves. USMSPC, Richmond City, Virginia, Ward 1, 1850, image 28; USMSSC, Richmond City, Virginia, 1850, image 7, an-cestry.com.

Chapter 4

1. See note 58, this chapter.

2. JCCASN, *Pride v. Pulliam*, N.C., 4 Hawks 49, December 1825, 2:49–50.

3. JCCASN, *Bazil v. Kennedy*, D.C., 2 Fed. Cas. 1096 (1 Cranch C. C. 199), November 1804, 4:156. GAA.

4. JCCASN, *Patton v. Patton*, Ky., 5 J. J. Marsh. 389, April 1831, 1:318. DAA.

5. Petition of Maria to the Parish Court of Orleans Parish, Louisiana, 24 November 1818, in Supreme Court of Louisiana Collection, *Maria, a slave, v. Robert Avart*, Books 352 and 488, UNO; Related Documents: Transcript of Parish Court Records, 25 November 1818–16 April 1819, including: Opinion of the Court, 5 April 1819, and Judgment, 16 April 1819; Transcript of Parish and Supreme Court Records, 25 November 1818–26 May 1820, in-cluding: Mandate of the Supreme Court, 18 June 1819, Remanded Parish Court Order, 24 May 1820, and Supplemental Petition, ca. 24 May 1820; Last Will and Testament, Erasmus Robert Avart, 6 October 1818 [text in French], certified 9 October 1818, filed 17 May 1820, with *Marie v. Avart*. PAR 20881875.JCCASN, *Marie v. Avart*, 6 Mart. La. 731, June 1819, 3:461–462; *Marie v. Avart's Heirs*, 8 Mart. La. 512, July 1820, 3:466; Judith Kelleher Schafer,

Slavery, the Civil Law and the Supreme Court of Louisiana (Baton Rouge: Louisiana State University Press, 1994), 9. D GARR.

6. JCCASN, *Patton v. Patton*, Ky., 5 J. J. Marsh. 389, April 1831, 1:318; *Hubbard's Will*, Ky., 6 J. J. Marsh. 58, April 1831, 1:318–319; *Singleton's Will*, Ky., 8 Dana 315, June 1839, 1:345–347; *John v. Morton*, Md., 8 Gill and John. 391, December 1836, 4:85; Petition of John Sr., Henry Johnson, Henry Grosher, Frank, Tom Sr., et al., to the County Court of Montgomery County, Maryland, 1 December 1835, in SC, *John Sr., Henry Johnson, Henry Grosher, Frank, Tom Sr., et al. v. William Morton*, Microfilm M 11014, Volume 4239-3, Document/Case 134, MSA; Related Documents: Court Record, 14 November 1836-8 December 1836; Correspondence, R. Forrest to Thomas A. Alexander, 17 January 1837, with *John, et al. v. Morton*. PAR 20983516. DAA.

7. Petition of Dick to the Circuit Court of Boyle County, Kentucky, 22 May 1844, in Records of the Circuit Court, Equity/Chancery Cases, *Dick v. John Pratt, Michael Hope, Rebecca Reed, et al.*, Box/Drawer 44, KDLA; Related Documents: Bond, Dick, June 1844; Injunction, 30 May 1844, with *Dick v. Pratt* PAR 20784407. Injunction granted.

8. JCCASN, *Weir's Will*, Ky., 9 Dana 434, May 1840, 1:352–353. The appeals court ruled that Weir was clearly "an emancipator." G DARev.

9. JCCASN, *Nicholas v. Burruss*, Vir., 4 Leigh 289, February 1833, 1:172–173. GAA. *Hughes v. Negro Milly*, Md., 5 Mar. and John 310, June 1821, 4:71. GAA. *Emory v. Erskine*, Va., 7 Leigh 2677, February 1836, 1:180–181; *Erskine v. Henry*, Vir., 9 Leigh 188, February 1838, 1:189–190; *Reports of Cases Argued and Determined in the Court of Appeals, and in the General Court of Virginia* (Charlottesville, VA: Michie, 1902), 9:188–99. DAA. JCCASN, *White v. Turner (a man of color)*, Ky., 1 B. Mon. 130, December 1840, 1:355. GAA. JCCASN, *Campbell v. Street*, N.C., 1 Iredell 109, June 1840, 2:89–190. GAA. Petition of Gideon, Peter, Abraham, James, Rosannah, Lewis, Jude, Sabre, Eliza, Andrew, Sinda, Jonathan, Malinda, and Elias Arterburn, next friend, to the Chancery Court of Washington County, Tennessee, 17 December 1849, in Washington County Court Records, Chancery Court, *Gideon, Peter, Abraham, and Elias Arterburn, et al. v. William Jones, James F. Gammon, et al.*, Box/Drawer 166, Entry Folder 17, Document/Case 18, AAETSU; Related Documents: Decrees, 15 November 1855, ca. November 1855; Clerk and Master's Report No. 6, 3 May 1861; Decree, 12 May 1865, with *Gideon et al. v Jones et al.* PAR 21484901. D GARR. Freed with general emancipation and compensated for hire.

10. Petition of Philis to the Circuit Court of Jefferson County, Kentucky, 8 June 1833, in Records of the Circuit Court, Case Files, *Philis v. John Shadburn*, Box/Drawer 1-41, Document/Case 2929, KDLA; Related Documents: Decree, 4 December 1834; Last Will and Testament, Charles Withers, 1 June 1830, with *Philis v. Shadburn*. PAR 20783308. Granted.

11. JCCASN, *Mahan v. Jane*, Ky., 2 Bibb 32, Spring 1810, 1:285. D GARev.

12. JCCASN, *Rucker v. Gilbert*, Vir., 3 Leigh 8, May 1831, 1:166; *Reports of Cases Argued and Determined in the Court of Appeals and in the General Court of Virginia*, vol. 3, comp. Benjamin Watkins Leigh (Richmond, VA: Samuel Shepherd, 1833), 8–11. D GARev.

13. JCCASN, *Jordan v. Bradley*, Dudl. Ga. 170, October 1830, 3:12; *Cleland v. Waters*, 16 Ga. 496, October 1854, 3:38; *Curry v. Curry*, 30 Ga. 253, March 1860, 3:76–77.

14. *Prudence v. Bermodi*, No. 1888, 1 La. 234 (1830), in Schaffer, *Slavery, the Civil Law*, 185–187. DAA. There were a number of cases in Louisiana where executors, heirs, and others sued one another to assist or prevent a paramour's freedom. *Bird v. Vail*, No. 3554, 9 La. Ann. 174 (1854), in Schaffer, *Slavery, the Civil Law*, 188. D GARev. The slave daughters of Jean Baptiste Lagarde, a white overseer, in a suit brought by a free black woman who cared for them, were declared free because of Lagarde's will and the fact that they had lived as free persons, in "good-faith possession of *themselves*," for more than ten years. The Civil Code, article 3510, allowed for their freedom. *Audat v. Gilly*, No. 5337, 12 Rob. 323 (La 1845), in Schafer, *Slavery, the Civil Law*, 193–194. GAA.

15. For appellate cases involving single, white men who provided for their mixed-race slave children and black paramours, see Bernie D. Jones, *Fathers of Conscience: Mixed-Race Inheritance in the Antebellum South* (Athens: University of Georgia Press, 2009), 7–15.

16. Petition of Ann W. Wood to the Equity Court of Charles County, Maryland, 20 September 1824, in SC, *Ann W. Wood v. William Strickland and Thomas Bruce*, Microfilm M 11018, Volume

4239-5, Document/Case 12352, MSA; Related Documents: PARs 20982402, 20983718; Copy of Last Will and Testament, John Perrie, Prince George's County, 31 March 1791; Copy of Probate, Prince George's County, 1 September 1794; Register of Wills' Certification, Prince George's County, 22 September 1824; Supplemental Bill of Complaint, Ann Wood, Court of Chancery, 1 December 1837; Order, Court of Chancery, 27 December 1837, with *Wood v. Strickland et al.* PAR 20982401. Injunction granted; injunction dissolved; transferred to chancery; continued. Petition of Clarissa Highland to the County Court of Charles County, Maryland, 17 September 1824, in SC, *Clarissa Highland v. Ann W. Wood,* Microfilm M 11018, Volume 4239-5, Document/Case 12352, MSA; Related Documents: PARs 20982401, 20983718; Copy of Court Record, 17 September 1824–ca. 27 March 1828; Copy of List of Sales, John Perrie, Prince George's County, 1795; Clerk's Certification, 14 October 1837, with *Highland v. Wood.* PAR 20982402. Granted.

17. Petition of Milly, Hannah, Washington, Henry, Joseph, Susan, Betty, Fanny, Hannah, and Susan to the County Court of Harford County, Maryland, 3 March 1819, in SC, *Milly, Hannah, Washington, et al. v. William Hughes,* Microfilm M 11014, Volume 4239-3, Document/Case 34, MSA; Related Documents: Court Record, 18 May 1819; Last Will and Testament, Margaret Coale, 23 July 1776; Deed of Manumission, 3 March 1819, with *Milly et al. v. Hughes.* PAR 20981906. GAA. Petition of Jonas to the Chancery Court of Jefferson County, Kentucky, 14 October 1837, in Records of the Circuit Court, Case Files, *Jonas v. Sally White, Robert Glass, Sarah Blackburn, et al.,* Box/Drawer 2-19, Document/Case 915, KDLA; Related Documents: Order, 11 October 1837; Answer, Robert W. Glass, 3 April 1838; Answer, Robert G. Vance, 19 April 1838; Deposition, Silas M. Noel, 24 November 1838; Decree, 24 February 1840, with *Jonas v. White et al.* PAR 20783714. Granted.

18. Petition of George, David, Jim, Harry, Maria, Beck, and Mary to the County Court of Kent County, Maryland, 20 March 1826, in SC, *George, et al. v. Thomas C. Kennard,* Microfilm M 11014, Volume 4239-1, Document/Case 29, MSA; Related Documents: Transcript of Court Record, 20 March 1826; Bill of Exceptions, George, et al., 20 March 1826; Clerk's Certification, 18 May 1826; Appellants' Statement, 25 May 1827; Ruling, June Term 1827, with *George v. Kennard.* PAR 20982607. JCCASN, *Negro George v. Corse,* 2 Har. and Gill, 1, June 1827, 4:76. DAA.

19. Petition of Samuel to the Chancery Court of Fluvanna County, Virginia, 7 April 1813, in Ended Chancery Court Causes, *Samuel v. Elijah May, Alexander Crawford, and John Quarles,* Box/Drawer 10, LV; Related Documents: Court Record, January 1813–July 1821; Answer, Elijah May, June 1821; Court Record, September 1821–October 1832; Order, 7 April 1826, with *Samuel v. May, et al.* PAR 21681309. Injunction granted.

20. JCCASN, *Caleb v. Field,* Ky., 9 Dana 346, May 1840, 1:350. G DARev.

21. Petition of Nancy, a slave, and Ira Garrett to the Circuit Superior Court of Albemarle County, Virginia, 12 October 1843, in Ended Chancery Court Causes, *Nancy and Ira Garrett v. Charles Carter, Samuel O. Moon, William Moon, Martha Judy, and Elizabeth Moon,* Box/Drawer 617, Document/Case 234, LV; Related Documents: PARs 21683520, 21684310; Answer, Charles Carter, 23 January 1844; Order, 27 October 1845; Court Record, 13 October 1843–22 October 1845, with *Nancy et al. v. Ira Garrett, et al* [*fierii facias*]. PAR 21684313. Injunction granted. Dissolved.

22. JCCASN, *Chambers v. Davis,* Ky., 15 B. Mon. 522, February 1855, 1:417 [create a fund]; *Bank v. Benham,* 23 Ala. 143, June 1853, 1:127–128, 188–189; *Nicholas v. Burruss,* Vir., 4 Leigh 289, February 1833, 1:172–173 [liens]; Petition of Jane to the Superior Court of Sussex County, Virginia, 11 June 1836, found in Records of the Circuit Superior Court of Chancery, Petersburg, *Jane v. Thomas Hunt, Jeremiah Cobbs, and Lewis Lanier,* Box/Drawer 38-40, Circuit Court Clerk's Office, Petersburg, Virginia; Related Documents: Answer, Lewis Lanier, 11 June 1836; Copy of Last Will and Testament, Buckner Lanier, 18 May 1811; Report, Jordan Branch, 1 June 1840; Decree, November 1840; Receipt, Jordan Branch to David May, 17 November 1840; Statement, Jordan Branch, 24 April 1841, with *Jane v. Hunt et al.* PAR 21683629. Granted.

23. Randall M. Miller, "'Home as Found': Ex-Slaves in Liberia," *Liberian Studies Journal* 6, no. 2 (1975): 92–108; Randall M. Miller, ed., *"Dear Master": Letters of a Slave Family* (Ithaca, NY: Cornell University Press, 1978), 24–36; Tom W. Shick, *Behold the Promised Land: A*

History of Afro-American Settler Society in Nineteenth-Century Liberia (Baltimore: Johns Hopkins University Press, 1980); Penelope Campbell, *Maryland in Africa: The Maryland State Colonization Society, 1831–1857* (Urbana: University of Illinois Press, 1971); Claude A. Clegg III, *The Price of Liberty: African Americans and the Making of Liberia* (Chapel Hill: University of North Carolina Press, 2004), chap. 2; JCCASN, *Elder v. Elder*, Vir., 4 Leigh 252, February 1833, 1:171–172; *Isaac v. West*, Vir., 6 Randolph 652, December 1828, 1:157–158 [freed and then pay estate debts]. G DARev. Petition of Moses to the Orphans' Court of Anne Arundel County, Maryland, 18 September 1838, in Register of Wills, 1820–1851 (Petitions and Orders), *Moses v. John Collinson*, Microfilm CR 63,127, Frame/Pages 579–580, MSA; Related Documents: Order, 18 September 1838, with *Moses v. Collinson*. PAR 20983816. Granted. JCCASN, *Henry v. Hogan*, Tenn., 4 Humphreys 208, July 1843, 2:518–519.

24. JCCASN, *Vance v. Crawford*, 4 Ga. 445, May 1848, 3:19; *American Colonization Society v. Gartrell*, 23 Ga. 448, August 1857, 3:58; *Cooper v. Blakey*, 10 Ga. 263, July 1851, 3:28; JCCASN, *Cooper v. Blakey*, 10 Ga. 263, July 1851, 3:28; *Cleland v. Waters*, 16 Ga. 496, October 1845, 3:38; *Cleland v. Waters*, 19 Ga. 35, September 1855, 3:46; *Atwood's Heirs, v. Beck, Administrator*, 21 Ala. 590, December 1852, 3:183–185; *Leech v. Cooley*, Miss., 6 S. and M. 93, January 1846, 3:305; JCCASN, *Thompson v. Newlin*, N.C., 6 Ired. Eq. 380, December 1849, 2:141–142; *Thompson v. Newlin*, N.C., 6 Ired. Eq. 380, December 1849, 2:141–142; *Myers v. Williams*, N.C., 5 Jones Eq. 362, June 1860, 2:239–40 [created a perpetuity]; *Purvis et al. v. Sherrod, Executor*, 12 Tex. 140, 1854, 5:287–88.

25. JCCASN, *Patty and others (paupers) v. Colin*, Vir., 1 Hen and M. 519, November 1807, 1:115; *Reports of Cases Argued and Determined in the Supreme Court of Virginia: With Select Cases, Relating Chiefly to Points of Practice, Decided by the Superior Court of Chancery for the Richmond District* (Flatbush, NY: I. Riley, 1809), 519–530. G DARR. JCCASN, *Nicholas v. Burruss*, Vir., 4 Leigh 289, February 1833, 1:172–173; *Reports of Cases Argued and Determined in the Court of Appeals and in the General Court of Virginia*, vol. 4, comp. Benjamin Watkins Leigh (Richmond, VA: Samuel Shepherd, 1834), 89–303 [vouching for title]. GAA. Petition of Sally, Hester, Sarah, Kitty, John, Ben, Jeremiah, Joe, Sampson, James, Vachel, Anthony, Charles Lamar, Grace, Patty, Patty, Bill, Joe, John, Henny, Ann, Jenny, Betty, Jenny, and Emily to the Orphans' Court of Anne Arundel County, Maryland, November 1831, in Register of Wills, 1820–1851 (Petitions and Orders), Microfilm CR 63,127, MSA; Related Documents: PAR 20983111; Order, ca. November 1831 [swore out arrest warrants], with Petition of Sally et al., PAR 20983112. Granted. Petition of Bill, Tom, Suckey, and Nelly to the Orphans' Court of Anne Arundel County, Maryland, April 1831, in Register of Wills, 1820–1851 (Petitions and Orders), *Bill, Tom, Suckey, and Nelly v. Joseph J. Hopkins*, Microfilm CR 63,127, MSA; Related Documents: PAR 20983114; Order, ca. April 1831, with *Bill et al. v. Hopkins*. PAR 20983113. Granted. Petition of Osborne, Oscar, Isaac, Basil, Henry, and Dinah to the Orphans' Court of Anne Arundel County, Maryland, April 1831, in Register of Wills, 1820–1851 (Petitions and Orders), *Osborne, Oscar, Isaac, et al. v. Joseph J. Hopkins*, Microfilm CR 63,127, MSA; Related Documents: PAR 20983113; Order, ca. April 1831, with *Osborne et al. v. Hopkins* [two estates]. PAR 20983114. Granted.

26. JCCASN, *Bostick v. Keizer*, Ky., 4 J. J. Marsh. 597, October 1830, 1:317.

27. JCCASN, *Bostick v. Keizer*, Ky., 4 J. J. Marsh. 597, October 1830, 1:317; Last Will and Testament, James Eppes, 11 August 1789, with *Bostick v. Keizer*; also see note 53, this chapter. Petition of Anna Barnet to the City Court of Baltimore City, Maryland, 12 October 1836, in SC, *Anna Barnet v. Thomas S. Wilson*, Microfilm M 11014, Volume 4239-3, Document/Case 97, MSA; Related Documents: Transcript of Court Record, 12–27 October 1836; Copy of Will, Elizabeth Richmond, 22 October 1831; Copy of Inventory, Estate of Elizabeth Richmond, 13 June 1832; Order for Sale, August Term 1836; Clerk's Certification, 14 November 1836; Court Record and Writ of *Procedendo*, 5 December 1836; Clerk's Notation, January 1837, with *Barnet v Wilson*. PAR 20983620; JCCASN, *Wilson v. Negro Ann Barnet*, Md., 8 Gill and John. 159, December 1836, 4:83–84; see: *Wilson v. Negro Ann Barnett*, Md., 9 Gill and John, 158, December 1837, 4:88. GAA.

28. T. Stephen Whitman, *The Price of Freedom: Slavery and Manumission in Baltimore and Early National Maryland* (Frankfort: University of Kentucky Press, 1987).

29. Sean Condon, "The Significance of Group Manumissions in Post-Revolutionary Rural Maryland," *Slavery & Abolition* 32 (2011): 84.

NOTES TO PAGES 81-84

30. Deed of Manumission, John Elliott, 28 October 1784, PAR 20978505. JCCASN, *Negroes Peter and Others v. Elliott*, Md., 2 Har. and McH. 199, November 1793, 4:51-52.
31. Found in JCCASN, *Fanny v. Bryant*, Ky., 4 J. J. Marsh 368, October 1830, 1:317. G DARev.
32. JCCASN, *Charles (a man of color) v. French*, Ky., 6 J. J. Marsh. 331, June 1831, 1:319-320 ["freely and immediately liberate"]. G DARev. For bills of sale and bonds as devices for emancipation, see JCCASN, *Sarah Thoroughgood, Negro v. Anderson*, Del., 5 Harrington 97, October 1848, 4:232-233. GAA.
33. Petition of Stephen Faris, Ebby Faris, and Asbury to the Chancery Court of Talbot County, Maryland, 7 July 1826, in SC, *Stephen Faris, Ebby Faris, and Asbury v. Solomon Lowe*, Microfilm M 11017, Volume 4239-5, Document/Case 7910, MSA; Related Documents: Decree, 7 July 1826; Copy of Deed of Manumission, Jacob Handy to Rachel, et al., 12 July 1797; Clerk's Certification, 9 September 1823, with *Faris et al. v. Lowe*. PAR 20982602. Injunction denied. JCCASN, *Fanny v. Bryant*, Ky., 4 J. J. Marsh 368, October 1830, 1:317 [bill of rights]. G DARev.
34. Petition of Thomas Johnson to the Circuit Court of the District of Columbia, 1 June 1814, *Thomas Johnson v. John P. Van Ness*, in RUSCC-CDRCF, Record Group 21, Docket 2, Box/Drawer 13, Document/Case 54, NA; Related Documents: Copy of Deed of Manumission, John P. Van Ness, 26 June 1807, with *Johnson v. Van Ness*. PAR 20481402. Granted. Orville W. Taylor, *Negro Slavery in Arkansas* (Durham, NC: Duke University Press, 1958; reprint, Arkansas University Press, 2000), 239; JCCASN, *Harriet and others v. Swan*, 18 Ark. 495, January 1857, 5:251-252. DAA.
35. Frederick Douglass, *My Bondage and My Freedom* (New York: Miller, Orton and Mulligan, 1855), 328-329, http://docsouth.unc.edu/neh/douglass55/douglass55.html; *Laws Made and Passed of the General Assembly of the State of Maryland, at a Session Begun and Held at Annapolis, on Monday the 26th Day of December, 1831, and Ended on Wednesday the 14th Day of March, 1832* (Annapolis, MD: J. Hughes: 1832) chap. 281, sections 1 and 4; Petition of Dennis to the Chancery Court of Jefferson County, Kentucky, 29 March 1842, in Records of the Circuit Court, Case Files, *Dennis v. Evans C. Beard*, Box/Drawer 2-62, Document/Case 3522, KDLA; Related Documents: Answer, Evans Beard, 20 May 1842; Replication, Dennis, 20 September 1842; Depositions, Spilman Hord and Christopher Graham, 28 June 1843; Correspondence, James Taylor to Dennis Isom, 7 April 1841; Decree, 18 July 1843, with *Dennis v. Beard* [virtual freedom]. PAR 20784206. Granted.
36. JCCASN, *Johnson v. Negro Lish*, Md., 4 Har. and John. 441, June 1819, 4:66-67. GAA. Petition of Rachel Furley to the Circuit Court of the District of Columbia, 16 February 1819, in RUSDC-SHCP, *Rachel Furley v. Nehemiah Baden and Benjamin Baden*, Record Group 21, Box/Drawer 14, Entry Folder 20, Document/Case 194, NA [freedom deferred]. PAR 20481901. Injunction granted.
37. Eva Sheppard Wolf, *Race and Liberty in the New Nation: Emancipation in Virginia from the American Revolution to Nat Turner's Rebellion* (Baton Rouge: Louisiana State University Press, 2006), 50-53, 63-65.
38. JCCASN, *Fidelio v. Dermott*, D.C., 8 Fed. Cas 1175 (1 Cranch C. C. 405), June 1807, 4:160; Letitia Woods Brown, *Free Negroes in the District of Columbia, 1790-1846* (New York: Oxford University Press, 1974), 91, 201. Granted.
39. JCCASN, *Mayho v. Sears*, N.C., 3 Iredell 224, December 1842, 2:99-100. DAA; *Young v. Small*, Ky., 4 B. Mon. 220, October 1843, 1:362-363. G DARev.
40. Petition of Charles Henry Wood and Betsy Wood to the Circuit Court of the District of Columbia, 7 May 1836, in RUSCC-CDRCF, *Charles Henry Wood and Betsy Wood v. John Gadsby*, Record Group 21, Rules 3, Box/Drawer 44, Entry Folder 20, Document/Case 489, NA; Related Documents: Answer, John Gadsby, 17 May 1836; Injunction, John Gadsby and Edward Dyer, 7 May 1836; Deed of Manumission, Ann Key, 13 May 1828, with *Wood et al. v Gadsby*. PAR 20483614. Injunction granted. Petition of Dennis, Mingo, Dick, Joice, Esther, Demos, Tilday, Jacob, and Jim to the Chancery Court of Southampton County, Virginia, March 1808, in Chancery Court Papers, *Dennis, Mingo, Dick, et al. v. James Sebrell, Jethro Joyner, William Joyner, and James Jones*, Box/Drawer 19, Entry Folder 1814-69, LV; Related Documents: Order, ca. March 1808; Answer, James Sebrell, 19 December 1808; Answers, William Joyner, James Jones, ca. December 1808; Depositions, Presley [Presly] Barrett,

Micajah Joyner, 16 October 1809; Copy of Petition to sue *in forma pauperis*, 18 June 1807, with *Dennis et al. v Jones*. PAR 21680803. Petition to sue granted; case dismissed in 1814.

41. JCCASN, *Milly (a woman of color) v. Smith*, 2 Mo. 36, May 1828, 5:130–31; JCCASN, *Milly v. Smith*, 2 Mo. 171, September 1829, 5:137; Petition of Milly, Harry, Dick, William, and David Shipman to the Circuit Court of St. Louis County, Missouri, 9 May 1827, in Records of the Circuit Court, *Milly et al. and David Shipman v. Stephen Smith*, CCBSL; Related Documents: Order, 9 May 1827; Deposition, Nathan Dillon, 9 May 1827; Request for Transcript, State Supreme Court, 18 August 1829; Clerk's Notation, ca. 27 August 1829; Transcript of Court Record, *Milly v. Stephen Smith*, Circuit Court, 9 May 1827–11 August 1829; Copy of Deed of Mortgage, David Shipman to Stephen Smith, Shelby County, Kentucky, 17 October 1826; Copy of Deed of Emancipation, David Shipman, Jefferson County, Indiana, 3 October 1826; Clerk's Certification, Circuit Court, St. Louis County, Missouri, 27 August 1829; Opinion of Court, *Milly v. Smith*, State Supreme Court, 13 May 1828, with *Milly, et al. v. Smith*. PAR 21182708 [petition granted; plea of trespass filed, denied, appealed, reversed, remanded, retried, denied, appealed, reversed]. G DARR. JCCASN, *Foster v. Fosters*, Va., 10 Grattan 485, November 1853, 1:227–229; *Reports of Cases Decided in the Supreme Court of Appeals of Virginia*, vol. 10: *From April 1, 1853, to April 1, 1854*, comp. Peachy R. Gratten (Richmond, VA: Richie & Dunnavant, 1855), 485–493 [*Foster's adm'r v. Fosters*]. GAA.

42. Elizabeth Warbasse, *The Changing Legal Rights of Married Women, 1800–1861* (New York: Garland, 1987), 5–6, 48; Sally G. McMillen, *Southern Women: Black and White in the Old South* (Arlington Heights, IL: Harlan Davidson, 1992), 43. For dower rights, see Morris, *Southern Slavery and the Law*, 93–96; for Louisiana, see *The Replication of the Project of the Civil Code of Louisiana 1825* (New Orleans: Thomas J. Moran's Sons, 1937), 298; *Civil Code of the State of Louisiana, Preceded by the Treaty of Cession with France* (n.p.: Published by a Citizen of Louisiana, 1825), 511–512; for Mississippi, see *Laws of the State of Mississippi: Passed at an Adjourned Session of the Legislature, Held in the City of Jackson, From January 7, to February 16, A. D. 1839* (Jackson, MI: B. D. Howard, State Printer, 1839), 72; Loren Schweninger, *Families in Crisis in the Old South: Divorce, Slavery, and the Law* (Chapel Hill: University of North Carolina Press, 2012), chap. 5.

43. Kirsten E. Wood, *Masterful Women: Slaveholding Widows from the American Revolution through the Civil War* (Chapel Hill: University of North Carolina Press, 2004), 150–157; Martha Cocke to Caroline Cocke, April 9 [1811?], Cocke Family Papers, quoted in Kirsten Wood, "'The Strongest Ties That Bind Poor Mortals Together'": Slaveholding Widows and Family in the Old Southeast," in *Negotiating Boundaries of Southern Womanhood: Dealing with the Powers That Be*, ed. Janet L. Coryell, Thomas H. Appleton Jr., Anastatia Sims, and Sandra Gioia Treadway (Columbia: University of Missouri Press, 2000), 135; JCCASN, *Drury v. Negro Grace*, Md., 2 Har. and John 356, December 1808, 4:61. D GARev.

44. Petition of William to the County Court of Somerset County, Maryland, 24 May 1819, in SC, *William v. William Kelly*, Microfilm M 11014, Volume 4239–1, Document/Case 20, MSA; Related Documents: Court Record, 24 May 1819; Commissioners' Report, 20 January 1817, with *William v. Kelly*. PAR 20981905. DAA. JCCASN, *Negro William v. Kelly*, Md., 5 Har.and John. 59, June 1820, 4:69, DAA; *Caleb v. Field*, Ky., 9 Dana 346, May 1840, 1:350 [renounce will]. G DARR.

45. Christopher Doyle, "Judge St. George Tucker and the Case of *Tom v. Roberts*: Blunting the Revolution's Radicalism from Virginia's District Courts," *Virginia Magazine of History and Biography* 106 (Autumn 1998): 440; T. Stephen Whitman, *Challenging Slavery in the Chesapeake: Black and White Resistance to Human Bondage, 1775–1865* (Baltimore: Maryland Historical Society, 2007), 64–65.

46. Petition of Jack to the Circuit Court of St. Louis County, Missouri, 9 June 1818, in Records of the Circuit Court, *Jack v. Barnabas Harris*, Document/Case 111, CCBSL; Related Documents: PARs 21181803, 21185408; Copy of Indenture, Eusebius Hubbard, et al., 11 October 1811; Deposition, Wallis Estell, 10 April 1819, with *Jack v. Harris*. PAR 21181802. Denied.

47. Petition of Peter, Will, Jack, Amos, Joe, Job, Sam, Cesar, Phillis, Violet, Sabina, Sal, Darky, Rose, Peg, Nan, Esther, Dinah, Andrew, Fann, Sue, and Daniel to the General Court of Queen

Anne's County, Maryland, 12 April 1785, in SC, *Peter, Will, Jack, et al. v. Susannah Elliott and Rachel Elliott*, Microfilm M 11015, Frame/Pages 23, Volume 4239-2, Document/Case 3, MSA; Related Documents: Court Records, September 1786, 12 April 1785, September 1785 and April 1786; Deed of Manumission, John Elliott, 28 October 1784; Depositions, Dr. Jacob Ringgold and Susannah Cockey, 17 April 1786; Testimony, Henry Carter Jr., September Term 1785; Testimony, Henry Carter, 17 April 1786; Testimony, William Errickson and Thomas Elliott, ca. 1786; Court Record, September 1786; Copy of Court Records and Petition; Court of Appeals Record and Costs, ca. 1793, with *Peter et al. v Elliott et al.* PAR 20978505. The 1752 law was repealed 1796. JCCASN, *Negroes Peter and others v. Elliott*, Md., 2 Har. And McH. 199, November 1793, 4:51–52. DAA.

48. Petition of Clara to the City Court of Baltimore, Maryland, June 1818, in SC, *Clara v. Timothy D. Meagher*, Microfilm M 11014, Frame/Pages 17, Volume 4239-3, Document/Case 47, MSA; Related Documents: Transcript of Court Record, June 1818–November 1818; Clerk's Certification, 5 December 1818; Copy of Deed of Manumission, Sussex County, Delaware, Prettyman Boyce to his Slaves, 12 October 1801; Affidavit and Certifications, 18 November 1801, 4 July 1816, 10 August 1816, 12 August 1816; Attorneys' Agreement, ca. 1818; Correction to Court Record, 22 May 1819, with *Clara v. Meagher* [one witness; two required]. PAR 20981816. DAA. JCCASN, *Negro James v. Gaither*, Md., 2 Har. and John. 176, December 1807, 4:60. In 1802, the county court issued a judgment for petitioner; in 1804 the General Court reversed the verdict, noting the petitioner was a slave because the deed was not "evidenced" by two witnesses according to the Maryland law of 1752. D GARev.

49. JCCASN, *Maria and another v. Edwards*, 1 Rob. La. 359, February 1842, 3:543. G DARev. For this and other appeals cases see the Historical Archives of the Supreme Court of Louisiana, http://libweb.uno.edu/jspui/handle/123456789/1; Petition of Alice, Peter, and Charles to the Common Pleas Court of Kent County, Delaware, 28 November 1782, in Records of the Court of Common Pleas, *Alice, Peter, and Charles v. John Thompson*, Microfilm Reel 1, Frame/Pages 8–9 [oral manumission], DSA. PAR 20378201. Denied, appealed.

50. Petition of Anna to the County Court of St. Mary's County, Maryland, 7 August 1815, in SC, *Anna v. Jonathan Woodburn*, Microfilm M 11014, Frame/Pages 30, Volume 4239-3, Document/Case 36, MSA; Related Documents: PAR 20981701; Transcript of Court Record, August–December 1815; Copy of Will, Leonard Burroughs, 12 September 1811, with *Anna v. Woodburn*. PAR 20981508. JCCASN, *Burroughs v. Negro Anna*, Md., 4 Har. and John. 262, June 1817, 4:65. D GARev.

51. Petition of Daniel Nelson to the County Court of Craven County, North Carolina, June 1811, in Records of the County Court, Slaves and Free Negroes 1775–1861, NCDAH; Related Documents: Certificate, John S. Nelson, 16 November 1808, with petition of Nelson. Daniel's owner was Benjamin Nelson. PAR 21281106. Granted.

52. JCCASN, *Hannah et al (paupers) v. Peake*, Ky., 2 A. K. Marsh. 133, December 1819, 1:293; *A. K. Marshall's Reports of the Court of Appeals of Kentucky, Commencing with the Fall Term, 1817, and Ending with the Fall Term, 1821*, 3 vols. (Cincinnati, OH: Henry W. Derby, 1848), 2:566–568. GAA.

53. Petition of Will, Burwell, Jane, and Lucy to the Court of Chancery, Sussex County, Virginia, *Will, Burwell, Jane, and Lucy v. Charles Harrison*, Court Record, November 1795–November 1797; Order, 27 May 1797; Last Will and Testament, James Eppes, 11 August 1789, Loose Court Papers, LV, *Will et al. v. Harrison*. PAR 21679503. Granted. The heirs failed to contest the suit. For a slave held for fourteen years after he should have been freed, see Petition of Tom to the Circuit Court of Jefferson County, Kentucky, 14 October 1805, in Records of the Circuit Court, Case Files, *Tom v. William Lynn*, Box/Drawer 1-2, Document/Case 280, KDLA; Related Documents: Injunction, 26 September 1805; Decree, ca. 1805, with *Tom v. Lynn*. PAR 20780501. Granted.

54. Petition of Eliza Chapman and Robert Chapman to the Circuit Court of the District of Columbia, 17 August 1833, in RUSCC-CDRCF, *Eliza Chapman and Robert Chapman v. Robert Fenwick*, Record Group 21, Rules 3, Box/Drawer 40, Entry Folder 20, Document/Case 250, NA; Related Documents: Subpoena, Robert Fenwick, 17 August 1833; Injunction, Robert Fenwick, 17 August 1833; Correspondence, Robert Dunlap to William Cranch, 17 August 1833, with *Chapman et al. v. Fenwick*. PAR 20483303. Granted. Brown, *The Free Negro*

in the District of Columbia, 94–95; JCCASN, *Fenwick v. Chapman*, 9 Peters 461, January 1835, 4:191–192; *Reports of Cases Civil and Criminal in the United States Circuit Court of the District of Columbia, 1801–1841*, 6 vols., comp. William Cranch (Boston: Little, Brown, 1852), 4:431–438. Granted. Their mother was Kitty Chapman.

55. Petition of Dennis to the Baltimore County Court, 3 September 1849, in SC, *Dennis v. Perry Spencer*, Microfilm M 11014, Volume 4239-3, Document/Case 241, MSA; Related Documents: Copy and Certification of Last Will and Testament, Samuel Brohawn, 19 October 1831; Subpoena and Sheriff's Return, 3 September 1849; Testimony, Thomas Hicks, 19 December 1845; Statements of Evidence, October 1849; Order and Notice of Appeal, 20 October 1849, with *Dennis v. Spencer*. PAR 20984919. JCCASN, *Spencer v. Negro Dennis*, Md., 8 Gill 314, December 1849, 4:109–110. GAA.

56. Petition of Nancy Green, Benjamin Green, and Mary Green to the County Court of Kent County, Maryland, 4 April 1806, in SC, *Nancy Green, Benjamin Green, and Mary Green v. Philip Crisfield*, Microfilm M 11014, Frame/Pages 3, Volume 4239-1, Document/Case 2, MSA; Related Documents: Court Record, 1806–1808; Deed of Manumission, Edward Green, 10 February 1801; Transcript of Court Record, 1806–1808; Order, 21 July 1812; Appeal's judgment affirmed, June Term, 1813, with *Green, et al. v. Crisfield*. PAR 20980602. GAA. Crisfield possessed six slaves. USMSPC, Kent County, Maryland, 1810, image 12, ancestry.com.

57. Arthur Howington, "'A Property of Special and Peculiar Value': The Tennessee Supreme Court and the Law of Manumission," *Tennessee Historical Quarterly* 44 (Fall 1985): 310.

58. Petition of Samuel Holbrook, Jane L. Holbrook, Matilda Hyland, and David, Dick, Peter, et al. to the Orphans' Court of Somerset County, Maryland, 21 August 1810, in SC, *Samuel Holbrook, Dick, Peter, et al. v. Nicholas Dashiell, Eleanor Collier, James Evans, et al.*, Microfilm M 11014, Volume 4239-1, MSA; Related Documents: Testimony for libellants, John H. Anderson, Tubman Lowes, Littleton D. Teackle, Littleton Aires, 28 November 1810; Josiah Polk, William Conway, Thomas Jones, 29 November 1810. Testimony for respondents, Jesse Dashiell, Doctor Matthias Jones [frames 985–986, 991–992], Thomas Jones, John Collman, 30 November 1810 [frames 987–991, 997–998]. Testimony for libellants, Levin D. Collier [frames 992–996], Thomas Jones, 1 December 1810; John Collman, 3 December 1810. Testimony for respondents, Benjamin Dashiell, 3 December 1810. Testimony for libellants, George D. Atkinson, 4 December 1810 [frames 998–1001]. Orphans' Court Transcript, 21 August 1810–June 1813 (missing pages 14 and 15); the contested wills of Alexander Stewart are included in Orphans' Court Transcript, including the first will as Exhibit 1 [frames 940–943], the second will as Exhibit 2 [frames 962–963], and the third will as Exhibit 3 [frames 987–988], with *Dick et al. v. Dashiell et al.* PAR 20981009. D GARev.

Chapter 5

1. Petition of Mary B. Duvall to the Orphans Court of Baltimore City, Maryland, 11 February 1855, in SC, *Mary B. Duvall v. Delia*, Microfilm M 11026, Frame/Pages 273, Volume 4239-14, MSA; Related Documents: PARs 21485629, 21485733, 21485746; Order, 11 February 1856, with *Duvall v. Delia*. PAR 20985577. Granted.

2. In 1850, Cheatham owned six slaves and real estate valued at $6,000. USMSPC, Davidson County, Tennessee, 1850, p. 120; USMSSC, Davidson County, Tennessee, 1850, p. 645.

3. USMSPC, Davidson County, Tennessee, 1850, p. 275; USMSSC, Davidson County, Tennessee, 1850, n.p.; USMSSC, Davidson County, Tennessee, 11th District, 1860, p. 2. Harrison owned three slaves in 1850 and five slaves in 1860. They worked on his farm.

4. For several years Porter and his partner William A. Bush "clandestinely ran" slaves from Kentucky to Tennessee and sold them without proper titles. Petition of James Jenkens to the Chancery Court of Davidson County, Tennessee, 15 June 1855, in Records of the Chancery Court, Case Files, *James Jenkens v. Reese W. Porter and William A. Bush*, Box/Drawer 13, Document/Case 1420, MNDCA; Related Documents: Order, 15 June 1855; Bill of Review, *Reese W. Porter and William A. Bush v. James Jenkins*; Decree, 13 May 1856, with *Porter v. Bush*. PAR 21485530.

5. Petition of Delia Larkins to the Chancery Court of Davidson County, Tennessee, 9 September 1856, in Records of the Chancery Court, Case Files, *Delia Larkins v. Mary B. Devough [Duvall], William Summerhill, Benjamin Campbell, and Landon Harrison,* Box/Drawer 15, Document/Case 1701, MNDCA; Related Documents: PARs 20985577, 21485530, 21485620, 21485630, 21485706, 21485733, 21485746, 21485828; Order, 9 September 1856; Printed Notice, Chancery Court Case of *Delia Larkins v. Mary Devough [Duvall], et al.,* 9 September 1856; Decree, 30 May 1857; Copy of Order, Orphans Court of Baltimore City, *Mary B. Duvall v. Negress Delia,* 11 February 1856; Certification of Copy, 16 July 1856, with *Delia v. Duvall et al.* PAR 21485629. Granted.

6. The will was dated 1821. Cases often ended up in different states many years after a will or deed was created. In this case Harriet went from Tennessee to Alabama. Petition of Harriett to the Circuit Court of Shelby County, Alabama, 24 January 1857, in Records of the Circuit Court, Estate Papers, *Harriett v. Alexander Nelson,* Box/Drawer 31, Document/Case 34, 34A, Shelby County Archives, Columbiana, Alabama; Affidavit, D. W. Prentice, 18 March 1857; Order, 20 March 1857; Agreement, 17 March 1858, with *Harriett v. Nelson.* PAR 20185722. No decree with petition. For another freedom suit filed in the state, which ended with a dismissal after six years, see James Benson Sellers, *Slavery in Alabama* (Tuscaloosa: University of Alabama Press, 1950), 157.

7. Petition of Malinda and Mary Ann [her daughter] to the Chancery Court of Davidson County, Tennessee, 9 July 1853, in Records of the Chancery Court, Case Files, *Malinda and Mary Ann v. Elizabeth Smith,* Box/Drawer 10, Document/Case 1048, MNDCA; Related Documents: Pledge for Security, William Phillips, 8 July 1853; Order, 9 July 1853; Writ of Attachment, 18 November 1853, with *Malinda et al. v. Smith.* PAR 21485324. No decree with petition.

8. In 1840–1842, descendants of the term slaves were still seeking free status. Petition of Robert Christian, Nancy Ann Brown Christian, Joice Brown Christian, and Isaac Brown Christian to the Circuit Superior Court of Campbell County, Virginia, 1840, in Records of the Circuit Superior Court of Chancery, *Robert Christian, Nancy Ann Brown Christian, et al. v. Henry A. Christian and Reuben D. Palmer,* Box/Drawer 1842, Circuit Court Building, Rustburg, Virginia; Related Documents: Preliminary Version of Petition, ca. 1838; Answer, Reuben D. Palmer, 2 November 1840, filed 4 January 1841; Answer, Henry A. Christian, 9 February 1842; Copy of Decree of High Court of Chancery, Richmond, Virginia, 2 March 1803, with *Christian et al. v. Christian et al.* PAR 21684024. Dismissed.

9. Petition of Lucy Brown to the District Court of Orleans Parish, Louisiana, 8 March 1851, in Supreme Court of Louisiana Collection, *Lucy Brown v. Persifor F. Smith and Howard Smith,* Book 2,761, University of New Orleans; Related Documents: Transcript of Court Records, 10 March 1851–7 June 1852, including Act of Sale, Sewell Turpin Taylor to Persifor F. Smith, 22 September 1843; Testimonies, M. C. Edwards et al., 11–12 May 1852; Copy of Laws of Maryland, 31 December 1796, certified 17 March 1852; Verdict and Judgment, 13 May 1852; and Court Record of Appeal, 7 June 1852; Supreme Court Opinion and Decree, 10 January 1853, with *Brown v. Smith et al.* PAR 20885150. JCCASN, *Lucy Brown (f.w.c.) v. Smith,* 8 La. An. 59, February 1853, 3:226–227. GAA. Judith Kelleher Schafer, *Slavery, the Civil Law, and the Supreme Court of Louisiana* (Baton Rouge: Louisiana State University Press, 1994), 29. The Louisiana Supreme Court awarded Brown five dollars a month wages from the date of filing her suit to the date of the judgment.

10. Four petitions by sixteen slaves, Jack, Frank, and others, were filed in the County Court of St. Mary's County, Maryland, against Hugh Hopewell and Elizabeth Hopewell, 4 November 1779, regarding the 1732 will of William Cole. Related Documents: Court Records, 1 May 1780, 22 May 1780; Last Will and Testament, William Cole, 7 February 1732; Copy of Deed of Gift, William Cole to Elizabeth Cole, 2 November 1732; Depositions, James Chizum, Martha Chizum, John Beale [Beal], Joseph Bennett, 29 September 1780; Appeal Bond, James Hopewell and Uriah Forrest, 17 May 1781; Certification of Copy, 2 May 1782, with petitions. PARs 20977901, 20977902, 20977903, 20977904. Maryland Court of Appeals, Judgments 8, *James Hopewell vs. Negroes Frank et al.,* 7 May 1782, lower court [General Court] judgment affirmed, May Term 1784; [Docket, p. 139], Case S381-128, MSA; JCCASN, *Negro Jack*

v. Hopewell, Md., 6 Har. and John. 20 n., May 1784, 4:50. The high court of appeals "allowed 10 pounds each for wages; Negro Frank 1f. Isaac & George 20 pounds each." G DARev.

11. Max Grivno, *Gleanings of Freedom: Free and Slave Labor along the Mason-Dixon Line, 1790–1860* (Urbana: University of Illinois Press, 2011), 13.

12. Petition of Anthony to the County Court of Frederick County, Maryland, 23 November 1791, in SC, *Anthony v. Michael Null*, Microfilm M 11024, Frame/Pages 3, Volume 4239-22, MSA; Related Documents: Deposition, Margaret Shaw, 22 March 1792; Notation, ca. 1792, with *Anthony v. Null*. PAR 20979109. No decree with petition.

13. Petition of Delia, Statia, Edmund, and Madison to the Circuit Court of the District of Columbia, 25 April 1814, in RUSCC-CDRCF, *Delia [Statia?], Edmund, and Madison v. Thomas Offutt and John Wiley*, Record Group 21, Box/Drawer 11, Document/Case 182, NA. PAR 20481401. Granted.

14. Petition of Helen to the Circuit Court of the District of Columbia, 24 September 1825, in RUSCC-CDRCF, *Helen v. Henry Drain*, Record Group 21, Rules 2, Box/Drawer 31, Entry Folder 20, Document/Case 130, NA; Related Documents: Decree, 24 September 1825; Opinion, Buckner Thurston, 25 October 1825; Bond, Fleet Smith, 12 November 1825, with *Helen v. Drain*. PAR 20482501. Injunction granted.

15. Petition of John to the County Court of Frederick County, Maryland, 10 November 1838, in SC, Microfilm M 11024, Frame/Pages 12, Volume 4239-22, MSA; Related Documents: Copy of Deed of Manumission, 3 May 1828; Writ of *Habeas Corpus*, John, 10 November 1838; Summons, Joseph Wagner, 10 November 1838; Answer, Joseph Wagner, 12 November 1838; Order, 12 November 1838, with petition. PAR 20983803. Granted. Petition of Perry to the Chancery Court of Jefferson County, Kentucky, 13 August 1836, in Records of the Circuit Court, Case Files, *Perry v. John B. Hundley, Basil N. Hobbs, and Thomas Batman*, Box/Drawer 2-9, Document/Case 488, KDLA; Related Documents: Order, 31 August 1836; Amended Bill, 2 September 1836; Copy of Deed of Emancipation, 7 May 1802; Court Record, 14 October 1822; Appellate Decree, 1 November 1838, with *Perry v. Hundley et al.* PAR 20783620. GAA. For Louisiana, see: JCCASN, *Fernandez v. Bein*, 1 La. An. 32, April 1846, 3:576.

16. Petition of Simeon Clark to the Circuit Court of Todd County, Kentucky, 16 October 1832, in Records of the Circuit Court, Equity Case Files, *Simeon Clark v. Henry Carpenter and Henry Keener*, Box/Drawer 12, KDLA; Related Documents: Order, 16 October 1832; Answer, Henry Carpenter, 20 October 1832; Depositions, Nathaniel Burrus and H. B. Grooms, 13 April 1833; Notice, Simeon Clark, 21 January 1833; Deposition, Joshua D. Austin, 20 March 1833; Sheriff's Report, 17 April 1833; Agreement, April 1833; Decree, 29 April 1835, with *Clark v Carpenter et al.* PAR 20783210. Injunction granted; freedom granted in 1835.

17. JCCASN, *Ponder v. Cole*, 26 Ga. 485, November 1858, 3:65–66. It appears that the plaintiff's suit was granted, appealed, and affirmed. The suit was described in the case of the purchaser of Price against the slave trader who sold him.

18. JCCASN, *Negro Cato v. Howard*, Md., 2 Har. and John. 323, June 1808, 4:60; *A Practical Treatise on the Law of Slavery, Being a Compilation of All the Decisions Made on that Subject, in the Several Courts of the United States, and State Courts*, comp. Jacob D. Wheeler (New York: Allan Pollack Jr., 1837), 332. G DARev.

19. JCCASN, *White v. Turner (a man of color)*, Ky., 1 B. Mon. 130, December 1840, 1:355; Arnold Taylor, *Suing for Freedom in Kentucky* (Bangor, ME: BookLocker.com, 2010), 151–161. GAA.

20. See, for example, Petition of Rebecca Rathal, Araminta Kimmey, and Sally Kimmey to the Common Pleas Court of Kent County, Delaware, 1824, in Records of the Court of Common Pleas, *Rebecca Rathal, Araminta Kimmey, and Sally Kimmey v. Philip Fiddeman*, Microfilm Reel 1, Frame/Pages 312–13, DSA; Related Documents: PARs 20382209, 20382304, 20382803; Affidavit, John Rathal [spelled several different ways], 18 December 1824; Depositions, John Rathal, Thomas Rathal, William Rathal, Sinai Wyatt, 22 May 1824; Deposition, Thomas Rathal, 15 December 1824; Deposition, Daniel Stapleford, 18 December 1824; Bill of Sale, Rebecca Rathal to John Rathal, 21 May 1820; Bill of Sale, Rebecca Rathal to Richard Tilghman, Queen Anne's County, Maryland, 23 December 1820, with *Rathal et al. v. Fiddleman*. PAR 20382409. KCCCP-CJD, May Term 1825, Record Group 3815, Microfilm Reel 7, pp. 45, 60, DSA. Granted.

21. Petition of Catherine Henderson and Benjamin Henderson to the Circuit Court of the District of Columbia, 9 December 1833, in RUSCC-CDRCF, *Catherine Henderson and Benjamin Henderson v. Harriet Lloyd and Mr. Freeman*, Record Group 21, Rule 3, Box/Drawer 41, Entry Folder 20, Document/Case 274, NA; Related Documents: Deposition, Hugh Smith, 9 December 1833, with *Henderson et al. v. Lloyd et al.* PAR 20483302. Granted.

22. Petition of Charity, Mary, and Kitty to the Equity Court of Montgomery County, Maryland, 10 October 1818, in SC, *Charity, Mary, and Kitty v. Adam Robb, Henry Lansdale, and Alexander Robb*, Microfilm M 11024, Frame/Pages 1, Volume 4239-25, MSA; Related Documents: Answer, Adam Robb, 19 May 1819; Affidavit, William Campbell, 10 October 1818; Attorneys' Agreement, July Term 1820, with *Charity et al. v. Robb et al.* PAR 20981813. Injunction granted. USMSPC, Montgomery County, Maryland, 3rd Election District, 1820, image 10 [William Campbell] ancestry.com; see also Petition of Grace Travers to the Court of Common Pleas, Kent County, Delaware, 12 May 1820, in Records of the Court of Common Pleas, *Grace Travers v. Joshua B. Shockley*, DSA; Related Documents: Depositions, John Cooper, Eugene Cooper Jr., William Hall, Asa Willoughby, ca. 1820, with *Travers v. Shockley*. PAR 20382004. Granted.

23. Petition of Easter, Susan, and Charlotte to the Orphans Court of Baltimore County, Maryland, 1 September 1827, in SC, *Easter, Susan, and Charlotte v. William Bosley and Amos Ogden Jr.*, Microfilm M 11025, Frame/Pages 129, Volume 4239-14, MSA; Related Documents: PARs 20982705, 20982708, 20982710, 20982711, with *Susan et al. v. Bosley et al.* PAR 20982713. No decree with petition.

24. JCCASN, *Stephen Smith, negro, by a next friend, v. Milman*, Del., 2 Harrington 497, Spring 1839, 4:226–227. GAA.

25. JCCASN, *Boyce v. Nancy*, Ky., 4 Dana 236, June 1836, 1:333. GAA.

26. *Reports of Cases Decided in the Supreme Court of Appeals of Virginia*, vol. 14: *From October 1, 1858, to July 1, 1860*, 2nd ed., comp. Peachy R. Gratten (Richmond, VA: Richie & Dunnavant, 1860), 314–328; JCCASN, *Fulton v. Gracey*, Va., 15 Grattan 314, September 1859, 1:250–251. GAA.

27. Judith Kelleher Schafer, *Becoming Free, Remaining Free: Manumission and Enslavement in New Orleans, 1846–1862* (Baton Rouge: Louisiana State University Press, 2003), 4–5; JCCASN, *Dolliole (f. m. c.) v. White*, 5 La. An. 98, January 1850, 3:602. DAA.

28. JCCASN, *Pleasants v. Pleasants*, Vir., 2 Call 319, May 1799, 1:105–106; William Fernandez Hardin, "Litigating the Lash: Quaker Emancipator Robert Pleasants, the Law of Slavery, and the Meaning of Manumission in Revolutionary and Early National Virginia" (PhD diss., Vanderbilt University, 2013), chap. 6; JCCASN, *Maria v. Surbaugh*, Va., 2 Randolph 228, February 1824, 1:74, 138–139; cited 180, 193, 194, 202, 204, 237, 246, 278; *Reports of Cases Argued and Determined in the Supreme Court of Virginia*, vol. 2, comp. Peyton Randolph (Richmond: Shepard and Pollard, 1824), *Maria v. Surbaugh*, 228–246. DAA.

29. *Crenshaw v. Matilda* (1827). The case was not reported but the judge's notes are examined in Theodore Brown Jr., "The Formative Period in the History of the Supreme Court of Tennessee, 1796–1835," in *A History of the Tennessee Supreme Court*, ed. James W. Ely Jr. (Knoxville: University of Tennessee Press, 2002), 30. GAA.

30. JCCASN, *Harris V. Clarissa, et al.*, Tenn., 16 Yerger 227, March 1834, 2:500. GAA. Arthur Howington, "'A property of special and peculiar value': The Tennessee Supreme Court and the Law of Manumission," *Tennessee Historical Quarterly* 44, no. 3 (Fall 1985): 305; *A Practical Treatise on the Law of Slavery Being a Compilation of All the Decisions Made on that Subject, in the Several Courts of the United States, and State Courts*, comp. Jacob D. Wheeler (New York: Allan Pollock Jr., 1837), 390–391; Thomas D. Morris, *Southern Slavery and the Law, 1619–1860* (Chapel Hill: University of North Carolina Press, 1996), 413–414.

31. JCCASN, *Will (a negro) v. Thompson*, Ken., Hardin 52 n., May 1805, 1:280; *Thompson v. Wilmot*, Ken., 1 Bibb 422, June 1809, 1:282–283. G DARev.

32. JCCASN, *Negro Cato v. Howard*, Md., 2 Har. and John. 323, June 1808, 4:60 [oral agreement]. G DARev.

33. Edward M. Post, "Kentucky Law Concerning Emancipation and Freedom of Slaves," *The Filson Club History Quarterly* 59 (July 1985): 259; JCCASN, *Fanny v. Bryant*, Ky., 4 J. J. Marsh. 368, October 1830, 1:317. G DARev.

34. JCCASN, *Sarah v. Taylor,* 21 Fed. Cas. 431 (2 Cranch C. C. 155), December 1819, 4:170. GAA.

35. JCCASN, "Virginia: Introduction," 1:73n160.

36. JCCASN, *Negro Benjamin Jones v. Wooten,* Del., 1 Harrington 77, April 1833, 4:219–220. DAA. *Negro Ann Elliott v. Twilley,* Del., 5 Harrington 192, June 1849, 4:234. G DARev.

37. JCCASN, *Fanny v. Kell,* D.C., 8 Fed. Cas. 995 (2 Cranch C. C. 412), May 1824, 4:175. DAA.

38. JCCASN, *Peter v. Cureton,* D.C., 19 Fed. Cas. 312 (2 Cranch C. C. 561), April 1825, 4:176. The case was dismissed because neither Peter nor his brother had reached age thirty-one. DAA

39. Petition of Delia, Charlotte, Maria, and Ambrose to the Circuit Court of the District of Columbia, 22 February 1821, in RUSCC-CDRCF, *Charlotte, Maria, Ambrose, and Delia v. Jonathan T. Burch,* Record Group 21, Rule 2, Entry Folder 20, Document/Case 284, NA; Related Documents: Deposition, Benjamin Ringgold, 22 February 1821 [*sic*]; Letter, Singleton Townshend, 4 March 1821; Bond, Singleton Townshend, 3 March 1821; Jail Receipt, George Miller, ca. 1821; Bill of Sale, Urban Hollyday, 14 February 1821; Bond Receipt, Singleton Townshend, 5 March 1821; Decree, 22 February 1821, with *Charlotte et al. v. Burch.* PAR 20482101. Granted.

40. JCCASN, *Samuel v. Childs,* 21 Fed. Cas 306 (4 Cranch C. C. 189), December 1831, 4:186–87; *Reports of Cases Civil and Criminal in the United States Circuit Court of the District of Columbia, 1801–1841,* 6 vols., comp. William Cranch (Boston: Little, Brown, 1852), 4:189–190. DAA.

41. *Wood v. Humphreys,* May 1855, in *Reports of Cases Decided in the Supreme Court of Appeals of Virginia,* vol. 12: *From January 1, to October 1, 1855,* comp. Peachy R. Gratten (Richmond, VA: Richie & Dunnavant, 1856), 333–362; Morris, *Southern Slavery and the Law,* 411; JCCASN, *Wood v. Humphreys,* Vir., 12 Grattan 333, May 1855, 1:236–237. The appeals judge noted that the testator's intention in his will to free the mother and all of her descendants took the document "out of the operation of the principle" set forth in *Maria v. Surbaugh,* which ruled children of term slave women were not entitled to their freedom if born during the mother's term of servitude unless specifically indicated in the will. G DARev.

42. JCCASN, *Kitty v. McPherson,* D.C., 14 Fed. Cas. 709 (4 Cranch C. C. 172), May 1831, 4:186. Injunction granted. The defendant posted the bond.

43. JCCASN, *Hundley v. Perry,* Ky., 7 Dana 359, November 1838, 1:342–343. GAA.

44. JCCASN, *Will (a negro) v. Thompson,* Ky., Hardin 52 n., May 1805, 1:280; *Thompson v. Wilmot,* Ky., I Bibb 422, June 1809, 1:282–283. GAA.

45. Petition of Wesley Brown to the Chancery Court of Jefferson County, Kentucky, 3 August 1841, in Records of the Circuit Court, Case Files, *Wesley Brown v. Thomas J. Godwin, Francis Brumaker, and T. L. Huff,* Box/Drawer 2-54, Document/Case 3150, KDLA; Related Documents: Amended Bills, 17 September 1841, 18 October 1842, 1 October 1844; Answer, Thomas Godman, 24 January 1842; Copy of Last Will and Testament, Stephen Donaldson, 26 October 1841; Decree, 14 October 1845, with *Brown v. Godwin et al.* PAR 20784113. Granted.

46. Petition of Comfort to the Court of Common Pleas, Kent County, Delaware, 9 December 1796, in Records of the Court of Common Pleas, *Comfort v. Thomas Smith,* DSA; Related Documents: PARs 20379609, 20379610; Court Record, ca. 1796; Deposition, John Walker, 7 December 1798; Depositions; Holliday Smith, Solomon Cahall, Olive Jump, 8 December 1798; Depositions, Manlove Adams, James Adams, Caroline County, Maryland, 5 December 1798; Deposition, George Turner, 8 December 1798, with *Comfort v Smith.* PAR 20379611. Granted. The defendant was a new owner of Comfort. It was against the law in Delaware to export slaves without a special license. In 1800, free black Comfort headed a household with three other blacks. USMSPC, Kent County, Delaware, Mispillion Hundred, Milford, 1800, p. 85.

47. *Laws Made and Passed by the General Assembly of the State of Maryland, at a Session Begun and Held in the City of Annapolis, on Monday the Second Day of December, Eighteen Hundred and Sixteen* (Annapolis, MD: Jonas Green, 1817), 116–121.

48. Petition of William and Leroy Cole to the Circuit Court of Harrison County, Kentucky, 14 October 1829, in Records of the Circuit Court, Case Files, *William and Leroy Cole v. James Miller,* Box/Drawer 198-200, Document/Case 5282, Harrison County Courthouse, Cynthiana, Kentucky; Related Documents: Order, 12 October 1829; Bond, Leroy Cole and

James P. Curry, 14 October 1829; Order, 14 October 1829; Memo, March 1830, with *Cole et al. v. Miller.* PAR 20782918. Granted.

49. JCCASN, *Williams v. Manuel,* 1 Rob. Va. 674, March 1843, 1:203; *Reports of Cases Decided in the Supreme Court of Appeals and in the General Court of Virginia,* vol. 1: *From April 1, 1842, to April 1, 1843,* 2nd ed., comp. Conway Robinson (Richmond, VA: J. E. Goode, 1842), 674–688. Injunction granted and dissolved. Manuel was ordered to serve as a term slave until the end of his term; it did not appear that the owner contemplated removing the plaintiff beyond the jurisdiction of the court before that time.

50. Petition of Ann Lee to the Circuit Court of Washington, DC 6 July 1826, in RUSCC-CDRCF, *Ann Lee v. Ann Hutchinson and Joseph Venable,* Record Group 21, Rules 2, Box/Drawer 31, Entry Folder 20, Document/Case 195, NA; Related Documents: Order, ca. 1826, with *Lee v. Hutchinson et al.* PAR 20482606. Granted.

51. Petition of Anne Green to the County Court of Anne Arundel County, Maryland, 11 August 1851, in SC, *Anne Green v. Landy Linstead,* Microfilm M 11015, Frame/Pages 14, Volume 4239-2, Document/Case 138, MSA; Related Documents: PARs 20984931, 20985327, 20985328, 20985329, 20985642; Court Transcript, June Term 1852, includes Copy of the Last Will and Testament, Ignatius Brite, 19 August 1823, with *Green v. Linstead.* PAR 20985111. JCCASN, *Linstead v. Green,* 2 Md. 82, June 1852, 4:117. D GARev.

52. JCCASN, *Carmelite (a slave) v. Lacaze,* 7 La. An. 629, November 1852, 3:625; Petition of Carmélite to the District Court of Orleans Parish, Louisiana, 30 July 1851, in Supreme Court of Louisiana Collection, *Carmélite v. Jean Lacaze,* Book 2, 506, UNO; Related Documents: Affidavit, Carmélite, 30 July 1851; Order, 19 August 1851; Bond, 25 November 1851; Testimonies, Mme. Somer, et al., 26 November 1851, 20 December 1851; Reasons for Judgment, 6 December 1851; Judgment, 6 December 1851; Order, 4 December 1851; Rule for a New Trial, 8 December 1851; Sheriff's Return, 11 December 1851; Court Record of Order on Rule, 13 December 1851; Judgment on Rule, 15 December 1851; Petition of Appeal, 23 December 1851; Order, 23 December 1851; Bond, 23 December 1851; Citation, 25 December 1851; Sheriff's Return, 24 December 1851; List of Court Records, n.d.; Supreme Court Record of Appeal, 28 January 1852; Supreme Court Opinion and Decree, 26 April 1852; Supreme Court Decree on Rehearing, 22 November 1852, with *Carmelite v. Lacaze.* PAR 20885148. DAA. Schafer, *Slavery, the Civil Law,* 238–239; Schafer, *Brothels, Depravity, and Abandoned Women: Illegal Sex in Antebellum New Orleans* (Baton Rouge: Louisiana State University Press, 2009), 43. Schafer considered the case "the most outrageous" denial of emancipation in the state's history. See also: Schafer "'Open and Notorious Concubinage': The Emancipation of Slave Mistresses by Will and the Supreme Court in Antebellum Louisiana," *Louisiana History* 28 (Spring 1987): 165–182.

53. JCCASN, *Vigel v. Naylor,* D.C., 24 Howard 208, December 1860, 4:208. G DARR.

54. James M. Wright, *The Free Negro in Maryland, 1634–1860* (New York: Columbia University Press, 1921; reprint, New York: Octagon Books, 1971), 58.

55. *The Revised Statutes of Missouri* (St. Louis: Chambers & Knapp, 1845), 283–284; Kelly Marie Kennington, "River of Injustice: St. Louis's Freedom Suits and the Changing Nature of Legal Slavery in Antebellum America" (PhD diss., Duke University, 2009), 28; Kelly Marie Kennington, "Law, Geography, and Mobility: Suing for Freedom in Antebellum St. Louis," *Journal of Southern History* 80, no. 3 (August 2014): 584; Lea VanderVelde, *Redemption Songs: Suing for Freedom before Dred Scott* (New York: Oxford University Press, 2014), 6. The 1845 law made reference to an 1835 statute prohibiting plaintiffs in freedom suits from recovering monetary damages if their suit succeeded.

56. *Jerry v. Charles Hatton,* July 1826 and November 1826, 39 and 42, Circuit Court Case Files, Office of the Circuit Clerk of St. Louis, Missouri State Archives-St. Louis, Office of the Secretary of State. Granted.

57. JCCASN, *Paup v. Mingo,* Vir., 4 Leigh 163, January 1833, 1:169–170; *Negro Andrew Franklin v. Waters,* Md., 8 Gill 322, December 1849, 4:110.

58. Petition of Philis to the Circuit Court of Jefferson County, Kentucky, 8 June 1833, in Records of the Circuit Court, Case Files, *Philis v. John Shadburn,* Box/Drawer 1-41, Document/Case 2929, KDLA; Related Documents: Decree, 4 December 1834; Copy of the Last Will and Testament, Charles Withers, 1 June 1830, with *Philis v. Shadburn.* PAR 20783308. Granted.

59. Petition of Lavina, Jackson, and James McCombs to the Chancery Court of Giles County, Tennessee, 6 August 1836, in Supreme Court Cases, Middle Tennessee, *Lavina, Jackson, and James McCombs v. John Goff, William Porter, and John Porter,* Box/Drawer 58, TSLA; Related Documents: Bond, 5 August 1836; Demurrer, John Goff, 21 February 1837; Orders, March Term 1837, September Term 1836 [1837]; Answers, William Porter, 10 March 1837; John Goff, April Term 1837; Record of Proceedings, February 1837 to September Terms 1837; Decree and Appeal, September Term 1837; Depositions, Thomas C. Porter, 6 May 1837; William R. Davis, Thomas C. Porter, Burnurd M. Burch, 7 August 1837; William Conner, John Kenan, 1 September 1837; Last Wills and Testaments, John Duffield, 6 March 1807; Elizabeth Duffield, 7 October 1826; Decree and Opinion, 3 March 1838, with *Lavina et al. v Goff et al.* PAR 21483614. JCCASN, *Lavina v. Duffield's Executors,* Tenn., Meigs 117n, March 1838, 2:506. G DARev.

60. JCCASN, *Matilda v. Crenshaw,* Tenn. 4 Yerger 209, March 1833, 2:496–497. Granted. Her freedom suit was filed in 1825; her award was granted in 1833.

61. Petition of John Johnson to the District Court of Orleans Parish, Louisiana, 10 April 1816, in Records of the First Judicial District Court, Case Records, *John Johnson v. Sosthene Allen,* Microfilm Reel 1A, Louisiana Collection, Document/Case 1,043, NOPL; Related Documents: Order, 10 April 1816; Opinion, 4 July 1817; Copy of Opinion, 4 August 1817, with *Johnson v Allen.* PAR 20881603. Granted.

62. Schafer, *Becoming Free,* 20–21.

63. Petition of Anthony to the Circuit Court of Cumberland County, Kentucky, 24 May 1848, in Records of the Circuit Court, Equity Judgments, *Anthony v. Josiah Brummall and Nicholas C. Robinson,* Microfilm Reel 218723, Document/Case 1707, KDLA; Related Documents: Order, 24 May 1848; Amended Bill, July Term 1848; Answer, Josiah Brummal, 16 May 1849; Depositions, Milton King, Elam F. Boles, and F. W. Alexander, 30 March 1850; Summons, Elam F. Boles, 30 March 1850; Deed of Emancipation, 23 March 1793; Orders, July Term 1848, October Term 1848, 14 April 1849, 12 October 1849, April Term 1850 and 12 July 1850; Decree, September 1850, with *Anthony v. Brummall et al.* PAR 20784805. Granted.

64. Taylor, *Suing for Freedom in Kentucky,* 60–62.

65. Wright, *The Free Negro in Maryland,* 59.

66. Petition of Peter Robinson, Sarah Robinson, Samuel Redden, Rachel Redden, Jack, Isaac, Lizey, Phillis Williams, Mahaley, Jesse, Maryatta, and Peter Robinson Sr. to the County Court of Sussex County, Delaware, 3 July 1820, in Records of the Chancery Court, Case Files, *Peter Robinson, Sarah Robinson, Samuel Redden, et al. v. Sally Kershaw,* Microfilm Reel 8, Record Group 4835, Entry Folder 292, Document/Case P22, DSA; Related Documents: Answer, Sarah Kershaw, 29 November 1820; Agreement, Peter Robinson, et al., and Thomas Cooper and John L. Wells, ca. 1820; Interrogatories, 28 June 1821; Exceptions, Peter Robinson, 19 June 1821; Depositions, Thomas O'Neal, Solomon Short, 10 July 1821; Correspondence, Samuel Redding to Solicitors of Complainants, ca. 1821; Account, Estate of Mitchell Kershaw, 6 March 1823, with *Robinson et al. v Kershaw.* PAR 20382003. Granted.

67. Petition of Eleanor Gray to the Circuit Court of the District of Columbia, 29 April 1828, in RUSCC-CDRCF, *Eleanor Gray v. David English and Charles Burnett,* Record Group 21, Rules 2, Box/Drawer 32, Entry Folder 20, Document/Case 295, NA; Related Documents: PAR 20482702; Answer, David English and Charles Burnett [Burnet], ca. 1828; Affidavit, Sarah [Sally] Wood, 5 March 1828; Decree, 7 June 1828, with *Gray v. English et al.* PAR 20482803. Granted. JCCASN, *Barnes v. Barnes,* 2 Fed. Cas. 855 (3 Cranch C. C. 269), December 1827, 4:182.

68. Petition of George to the Circuit Court of Jefferson County, Kentucky, 28 August 1848, in Records of the Circuit Court, Case Files, *George v. Thomas Powell, Robert Cooper, and Joseph Kean,* Box/Drawer 2-101, Document/Case 6053, KDLA; Related Documents: Order, 28 August 1848; Amended Bill, 31 August 1848; Answer, Robert Cooper and James McMillan, 15 September 1848; Answer, Joseph A. Keen, 8 September 1848; Receipt, 1848, with *George v. Powell et al.* PAR 20784807. Injunction granted.

69. Petition of Sarah Blackiston to the County Court, Kent County, Delaware, 1821, in Court Papers ca. 1776–1867, DSA; Related Documents: PAR 20382106; Certificate, Alexander

McClyment, 11 December 1821; Orders, 12 December 1821, 18 June 1822. Granted, rescinded, with petition of Blackiston. PAR 20382107. Petition of Abel Harris to the County Court, Kent County, Delaware, 26 November 1821, in Court Papers ca. 1776–1867, DSA; Related Documents: PAR 20382107; Statement, James Greenwood, Samuel Patterson, Solomon Conner, et al., ca. November 1821; Order, 7 December 1821, with petition of Harris. PAR 20382106. Granted. The case was found with the petition of Jacob's wife, a term slave, to go with her husband who was about to be sold out of the state. The court ruled that the law prohibiting exportation could not be implemented in her case because she was not the reason for the court action. Jacob was captured and his owner's petition to export him was granted.

70. Schafer, *Slavery and the Civil Law*, 259–260; JCCASN, *Louisa Marshall v. Mrs. Charles Watrigant et al.*, 13 La. An. 619, June 1858, 3:663. D GARev

71. Kenneth Stampp, *The Peculiar Institution: Slavery in the Ante-Bellum South* (New York: Knopf, 1956), 95–96.

72. Herman Cox, age thirty-four in 1860, owned real estate worth $10,800 and two slaves. USMSPC, Davidson County, Tennessee, 8th Ward, 1860, p. 479; USMSSC, Davidson County, Tennessee, 8th Ward, 1860, p. 258.

73. Petition of Delia Larkins to the Chancery Court of Davidson County, Tennessee, 29 November 1857, in Records of the Chancery Court, Case Files, *Delia Larkins ex parte*, MNDCA; Related Documents: PARs 20985577, 21485629, 21485733, 21485734, with Larkins petition. Granted to serve out her term. PAR 21485746.

74. Affidavit of R. J. Meigs to the Chancery Court of Davidson County, Tennessee, 27 November 1857, in Records of the Chancery Court, Case Files, *R. J. Meigs v. H. H. Haynes and Thomas Smith*, Box/Drawer 15, Document/Case 1701, MNDCA; Related Documents: PARs 20985577, 21485629, 21485719, 21485733, 21485746; Writ of Attachment Nisi for Contempt, Thomas Smith and H. H. Haynes, 27 November 1857; Sheriff's Returns, 28 and 30 November 1857; Answer, H. H. Haynes, 28 1857, with *Meigs v. Haynes et al.* The court issued an arrest warrant. The defendant could not be found. PAR 21485734. In 1860, Rettson J. Meigs owned realty valued at $30,000 and five slaves between twelve and eighteen years old. USMSPC, Davidson County, Tennessee, 5th Ward, 1860, p. 416; USMSSC, Davidson County, Tennessee, 5th Ward, 1860, p. 253.

75. In 1860, North Carolina-born Thomas Smith, age fifty-eight, owned $144,000 in realty and $110,000 personal property, including five slaves in the city. USMSPC, Davidson County, Tennessee, 1840, p. 361; USMSPC, Davidson County, 1850, p. 92; USMSPC, Davidson County, 3rd Ward, 1860, p. 92; USMSSC, Davidson County, 23rd Dist., 1850, p. 617; USMSSC, Davidson County, Wards 1–4, 1860, p. 16; H. H. Haynes, a clerk, lived at 33 Cedar Street; Tom Smith lived at 34 Cherry Street. *Nashville Business Directory, 1855-6*, comp. John P. Campbell (Nashville: Printed for the Author, 1855), 55, 107.

76. USMSPC, Baltimore City, Maryland, 11th Ward, 1860, p. 174. They were all born in Maryland.

Chapter 6

1. Petition of Nicholas Tachaud to the District Court of Orleans Parish, Louisiana, 24 May 1822, in Records of the First Judicial District Court, Case Records, *Nicholas Tachaud v. Richard Richardson*, Microfilm Reel 10, Louisiana Collection, Document/Case 4,696, NOPL; Related Documents: Order, 24 May 1822; Jury Verdict, 24 April 1823; Judgment, 24 April 1823; Testimony in open court: free women of color Hermine Boiredan, M. Savary, Justine Layeux, C Mandeville; free man of color, Joseph Savoy, and a white woman, C. Mandeville, 24 April 1823, with *Tachaud v. Richardson*. PAR 20882219. Granted. In 1830, lawyer Henry R. Denis headed a household in New Orleans with six other whites, five slaves, and a free woman of color over age fifty-five. USMSPC, Orleans Parish, Lousiana, 1830, image 47, ancestry.com.

2. JCCASN, *Gary v. Stevenson*, 19 Ark. 580, January 1848, 5:255; Jason A. Gillmer, "Suing for Freedom: Interracial Sex, Slave Law, and Racial Identity in the Post-Revolutionary

and Antebellum South," *North Carolina Law Review* 82, part 2 (January 2004): 537–538, 596. DAA.

3. Petition of Caroline or Catharine and William Gilless to the Chancery Court of Jefferson County, Kentucky, 21 October 1845, in Records of the Circuit Court, Case Files, *Caroline and William Gilless v. William Kelly, John Price, Stephen Chenoworth* [original case], Box/Drawer 2-85, Document/Case 4883, KDLA; Related Documents: PAR 2074716; Amended Bill, 31 October 1845; Answer, J. W. Browner, 1 March 1846; Answer, William Kelly, 27 October 1845; Deposition, Isaac Everett, 9 December 1847, with *Gilless v. Kelly et al.* PAR 20784508. Petition of Caroline and William Gilless to the Chancery Court of Jefferson County, Kentucky, 24 December 1847, in Records of the Circuit Court, Case Files, *Caroline and William Gillis v. William H. Kelly, Levi Tyler, J. W. Brawner, and James Quarles* [second suit], Box/Drawer 2-97, Document/Case 5775, KDLA; Related Documents: PARs 20781802, 20782610, 20785107; Answer, W. H. Kelly, 29 December 1847; Bill of Revivor, 30 June 1848; Affidavit, William B. Henderson, 30 June 1848; Copy of Interrogatories, ca. 1848; Depositions, Ann Finley, William S. Cook, 24 August 1848; Order, 21 July 1848; Decree, 11 October 1850, with *Gilles et al. v. Tyler et al.* PAR 20784716. Granted.

4. Peter Wallenstein, *Tell the Court I Love My Wife: Race, Marriage, and Law—An American History* (New York: Palgrave Macmillan, 2002), 24; JCCASN, *Shorter v. Rozier*, Md., 3 Har. and McH. 238, October 1794, 4:52. GAA.

5. JCCASN, *Hook v. Nanny Pagee and her children*, Vir., 2 Munford 379, June 1811, 1:121; *Reports of Cases Argued and Determined in the Supreme Court of Appeals of Virginia*, vol. 2 (New York: I. Riley, 1814); *Hook against Nanny Pagee and her children*, June 1811, 379–87. GAA. In this case, the court ruled that it was incumbent on the defendant to prove "that the plaintiff was descended in the maternal line from a slave."

6. JCCASN, *Henry V. Bollar*, Vir., 7 Leigh 19, January 1836, 1:179. GAA.

7. JCCASN, *Gentry v. McMinnis*, Ky., 3 Dana 382, October 1835, 1:330. GAA.

8. Petition of Martha Drusilla to the Circuit Court of St. Louis County, Missouri, 27 October 1844, in Records of the Circuit Court, *Martha Drusilla v. Richmond J. Curle*, CCBSL, J. Curle, 28 October 1844; Order, 28 October 1844; Plea of Trespass, Martha Drusilla, November Term 1844; Copy of Order, ca. 27 October 1844; Sheriff's Report, 28 October 1844; Copy of Writ of *Habeas Corpus*, Martha Drusilla, 28 October 1844; Sheriff's Return, 4 November 1844; Notice, Martha Drusilla, 28 October 1844; Sheriff's Return, 4 November 1844; Plea, Richmond J. Curle, 19 November 1844; Motion, Richmond J. Curle, 7 March 1845; Summons to Testify, John Watson, 5 May 1845; Notice, Richmond J. Curle, April Term 1845; Deposition, James A. Little, 5 May 1845; Affidavit, John Watson, 7 May 1845; Bill of Exceptions, Richmond J. Curle, 8 May 1845; Motion, Richmond J. Curle, 7 June 1845; Summons, James Little, Francis Murdock, 7 February 1846; Summons, Lewis Newell, et al., 7 February 1846; Summons, Richmond Curl, 7 February 1846; Affidavit, Richmond J. Curle, 10 February 1846; Instructions to Jury Refused, ca. 13 February 1846; Instructions to Jury, 13 February 1846, with *Drusilla v. Curle*. PAR 21184427. Granted.

9. *Report of Cases Civil and Criminal Argued and Adjudged in the Circuit Court of the District of Columbia for the County of Washington, From March Term, 1840, to March Term 1850, A Continuation of Cranch's Circuit Court Reports of the District of Columbia*, ed. John A. Hayward and George C. Hazelton (Chicago: T. H. Flood, 1907), 369. The statement was made in the case *Drayton v. United States*, February 1849.

10. JCCASN, *Gobu v. E. Gobu*, Taylor N.C. 164 [100], April 1802, 2:18–19. GAA. John Hope Franklin, *The Free Negro in North Carolina, 1790–1860* (Chapel Hill: University of North Carolina Press 1943), 53; see also *Alfred Nichols v. William F. Bell*, December Term 1853, in *North Carolina Reports*, vol. 46: *Cases Argued and Determined in the Supreme Court of North Carolina, from December Term, 1853, to August Term, 1854, Both Inclusive* (Raleigh: E. M. Uzzell, 1906), 43–45.

11. Stanley Harrold, *Border War: Fighting over Slavery before the Civil War* (Chapel Hill: University of North Carolina Press, 2010), 1–16.

12. *Adèle v. Beauregard*, Orleans Parish, 1810, in Judith Kelleher Schafer, *Slavery, the Civil Law, and the Supreme Court of Louisiana* (Baton Rouge: Louisiana State University Press, 1994), 20, 144, 158, 264 n19, 267. GAA. JCCASN, *Sally Miller [Müller] v. Belmonti*, La., 11 Rob. La. 302,

July 1845, 3:392–393, 570–571. G DARev. Walter Johnson, "The Slave Trader, the White Slave, and the Politics of Racial Determination in the 1850s," *The Journal of American History*, 87, part 1 (June 2000): 13–38; Carol Wilson, *The Two Lives of Sally Miller: A Case of Mistaken Racial Identity in Antebellum New Orleans* (New Brunswick, NJ: Rutgers University Press, 2007); JCCASN, *Morrison v. White*, 16 La. An. 100, February 1861, 3:687. D GARev. For other states, see: JCCASN, *Davis, Guardian of Erasmus, claiming his freedom v. Hale*, Ga., Dec. (Part II) 82, January 1843, 3:16. GAA. Martha Hodes, *White Women, Black Men: Illicit Sex in the Nineteenth-Century South* (New Haven, CT: Yale University Press, 1997), 117; JCCASN, *Clark v. Gautier, in behalf of Dick (a person of color)*, 8 Fla. 360, 1859, 3:120. D GARev.

13. Petition of John to the Circuit Court of Ray County, Missouri, 11 November 1841, in Records of the Supreme Court, Case Files, *John v. James Offutt*, Box/Drawer 32, Document/ Case 1343, MoSA; Related Documents: Transcript of Court Record [pages missing], *John v. James Offutt*, 11 November 1841–ca. May 1843; Depositions, Eli Offutt, William M. Offutt, 12 October 1829; Opinion, Missouri Supreme Court, ca. July 1843, with *John v. Offutt*. PAR 21184121. JCCASN, *Offutt v. John (a mulatto)*, Mo., 8 Mo. 120, July 1843, 5:161. D GARR. For other failed suits, see: Petition of James Martin to the Circuit Court of Jefferson County, Kentucky, 30 May 1828, in Records of the Circuit Court, Case Files, *James Martin v. Betsy Wells*, Box/Drawer 1-21, Document/Case 1538, KDLA. PAR 20782806. Discontinued. JCCASN, *Chancellor v. Milly*, Ky., 9 Dana 23, October 1839, 1:347. D GARR. *Heirn, Executor v. Bridault and Wife*, 37 Miss. 209, April 1859, 3:359–360. D GARev; *Gary v. Stevenson*, 19 Ark. 580, January 1848, 5:255–256. DAA; Gillmer, "Suing for Freedom," 537–538.

14. JCCASN, *Daniel v. Guy*, 19 Ark. 121, July 1857, 5:252–253, 226–227, 261–262; Gillmer, "Suing for Freedom," 618–619. The plea was granted, reversed, remanded; granted again after jury examined plaintiff's foot and determined it was not a *"negro foot."* GAA.

15. JCCASN, *Gary v. Stevenson*, 19 Ark. 580, January 1848, 5:255–256. DAA. Gilmer, "Suing for Freedom," 537–538.

16. For views of how illicit sexual relations between whites and blacks were not only deemed the height of infamy but also as undermining the fabric of southern civilization, see Diane Miller Sommerville, *Rape & Race in the Nineteenth Century South* (Chapel Hill: University of North Carolina Press, 2004); Joshua D. Rothman, *Notorious in the Neighborhood: Sex and Families across the Color Line in Virginia, 1787–1861* (Chapel Hill: University of North Carolina Press, 2003); John Rankin, *Letters on American Slavery, Addressed to Mr. Thomas Rankin, Merchant at Middlebrook, Augusta Co., Va.,* 5th ed. (Boston: Garrison and Knapp, 1839), 63; Loren Schweninger, *Families in Crisis in the Old South: Divorce, Slavery, and the Law* (Chapel Hill: University of North Carolina Press, 2012), chap. 6.

17. Petition of Stephen Kindrall to the Circuit Court of Bibb County, Alabama, 13 April 1831, in Records of the Circuit Court, Record Book 1826–1836, *Stephen Kindrall v. Anthony Stoutenborough*, Frame/Pages 169–172, Bibb County Courthouse, Centreville, Alabama; Related Documents: Bond Order, Stephen Kindrall, 13 April 1831; Answer, Anthony Stoutenborough, n.d.; Order, 14 April 1831; Order, 13 May 1831; Bond, Anthony Stoutenborough, et al., 22 April 1831; Jury Verdict, October 1831, with *Kindrall v. Stoutenborough*. PAR 20183101. Dismissed.

18. See JCCASN, *Samuel Scott v. Williams*, N.C. 1 Devereux 276, June 1828, 2:54. GAA. *Nichols v. Bell*, 1 Jones N.C. 32, December 1853, 2:176, an action involving a contract between a "brown" person and white man.

19. Petition of Henrietta Bell to the Circuit Court of Jefferson County, Kentucky, 19 December 1827, in Records of the Circuit Court, Case Files, *Henrietta Bell v. James Cummins*, Box/Drawer 1-12, Document/Case 900, KDLA; Related Documents: Order, ca. 1827; Final Decree, 14 November 1829, with *Bell v. Cummins*. Subpoena issued. PAR 20782721. Dismissed by complainant; settled in 1829.

20. Petition of Gus and Anderson Brown to the Circuit Court of Woodford County, Kentucky, 28 June 1852, in Records of the Circuit Court, Case Files, *Gus and Anderson Brown v. Thomas P. Porter, Henry Moss, and William Brown*, Box/Drawer 130, KDLA; Related Documents: Order, 28 June 1852; Answer, Thomas Porter and Henry Moss, 5 July 1852; Answer, William Brown, 27 July 1852; Deposition, George D. Brown, 13 September 1854; Notice, 23 August 1852; Acknowledgment, M. Polk, 3 September 1852; Acknowledgment,

Thomas Porter, ca. 1852; Depositions, Richard Thomasson, Zachariah Herndon, and John R. Ferguson, 3 September 1852; Account of Hire, 1849–1854; Decree, 4 October 1854, with *Gus et al. v. Porter et al.* PAR 20785204. Granted.

21. *Davis (a man of color) v. Curry,* Ky., 2 Bib 238, Fall 1810, in *A Practical Treatise on the Law of Slavery: Being a Compilation of All the Decisions Made on That Subject, in the Several Courts of the United States, and State Courts,* comp. Jacob D. Wheeler (New Orleans: Benjamin Levy, 1837), 5–6. DAA.

22. JCCASN, *Robert Thomas v. the Reverend Henry Pile,* Md., 3 Har. and McH. 241, October 1794, 4:52; Sweet, *Legal History of the Color Line,* 176–177; *Maryland Reports, Being a Series of the Most Important Law Cases Argued and Determined in the General Court and Court of Appeals of the State of Maryland, from October, 1790, to May 1797,* 3 vols., comp. Thomas Harris and John McHenry (New York: I. Riley, 1813), 3:241. GAA.

23. Petition of Richard Booth, Ann Arundel County, Maryland, to the General Court, 12 May 1789, in SC, *Richard Booth v. David Weems,* Microfilm M 11015, Frame/Pages 4, Volume 4239-2, MSA; Related Documents: PARs 20979902, 20981109, 20981825; Court Record, 9 October 1789; Order, 29 July 1789; Deposition, John Batson, 26 September 1789; Court Records, 1789–1792; Depositions, Eleanor King, Joseph Mumford, and Edward Booth [alias Brown], 3 June 1791, Alice Taylor, 14 October 1791, John Wood, 3 May 1792, Mary McKinsey, 20 May 1792, Henry Wilson, 27 May 1790, John Welch, 25 May 1792; Interrogatories, ca. 1792; Depositions, John Carr, John King, James Gibson Sr., William Armogater, Mary Brown, Philemon Lloyd Chew, Thomas Lane, Joseph Crandele, 3 May 1792, William Wood, ca. May 1792, Nehemiah Birckhead, Morgan Wood, Robert Ward, 18 May 1792, Elizabeth Batson, 24 May 1792; Copy of Last Will and Testament, Richard Harrison, 10 July 1713; Inventory, Estate of Richard Harrison, 9 April 1717; Depositions, Mary McKenzie, 31 May 1792, Richard Harrison, 2 June 1792; Court Record, Order, and Appeal, 9 October 1792; Request for Records, 12 November 1793; Certification of Copy, 10 May 1794; Plaintiff's Costs, ca. June 1794; Copy of Petition, Depositions, Orders, Court Records, with *Booth v. Weems.* PAR 20978908. Court of Appeals (Judgments) No. 4 *Richard Booth vs. David Weems;* transcript on diminution June 1794; transcript 14 November 1792; "That your Petitioner is descended from a free Woman and is unjustly deprived of his Liberty by David Weems of said [Anne Arundel] County who holds and claims your Petitioner as a slave—"; judgment reversed; freedom granted, June Term 1794, signed 30 September 1796 [Docket 307], S381-13, Microfilm: M 11015, Accession No.: SC 4239-2-4 Location: 01/ 62/06/14, MSA. G DARev.

24. *Justina v. Mary Hutchinson,* 1782, Records of the Court of Common Pleas of Kent County, Delaware, Microfilm Reel 1, Frame/Pages 25–46, DSA; Related Documents: Deposition, James Morris, 17 December 1782; Depositions, Rebecca Steel, Philadelphia, Pennsylvania, 7 February 1782, 22 April 1782; Depositions, Miers Fisher, N. Hammond, Philadelphia, Pennsylvania, 4November 1782; Depositions, John Clayton, Silas Snow, Gunning Bedford Jr., John Vining, Richard Bassett (twice), Edward Tilghman Jr.,16 May 1783 [twice]; Deposition, John Clayton, 1783; Deposition, John Freedman, ca. 1782, with *Justina v. Hutchinson.* PAR 20378202. No petition or decree with the court record.

25. JCCASN, *Davis v. Forrest,* D.C., 7 Fed. Cas. 129 (2 Cranch C. C. 23), June 1811, 4:164. GAA [Susan and Airy Davis, Rosamund Bentley]; *Wood v. John Davis,* D. C. 7 Cranch 271, March 1812, 4:164–65. D GARev. *Mima Queen and Child v. Hepburn,* 7 Cranch 290, February 1813, 4:165–66. DAA. The Queens claimed descent from "a yellow woman, a native of South America." Letitia Woods Brown, *The Free Negro in the District of Columbia, 1790–1846* (New York: Oxford University Press, 1972), 30–31, 68–69, 70–74, 193–197, Appendix 1; Petition of Ruth Tillet to the County Court of Pasquotank County, North Carolina, March 1783, in Records of the County Court, Slaves and Free Persons of Color 1733–1866, NCDAH; Related Documents: Ruling, March 1783, with Tillet plea. PAR 21278301. Granted.

26. JCCASN, *Gregory v. Baugh,* Va., 2 Leigh 665, March 1831, 1:163–166; *Gregory v. Baugh,* February 1827, in *Reports of Cases Decided in the Supreme Court of Appeals in Virginia,* vol. 4, comp. Peyton Randolph (Richmond, VA: Peter Cottom, 1827), 611–659. D GARev.

27. Edmund S. Morgan, *American Slavery American Freedom: The Ordeal of Colonial Virginia* (New York: W. W. Norton, 1975), 330.

28 "Indian Slaves in Maryland and Virginia," Native Heritage Project, 27 June 2012, http://nativeheritageproject.com/2012/06/27/indian-slaves-in-maryland-and-virginia/; JCCASN, "Virginia: Introduction," 1:61, 66 [Virginia], 63–64 [Maryland]; C. S. Everett, "'They shalbe slaves for their lives: Indian Slavery in Colonial Virginia," in *Indian Slavery in Colonial America*, ed. Allan Gallay (Lincoln: University of Nebraska Press, 2009), 70–71.

29. JCCASN, *Tayon v. Celeste and others*, 1 Mo., 608, June 1806, 5:103–108, 123–124; the early testimony can be found in *Marguerite v. Pierre Chouteau*, 2 Mo. 71, May 1828, 5:132–135; *Marguerite v. Chouteau*, 3 Mo. 540, October 1834, 5:109–111, 143–145. Granted, denied, appealed, change of venue.

30. *Virginia Reports, Jefferson—Grattan 1730–1880, Annotated and under the Supervision of Thomas Johnson Michie* (Charlottesville, VA: Michie Co., 1903), 647; JCCASN, *Pallas, Bridget, James, Tabb, Hannah, Sam, and others (Indians and paupers) v. Hill and others*, Va., 2 Hen. 149, March 1808, 1:116–117. G DARR. Edward Dumbuald, "A Manuscript from Monticello: Jefferson's Law Library and Legal History," *American Bar Association Journal*, 38 (May 1952): 389–391. The 1691 law was brought to the fore in 1808 when "three copies of the same act agreeing in every essential point" were found.

31. JCCASN, *Hannah and other Indians v. Davis*, Va., 2 Tucker, App. 47, April 1787, 1:94–95. GAA; *Jenkins v. Tom*, 1 Wash. Va. 123, Fall 1792, 1:99–100. GAA. *Reports of Cases Argued and Determined in the Court of Appeals of Virginia*, vol. 1, comp. Bushrod Washington (Richmond, VA: Thomas Richardson, 1798), 123–124; JCCASN, *Coleman v. Dick and Pat*, 1 Wash. Va., 233, Fall 1793, 1:101–102. GAA. *Reports of Cases Argued and Determined in the Court of Appeals of Virginia*, , 233–239; Peter Wallenstein, "Indian Foremothers: Race, Sex, Slavery and Freedom in Early Virginia," in *The Devil's Lane: Sex and Race in the Early South*, ed. Catherine Clinton and Michele Gillespie (New York: Oxford University Press, 1997), 63–64; Peter Wallenstein, *Tell the Court I Love My Wife: Race, Marriage, and Law—An American History* (New York: Palgrave Macmillan, 2002), 30.

32. Robert M. Cover, *Justice Accused: Antislavery and the Judicial Process* (New Haven, CT: Yale University Press, 1975), 51; Eva Sheppard Wolf, *Race and Liberty in the New Nation: Emancipation in Virginia from the American Revolution to Nat Turner's Rebellion* (Baton Rouge: Louisiana State University Press, 2006), 147–149; JCCASN, *Hudgins v. Wrights*, Va., 1 Hen. and M. 134, November 1806, 1:112–113. GAA. JCCASN, "Virginia: Introduction," 1:64–66: Suzanna Sherry, "The Early Virginia Tradition of Extra-textual Interpretation," in *Toward a Usable Past: Liberty under State Constitutions*, ed. Paul Finkelman and Stephen E. Gottlieb (Athens: University of Georgia Press, 1991), 306–307; Gillmer, "Suing for Freedom," 601–602; Christopher Doyle, "Judge St. George Tucker and the Case of *Tom v. Roberts*: Blunting the Revolution's Radicalism from Virginia's District Courts," *Virginia Magazine of History and Biography* 106 (Autumn 1998): 432. The other plaintiffs included Jackey Wright, Maria Wright, John Wright, and Spsabar Wright. See also: Gregory Ablavsky, "'Making Indians White'; The Judicial Abolitions of Native Slavery in Revolutionary Virginia and Its Racial Legacy." *University of Pennsylvania Law Review* 159 (2011): 1457–1531.

33. Petition of Robert Moody to the County Court of Queen Anne's County, Maryland, May 1803, in SC, *Robert Moody v. Richard J. Jones*, Microfilm M 11014, Frame/Pages 5, Volume 4239-1, Document/Case 19, MSA; Related Documents: PARs 20979204, 20979704, 20980003; Transcript of Court Record, May 1803-ca. 13 May 1812; Clerk's Certification, 20 May 1812 [Moody filed transcripts of the three earlier cases as evidence in his own freedom suit], with *Moody v. Jones*. PAR 20980305. GAA. Petition of Margaret Creek to the Oyer and Terminer Court of Baltimore County, Maryland, November 1797, in SC, *Margaret Creek v. William Wilkins*, Microfilm M 11014, Frame/Pages 5, Volume 4239-1, Document/Case 19, MSA; Related Documents: PARs 20979204, 20980003, 20980305; Transcript of Court Record, November 1797–March 1800; Clerk's Certification, 29 October 1800, with *Creek v. Wilkins*. PAR 20979704. Granted.

34. JCCASN, *Ulzere v. Poeyfarré*, 8 Mart. La. 155, 1820, 3:464–65 and 2 Mart. N. S. 504, May 1824, 3:476. GAA. Schafer, *Slavery, the Civil Law*, 20; JCCASN, *Tayon v. Celeste and others*, 1 Mo., 608, June 1806, 5:103–108, 123–124. Granted. *Marguerite v. Pierre Chouteau*, 2 Mo. 71, May 1828, 5:109–111, 132–135, 152; *Marguerite v. Chouteau*, 3 Mo. 540, October 1834, 5:109–111, 143–145. Granted, denied, appealed, change of venue.

35. Petition of Phillis to the Common Pleas Court of Kent County, Delaware, 1795, in Records of the Court of Common Pleas, *Phillis v. Evan Lewis*, Microfilm Reel 1, Frame/Pages 202–208, DSA; Related Documents: Commission, 12 December 1795; Certificate, Martin Luther Haynie and Isaac Henry, Somerset County, Maryland, 4 April 1796; Deposition, Sarah Ward, Somerset County, Maryland, 4 April 1796, with *Phillis v. Lewis*. PAR 20379522. KCCCP-CJD, August 1793 through May 1794, p. 143, Reel 4, Frame 1463, continued; filed August 1793; *Phyllis v. Lewis*, December Term 1793, p. 83, Reel 4, Frame 263, freed December 3, 1796. Granted.

36. Petition of Robert Moody to the County Court of Queen Anne's County, Maryland, May 1803, in SC, *Robert Moody v. Richard J. Jones*, Microfilm M 11014, Frame/Pages 5, Volume 4239-1, Document/Case 19, MSA; Related Documents: PARs 20979204, 20979704, 20980003; Transcript of Court Record, May 1803–ca. 13 May 1812; Clerk's Certification, 20 May 1812 [Moody filed transcripts of three earlier cases, including the plea of as evidence in his own freedom suit]. PAR 20980305. Granted.

37. *Vaughn v. Phebe, a woman of color,* January 1827, in *A Practical Treatise on the Law of Slavery: Being a Compilation of All the Decisions Made on That Subject, in the Several Courts of the United States, and State Courts,* comp. Jacob D. Wheeler (New Orleans: Benjamin Levy, 1837), 395–404; JCCASN, *Vaughan v. Phebe (a woman of color),* Tenn., Mart. and Yerg. 5, January 1827, 2:479, 492–493. G GARR. Eight years later, a judge on the same court admitted that the case involving Phebe extended "the right to introduce hearsay evidence to the utmost limit, and further than other high courts have gone," but that Tennessee should not disturb that principle. JCCASN, *Miller v. Denman,* Tenn., 8 Yerger 233, July 1835, 2:502–503.

38. Petition of Charles Evans, Amey Evans, Sukey Evans, Sinar Evans, Solomon Evans, Frankey Evans, Sally Evans, Milly Evans, Adam Evans, and Hannah Evans to the Superior Court of Richmond County, Virginia, 7 May 1805, in Records of the Circuit Superior Court of Chancery, *Charles Evans, Amey Evans, Sukey Evans, et al. v. Lewis B. Allen,* Box/Drawer 4, Document/Case 236, LV; Related Documents: PAR 21680401; Answer, Lewis B. Allen, 20 January 1809; Copies of Depositions, Robert Wills, 25 June, 9 July 1791; John Meriwether, 13 November 1790; Copy of Jury Verdicts, April 1792, 4 April 1795; Genealogy of Family of Slaves Claiming their Freedom, ca. 1795, with *Evans et al. v. Allen.* PAR 21680501. Granted. Including the two earlier cases, a total of twenty-five Indian slaves were freed. See Loren Schweninger, ed., Marguerite Howell and Nicole Mazgaj, asst. eds., *The Southern Debate Over Slavery: Petitions for Southern County Courts, 1775-1867* (Urbana: University of Illinois Press, 2008), 78–80.

39. Edmund Randolph, Certificate to the Superior Court Judge, Richmond City, May 5, 1805. PAR 21680501. *Charles Evans and others v. Lewis B. Allen,* Lynchburg City Chancery Court, 1814, http://www.virginiamemory.com/online_classroom/shaping_the_constitution/doc/freedomsuit; Randolph represented the slaveholding interests in the important appellate case of *Pleasants v. Pleasants* decided in 1799, concerning the manumission of 431 slaves. The court ruled against the appellants (Randolph's clients) who sought to undermine the 1771 will of Quaker John Pleasants. James H. Kettner, "Persons or Property? The Pleasants Slaves in the Virginia Courts, 1792-1799," in *Launching the "Extended Republic:" The Federalist Era,* ed. Ronald Hoffman and Peter J. Albert (Charlottesville: University Press of Virginia, 1996), 148–149; JCCASN, *Pleasants v. Pleasants,* Vir., 2 Call 319, May 1799, 1:105–106.

40. Petition of Mima, Sylla, Maria, Joe, Cynthia, and Alfred to the District Court of Richmond City, Virginia, 26 September 1811, in Records of the Circuit Court, Equity Judgments, Barren County, Kentucky, *Persons of Color v. Boyles,* 25 March 1841, *Mima, Sylla, Maria, et al. v. Elizabeth Manson Hardaway,* Microfilm Reel 218692, KDAH; Related Documents: Court Transcript, 18 September 1810-1821, January 1815; Supplemental Bill, 2 June 1814; Decree, 21 January 1815; Certification of Transcript, 16 November 1841, with *Mima et al. v. Hardaway.* PAR 21681109. Granted. In 1811, Mima's children were cited as "Sylla, Maria, Joe, Cynthia and Alfred." In 1814, her children were listed as "Siller, Maria, Joe, Synthia, and Harriet."

41. *Marguerite, a free woman of color v. Chouteau, Pierre, Sr.,* 1825, Case 26, in Circuit Court Case Files, Office of the Circuit Clerk, St. Louis, Missouri State Archives, St. Louis Office of the Secretary of State; JCCASN, *Marguerite v. Pierre Chouteau,* 2 Mo 71, May 1828, 5:109–111; 132–135, 152. Granted, denied, appealed, CV. Foley, "Slave Freedom Suits before Dred Scott,"

4; Lea VanderVelde, *Redemption Songs: Suing for Freedom before Dred Scott* (New York: Oxford Press, 2014), chap. 3.

42. Petition of Nanny and Moses Lawson to the County Court of Henrico County, Virginia, 4 March 1807, in Ended Chancery Court Causes, *Nanny and Moses Lawson v. Betsey DuVal*, Box/Drawer 79-5, Entry Folder 1813, LV; Related Documents: Jury Verdict, 5 March 1813; Court Record, 4 March 1807–9 August 1811; Deposition, Sarah Anderson Thomson, 11 April 1810; Notes on Case, ca. 1810; Deposition, Vincent Oliver, ca. 1807; Notes on Case, ca. 1807; Depositions, Martha Cottrel, 22 December 1806; Elliot Lacy, 24 December 1806; Elisha Price, 11 February 1807; Drury Wood, 25 November 1809, with *Nanny et al. v. Duval*. PAR 21680713. Dismissed.

43. JCCASN, *Seville v. Chretien*, 5 Mart. La. 275, September 1817, 3:456–457. D GARev. Schafer, *Slavery, the Civil Law*, 222–223.

44. JCCASN, *Ulzere et al. v. Poeyfarre*, 8 Mart. La. 155, May 1820 3:464; *Ulzire [sic] et al. v. Poeyfarre*, 2 Mart. N. S. 504, May 1824, 5:476. There were two trials with juries, the first won by plaintiffs, appealed, reversed, and remanded; the second won by the slaves, appealed and affirmed. The defendant did not have legal title to the plaintiffs. GAA

45. Arnold Taylor, *Rose, a Woman of Colour: A Slave's Struggle for Freedom in the Courts of Kentucky* (Bloomington, IN: iUniverse Books, 2008); JCCASN, *Gatliff v. Rose*, Ky., 8 B. Mon. 629, September 1848, 1:388–389. G GARR.

46. See note 53, chap. 2, this volume.

47. Petition of Philis Thomas Sr., Ann Thomas, Charles Thomas, John Thomas, Sarah Thomas, William Thomas, George Thomas, Philis Thomas Jr., and Morris Thomas to the Circuit Court of Jefferson County, Kentucky, 11 September 1833, in Records of the Circuit Court, Case Files, *Philis Thomas Sr., Ann Thomas, Charles Thomas, et al. v. William Hunt*, Box/Drawer 1-44, Document/Case 3181, KDAH; Related Documents: PAR 20783316; Order, 11 September 1833; Answer, William Hunt, 26 September 1833; Court Opinion, 30 September 1833; Court Record, St. Mary's County, Maryland, August Term 1810 and March Term 1813; Certificate, 19 July 1822, with *Thomas v. Hunt*. Injunction granted; injunction dismissed. PAR 20783315.

48. JCCASN, *Jackson v. Bridges*, 1 Rob. La. 172, November 1841, 3:541–542. DAA.

49. Petition of Charles Beall, Frank Beall, and Bacchus Beall to the County Court of Prince George's County, Maryland, 4 March 1843, in SC, *Charles Beall, et al. v. Joseph J. Jones*, Microfilm M 11014, Volume 4239-3, MSA; Related Documents: Court Transcript, 3 April 1848 to 7 August 1848, includes Last Will and Testament, Nathaniel Chew, 30 May 1826, Deposition, Robert Clarke, 3 April 1847; Appellate Court Opinion, 3 December 1849, with *Beall et al. v. Jones*. PAR 20984307. D GARR.

50. In an action of trespass *vi et armis* and false imprisonment, for example, a plaintiff, Jonathan Stanton of North Carolina, introduced evidence that for more than thirty years prior to his birth his maternal grandmother and mother were recognized as free persons of color living in Carteret and Hyde Counties. The owner, however, presented a copy of an attachment levied against Beck, the plaintiff's grandmother and her children. The lower court ignored the attachment. The verdict for the plaintiff was reversed and remanded because the attachment showed that Beck was a slave. Franklin, *The Free Negro in North Carolina*, 86; Guion Griffis Johnson, *Ante-Bellum North Carolina: A Social History* (Chapel Hill: University of North Carolina Press, 1937), 598 [results of case]; JCCASN *[William] Brookfiled v [Jonathan] Stanton*, NC, 6 Jones N.C. 156, December 1858, 2:220–221. D GARR.

51. JCCASN, *Spurrier v. Parker*, Ky., 16, B. Mon. 274, October 1855, 1:421–422. D GARev.

52. JCCASN, *Lewis v. Fullerton*, Va., 1 Randolph 15, December 1821, 1:135–136. DAA. Conway Robinson, *The Practice in the Courts of Law and Equity of Virginia*, vol. 1: *Containing Practice in the Courts of Law in Civil Cases* (Richmond, VA: Samuel Shepherd, 1832), 429 [precedent].

53. JCCASN, *Charlton v. Unis*, Va., 4 Grattan 58, July 1847, 1: 212; *Unis v. Charlton*, 12 Grattan 484, August 1855, 1:238–239 [four actions combined in an 1855 appeal]; *Reports of Cases Argued and Determined in the Supreme Court of Virginia*, vol. 12: *From January 1 to October 1 1855*, comp. Peachey R Grattan (Richmond, VA: Richie and Dunnavant, 1856), *Unis v. Charlton*, August 1855, 484–489. DAA. The trials took place in Montgomery and Rockbridge Counties.

54. Petition of Charles Smith to the Court of Common Pleas, Kent County, Delaware, 14 April 1824, in Records of the Court of Common Pleas, *Charles Smith v. Daniel Walker*, DSA; Related Documents: Depositions, John Voshell, Augustus Short, 17 December 1824; Deposition, Daniel Hayden [Haden], 18 December 1824, with *Smith v. Walker*. PAR 20382408.KCCCP-CJD, May Term 1824, p. 72, Microfilm Reel 7, p. 51, Record Group 3815, DSA. Granted.

55. Petition of Anson, Michael, and William Clark to the Circuit Court of St. Louis County, Missouri, 2 May 1832, in Records of the Circuit Court, *Anson, Michael, and William Clark v. Henry Mitchell and Henry Russell*, Document/Case 57, CCBSL; Related Documents: Order, 23 May 1832; Plea of Trespass, *Anson vs. Henry G. Mitchel and Henry C. Russel [Russell]*, ca. 25 May 1832; Subpoena, Henry G. Mitchell and Henry C. Russell, ca. 25 May 1832; Copy of Order, 23 May 1832; Sheriff's Return, 28 May 1832; Order for Hiring Out, 30 May 1832; Plea, Henry G. Mitchel and Henry C. Russell, 26 July 1832, with *Anson et al. v. Mitchel et al.* PAR 21183201. William King, next friend, possessed thirteen slaves. USMSPC, St. Louis County, Missouri, St. Louis Upper Ward, 1830, image 1, ancestry.com; *Anson, a boy of color, v. Elijah Mitchell* and *Anson, a boy of color, v. Henry Mitchell and Henry Russell*, July 1832, Cases 48 and 57, Circuit Court Case Files, Office of the Circuit Clerk, St. Louis, Missouri State Archives, St. Louis Office of the Secretary of State. Granted. Lawyer Joseph Strother possessed five slaves. USMSPC, St. Louis County, Missouri, St. Louis Upper Ward, 1830, image 15, ancestry.com.

56. *Henry James, a boy of color, v. William Walker*, November 1834, Case 83, Circuit Court Case Files, Office of the Circuit Clerk, St. Louis, Missouri State Archives, St. Louis, Office of the Secretary of State. G DARR.

57. Petition of Sanford to the Circuit Court of Boone County, Missouri, 17 July 1833, in Records of the Circuit Court, *Sanford v. Mark Reavis*, Microfilm Reel C 16664, Document/Case 518, MoSA; Related Documents: PARs 21182304, 21183401; Affidavit, Sarah Reavis, 12 July 1833; Plea of Trespass, *Sanford vs. Mark Reavis*, ca. 18 July 1833; Copy of Order, 18 July 1833; Writ of *Habeas Corpus* to Mark Reavis for Sanford, 18 July 1833; Sheriff's Return, 23 July 1833; Reply to Writ, Mark Reavis, 24 July 1833; Bond, Mark Reavis, and William S. Burch, 7 August 1833; Plea, Mark Reavis, 30 October 1833; Jury Verdict, ca. February Term 1834; Bill of Exceptions, Mark Reavis, February Term 1834; Decree, Supreme Court, May 1834; Clerk's Certification, Supreme Court, 30 May 1834; Note and Request, Clerk of Supreme Court to Clerk of Circuit Court, 30 May 1834, with *Sanford v. Reavis*. PAR 21183309. GAA.

58. JCCASN, *Pepoon, Guardian of Phebe (a woman of color) v. Clark*, S.C. 1 Mill 137, May 1817, 2:301–302; *Reports of the Judicial Decisions in the Constitutional Court of South Carolina, Held in Charleston and Columbia, 1817 and 1818*, 2 vols. (Charleston: John Mill, 1819), *Joseph Pepoon, Guardian of Phebe (a woman of Color) v. Bartholomew Clark*, 1:137–142. GAA.

59. For North Carolina, see: Petition of Lydia Campbell to the County Court of Person County, North Carolina, 1835, in Records of the North Carolina Supreme Court, *Lydia Campbell v. James Street*, Box/Drawer 2509, NCDAH; Related Documents: Record, March 1835; Copy of Last Will and Testament, Thomas Campbell, 23 October 1797; Record, 12 February 1798; Copy of Letters of Administration, 11 November 1833; Decree, 11 April 1837; North Carolina Reports, Supreme Court, June Term 1840–June 1841, pp. 86–88, with *Campbell v. Street*. PAR 21283501. JCCASN, *Campbell v. Street*, N.C., 1 Iredell 109, June 1840, 2:89–90. GAA. The court reporter noted, "This case was decided several terms ago, but was overlooked by the Reporters." For Florida, see Petition of Sarah Frazier, Antony Frazier, Nat Frazier, Fanny Frazier, Francis Frazier, Lucy Frazier, Bill Frazier, Tom Frazier, George Frazier, July Ann Frazier, Elizabeth Frazier, and Mary June Frazier to the Circuit Court of Leon County, Florida, 1855, in Chancery Case Files, *Sarah Frazier, Antony Frazier, Nat Frazier, et al., v. George T. Ward*, Record Group Series L60, Box/Drawer 7, Entry Folder 451, Tallahassee, Florida State Archives; Related Documents: Answer, George T. Ward, 19 March 1856; Copy of Indenture, 30 October 1824; Decree, 19 March 1857; Amendment of Decree, 9 June 1857, with *Frazier et al. v. Ward*. PAR 20585507. Granted. For Alabama, see JCCASN, *Field v. Milly Walker*, 17 Ala. 80, June 1849 [*Habeas Corpus*] 3:172; JCCASN, *Field v. Walker*, 23 Ala. 155, June 1853, 3:189–190; *Cases Argued and Determined in the Supreme Court of Alabama, during the June Term, 1853*, vol. 23 (Montgomery, AL: J. H. and T. F. Martin, 1854), 155–168. GAA.

60. Petition of Almira and Carlo Bastia to the District Court of Orleans Parish, Louisiana, 6 December 1816, in Records of the First Judicial District Court, Case Records, *Almira and*

Carlo Bastia v. Page and Genevieve Barlatier Rabouen, Microfilm Reel 2, Louisiana Collection, Document/Case 1,261, NOPL; Related Documents: Court Records, 13 December 1816, 6 February 1817, 15 February 1817; Judgment, 1 March 1819, with *Almira et al. v. Rabouen et al.* PAR 20881614. Granted.

61. Petition of Daniel Hancock to the District Court of St. Landry Parish, Louisiana, 20 December 1823, in Records of the Fifth Judicial District Court, *Daniel Hancock v. John Davis,* Document/Case 834, St. Landry Parish Courthouse, Opelousas, Louisiana; Related Documents: Depositions, Obediah Pearson and Alexander Robb, 20 December 1823, John Doty, ca. 1823, Mary, ca. 1824; Copy of Petition, 20 December 1823; Bond, 29 December 1823; Oath, Daniel Hancock, December 20, 1823; Amended Petition, 1824; Supplemental Petition, ca. 1824; Supplemental Petition, 15 May 1824; Order, June 1825; Order, 14 June 1825; Answer, John Davis, 12 May 1824; Judgment, November Term 1826, with *Hancock v. Davis.* PAR 20882322. Granted. In 1820, Alexander Robb headed a household (alone) with seven slaves. USMSPC, St. Landry Parish, Louisiana, 1820, image 11, ancestry.com.

62. In *Lydia Campbell v. James Street,* see note 59, this chapter.

63. See note 1, this chapter.

Chapter 7

1. See note 99, this chapter.

2. "The Somerset Case," National Arrchives, UK, n.d., http://www.nationalarchives.gov.uk/pathways/blackhistory/rights/docs/state_trials.htm.

3. JCCASN, "Louisiana: Introduction," 3:389; Judith Kelleher Schafer, *Becoming Free, Remaining Free: Manumission and Enslavement in New Orleans, 1846–1862* (Baton Rouge: Louisiana State University Press, 2003), 15; Sue Peabody, *"There Are No Slaves in France": The Political Culture of Race and Slavery in the* Ancien Regime (New York: Oxford University Press, 1996), 131–132.

4. Henry W. Farnam, *Chapters in the History of Social Legislation in the United States to 1860* (Washington, DC: Carnegie Institution, 1938), 211–212; Lorenzo Johnston Greene, *The Negro in Colonial New England, 1620–1776* (New York: Columbia University Press, 1942), 76–77.

5. Robert Pierce Forbes, *The Missouri Compromise and Its Aftermath: Slavery and the Meaning of America* (Chapel Hill: University of North Carolina Press, 2007).

6. Eric Foner, *Gateway to Freedom: The Hidden History of the Underground Railroad* (New York: W. W. Norton, 2015), 44.

7. John Hope Franklin, *A Southern Odyssey: Travelers in the Antebellum North* (Baton Rouge: Louisiana State University Press, 1975), 1–3; John Hope Franklin and Loren Schweninger, *In Search of the Promised Land: A Slave Family in the Old South* (New York: Oxford University Press, 2006), 75–86.

8. Petition of Julia to the Circuit Court of St. Louis County, Missouri, 10 March 1831, in Records of the Supreme Court, Case Files, *Julia v. Samuel McKinney,* Box/Drawer 537, Document/Case 5, MoSA; Related Documents: PARs 21183104, 21183305; Transcript of Court Record, 10 March 1831–8 April 1833; Clerk's Certification, 1833; Opinion, Supreme Court, 26 November 1833, with *Julia v. McKinney.* PAR 21183109. GAA. JCCASN, *Julia (a woman of color) v. McKinney,* 3 Mo. 270, October 1833, 5:141–142; see also JCCASN, *Bush v. White,* Ky., 3 T. B. Mon. 100, November 1825, 1:306. GAA.

9. JCCASN, *Rankin v. Lydia (a pauper),* Ky., 2 A. K. Marsh. 467, October 1820, 1: 294–295. GAA. Indeed, most judges and juries in Kentucky and elsewhere agreed with this precept. *The Civil Code of the State of Louisiana, Preceded by the Treaty of Cession with France, the Constitution of the United States of America, and the State* (Published by a Citizen of Louisiana, 1825), 93; Paul Finkelman, *An Imperfection Union: Slavery, Federalism, and Comity* (Chapel Hill: University of North Carolina Press, 1981), 181–182.

10. JCCASN, *Griffith v. Fanny,* Va., Gilmer 143, December 1820, 1:133–134; *Virginia Reports, Jefferson—Grattan 1730–1880, Annotated and under the Supervision of Thomas Johnson Michie* (Charlottesville, VA: Michie Co., 1903), 863–864. GAA.

11. Petition of Mary to the Circuit Court of Jefferson County, Kentucky, 26 November 1807, in Records of the Circuit Court, Case Files, *Mary v. Jacob Fenton and William Trigg*, Box/ Drawer 1-1, Document/Case 181, KDLA; Related Documents: Summons, Jacob Fenton, 26 November 1807; Sheriff's Returns, ca. 1807; Amended Bill, ca. 1810; Answer, William Trigg, 18 May 1810, with *Mary v. Fenton et al.* PAR 20780707. Dismissed.

12. JCCASN, *Harry et al. v. Decker and Hopkins*, Walk. Miss. 36, June 1818, 3:283. GAA. Also see JCCASN, *Guillemette v. Harper*, S.C., 4 Richardson 186, November 1850, 2:418–419; *Charles Guillemette, & Eugenia, his wife, v. James Harper*, in *Reports of Cases at Law, Argued and Determined in the Court of Appeals and Court of Errors of*, vol 4: *From November, 1850, to May, 1851, Both Inclusive* (Columbia, SC: A. S. Johnson, 1851), 186–192. GAA. JCCASN, *Glover v. Millings*, Ala., 2 Stew. and P. 28, January 1832, 3:136. D GARR.

13. Petition of Israel to the Circuit Court of St. Louis County, Missouri, 3 December 1825, in Records of the Circuit Court, *Israel v. William Rector and Isaac A. Litcher*, Document/Case 21, CCBSL; Related Documents: PAR 21182505; Plea of Trespass, Israel, 14 February 1826; Summons, William Rector, 14 February 1826; Sheriff's Return, 11 March 1826; Plea, Isaac A. Litcher, 25 July 1826; Amended Declaration, Israel, 26 July 1826; Plea, Isaac A. Litcher, 27 July 1826; Statement, Israel, August Term 1826; Summons, Ichabud Allen, John Hunter, 4 August 1826; Sheriff's Return, 10 August 1826; Summons, James Milligan, John B. Areot, 16 August 1826; Sheriff's Return, 16 August 1826; Summons, Thomas Thruston, 22 August 1826; Sheriff's Return, 23 August 1826, with *Israel v. Rector et al*. PAR 21182504. Granted. Petition of Martha Ann to the Circuit Court of St. Louis County, Missouri, 18 April 1844, in Records of the Circuit Court, *Martha Ann v. Hiram Cordell*, Document/Case 9, CCBSL; Related Documents: PAR 21184418; Plea, Hiram Cordell, 20 November 1844; Plea of Trespass, Martha Ann, November Term 1844; Summons and Copy of Summons, Hiram Cordell, 18 April 1844; Copy of Order, ca. 18 April 1844; Sheriff's Return, 19 September 1844; Jury Verdict, n.d., with *Martha Ann v. Cordell*. PAR 21184416. Granted. For other suits in Missouri, see Kelly Marie Kennington, "Law, Geography, and Mobility: Suing for Freedom in Antebellum St. Louis," *Journal of Southern History* 80 (August 2014): 575–604; Kelly Marie Kennington, "River of Injustice: St. Louis's Freedom Suits and the Changing Nature of Legal Slavery in Antebellum America" (PhD diss., Duke University, 2009); Kelly Marie Kennington, *In the Shadow of Dred Scott: St. Louis Freedom Suits and the Legal Culture of Slavery in Antebellum America* (Athens: University of Georgia Press, 2017); Lea VanderVelde, *Redemption Songs: Suing for Freedom before Dred Scott* (New York: Oxford University Press, 2014).

14. Petition of Winney, Jerry, Daniel, Jenny, Nancy, Lydia, Sarah, Hannah, Lewis, and Malinda to the Superior Court of St. Louis County, Missouri, June 1818, in Records of the Circuit Court, Certified Copy of Petition and Related Documents, Supreme Court Cases, Box 541, Case 18, MSA; *Winney, Jerry, Daniel, et al. v. Phebe Whitesides, Representatives of Thomas Whitesides, John Whitesides, Robert Musick, et al.*, Document/Case 190, CCBSL; Related Documents: PAR 21182502; Plea of Trespass, Winny, March Term 1819; Summons, Phebe Whitesides, 14 December 1818; Sheriff's Return, 9 February 1819; Deposition, Francis [Frances] Collard, 8 June 1818; Deposition, Thomas R. Musick, 7 February 1822; Copy of Petition, Winney, et al., 2 November 1824; Assignment of Errors, Phebe Whitesides, 7 May 1822; Writ of Error, 11 November 1823; Copy of Plea of Trespass, Winny, March Term 1819; Copy of Summons, Phebe Whitesides, 14 December 1818; Copy of Plea, Phebe Whitesides, April Term 1819; Copy of Replication, Winny, April Term 1819; Copy of Jury Verdict, February Term 1822; Copy of Bill of Exceptions, Phebe Whitesides, 15 February 1822; Supreme Court Opinion, 8 November 1824, with *Winny et al. v. Whitesides et al.* PAR 21181801. JCCASN, *Winny (a free woman held in slavery) v. Whitesides*, 1 Mo. 472, November 1824, 5:125. GAA.

15. Petition of Rachel to the Circuit Court of St. Louis County, Missouri, 4 November 1834, in Records of the Supreme Court, Case Files, *Rachel v. William Walker*, Box/Drawer 545, Document/Case 25, MoSA; Related Documents: Transcript of Court Record, *Rachel v. William Walker*, 4 November 1834–6 April 1836; Reasons for New Trial, Rachel, 5 April 1836; Clerk's Certification, 16 May 1836; Opinion, Missouri Supreme Court, ca. 5 July 1836, with *Rachel v. Walker*. Petition granted; plea of trespass filed; judgment by default; judgment set aside, denied; motion for new trial denied, appealed, reversed, and remanded. PAR

21183404. JCCASN, *Rachel (a woman of color) v. Walker*, 4 Mo. 350, June 1836, 5:116–117, 148. G DARR.

16. JCCASN, *Amy (a woman of color) v. Smith*, Ky., 1 Littell 326, June 1822, 1:301. DAA.

17. Petition of Amy Moore to the Circuit Court of St. Louis County, Missouri, 24 September 1844, in Records of the Circuit Court, *Amy Moore v. Robert N. Moore*, CCBSL; Related Documents: Summons, Robert N. Moore, 7 October 1844; Sheriff's Return, 7 October 1844; Copy of Order, 25 September 1844; Plea, Robert N. Moore, 19 November 1844; Continuance, 21 January 1846; Agreement, Amy Moore, Robert Moore, 17 May 1847; Plea of Trespass, Amy Moore, 24 September 1844; Copy of Order, 25 September 1844, with *Moore v Moore*. PAR 21184408. Denied.

18. JCCASN, *Collins v. America (a woman of color)*, Ky., 9 B. Mon. 565, September 1849, 1:391. D GARR. Edward M. Post, "Kentucky Law Concerning Emancipation and Freedom of Slaves," *Filson Club History Quarterly* 59 (July 1985): 362.

19. Petition of Henry to the Chancery Court of Jefferson County, Kentucky, 3 May 1837, in Records of the Circuit Court, Case Files, *Henry v. Simon Moses and Benjamin Ballard*, Box/ Drawer 2-14, Document/Case 717, KDLA; Related Documents: PAR 20783704; Affidavits, James Richey and A. Thompson, 3 May 1837; Order, 3 May 1837; Answer, Simon Moses, 6 May 1837; Deposition, Tabitha Wren, 8 June 1837; Deposition, James Chenowith, 28 June 1837; Decree, 2 March 1841, with *Henry v. Moses et al*. PAR 20783703. Granted.

20. JCCASN, *Spotts v. Gillaspie*, Va., 6 Randolph 566, November 1828, 1:156. GAA.

21. JCCASN, *Betty v. Horton*, Va., 5 Leigh 615, July 1833, 1:175. G DARev.

22. JCCASN, *Elizabeth Thomas (f. w. c.) v. Generis et al.*, 16 La. 483, December 1840, 3:390, 529. GAA.

23. Paul Finkelman, *Slavery and the Founders: Race and Liberty in the Age of Jefferson*, 3rd ed. (Armonk, NY: M. E. Sharp, 2014), 82; in its 1818 constitution, Illinois indicated that "no person bound to labor in any other state shall be hired to labor in this state, except within the tract reserved for the salt works near Shawneetown" in Massac County where hirelings could work for up to one year. For Illinois slavery in subsequent years, see VanderVelde, *Redemption Songs*, 134–137; Harrison Anthony Trexler, *Slavery in Missouri, 1804–1865* (Baltimore: Johns Hopkins University Press, 1914), 35, 216–217.

24. JCCASN, *Negro David v. Porter*, Md., 4 Har. and McH. 418, October 1799, 4:56; *Maryland Reports, Being a Series of the Most Important Law Cases Argued and Determined in the General Court and Court of Appeals of the State of Maryland, from May, 1797, to the End of 1799*, vol. 4, comp. Thomas Harris and John McHenry (Annapolis, MD: Jonas Green, 1818), 415–418. GAA. Max Grivno, *Gleanings of Freedom: Free and Slave Labor along the Mason-Dixon Line, 1790–1860* (Urbana: University of Illinois Press, 2011), 45.

25. Petition of Vincent to the Circuit Court of St. Louis County, Missouri, 6 November 1829, in Records of the Circuit Court, Supreme Court Cases, Box 542, 10, *Vincent v. James Duncan*, 3 September 1830; MoSA; *Vincent v. James Duncan, John Duncan, and Coleman Duncan*, Document/Case 14, CCBSL; Related Documents: Order, 6 November 1829; Plea of Trespass, 6 November 1829; Subpoena, James Duncan, 6 November 1829; Copy of Order, 6 November 1829; Sheriff's Return, 6 November 1829; Plea, James Duncan, 26 November 1829; Court Record, ca. 26 November 1829–ca. November 1832; Depositions, Abner West, Alexander Miller, and Benjamin Pritchett, Hopkins County, Kentucky, 3 January 1830; Deposition, John Duncan, Hopkins County, Kentucky, 4 February 1830; Depositions, Willis Hargrave, Marmaduke S. Ensminger, and Lee Hargrave, Gallatin County, Illinois, 15 March 1830; Deposition, Timothy Guard, Gallatin County, Illinois, 16 March 1830; Judge's Certifications, Gallatin County, Illinois, 15, 16, and 19 March 1830; Clerk's Certification, Gallatin County, Illinois, 19 March 1830; Notices of Taking Depositions, *Vincent vs. James Duncan, Ralph vs. Coleman Duncan*, 11 October 1831; Attorney's Acknowledgments, 11 October 1831; Deposition, Samuel Stebbins, 14 October 1831; Copy of Judgment, Missouri Supreme Court, September 1830; Clerk's Certification, Missouri Supreme Court, 16 February 1831, with *Vincent v. Duncan et al*. PAR 21182903. JCCASN, *Vincent (a man of color) v. James Duncan*, 2 Mo. 214, September 1830, 5:137–138. D DARR.

26. Petition of Ben to the Circuit Court of St. Louis County, Missouri, 18 January 1836, in Records of the Circuit Court, *Ben v. Thomas J. White and William L. Woods*, Document/Case

50, CCBSL; Related Documents: Order, 18 January 1836; Plea of Trespass, Ben, 19 January 1836; Copy of Order, 18 January 1836; Subpoena, Thomas J. White, William L. Woods, 19 January 1836; Sheriff's Return, 20 January 1836; Depositions, John Holtz, Samuel Swagart, George W. Howard, Eliza Howard, 30 October 1838; Plea, Thomas J. White, 16 March 1836; Case Summary, 28 December 1838, with *Ben v. White et al.* PAR 21183614. Granted.

27. Petition of Squire Brown to the Circuit Court of St. Louis County, Missouri, 27 June 1841, in Records of the Circuit Court, *Squire Brown v. William C. Anderson,* CCBSL; Related Documents: Order, 28 June 1841; Plea of Trespass, *Squire Brown v. William C. Anderson,* 1 July 1841; Subpoena, William C. Anderson, 1 July 1841; Copy of Order, 28 June 1841; Sheriff's Return, 3 July 1841; Plea, William C. Anderson, 20 July 1841, with *Brown v. Anderson.* Petition granted, plea of trespass filed, dismissed. PAR 21184107. Petition of Squire Brown to the Circuit Court of St. Louis County, Missouri, 17 January 1844, in Records of the Circuit Court, *Squire Brown v. Charles R. Anderson and Israel Morris,* Document/Case 328, CCBSL; Related Documents: PAR 21184107; Plea of Trespass, Squire Brown, November Term 1843; Plea, Charles R. Anderson, 17 January 1844; Order, 17 January 1844; Deposition, Buyram B. Dayton, 19 January 1844; Warrant, Squire Brown, 19 January 1844; Sheriff's Return, 20 January 1844; Order, ca. January 1844; Motions, Charles R. Anderson, 12 and 29 February 1844; Bill of Exceptions, Charles R. Anderson, 15 March 1844, with *Brown v. Anderson.* PAR 21184424. JCCASN, *Anderson v. Brown (of color),* 9 Mo. 646, October 1845, 5:167. CV to court of common pleas regarding court costs; Brown was released from jail.

28. JCCASN, *Ralph (a man of color) v. C. Duncan,* 3 Mo. 194, May 1833, 5:139–140. G DARR.

29. JCCASN, *Hay v. Dunky,* 3 Mo. 588, October 1834, 5:145–146. GAA.

30. Petition of Frank Irwin to the District Court of West Feliciana Parish, Louisiana, 6 February 1837, in Records of the Third Judicial District Court and Supreme Court, Louisiana Collection, *Frank Irwin v. Thomas Powell,* Book 3, 280, Document/Case 1,635, West Feliciana Parish Courthouse, St. Francisville, Louisiana; Related Documents: Order, 6 February 1837; Answer, Thomas Powell, 6 May 1837; Testimonies, General Taylor, et al., 19 September 1837–6 December 1837; Judgment, 22 December 1837, Records of the Third Judicial District Court at West Feliciana Parish Courthouse, St. Francisville, Louisiana; Transcript of Court Records, 6 February 1837–15 November 1837, including Copy of Petition and Order, 6 February 1837; and Testimonies, R. A. Madison, et al., 14 November 1837, certified 15 November 1837; Petition of Appeal, 26 December 1837; Order, 26 December 1837; Supreme Court Opinion and Decree, 5 February 1838, Supreme Court of Louisiana Collection UNO, with *Irwin v Powell.* PAR 20883713. JCCASN, *Frank (f.m.c.) v. Powell,* 11 La. 499, January 1838, 3:516; Judith Kelleher Schafer, *Slavery, the Civil Law, and the Supreme Court of Louisiana* (Baton Rouge: Louisiana State University Press, 1994), 271–272, 274. GAA.

31. Petition of Andrean Paschall to the Circuit Court of St. Louis County, Missouri, 13 March 1844, in Records of the Circuit Court, *Andrean Paschall v. Richard W. Ulrici,* Document/Case 340, CCBSL; Related Documents: Order, ca. 13 March 1844; Warrant, Andrean Paschall, 13 March 1844; Plea of Trespass, Andrean Paschall, 19 March 1844; Sheriff's Return, 18 and 19 March 1844; Notice, Andrean Paschall, 10 December 1844; Sheriff's Return, 9 December 1844; Statement, Richard Ulrici, 13 December 1844; Deposition, Gabriel Paul, 14 December 1844; Certification of Deposition, 14 December 1844; Plea, Richard W. Ulrici, 29 April 1844, with *Paschall v. Ulrici.* PAR 21184415. Denied.

32. Petition of Thomas Jefferson to the Circuit Court of St. Louis County, Missouri, 12 December 1842, in Records of the Circuit Court, *Thomas Jefferson v. Milton W. Hopkins,* Document/Case 219, CCBSL; Related Documents: PAR 21184517; Transcript of Court Record, 10 December 1842–27 May 1844; Certification, 5 July 1844; Summons, William Carr Lane, et al., 22 October 1844; Summons, William Carr Lane, 24 October 1844; Sheriff's Return, 24 October 1844; Attachment, William Carr Lane, 25 October 1844; Motion, Thomas Jefferson, 28 October 1844; Bill of Sale, Charles W. Drechler, William Carr Lane, 19 March 1840; Jury Instructions, n.d.; Jury Verdict, n.d., with *Jefferson v. Hopkins.* PAR 21184219. Denied.

33. JCCASN, *Nat (a man of color) v. Ruddle,* 3 Mo. 400, June 1834, 5:143. DAA.

34. JCCASN, *François La Grange (alias Isidore) v. Pierre Chouteau,* 2 Mo. 20, May 1823, 5:129–130. DAA.

35. JCCASN, *Mahoney v. Ashton*, Md., 4 Har. and McH. 63, October 1797, June 1802, 4:5, 53–
    55. The High Court of Appeals explained that in the Somerset case of 1772, Lord Mansfield
    of the King's Bench said slavery was "so odious that nothing can be suffered to support it
    but positive law." England had no such laws. Maryland had a positive law enacted in 1715.
    The court could have also have cited acts passed in 1664 and 1681. *Proceedings and Acts of
    the General Assembly of Maryland, at a Session Held at St. Marys, September 13–21, 1664*,
    p. 533, Archives of Maryland Online, http://aomol.msa.maryland.gov/000001/000001/
    html/am1--507.html *Proceedings and Acts of the General Assembly of Maryland, October
    1678-November 1683*, p. 203, http://aomol.net/000001/000007/html/am7--203.html;
    Eric Robert Papenfuse, "From Recompense to Revolution," *Mahoney v. Ashton* and the
    Transfiguration of Maryland Culture, 1791–1802, *Slavery and Abolition* 15 (December
    1994): 54. D GARev.
36. Bernard Moitt, "Slave Women and Resistance in the French Caribbean," in *More Than
    Chattel: Black Women and Slavery in the Americas*, ed. David Barry Gaspar and Darlene Clarke
    Hine (Bloomington: Indiana University Press, 1996), 241; slavery was re-imposed in French
    territories in 1802.
37. Sue Peabody, "'Free upon Higher Ground': Saint Domingue Slave Suits for Freedom in
    U.S. Courts," in *The World of the Haitian Revolution*, ed. David Geggus and Norman Fiering
    (Bloomington: Indiana University Press, 2009), 267–268.
38. *Laws of Maryland Made and Passed at a Session of the Assembly, Begun and Held in the City
    of Annapolis on the Fifth of November, in the Year of Our Lord One Thousand Seven Hundred
    and Ninety-Two* (Annapolis, MD: Frederick Green, 1793), 164–165; Papenfuse, "From
    Recompense to Revolution," 38.
39. JCCASN, *Boisneuf v. Lewis*, Md., 4 Har. and McH. 414, October 1799, 4:55–56; *Being a Series
    of the Most Important Law Cases Argued and Determined in the General Court and Court of
    Appeals of the State of Maryland, from October, 1790, to May, 1797*, 3 vols., comp. Thomas
    Harris Jr. and Tom McHenry (New York: I. Riley, 1813), 3:185–197. GAA.
40. Petition of Marine De Fontaine and Betsy De Fontaine to the Court of Oyer and Terminer,
    Baltimore County, Maryland, July 1816, in SC, *Marine De Fontaine and Betsy De Fontaine
    v. John P. Bonard*, Microfilm M 11014, Volume 4239-3, Document/Case 79, MSA; Related
    Documents: Court Record, 28 November 1816; Transcript of Court of Appeals, 9 June
    1817-27 June 1818, with *De Fontaine et al. v Bonard*. PAR 20981606. JCCASN, *De Fontaine
    v. De Fontaine*, Md., 5 Har. and John. 99 n., June 1818, 4:66. DAA. *Digest of Maryland Reports*,
    2 vols. (Baltimore: Cushing and Brother, 1847), 2:726; for another case where the court ruled
    that the owner was a sojourner, see JCCASN, *Baptiste v. De Volunbrun*, Md., 5 Har. and John.
    86, June 1820, 4:69. DAA.
41. JCCANS, *Clarissa v. Edwards*, Tn., 1 Overton 393, May 1809, 2:484; JCCANS, *Edwards
    v. M'Connel*, Tn., Cook 305, February 1813, 2:484–485; *Tennessee Reports: Reports
    of Cases Argued and Determined in the Highest Courts of Law and Equity of the State of
    Tennessee*, 10, vols., comp. William Frierson Cooper (St. Louis: Soule, Thomas and
    Winsor, 1870), 1:392–395; Peabody, "'Free upon Higher Ground,'" 278. G DARev
    [Clarissa]. In Clarissa's suit the anti-importation law of Virginia was not mentioned. In
    an action of detinue [the wrongful taking of personal property] by the owner to recover
    Clarissa's son, the lower court ruled in sixteen-year-old Sac's favor, but the appeals court
    could not determine whether Clarissa was free at the time of Sac's birth and reversed the
    lower court's decision.
42. Between May 1809 and January 1810, the mayor of New Orleans listed 9,059 Cuban refugees,
    including 2,731 white, 3,102 free persons of color, and 3,225 slaves. Paul F. Lachance, "The
    Politics of Fear: French Louisianans and the Slave Trade, 1706–1809," in *The Louisiana Purchase
    Bicentennial Series in Louisiana History*, vol. 11: *The African American Experience in Louisiana,
    Part A, From Africa to the Civil War*, ed. Charles Vincent (Lafayette: Center for Louisiana
    Studies, 1999), 138. Petition of Castor to the Parish Court of Orleans Parish, Louisiana, 11
    October 1813, in Records of the Parish Court, *Castor v. Claire L'Eveque*, Microfilm Reel 2,
    Louisiana Collection, Document/Case 160, NOPL; Related Documents: Sheriff's Return,
    12 October 1813, with *Castor v. L'Eveque* [Cuba]. In 1820, Castor was listed as a white man.
    PAR 20881318. No decree with petition.

43. JCCASN, *Metayer v. Noret*, La., 5 Mart. La. 566, June 1818, 3:459; *Metayer v. Metayer*, La., 6 Mart. La. 16, January 1819, 3:459–460. GAA. Peabody, "'Free upon Higher Ground,'" 271–272; Schafer, *Slavery, the Civil Law*, 308.

44. Petition of Pierre to the Circuit Court of St. Louis County, Missouri, 5 November 1842, in Records of the Supreme Court, Case Files, *Pierre v. Gabriel L. Chouteau*, Box/Drawer 34, Document/Case 34, MoSA. PAR 21184310. Granted.

45. JCCASN, *Isabella v. Pecot*, La., 2 La. An. 387, April 1847, 3:581–582; Petition of Isabella to the District Court of St. Mary Parish, Louisiana, 20 March 1843, in Supreme Court of Louisiana Collection, *Isabella v. Peter Pecot*, Book 373, Document/Case 3,092, UNO; Related Documents: Transcript of Supreme Court Records, 20 March 1843–24 October 1846, including: Deposition, John A. Dwight, ca. 1845, with *Isabella v. Pecot*. PAR 20884309. DAA.

46. Melville Herskovits, *The Myth of the Negro Past* (Boston: Beacon Press, 1941), 47–48; Virginia Bever Platt, "The East India Company and the Madagascar Slave Trade," *William and Mary Quarterly* 26, no. 4 (October 1969): 576; JCCASN, *Negro Mary v. Vestry of William and Mary's Parish*, Md., 3 Har. and McH. 501, October 1796, 4:53. DAA.

47. Petition of Priscilla Smith to the Parish Court of Orleans Parish, Louisiana, 23 January 1837, in Supreme Court of Louisiana Collection, *Priscilla Smith v. Smith*, Book 3, 314, UNO; Related Documents: Transcript of Court Records, 18 April 1837–15 March 1838, including Testimony, E. Caillard et al., 18 April 1837; Judgment [some text in French], 12 February 1838; Petition of Appeal, 21 February 1838; Order, 21 February 1838; Points and Authorities of Appeal [some text in French; passport], 3 April 1838, with *Smith v. Smith*. PAR 20883742. JCCASN, "Introduction: Louisiana," 3:389; *Pricilla Smith (f.w.c.) v. Smith*, 13 La. 441, April 1839, 3:520–521; Schafer, *Slavery, the Civil Law*, 273–274. G DARev.

48. Petition of Arséne to the District Court of Orleans Parish, Louisiana, 1847, in Supreme Court of Louisiana Collection, *Arséne v. Louis Aimé Pignéguy*, Book 459, UNO; Related Documents: Testimonies, J. Ducourneau, et al., ca. 1847; Court Record of Case No. 395, 24 October 1846–24 December 1846, including *Arséne alias Cora v. Louis Arséne Pignéguy [Aimé Pignéguy]*, 24 October 1846; and Opinion, 4 November 1846; Supreme Court Opinion and Decree, 14 June 1847, with *Arséne v. Pignéguy*. GAA. PAR 20884746. JCCASN, *Arséne v. Pignéguy*, 2 La. An. 629, June 1847 [621], 3:390, 582–583; Schafer, *Slavery, the Civil Law*, 277; Schafer, *Becoming Free*, 22. Granted. Arséne received approximately fifty-six dollars and her freedom.

49. *Phany v. Bouny and Poincy*, No. 1421, First District Court of New Orleans, 20 November 1847, in Schafer, *Becoming Free*, 19–20. Granted.

50. *Aurore v. Decuir*, No. 1919, First District Court of New Orleans, 16 October 1848, in Schafer, *Becoming Free*, 20, 23. Granted. It was not unusual for free women of color in Louisiana to own slaves, but it was very unusual for them to sell their own kin. When Aurore returned to Louisiana she was purchased by her sister who after some years sold her to the current owner.

51. Petition of Marie to the District Court of West Baton Rouge Parish, Louisiana, 4 September 1848, in Records of the Sixth Judicial District Court, *Marie v. Doussan Dr. and Doussan Mrs.*, Document/Case 1,007, West Baton Rouge Parish Courthouse, Port Allen, Louisiana; Related Documents: Judgment, 27 September 1848; Answer, 14 September 1848; Answer to Interrogatories, 7 September 1848, with *Marie v. Doussan, et al.* PAR 20884843. Granted.

52. *Tabé v. Vidal*, No. 1584, First District Court of New Orleans, 26 November 1847, in Schafer, *Becoming Free*, 20. Granted. *Ann alias Anna v. Durel*, No. 1281, Second District Court of New Orleans, 5 March 1857, in Schafer, *Becoming Free*, 31–32. Granted. For a chapter about his seeking out slave plaintiffs, see "'Voleur de Negres': The Strange Career of Jean Charles David," in Schafer, *Becoming Free*, 34–44.

53. Schafer, *Becoming Free*, 15–16; *Acts Passed at the First Session of the First Legislature of the State of Louisiana, Begun and Held in the City of New Orleans, on the 9th day of February, 1846* (New Orleans: W. Van Bethhuysen and Besancon Jr., 1846), 163.

54. JCCASN, *Liza (c. w.) v. Dr. Puissant et al.*, La., 7 La. An. 80, February 1852, 3:622; Petition of Liza to the District Court of Orleans Parish, Louisiana, 29 November 1850, in Supreme Court of Louisiana Collection, *Liza v. Puissant and Felicie Norbert Fortier Puissant*, Book 2,326, University of New Orleans; Related Documents: Order, 29 November 1850; Judgment, 14 April 1851; Sheriff's Return, 23 October 1850; Court Record, 14 April 1851; Opinion of the

Court [some text in French], 14 April 1851; Court Record of Appeal, 16 May 1851; Bond, 2 June 1851; Supreme Court Opinion and Decree, February 1852, with *Liza v. Puissant et al.* PAR 20885043. DAA. Schafer, *Slavery, the Civil Law,* 279–282; Schafer, *Becoming Free,* 27–28.

55. Stephen Deyle, *Carry Me Back: The Domestic Slave Trade in American Life* (New York: Oxford University Press, 2005), 52; US House of Representatives, *The Federal and State Constitutions, Colonial Charters, and Other Organic Laws of the States Territories, and Colonies,* 59th Cong., 2nd sess., 1909, 7 vols. (Washington, DC: Government Printing Office, 1909), 4:2062 [Mississippi Constitution of 1832].

56. The states with importation laws included Virginia in 1778, 1785, 1788, 1789, 1790, 1792, etc.; Kentucky in 1794; Tennessee in 1812; Georgia in 1798; Delaware in 1789; Maryland in 1783 and 1796; North Carolina in 1794; South Carolina in 1800, 1801, 1802; Missouri in 1835; Arkansas in 1838; Mississippi in 1837; and Louisiana in 1826. At least six states affirmed in their constitutions the authority of the general assembly to pass importation laws.

57. Petition of Robert Wright to the Delaware General Assembly, 22 January 1819, in General Assembly, Legislative Papers, Record Group 1111, Frame/Pages 517–520, DSA; House: read, referred; denied. PAR 10381906. Congress acknowledged the rights of states to pass such statutes and conceded that the southern constitutions with importation laws were "not repugnant to the Constitution of the United States." In 1841, the US Supreme Court, in *Groves v. Slaughter,* agreed: the cases arising from the domestic slave trade were state issues. JCCASN, *Groves v. Slaughter,* La., 15 Peters (U. S.) 449, January 1841, 3:534–535; JCCASN, "Introduction: Mississippi," 3:277.

58. JCCASN, *Commonwealth v. Griffin,* Ky., 3 B. Mon. 208, October 1842, 1:361–362. Arrested for illegally importing a slave and fined $600, Griffin was jailed until he paid the fine as required by state law. See also JCCASN, *Commonwealth v. Young,* Ky., 7 B. Mon. 1 September 1846, 1:376; David Lightner, *Slavery and the Commerce Power: How the Struggle against the Interstate Slave Trade Led to the Civil War* (New Haven, CT: Yale University Press, 2006), chap. 4; Earle M. Maltz, "Slavery, Federalism and the Structure of the Constitution," *American Journal of Legal History* 36 (October 1992): 471–473.

59. For example, see the laws passed in Kentucky. *Acts Passed at the First Session of the Twenty Third General Assembly for the Commonwealth of Kentucky, Begun and Held in the Town of Frankford, on Monday the Fifth Day of December, One Thousand Eight Hundred and Fourteen, and of the Commonwealth the Twenty-Third* (Frankfort, KY: Gerard & Berry, 1815), 435–437 [1814 law]; *A Digest of the Statute Laws of Kentucky, of a Public and Permanent Nature, from the Commending of the Government to the Session of the Legislature, Ending on the 24th February, 1834, with References to Judicial Decisions,* 2 vols. (Frankfort, KY: Albert G. Hodges, 1834), 2:1482–1484; *Digest of the Statute Laws of Kentucky, of a Public and Permanent Nature Passed Since 1834, with References to Judicial Decisions* (Frankfort, KY: Albert G. Hodges, 1842), 555–557; JCCASN, *Commonwealth v. Jackson,* Ky, 2 B. Mon. 402, May 1842, 1:359.

60. JCCASN, *Commonwealth v. Griffin,* Ky., 7 J.J. Marsh. 588, October 1832, 1:323; *Commonwealth v. Greathouse,* 7 J. J. Marsh, 590, October 1832 [importation constituted one offense; sale of a slave constituted a second offense].

61. *Laws of Maryland, Made and Passed at a Session of Assembly, Begun and Held in the City of Annapolis on Monday the Seventh of November, in the Year of Our Lord One Thousand Seven Hundred and Ninety-Six* (Annapolis, MD: Frederick Green, 1796), chap. 67.

62. For Florida, see Farnam, *Chapters in the History of Social Legislation,* 335.

63. *Acts Passed at the First Session of the Twenty Third General Assembly for the Commonwealth of Kentucky,* 435–437.

64. *Code of Laws of the District of Columbia: Prepared under the Authority of the Act of Congress of the 29th of April 1816* (Washington, DC: Davis and Force, 1819), 197–199; *The Revised Code of the District of Columbia, Prepared under the Authority of the Act of Congress, Entitled An Act to Improve the Laws of the District of Columbia, and to Codify the Same, Approved March 5, 1855* (Washington, DC: A. O. P. Nicholson, 1857), 165.

65. John Codman Hurd, *The Law of Freedom and Bondage in the United States,* 2 vols. (Boston: Little, Brown, 1862; reprint, New York: Negro Universities Press, 1968): 2:74–76, 76n1.

66. JCCASN, "Introduction: Delaware," 4:213; *Laws of the State of Delaware, from the Fourteenth Day of October, One Thousand Seven Hundred, to the Eighteen Day of August,*

One Thousand Seen Hundred and Ninety-Seven, 2 vols. (New-Castle, DE: Samuel and John Adams, 1797), 2:884–885 [1793 Delaware law]. An act of 1827 permitted slave owners on Maryland farms "through which the line of the State runs" to employ slaves in both Delaware and Maryland. *Laws of Maryland, Made and Passed at a Session of Assembly Begun and Held in the City of Annapolis, on Monday the Twenty-first of April, in the Year of Our Lord One Thousand Seven Hundred and Eighty-Three* (Annapolis, MD: Frederick Green, 1784), chap. 23; *The Statutes at Large; Being a Collection of all the Laws of Virginia from the First Session of the Legislature in the Year 1619*, 13 vols. comp. William Waller Hening (Richmond, VA ,1823), 12:182 [1785 law], http://vagenweb.org/hening/; Hurd, *The Law of Freedom and Bondage*, 2:2, 74–75 [1778 Virginia law; 1787 Delaware law]. For a copy of the Virginia oath, see JCCASN, *Murray (a pauper) v. M'Carty*, Va., 2 Munford 393, June 1811, 1:121.

67. June Purcell Guild, ed., *Black Laws of Virginia: A Summary of the Legislative Acts of Virginia Concerning Negroes from Earliest Times to the Present* (Richmond, VA: Whittet & Shepperson, 1936; reprint, New York: Negro Universities Press, 1969), 72, 106; *Acts Passed by the General Assembly of the Commonwealth of Virginia, Begun and Held at the Capitol, in the City of Richmond, on Monday the Second Day of December, One Thousand Eight Hundred and Five* (Richmond, VA: Samuel Pleasants, 1806), p. 36; John Henderson Russell, *The Free Negro in Virginia 1619–1865* (Baltimore: Johns Hopkins University Press, 1913), 70–71; *Laws Made and Passed by the General Assembly of the State of Maryland at a Session of the Said Assembly, Which Was Begun and Held in the State House, at the City of Annapolis, in the County of Anne Arundel, on the Last Monday of December... and Concluded on Thursday the Twenty-fourth Day of February, A. D. 1831, in the 55th Year of the Independence of the United States of America* (Annapolis, MD: J. Green, 1831), 1068–1070.

68. Petition of James Denby to the Common Pleas Court of Kent County, Delaware, 1814, in Records of the Court of Common Pleas, *James Denby v. Francis Hall*, Microfilm Reel 1, Frames 296–297, DSA. PAR 20380020. KCCCP-CJD, November Term 1814, p. 53, Reel 6, Frame 49, filed June 20, 1814, dismissed May 15, 1815 "for want of prosecution," Record Group 3815, DSA. Dismissed. In this case, the court issued commissions to John Reed to oversee testimony in Philadelphia, and to Kensey Harrison to oversee testimony in Centreville, Maryland; witnesses were required to respond to interrogatories.

69. Petition of David to the Common Pleas Court of Kent County, Delaware, 6 April 1803, in Records of the Court of Common Pleas, *David v. Nathan Baynard*, Microfilm Reel 2, Frames 34–35, DSA. PAR 20380304. KCCCP-CJD, May Term 1803, p. 82, Mircofilm Reel 5, Frame 224, Record Group 3815, filed 6 April, 1803, dismissed 11 May, 1805, DSA. Complainant did not appear.

70. Petition of Eli to the County Court of Somerset County, Maryland, 13 April 1807, in SC, *Eli v. William Anderson*, Microfilm M 11014, Volume 4239-1, MSA; Related Documents: Court Record, 13 April 1807; Copy of Apprenticeship Agreement, 1 January 1779; Bill of Exceptions, ca. 1807, with *Eli v. Anderson*. PAR 20980710. Granted, appealed.

71. JCCASN, *M'Michen v. Amos*, Va., 4 Randolph 134, March 1826, 1:144. GAA.

72. Petition of Rebecca Ringgold, Araminta Ringgold, and William Ringgold to the Circuit Court of Kent County, Maryland, 14 June 1851, in SC, *Rebecca Ringgold, et al. v. David Barley*, Microfilm M 11015, Volume 4239-2, Document/Case 151, MSA; Related Documents: Circuit Court Record, December Term 1852, includes Record of Negroes Registered, Cornelius Money, 19 March 1832; Copy of Circuit Court Record, December Term 1853, with *Ringgold et al. v. Barley*. Denied, appealed, reversed. PAR 20985110. Rebecca's lawyer cited the Maryland act 1831, chap. 323, sect.4. JCCASN, *Rebecca Rinngold and others (negroes) v. Barley*, 5 Md. 186, December 1853, 4:124. G DARev.

73. JCCASN, *Battles v. Miller*, D.C., 2 Fed. Cas. 1037 (3 Cranch C. C. 294), May 1828, 4:182. GAA. JCCASN, *Crawford v. Slye*, D.C., 6 Fed. Cas. 778 (4 Cranch C. C. 457), March 1834, 4:190. GAA. *Burr v. Dunnahoo*, D.C., 4 Fed.Cas. 806 (1 Cranch C. C. 370), December 1806, 4:160; *Reports of Cases Civil and Criminal in the United States Circuit Court of the District of Columbia, 1801-1841*, 6 vols., comp. William Cranch (Boston: Little, Brown, 1852), 1:370; Letitia Woods Brown, *The Free Negro in the District of Columbia, 1790-1846* (New York: Oxford University Press, 1972), 123. GAA. JCCASN, *Foster V. Simmons*, 9 Fed. Cas. 579 (1 Cranch 316), June 1806, 4:158–159. GAA.

74. Petition of Robert Oakes to the Oyer and Terminer Court of Baltimore County, Maryland, 8 July 1805, in SC, *Robert Oakes v. Robert Stewart*, Microfilm M 11014, Volume 4239-3, Document/Case 12, MSA; Related Documents: Court Record, 1805-1806; Admission, Robert Stewart, March 1806; Copy of the *Act of the Virginia General Assembly*, 17 December 1792; Decree and Appeal, March 1806; Court Record, 1808–1813; Decree, 6 December 1813, with *Oakes v. Stewart*. PAR 20980507. GAA. JCCASN, *Stewart v. Oakes*, Md., 3 Har. and John. 491, December 1814, 4:62; Court of Appeals (Judgments, Western Shore) No. 12 *Robert Stewart vs. Robert Oakes*; transcript 10 December 1808; record of appeals court 15 December 1811; judgment affirmed by the appeals court with costs December Term 1813 [Docket]; MSA S382-143, Microfilm: M 11014, Accession No.: MSA SC 4239-3-26, Location: 01/62/14/34; for Virginia, see *N Y Court of Appeals: Report of the Lemmon Slave Case, Containing Points and Arguments of Counsel on Both Sides, with Opinions of All the Judges* (New York: Horace Greeley, 1861), 55, citing *Wilson v. Isbell* and *Hunter v. Hulcher*.

75. William H. Williams, *Slavery and Freedom in Delaware, 1639-1865* (Wilmington, DE: Scholarly Resources, 1996), 152–153; Petition of Abraham to the Common Pleas Court of Kent County, Delaware, 11 May 1804, in Records of the Court of Common Pleas, *Abraham v. Edward Burrows*, Microfilm Reel 2, Frame/Pages 75–76, DSA. PAR 20380402. JCCASN, *Negro Abram v. Burrows*, Del., 5 Harrington, 102 n., November 1804, 4:218. GAA.

76. Petition of Beck to the Common Pleas Court of Kent County, Delaware, 11 March 1803, in Records of the Court of Common Pleas, *Beck v. Edward Holliday*, Microfilm Reel 2, Frame/ Pages 30–31, DSA. PAR 20380301. JCCASN, *Negro Beck v. Holiday*, Del., 5 Harrington 101, November 1805, 4:218. GAA.

77. JCCASN, "Delaware: Introduction," 4:213.

78. *Laws of the State of Delaware,* , 2:884–885, 885n. a; JCCASN, "Delaware: Introduction," 4:212.

79. Petition of David Eastburn, Nathanel Kinsey, Eli Evans, William D. Phillips, Thomas Evans, et al., to the Delaware General Assembly, 1801, Legislative Papers, Microfilm, Frame 207–211, DSA. No act with petition. PAR 10380101. Petition of Caleb Rooney, Jacob West, John M. West, James Wilson, and Joseph H. Thompson to the Delaware General Assembly, January 1817, Legislative Papers, Record Group 1111, Microfilm Frame 394–396, DSA. PAR 10381705. No act with petition.

80. *Laws of the State of Delaware*, 2:884–885 [the law was passed 14 June 1793]; JCCASN, "Delaware: Introduction," 4:212.

81. Petition of Minus Brown to the Court of Common Pleas, Kent County, Delaware, May 1825, in Records of the Court of Common Pleas, *Minus Brown v. George Magee*, DSA; Related Documents: PAR 20382508; Deposition, John Noble, Sussex County, 12 December 1825, with *Brown v. Magee*. PAR 20382507. Petition of Minus Brown to the Court of Common Pleas, Kent County, Delaware, May 1825, in Records of the Court of Common Pleas, *Minus Brown v. Stanford Banning*, DSA. PAR 20382508. KCCCP-CJD, December 1822 to December 1828, *Minus Brown Negro v. Stanford Banning*, May 1825, p. 136, Record Group 3815, Microfilm Reel 7, p. 86, DSA. Granted.

82. Petition of Sarah, Phebe, George, Polly, Amy, Grace, Michael, Milley, Levin, John, Bayard, and Jonathan Turner, Next Friend, to the Superior Court of Kent County, Delaware, 24 May 1834, in Records of the Superior Court, *Sarah, et al. v. Andrew Allen*, Microfilm Reel R79.3, DSA; PAR 20383402. JCCASN, *Allen v. Negro Sarah*, Del., 2 Harrington 434, June 1838, 4:224–225. GAA.

83. Petition of Rosa Rathel to the Court of Common Pleas, Kent County, Delaware, 5 July 1830, in Records of the Court of Common Pleas, *Rosa Rathel v. Winlock Hall*, DSA; Related Documents: *Rosa Rathal v. Winlock Hall*, November Term 1830, p. 91, Reel 7, Frame 327, Summons July 5, 1830, KCCCP-CJD; Hall disclaimed "any title" to the plaintiff; freed 9 December 1830. PAR 20383001, PAR 20383004. Granted.

84. *Laws Made and Passed by the General Assembly of the State of Maryland*, 1068–1070; Petition of David Cross, Airy Cross, Charles Cross, David Cross, Perry Cross, Mary Cross, Harriet Cross, and James Cross to the County Court of Anne Arundel County, Maryland, 23 March 1836, in SC, *David Cross, Airy Cross, Charles Cross, et al. v. William Black*, Microfilm M 11014, Volume 4239-3, Document/Case 153, MSA; Related Documents: Transcript

of Court Record, 23 March 1836–23 October 1837 [pp. 16–17 missing]; Exhibit No. 1, William and Sarah Black to Maria Thornton, Portage County, Ohio, 21 November 1835; Clerk's Certification, 20 November 1837, with *Cross et al. v. Black*. PAR 20983601. A lengthy summary with depositions and opinion is found in JCCASN, *Cross v. Black*, Md., 19 Gill and John. 198, December 1837, 4:89–93. DAA.

85. JCCASN, *Barnett v. Sam*, Vir., Gilmer 232, April 1821, 1:134; *Reports of Cases Decided in the Court of Appeals of Virginia, from April 10th 1820, to June 28th 1821* (Richmond, VA: N. Pollard-Franklin Press, 1821), 232–234. D GARev.

86. JCCASN, *Tarlton v. Tippett*, D.C., 23 Fed. Cas. 702 (2 Cranch C. C. 463), April 1824, 4:174–175. DAA.

87. Petition of Henry Ward Pearce to the Delaware General Assembly, 6 June 1788, in General Assembly, Legislative Papers, Record Group 1111, Frame/Pages 97–99, DSA. Referred to committee. PAR 10378805. See also petition of Sluyter Bouchell to the Delaware General Assembly, New Castle County, Delaware, 22 October 1790, in General Assembly, Legislative Papers, Record Group 1111, pp. 109–113, DSA; Related Documents: Summary, *Abram v. John Moody* 1789. PAR 10379002. No act with petition.

88. JCCASN, *Negro Plato v. Bainbridge*, Md., 4 Har. and McH. 416, October 1799, 4:56. DAA. JCCASN, *Negro Harry v. Lyles*, Md., 4 Har. and McH. 215, June 1800, 4:57. DAA. *Maryland Reports, Being a Series of the Most Important Law Cases Argued and Determined in the General Court and Court of Appeals of the State of Maryland, from May, 1797, to the End of 1799*, vol. 4, comp. Thomas Harris and John McHenry (Annapolis, MD: Jonas Green, 1818), 215–218; *Laws of Maryland* (Annapolis, MD: Frederick Green, 1784), chap. 23.

89. JCCASN, *Violette v. Ball*, D.C., 28 Fed. Cas. 1218 (2 Cranch C. C. 102), June 1814, 4:167. DAA.

90. JCCASN, *South v. Solomon*, Vir., 6 Munford 12, October 1817, 1:128–129. D GARev.

91. JCCASN, *London v. Scott*, D.C., 15 Fed. Cas. 940 (1 Cranch C. C. 264), November 1805, 4:157; *Scott v. Negro London*, D.C., 3 Cranch 324, February 1806, 4:158. G GARR. Michael L. Nicholls, " 'The squint of freedom': African-American Freedom Suits in Post-Revolutionary Virginia," *Slavery and Abolition* 20 (August 1999): 52–53; *Reports of Cases Civil and Criminal in the United States Circuit Court of the District of Columbia, 1801-1841*, November 1805, 1:264–265; The Supreme Court reversed the lower court's decision; the Alexandria court re-docked case in 1807; case called in July 1808; accommodation reached "as both parties agreed to dismiss the cause." For a successful case, see JCCASN, *Scott v. Negro Ben*, D.C., 6 Cranch 3, February 1810, 4:163. G GARR.

92. JCCASN, *Matilda v. Mason*, D.C., 16 Fed. Cas. 1106 (2 Cranch C. C. 343), April 1823, 4:173; JCCASN, *Mason v. Matilda*, D.C., 12 Wheaton 590, March 1827, 4:179. D GARR. http://supreme.justia.com/us/25/590/case.html. Also see JCCASN, *Negress Sally Henry, by William Henry, her father and next friend, v. Ball*, D.C., 1 Wheaton 1, February 1816, 4:168. DAA. The US Supreme Court affirmed the circuit court's decision. http://law.onecle.com/ussc/14/14-us-1.html.

93. JCCASN, *Lee v. Lee*, D.C. 8 Peters 44, January 1834, 4:188, 195–196; US Supreme Court, *Lee v. Lee*, 33 U.S. 44 (1834), http://supreme.justia.com/cases/federal/us/33/44/; *Reports of Cases Civil and Criminal*, November 1835, 4:643–644. D DARR. There was no new trial.

94. JCCASN, *Negro Isaac V. Ferguson*, Del., 5 Harrington 102, November 1794, 4:217. GAA. *Jemima v. Ross*, Del., 5 Harrington 102, 1796, n.8. GAA. John B. Parks, "Freedom v. Slavery: Lawsuits, Petitions and the Legitimacy of Slavery in British Colonies and the United States" (PhD diss., Howard University, 2008), 212; Petition of Abraham to the Common Pleas Court of Kent County, Delaware, 11 May 1804, in Records of the Court of Common Pleas, *Abraham v. Edward Burrows*, Microfilm Reel 2, Frame/Pages 75–76, DSA. PAR 20380402. KCCCP-CDJ, May Term 1804, p. 128, Reel 5, Frame 247, filed May 1804, freed 1 December, 1804. Granted. JCCASN, *Negro Abram v. Burrows*, Del., 5 Harrington 102n, November 1804, 4:218. GAA. JCCASN, *U.S. v. Davis*, D.C., 25 Fed. Cas. 775 (5 Cranch C. C. 622), January 1840, 4:203. The case involved slaves Emanuel Price and Maria Corse who were removed "beyond the District of Columbia" and afterward won their freedom. The defendant was the jailor; this suit awarded *habeas corpus ad subjiciendum* directed at Davis. JCCASN, *Henderson v. Negro Tom*, Md., 4, Har. and John. 282, June 1817, 4:65. GAA. *M'Michen v. Amos*, Va., 4 Randolph

134, March 1826, 1:144; *Reports of Cases Decided in the Supreme Court of Appeals in Virginia*, vol. 4, comp. Peyton Randolph (Richmond, VA: Peter Cottom, 1827), 134–143. GAA.

95. Don E. Fehrenbacher, *Slavery, Law, and Politics: The Dred Scott Case in Historical Perspective* (New York: Oxford University Press, 1981), 243–247; Roger B. Taney, "The Dred Scott Decision," 1857, http://www.digitalhistory.uh.edu/disp_textbook.cfm?smtID=3&psid=293 [quote]; Christopher Tomlins, *Freedom Bound: Law, Labor, and Civic Identity in Colonizing English America, 1580–1865* (Cambridge: Cambridge University Press, 2010), 512–522; Mark Graber, *Dred Scott and the Problem of Constitutional Evil* (Cambridge: Cambridge University Press, 2008).

96. JCCASN, *Ralph (a man of color) v. C. Duncan*, 3 Mo. 194, May 1833, 5:139–140. G DARR. *Julia (a woman of color) v. McKinney*, 3 Mo. 270, October 1833, 5:141–142. G DARR. *Hay v. Dunky*, 3 Mo. 588, October 1834, 5:145–146. GAA. *Rachel (a woman of color) v. Walker*, 4 Mo. 350, June 1836, 5:148. G DARR. *Wilson (a colored man) v. Melvin* 4 Mo. 592, June 1837, 5:150–151. G DARR. *Randolph v. Alsey (a person of color)*, 8 Mo. 656, July 1844, 5:162. GAA.

97. Petition of Silvia to the Circuit Court of McDonald County, Missouri, 5 May 1849, in Records of the Supreme Court, Case Files, *Silvia v. Joel Kirby*, Box/Drawer 63, MoSA; Related Documents: Transcript of Circuit Court Record, 5 May 1849–11 December 1851; Clerk's Certificate, 26 January 1852; Copy of Bill of Costs, n.d.; Opinion of the Supreme Court, 29 January 1853, with *Silvia v. Kirby*. Petition granted; plea of trespass filed, denied, appealed, affirmed. PAR 21184902. JCCASN, *Sylvia (a slave) v. Kirby*, 17 Mo. 434, January 1853, 5:188. DAA.

98. JCCASN, *Bush v. White*, Ky., 3 T. B. Mon. 100, November 1825, 1:306. GAA. JCCASN, *Winny (a free woman held in slavery) v. Whitesides*, Mo., 1 Mo. 472, November 1824, 5:125. GAA.

99. Petition of John Merry to the Circuit Court of St. Louis County, Missouri, 30 September 1826, in Records of the Circuit Court, *John Merry v. Louis Menard and Clayton Tiffin*, Document/Case 18, CCBSL; Related Documents: PARs 20882930, 21183108, 21184114; Order, 30 September 1826; Summons, Clayton Tiffin, Louis Menard, 11 October 1826; Plea of Trespass, *John Merry vs. Louis Menard and Clayton Tiffin*, 7 October 1826; Sheriff's Return, 11 October 1826; Depositions: Augustus Trotlier, 6 April 1827; Julie Bourdeau, 12 April 1827; Louis [Pinconeau?], 6 April 1827; John Merry, Oath in Open Court, Request Appeal to the Missouri Supreme Court; Copy of Supreme Court Opinion, May Term 1827; Certification of Copy, 25 July 1827, with *Merry v. Menard et al.* PAR 21182606. JCCASN, *Merry v. Tiffin and Menard*, 1 Mo. 725, May 1827, 5:128–129. G DARev.

Chapter 8

1. Frederic Bancroft, *Slave-Trading in the Old South* (Baltimore: J. H. Furst, 1931), 43; Steven Deyle, *Carry Me Back: The Domestic Slave Trade in American Life* (New York: Oxford University Press, 2005), 98–100; Stanley Harrold, *Subversives: Antislavery Community in Washington, D.C., 1828–1865* (Baton Rouge: Louisiana State University Press, 2003), 30; USMSPC, Baltimore City, Maryland, 7th Ward, 1840, image 41, ancestry.com [Jerome Bonaparte];USMSPC, 7th Ward, 1840, image 29, ancestry.com [James O. Law].

2. Petition of Beverly Dowling to the City Court of Baltimore City, Maryland, 31 October 1835, in SC, *Beverly Dowling v. Sophia Bland and Austin T. Woolfolk*, Microfilm M 11014, Volume 4239-3, Document/Case 110, MSA; Related Documents: PAR 20983509; City Court Transcript, 5 October 1835–2 May 1836, includes Bills of Exceptions, Sophia Bland, October Term 1835; Correspondence, James Law to Sophia Bland, 26 October 1833, 23 December 1833, 7 June 1834; Court Costs, October Term 1835, with *Dowling v. Bland*. PAR 20983515. *The Report of and Testimony Taken before the Joint Committee of the Senate and House of Delegates of Maryland* (Annapolis, MD: William M'Neir, Printer, 1836), 66; JCCASN, *Bland v. Negro Beverly Dowling*, Md., 9 Gill and John. 19, June 1837, 4:87. GAA.

3. Frederick Douglass, *My Bondage and My Freedom* (New York: Miller, Orton and Milligan, 1855), 328–329; Jonathan D. Martin, *Divided Mastery: Slave Hiring in the American South* (Cambridge: Harvard University Press, 2004), 166 [quote], 181–182, 187; Charles C. Jones Jr. to Charles C. Jones Sr., 1 October 1856, in *Children of Pride: A True Story of Georgia and*

the *Civil War*, ed. Robert Mason Myers (New Haven, CT: Yale University Press, 1972), 240–243; T. Stephen Whiteman, *Challenging Slavery in the Chesapeake: Black and White Resistance to Human Bondage, 1775–1865* (Baltimore: Maryland Historical Society, 2007), 80; Christopher Phillips, *Freedom's Port: The African American Community of Baltimore, 1790–1860* (Urbana: University of Illinois Press, 1997), chap. 2.

4. Calvin Schermerhorn, *Money over Mastery, Family over Freedom: Slavery in the Antebellum Upper South* (Baltimore: Johns Hopkins University Press, 2011), 137–139.

5. John Codman Hurd, *The Law of Freedom and Bondage in the United States*, 2 vols. (Boston: Little, Brown, 1862; reprint, New York: Negro University Press, 1968), 2:85; *The Public Acts of the General Assembly of North Carolina Containing the Acts from 1790–1803* (New Bern: Martin and Ogden, 1804), 120–121; *Acts and Resolutions of the General Assembly, of the State of South-Carolina Passed in December, 1800* (Columbia: Daniel and J. J. Faust, 1801), 39–41; *Supplement to the Revised Code of the Laws of Virginia: Being a Collection of All the Acts of the General Assembly of a Public and Permanent Nature Passed Since the Year 1819* (Richmond, VA: Samuel Shepherd, 1833), 236. The five states included North Carolina, South Carolina, Virginia, Georgia, and Tennessee. John Hope Franklin and Loren Schweninger, *Runaway Slaves: Rebels on the Plantation* (New York: Oxford University Press, 1999), 258.

6. Petition of Gibson Keadle to the Chancery Court of Prince George's County, Maryland, 21 February 1810, in SC, *Gibson Keadle v. Ninian T. Willett*, Microfilm M 11081, Frame/Pages 50, Volume 4239-5, Document/Case 2918, MSA; Related Documents: Agreement, Negro John and Ninian T. Willett, 30 December 1800; Statement, Baker, 1 June 1816, with *Keadle v. Willett*. PAR 20981004. No decree with petition. For a discussion of self-purchase in Louisiana, see Judith Kelleher Schaffer, *Becoming Free, Remaining Free: Manumission and Enslavement in New Orleans, 1846–1862* (Baton Rouge: Louisiana State University Press, 2003), chap. 3.

7. Matthew Salafia, *Slavery's Borderlands: Freedom and Bondage along the Ohio River* (Philadelphia: University of Pennsylvania Press, 2013), 126–127.

8. Petition of Patience, Juliet, Levin, George, Rhoda, Arthur, Nathan, Peggy, and David to the County Court of Somerset County, Maryland, 23 April 1825, in SC, *Patience, Juliet, Levin, George, et al. v. Isaac Morris, Joshua Morris, John Morris, Isaac, et al.*, Microfilm M 11014, Frame/Page 11, Volume 4239-1, Document/Case 8, MSA; Related Documents: Transcript of Court Record, Somerset County Court, 23 April 1825–31 May 1827; Copy of Deed of Manumission, Joshua Morris Sr., Worcester County, 11 October 1806; Clerk's Certification, Worcester County Court, 15 April 1825; Copy of Will, Joshua Morris Sr., Worcester County, 23 January 1819; Copy of Probate Record, Worcester County, 2 March 1819; Register of Wills Certification, Worcester County, 15 April 1825; Clerk's Certification, Somerset County Court, 27 July 1827; Agreement, Somerset County, ca. 1829; Appellants' Statements, Court of Appeals for the Eastern Shore, 1 June 1829, 5 June 1830, with *Patience et al. v. Morris et al.* PAR 20982503. GAA.

9. Petition of Adam Johnson to the Circuit Court of the District of Columbia, 25 June 1822, in RUSCC-CDRCF, *Adam Johnson v. George Clarke*, Record Group 21, Book 3, Box/Drawer 18, Entry Folder 20, Document/Case 40, NA; Related Documents: Answer, George Clarke, 12 October 1822; Injunction, George Clarke, 11 June 1822; Deed of Manumission, Adam Johnson, 17 June 1822; Receipt of Adam Johnson, 23 June 1822; Summons, George Clarke, 26 June 1822; Order, 12 October 1822, with *Johnson v. Clarke*. PAR 20482201. Granted.

10. JCCASN, *Doubrere v. Grillier's Syndic*, La., 2 Mart. N. S. 171, February 1824, 3:474. G DARev.

11. Petition of Samuel Wilkinson to the Chancery Court of Jefferson County, Kentucky, 15 September 1837, in Records of the Circuit Court, Case Files, *Samuel Wilkinson v. James Roberts*, Box/Drawer 2-18, Document/Case 855, KDLA; Related Documents: Permission to Labor, Samuel Wilkinson, 10 January 1836; Amended Bill, 22 September 1837; Answer, James Roberts, 27 October 1837; Deposition, Joseph Stephens, 25 January 1838; Court Record and Decree, 21 May 1838, with *Wilkinson v. Roberts*. PAR 20783711. Granted.

12. Petition of Reuben to the Common Pleas Court of Kent County, Delaware, 10 December 1795, in Records of the Court of Common Pleas, *Reuben v. Daniel James*, Microfilm Reel 1, Frame/Pages 217–229, DSA; Related Documents: Interrogatories, George Ferguson, May

1796, 1797; Affirmation, George Ferguson, 3 May 1797; Commission, Caleb Boyer and Matthew Driver, May 1797, with *Reuben v. James*. PAR 20379523. Dismissed.

13. JCCASN, *François v. Lobrano*, 10 Rob. La. 450, April 1845, 3:569. DAA. Judith Kelleher Schafer, *Slavery, the Civil Law, and the Supreme Court of Louisiana* (Baton Rouge: Louisiana State University Press, 1994), 228–229.

14. Thomas D. Morris, *Southern Slavery and the Law, 1619–1860* (Chapel Hill: University of North Carolina Press, 1996), 380–385; JCCASN, *The Guardian of Sally (a negro) v. Beaty*, S.C., 1 Bay 260, May 1792, 2:267, 275–276. GAA. See also an action of trover [recover the value of personal property that has been wrongfully disposed of by another person] in favor of a quasi-free, self-purchased slave, JCCASN, *Linam v. Johnson*, S.C., 2 Bailey 137, January 1831, 2:344. GAA.

15. Petition of Rebecca Garrett, Richard Garrett, Sarah Jane Garrett, Joseph Franklin Garrett, Matilda Garrett, Maria Garrett, and Benjamin Presslman, attorney, to the Court of Baltimore County, Maryland, 8 March 1849, in SC, *Rebecca Garrett, Richard Garrett, Sarah Jane Garrett, et al. v. Thomas Anderson*, Microfilm M 11014, Frame/Pages 3, Volume 4239-3, Document/ Case 164, MSA; Related Documents: Transcript of Court Proceedings, 8 March 1849–3 June 1850; Testimony, Captain Hewett, Mr. Presslman, ca. September 1849; Testimony, Lewis Maller, 27 May 1850; Order, 30 May 1850; Copy of Will of Sarah Cord, 10 September 1804; Appellate Court Ruling, 28 June 1850, with *Garrett et al. v. Anderson*. PAR 20984917. JCCASN, *Anderson v. Garrett*, Md., 9 Gill 120, June 1850, 4:112–113. D GARev.

16. JCCASN, *Contee v. Garner*, D.C., 6 Fed. Cas. 361 (2 Cranch C. C. 162), December 1818, 4:170. DAA. In this case, a slave signed a bond to pay his master for his freedom. The judge ruled that it was *non est factum* ["it is not [my] deed"]; slaves did not have the legal right to make such a contract.

17. JCCASN, *Beall v. Joseph (a negro)*, Ky., Hardin 51, May 1806, 1:281. D GARev. Mark Tushnet, *The American Law of Slavery, 1810–1860: Considerations of Humanity and Interest* (Princeton, NJ: Princeton University Press, 1981), 196–197; Marlin Christopher Barber, "Citizens under the Law: African Americans Confront the Justice System in Kentucky, Missouri, and Texas" (PhD diss., University of Missouri, 2011), 95–96.

18. JCCASN, *Richard v. Van Meter*, D.C., 20 Fed. Cas. 682 (2 Cranch C. C. 214), December 1827, 4:180; *Reports of Cases Civil and Criminal in the United States Circuit Court of the District of Columbia, 1801–1841*, 6 vols., comp. William Cranch (Boston: Little, Brown, 1852), 3:214–216. DAA.

19. James Benson Sellers, *Slavery in Alabama* (Tuscaloosa: University of Alabama Press, 1950), 232; for other states, see JCCASN, *Nat (a man of color) v. Ruddle*, 3 Mo. 400, June 1834, 5:143. DAA. *Redmond (of color) v. Murray*, Mo., 30 Mo. 570, October 1860, 5:213–214. DAA. PAR 20285101. *Jackson v. Bob*, 18 Ark. 399, January 1857, 5:250–251. D GARR.

20. Petition of Moses to the Circuit Court of Barren County, Kentucky, 12 June 1844, in Records of the Circuit Court, Equity Judgments, *Moses v. George Wilcoxen, Catharine Wilcoxen, Daniel Wilcoxen, et al., Heirs of Isaac Wilcoxen*, Microfilm Reel 218714, Document/Case 1505, KDLA; Related Documents: PARs 20782904, 20783822, 20783922; Amended Bill, 18 September 1845; Depositions, James Hardy, Elias Smith, William Harlow and Drewery Roberts, 1 September 1846; Decree, ca. June 1847, with *Moses v. Wilcoxen et al*. PAR 20784408. Granted.

21. Petition of Adam Smith and William Garrett, next friend, to the Chancery Court of Williamson County, Tennessee, 31 October 1843, in Records of the Chancery Court, *Adam and William Garrett v. Michael Garrett, Overton Kennedy, and Amos Hurley*, Williamson County Archives, Franklin, Tennessee; Related Documents: Answer, Amos Hurly, ca. 1843 [incomplete]; Decree, 9 May 1845, with *Garrett v. Garrett et al*. PAR 21484311. Granted.

22. For mixed results, see JCCASN, *Major (of color) v. Winn*, Ky., 13 B. Mon. 250, September 1852, 1:406. DAA. *Norris (of color) v. Patton*, Ky., 15 B. Mon. 575, June 1855, 1:418–419. DAA.

23. Petition of James King and Mary King to the Chancery Court of Jefferson County, Kentucky, 18 July 1835, in Records of the Circuit Court, Case Files, *James King and Mary King v. Henry C. Pope*, Box/Drawer 2-3, Document/Case 128, KDLA; Related Documents: Answer, Henry C. Pope, 21 July 1835; Deed of Emancipation, Henry C. Pope to Mary King, 22 June 1837; Writ of *Habeas Corpus*, 18 July 1835; Orders, 18 July 1835, with *King et al. v. Pope*. PAR 20783501. Granted.

24. Petition of Daphne Lawson to the Chancery Court of Henrico County, Virginia, 9 March 1820, in Ended Chancery Court Causes, *Daphne Lawson v. Robert McCracken*, Box/Drawer 79-7, LV; Related Documents: Conditional Agreement of Emancipation, Robert McCracken, October 1808; Hiring Permit, Robert McCracken to Daphne, 29 January 1814; Receipt, 18 August 1819; Bill of Sale, Robert McCracken, 14 May 1808; Supplemental Petition, 9 March 1820; Court Record, 9 March 1820 to 4 December 1820; Affidavit, Peyton Drew, 8 August 1820; Decree, 9 August 1820; Sheriff's Return, 19 October 1820; Answer, Robert McCracken, 30 June 1820, with *Lawson v. McCracken*. PAR 21682017. Granted.

25. Petition of Joseph Cooke to the Circuit Court of the District of Columbia, 27 March 1827, in RUSCC-CDRCF, *Joseph Cooke v. John Davidson and Thomas Wilson*, Record Group 21, Box/Drawer 1, Entry Folder 20, NA; Related Documents: Affidavit, Lund Washington, 27 March 1827, with *Cooke v. Davidson et al.* PAR 20482701. Injunction granted.

26. JCCASN, *Brown v. Wingard*, D.C., 4 Fed. Cas. 438 (2 Cranch C. C. 300), April 1822, 4:172; *Brown v. Wingard*, 4 Fed. Cas. 438, 2 Cranch C. C. 300, 2 D.C. 300, No. 2034 (C. C. Dist. Col., 1822); *Reports of Cases Civil and Criminal in the United States Circuit Court of the District of Columbia, 1801–1841*, 2:261–262; *Joseph Brown, (Negro,) v. Mary Wigard*. DAA.

27. Letitia Woods Brown, *Free Negroes in the District of Columbia, 1790–1846* (New York: Oxford University Press, 1972), 109; *Letty v. Lowe*, December 1825, in *Reports of Cases Civil and Criminal in the United States Circuit Court of the District of Columbia*, 2:634–636; JCCASN, *Letty v Lowe*, D.C., 15 Fed. Cas. 411 (2 Cranch C. C. 634), May 1826, 4:177–178. DAA. Cranch sympathized with the plaintiffs, however. In response to Letty's freedom suit claiming she owed only thirty-six dollars, the court issued judgment for defendant upon demurrer, "without prejudice" concerning a "self-purchase agreement."

28. Petition of Jeremiah Drummond to the Circuit Court of Fayette County, Kentucky, 8 March 1816, in Records of the Circuit Court, Case Files, *Jeremiah Drummond v. Francis Carlton and Benjamin Stout*, Box/Drawer 40, Document/Case 362, KDLA; Related Documents: Deposition, John D. Young, 13 January 1817, with *Drummond v. Carlton et al.* PAR 20781605. Dismissed, agreement.

29. Petition of Tom to the District Court of Pointe Coupee Parish, Louisiana, 18 May 1854, in Records of the Ninth Judicial District Court, *Tom v. René Porche*, Document/Case 1,126, Pointe Coupee Parish Courthouse, New Roads, Louisiana; Related Documents: Amended Petition, 6 June 1854; Testimony of Emile Jarreau, et al [text in English and French], 20 March 1855; Judgment, 6 June 1855, with *Tom v. Porche*. PAR 20885414. Nonsuit. Schafer, *Becoming Free*, 11–12.

30. *Acts Passed at the First Session of the Twentieth General Assembly of the State of Tennessee, 1833* (Nashville: Allen A. Hall & Frederick S. Heiskell, 1833), 99–100 [contracts for freedom]; Timothy S. Huebner, "Judicial Independence in an Age of Democracy, Sectionalism, and War, 1835–1865," in *A History of the Tennessee Supreme Court*, ed. James W. Ely (Knoxville: University of Tennessee Press, 2002), 93–94; JCCASN, *Greenlow v. Rawlings*, Tenn., 3 Humphreys 90, April 1842, 2:514–515. GAA. *Lewis v. Simonton*, Tenn., 8 Humphreys 185, December 1847, 2:534–535. GAA. *Ford v. Ford*, Tenn. 7 Humphreys 92, September 1846, 2:479, 530 [quote of Nathan Green]. GAA. Arthur F. Howington, "'Not in the Condition of a Horse or an Ox': *Ford v. Ford*, the Law and Testamentary Manumission, and the Tennessee Courts' Recognitions of Slave Humanity," *Tennessee Historical Quarterly* 34, no. 3 (1975): 249–263; JCCASN, *Isaac (a man of color) v. Farnsworth*, Tenn., 3 Head 275, September 1859, 2:574; *Isaac (a man of color), by Next Friend v. Henry Farnsworth, et al.*, September 1859, in *Reports of Cases Argued and Determined in the Supreme Court of Tennessee During the Years 1859–1860*, comp. John W. Head (Nashville: S. C. Mercer, 1866), 275–280. GAA.

31. Schafer, *Becoming Free*, 51; Petition of Austin Tripplet to the Circuit Court of the District of Columbia, 19 November 1845, in RUSCC-CDRCF, *Austin Tripplet v. Henry Lloyd*, Record Group 21, Rules 4, Box/Drawer 59, Entry Folder 20, Document/Case 394, NA; Related Documents: Order, 19 November 1945; Receipts, Henry Lloyd, 22 May 1845, 26 March 1845, 6 September 1845, 1 November 1845, 19 July 1845, 14 April 1845, 7 September 1845, with *Tripplet v. Lloyd*. PAR 20484502. Granted.

32. Petition of Eliza Brooks the Elder, Sarah Brooks, Eliza Brooks the Younger, and Robert S. Ferguson to the Chancery Court of Washington County, Tennessee, 15 April 1850, in

Washington County Court Records, Chancery Court, *Eliza Brooks the Elder, Sarah Brooks, Eliza Brooks the Younger, and Robert S. Ferguson v. Charles Greene, Richard H. Deakins, and Robert Brooks*, Record Group 18, Box/Drawer 153B, Entry Folder 6, AAETSU; Related Documents: Order, 15 April 1850; Decree, 17 May 1852; Writ of *Fieri Facias* and Bill of Costs, May 1852, with *Brooks et al. v. Green et al.* PAR 21485016. Settled in favor of plaintiffs. In 1850, Robert Brooks, age sixty-one, headed a family with Mary Brooks, age forty-eight, listed as mulatto, Sarah Brooks, age fifteen, and Robert Brooks, age seven. USMSPC, Washington County, Tennessee, Swinneys Subdivision, 1850, ancestry.com; in 1860, the census listed Eliza age thirty-three, Robert age forty-one, Sarah age six, and Eliza age two; Robert possessed no property. USMSPC, Washington County, Tennessee, Subdivision 4, image 100, ancestry.com.

33. Petition of Emily, Betsy, Spicy, Edmund, and Quisen [Levi?] B. Jones to the Circuit Court of Woodford County, Kentucky, 1 September 1845, in Records of the Circuit Court, Case Files, *Emily, Betsy, Spicy, et al. v. Robert Adams, Benjamin Bailey, and George McConnel*, Box/Drawer 134, KDLA; Related Documents: Answer, Robert Adams, 3 March 1846; Order, ca. 1848; Amended Bill, 30 March 1848; Answer, Waller Chenault, 27 December 1848; Abstract, March 1848, Bill of Revivor, ca. 1850; Answer to Bill of Revivor, David Adams, 7 September 1850, with *Emily et al. v. Adams et al.* PAR 20784506. Granted. JCCASN, *Jones v. Bennet*, Ken., 9 Dana 333, May 1840, 1:339–340. G GARR. Edward M. Post, "Kentucky Law Concerning Emancipation and Freedom of Slaves," *Filson Club History Quarterly* 59 (July 1985): 362–363; Arnold Taylor, *Suing for Freedom in Kentucky* (Bangor, ME: BookLocker.com, 2010), 50–54.

34. Petition of Susannah Williams to the Chancery Court of Anne Arundel County, Maryland, 26 February 1806, in SC, Microfilm M 11081, Volume 4239-5, Document/Case 4015, MSA. PAR20980604. Granted.

35. Petition of Susan Philips, Samuel Franklin Philips, and Catherine Philips to the County Court of Williamson County, Tennessee, 20 January 1846, in Records of the County Court, Emancipations, Williamson County Archives, Franklin, Tennessee. PAR 21484603. Granted. USMSPC, Williamson County, Tennessee, Ninth Civil District, 1850, p. 502 [handwritten number]. It took Susan Phillips sixteen years to pay for herself and save enough for her son's purchase price of $400. By then she also had a daughter.

36. JCCASN, *David Jarman v. Humphrey*, NC, 6 Jones N. C. 28, December 1858, 2:218. GAA.

37. Patience Essah, *A House Divided: Slavery and Emancipation in Delaware, 1638–1865* (Charlottesville: University Press of Virginia, 1996), 38–41, 44–45; William H. Williams, *Slavery and Freedom in Delaware, 1693–1865* (Wilmington, DE: Scholarly Resources, 1996), 186, 250.

38. Petition of Robert Hammond and Peter Hammond to the Common Pleas Court of Kent County, Delaware, 24 April 1811, in Records of the Court of Common Pleas, *Robert Hammond and Peter Hammond v. William Hazzard*, Microfilm Reel R79.2, Record Group 1325, DSA. PAR 20381105. No decree with petition. Result not found in KCCCP-CJD.

39. JCCASN, *Isaac Tindal v. Hudson*, Del., 2 Harrington 441, Fall 1838, 4:215. GAA.

40. Max Grivno, *Gleanings of Freedom: Free and Slave Labor along the Mason Dixon Line, 1790–1860* (Urbana: University of Illinois Press, 2011), 179. For a free black father working to free his daughter and probably paying the owner for her freedom, see Petition of Rebecca and B. F. Graves to the Circuit Court of Fayette County, Kentucky, 21 January 1850, in Records of the Circuit Court, Case Files, *Rebecca and B. F. Graves v. Venus Breckenridge and John Gilbert*, Box/Drawer 132, Document/Case 686, KDLA; Related Documents: Answer, John Gilbert, 8 March 1850; Bill of Sale, Edward Allender to John Gilbert, 26 May 1835; Commissioner's Report, 3 August 1839; Statement, John Gilbert, 29 February 1839; Answer, Venus Breckenridge, 14 February 1850; Deposition, John Gilbert, 7 September 1850; Decree, 30 November 1850, with *Graves et al. v. Breckenridge et al.* PAR 20785002. Granted.

41. Petition of John H. Gray and Billy Armour to the County Court of Shelby County, Tennessee, January 1850, in Records of the County Court, Document/Case 557, Memphis and Shelby County Archives, Memphis, Tennessee; Related Documents: Report, January Term 1850; Bill of Sale, John D. Armour to Rev. John H. Gray, 5 July 1846; Acknowledgment, John D. Armour, 5 January 1850; Receipts, Billy to J. B. Kirtland, 5 July 1848 and 7 November 1848; Notice of Emancipation for Billy Armour, John H. Gray, 4 January 1850; Solicitor's Memorandum, January 1850; Affidavit, William Armour Jr., 7 January 1850; Bond, John

H. Gray, Billy Armour, Isaac R. Kirtland, J. T. Swayne, January 1850; Decree, January Term 1850, with petition of Amour. Granted. PAR 21485057. In 1850, William Armour was cited in the census as a forty-four-year-old shoemaker living with his wife Rachel. USMSPC, Shelby County, Tennessee, Memphis, 4th Ward, 1850, image 13, ancestry.com.

42. JCCASN, "South Carolina: Introduction," 2:267–268.

43. Amrita Chakrabarti Myers, *Forging Freedom: Black Women and the Pursuit of Liberty in Antebellum Charleston* (Chapel Hill: University of North Carolina Press, 2011), 1; Petition of J. E. Holmes to the President of the South Carolina Senate, in Records of the General Assembly, ca. 1822, Document ND 1751, SCDAH; Related Documents: Sponsor: William Crafts Jr., Senate, St. Philip and St. Michael Parish, with petition of Holmes. PAR 11382227. Granted.

44. Petition of Mary Donoho to the Circuit Court of the District of Columbia, 8 September 1828, in RUSCC-CDRCF, *Mary Donoho v. Archibald Thompson and Henry Ryan*, Record Group 21, Rules 2, Box/Drawer 33, Document/Case 307, NA; Related Documents: Bond, Mary Donoho and John Baker, 8 September 1828; Injunction, Archibald Thompson and Henry Ryan, 8 September 1828, with *Donoho v. Thompson et al.* PAR 20482801. Granted.

45. Petition of Dicey to the Chancery Court of Jefferson County, Kentucky, 17 February 1838, in Records of the Circuit Court, Case Files, *Dicey v. Michael McMann*, Box/Drawer 2-23, Document/Case 1116, KDLA; Related Documents: Affidavit, Sarah Christopher, 17 July 1838; Order, 17 February 1838; Answer, Michael McMann, 2 March 1838; Bill of Sale, John Edwards and Jacob Geiger to Michael McMann, 26 November 1832; Decree, 12 February 1839, with *Dicey v. McMann*. PAR 20783802. Granted.

46. Petition of William Kennedy to the Circuit Court of the District of Columbia, 23 March 1828, in RUSCC-CDRCF, *William Kennedy v. William Gadsly, Augustus Newton, J. Purnell Pendleton, and William H. Williams*, Record Group 21, Rules 3, Box/Drawer 46, Entry Folder 20, Document/Case 478, NA; Related Documents: Injunction, William Gadsly, Augustus Newton, William H. Williams, and J. Purnell Pendleton, 23 March 1838; Summons, William Gadsly, Augustus Newton, William H. Williams, and J. Purnell Pendleton, 23 March 1838, with *Kennedy v. Gadsly et al.* PAR 20483805. Granted.

47. JCCASN, *Rosine and others v. Bonnabel*, 5 Rob. La. 163, June 1843, 3:553. G DARR.

48. Harrold, *Subversives: Anti-Slavery Community*, 94, 98, 103–104, 114; Petition of Lucy Crawford to the Circuit Court of the District of Columbia, 18 October 1845, in RUSCC-CDRCF, *Lucy Crawford v. Martha A. Scott and Alexander Hunter*, Record Group 21, Rules 4, Box/Drawer 58, Entry Folder 20, Document/Case 387, NA; Related Documents: Injunction, Martha Scott, 18 October 1845; Request for Dismissal, J. Hellen for complainant, 21 October 1845, with *Crawford v. Scott et al.* PAR 20484503. Granted.

49. Petition of Adam Johnson to the Circuit Court of the District of Columbia, 25 June 1822, in RUSCC-CDRCF, *Adam Johnson v. George Clarke*, Record Group 21, Book 3, Box/Drawer 18, Entry Folder 20, Document/Case 40, NA; Related Documents: Answer, George Clarke, 12 October 1822; Injunction, George Clarke, 11 June 1822; Deed of Manumission, Adam Johnson, 17 June 1822; Receipt of Adam Johnson, 23 June 1822; Summons, George Clarke, 26 June 1822; Order, 12 October 1822, with *Johnson v. Clarke*. PAR 20482201. Granted. JCCASN, *Letty v. Low*, D.C. 15 Fed. Cas. 411 (2 Cranch C. C. 634), May 1826, 4:177–178; *Reports of Cases Civil and Criminal in the United States Circuit Court of the District of Columbia*, 2:634–636; Brown, *The Free Negro in the District of Columbia, 1790–1846*, 109. DAA.

50. Petition of Nancy Ann to the Chancery Court of Jefferson County, Kentucky, 22 November 1844, in Records of the Circuit Court, Case Files, *Nancy Ann v. Peter Talbott and William Shephard*, Box/Drawer 2-78, Document/Case 4491, KDLA; Related Documents: Amended Bill, 28 January 1845; Receipt, Peter Talbot to Lewis Thomas, 20 April 1840; Amended Bill, 8 April 1845; Decree, 23 March 1845, with *Nancy Ann v. Talbott et al.* PAR 20784416. Granted. The judge indicated importance of witness testimony in rendering his decision.

51. Schafer, *Slavery, the Civil Law*, 229–230; JCCASN, *Gaudet v. Gourdain*, et al., 3 La. An. 136, February 1848, 3:588; Petition of Azéla Gaudet to the District Court of St. James Parish, Louisiana, 21 October 1846, in Supreme Court of Louisiana Collection, *Azéla Gaudet v. Jean Gourdain and Joseph Marcel Braud*, Book 364, Document/Case 714, UNO; Related

Documents: Order, 21 October 1846; Verdict, 11 January 1847; Testimonies, Valery Gaudet, et al [text in French], ca. January 1847; Judgment, 11 January 1847; Motion for New Trial, ca. January 1847; Order, ca. January 1847; Supreme Court Opinion and Decree, 3 February 1848; Petition of Opposition, Jean Gourdain, n.d.; Copy of Supreme Court Opinion and Decree, 14 February 1848, with *Gaudet v. Gourdain*. PAR 20884624. G DARev.

52. JCCASN, *Willis (of color) v. Bruce*, Ky., 8 B. Mon. 548, September 1848, 1:387–388. DAA.

53. Petition of Billey Kelley to the Chancery Court of Warren County, Tennessee, 5 January 1852, in Supreme Court Cases, Middle Tennessee, *Billey Kelley v. Thomas C. Smartt and Abner Kelly [Kelley]*, Box/Drawer 99A, TSLA; Related Documents: Order, 3 January 1852; Answer, Abner Smartt, 5 April 1852; Copy of Bill of Sale, Trott to Laughlin, 17 April 1853; Replication, Billey Kelley, ca. April 1852; Depositions, Elijah Stephens and Henry D. McBroom, 9 September 1853; Decree, March Term, 1852; Decree, September Term 1852; Decree, March Term 1853, with *Kelley v. Smartt et al.* PAR 21485225. No final decree with case file.

54. See note 2, this chapter. The appeals court noted that a slave could not enter into a contract with his master, but the owner sanctioned his going at large for an extended period. She must therefore bear the consequences his "seizure and sale amounting to an importation within the meaning of the act of 1796, ch. 67," despite his return to Maryland not being condoned by his owner. USMSPC, New York City, New York, 5th Ward, 1840, image 221, ancestery.com.

Chapter 9

1. See note 64, this chapter.

2. Loren Schweninger, *Black Property Owners in the South, 1790-1915* (Urbana: University of Illinois Press, 1990), 135.

3. Quoted in Carol Wilson, *Freedom at Risk: The Kidnapping of Free Blacks in America, 1780-1865* (Frankfort: University of Kentucky Press, 1994), 43.

4. *Richmond Enquirer*, July 5, 1850.

5. *Nashville Whig*, December 25, 1816.

6. *New Orleans Bee*, October 7, 1833. See John Hope Franklin and Loren Schweninger, *Runaway Slaves: Rebels on the Plantation* (New York: Oxford University Press, 1999), 184.

7. Petition of Ceasar or Casar Colick to the Court of General Sessions, Kent County, Delaware, 7 December 1795, in Court Papers ca. 1776–1867. DSA. PAR 20379502.

8. Petition of Samuel Legg to Court of General Sessions, Kent County, Delaware, 10 December 1795, in Court Papers ca. 1776–1867. DSA. PAR 20379506. Petition of Jesse Brooks to Court of General Sessions, Kent County, Delaware, 1 December 1795, in Court Papers ca. 1776–1867, DSA. PAR 20379505.

9. Petition of Peter Sweeper to the Circuit Court of Jackson County, Tennessee, March 1839, in Supreme Court Cases, Middle Tennessee, *Peter Sweeper v. William Woodfolk*, Box/Drawer 63, TSLA; Related Documents: Court Transcript, ca. 21 September 1835–25 November 1840; Copy of Baltimore County Court Records, *State v. Peter Sweeper*, September Term 1826; Copy of Petition, ca. 21 September 1835; Copy of Plea of Trespass, March Term 1836, with *Sweeper v. Woodfolk*. PAR 21483921. He won a verdict in the lower court for his freedom and for $743 in damages. The appeals court ruled that Sweeper was entitled to his freedom but not entitled to the damages but could file a separate suit for payment. JCCASN, *Woodfolk v. Sweeper*, Tenn., 2 Humphreys 88, December 1840, 2:511; *Reports of Cases Argued and Determined in the Supreme Court of Tennessee*, vol. 2, comp. West H. Humphreys; new edition with notes and references (St. Louis: G. I. Jones and Company, 1872), 88–96. GAA.

10. "List of free negroes to be Sold for taxes," Records of the County Court, Prince Edward County, Virginia, Box 41, Packet January–April 1847, LV.

11. Petition of Louisa Alexander and Eliza Alexander to the Circuit Superior Court of Campbell County, Virginia, 23 January 1840, in Records of the Circuit Superior Court of Chancery, *Louisa Alexander and Eliza Alexander v. John P. White and Adam Clement*, Box/Drawer 1853, Circuit Court Building, Rustburg, Virginia; Related Documents: Order, 27 January 1840; Answer and Affidavit, John P. White, 10 March 1840, with *Alexander et al. v. White et al.* PAR 21684008. Suit abated with Louisa's death.

12. Article 1, Section 9, in http://www.usconstitution.net/xconst_A1Sec9.html.

13. Petition of John J. Robinson to the Criminal Court of Warren County, Mississippi, 4 November 1836, in Natchez Trace Slaves and Slavery Collection, *John J. Robinson v. State of Mississippi*, Box/Drawer 2E773, CAHUT; Related Document: Order, 5 November 1836, with *Robinson v. State*. PAR 21083606. Granted.

14. Petition of Edward Hammons to the Superior Court of Craven County, North Carolina, 3 June 1841, in Records of the County Court, Slaves and Free Negroes 1775–1861, NCDAH; Related Documents: Writ of *Habeas Corpus*, 4 June 1841; Sheriff's Report, 8 June 1841; Authorization, 10 December 1840; Order, 4 June 1841, with petition of Hammons. PAR 21284115. Granted. Hammons remained in jail for six months.

15. Petition of John McKenney to the Circuit Court of the District of Columbia, 31 October 1820, in RUSDC-SHCP, Record Group 21, Box/Drawer 1, Entry Folder 28, NA.PAR 20482002. Granted. See also Petition of Robert Henry Jackson to the Chancery Court of Jefferson County, Kentucky, 8 December 1860, in Records of the Circuit Court, Case Files, *Robert Henry Jackson v. William K. Thomas and John Lambert*, Box/Drawer 2-216, Document/Case 16279, KDAH; Related Documents: Answers, William K. Thomas, John Lamborn, 11 January 1861; Order and Opinion, ca. 1861, with *Jackson v. Thomas et al*. PAR 20786012. Granted.

16. Ira Berlin, *Slaves without Masters: The Free Negro in the Antebellum South* (New York: Pantheon, 1974), 136, 176–177.

17. Petition of Thomas Waddle to the County Court of Baltimore County, Maryland, March 1811, in SC, *Thomas Waddle v. Samuel Haney and Robert Long*, Microfilm M 11014, Frame/Pages 10, Volume 4239-3, Document/Case 62, MSA; Related Documents: Court Record, March 1811–8 May 1811, with *Waddle v. Haney et al*. PAR 20981115. JCCASN, *Haney v. Waddle*, 3 Har. and John. 557 March 1815, 4:64 "a minor could do no act to affect his rights, nor could his guardian for him." D GARev. Petition of John Singleton to the Circuit Court of St. Louis County, Missouri, 30 August 1827, in Records of the Circuit Court, *John Singleton v. Alexander Scott and Robert Lewis*, Document/Case 23, CCBSL; Related Documents: Order, 31 August 1827; Plea of Trespass and Copy of Plea of Trespass, 3 September 1827; Sheriff's Return, 5 September 1827; Copy of Order, 31 August 1827; Subpoena, Alexander Scott and Robert Lewis, 3 September 1827, with *Singleton v. Scott et al*. PAR 21182704. Granted. Petition of Caroline Brooks to the Circuit Court of the District of Columbia, 5 April 1834, in RUSDC-SHCP, Record Group 21, Box/Drawer 1, Entry Folder 28, NA; PAR 20483401. Granted. Petition of Katharine Smith to the Circuit Court of theDistrict of Columbia, 10 November 1834, in, RUSDC-SHCP, Record Group 21, Box/Drawer 1, Entry Folder 28, NA. PAR 20483405. Granted.

18. Petition of Richard Coleman to the Criminal Court of Warren County, Mississippi, 30 January 1837, in Natchez Trace Slaves and Slavery Collection, Box/Drawer 2E773, Entry Folder 3, Document/Case 30, CAHUT; Related Documents: Order, 31 January 1837; Sheriff's Return, 31 January 1837; Order, ca. 1837; Affidavit, David Atway, Henderson County, Tennessee, 24 August 1836; Order, 31 January 1837; Rough Minutes, 31 January 1837, with petition of Coleman. Granted. PAR 21083705. Coleman was "legally discharged." In the census, David Attaway [or Allaway], a non-slave owner in his twenties, headed a household with his wife and their five children. USMSPC, Henderson County, Tennessee, 1830, image 3, ancestry.com.

19. Petition of Thornton Kinney to the Circuit Court of St. Louis County, Missouri, July 1853, in Records of the Circuit Court, *Thornton Kinney v. John F. Hatcher and Charles C. Bridges*, Document/Case 35, CCBSL; Related Documents: PARs 21185501, 21185801; Affidavits, Enos L. Litchfield, James Harrison, Charles H. Haven, 23 July 1853; Supplemental Petition, 22 October 1853; Declaration, Thornton Kinney, 25 July 1853; Subpoena, John F. Hatcher, Charles C. Bridges, 25 July 1853; Sheriff's Return, 25 July 1853; Court Record, April Term 1853–March 1856, with *Kinney v. Hatcher, et al*. Hatcher not found in the county. Court dismissed the case because the plaintiff could not provide security. PAR 21185311. Dismissed. In 1856, the plaintiff's lawyer unsuccessfully sought to reinstate the suit. Petition of Margaret Dorsey to the Circuit Court of the District of Columbia, 27 July 1836, in SCBSL, Record Group 21, Box/Drawer 28, Entry Folder 28, NA; Related Documents: Affidavit, William

P. Palmer, 25 July 1836; Writ of *Habeas Corpus*, Margaret Dorsey, 27 July 1836; Marshal's Return, ca. 1836; Order, 27 July 1836, with petition of Dorsey. PAR 20483601. Granted.

20. Petition of Adaline to the District Court of East Baton Rouge Parish, Louisiana, 27 June 1851, in Records of the Sixth Judicial District Court, Document/Case 853, East Baton Rouge Parish, Clerk of Court Archives, Baton Rouge, Louisiana; Related Documents: Order, 27 June 1851; Judgment, 27 June 1851, with petition of Adaline. PAR 20885127. Granted.

21. Petition of Hamilton [also spelled Hambleton] Russel to the Circuit Court of the District of Columbia, 5 August 1835, in RUSDC-SHCP, Record Group 21, Box/Drawer 1, Entry Folder 28, NA; Related Documents: Marshal's Report, 5 August 1835; Writ of *Habeas Corpus*, Hamilton Russell, 5 August 1835; Letter, John Adams, 20 June 1835, with petition of Hamilton. PAR 20483502. Granted.

22. Petition of Jones H. Jenkins to the Circuit Court of the District of Columbia, 27 July 1835, in RUSDC-SHCP, Record Group 21, Box/Drawer 1, Entry Folder 28, NA; Related Documents: Correspondence, Robert Leslie to William Brent, 24 July 1835; Copy of Freedom Certificate, Jones H. Jenkins, 23 July 1835; Confinement Note, Samuel Stettinius, 20 June 1835; Writ of *Habeas Corpus*, 28 July 1835; Marshal's Report, 29 July 1835; Decree, 29 July 1835, with petition of Jenkins. PAR 20483501. Granted.

23. *Laws Made and Passed by the General Assembly of the State of Maryland, at a Session Begun and Held in the City of Annapolis, on Monday the Sixth Day of December, Eighteen Hundred and Twenty-Four* (Annapolis, MD: J. Hughes, 1824), 132–133.

24. Baltimore County Register of Wills (Petitions and Orders), Petition of Frances B [Eoff?], 24 October 1856, Microfilm M-11,020, SC, MSA; Indenture of John Henry Doman to John Breckinridge, 23 October 1856, with petition of [Eoff?]. Franklin and Schweninger, *Runaway Slaves*, 189.

25. Solomon Northrup, *Narrative of Solomon Northrup, a Citizen of New-York, Kidnapped in Washington City in 1841 and Rescued in 1853, from a Cotton Plantation Near the Red River in Louisiana* (Buffalo, NY: Derby, Orton and Mulligan, 1853); Wilson, *Freedom at Risk*, chap. 1.

26. Wilson, *Freedom at Risk*, 68–69; William H. Williams, *Slavery and Freedom in Delaware, 1639–1865* (Wilmington, DE: Scholarly Resources, 1996), 238; Act of 8 February 1826, in *Revised Laws of Delaware*, p. 131; Act of 18 February 1841, in *Session Laws of Delaware*, p. 400.

27. Max Grivno, *Gleanings of Freedom: Free and Slavery Labor along the Mason-Dixon Line, 1790-1860* (Urbana: University of Illinois press, 2011), 136.

28. Quotes in Berlin, *Slaves without Masters*, 99, 160.

29. Petition of Frank Irwin to the District Court of West Feliciana Parish, Louisiana, 6 February 1837, in Records of the Third Judicial District Court and Supreme Court of Louisiana Collection, *Frank Irwin v. Thomas Powell*, Book 3, 280, Document/Case 1,635, West Feliciana Parish Courthouse, St. Francisville, Louisiana; Related Documents: Order, 6 February 1837; Answer, Thomas Powell, 6 May 1837; Testimonies, General Taylor, et al., 19 September 1837–6 December 1837; Judgment, 22 December 1837, Records of the Third Judicial District Court, West Feliciana Parish Courthouse, St. Francisville, Louisiana, with *Irwin v. Powell*. Transcript of Court Records, 6 February 1837–15 November 1837, including Copy of Petition and Order, 6 February 1837; and Testimonies, R. A. Madison, et al., 14 November 1837, certified 15 November 1837; Petition of Appeal, 26 December 1837; Order, 26 December 1837; Supreme Court Opinion and Decree, 5 February 1838, Supreme Court of Louisiana Collection, UNO. PAR 20883713. JCCASN, *Frank (f.m.c.) v. Powell*, 11 La. 499, January 1838, 3:389, 516. GAA. Judith Kelleher Schafer, *Slavery, the Civil Law, and the Supreme Court of Louisiana* (Baton Rouge: Louisiana State University Press, 1994), 262, 271–272; JCCASN, *Julia Arbuckle (f.w.c.) v. Bonny et al.*, 5 La, An. 699, November 1850, 3:608. GAA. *Foster v. Mish*, 15 La. An. 199, April 1860, 3:679. GAA. Judith Kelleher Schafer, *Becoming Free, Remaining Free: Manumission and Enslavement in New Orleans, 1846–1862* (Baton Rouge, Louisiana State University Press, 2003), 119–121, 126; Grivno, *Gleanings of Freedom*, 21–14, 136, 189, 192; Patience Essah, *A House Divided: Slavery and Emancipation in Delaware, 1638–1865* (Charlottesville: University Press of Virginia, 1996), 14, 121–123; Wilson, *Freedom at Risk*, 59, 61, 63.

30. Petition of Harriett Scott to the District Court of St. Landry Parish, Louisiana, 16 May 1829, in Records of the Fifth Judicial District Court, *Harriett Scott v. George Jackson*, Document/

Case 1,514, St. Landry Parish Courthouse, Opelousas, Louisiana; Related Documents: Court Record, 16 May 1829; Answer, Sheriff George Jackson, 16 May 1829; Judgment, 16 November 1830; Supplemental Petition, 27 January 1831; Writ of *Habeas Corpus*, ca. 28 January 1831; Sheriff's Return, 28 January 1831, with *Scott v. Jackson*. PAR 20882912. Granted.

31. Petition of John Roach to the District Court of Orleans Parish, Louisiana, 20 February 1817, in Records of the First Judicial District Court, Case Records, *John Roach v. J. H. Holland*, Microfilm Reel 3, Louisiana Collection, Document/Case 1,353, NOPL; Related Documents: PARs 20881324, 20881533, 20881803, 30882903, 20883458; Order, 20 February 1817; Judgment, 27 November 1817; Answer, J. H. Holland, ca. February 1817; Supplemental Petition, ca. 1817; Deposition, William D. Dixon, 17 April 1817; Countersuit, 19 July 1817; Order 19 July 1817, with *Roach v. Holland*. PAR 20881703. Granted.

32. Schafter, *Becoming Free*, 24–25, 115–116, 118–128; Orville W. Taylor, *Negro Slavery in Arkansas* (Durham, NC: Duke University Press, 1958; reprint, Arkansas University Press, 2000), 74; JCCASN, *Strayhorn v. Giles*, 22 Ark. 517, January 1861 [519], 5:261. GAA. Petition of Henrietta Norris and Flora Moore to the Circuit Court the District of Columbia, 23 May 1835, in RUSCC-CDRCF, *Henrietta Norris and Flora Moore v. George W. Gray and Washington Robey*, Record Group 21, Rules 3, Box/Drawer 43, Document/Case 350, NA; Related Documents: Affidavit, Flora Moore, 23 May 1835; Injunction, George M. Gray and Washington Robey, 23 May 1835, with *Norris v. Gray*. PAR 20483513. Granted. Four Delaware blacks who were freed or about to be freed petitioned the District Court in the District of Columbia. See Petition of Joseph Armstrong, Peter Butler, Emanuel Price, and Maria Coase to the Circuit Court of the District of Columbia, 14 January 1840, in RUSDC-SHCP, Record Group 21, Box/Drawer 1, Entry Folder 28, NA; Related Documents: PARs 20484006, 20484007, 20484008; Affidavit, Francis S. Key, 14 January 1840, with petition of Armstrong et al. PAR 20484002. Granted. Petition of Jim Morton to the Chancery Court of Jefferson County, Kentucky, 26 April 1845, in Records of the Circuit Court, Case Files, *Jim Morton v. Bernard Dougherty*, Box/Drawer 2-82, Document/Case 4693, KDLA; Related Documents: Order, ca. 1845; Amended Bill, 30 April 1845; Order, ca. 1845; Marshal's Report, 22 May 1845; Summons, Bernard Dougherty, 26 April 1845; Order, ca. 1845, with *Morton v. Dougherty*. PAR 20784503. Granted.

33. *Acts and Resolutions of the General Assembly, of the State of South-Carolina, Passed in December, 1800* (Columbia: Daniel & J. J. Faust, 1801), 39–41; Thomas Gibbs Morgan, comp. and ed., *Civil Code of the State of Louisiana: With Statutory Amendments, from 1825 to 1853, Inclusive; and References to the Decisions of the Supreme Court of Louisiana to the Sixth Volume of Annual Reports* (New Orleans: J. B. Steel, 1853), 30–31. They were also required to be age thirty or older. In 1827, the age limit was revised when the assembly permitted judges and police juries in the parishes to decide on the manumission of slaves under age thirty, but only for resident slaves (those born in Louisiana). *Acts Passed at the First Session of the Eighth Legislature of the State of Louisiana, Begun and Held in the City of New-Orleans, on Monday, the First Day of January, in the Year of Our Lord One Thousand Eight Hundred and Twenty-Seven, and of the Independence of the United States of America, the Fifty-First* (New Orleans: John Gibson, 1827), 12, 14.

34. *Acts Passed at a General Assembly of the Commonwealth of Virginia, Begun and Held at the Capitol in the City of Richmond, on Monday the Fourth Day of December, in the Year of Our Lord, One Thousand Eight Hundred and Fifteen, and of the Commonwealth, the Fortieth* (Richmond, VA: Thomas Ritchie, 1816), 51–52; *Acts Passed at the First Session of the Twenty-Fourth General Assembly of the State of Tennessee, 1841–42* (Murfreesborough, TN: D. Cameron, 1842), 229.

35. John Hope Franklin, *The Free Negro in North Carolina, 1790–1860* (Chapel Hill: University of North Carolina Press, 1943), 20–21; Henry W. Farnam, *Chapters in the History of Social Legislation in the United States to 1860* (Washington, DC: Carnegie Institution, 1938), 381.

36. Petition of Joseph Antoine to the Circuit Court of Jefferson County, Kentucky, 19 September 1804, in Records of the Circuit Court, Case Files, *Joseph Antoine v. Emanuel Lacey, Jonathan Purcel, and Davis Floyd*, Document/Case 10, KDLA. PAR 20780403. Granted. Antoine's petition was among the few that were written by a plaintiff.

37. Petition of Esther to the Common Pleas Court of Kent County, Delaware, 8 December 1796, in Records of the Court of Common Pleas, *Esther v. James Johnston and Curtis Morris*, Microfilm Reel 1, Frame/Pages 175–176, DSA. PAR 20379606. KCCCP, May 1797, p. 202, Reel 4, Frame 327, continued. No result.

38. JCCASN, *Lee v. Preuss*, D.C. 15 Fed. Cas. 223 (3 Cranch C. C. 112) May 1827, 4:201. DAA.

39. JCCASN, *Fidelio v. Dermott*, D.C., 8 Fed. Cas. 1175 (1 Cranch C.C. 405), June 1807, 4:160; *Reports of Cases Civil and Criminal in the United States Circuit Court of the District of Columbia, 1801–1841*, 6 vols. comp. William Cranch (Boston: Little, Brown, 1852), 1:405–406. GAA. Letitia Woods Brown, *The Free Negroes in the District of Columbia, 1790–1846* (New York: Oxford University Press, 1972) 201 n.85 [advertisements].

40. JCCASN, *Brown v. Shields*, Va., 6 Leigh 440, May 1835, 1:177; *Reports of Cases Argued and Determined in the Court of Appeals and in the General Court of Virginia*, vol. 6, comp. Benjamin Watkins Leigh (Richmond, VA: Shepherd & Colin, 1837), *Brown v. Shields*, May 1835, 440–456 [revealed the 1824 case of Edmund who ran away to his home county of Rockingham. With the assistance of a number of whites who testified on his behalf, Edmond won his freedom]. Granted. Petition of Jim Morton to the Chancery Court of Jefferson County, Kentucky, 26 April 1845, in Records of the Circuit Court, Case Files, *Jim Morton v. Bernard Dougherty*, Box/Drawer 2-82, Document/Case 4693, KDLA; Related Documents: Order, ca. 1845; Amended Bill, 30 April 1845; Order, ca. 1845; Marshal's Report, 22 May 1845; Summons, Bernard Dougherty, 26 April 1845; Order, ca. 1845, with *Morton v. Dougherty*. PAR 20784503. Granted.

41. JCCASN, *Coots v. Morton*, D.C., 6 Fed. Cas. 496 (5 Cranch C. C. 409), March 1838, 4:201. Granted.

42. JCCASN, *Lee v. Preuss*, 15 Fed. Cas. 223 (3 Cranch C. C. 112), May 1827, 4:179–180. DAA.

43. Petition of Hannah West and Sarah West to the Common Pleas Court of Sussex County, Delaware, 17 November 1818, in Records of the Court of Common Pleas, *Hannah West and Sarah West v. James Jones and Job Ingram*, Microfilm Reel R79.2 or R79.3, DSA; Related Documents: Commission, Jehu Stockley, James Anderson, and Watson Pepper, 25 October 1821; Depositions, Jehu West, Levin M. Coston, Philip Marvel, James P. W. Kollock, Robert Barr, Josiah Marvel, John Kollock, Thomas Scott, William B. Spicer, 9 November 1821, with *West et al. v. Jones et al.* PAR 20381810. Granted.

44. Frederick Law Olmsted, *A Journey in the Seaboard Slave States, with Remarks on Their Economy* (New York: Dix and Edwards, 1856), 82–85; Schweninger, *Black Property Owners in the South*, 36–47.

45. Petition of Adam Johnson to the Circuit Court of the District of Columbia, 25 June 1822, in RUSCC-CDRCF, *Adam Johnson v. George Clarke*, Record Group 21, Book 3, Box/Drawer 18, Entry Folder 20, Document/Case 40, NA; Related Documents: Answer, George Clarke, 12 October 1822; Injunction, George Clarke, 11 June 1822; Deed of Manumission, Adam Johnson, 17 June 1822; Receipt of Adam Johnson, 23 June 1822; Summons, George Clarke, 26 June 1822; Order, 12 October 1822, with *Johnson v. Clarke*. PAR 20482201. Granted. In 1830, Adam Johnson, free person of color age thirty-six to fifty-four, headed a free black family in Talbot County, Maryland, with his wife (same age group) and their four children under age ten. USMSPC, Talbot County, Maryland, 1830, image 73, ancestry.com.

46. Arnold Taylor, *Suing for Freedom in Kentucky* (Bangor, ME: BookLocker.com, 2010), 227–232; JCCASN, *Graham v. Kinder*, Ken., 11 B. Mon. 60, December 1850, 1:396. GAA.

47. JCCASN, *François v. Lobrando*, 10 Rob. La. 450, April 1845, 3:569; Schafer, *Slavery, the Civil Law*, 228–229. DAA.

48. Petition of Bob to the Circuit Court of Sevier County, Arkansas, 20 August 1851, in Arkansas Supreme Court, Records and Briefs, *Bob v. Isaac Jackson*, Document/Case 850, UArLRSL; Related Documents: Court Order, 20 August 1851; Declaration, 22 August 1851; Summons, 21 August 1851; Answer, Isaac Jackson, 23 August 1851; Bill of Exceptions, 23 August 1851; Court Order, 22 August 1851; Statement, 18 August 1852; Answer to Statement, 18 August 1852; Answer, Isaac Jackson, 18 August 1852; Amended Bill, 19 August 1852; Continuances, 29 August 1852, 23 February 1853; Summons and Deposition, George A. Brown, 25 February 1853; Depositions, Isaac A. Fishback, Loliver Neville, 10 August 1853; Interrogatories, February 1853; Deposition, George A. Brown, 9 May 1853; Statement,

16 August 1853; Continuance, 19 August 1853; Verdict, 20 August 1853; Appeal, 20 August 1853; Bill of Exceptions, 20 August 1853; Testimony, David Horan, 8 May 1846; Testimony, George Turrentine, William Bizzell, n. d.; Instructions to Jury, 23 August 1853; Index to Transcript, with *Bob v. Jackson*. JCCASN, *Jackson v. Bob*, 18 Ark 199, January 1857 [402], 5:250. D GARR. The Arkansas Supreme Court ruled that a slave may "pay the money or perform the labor, yet he cannot compel his master to execute the contract, because both the money and the labor of the slave belong to the master and could constitute no legal consideration for the contract."

49. JCCASN, *Emmanuel v. Ball*, 8 Fed. Cas. 611 (2 Cranch C. C. 101, June 1814), 4:167; *Emanuel v. Ball*, 8 Fed. Cas. 611, 2 Cranch C.C. 101, 2 D.C. 101, No. 4433 (C.C. Dist. Col., 1814); *Reports of Cases Civil and Criminal in the United States Circuit Court of the District of Columbia*, 2:101. DAA.

50. Petition of Pelagie Brown to the District Court of Orleans Parish, Louisiana, 5 September 1854, in Supreme Court of Louisiana Collection, *Pelagie Brown v. Ursin Raby*, Book 5,797, Document/Case 7, 854, UNO; Related Documents: Sheriff's Return, 5 October 1854; Note of Evidence and Testimony, Sheriff Pellerin, et al., 9 October 1854; Affidavit, Ursin Raby, n.d., filed 9 October 1854; Recorder's Order for Slave, 5 October 1854; Record of Order Rule, 9 October 1854; Judge's Opinion [fragment], 14 May 1858; Judgment, 14 May 1858; Record of Motion and Order for Appeal, 19 May 1858; Supreme Court's Opinion and Decree, 24 January 1859, with *Brown v. Raby*. PAR 20885451. JCCASN, *Brown (f. w. c.) v. Raby*, 14 La.An 41, January 1859, 3:668. DAA. *New Orleans Daily Picayune*, September 1854, pp. 7, 8, in Schafer, *Becoming Free*, 104.

51. Petition of Mary Donoho to the Circuit Court of the District of Columbia, 8 September 1828, in RUSCC-CDRCF, *Mary Donoho v. Archibald Thompson and Henry Ryan*, Record Group 21, Rules 2, Box/Drawer 33, Document/Case 307, NA; Related Documents: Bond, Mary Donoho and John Baker, 8 September 1828; Injunction, Archibald Thompson and Henry Ryan, 8 September 1828, with *Donoho v. Thompson et al.* PAR 20482801. Injunction granted.

52. Legislative records, petition of Israel Leonard to the legislative council of the Mississippi Territory, ca. 1806, Record Group 5, Series 524, Box 27, MDAH.

53. Petition of Ann Barnet [Barnett] to the Baltimore City Court, Maryland, 12 October 1836, in SC, *Ann Barnet v. Thomas S. Wilson*, Microfilm M 11014, Frame/Pages 32, Volume 4239-3, Document/Case 97, MSA; Related Documents: Transcript of Court Record, 12–27 October 1836; Copy of Will, Elizabeth Richmond, 22 October 1831; Copy of Inventory, Estate of Elizabeth Richmond, 13 June 1832; Order for Sale, August Term 1836; Clerk's Certification, 14 November 1836; Court Record and Writ of Procedendo, 5 December 1836; Clerk's Notation, January 1837, with *Barnet v. Wilson*; JCCASN, *Wilson v. Negro Ann Barnet*, Md., 8 Gill and John. 159, December 1836, 4:83–84; *Wilson v. Negro Ann Barnet*, Md., Gill and John. 158, December 1837, 4:88. PAR 20983620. GAA.

54. JCCASN, *Nolé v. de St. Romes and Wife*, 3 Rob. La. 484, January 1843, 3:549; Schafer, *Slavery, the Civil Law*, 237–238. DAA.

55. Petition of John Peck to the District Court of Orleans Parish, Louisiana, 24 September 1816, in Records of the First Judicial District Court, Case Records, *John Peck v. Mr. Burton and Mr. Gorham*, Microfilm Reel 2, Louisiana Collection, Document/Case 1,179, NOPL; Deposition, William Burton, 21 September 1816; Order, ca. September 1816; Court Record, 7 October 1816; Testimony, Col. John Taylor, 3 November 1817; Judgment, 9 March 1818, with *Peck v. Burton et al.* PAR 20881607. Denied.

56. Petition of Nat to the Circuit Court of St. Louis County, Missouri, 6 May 1833, in Records of the Supreme Court, Case Files, *Nat v. Stephen Ruddle*, Box/Drawer 538, Document/Case 21, MoSA; Related Documents: Transcript of Court Record, 6 May 1833–7 May 1834; Certification, 23 May 1834; Copy of Depositions, Hans Patton, et al., 28 October 1833–10 April 1834; Assignment of Errors, Nat, ca. 23 May 1834, with *Nat v. Ruddle*. PAR 21183303. JCCASN, *Nat (a man of color) v. Ruddle*, 3 Mo. 400, June 1834, 5:143. DAA.

57. Petition of Laura Lyles, Henny Lyles, Richard Lyles, Charles Lyles, Sylvester Lyles, William Lyles, Albert Lyles, and Washington Lyles to the Circuit Court of the District of Columbia, 7 October 1856, in RUSCC-CDRCF, *Laura Lyles, Henny Lyles, Richard Lyles, et al. v. Christopher C. Hyatt and Dionysius Sheriff*, Record Group 21, Rules 5, Box/Drawer 91, Entry Folder 20,

Document/Case 1205, NA; Related Documents: Amended Bill, ca. 1856; Order, 7 October 1856, with *Lyles et al. v. Hyatt et al.* "Injunction refused this 13 of October AD 1856 upon the ground not the case." PAR 20485604. Injunction denied. JCCASN, *Negroes Charles and others v. Sheriff,* 12 Md. 274, July 1858, 4:135; *Sheriff v. negroes Charles and others,* 12 Md. 280, July 1858, 4:136. There were several suits involving this case: one by slave plaintiffs in the District of Columbia seeking a protective injunction that was denied; another by the slave plaintiffs in Maryland asking for a report on the assets in their owner's estate. The lower court refused to grant the request because no affidavit was presented with the bill of complaint. The appeals court reversed this decision: slave plaintiffs could not sign an affidavit because blacks were not capable of testifying against whites (Maryland act of 1846) and reversed the ruling; a third suit in Maryland was filed by the executor of the owner's estate which was dismissed, appealed, and affirmed. There was no final decree presented regarding freedom in the three suits. Numerous records were checked to uncover what happened to the family but to no avail. They may have changed their name or migrated to Liberia.

58. JCCASN, *Battles v. Miller,* D.C., 2 Fed. Cas. 1047 (3 Cranch C. C. 296), May 1828, 4:182; *Reports of Cases Civil and Criminal in the United States Circuit Court of the District of Columbia,* 3:296–298. GAA.

59. Petition of Vina to the Circuit Court of St. Louis County, Missouri, 10 December 1831, in Records of the Circuit Court, *Vina v. Martin Mitchel,* Document/Case 19, CCBSL; Related Documents: PARs 21381602, 21183201, 21183202, 21183203, 21183208, 21383213, 21183215; Plea of Trespass, *Vina vs. Martin Mitchel,* 20 December 1831; Subpoena, Martin Mitchell, 23 December 1831; Sheriff's Return, ca. 1831; Plea of Trespass, 4 May 1833, with *Vina v.Mitchel.* PAR 21183111. Granted. The court awarded the plaintiff $250 in damages.

60. JCCASN, *Mary v. Talburt,* 16 Fed. Cas. 949 (4 Cranch C. C. 187), December 1831, 4:186; Minutes, December 31, 1831, Microfilm Reel 3, Frame 449, at NA [National Archives]; *Reports of Cases Civil and Criminal in the United States Circuit Court of the District of Columbia,* 4:187–188. Granted.

61. Petitions of Jonas, Charles, Turner, and Willis to the Chancery Court of Jefferson County, Kentucky, 14 October 1837, in Records of the Circuit Court, Case Files, *Jonas, Charles, Turner, and Willis v. Sally White, Robert Glass, Sarah Blackburn, et al.,* Box/Drawer 2-19, Document/Case 915, KDLA; Related Documents: Order, 11 October 1837; Answer, Robert W. Glass, 3 April 1838; Answer, Robert G. Vance, 19 April 1838; Deposition, Silas M. Noel, 24 November 1838; Decree, 24 February 1840, with *Jonas et al. v. White et al.* PARs 20783714, 20783715, 20783716, 20783717. JCCASN, *White v. Turner* (a man of color), Ky., 1 B. Mon. 130, December 1840), 1:355. GAA. Taylor, *Suing for Freedom in Kentucky,* 151–161 ["absconded" quote, p. 156]. The suit by Charles was abated due to his death.

62. Petition of Jane Millis to the Court of Common Pleas, Kent County, Delaware, 1822, in Records of the Court of Common Pleas, *Jane Millis v. William Spear,* DSA; Related Documents: Depositions sworn in open court: James Cheffins, James Wright, John Denning, 11 May 1822 [Depositions on Reel 2], with *Millis v. Spear.* PAR 20382215. Also see: *Negro Jane Millis v. William Spear,* in CCBSL, November Term 1821, p. 234, Record Group 3815, Microfilm Reel 6, p. 464, DSA. Granted.

63. Petition of Milly, Eliza, and Bob to the Circuit Court of St. Louis County, Missouri, 21 April 1819, in Records of the Circuit Court, *Milly, Eliza, and Bob v. Mathias Rose,* Document/Case 20, CCBSL; Related Documents: Pleas, Mathias Rose, 3 August 1819; Statement, Mathias Rose, 17 August 1819; Writ of *Habeas Corpus,* Milly, 14 August 1819, with *Milly et al. v. Rose.* PAR 21181902. Writ granted. In 1830, Mathias Rose, in his sixties, headed a household with four slaves, among them a girl and a boy between the ages of ten and twenty-three and a boy and girl under the age of ten. In that year, Milly's children would have been teenagers and Milly would have been forty-one. USMSPC, St. Louis, Missouri, St. Ferdinand, 1830, image 17, ancestry.com.

64. Petition of Abraham Carpenter to the County Court of Craven County, North Carolina, 5 February 1830, in Records of the County Court, Slaves and Free Negroes, NCDAH; Related Documents: Ard Reynolds to Thomas Watson, 18 February 1830. Reynolds lamented that several months before he had received a letter so poorly written that he thought it was re-garding a runaway who had fled from North Carolina to Connecticut. He failed to re-spond. Depositions, Jacob Dayton, Abraham Hubbard, Fairfield County, Connecticut, 17

February 1830; Certificate, Samuel Close, Fairfield County, Connecticut, 18 February 1830; Certificate, Inhabitants of Greenwich, Connecticut, [1830]; Writ of *Habeas Corpus*, 9 March 1830; Order, 9 March 1830, with petition of Carpenter. PAR 21283005. Granted.

Chapter 10

1. Edward Noble et al., *The History of Caroline County, Maryland, from Its Beginning* (Fredericksburg, MD: J. W. Stowell, 1920), 94–99.
2. *Journal and Correspondence of the Council of Maryland, April 1, 1778 through October 26, 1779*, 23, 249, http://msa.maryland.gov/megafile/msa/speccol/sc2900/sc2908/000001/000021/html/am21--23.html.
3. William M. Hardcastle (1778–1874) SC 5496-51532, MSA.
4. Noble et al., *The History of Caroline County*, 165–166, https://archive.org/details/historyofcarolin00nobl.
5. In 1800, seven members of the Hardcastle family owned these slaves, including Thomas Hardcastle Sr., who owned twenty-three; Robert Jr., who owned nine with three free blacks in his household; Annabella, who owned seven; John, who owned eight; William, who owned four; Thomas Jr., who owned sixteen; and Philomon, who owned four. USMSPC, Caroline County, Maryland, 1800, images 6, 10, 11, ancestry.com.
6. Hawkins was born on the Dixon farm about 1782. In 1790, Dixon owned five slaves, including Hawkins. Depositions of Betsey Faulkner and John Bennett, 4 May, 1822, in note 11 this chapter and *1790 Caroline Co., Maryland Federal Census*, http://usgwcensus.org/cenfiles/md/caroline/1790/pg0035.txt. The family of John's owner was spelled "Hughett" in the 1800 census. USMSPC, Caroline County, Maryland, 1800, image 11, ancestry.com.
7. Deposition, John Conner, May 4, 1822, in note 11, this chapter.
8. The marriage of slaves was a civil contract and slaves had no civil standing; thus their vows were null and void in law. Tera W. Hunter, *Bound in Wedlock: Slave and Free Black Marriage in the Nineteenth Century* (Cambridge, MA: Belknap Press of Harvard University Press, 2017), 12. The deed also freed twenty-four other slaves at various times in the future. A copy of the deed can be found with Petition of John Hawkins to the Delaware General Assembly, 17 February 1837, in General Assembly, Legislative Papers, Record Group 1111, Microfilm 250–253, 258–263, Frame/Pages 250–253, 258–263, DSA; Related Documents: Records of the Caroline County Court, Maryland, Copy of Bill of Sale, John Cooper to Samuel B. Cooper, et al., 7 July 1826; Affidavit of Samuel B. Cooper, 15 February 1837; Records of the Kent County, Delaware, County Court, Deed of Manumission, John Cooper to [twenty-five] Negro Slaves, 29 December 1809, with Hawkins to General Assembly. House: presented, read, referred. PAR 10383702. No private act was passed in Delaware in 1837 or 1838 on their behalf.
9. Depositions of Thomas M. Cooper, 7 December 1822, William Bell, 6 May 1822, and John Burnett, 18 May 1821, in note 11, this chapter.
10. Deposition of John Conner, May 4, 1822, in note 11, this chapter. Later, however, Richard returned to Maryland with the two Hawkins children.
11. Petition of Benjamin Hawkins, Anna Hawkins, and John Hawkins to the Common Pleas Court of Kent County, Delaware, November 1820, in Records of the Court of Common Pleas, *Benjamin Hawkins, Anna Hawkins, and John Hawkins v. Samuel Cooper*, Microfilm Reel 1, Frames 304–305, DSA; Related Documents: PAR 20382111; Depositions, John Bennett, Betsey Faulkner, John Conner, 4 May 1822; Deposition, Daniel Hill, 9 May 1822; Deposition, Thomas Cooper, 7 December 1822; Deposition, William Bell, 6 May 1822; Deposition, John Burnett, 18 May 1821; Deposition, Ephraim Draper, ca. 1821; Deposition, John Conner, 18 May 1821; Deposition, John Cooper, 4 May 1822; Deposition, William Dill, ca. 1822; Deposition, Ebenezer Barcus, ca. 1822 [Depositions on Reel 2], with *Hawkins et al. v. Samuel Cooper*. No decree with petition. PAR 20382110. Petition of William Hawkins, Nancy Hawkins, and John Hawkins to the Common Pleas Court of Kent County, Delaware, 1820, in Records of the Court of Common Pleas, *William Hawkins, Nancy Hawkins, and John Hawkins v. Richard Cooper*, Microfilm Reel 1, Frames 306–307, DSA; Related Documents: PAR 20382110, with *Hawkins et al. v. Richard Cooper*. PAR 20382111.KCCCP-CJD, November

Term 1820, p. 193, Reel 6, Frame 443, Summons August 25, 1820, continued thru May 1824, discontinued in November 1824, DSA.

12. Michael Tadman, *Speculators and Slaves: Masters, Traders, and Slaves in the Old South* (Madison: University of Wisconsin Press, 1989), 147–151; Frederic Bancroft, *Slave-Trading in the Old South* (Baltimore: J. H. Furst, 1931), 3–22; Walter Johnson, *Soul by Soul: Life Inside the Antebellum Slave Market* (Cambridge, MA: Harvard University Press, 1999), 19; Steven Deyle, *Carry Me Back: The Domestic Slave Trade in American Life* (New York: Oxford University Press, 2005), 39; Loren Schweninger, ed., *From Tennessee Slave to St. Louis Entrepreneur: The Autobiography of James Thomas*, foreword by John Hope Franklin (Columbia: University of Missouri Press, 1984), 61; John Hope Franklin and Loren Schweninger, *In Search of the Promised Land: A Slave Family in the Old South* (New York: Oxford University Press, 2006), 51–54; Donald R. Wright, *African Americans in the Early Republic, 1789–1831* (Arlington Heights, IL: Harlan Davidson, 1993), 12, 23, 26.

13. Petition of Clara, Frank, Maria, Sophia, Eliza, and Lewis to the Circuit Court of the District of Columbia, 12 April 1820, in RUSCC-CDRCF, *Clara, Frank, Maria, Sophia, Eliza, and Lewis v. Thomas Ewell*, Record Group 21, Box/Drawer 11, Document/Case 251, NA; Related Documents: Copy of Note, John Peltz to Charles Varden, 24 May 1815; Deposition, John Margert, 9 June 1815; Summons and Court Order, Thomas Ewell, 12 April 1820, with *Clara et al. v. Ewell*. PAR 20482001. Granted.

14. Petition of Andrew Ross to the Circuit Court of the District of Columbia, 12 August 1807, in RUSCC-CDRCF, *Andrew Ross v. Sarah Foushee and Sarah Chambers*, Record Group 21, Box/Drawer 6, Entry Folder 20, NA. Granted. PAR 20480701. See also: Petition of Sally Henry and Sally Henry [daughter] to the Circuit Court of the District of Columbia, 22 July 1814, in RUSCC-CDRCF, *Sally Henry and Sally Henry v. Henry W. Ball and Spencer Ball*, Record Group 21, Box/Drawer 11, Document/Case 199, NA. PAR 20481403. Granted.

15. Petition of Benjamin Hacket to the County Court of Baltimore County, Maryland, 7 November 1818, in SC, *Benjamin Hacket v. Alexander Briscoe, Maria Briscoe Raine, and James Briscoe*, Microfilm M 11019, Frame/Pages 2, Volume 4239-15, Document/Case C5, MSA; Related Documents: Bond, Benjamin Hacket, Shepwith H. Coale, Amos Bullock, 7 November 1818; Answer, Maria Raine, Alexander Briscoe, James Briscoe, 30 April 1819; Order, 20 May 1825, with *Hacket v. Briscoe et al.* PAR 20981811. Injunction dissolved.

16. Petition of Margaret, Frank, and Titus to the Circuit Court of Jefferson County, Kentucky, 24 September 1828, in Records of the Circuit Court, Case Files, *Margaret, Frank, and Titus v. William Duvall*, Box/Drawer 1-16, Document/Case 1232, KDLA; Related Documents: Order, 24 September 1828; Answer, William Duvall, 25 September 1828, with *Frank et al. v. Duvall*. PAR 20782815. Dismissed.

17. Petition of Sally Baker, Jeffery Baker, and Mary Baker to the Circuit Court of the District of Columbia, 28 October 1825, in RUSCC-CDRCF, *Sally Baker, Jeffery Baker, and Mary Baker v. Charles Hay and Thomas Cayce*, Record Group 21, Rules 2, Box/Drawer 31, Entry Folder 20, Document/Case 136, NA; Related Documents: Affidavit, Henry B. Robinson, 28 October 1825; Injunction, Charles Hay and Thomas Cayce, 28 October 1825, with *Baker et al. v. Hay et al.* PAR 20482502. Granted.

18. Petition of Charity, Mary, and Kitty to the Equity Court of Montgomery County, Maryland, 10 October 1818, in SC, *Charity, Mary, and Kitty v. Adam Robb, Henry Lansdale, and Alexander Robb*, Microfilm M 11024, Frame/Pages 1, Volume 4239-25, MSA; Related Documents: Answer, Adam Robb, 19 May 1819; Affidavit, William Campbell, 10 October 1818; Attorneys' Agreement, July Term 1820, with *Charity et al. v. Robb et al.* PAR 20981813. Injunction granted. See also: Petition of Beale to the Circuit Court of the District of Columbia, 10 January 1826, in RUSCC-CDRCF, *Beale v. Edward Calvert and George Calvert Jr.*, Record Group 21, Rules 2, Box/Drawer 31, Entry Folder 20, Document/Case 163, NA; Related Documents: Injunction, Edward Calvert and George Calvert Jr., 10 January 1826; Summons, Edward Calvert and George Calvert Jr., 10 January 1826, with *Beale v. Calvert et al.* PAR 20482601. Injunction granted.

19. See note 47, chap. 12, this volume.

20. Petition of Margaret, Frank, and Titus to the Circuit Court of Jefferson County, Kentucky, 24 September 1828, in Records of the Circuit Court, Case Files, *Margaret, Frank, and*

Titus v. William Duvall, Box/Drawer 1-16, Document/Case 1232, KDLA; Related Documents: Order, 24 September 1828; Answer, William Duvall, 25 September 1828, with *Margaret et al. v. Duvall*. PAR 20782815. Dismissed.

21. Petition of Charlotte, James, Edmund, Emaline, Flora, Elias, Frank, Charles, Cyrus, and Alexander to the Chancery Court of Jefferson County, Kentucky, 19 September 1845, in Records of the Circuit Court, Case Files, *Charlotte, James, Edmund, et al. v. William Trigg*, Box/Drawer 2-84, Document/Case 4842, KDLA; Related Documents: Order, ca. September 1845; Summons, William Trigg and Hannah, George, Nelson, and Cressa, persons of color, 19 September 1845; Order, ca. September 1845; Sheriff's Return, 20 September 1845, with *Charlotte et al. v. Trigg*. PAR 20784507. Injunction granted.

22. Petition of Sally Toogood and Martha Toogood to the Equity Court of Montgomery County, Maryland, 20 February 1822, in SC, *Sally Toogood and Martha Toogood v. Andrew Graff, Walter Stewart, and Daniel Grant*, Microfilm M 11024, Frame/Pages 2, Volume 4239-25, MSA; Related Documents: PARs 20982202, 209828; Answer, Walter Stewart, 6 March 1822; Order, 19 February 1822, with *Toogood et al. v. Graff et al.* PAR 20982201. Granted.

23. Petition of Sam Davis, Elizabeth Davis, and Polly Davis to the Circuit Superior Court of Lynchburg County, Virginia, 25 September 1832, in Records of the Circuit Court of Chancery, *Sam Davis, Elizabeth Davis, and Polly Davis v. Mahlon Cadwallader*, Box/Drawer 25, Document/Case 1202, LV; Related Documents: PAR 21683226; Writ of Injunction, 25 September 1832; Decree, July Term 1833, with *Davis et al. v. Cadwallader*. PAR 21683231. Injunction granted.

24. Petition of Sally and Armistead to the Circuit Court of Jefferson County, Kentucky, 3 May 1822, in Records of the Circuit Court, Case Files, *Sally and Armistead v. Robert Turner*, Box/Drawer 1-11, Document/Case 837, KDLA; Related Documents: Order, 28 April 1822; Answer, Robert Turner, February 1824; Decree, 9 October 1827; Appellate Decree, 13 June 1827, with *Sally et al. v. Turner*. PAR 20782208. GAA.

25. Petition of Charles Henry Wood and Betsy Wood to the Circuit Court of the District of Columbia, 7 May 1836, in RUSCC-CDRCF, *Charles Henry Wood and Betsy Wood v. John Gadsby*, Record Group 21, Rules 3, Box/Drawer 44, Entry Folder 20, Document/Case 489, NA; Related Documents: Answer, John Gadsby, 17 May 1836; Injunction, John Gadsby and Edward Dyer, 7 May 1836; Deed of Manumission, Ann Key, 13 May 1828, with *Wood et al. v. Gadsby*. PAR 20483614. Injunction granted.

26. Petition of Charlotte, Ellen, George, and Jesse Williams to the County Court of Knox County, Tennessee, 10 November 1851, in Records of the Chancery Court, Loose Records, *Charlotte, Ellen, George, and Jesse Williams v. William Cain and B. M. Townsend*, Microfilm Reel 12, Document/Case 645, TSLA; Related Documents: Writ of Injunction and Attachment, 9 November 1851, with *Williams et al. v. Cain et al.* PAR 21485110. Granted. See also: Petition of Pauline to the District Court of Pointe Coupee Parish, Louisiana, 17 November 1857, in Supreme Court of Louisiana Collection, *Pauline v. Louis A. Hubert and Phillip M. Moore*, Book 6,012, Document/Case 1,850, UNO; Related Documents: Order, 9 November 1857; Testimonies, Zenon Porche Esq. and Simon Goudran, 31 December 1857; Judgment, 31 December 1857; Appeal, 12 August 1858; Order, 12 August 1858; Supreme Court Opinion and Decree, 28 March 1859; Supreme Court Dissenting Opinion, 14 April 1859; Transcript of Court Records, 18 December 1857–31 October 1857; Supreme Court Opinion [Original], 14 April 1859, with *Pauline v. Hubert et al.* PAR 20885717; JCCASN, *Pauline (f.W.C.) v. Hubert*, 14 La. An. 161, March 1859, 3:670; D GARev. Judith Kelleher Schafer, *Slavery, the Civil Law, and the Supreme Court of Louisiana* (Baton Rouge: Louisiana State University Press, 1994), 232–234.

27. Petition of Lewis Gassaway and Charity Gassaway to the Circuit Court of the District of Columbia, 8 October 1856, in RUSCC-CDRCF, *Lewis Gassaway and Charity Gassaway v. Adam Rose*, Record Group 21, Rules 5, Box/Drawer 91, Entry Folder 20, Document/Case 1206, NA; Related Documents: PAR 20485606; Copy of Order, 8 October 1856; Injunction, Adam Rose, 13 October 1856, with *Gassaway et al. v. Rose*. PAR 20485605. Injunction granted. Petition of Wiatt, Rebecca, Abner, Nathan, Nancy, Rebecca, and George W. Vaughan to the Chancery Court of Washington County, Tennessee, 10 February 1851, in Washington County Court Records, Chancery Court, *Wiatt, Rebecca, Abner, et al. and George*

W. Vaughan v. Right Light, John Easly, James Cole, et al., Record Group 18, Box/Drawer 205, Entry Folder 7, AAETSU; Related Documents: Will, Vachael Light, 11 March 1850; Order, 13 December 1850; Court Records, 10 February 1851, 5 June 1851, with *Wiatt et al. v. Light et al.* PAR 21485147. Injunction granted. Petition of Jim Hickey and Charles J. McClung to the Chancery Court of Knox County, Tennessee, January 1860, in Records of the Chancery Court, Loose Records, *Jim Hickey and Charles J. McClung v. M. W. Williams, The State of Tennessee, and William P. Crippen,* Microfilm Reel 24, Document/Case 1181, TSLA; Related Documents: Order, January 1860; Injunction, October 1860; Answer, W. P. Crippen, 4 April 1860; Answer, The State of Tennessee, n.d., with *Hickey et al. v. Williams et al.* PAR 21486004. Injunction granted.

28. Petition of Ralph, Jenny, and Jenny [daughter] to the Circuit Court of Jefferson County, Kentucky, 24 July 1807, in Records of the Circuit Court, Case Files, *Ralph, Jenny, and Jenny v. Richard Phillips,* Box/Drawer 1-2, Document/Case 242, KDLA; Related Documents: Court Record, 1807–1810; Answer, Richard Phillips, 3 November 1807; Order, November Term 1807, with *Ralph et al. v. Phillips.* PAR 20780702. Denied.

29. Petition of Toney Emory and Abraham Emory to the Common Pleas Court of Kent County, Delaware, 6 May 1795, in Records of the Court of Common Pleas, *Toney Emory and Abraham Emory v. Jacob Grewell,* Microfilm Reel 1, Frame/Pages 133–134, DSA; Related Documents: PAR 20379518, with *Emory et al. v. Grewell.* PAR 20379508. Granted. Petition of Phobe Emory and Abraham Emory to the Common Pleas Court of Kent County, Delaware, 6 May 1795, in Records of the Court of Common Pleas, *Phobe Emory and Abraham Emory v. Jacob Grewell,* Microfilm Reel 1, Frame/Pages 155–156, DSA. PAR 20379518. Granted.

30. Petition of Charles Beall, Frank Beall, and Bacchus Beall to the County Court of Prince George's County, Maryland, 4 March 1843, in SC, *Charles Beall, Frank Beall, and Bacchus Beall v. Joseph J. Jones,* Microfilm M 11014, Frame/Pages 15, Volume 4239-3, MSA; Related Documents: Court Transcript, 3 April 1848–7 August 1848, Copy of Last Will and Testament, Nathaniel Chew, 30 May 1826, Deposition, Robert Clarke, 3 April 1847; Appellate Court Opinion, 3 December 1849, with *Beall et al. v. Jones.* PAR 20984307. D GARR.

31. Petition of John L. Butler to the Circuit Court of the District of Columbia, June 1847, in RUSDC-SHCP, *John L. Butler v. Sampson Simms,* Record Group 21, Box/Drawer 2, Entry Folder 28, NA; Related Documents: Writ of *Habeas Corpus,* John L. Butler, June 1847; Copy of Writ of *Habeas Corpus,* John L. Butler, June 1847; Answer, Sampson Simms, ca. 1847; Indenture, Sampson Simms, 19 February 1846, with *Butler v. Simms.* PAR 20484710. Granted. In 1850, Simms owned a single slave, a forty-six-year-old black woman. USMSSC, District of Columbia, Ward 2, 1850, image 4, ancestry.com.

32. Wilma King, *Stolen Childhood: Slave Youth in Nineteenth Century America* (Bloomington: Indiana University Press, 1995), 205n45.

33. Petition of Henry Slim to the Circuit Court of the District of Columbia, 5 February 1817, in RUSCC-CDRCF, *Henry Slim v. Francis Jenkins, Edward Jenkins, and Thomas Jenkins,* Record Group 21, Box/Drawer 28, Entry Folder 20, Document/Case 33, NA. PAR 20481701. Granted.

34. Petition of Jacob Sampson to the Circuit Court of Jefferson County, Kentucky, 7 April 1829, in Records of the Circuit Court, Case Files, *Jacob Sampson v. James Wilson, Andrew Wilson, Lucy Taylor, et al.,* Box/Drawer 1-42, Document/Case 3020, KDLA; Related Documents: Court Record, 1829–1834, with *Sampson v. Wilson et al.* PAR 20782906. Dismissed.

35. Petition of Peter Dewees to the Equity Court of Charleston District, South Carolina, 24 April 1854, in Records of the Equity Court, Bills, *Peter Dewees v. Thomas J. Cumming,* Microfilm Order 343, Reel D1270, Document/Case 1854–1885, SCDAH; Related Documents: Order, 24 April 1854; Writ of *Fieri Facias,* 25 April 1854; Answer, Thomas J. Cumming, 1 May 1854; Copy of Bill of Sale, 2 May 1854; Order, 29 May 1854; Decree, 30 October 1855, with *Dewees v. Cumming.* PAR 21385446. Injunction granted, dissolved, dismissed; state laws prohibited such slave emancipations.

36. Petition of Eliza Brooks the Elder, Sarah Brooks, Eliza Brooks the Younger, and Robert S. Ferguson to the Chancery Court of Washington County, Tennessee, 15 April 1850, in Washington County Court Records, Chancery Court, *Eliza Brooks the Elder, Sarah Brooks, Eliza Brooks the Younger, and Robert S. Ferguson v. Charles Greene, Richard H. Deakins, and*

Robert Brooks, Record Group 18, Box/Drawer 153B, Entry Folder 6, AAETSU; Related Documents: Order, 15 April 1850; Decree, 17 May 1852; Writ of *Fieri Facias* and Bill of Costs, May 1852, with *Brooks et al. v. Greene et al.* PAR 21485016. Granted, settled in favor of the plaintiffs.

37. Inflation calculator: http://www.westegg.com/inflation; of course, the price of a loved one is incalculable. For other time-payment plans of free black fathers see: Petition of Walter Waterford and Lewis Garner to the Chancery Court of Washington County, Tennessee, 8 March 1837, in Washington County Court Records, Chancery Court, *Walter Waterford and Lewis Garner v. David Waterford the Younger*, Record Group 18, Box/Drawer 205, Entry Folder 8, AAETSU. PAR 21483715. GAA. Marie Tedesco, "A Free Black Slave Owner in East Tennessee: The Strange Case of Adam Waterford," in *Appalachians and Race: The Mountain South from Slavery to Segregation*, ed. John Inscoe (Lexington: University of Kentucky Press, 2001), 133–153. PAR 21485707. Partially granted; settled.

38. Petition of Jacob Jamieson to the County Court of Williamson County, Tennessee, 3 July 1843, in Records of the County Court, Emancipations, Williamson County Archives, Franklin, Tennessee; Related Documents: PAR 21484323; Report and Ruling, 3 July 1843; Bond, Jacob Jamieson, et al., to Gilbert Marshall, 3 July 1843, with petition of Jamieson. PAR 21484322. Granted.

39. Petition of Job Hazell to the Superior Court of Cumberland County, North Carolina, 21 May 1821, in Records of the County Court, Miscellaneous Records, NCDAH; Related Documents: Order, ca. 1821, with petition of Hazell. PAR 21282103. Granted. Also see: Petition of London Leonard to the County Court of Pasquotank County, North Carolina, June 1801, in Records of the County Court, Slaves and Free Persons of Color 1733–1866, NCDAH. PAR 21280110. Granted.

40. Petition of James Green to the County Court of Craven County, North Carolina, 1818, in Records of the County Court, Slaves and Free Negroes 1775–1861, Document/Case 9, NCDAH [mother]. PAR 21281808. Granted. Petition of Norbert Robert to the Parish Court of Orleans Parish, Louisiana, 11 July 18, in Records of the Parish Court, Emancipation Petitions 1813–1843, Microfilm Reel 98-2, Frame/Pages 32A, NOPL; Related Documents: PARs 20882738, 20882755; Order, 11 July 18; Sheriff's Return, 14 July 18, with petition of Robert [mother]. PAR 20882153. Granted. Petition of Phillip Thompson to the County Court of Shelby County, Tennessee, 1 February 1849, in Records of the County Court, Document/Case 540, Memphis and Shelby County Archives, Memphis, Tennessee; Related Documents: PARs 21484346, 21484953; Bond, Phillip Thompson, et al., to the State of Tennessee, 5 February 1849, with petition of Thompson [sister and nephews]. PAR 21484952. Granted.

41. Thomas Gibbs Morgan, comp. and ed., *Civil Code of the State of Louisiana: With Statutory Amendments, from 1825 to 1853, Inclusive; and References to the Decisions of the Supreme Court of Louisiana to the Sixth Volume of Annual Reports* (New Orleans: J. B. Steel, 1853), 30–31.

42. Petition of Eugène Alexis to the Police Jury Court of St. John the Baptist Parish, Louisiana, 7 June 1852, in Records of the Fourth Judicial District Court, St. John the Baptist Parish Courthouse, Edgard, Louisiana; Related Documents: Certificate [text in French], 7 June 1852; Petition to District Court, 12 July 1852; Order, 10 July 1852; Sheriff's Return, 20 August 1852; Notice of Emancipation [text in French and English], 16 July 1852; Supplemental Petition to District Court, 1 September 1852; Order, 31 August 1852; Certificate of No Opposition, 30 August 1852; Copy of Petition to District Court and Order, 10 July 1852, with petition of Alexis. PAR 20885202. Granted.

43. Laura Foner, "The Free People of Color in Louisiana and St. Domingue: A Comparative Portrait of Two Three-Caste Slave Societies," *Journal of Social History* 3, no. 4 (Summer 1970): 409; Petition of François Larche to the Parish Court of Orleans Parish, Louisiana, 12 September 1827, in Records of the Parish Court, Emancipation Petitions 1813–1843, Microfilm Reel 98-2, Frame/Pages 41G, NOPL; Related Documents: PAR 20882761; Order, 14 September 1827; Sheriff's Return, 15 September 1827, with petition of Larche. PAR 20882745. Granted.

44. Petition of Jean Bapitste Vasnier to the Police Jury Court of Orleans Parish, Louisiana, October 1832, in Records of the Parish Court, Emancipation Petitions 1813–1843, Microfilm Reel

98-1, Frame/Pages 21B, NOPL; Related Documents: Certificate [text in French], 13 April 1832; Extracts from Police Jury Deliberations, 6 October 1832, 2 March 1833, certified 4 March 1833; Order, 29 March 1834; Sheriff's Return, 2 April 1834, with petition of Vasnier. PAR 20883221. Granted.

45. See note 11, this chapter.

46. KCCCP-CJD, November Term, 1824, Microfilm Reel 6, p. 193, Microfilm Reel p. 443, 25 November 1824, Record Group 3815, DSA. Discontinued. John Hawkins signed with his X, attested by N. Smithers.

47. Petition of John Hawkins to the Delaware General Assembly, 17 February 1837, in General Assembly, Legislative Papers, Record Group 1111, Microfilm 250–253, 258–263, Frames 250–253, 258–263, DSA; Related Documents: Records of the Caroline County, Maryland, Court, Copy of Bill of Sale, John Cooper to Samuel B. Cooper, et al., 7 July 1826; Affidavit of Samuel B. Cooper, 15 February 1837; Records of the Kent County, Delaware, County Court, Deed of Manumission, John Cooper to Negro Slaves, 29 December 1809, with Hawkins to General Assembly. House: presented, read, and referred. No bill with petition. PAR 10383702. USMSPC, Caroline County, Maryland, 1840, image 3, ancestry.com [John Hawkins family]. The John Hawkins family should not be confused with the Hawkins family of Queen Anne's County who were assisted to freedom, in 1845, by Quaker-abolitionist Thomas Garrett, in *Archives of Maryland*, http://www.msa.md.gov/megafile/msa/speccol/sc5400/sc5496/008800/008849/html/008849bio.html.

Chapter 11

1. Petition of Anne Edinbro to the Circuit Court of District of Columbia, Washington County, 17 August 1838, in Records of the US Circuit Court, Chancery Dockets and Rules Case Files, *Anne Edinbro v. Robert Earle and David Waters*, Record Group 21, Rules 3, Box/Drawer 46, Entry Folder 20, Document/Case 489, NA; Related Documents: Depositions, Jane Edinbro [Edinburg], Mary Heugh, 17 August 1838; Answers, Robert Earle and David Waters, 30 November 1838; Affidavit, David Waters, 30 November 1838; Deposition, Jane Edinbro and Harriet Edinbro, 26 April 1839; Deposition, Jane Edinbro, 22 May 1839; Deposition, Mary Heugh, May 22, 1839; Deed of Manumission, Mary Heugh, 19 September 1829; Bill of Sale, Mary Heugh to Robert Earle, 10 September 1834, with *Edinbro v. Earle et al.* Injunction granted. PAR 20483807. For the deed of manumission, see Dorothy S. Provine, *The District of Columbia Free Negro Registers, 1821–1861* (Bowie, MD: Heritage Books, 2015 [1996]), 720, September 21, 1829.

2. Petition of William Hickman to the Circuit Court of Bourbon County, Kentucky, 6 June 1829, in Records of the Circuit Court, Case Files, *William Hickman v. Thomas Trundle*, Box/Drawer 718-722, Entry/Folder Packet 722, CCH, Paris, Kentucky; Related Documents: Order, 6 June 1829; Agreement to Dismiss, William Hickman and Thomas Trundle, 23 September 1829, with *Hickman v. Trundle*. PAR 20782909. Dismissed. Petition of Samuel Warren, Charles Steedman, and Laurens McGregor to the Equity Court of Charleston District, South Carolina, 15 April 1807, in Records of the Equity Court, Bills, *Samuel Warren, Charles Steedman, and Laurens McGregor v. Frederick Rutledge Jr., Elias Horry, and Mr. Rutledge*, Document/Case 1807-64, SCDAH; Related Documents: PARs 21380707, 21381612; Correspondence, Frederick Rutledge to Colonel Warren [Incomplete], 28 July 1806, with *Warren et al. v. Rutledge et al.* PAR 21380709. No decree with petition. See Loren Schweninger, ed., *The Southern Debate over Slavery*, vol. 2: *Petitions to Southern County Courts, 1775–1867* (Urbana: University of Illinois Press, 2008), 92–94; Petition of William Botkin to the Circuit Court, Harrison County, Kentucky, 28 March 1831, in Records of the Circuit Court, Case Files, Case 6080, *William Botkin v. Samuel Chambers, Martha L. Jordan, Lewis Slinker*, CCH, Cynthiana, Kentucky; Related Documents: Decree, June 1834, with *Botkin v. Chambers et al*. PAR 20783103. Granted.

3. Petition of Lucy Mitchell to the Orphans Court of Anne Arundel County, Maryland, 13 April 1859, in Register of Wills, 1851–1874 (Petitions and Orders), Microfilm Reel CR 63,128, Frames 289–290, 503–504, MSA; Related Documents: Certificate of Affidavit, 22 April

1859; Commissioners' Appointment, ca. January 1856; Commissioners' Oaths and Report, 28 January 1856, with petition of Lucy. PAR 20985952. No decree with petition.

4. Petition of Fleming Saunders to the Circuit Court of Campbell County, Virginia, October 1852, in Records of the Circuit Superior Court of Chancery, *Fleming Saunders v. William Watts and Edward Saunders*, Drawer 1855, Circuit Court Building, Rustburg, Virginia; Related Documents: PAR 21684926; Decree, May 1855; List of Dower Slaves of Mary Watts, ca. 1852, with *Saunders v. Watts et al.* PAR 21685219. Dismissed.

5. Petition of Jane to the Circuit Court of St. Louis County, Missouri, 15 April 1831, *Jane vs. William Dallam*, in Records of the Circuit Court, Document/Case 22, CCBSL; Related Documents: Copy of Order, 15 April 1831; Deposition, G. W. Call, 16 April 1831; Correspondence, Thomas M. Smith to James L. Murray, ca. 3 April 1831; Plea of Trespass, 10 May 1831; Subpoenas, William Dallam, 10 May and 23 September 1831; Sheriff's Returns, 9 July and 12 November 1831, with *Jane v. Dallam*. Petition to sue granted; plea of trespass filed. PAR 21183105. G DefNF. Jane's children, Henry, Margaret, and Sally, filed separately against Dallam who was not found in the county.

6. Petition of Jenney Ash to the County Court of Bertie County, North Carolina, 1785, in Records of the County Court, Slave Papers 1781–1786, *Jenney Ash v. John Gardner*, NCDAH; Related Documents: Answer, John Gardner, 12 May 1785, with *Ash v. Gardner* [Indian ancestry]. PAR 21278502. No decree with petition. For free members of the family, see: Paul Heinegg, *Free African Americans of North Carolina, Virginia, and South Carolina: From the Colonial Period to about 1820* (Baltimore: Clearfield, 2005), 84.

7. Petition of Rachel Baker, James, Isaac, Esther, Betty, John, Isaac, Tom, Phoebe, Benjamin, Caty, Henny Baker, Ibby, Harry, Nancy, Sarah, Charles, Henny, and Harry to the County Court of Queen Anne's County, Maryland, 26 October 1800, in SC, *Rachel Baker, James, Isaac, Esther, et al. v. John Paca*, Microfilm M 11014, Frame/Pages 5, Volume 4239-1, MSA; Related Documents: PARs 20979204, 20979704, 20980305; Transcript of Court Record, ca. 26 October 1800–October 1802; Clerk's Certification, 1 May 1812, with *Baker et al. v. Paca*. PAR 20980003. Granted.

8. Petition of Nathaniel Allen to the County Court of Anne Arundel County, Maryland, September 1794, in SC, *Nathaniel Allen v. Richard Higgins*, Microfilm M 11015, Frame/Pages 2, Volume 4239-2, Document/Case 28, MSA; Related Documents: Court Record, September 1794-1 November 1796; Appellate Court Ruling, June Term 1798, with *Allen v. Higgins*. PAR 20979401. D GARev. In this case, free black Jane Allen, the petitioner's mother, stated in a deposition that she had given birth to Nathaniel "by a Negro Man."

9. Petition of Fanny, Kitty, and Hercules to the Common Pleas Court of Kent County, Delaware, 12 December 1794, in Records of the Court of Common Pleas, *Fanny, Kitty, and Hercules v. James Huchins*, Microfilm Reel 1, Frame/Pages 119–20, DSA. PAR 20379402. Denied. KCCCP-CJD, May 1795, p. 123, Microfilm Reel 4, Frame 285, not summoned, appearance, continued through November 1797; KCCCP-CJD, p. 16, Microfilm Reel 4, Frame 453, August 3, 1798, "not to be brought forward."

10. Petition of Amey and [her son] Jacob to the Common Pleas Court of Kent County, Delaware, December 1794, in Records of the Court of Common Pleas, *Amey and Jacob v. John Young*, Microfilm Reel 3, Frame/Pages 21–23, DSA; Related Documents: Court Record, ca. 1794, with *Amey et al. v. Young*. PAR 20379409. KCCCP-CJD, December 1795, p. 17, Microfilm Reel 4, Frame 454, DSA. Granted. Petition of Hannah Hurt, Sarah Hurt, Minta Hurt, and Nathan Hurt to the Common Pleas Court of Kent County, Delaware, ca. 1800, in Records of the Court of Common Pleas, *Hannah Hurt, Sarah Hurt, Minta Hurt, and Nathan Hurt v. Lemuel Sappington and Thomas Sappington*, Microfilm Reel 1, Frame/Pages 310–311, DSA; Related Documents: PARs 20380040, 20381708, with *Hurt et al. v. Sappington et al.* PAR 20380027. No decree with petition. Petition of Margaret Gibbs to the Common Pleas Court of Kent County, Delaware, 5 May 1803, in Records of the Court of Common Pleas, *Margaret Gibbs v. John Graham*, Microfilm Reel 2, Frames, 46–47, DSA. PAR 20380308. Partially granted. Petitions of Margaret Gibbs, Charlotte Gibbs, Jacob Gibbs, Jonathan Gibbs, and Phillipa Gibbs, 5 May 1803, in Records of the Court of Common Pleas, *Margaret Gibbs, Charlotte Gibbs, Jacob Gibbs, et al. v. John Graham*, Microfilm Reel 2, Frames 36–37, 42–43, 44–45, 48–49, DSA. PARs 20380305, 20380306, 20380307, 20380309. Related documents: 20380501,

20380502. KCCCP-CJD, May Term 1803, pp. 91–92, Reel 5, Frame 229, filed May 6, 1803; "settled say Petitioner," 1 December 1804, DSA.

11. Petition of Nanny and Moses Lawson to the County Court of Henrico County, Virginia, 4 March 1807, in Ended Chancery Court Causes, *Nanny and Moses Lawson v. Betsey DuVal*, Box/Drawer 79-5, Entry Folder 1813, LV; Related Documents: Jury Verdict, 5 March 1813; Court Record, 4 March 1807–9 August 1811; Deposition, Sarah Anderson Thomson, 11 April 1810; Notes on Case, ca. 1810; Deposition, Vincent Oliver, ca. 1807; Notes on Case, ca. 1807; Depositions, Martha Cottrel, 22 December 1806; Elliot Lacy, 24 December 1806; Elisha Price, 11 February 1807; Drury Wood, 25 November 1809, with *Lawson et al. v. DuVal* [claimed descent from a Cherokee woman]. PAR 21680713. Dismissed. Petition of Mary Queen, Charles Queen, and Elizabeth Queen to the County Court of Charles County, Maryland, 1 May 1808, in SC, *Mary Queen, Charles Queen, and Elizabeth Queen v. Charles Neale*, Microfilm M 11014, Frame/Pages 24, Volume 4239-3, Document/Case 13, MSA; Related Documents: PAR 20980807; Court Record, 1 May 1808–10 December 1810, with *Queen et al. v. Neale* [claimed descent from a white women]. PAR 20980806. JCCASN, *Queen v. Neal*, Md., 3 Har. and John, 185, December 1810, 4:62. DAA. See note 66, chap. 2, this volume. *Betsy v. Latham* [descended from Cherokee woman]. PAR 20881205. Dismissed. Petition of Henny Hemsley, Susan Hemsley, Juliana Hemsley, and Priscilla Hemsley to the County Court of Queen Anne's County, Maryland, 1 May 1815, in SC, *Henny Hemsley, Susan Hemsley, Juliana Hemsley, and Priscilla Hemsley v. George Walls*, Microfilm M 11014, Frame/Pages 7, Volume 4239-1, Document/Case 21, MSA; Related Documents: Transcript of Court Record, 1 May 1815–June Term 1817, with *Hemsley et al. v. Walls* [claimed descent from a free woman of color]. PAR 20981505. JCCASN, *Walls v. Hemsley*, Md., 4 Har. and John. 243, June 1817, 4:64–65. D GARev.

12. Petition of Charity, Mary, and Kitty to the Equity Court of Montgomery County, Maryland, 10 October 1818, in SC, *Charity, Mary, and Kitty v. Adam Robb, Henry Lansdale, and Alexander Robb*, Microfilm M 11024, Frame/Pages 1, Volume 4239-25, MSA; Related Documents: Answer, Adam Robb, 19 May 1819; Affidavit, William Campbell, 10 October 1818; Attorneys' Agreement, July Term 1820, with *Charity et al. v. Robb et al.* PAR 20981813. Injunction granted.

13. Petition of Milly, Hannah, Washington, Henry, Joseph, Susan, Betty, Fanny, Hannah, and Susan to the County Court of Harford County, Maryland, 3 March 1819, in SC, *Milly, Hannah, Washington, et al. v. William Hughes*, Microfilm M 11014, Frame/Pages 11, Volume 4239-3, Document/Case 34, MSA; Related Documents: Court Record, 18 May 1819; Copy of Last Will and Testament, Margaret Coale, 23 July 1776; Deed of Manumission, 3 March 1819, with *Milly et al. v. Hughes*. PAR 20981906. JCCASN, *Hughes v. Negro Milly*, Md., 5 Har. and John 310, June 1821, 4:71. GAA.

14. Petition of Marie Coffy to the Parish Court of Orleans Parish, Louisiana, 1 July 1817, in Supreme Court of Louisiana Collection, *Marie Coffy v. Castillon Mrs., Pontalba Mr., and Pontalba Mrs.*, Book 255, UNO; Related Documents: Transcript of Court Records, 1 July 1817–8 December 1817, including: Orders, 29 July 1817, 9 August 1817; Petition of Appeal, 9 August 1817; Admission of Facts [text in English and French], ca. 1817; Record of Supreme Court Filing, 8 December 1817; Legislative Extract [text in French], with *Coffy v. Castillon, et al.* PAR 20881765. JCCASN, *Cuffy v. Castillon*, 5 Mart. La. 494, May 1818, 3:458–459. DAA. The Spanish court had, indeed, freed them, but their free black husband and father had paid the owner only a small portion of the $3,400 asking price, and "without payment, or an offer to pay the full amount," they could make no claim for benefit under the contract.

15. Petition of Lavina, Jackson, and James McCombs to the Chancery Court of Giles County, Tennessee, 6 August 1836, in Supreme Court Cases, Middle Tennessee, *Lavina, Jackson, and James McCombs v. John Goff, William Porter, and John Porter*, Box/Drawer 58, TSLA; Related Documents: Bond, 5 August 1836; Demurrer, John Goff, 21 February 1837; Orders, March Term 1837, September Term 1836 [1837]; Answers, William Porter, 10 March 1837; John Goff, April Term 1837; Record of Proceedings, February 1837 to September Terms 1837; Decree and Appeal, September Term 1837; Depositions, Thomas C. Porter, 6 May 1837; William R. Davis, Thomas C. Porter, Burnurd M. Burch, 7 August 1837; William Conner, John Kenan, 1 September 1837; Last Wills and Testaments, John Duffield, 6 March 1807;

Elizabeth Duffield, 7 October 1826; Decree and Opinion, 3 March 1838, with *Lavina et al. v. Goff et al.* PAR 21483614. JCCASN, *Lavina v. Duffield's Executors*, Tenn., Meigs 117n, March 1838, 2:506. G DARev.

16. Petition of Nancy, James, Mahala, Emeline, Abraham, Elizabeth, Jessee, and Francis Rogan to the Chancery Court of Sumner County, Tennessee, 10 March 1843, in Records of the County Court, Loose Record Lawsuits, *Nancy, James, Mahala, et al., and Francis Rogan v. James Mahan,* Frame/Pages pp. 324, 329–339, 345–354, Document/Case 393, TSLA; Related Documents: PAR 21484331; Oath, Nancy, 9 March 1843; Deposits, Elizabeth Barr, Barnard Rogan, David Mahan [Mahon], Martha Moncrieth [Morceff], Nancy Lea, William Parker, William S. Monday, and John McNeill [McNeal], 18 September 1843; Certification, 18 September 1843; Amended Bill, 25 March 1844, with *Nancy et al. v. Mahan.* PAR 21484330. No decree with petition. For the sale of Mahala, see Petition of Richmond C. Tyree to the Chancery Court of Sumner County, Tennessee, 19 April 1843, in Records of the Chancery Court, Loose Record Lawsuits, *Richmond C. Tyree v. James Mahan,* pp. 321–324, 329–339, 346–354, Document/Case 393, TSLA; Related Documents: PAR 21484330; Order, 14 April 1843; Copy of Last Will and Testament, Sally Mahan [Mahon], 7 April 1841; Copy of Probate Record, County Court, Estate of Sally Mahan, August Term 1842; Clerk's Certification of Copy, 23 March 1843; Docket Page of Writ of Attachment, 12 May 1843; Sheriff's Return, 18 May 1843; Statement of Court Costs, ca. May 1843, with *Tyree v. Mahan.* PAR 21484331. Granted.

17. Petition of Barbara to the Chancery Court of Scott County, Virginia, February 1823, in Determined Chancery Causes, *Barbara v. Comfort Osborne, Jonathan Osborne, John Osborne, Isaac Richmond, et al.,* Box/Drawer 23, Entry Folder 1836–1837, LV; Related Documents: PARs 21682318, 21682613, 21683111; Court Record, February 1823-January 1837; Answer, Isaac Richmond, 15 November 1823; Correspondence, William Kilgore to Colonel Andrew McHenry, 10 October 1823; Supplemental Bill, Barbara, free woman of color, 14 May 1829, with *Barbara v. Osborne et al.* PAR 21682320. Granted.

18. Petition of Belinda, Charlotte, and Thomas H. Haquer to the Superior Court of Leon County, Florida, 11 November 1839, in Chancery Case Files, *Belinda, Charlotte, and Thomas H. Haquer v. John Parkhill and Edward Loockerman,* Record Group Series L60, Box/Drawer 9, Entry Folder 603, Tallahassee, Florida State Archives; Related Documents: PARs 20583701, 20584001; Replication, Belinda and Charlotte, 1844; Decree, 4 May 1844; Oath, Thomas Haynes, 10 March 1842, with *Belinda et al. v. Parkhill et al.* PAR 20583904. Granted.

19. Lea VanderVelde, *Redemption Songs: Suing for Freedom before Dred Scott* (New York: Oxford University Press, 2014), 168; Petition of Malinda to the Circuit Court of St. Louis County, Missouri, 24 August 1845, in Records of the Circuit Court, *Malinda v. George W. Coons,* CCBSL; Related Documents: PARs 21184112, 21184113, 21184401, 21184420, 21184429, 21184512, 21184905 through 21184912; Affidavit, William Burchsted, 23 August 1845; Order, 25 August 1845; Plea of Trespass, 1 November 1845; Subpoena, George W. Coons, 1 November 1845; Copy of Order, 25 August 1845; Sheriff's Return, 4 November 1845; Plea, George W. Coons, 20 April 1846, with *Malinda v. Coons.* PAR 21184508. Dismissed by Plaintff.

20. Petition of Mary, Patsey, Thomas, and Joseph to the District Court of Concordia Parish, Louisiana, 9 March 1849, in Supreme Court of Louisiana Collection, *Mary, Patsey, Thomas, and Joseph v. Daniel L. Brown,* Book 1,640, Document/Case 1,366, UNO; Related Documents: Transcript of Court Records, 9 March 1849-9 January 1850, including: Act of Emancipation [fragment], 22 December 1846; Deed of Emancipation, 1 October 1845; Testimonies, James Nichols, et al., 26 October 1849, 31 October 1849; and Judgment, 16 November 1849; Supreme Court Decree, 25 February 1850, with *Mary et al. v. Brown.* PAR 20884944. JCCASN, *Mary (f.w.c.) et al. v. Brown,* 5 La. An. 269, April 1850, 3:604; Schafer, *Slavery, the Civil Law,* 255. D GARev.

21. Petition of Clara Fenwick to the Circuit Court of the District of Columbia, 5 November 1835, in RUSDC-SHCP, *Clara Fenwick v. Lansing Tooker and John A. Wilson,* Record Group 21, Box/Drawer 1, Entry Folder 28, NA; Related Documents: PAR 20483514; Testimony, Lansing Tooker, Mr. Barclay, Edmunds Hoffman, Mr. Tounnel, 9 November 1835; Writ of *Habeas Corpus,* William Fenwick, 6 November 1835; Summons, J. E. Hoffman, 7 November 1835,

with *Fenwick v. Tooker et al.* PAR 20483506. *Reports of Cases Civil and Criminal in the United States Circuit Court of the District of Columbia, 1801–1841,* 6 vols., comp. William Cranch (Boston: Little, Brown, 1852), 4:500–503; Minutes of the Circuit Court for the District of Columbia, 1801–1863, 2 January 1836, Reel 4, Frame 168, NA. Jury sworn and verdict for petitioner; injunction granted; injunction made perpetual; won freedom in the law court. Petition of Henny Taylor and [her son] Chester Taylor to the Circuit Court of the District of Columbia, 1 May 1839, in RUSDC-SHCP, Record Group 21, Box/Drawer 1, Entry Folder 28, NA; Related Documents: Affidavit, Joseph F. Daley, 30 April 1839; Return, 20 May 1839; Writ of *Habeas Corpus,* Henry Taylor, 1 May 1839, with petition of Henny Taylor. PAR 20483905. Granted.

22. Petition of Clara Thomas and Ann Thomas to the Circuit Court of Jefferson County, Kentucky, 28 March 1822, in Records of the Circuit Court, Case Files, *Clara Thomas and Ann Thomas v. William Taylor, Charles Taylor, and Worden Pope,* Box/Drawer 1-26, Document/Case 1934, KDLA; Related Documents: Order, 28 March 1822, with *Thomas et al. v Taylor et al.* PAR 20782205. Injunction granted; dismissed by plaintiff's attorney.

23. Petition of Marie Joseph to the District Court of Natchitoches Parish, Louisiana, 16 April 1823, in Records of the District Court, *Marie Joseph v. Magdelaine,* Entry Folder Bundle 20, Document/Case 619, Natchitoches Parish Courthouse, Natchitoches, Louisiana; Judgment, May Term 1823, with *Joseph v. Magdelaine.* PAR 20882307. Granted. See also: Petition of Celeste to the District Court of Natchitoches Parish, Louisiana, 16 April 1823, in Records of the District Court, *Celeste v. Amelie,* Entry Folder Bundle 18, Document/Case 620, Natchitoches Parish Courthouse, Natchitoches, Louisiana; Related Documents: PAR 20882307; Answer, Amelie, 5 May 1823; Judgment, May Term 1823, with *Celeste v. Amelie.* PAR 20882308. Granted.

24. Petition of Charlotte and Emily to the Circuit Court of Jefferson County, Kentucky, 23 March 1832, in Records of the Circuit Court, Case Files, *Charlotte and Emily v. Robert Ball and Richard Oldham,* Box/Drawer 1-32, Document/Case 2310, KDLA; Related Documents: PARs 20783004, 20783201; Court Record, 1832–1834; Order, 23 March 1832, with *Charlotte et al. v. Ball et al.* PAR 20783202. Injunction granted.

25. Petition of Louisa Alexander and Eliza Alexander to the Circuit Superior Court of Campbell County, Virginia, 23 January 1840, in Records of the Circuit Superior Court of Chancery, *Louisa Alexander and Eliza Alexander v. John P. White and Adam Clement,* Box/Drawer 1853, Circuit Court Building, Rustburg, Virginia; Related Documents: Order, 27 January 1840; Answer and Affidavit, John P. White, 10 March 1840, with *Alexander et al. v. White et al.* PAR 21684008. Injunction granted, case abated.

26. Petition of Lizzy, Narcissa, Stella, Rial, Penelope, and Snead to the Circuit Court of Jefferson County, Kentucky, 15 September 1834, in Records of the Circuit Court, Case Files, *Lizzy, Narcissa, Stella, et al., v. John H. Cutter, John Evans, and E. F. Atchison,* Box/Drawer 1-38, Document/Case 2727, KDLA; Related Documents: Order, 15 September 1834; Certificate, Isaac Carson, 12 August 1825; Copy of Last Will and Testament, Isaac Carson, 12 August 1825, with *Lizzy et al, v. Cutter et al.* PAR 20783410. Granted.

27. Petition of Winney, Jerry, Daniel, Jenny, Nancy, Lydia, Sarah, Hannah, Lewis, and Malinda to the Superior Court of St. Louis County, Missouri, June 1818, in Records of the Circuit Court; (Certified Copy of Petition and Related Documents found in Supreme Court Cases, Box 541, Case 18, MoSA), *Winny, Jerry, Daniel, Jenny, et al. v. Phebe Whitesides, Representatives of Thomas Whitesides, John Whitesides, Robert Musick, et al.,* Document/Case 190, CCBSL. In drawn-out litigation spanning seven years, Winny and her family eventually won their freedom. Winny's eight children filed separate suits.

28. Petition of Mary, Samuel, and Edward to the Circuit Court of St. Louis County, Missouri, 5 November 1850, in Records of the Circuit Court, *Mary, Samuel, and Edward v. Louncelot H. Calvert,* CCBSL; Related Documents: PAR 21183114; Order, 5 November 1850; Supplemental Petition, 5 November 1850; Copy of Order, 5 November 1850; Subpoena, Louncelot Calvert, 5 November 1850; Sheriff's Return, 5 November 1850; Depositions, James Hendrickson, Henry Hendrickson, William Maxwell, Henry Wise, 25 September 1851, with *Mary et al. v. Calvert.* PAR 21185012. G DisByPlff.

29. Petition of Nanette and Antoine La Cour to the Parish Court of Iberville Parish, Louisiana, 2 February 1829, in Records of the Old Parish Court, *Nanette and Antoine La Cour v [no named defendants]*, Document/Case 732, Iberville Parish Courthouse, Plaquemine, Louisiana; Related Documents: Affidavit [text in French], 3 October 1828; Order, 11 July 1829; Record of Police Jury Decision, 16 December 1828; Sheriff's Return, 1 April 1829; Order, 2 February 1829; Slave Title Transfer Agreement, 20 May 1819, with petition of Nanette La Cour. PAR 20882901. Granted. Antoine La Cour, a free person of color, owned eighteen slaves and headed a family of seven other free persons of color. USMSPC, Iberville Parish Louisiana, 1830, image 1, ancestry.com.

30. Petition of Henrietta Norris and Flora Moore to the Circuit Court of the District of Columbia, 23 May 1835, in RUSCC-CDRCF, *Henrietta Norris and Flora Moore v. George W. Gray and Washington Robey*, Record Group 21, Box/Drawer 43, Document/Case 350, NA; Related Documents: Affidavit, Flora Moore, 23 May 1835; Injunction, George M. Gray and Washington Robey, 23 May 1835, with *Norris, et al. v Gray, et al.* PAR 20483513. Injunction granted.

31. See note 69, chap. 3, this volume. For this and other District of Columbia freedom suits, see the O Say Can You See: Early Washington, DC, Law and Family website, http://earlywashingtondc.org/cases.

32. Amrita Chakrabarti Myers, *Forging Freedom: Black Women and the Pursuit of Liberty in Antebellum Charleston* (Chapel Hill: University of North Carolina Press, 2011) 48–50; Larry Koger, *Black Slaveowners: Free Black Slave Masters in South Carolina, 1790–1860* (Jefferson, NC: McFarland, 1985), 53; Max Grivno, *Gleanings of Freedom: Free and Slave Labor along the Mason Dixon Line, 1790–1860* (Lexington: University of Kentucky Press, 2011), 179–181.

33. Loren Schweninger, "John Carruthers Stanly and the Anomaly of Black Slaveholding," *The North Carolina Historical Review*, 67, no. 2 (April 1990): 159–192.

34. *Acts Passed at the First Session of the Eighth Legislature of the State of Louisiana, Begun and Held in the City of New-Orleans, on Monday, the First Day of January, in the Year of Our Lord One Thousand Eight Hundred and Twenty-Seven, and of the Independence of the United States of America, the Fifty-First* (New Orleans: John Gibson, 1827), 12, 14.

35. Petition of Damarisse Devel to the Parish Court of Orleans Parish, Louisiana, 14 July 1834, in Records of the Parish Court, Emancipation Petitions 1813–1843, Microfilm Reel 98-1, Frame/Pages 19K, NOPL; Related Documents: PAR 20882988; Order, 14 July 1834; Sheriff's Return, 17 July 1834, with petition of Devel. PAR 20883475. Granted.

36. Petition of Charlotte to the Parish Court of Orleans Parish, Louisiana, January 1829, in Records of the Parish Court, Emancipation Petitions 1813–1843, Microfilm Reel 98-1, Frame/Pages 11F, NOPL; Related Documents: Certificates, 15 November 1828; Extract from Police Jury Deliberations, 17 January 1829, certified ca. 17 January 1829; Order, January 1829; Sheriff's Return, January 1829, with petition of Charlotte. PAR 20882993. Granted [son was a shoemaker]; Petition of Victoire to the Police Jury Court of Orleans Parish, Louisiana, July 1829, in Records of the Parish Court, Emancipation Petitions 1813–1843, Microfilm Reel 98-1, Frame/Pages 31, NOPL; Related Documents: Certificate [text in French], 6 July 1829; Extract from Police Jury Deliberations, 19 July 1829, certified 20 July 1829; Petition to Parish Court, ca. 28 July 1829; Order, 28 July 1829; Sheriff's Return, 29 July 1829, with petition of Victoire. PAR 20882995. Granted [both young men were bricklayers].

37. Petitions of Affey White, Amy White, Joseph White, Samuel White, Sophia White, with free black Job White as Next Friend, to the Common Pleas Court of Kent County, Delaware, 22 April 1805, in Records of the Court of Common Pleas, *Affey White, Amy White, Joseph White, et al. v. George Dehorty*, Microfilm Reel 2, Frames 126–137, DSA. PAR 20380516, Related Documents: PARs20380517, 20380518, 20380519, 20380520, 20380521. KCCCP-CJD, May Term 1805, pp. 154–155, Reel 5, Frames 260–261, filed April 22, 1805; continued November 1806 on rule hearing; KCCCP-CJD., p. 4, Reel 5, Frame 383, May 13, 1807, plaintiffs and four children demur to possession of next friend; KCCCP-CJD, May Term 1806, p. 26, Reel 5, Frame 394, freed May 16, 1810. Granted. USMSPC, Kent County, Delaware, Murderkill Hundred, 1810, image 22 [free black Job White], ancestry.com.

38. Petition of Siller, Lucinda, Hetty, Thomas, Clara, Sylvia, Stephen, Joseph, and Doctor Franklin to the Circuit Court of Barren County, Kentucky, 25 March 1841, in Records of the Circuit

Court, Equity Judgments, *Siller, Lucinda, Hetty, et al. v. Anderson R. Bowles, Malinda Munday, and George Munday*, Microfilm Reel 218692, Case 1123, KDLA; the mother Siller as the next friend filed a series of individual suits for each child; these suits were apparently consolidated into a single suit. Related Documents: PAR 21681109; Affidavit, B. B. Crump, 24 March 1841; Decree, n.d.; Order, June 1841; Copy of Order, June 1841; Answer, Anderson R. Bowles, Malinda Munday, and George Munday, 24 June 1841; Deposition, James Cummins, 23 August 1842; Deposition, James Hicks, 25 April 1842, with *Siller et al. v. Bowles et al.* The court "doth adjudge, order and decree that the complainant [Siller] is a free person." PAR 20784116. Granted. Siller was the daughter of Mina, an Indian woman in Virginia. A decree in March 1845 favored defendant Bowles; it probably concerned hiring wages as damages as suggested in the depositions.

39. Petition of Catherine Henderson and Benjamin Henderson to the Circuit Court of the District of Columbia, 9 December 1833, in RUSCC-CDRCF, *Catherine Henderson and Benjamin Henderson v. Harriet Loyed and Mr. Freeman*, Record Group 21, Rules 3, Box/ Drawer 41, Entry Folder 20, Document/Case 274, NA; Related Documents: Deposition, Hugh Smith, 9 December 1833, with *Henderson et al. v. Loyed et al.* PAR 20483302. Granted.

40. See note 54, chap. 4, this volume. *Chapman et al. v. Fenwick.* PAR 20483303. Granted. *Reports of Cases Civil and Criminal in the United States*, Cranch, 4:431–438; Letitia Woods Brown, *The Free Negro in the District of Columbia, 1790–1846* (New York: Oxford University Press, 1972), 94–95.

41. Petition of Brunetta Barnes to the Circuit Court of St. Louis County, Missouri, 30 July 1840, in Records of the Circuit Court, *Brunetta Barnes, by her next friend Peter Charleville v. Berry Meachum*, Document/Case 40, CCBSL; Related Documents: Deposition, Jesse R. Grant, Clermont County, Ohio, 10 May 1841, with *Barnes v. Meachum*, PAR 21184003. Granted.

42. Petition of Appollonia Julia to the District Court of Orleans Parish, Louisiana, 29 April 1818, in Records of the First Judicial District Court, Case Records, *Appollonia Julia v. William Bertin*, Microfilm Reel 4, Louisiana Collection, Document/Case 1,837, NOPL; Related Documents: Order, ca. April 1818; Judgment, 17 June 1818, with *Julia v. Berlin.* PAR 20881804. Granted.

43. Petition of Almira, by her next friend Carlo Bastia, to the District Court of Orleans Parish, Louisiana, 6 December 1816, in Records of the First Judicial District Court, Case Records, *Almira and Carlo Bastia v. Page and Genevieve Barlatier Rabouen*, Microfilm Reel 2, Louisiana Collection, Document/Case 1,261, NOPL; Related Documents: Court Records, 13 December 1816, 6 February 1817, 15 February 1817; Judgment, 1 March 1819, with *Bastia v. Rabouen et al.* PAR 20881614. Granted.

44. Petition of Maria Townes to the District Court of Orleans Parish, Louisiana, 29 March 1824, in Records of the First Judicial District Court, Case Records, *Maria Townes v. Reed*, Microfilm Reel 14, Louisiana Collection, Document/Case 6,075, NOPL; Related Documents: Orders, 29 March 1824, 20 December 1824; Deposition, Garland Tate, 29 November 1824, with *Townes v. Reed.* PAR 20882415. Granted.

45. Petition of John Johnson, with his next friend N. Wheeler, to the District Court of Orleans Parish, Louisiana, 10 April 1816, in Records of the First Judicial District Court, Case Records, *John Johnson v. S. Allain*, Microfilm Reel 1A, Louisiana Collection, Document/Case 1,043, NOPL; Related Documents: Order, 10 April 1816; Opinion, 4 July 1817; Copy of Opinion, 4 August 1817, with *Johnson v. Allain.* PAR 20881603. Granted.

46. Minutes of the Circuit Court for the District of Columbia, April 27, 1835, Reel 4, Frame 125, juror withdrawn; Minutes of Circuit Court, June 3, 1835, Reel 4, Frame 136, jury sworn; verdict for petitioners, NA. JCCASN, *Wallingsford v. Allen*, D.C., 10 Peters 583, January 1836, 4:196–197; Supreme Court, *Wallingsford, plaintiff in error v. Sarah Ann Allen*, 35 U.S. 10 Pet. 583 (1836). *Reports of Decisions in the Supreme Court of the United States, with Notes and a Digest*, comp. B. R. Curtis, 22 vols. (Boston: Little, Brown, 1870), 2: 255–261. GAA.

47. Petition of John Griffin to the County Court of Williamson County, Tennessee, 3 April 1843, in Records of the County Court, Emancipations, *John Griffin v [no named defendants]*, Williamson County Archives, Franklin, Tennessee; Related Documents: PAR 21484354; Certification of Character, Thomas Green, Jeremiah Bennet, Leonard Vernon, et al., 4 April

1839; Decree, 3 April 1843, with suit of Griffin [seeks to remain the state with his slave family]. PAR 21484302. Granted.

48. Petition of Sophia Tydings to the Orphans Court of Anne Arundel County, Maryland, 17 September 1833, in Register of Wills, 1820–1851 (Petitions and Orders), Microfilm CR 63,127, Frame/Pages 436–437, MSA; Related Documents: Testimony, Thomas Franklin, 17 September 1833; Order, 17 September 1833, with petition of Tydings. PAR 20983324. Granted. The children were permitted to remain in the state for one year.

49. Petition of Peter Rollins to the Orphans Court of Anne Arundel County, Maryland, 2 April 1840, in SC, Microfilm M 11024, Frame/Pages 1, Volume 4329-24, MSA; Related Documents: PAR 20984105; Order, 14 April 1840, with petition of Rollins. PAR 20984006. Granted.

50. Petition of Dolly, Washington, Jefferson, Leo, and Caroline to the Circuit Court of the District of Columbia, 14 December 1824, in RUSCC-CDRCF, *Dolly, Washington, Jefferson, Leo, and Caroline v. Robert Brawner and Samuel Wheeler*, Record Group 21, Box/Drawer 29, Entry Folder 344, Document/Case 20, December 14 1824, NA; Related Documents: Affidavit, Francis Scott Key, 13–14 December 1824; Correspondence, Robert Brawner to Samuel Wheeler, 19 May 1825, with *Dolly et al. v. Brawner et al.* PAR 20482405. Granted. Petition of Bob, Milley, Harry, Fanny, Sam, Michael, Milley, Perry, and Bob to the District Court of Iberville Parish, Louisiana, 17 April 1833, in Records of the Fourth Judicial District Court, *Bob, Milley, Harry, et al. v. John Nugent, Louis De Saule, and David Chambers*, Document/Case 1,322, Iberville Parish Courthouse, Plaquemine, Louisiana; Related Documents: Supplemental Petition, 17 April 1837; Answer, Louis De Saule, 2 April 1835; Argument for Plaintiffs, n.d.; Petition of Appeal, ca. April 1839; Order, 27 April 1839; Supreme Court Decree, 20 April 1840, with *Bob, et al. v. Nugent, et al.* PAR 20883304. JCCASN, *Bob and Milly et al. v. Nugent's Syndics*, 15 La. 63, March 1840, 3:524–525. D GARev.

51. JCCASN, *Griffith v. Fanny*, Va., Gilmer 143, December 1820, 1:133–134; *Virginia Reports, Jefferson—Grattan 1730–1880, Annotated and under the Supervision of Thomas Johnson Michie* (Charlottesville, Virginia: Michie Co., 1903), 863–864. GAA. Petition of Sally and Armistead to the Circuit Court of Jefferson County, Kentucky, 3 May 1822, in Records of the Circuit Court, Case Files, *Sally and Armistead v. Robert Turner*, Box/Drawer 1-11, Document/Case 837, KDLA; Related Documents: Order, 28 April 1822; Answer, Robert Turner, 21 February 1824; Decree, 9 October 1827; Appellate Decree, 13 June 1827, with *Armistead v. Turner*. PAR 20782208. Granted.

52. Petition of Sally Toogood, Martha Toogood, Rachael Ann Toogood, Mary Toogood, and Susan Rebecca Toogood to the Equity Court of Montgomery County, Maryland, 30 November 1822, in SC, *Sally Toogood, Martha Toogood, Rachael Ann Toogood, Mary Toogood, and Susan Rebecca Toogood v. Andrew Graff and Henry Howard*, Microfilm M 11024, Frame/Pages 2, Volume 4239-25, MSA; Related Documents: Bond, Henry Toogood and John Owings to Andrew Graff and Henry Howard, 30 November 1822; Agreement between Counsel for sale, 4 August 1823; Order of sale, 4 August 1823, with *Toogood et al. v. Graff et al.* The wife and children argued they were freed in Deed of Manumission by their former owner Peter Gardner. PAR 20982202. The injunction was granted and later partially withdrawn as per agreement of counsel; two of the petitioners were sold. In 1820, Henry Toogood lived with his wife and three daughters in Kent County on the Eastern Shore, some one hundred miles from Montgomery County where the suits were filed. USMSPC, Kent County, Maryland, 1820, image 18, ancestry.com.

53. Petition of Allen, and Stephen to the Hustings Court of Lynchburg City, Virginia, 4 August 1831, in Records of the Circuit Court of Chancery, *Watt, Allen, and Stephen v. Nathaniel Manson*, Box/Drawer 25, Document/Case 1198, LV. PAR 21683125. Granted. Petition of Watt, Allen, and Stephen to the Hustings Court of Lynchburg County, Virginia, August 1832, in Records of the Circuit Court of Chancery, *Watt, Allen, and Stephen v. Nathaniel I. Manson*, Box/Drawer 25, Document/Case 1198, LV; Related Documents: Copy of Transcript of Court Proceedings, ca. 21 August 1832; Copy of Last Will and Testament, Addison Davies, 5 June 1817, with *Watt et al. v. Manson*. PAR 21683233. Granted for Allen; dismissed without prejudice for Watt.

54. T. Stephen Whitman, *The Price of Freedom: Slavery and Manumission in Baltimore and Early National Maryland* (Frankfort: University of Kentucky Press, 1987), 98 [Maryland law]; John Codman Hurd, *The Law of Freedom and Bondage in the United States*, 2 vols. (Boston: Little, Brown, 1862; reprint, New York: Negro University Press, 1968), 2:87; Petition of William Blake to the Alabama General Assembly, 1823, in Records of the Alabama Secretary of State, Legislative Bills and Resolutions, ADAH; Related Documents: Report of Select Committee, November 1826, with petition of Blake. No decree with petition [Alabama law]. PAR 10182301. In 1831, a Tennessee law required emancipated blacks to secure a manumission deed from the county court and "thereupon immediately leave Tennessee," later revised to ninety days. *A Compilation of the Statutes of Tennessee, of a General and Permanent Nature, from the Commencement of the Government to the Present Time* (Nashville: James Smith, 1836), 279; *Acts Passed at the First Session of the Ninth Legislature of the State of Louisiana, Begun and Held in Donaldsonville, on the Third Day of January, One Thousand Eight Hundred and Thirty-One, and of the Independence of the United States of America the Fifty-Fourth* (New Orleans: John Gibson, 1831), 98, 100; John Hope Franklin, *The Free Negro in North Carolina, 1790–1860* (Chapel Hill: University of North Carolina Press, 1943), 27; *Acts Passed by the General Assembly of the State of North Carolina, at the Session of 1830–31* (Raleigh, NC: Lawrence & Lemay, 1831), 12–14 [thirty days]; Petition of John Forsyth, Walter Irwin, Woodson Wren, John Carson, and Morris Whitney to the Mississippi General Assembly, 4 June 1822, in Legislative Papers, Petitions and Memorials 1822, Record Group 47, Volume 17, MDAH; Related Documents: Deed of Manumission, John Forsyth, 6 January 1823; John Forsyth to C. M. Norton, 8 January 1823, with petition of Forsyth et al [Mississippi law]. PAR 11082201.
55. Petition of Ambrose Lewis to the Missouri General Assembly, 24 December 1846, in Records of the House of Representatives, 14th General Assembly, 1st Session, 1846–1847, Record Group 550, MoSA; Related Documents: Certificates, Thomas Shore, et al., Ashton R. Johnson, Edward E. Archer, Thomas Wright, ca. 1846; Certificate, J. D. Osborne, 26 December 1846; Certificate, John Shore, 26 December 1846; Certificates, A. J. Coons, J. B Osborn, Willis L. Williams, ca. 1846; Copy of Act for the Benefit of Ambrose Lewis and others, ca. 1847, with petition of Lewis. PAR 11184605 [Missouri law]. Granted. *Acts Passed at the General Assembly for the Commonwealth of Kentucky, Passed at November Session, 1850* (Frankfort, KY: A. G. Hodges, 1851), 305–308.
56. US House of Representatives, *The Federal and State Constitutions, Colonial Charters, and Other Organic Laws of the States Territories, and Colonies*, 59th Cong., 2nd sess., 7 vols. (Washington, DC: Government Printing Office, 1909): 6:3539; JCCASN, "Texas: Introduction," 5:270; ibid., *Purvis et al. v. Sherrod, Executor*, 12 Tex. 140, 1854, 5:287 (n.2) [Texas law].
57. Petition of Elizabeth McClary, Clem McClary Sr., Rachel McClary, Peter McClary, Mary Ann McClary, Susan McClary, Eleanor McClary, and Clem McClary Jr., by their next friend Clem McClary Sr. to the County Court of Williamson County, Tennessee, 3 October 1842, in Records of the County Court, Emancipations, Williamson County Archives, Franklin, Tennessee; Related Documents: Report, 3 October 1842; Decree, 3 October 1842; Certification, Martin Clark, ca. October 1842, with petition of McClary, et al. PAR 21484220. Granted.
58. *Acts Passed by the General Assembly of the Commonwealth of Virginia, Begun and Held at the Capitol, in the City of Richmond, on Monday the Second Day of December, One Thousand Eight Hundred and Five* (Richmond, VA: Samuel Pleasants, 1806), 36; June Purcell Guild, ed., *Black Laws of Virginia: A Summary of the Legislative Acts of Virginia Concerning Negroes from Earliest Times to the Present* (Richmond, VA: Whittet & Shepperson, 1936; reprint, New York: Negro Universities Press, 1969), 72, 106, 117; Thomas Morris, *Southern Slavery and the Law, 1619–1860* (Chapel Hill: University of North Carolina Press, 1996), 372.
59. Petition of William Parker to the Mississippi General Assembly, in Legislative Papers, n.d., Petitions and Memorials 1817–1839, Record Group 47, Volume 17, MDAH. Referred to Committee. PAR 11000008.
60. Petition of James Butler to the Virginia General Assembly, Petersburg Corporation, 6 December 1810, in Legislative Petitions, LV; Related Documents: Testimonial, R. Bate, 6 May 1805; List of Subscribers, ca. 1810, with petition of Butler. Reasonable, reported ["considerably advanced in years"]. PAR 11681002.

61. Petition of John Malone to the North Carolina General Assembly, Wake County, 28 November 1846, in General Assembly, Session Records, Senate Committee Reports, November 1846–January 1847, NCDAH; Related Documents: Testimonials of Will A. Graham, 22 November 1846, Will H. Haywood Jr., et al., 18 November 1846; Notice of Petition for Emancipation of Cherry and Edmund Malone in *Raleigh Register and Star*, 26 August 1846; Grand Jury Report, November 1846; Report of the Committee on Propositions and Grievances, ca. 1846, with petition of Malone. Committee favorable; Laid on table [purchasing loved ones]. PAR 11284602. Petition J. R. Drake, E. Peebles, John W. Gay, and eighty-five other residents of Northampton County on behalf of James Langford to the North Carolina General Assembly, Session Records, NCDAH; No act with petition. Northampton County residents wrote that Langford purchased himself but that his wife and children remained enslaved. PAR 11285203. Petition of Temperance Crutcher to the Tennessee General Assembly, Davidson County, 2 December 1837, in Legislative Petitions, Microfilm Reel 15, Document/Case 155-1837, 1, 2, TSLA; Referred to committee ["kindred and friends"]. PAR 11483722.

62. Petition of Judith Hope to the Virginia General Assembly, Richmond City, 11 December 1820, in Legislative Petitions, LV; Related Documents: PAR 11681901, and PAR 11682111, with petition of Hope. Bill drawn. She was purchased by her mother but did not gain her freedom. PAR 11682002.

63. Petition of Dick to the Virginia General Assembly, Patrick County, 26 January 1837, in Legislative Petitions, LV; Related Documents: Certificate, David Ross, et al., ca. 1837; Copy of Deed of Emancipation, John Koger to Dick, 10 February 1835, with petition of Dick. referred to Committee for Courts of Justice ["sorrows and vicissitudes"]. PAR 11683713. Petition of Richard Gregory to the Virginia General Assembly, Chesterfield County, 15 February 1848, in Legislative Petitions, LV; Related Documents: PARs 11684808, 11684810, with petition of Gregory. Referred to Committee for Courts of Justice [severing the ties of "flesh and blood"]. PAR 11684809.

64. Petition of John Griffith, W. N. Brown, G. L. Henderson, G. R. Taylor, and William Dyer to the Tennessee General Assembly, Monroe County, 23 January 1858, in Legislative Petitions, Microfilm Reel 20, Document/Case 156-1858-1-2, TSLA. Referred to Judiciary Committee. PAR 11485801.

65. Petition of Milly Brown to the Shelby County Court, Tennessee, 2 July 1848, in Memphis and Shelby County Archives, Document/Case 508; Related Documents: Order, 3 July 1848; Bond, Milly Brown, et al., to the Chairman of the County Court of Shelby County, Tennessee, 2 July 1848; Notification, Milly Brown, 6 June 1848; Affidavit, Barton Richmond, 15 January 1847, with petition of Brown. PAR 21484802. Granted.

66. *Acts of the State of Tennessee, Passed at the First Session of the Thirtieth General Assembly, for the Years 1853–4* (Nashville: M'Kennie & Brown, 1854), 121–122.

67. Petition of Ellie, Jacob, Lizy, Bob, Susan, Violet, and Reynolds, to the Tennessee General Assembly, Stewart County, 13 December 1855, in Legislative Petitions, Microfilm Reel 20, Case 45-1855-2-1, TSLA; Related Documents: List of Subscribers, ca. 1855; PAR 11485504, with petition of Lizy et al. referred to Judiciary Committee. PAR 11485508.

68. See note 1, this chapter; for a description of Williams' slave pen, see Stanley Harrold, *Subversives: Antislavery Community in Washington, D.C., 1828–1865* (Baton Rouge: Louisiana State University Press, 2003), 104; Sue L Eakin and Joseph Logsdon, eds., *Twelve Years A Slave: Narrative Of Solomon Northup, a Citizen Of New-York, Kidnapped in Washington City in 1841, and Rescued in 1853, from a Cotton Plantation near the Red River, in Louisiana* (Baton Rouge: Louisiana State University Press, 1968), 21–23.

Chapter 12

1. USMSPC, Jefferson County, Kentucky, Louisville, 1840, image 259, ancestry.com; USMSPC, Jefferson County, Kentucky, Louisville, 1850, image 76, ancestry.com; USMSSC, Jefferson County, Kentucky, Louisville, District 2, 1850, image 4, ancestry.com.

2. See notes 81–83, this chapter.

3. For an overview of the legal profession, see Alfred S. Konefsky, "The Legal Profession: From the Revolution to the Civil War," in *The Cambridge History of Law in America*, vol. 2: *The Long Nineteenth Century (1789–1920)*, ed. Michael Grossberg and Christopher Tomlins (Cambridge: Cambridge University Press, 2008), 68–105.

4. Lea VanderVelde, *Redemption Songs: Suing for Freedom before Dred Scott* (New York: Oxford Press, 2014), 6; Kelly Marie Kennington, "River of Injustice: St. Louis's Freedom Suits and the Changing Nature of Legal Slavery in Antebellum America" (PhD diss., Duke University, 2009), 31–32.

5. Judith Kelleher Schafer, *Becoming Free, Remaining Free: Manumission and Enslavement in New Orleans, 1846–1862* (Baton Rouge: Louisiana State University Press, 2003), 16 [1846 law], 23–24; Petition of Arséne to the District Court of Orleans Parish, Louisiana, 1847, in Supreme Court of Louisiana Collection, *Arséne v. Louis Aimé Pineguy*, Book 459, UNO; Related Documents: Testimonies, J. Ducourneau, et al., ca. 1847; Court Record of Case No. 395, 24 October 1846–24 December 1846, including: *Arsene alias Cora vs. Louis Arsene Pigneguy [Aimé Pineguy]*, 24 October 1846; and Opinion, 4 November 1846; Supreme Court Opinion and Decree, 14 June 1847, with *Arséne v. Pineguy*. PAR 20884746. GAA. Petition of Marie to the District Court of West Baton Rouge Parish, Louisiana, 4 September 1848, in Records of the Sixth Judicial District Court, *Marie v. Doussan Dr. and Doussan Mrs.*, Document/Case 1,007, West Baton Rouge Parish Courthouse, Port Allen, Louisiana; Related Documents: Judgment, 27 September 1848; Answer, 14 September 1848; Answer to Interrogatories, 7 September 1848, with *Marie v. Doussan*. PAR 20884843. Granted.

6. Richard Bassett, Delaware, US Army Center of Military History, http://www.history.army. mil/books/RevWar/ss/Bassett.htm; William Williams, *Slavery and Freedom in Delaware 1639–1865* (Wilmington, DE: SR Books, 1996), 150; Robert Pattison, *The Life and Character of Richard Bassett (Papers of the Historical Society of Delaware)* (Wilmington, DE: Historical Society of Delaware, 1900), 3–9.

7. Petition of Mary Queen, Charles Queen, and Elizabeth Queen to the County Court of Charles County, Maryland, 1 May 1808, in SC, *Mary Queen, Charles Queen, and Elizabeth Queen v. Charles Neale*, Microfilm M 11014, Frame/Pages 24, Volume 4239-3, Document/ Case 13, MSA; Related Documents: Court Record, 1 May 1808–10 December 1810, with *Queen et al. v. Neale*. PAR 20980806. DisAA. Petition of Nancy Queen to the County Court of Charles County, Maryland, 1 May 1808, in SC, *Nancy Queen v. Charles Neale*, Microfilm M 11014, Frame/Pages 25, Volume 4239-3, MSA; Related Documents: Court Record, 1808–1810; Court Opinion, ca. 1810; Court of Appeals Opinion, 17 December 1810, with *Queen v. Neale*. PAR 20980807. DAA. They were not successful as the appeals court ruled a black petitioner for freedom could not file an affidavit for a CV under the Maryland act of 1804, chap. 55, sec. 2; such a case was *sub judice* [under justice] and slaves were excluded by the act of 1717, chap. 13. JCCASN, *Queen v. Neal*, Md., 3 Har. and John. 158, December 1810, 5:62.

8. USMSPC, Anne Arundel County, Maryland, Annapolis, 1820, p. 9; Anne Arundel County, Maryland, 1830, pp. 3–4; Anne Arundel County, Maryland, District 2, 1840, pp. 11–12; Anne Arundel County, Maryland, Annapolis, 1840, pp. 1–2; In 1840, Nicholas Brewer Jr. possessed twenty-one slaves. Conway Sams and Elihu Riley, *The Bench and Bar of Maryland: A History 1634-1901*, 2 vols. (Chicago: Lewis, 1901), 2:597–600.

9. *Negro Ben v. Sabbrett Scott*, June Term 1807, in *Reports of Cases Civil and Criminal in the United States Circuit Court of the District of Columbia, 1801–1841*, 6 vols., comp. William Cranch (Boston: Little, Brown, 1852), 1:407–408, 532–533; Letitia Woods Brown, *Free Negroes in the District of Columbia, 1790–1846* (New York: Oxford University Press, 1972), 209n.5; JCCASN, *Scott v. Negro Ben*, 10 US 6 Cranch 3, February 1810, 4:163. G GARR; appealed to the US Supreme Court, http://supreme.justia.com/cases/federal/us/10/3/. *Joseph Brown, (Negro,) v. Mary Wigard*, April Term 1822, in *Reports of Cases Civil and Criminal in the United States Circuit Court of the District of Columbia*, 2:261–262. DAA. In 1830, Key possessed six slaves. USMSPC, District of Columbia, Georgetown, 1830, image 61, ancestry.com; for abolitionists in the District of Columbia, see Stanley Harrold, *Subversives: Antislavery Community in Washington, D.C., 1828–1865* (Baton Rouge: Louisiana State University Press, 2003); Jefferson Morley, *Snow-Storm in August: Washington City, Francis Scott Key,*

and the Forgotten Race Riot of 1835 (New York: Doubleday, 2012), 40; Marc Leepson, What So Proudly We Hailed: Francis Scott Key A Life (New York: Palgrave Macmillan, 2014), xi–xii, 25, 27, 38, 95, 130–31, 187, 191. For many of his cases, see: O Say Can You See: Early Washington, D.C., Law and Family website http://earlywashingtondc.org.

10. Crenshaw owned eight slaves in 1840. USMSPC, Barren County, Kentucky, 1840, p. 140; H. Levin, ed., Lawyers and Lawmakers of Kentucky (Chicago: Lewis, 1897), 87 in www.usbiographies.org/biographies/read.php?365,612.

11. John Hope Franklin and Loren Schweninger, In Search of the Promised Land: A Slave Family in the Old South (New York: Oxford University Press, 2006), 91, 269.

12. JCCASN, Barclay (f.w.c.) v. Sewell, 12 La. An. 262, April 1857, 3:653–4. GAA. Schafer, Becoming Free, 32. In 1850, Roselius owned five slaves, three adults, ages twenty-five to forty, a black girl age thirteen, and an eight-year-old mulatto boy. USMSSC, New Orleans, Louisiana, 1st Municipality, 4th ward, 1850, image 7, ancestry.com.

13. Petition of Matilda to the Superior Court of St. Louis County, Missouri, 4 April 1816, in Records of the Supreme Court, Case Files, Matilda v. Isaac Vanbibber, Box/Drawer 41, Entry Folder 35, Document/Case 3, MoSA; Related Documents: Plea of Trespass, Matilda, 17 September 1816; Sheriff's Return, 14 August 1816; Deposition, William Everitt, 5 March 1817; Affidavit, Joseph Philips, 18 March 1817; Deposition, Matthias M. Girk, 4 April 1816; Declaration, Matilda, September Term 1817; Pleas, Isaac Vanbibber, 3 September 1817; Replication, Matilda, 3 September 1817, with Matilda v. Vanbibber [Mathias McGirk] PAR 21181602. No decree with petition. Petition of Susan to the Circuit Court of St. Charles County, Missouri, 2 May 1817, in Records of the Circuit Court, Susan v. Henry Hight, Document/Case 127, CCBSL; Related Documents: Supreme Court Record, 25 September 1821; Supreme Court Opinion [incomplete], 27 September 1821; Supreme Court Records, 24 September 1821, 13 October 1821; Plea of Trespass, Susan, ca. May 1817; Summons, Henry Hight, 9 June 1817; Sheriff's Return, 24 July 1817; Summons, William Thompson, 16 January 1818; Action of Assault and Battery, Susan, ca. May 1817; Jury Verdict, ca. May 1817, with Susan v. Hight. PAR 21181701. JCCASN, Susan (a black woman) v. Hight, 1 Mo. 118, September 1821, 5:124. G DARR. William Van Ness Bay, Reminiscences of the Bench and Bar of Missouri, with an Appendix, Containing Biographical Sketches of Nearly All of the Judges and Lawyers who have Passed Away ... (St. Louis: F. H. Thomas, 1878), 536–537. As a young man Bey met Mathias McGirk (1783–1842) who was then at the end of his life.

14. See note 14, chap. 7, this volume. Petition of Winny [Winney], et al. to the Superior Court of St. Louis County, Missouri, June 1818, in Records of the Circuit Court; (Certified Copy of Petition and Related Documents found in Supreme Court Cases, Box 541, Case 18, MoSA), Winney, et al., v. Whitesides, et al., Document/Case 190, CCBSL; Supreme Court Opinion, 8 November 1824, with Winney, et al. v. Whitesides [J. Barton and Henry Geyer, attorneys]. PAR 21181801. GAA.

15. Petition of Jenney to the Supreme Court of St. Louis County, Missouri, 4 May 1825, in Records of the Supreme Court, Case Files, Jenney v. Ephraim Musick, Box/Drawer 23, Document/Case 68, MoSA; Related Documents: PAR 21181801; Affidavit, Jenny, 3 May 1825; Writ of Habeas Corpus, Jenny, 4 May 1825; Return to Writ of Habeas Corpus, Ephraim Musick, 4 May 1825; Suggestions Against the Return to the Writ of Habeas Corpus, Jenny, 5 May 1825; Supplemental Return, Ephraim Musick, 6 May 1825, with Jenney v. Musick. PAR 21182502. Granted [Edward Bates attorney]. William E. Foley, "Slave Freedom Suits before Dred Scott: The Case of Marie Jean Scypion's Descendants," Missouri Historical Review 79 (1984–1985): 15; Petition of Henry Jackson, Margarett Jackson, Sally Jackson, Anne Maria, William Henry, and Smith to the Circuit Court of St. Louis County, Missouri, 23 March 1842, in Records of the Circuit Court, Henry Jackson, Margarett Jackson, Sally Jackson, et al., v. James V. Frazier, Document/Case 102, CCBSL; Related Documents: PARs 21183105, 21183113, 21183406, 21184209; Order, ca. 23 March 1842; Writ of Habeas Corpus, Henry Jackson, et al., 30 March 1842; Sheriff's Return, 30 March 1842, with Jackson et al. v. Frazier [Hamilton R. Gamble, attorney]. PAR 21184208. Granted.

16. J. Thomas Scharf, History of St. Louis City and County from the Earliest Period to the Present Day, Including Biographical Sketches of Representative Men, 2 vols. (Philadelphia: Louis H. Everts, 1883), 2:1463.

17. Created from an Excel file on the freedom suits in this study, Denise Johnson found 689 lawyers prosecuting freedom suits in 1,452 cases. The records of county courts, appeals courts, and various secondary sources failed to cite counsel in about 571 cases, thus the conservative estimate of more than one thousand lawyers.

18. Kennington, "River of Injustice," 118–120.

19. Petition of John Thornton to the Circuit Court of the District of Columbia, 11 March 1835, in RUSCC-CDRCF, *John Thornton v. Orrin Davis*, Record Group 21, Rules 3, Box/Drawer 43, Entry Folder 330, NA; Related Documents: Depositions, Orrin Davis, James Long, 24 March 1835; Injunction, Orrin Davis, ca. 1835; Court Record, ca. 1835, with *Thornton v. Davis*. PAR 20483505. Injunction granted. Gilbert Giberson, in his forties, headed a household in 1840 with two women, one in her thirties the other in her twenties, and a girl between ten and fifteen. He possessed no slaves. USMSPC, District of Columbia, 1840, p. 26.

20. Ira Berlin, *Slaves without Masters: The Free Negro in the Antebellum South* (New York: Pantheon, 1974), 102; John Hope Franklin, *The Militant South, 1800–1861* (Cambridge: Harvard University Press, 1956), chap. 1; Elizabeth Fox-Genovese, *Within the Plantation Household: Black and White Women of the Old South* (Chapel Hill: University of North Carolina Press, 1988), 9, 16–17, 24, 94, 132, 308–316; Bertram Wyatt-Brown, *Honor and Violence in the Old South* (New York: Oxford University Press, 1986), xiii, 34, 43.

21. Petition of Prince Gray to the Circuit Court of the District of Columbia, 4 September 1820, in RUSCC-CDRCF, *Prince Gray v. Joel Gustine*, Record Group 21, Rules 1, Box/Drawer 28, Entry Folder 20, Document/Case 98, NA; Related Documents: Opinion of Counsel, B. Thurston, 4 September 1820; Opinion of Counsel, David M. Forrest, 4 September 1820, with *Gray v. Gustine*. PAR 20482005. Granted.

22. Petition of Eliza Chapman and Robert Chapman to the Circuit Court of the District of Columbia, 17 August 1833, in RUSCC-CDRCF, *Eliza Chapman and Robert Chapman v. Robert Fenwick*, Record Group 21, Book Rules 3, Box/Drawer 40, Entry Folder 20, Document/Case 250, NA; Related Documents: Subpoena, Robert Fenwick, 17 August 1833; Injunction, Robert Fenwick, 17 August 1833; Correspondence, Robert Dunlop to William Cranch, 17 August 1833, with *Chapman v. Fenwick*. PAR 20483303. Granted.

23. Petition of Guy to the Common Pleas Court of Kent County, Delaware, ca. 1800, in Records of the Court of Common Pleas, *Guy v. James Hutchins*, Microfilm Reel 1, Frame/Pages 302–303, DSA [illegal importation]. PAR 20380023. GAA. Petition of Charlotte, Maria, Ambrose, and Delia to the Circuit Court of the District of Columbia, 22 February 1821, in RUSCC-CDRCF, *Charlotte, Maria, Ambrose, and Delia v. Jonathan T. Burch*, Record Group 21, Entry Folder 20, Document/Case 284, NA; Related Documents: Deposition, Benjamin Ringgold, 22 February 1823; Letter, Singleton Townshend, 4 March 1821; Bond, Singleton Townshend, 3 March 1821; Jail Receipt, George Miller, ca. 1821; Bill of Sale, Urban Hollyday, 14 February 1821; Bond Receipt, Singleton Townshend, 5 March 1821; Decree, 22 February 1821, with *Charlotte et al. v. Burch* [term slave ten years; children to be freed at age thirty-five]. PAR 20482101. Granted. See Note 28, chap. 10, this volume; Answer, Richard Phillips, 3 November 1807; Order, November Term 1807, with *Ralph et al. v. Phillips* [Virginia owner signed deed of emancipation; lawyer could not produce a copy of the deed]. PAR 20780702. Denied.

24. Petition of John and Margarett Sarpee to the Circuit Court of St. Louis County, Missouri, 19 November 1831, in Records of the Circuit Court, *John and Margarett Sarpee v. William Campbell*, Document/Case 6, CCBSL; Related Documents: PARs 21182606, 21184114; Order, 19 November 1831; Plea of Trespass, John vs. William Campbell, 19 November 1831; Subpoena, William Campbell, 19 November 1831; Sheriff's Return, 19 November 1831; Copy of Order, 19 November 1831; Writ of *Habeas Corpus*, John, 20 November 1831; Sheriff's Return, 20 November 1831; Plea, William Campbell, 27 March 1832; Statement, John, ca. 27 March 1832; Notice to Take Depositions, John to William Campbell, 9 July 1832; Sheriff's Return, 9 July 1832; Order, 9 July 1832; Subpoena, Clayton and Eliza Tiffin, 13 July 1832; Sheriff's Returns, 16 and 21 July 1832; Deposition, Francis Jarrot, St. Clair County, Illinois, 14 July 1832; Justice's Certification, St. Clair County, Illinois, 16 July 1832; Clerk's Certification, County Court, St. Clair County, Illinois, 17 July 1832; Subpoenas, Clayton and Eliza Tiffin, 6 November 1832, 26 February 1833; Sheriff's Returns, 12 November 1832, 1

March 1833; Warrant, Clayton Tiffin, 22 April 1833; Sheriff's Return, ca. 22–23 April 1833, with *Sarpee et al. v. Campbell*. PAR 21183108. Granted.

25. Petition of Maria to the Circuit Court of Fayette County, Kentucky, 4 January 1850, in Records of the Circuit Court, Case Files, *Maria v. Rebecca Kirby*, Box/Drawer 143, Document/Case 711, KDLA; Related Documents: Answer, Rebecca Kirby, 15 January 1850; Interrogatories, July 1850; Deposition, Joseph Boyd, 16 July 1850; Decree, 31 March 1857, with *Maria v. Kirby*. PAR 20785001. Dismissed.

26. Petition of Caroline to the Circuit Court of St. Louis County, Missouri, 26 December 1845, in Records of the Circuit Court, *Caroline v. John H. Ferguson*, Document/Case 20, CCBSL; Related Documents: Affidavit, Caleb Lockwood, 24 December 1845; Order, 26 December 1845; Copy of Order, 26 December 1845; Sheriff's Return, 31 December 1845, with *Caroline v. Ferguson*. PAR 21184519. Granted.

27. Petition of Margaret Lee, Maria Lee, and Abraham Lee to the Superior Court of Washington County, Tennessee, 18 September 1795, in Washington County Court Records, Superior Court, Record Group 18, Box/Drawer 2, Entry Folder 7, AAETSU. PAR 21479502. No decree with petition.

28. Petition of Jenney Ash to the County Court of Bertie County, North Carolina, 1785, in Records of the County Court, Slave Papers 1781–1786, *Jenney Ash v. John Gardner*, NCDAH; Related Documents: Answer, John Gardner, 12 May 1785, with *Ash v. Gardner*. PAR 21278502 [children illegally enslaved]. No decree with petition. JCCASN, *Charlton v. Unis*, Vir., 4 Grattan 58, July 1847, 1:212; JCCASN, *Unis v. Charlton*, Vir., 12 Grattan 484, August 1855; JCCASN, 1:238; *Reports of Cases Argued and Determined in the Supreme Court of Virginia*, vol. 12: *From January 1 to October 1 1855*, comp. Peachey R Grattan (Richmond, VA: Richie and Dunnavant, 1856), 484–498 [kidnapped in North]. DAA. See note 17, chap. 6, this volume.

29. Petition of Clarissa Highland to the County Court of Charles County, Maryland, 17 September 1824, in SC, *Clarissa Highland v. Ann W. Wood*, Microfilm M 11018, Volume 4239-5, Document/Case 12352, MSA; Related Documents: PARs 20982401, 20983718; Copy of Court Record, 17 September 1824-ca. 27 March 1828; Copy of List of Sales, John Perrie, Prince George's County, 1795; Clerk's Certification, 14 October 1837, with *Highland v. Wood*. PAR 20982402. Granted. Petition of Lemman Dutton and Grace Dutton, free person of color and next friend, to the Circuit Court of St. Louis County, Missouri, 12 July 1834, in Records of the Supreme Court, Case Files, *Lemman Dutton and Grace Dutton v. John Paca*, Box/Drawer 545, Document/Case 22, MoSA; Related Documents: PARs 21183105, 21183113, 21184208, 21184209; Transcript of Court Record, *Lemman Dutton vs. John Paca*, 12 July 1834-8 April 1836; Clerk's Certification, 31 May 1836; Copy of Petition, 12 July 1834; Copy of Deed of Manumission, Josiah William Dallam, Harford County, Maryland, 13 March 1787; Bill of Exceptions, John Paca, 8 April 1836; Writ of Error, Missouri Supreme Court, 21 April 1836; Reply to Writ, Clerk of Circuit Court, 1 June 1836; Opinion, Missouri Supreme Court, ca. 5 July 1836, with *Dutton v. Paca*. PAR 21183406. JCCASN, *Paca v. Dutton*, Mo., 4 Mo. 371, June 1836, 5:149. GAA. Petition of Elizabeth, John, and Beverly to the Circuit Court of Chesterfield County, Virginia, May 1853, in Ended Chancery Court Causes, *Elizabeth, John, and Beverly v. Higgison Hancock [and minors] Mary, Robert, James, Washington, and Martha*, Entry Folder C-E May 1853–1854, LV; Related Documents: PAR 21684603; Amended Bill, ca. May 1853; Answer, Mary, Robert, James, Washington and Martha, May 1853; Answer, Higgison Hancock, May 1853; Order, May 1853; Decree, October Term 1853; Commissioner's Report, 31 March 1854; Final Decree, 4 May 1854, with *Elizabeth et al. v. Hancock et al.* PAR 21685305. Granted.

30. Petition of Rachel Steel to the Circuit Court of St. Louis County, Missouri, 15 March 1845, in Records of the Circuit Court, *Rachel Steel v. Thomas Taylor*, Document/Case 187, CCBSL; Related Documents: Order, 25 March 1845; Certificate of Character, Charlotte Grimes, 25 March 1845; Copy of Order, 25 March 1845; Plea of Trespass, *Rachel Steel v. Thomas Taylor*, April Term 1845; Summons, Thomas Taylor, 3 April 1845; Sheriff's Return, ca. 1845, with *Steel v. Taylor*. PAR 21184510 [dismissed when defendant failed to appear]. Granted, dismissed by plaintiff.

31. Petition of Margaret to the Circuit Court of Perry County, Missouri, 14 April 1836, in Records of the Circuit Court, *Margaret v. Leo Fenwick*, Document/Case 344, MoSA; Related

Documents: Order, 14 April 1836; Subpoena, Robert Manning, 24 August 1838; Subpoena, Wilson Brown and Robert Brown, 28 May 1838; Sheriff's Return, 28 May 1838; Subpoena, John Simon, J. M. Odin, 15 December 1838; Sheriff's Returns, 24 November 1838, 4 January 1839, 26 January 1839; Deposition, Edward M. Holden, 31 May 1838; Subpoena, Thomas Tevyman, Robert Manning, Joseph James, 15 May 1838; Sheriff's Return, 17 May 1838; Plea of Trespass, Margaret, 14 April 1836; Summons, Leo Fenwick, 11 May 1836; Copy of Order, 14 April 1836; Sheriff's Return, 17 July 1836; Subpoena, Joseph James, Fenwick J. Hamilton, Thomas Tevyman, 11 January 1838; Affidavit, Edward M. Holden, 27 September 1838; Subpoena, Joseph James, Fenwick J. Hamilton, Thomas Tevyman, 15 September 1837; Sheriff's Returns, 18 and 19 September 1837; Subpoena, Joseph James, Fenwick J. Hamilton, Thomas Tevyman, 30 May 1837; Sheriff's Returns, 3 and 21 June 1837; Subpoena, Joseph James, Fenwick Hamilton, 31 January 1837; Sheriff's Returns, 7 February 1837, 17 March 1837; Memorandum, 26 November 1836; Plea, Leo Fenwick, 9 August 1836; Subpoena, Joseph James, Fenwick J. Hamilton, 26 November 1836; Sheriff's Return, 3 December 1836, with *Margaret v. Fenwick.* PAR 21183610. Petition to sue granted; plea of trespass filed; no final result. In 1840, lawyer Edward Holden owned one slave. USMSPC, Perry County, Missouri, 1840, image 57, ancestry.com.

32. Petition of Daniel Hancock to the District Court of St. Landry Parish, Louisiana, 20 December 1823, in Records of the Fifth Judicial District Court, *Daniel Hancock v. John Davis,* Document/Case 834, St. Landry Parish Courthouse, Opelousas, Louisiana; Related Documents: Depositions, Obediah Pearson and Alexander Robb, 20 December 1823; Deposition of Mary, free woman of color, New York City, ca. 1824 [summarized by the judge in his decree]; Copy of Petition, 20 December 1823; Bond, 29 December 1823; Amended Petition, 1824; Supplemental Petition, ca. 1824; Supplemental Petition, 15 May 1824; Order, June 1825; Order, 14 June 1825; Answer, John Davis, 12 May 1824; Judgment, November Term 1826, with *Hancock v. Davis.* PAR 20882322. Granted.

33. Petition of James Becket to the Circuit Court of the District of Columbia, 28 August 1845, in RUSCC-CDRCF, *James Becket v. William Glover, Thomas Williams, and Agnes Clarke,* Record Group 21, Files 4, Box/Drawer 58, Entry Folder 20, Document/Case 382, NA; Related Documents: Sworn Statement, J. M. Carlisle, ca. 28 August 1845; Answer, William Glover, 23 March 1846; Copy of Last Will and Testament, John Chew, 9 May 1815; Oath, Jasper M. Jackson Sr., 28 March 1850; Testimony, Solomon Sibley, 28 March 1850; Injunction, William Glover, Thomas Williams and Agnes Clarke, 28 August 1845, with *Becket v. Glover.* PAR 20484504. Granted. Carlisle was listed as solicitor at the beginning of the case. Although no solicitor was cited with Sibley's affidavit, if a different lawyer had taken over he probably would have been cited.

34. Petition of Anthony to the Circuit Court of Cumberland County, Kentucky, 24 May 1848, in Records of the Circuit Court, Equity Judgments, *Anthony v. Josiah Brummall and Nicholas C. Robinson,* Microfilm Reel 218723, Document/Case 1707, KDLA; Related Documents: Order, 24 May 1848; Amended Bill, July Term 1848; Answer, Josiah Brummal, 16 May 1849; Depositions, Milton King, Elam F. Boles, and F. W. Alexander, 30 March 1850; Summons, Elam F. Boles, 30 March 1850; Copy of Deed of Emancipation, 23 March 1793; Orders, July Term 1848, October Term 1848, 14 April 1849, 12 October 1849, April Term 1850 and 12 July 1850; Decree, September 1850, with *Anthony v. Brummall et al.* PAR 20784805. Granted.

35. Petition of Fortune Scott to the Circuit Court of the District of Columbia, 20 January 1836, in RUSCC-CDRCF, *Fortune Scott v. William F. Masters,* Record Group 21, Rules 3, Box/Drawer 44, Entry Folder 20, Document/Case 371, NA; Related Documents: Injunction, William F. Masters, 20 January 1836, with *Scott v. Masters.* PAR 20483611. Granted.

36. Petition of Lucy Crawford to the City Court of Baltimore City, Maryland, 7 November 1845, in SC, *Lucy Crawford v. Hope H. Slatter,* Microfilm M 11024, Volume 4239-26, MSA; Related Documents: PARs 20484205, 20984308, 20984508, 20985117; Transcript of Baltimore City Court Proceedings, 6 October 1845–23 March 1848, with *Crawford v. Hope H. Slatter.* PAR 20984507. GAA. District of Columbia lawyer John Hellen filed a complaint against Crawford's owner in the District a few weeks before McCulloch submitted his petition in Baltimore. Petition of Lucy Crawford to the Circuit Court of the District of Columbia, 18

October 1845, in RUSCC-CDRCF, *Lucy Crawford v. Martha A. Scott and Alexander Hunter*, Record Group 21, Rules 4, Box/Drawer 58, Entry Folder 20, Document/Case 387, NA; Related Documents: Injunction, Martha Scott, 18 October 1845; Request for Dismissal, J. Hellen for complainant, 21 October 1845, with *Crawford v. Scott et al.* PAR 20484503. Granted. Stanley Harrold, *Subversives: Antislavery Community in Washington, D.C., 1828–1865* (Baton Rouge: Louisiana State University Press, 2003), 114; Frederic Bancroft, *Slave-Trading in the Old South* (Baltimore: J. H. Furst, 1931), 37–38.

37. Petition of Dennis, Mingo, Dick, Joice, Esther, Demos, Tilday, Jacob, and Jim to the Chancery Court of Southampton County, Virginia, March 1808, in Chancery Court Papers, *Dennis, et al. v. James Sebrell, Jethro Joyner, William Joyner, and James Jones*, Box/Drawer 19, Entry Folder 1814-69, LV; Related Documents: Order, ca. March 1808; Answer, James Sebrell, 19 December 1808; Answers, William Joyner, James Jones, ca. December 1808; Depositions, Presley [Presly] Barrett, Micajah Joyner, 16 October 1809; Copy of Petition to sue *in forma pauperus*, 18 June 1807, with *Dennis et al. v. Sebrell et al.* PAR 21680803. Petition to sue granted; case dismissed in 1814. See also: Petition of Charles Evans, Amey Evans, Sukey Evans, Sinar Evans, Solomon Evans, Frankey Evans, Sally Evans, Milly Evans, Adam Evans, and Hannah Evans to the Chancery Court of Richmond City, Virginia, 5 March 1804, in Records of the Circuit Superior Court of Chancery, *Charles Evans, Amey Evans, Sukey Evans, et al. v. Lewis B. Allen*, Box/Drawer 4, Document/Case 236, LV; Related Documents: Statement, Edmund Randolph, attorney, 5 March 1804; Order, March 1804, with *Evans et al. v. Allen.* PAR 21680501. Granted. Robert McColley, *Slavery in Jeffersonian Virginia*, 2nd ed. (Urbana: University of Illinois Press, 1973), 160 [Virginia law].

38. Petition of Rebecca Petition of Bett, Ben, Mary, Eliza, and Jack to the Superior Court of Winchester County, Virginia, 15 December 1818, in Ended Superior Court Cases, Frederick County, *Bett, Ben, Mary, Eliza, and Jack v. Charles Lewis and John Wimbish*, Box/Drawer 33, Entry Folder 1820, LV; Related Documents: Order, 17 December 1818; Amended Bill, April 1819; Answer, Charles Lewis, 22 November 1819; Court Notes, ca. April 1820; Decree and Copy of Decree, April 1820, 15 April 1820; Commissioners' Report, ca. July 1820; Final Decrees, November 1821, with *Bett et al. v. Lewis et al* [court process]. PAR 21681815. Granted.

39. For nuncupative wills, see Petition of Sophie to the Parish Court of Plaquemines Parish, Louisiana, 17 May 1845, in Supreme Court of Louisiana Collection, *Sophie v. Manette Duplessis, Casimir Duplessis, Virginie Duplessis Lafrance, et al.*, Book 424, Document/Case 258, UNO; Related Documents: Court Records, 3 February 1845, 10 February 1847; Supplemental Petition [text in English and partial text in French], 22 June 1846; Partition Suit Judgment, 26 March 1842, certified 9 April 1842; Adjudication of Slaves [partial], ca. 1842; Supreme Court Opinion [some text in French], 24 June 1847, with *Sophie v. Duplessis et al.* PAR 20884537. D GARev.

40. Petition of Margaret, Henry, Sally, and George Brown to the Circuit Court of St. Louis County, Missouri, 22 July 1831, in Records of the Circuit Court, *Margaret, Henry, Sally, and George Brown v. William Dallam*, CCBSL; Related Documents: PARs 21183105, 21183406, 21184208, 21184209; Letter, Thomas M. Smith to James L. Murray, ca. 1831; Order, 22 July 1831; Plea of Trespass, Henry by George Brown vs. William Dallam, 22 July 1831; Subpoena, William Dallam, 26 July 1831; Copy of Order, 22 July 1831; Plea of Trespass, 23 July 1831; Subpoena, William Dallam, 22 [23] July 1831; Copy of Order, 22 July 1831; Sheriff's Return, 12 November 1831; Plea of Trespass, *Sally by George Brown v. William Dallam*, 26 July 1831; Subpoena, William Dallam, 26 July 1831; Copy of Order, 22 July 1831; Sheriff's Return, 12 November 1831, with *Brown et al. v. Dallam*. Petition granted; separate pleas of trespass filed for *Margaret, Henry, and Sally vs. William Dallam*. PAR 21183113. Granted, DefNF. Petition of Jane to the Circuit Court of St. Louis County, Missouri, 15 April 1831, in Records of the Circuit Court, Document/Case 22, CCBSL; Related Documents: Copy of Order, 15 April 1831; Deposition, G. W. Call, 16 April 1831; Letter, Thomas M. Smith to James L. Murray, ca. 3 April 1831; Plea of Trespass, *Jane v. William Dallam*, 10 May 1831; Subpoenas, William Dallam, 10 May and 23 September 1831; Sheriff's Returns, 9 July and 12 November 1831, with *Jane v. Dallam*. PAR 21183105.

Granted, DefNF. Lawyer Thomas Smith possessed five slaves. USMSPC, Logan County, Kentucky, Russellville, 1830, image 5, ancestry.com.

41. Suit of Justina in the Court of Common Pleas, Kent County, Delaware, 1782 [petition missing] in Records of the Court of Common Pleas, *Justina v. Mary Hutchinson*, DSA; Related Documents: Deposition, James Morris, 17 December 1782; Depositions, Rebecca Steel, Philadelphia, Pennsylvania, 7 February 1782, 22 April 1782; Depositions, Miers Fisher, N. Hammond, Philadelphia, Pennsylvania, 4 November 1782; Depositions, four citizens testified about the prior testimony of a deceased witness, including Gunning Bedford Jr., John Vining, Richard Bassett, and Edward Tilghman Jr., 16 May 1783; Depositions, Silas Snow, lawyer Richard Bassett, and lawyer John Clayton, 16 May 1783, with *Justina v. Hutchinson*. PAR 20378202. No decree in case file.

42. Petition of Mahala to the County Court of Anne Arundel County, Maryland, 28 March 1825, in SC, *Mahala v. Charles Boone*, Microfilm M 11014, Frame/Pages 18, Volume 4239-3, Document/Case 152, MSA; Related Documents: Transcript of Court Record, 28 March 1825—28 May 1827; Clerk's Certification, 28 May 1827, with *Mahala v. Boone*. DAA. PAR 20982504. Plaintiff failed to appear. Court of Appeals (Judgments, Western Shore) No. 152, *Negro Mahala vs. Charles Boone*, transcript 7 June 1827, Anne Arundel County, appeal dismissed by the court June Term 1829 [Docket]; MSA S382-123, Microfilm: M 11014, Accession No.: MSA SC 4239-3-18.

43. See note 25, chap. 7, this volume.

44. For Louisiana, see Schafer, *Becoming Free*, 98.

45. Eric Robert Papenfuse, "From Recompense to Revolution":*Mahoney v. Ashton* and the Transfiguration of Maryland Culture, 1791-1802," *Slavery and Abolition* 15 (December 1994): 56n9; JCCASN, *Sprigg v. Negro Mary*, Md., 3 Har. and John. 491, December 1814, 4:62. D GARR.

46. KCCCP-CJD, December 1800 Term (filed May 1800), p. 76, Reel 5, Frame 42,; December Term 1801, p. 131, Reel 5, Frame 72, dismissed on 4 December 1802; verdict appealed. Petition of Solomon to the Common Pleas Court of Kent County, Delaware, 1 October 1800, in Records of the Court of Common Pleas, *Solomon v. William Banks*, Microfilm Reel 1, Frame/Pages 402-403, DSA; Related Documents [related documents are located on Reel 2]: Deposition, Solomon, 8 May 1802; Interrogatories, 11 November 1800; Summons, Caleb Boyer, Caroline County, Maryland, 1802, with *Solomon v. William Banks*. PAR 20380054. Dismissed on 4 December 1802. Dismissed, appealed.

47. Petition of Jane Dawson to the Superior Court of Randolph County, North Carolina, ca. July 1830, in Records of the County Court, Slaves and Free Persons of Color, *Jane Dawson v. Joshua Swain and William Hogan*, NCDAH; Related Documents: Bond, William Hogan, et al., to William Norwood, et al., 4 November [1830]; Depositions, Barbara Westmoreland, 4 August 1830; Jinny Dawson (alias Jones), 5 August 1830; Thomas Creekmore, Nancy Creekmore, 12 August 1830; Courtney Beason, 13 August 1830; Court Order, 13 August 1830; Record, 6 October 1831; Depositions, John Koen, John Spence, Kelly Roads, Nancy Burnham, Owen Williams, 18 October 1831; Affidavit of Jane Dawson, September 1833, with *Dawson v. Swain*. Injunction granted; no final verdict. PAR 21283008. USMSPC, Guilford County, North Carolina, 1830, image 35, ancestry.com [Morehead]; in 1850, Robert Dawson, free person of color over age fifty-five, lived alone in Randolph County. USMSPC, Randolph County, North Carolina, Regiment 2, 1850, image 17, ancestry.com. It appears that neither the testimony of whites corroborating Jane's account, nor her outstanding lawyer swayed the court in her favor. USMSPC, Guilford County, North Carolina, 1830, image 35, ancestry.com; at the time Morehead possessed eleven slaves. For free black testimony in North Carolina and other southern states see John Hope Franklin, *The Free Negro in North Carolina, 1790-1860* (Chapel Hill: University of North Carolina Press, 1943), 82-84.

48. Arnold Taylor, *Rose, a Woman of Colour: A Slave's Struggle from Freedom in the Courts of Kentucky* (New York: iUniverse, 2008), 30.

49. Affidavit, Rose, July 20, 1836, in Taylor, *Rose, a Woman of Colour*, 11-12; Thomas F. Brown and Leah C. Sims, "'To Swear Him Free': Ethnic Memory as Social Capital in Eighteenth-Century Freedom Petitions," in *Colonial Chesapeake: New Perspectives*, ed. Debra Myers

and Melanie Perrault (Lanham, MD: Lexington, 2006), 101–102. See note 46, chap. 2, this volume.

50. Petition of Mary Vance and Samuel Jones to the Chancery Court of Bedford County, Tennessee, 14 July 1853, in Supreme Court Cases, Middle Tennessee, *Mary Vance and Samuel Jones v. Nathaniel Porter*, Box/Drawer 116, TSLA; Related Documents: Order, 14 July 1853; Answer, Nathaniel Porter, 27 August 1853; Petition for Receiver, Mary Vance, 13 August 1853; Order, 13 August 1853; Supplemental Petition, ca. 6 August 1853; Order, 6 August 1853; Petition, Nathaniel Porter v. Mary Vance and Samuel Jones, 5 October 1854; Order, 5 October 1854; Supplemental Petition, 12 October 1854; Order, 12 October, 1854; Statement, John P. Steel, 12 October 1854; Report of Clerk and Master, 13 February 1854; Clerk and Master's, 16 August 1854; Depositions, Rosana Porter, Lewis Cotner, 27 July 1854; Decrees, ca. August 1854; Continuance, Samuel Jones; Final Decree, 1 September 1854; Appeal Bond, Mary Vance, George Porter, Garrett Philips to Nathaniel Porter, 2 September 1856; Supreme Court Decree, ca. 2 September 1856, with *Vance et al. v. Jones et al.* PAR 21485301. DAA.

51. Petition of Peter to the Circuit Court of St. Louis County, Missouri, 27 November 1827, in Records of the Circuit Court, *Peter v. James Walton*, Document/Case 67, CCBSL; Related Documents: PAR 21182901; Plea of Trespass, *Peter v. James Walton*, 31 December 1827; Plea, James Walton, 25 March 1828; Subpoena, James Walton, 31 December 1827; Sheriff's Returns, 30 January and 1 February 1828; Affidavit, Peter, 28 January 1828; Writ of *Habeas Corpus*, Peter, 28 January 1828; Sheriff's Return, 30 January 1828; Affidavit and Motion for New Trial, Peter, 15 December 1828 [page(s) missing], with *Peter v. Walton*. PAR 21182707. Denied.

52. Petition of Carey Ewton to the Circuit Court of St. Louis County, Missouri, 11 August 1829, in Records of the Circuit Court, *Carey Ewton v. Benjamin Wilder*, Document/Case 10, CCBSL; Related Documents: PAR 21183103; Affidavit, Cary Ewton, August 10, 1829; Copy of Order, 11 August 1829; Plea of Trespass, Carey Ewton vs. Benjamin Wilder, 11 August 1829; Subpoena, Benjamin Wilder, 11 August 1829; Sheriff's Return, 13 August 1829; Court Record, 24 November 1829, with ibid. PAR 21182905. Petition of Carey to the Circuit Court of St. Louis County, Missouri, 8 March 1831, in Records of the Circuit Court, *Carey Ewton v. Benjamin Wilder*, Document/Case 53, CCBSL; Related Documents: PAR 21182905; Order, 8 March 1831; Plea of Trespass, 8 March 1831; Subpoena, Benjamin Wilder, 8 May [March] 1831; Copy of Order, 8 March 1831; Sheriff's Return, 8 March 1831; Plea, Benjamin Wilder, 1 April 1831; Affidavit and Motion, Carey Ewton, 22 August 1831; Bill of Exceptions, Carey, 22 August 1831, with *Ewton v. Wilder*. Non suit declared; motion to set aside judgment denied.

53. For testimony on behalf of owners see note 66, chap. 3, this volume; *Betsy v. Lewis Latham*.

54. Petition of Simeon Clark to the Circuit Court of Todd County, Kentucky, 16 October 1832, in Records of the Circuit Court, Equity Case Files, *Simeon Clark v. Henry Carpenter and Henry Keener*, Box/Drawer 12, KDLA; Related Documents: Order, 16 October 1832; Answer, Henry Carpenter, 20 October 1832; Depositions, Nathaniel Burrus and H. B. Grooms, 13 April 1833; Notice, Simeon Clark, 21 January 1833; Deposition, Joshua D. Austin, 20 March 1833; Sheriff's Report, 17 April 1833; Agreement, April 1833; Decree, 29 April 1835, with *Clark v. Carpenter et al.* PAR 20783210. Injunction granted; Freedom Granted in 1835.

55. Petition of Moses to the Circuit Court of Barren County, Kentucky, 12 June 1844, in Records of the Circuit Court, Equity Judgments, *Moses v. George Wilcoxen, Catharine Wilcoxen, Daniel Wilcoxen, et al.*, Microfilm Reel 218714, Document/Case 1505, KDLA; Related Documents: PARs 20782904, 20783822, 20783922; Amended Bill, 18 September 1845; Depositions, James Hardy, Elias Smith, William Harlow, and Drewry Roberts, 1 September 1846; Decree, ca. June 1847, with *Moses v. Wilcoxen et al.* PAR 20784408. Granted.

56. Petition of Henry Brown to the Circuit Court of Woodford County, Kentucky, 4 January 1851, in Records of the Circuit Court, Case Files, *Henry Brown v. Eleanor Bullock*, Box/Drawer 128, KDLA; Related Documents: Order, 3 January 1851; Bill of Revivor, 17 December 1851; Amended Bill, 6 March 1852; Answer, Eleanor Bullock, 20 January 1851; Answer, William Bullock, 28 January 1852; Depositions, James W. Redd and Bird P. Smith, 25 August 1851; Decree, 11 March 1853; Commissioner's Reports, 25 August 1853 and 8 September 1853; Abstract, 1851–1852, with *Henry Brown v. Bullock*. PAR 20785124. Granted. For Thomas

Bullock's estate see Petition of William Brown to the Circuit Court of Woodford County, Kentucky, 4 January 1851, in Records of the Circuit Court, Case Files, Box/Drawer 128, Document/Case 53, KDLA; Related Documents: Inventory, Estate of Thomas Bullock, 23 September 1841; Commissioner's Report, 8 September 1853, with petition of William Brown. PAR 20785126. Granted. Kentucky-born lawyer Thomas F. Marshall, age forty-nine, lived with his father, Virginia-born Lewis Marshall, age seventy-six. The father owned $27,500 worth of land and seventeen slaves. Thomas Marshall was not listed as a slaveholder. USMSPC, Woodford County, Kentucky, 1st District, 1850, p. 439; USMSSC, Woodford County, Kentucky, 1st District, 1850, n.p. Marshall was assisted in contacting witnesses by twenty-four-year-old lawyer Joshua Tevis. USMSPC, Woodford County, Kentucky, 2nd District, 1850, p. 460.

57. Petition of George Pinkston to the Court of Common Pleas Kent County, Delaware, 2 March 1792, in Records of the Court of Common Pleas, *George Pinkston v. David Maxwell*, DSA; Related Documents: Subpoena, David Maxwell, May 1792; Depositions, Lemuel Cohee, Mark Foster, Sarah Rous, 6 December 1794; Deposition, Joseph Dixon, 10 May 1794, with *Pinkston v. Maxwell*. KCCCP-CJD, May 1792 through May 1794, p. 86, Reel 4, Frame 88, continued rule hearing; KCCCP-CJD, May Term 1792, p. 44, Reel 4, Frame 244, freed December 1794. PAR 20379205. Granted. For the 1793 law, see John Codman Hurd, *The Law of Freedom and Bondage in the United States*, 2 vols. (Boston: Little, Brown, 1862; reprint, New York: Negro University Press, 1968), 2:76.

58. Petition of Billey Kelley to the Chancery Court of Warren County, Tennessee, 5 January 1852, in Supreme Court Cases, Middle Tennessee, *Billey Kelley v. Thomas C. Smartt and Abner Kelly [Kelley]*, Box/Drawer 99A, TSLA; Related Documents: Order, 3 January 1852; Answer, Thomas C. Smartt, 5 April 1852; Copy of Bill of Sale, Trott to Laughlin, 17 April 1853; Replication, Billey Kelley, ca. April 1852; Deposition, Elijah Stephens, 9 September 1853; Deposition, Henry D. McBroom, 9 September 1853; Decree, March Term 1852; Decree, September Term 1852; Decree, March Term 1853, with *Kelley v. Smartt et al.* PAR 21485225. No decree with petition. Deposition corroborated Kelley's story. Decrees in September 1852 and March 1853 were to permit the sheriff to hire the plaintiff out pending the appeal. The results of the appeal were not found in JCCASL or the *Tennessee Reports* for 1854.

59. Petition of Siller, Lucinda, Doctor, Frankin, Hetty, Thomas, Clara, Sylvia, Stephen, and Joseph to the Circuit Court of Barren County, Kentucky, 25 March 1841, in Records of the Circuit Court, Equity Judgments, *Siller, Lucinda, Doctor,et al. v. Anderson R. Bowles, Malinda Munday, and George Munday*, Microfilm Reel 218692, Document/Case 1123, KDAH; Order, June 1841; Copy of Order, June 1841; Answer, Anderson R. Bowles, Malinda Bowles Munday, and George Munday, 24 June 1841; Deposition, James Hicks, 25 April 1842, Decree, ca. 1842, with *Siller et al. v. Bowles et al.* PAR 20784116. Granted. Transcript of court proceedings with above: Petition of Mima, Sylla, Maria, Joe, Cynthia, and Alfred to the Superior Court of Chancery, Richmond, Virginia, 26 September 1811, in Records of the Circuit Court, Equity Judgments, Barren County, Kentucky, Supplemental Bill, 2 June 1814; Decree, 21 January 1815; Certification of Transcript, 16 November 1814, with petition of Mima, et al. PAR 21681109. Granted. USMSPC, Barren County, Barren, Kentucky, 1840, p. 140 [Crenshaw possessed eight slaves; Cummins possessed one slave; same census citation].

60. Petition of Dolly to the Circuit Court of St. Louis County, Missouri, 26 March 1828, in Records of the Circuit Court, *Dolly v. John Young*, CCBSL; Related Documents: Copy of Order, 26 March 1828; Plea of Trespass, *Dolly vs. John Young*, 1 April 1828; Subpoena, John Young, 1 April 1828; Sheriff's Return, 12 April 1828; Plea, John Young, 28 November 1828; Subpoenas, William Skinner, Herman L. Hoffman, Otis Reynolds, Thomas Cohen, 4 April 1829, 3 June 1829, 27 October 1829; Sheriff's Returns, 6 April 1829, 5 June 1829, 3–4 November 1829, with *Dolly v. Young*. PAR 21182805. Granted.

61. Petition of Betsey Burk to the Circuit Court of the District of Columbia, 12 February 1847, in RUSCC-CDRCF, *Betsey Burk v. Ann Turner, John M. Barnaclo, and John Adams*, Record Group 21, Book Rules 4, Box/Drawer 60, Entry Folder 20, Document/Case 457, NA; Related Documents: Order, 12 February 1847; Affidavit, William Brent, 12 February 1847; Opinion, J. M. Carlisle, ca. 1847, with *Burk v. Turner et al.* PAR 20484706. Granted. For District of

Columbia laws, see *The Slavery Code of the District of Columbia, Together with Notes and Judicial Decision Explanatory of the Same* (Washington, DC: L. Towers, 1862).

62. JCCASN, *Negroes Louisa Bell and others v. Jones*, 10 Md. 322, December 1856, 4:131–132.
63. KCCCP-CJD, November Term 1814, p. 63, Microfilm Reel 6, p. 57, Record Group 3815, DSA; Petition of Minus Brown to the Court of Common Pleas, Kent County, Delaware, May 1825, in Records of the Court of Common Pleas, *Minus Brown v. George Magee*, DSA; Related Documents: PAR 20382508; Deposition, John Noble, Sussex County, 12 December 1825, with *Brown v. Magee*. PAR 20382507. KCCCP-CJD, May 1825, p. 136, Microfilm Reel 7, p. 86, Record Group 3815, DSA. Granted.
64. JCCASN, *Negro George v. Dennis*, Md., 2 Har.and John. 454, December 1809, 4:62. DAA. Petition of George to the County Court of Somerset County, Maryland, September 1807, in SC, *George v. Abraham Dennis*, Microfilm M 11014, Volume 4239-1, Document/Case 24, MSA; Related Documents: Court Record, September Term 1807 to 6 May 1808; Court Costs, on docket page, with *George v. Dennis*. PAR 20980701. DAA. Petition of Betty to the County Court of Worcester County, Maryland, November 1813, in SC, *Betty v. William Patterson*, Microfilm M 11014, Volume 4239-1, Document/Case 32, MSA; Related Documents: Court Transcript, November Term 1813-November 1814, with *Betty v. Patterson*. PAR 20981306. DAA.
65. *Gustavus Bird v. Lydia Titus, a free woman of color*, July 1833, Case No. 44, Circuit Court Case Files, Office of the Circuit Clerk, MoSA; Kennington, "River of Injustice," 73; Schafer, *Becoming Free*, 49–51.
66. Petition of Peter Sweeper to the Circuit Court of Jackson County, Tennessee, March 1839, in Supreme Court Cases, Middle Tennessee, *Peter Sweeper v. William Woodfolk*, Box/Drawer 63, TSLA. PAR 21483921. GAA.
67. Petition of Jane to the Superior Court of Sussex County, Virginia, 11 June 1836, in Records of the Circuit Superior Court of Chancery, Petersburg, *Jane v. Thomas Hunt, Jeremiah Cobbs, and Lewis Lanier*, Box/Drawer 38-40, Circuit Court Clerk's Office, Petersburg, Virginia. Granted.
68. Petition of Sarah, Hannah, Samuel, James, Fanny, Sis, Martha, Joseph, Clara, Mill, Elbert, Amanda, R. S. Ferguson, next friend, to the Chancery Court of Washington County, Tennessee, 14 August 1858, in Washington County Court Records, Chancery Court, *Sarah, Hannah, Samuel, et al., v. James Fitzgerald, Charles Cox, Melinda Cox, et al.*, Box/Drawer 201–213, AAETSU; Related Documents: Orders, 14 August and 17 August 1858; Writ of Delivery, 17 August 1858; Sheriff's Return, 21 August 1858; Injunction, James Fitzgerald, Charles Cox, Melinda Cox, et al., 14 August 1858; Sheriff's Return, 16 August 1858; Agreement, 29 October 1858; Acknowledgments of Executions, 9 April and 21 April 1859; Decrees, 16 November 1859, 16 May 1861, November Term 1861, 18 November 1865; Draft of Decree, May 1868, with *Sarah et al. v. Fitzgerald et al.* PAR 21485829. Granted. Timothy S. Huebner, "Judicial Independence in an Age of Democracy, Sectionalism, and War, 1835–1865," in *A History of the Tennessee Supreme Court*, ed. James W. Ely (Knoxville: University of Tennessee, 2002), 93.
69. "Narrative of James Fisher," in *National Anti-Slavery Standard*, April 13, 1843, found in *Slave Testimony: Two Centuries of Letters, Speeches, Interviews, and Autobiographies*, ed. John W. Blassingame (Baton Rouge: Louisiana State University Press, 1977), 230–231. At the outset of his narrative, Fisher noted that his mother remained in bondage during her entire life but later explained how she had purchased herself and her two daughters, indicating that she did not achieve legal freedom through the courts.
70. *Samuel, an infant of color v. Bernard T. Lynch*, November 1851, Case 29, pp. 9–10, Circuit Court Case Files, Office of the Circuit Clerk—St. Louis, St. Louis Circuit Court Historical Records Project, http://stlcourtrecords.wustl.edu.
71. Petition of Joshua to the Circuit Court of Pike County, Missouri, 30 November 1860, in Records of the Supreme Court, Case Files, *Joshua v. William Purse and R. M. Penn*, Box/Drawer 624, Document/Case 10, MoSA; Related Documents: Transcript of Circuit Court Record with Index, 30 November 1860-ca. 9 February 1861; Clerk's Certificate, 24 September 1864; Supreme Court Opinion, 7 December 1863; Writ of Error, 28 September 1863, with *Joshua v. Purse et al.* PAR 21186003. JCCASN, *Joshua (a man of color) v. Purse*, 34 Mo. 209, October 1863, 5:218–219. D DARR.

72. JCCASN, *Sam v. Green*, D.C., 21 Fed.Cas. 431 (2 Cranch C. C. 162), April 1819, 4:170 [wording of the law]; Petition of Francis Moore to the Circuit Court of Woodford County, Kentucky, 13 April 1830, in Records of the Circuit Court, Case Files, *Francis Moore v. Thomas Bullock*, Record Group Bundle 197, Box/Drawer 66, KDLA; for the many related PARs, see UNCG: Digital Library on American Slavery, https://library.uncg.edu/slavery/; Order, 12 April 1830, with ibid [failure to appeal verdict]. PAR 20783010. Dismissed.

73. JCCASN, *Pegram v. Isabell*, Va., 1 Hen. and M. 387, July 1807, 1:114; *Pegram v. Isabell*, Va., 2 Hen. and M. 193, March 1808, JCCASN, 1:117; *Reports of Cases Argued and Determined in the Supreme Court of Appeals in Virginia: With Selected Cases, Relating Chiefly to Points of Practice, Decided by the Superior Court of Chancery for the Richmond District*, vol. 2, comp. William W. Hening and William Munford (New York: I Riley, 1809), 193–211. D GARR.

74. Petition of Francis Scott Key to the Circuit Court of the District of Columbia, 14 January 1840, in RUSDC-SHCP, Record Group 21, Box/Drawer 1, Entry Folder 28, NA; Related Documents: Statement, Francis Scott Key, 14 January 1840; Writ of *Habeas Corpus*, Emmanuel Price and Maria Course, 18 January 1840, with ibid. PAR 20484008. Granted. Petition of Joseph Armstrong, Peter Butler, Emanuel Price, and Maria Coase to the Circuit Court of the District of Columbia, 14 January 1840, in RUSDC-SHCP, Record Group 21, Box/Drawer 1, Entry Folder 28, NA; Related Documents: PARs 20484006, 20484007, 20484008; Affidavit, Francis S. Key, 14 January 1840, with petition of Key. PAR 20484002. Granted.

75. JCCASN, *Beaty v. Judy and her children (persons of color)*, Ky., 1 Dana 101, April 1833, 1:323–24. Granted, appealed, reversed and remanded "with instructions to set aside the verdict, and dismiss the suit without prejudice."

76. Petitions of Dick, Bartlett, and Harry to the Circuit Court of Fayette County, Kentucky, 17 September 1813, in Records of the Circuit Court, Case Files, *Dick, Bartlett, and Harry v. Benjamin Clarke*, Box/Drawer 32, KDLA; Related Documents: PARs Orders, ca. 1813; Jury Verdicts, ca. 1813; Pleas of Trespass, ca. 1813; Will, Mildred Clark, 7 November 1807; Instrument of Emancipation, 3 March 1811, with *Dick et al. v. Clarke*. PARs 20781304, 20781306, 20781308. No final decrees with petition. For a suit improperly filed in a probate court, see: JCCASN, *Aramynta v. Woodruff*, Ar., 7 Ark. 422, January 1847, 5:232; Orville W. Taylor, *Negro Slavery in Arkansas* (Durham, NC: Duke University Press, 1958; reprint, Arkansas University Press, 2000), 239; *Reports of Cases in Law and in Equity, Argued and Determined in the Supreme Court of Arkansas During the January and July Terms, Eighteen Hundred and Forty-Six, and January Term Eighteen Hundred and Forty-Seven* (Little Rock, AR: B. J. Borden, 1847), 422–424.

77. JCCASN, *Bell v. McCormick*, D.C., 3 Fed. Cas. 107 (5 Cranch C. C.), March 1838, 4:201. DAA. *Jones v. Lipscomb*, Ky., 14 B. Mon. 296, January 1854, 1:410. D GARev.

78. JCCASN, *Henry v. Nunn*, Ky., 11 B. Mon. 239, January 1851, 1:398–399: Arnold Taylor, *Suing for Freedom in Kentucky* (Bangor, ME: BookLocker.com, 2010), 162–174. DAA.

79. JCCASN, *John, James, etc. (of color) v. Walker*, Ky., 8 B. Mon. 605, September 1848, 1:388. DAA.

80. There is no study of the results of freedom suits in the southern county courts. The few studies that have examined outcomes have done so for appellate cases. Their findings are close to the results of appeals cases in this study. See: John B. Parks, "Freedom v. Slavery: Lawsuits, Petitions and the Legitimacy of Slavery in British Colonies and the United States" (PhD diss., Howard University, 2008), 221; Marion J. Russell, "American Slave Discontent in Records of the High Courts," *Journal of Negro History* 31, no. 4 (October 1946): 418.

81. In 1840, A. J. Ballard, in his twenties, headed a household with another male in his twenties. In 1850, at age thirty-four, listed as a lawyer with $3,500 in realty, Ballard headed a household with his wife Francis, age twenty-three, and a one-month-old son Charles T. Ballard. USMSPC, Jefferson County, Kentucky, Louisville, 1840, image 191–192, ancestry.com; USMSPC, Jefferson County, Kentucky, Louisville, District 2, 1850, image 143, ancestry.com. In 1860, age forty-three, Ballard was listed as a lawyer with $18,000 in realty and $4,000 in personal property, heading a household with his wife Francis and their children. He owned nine slaves, six ages eighteen to eighty. USMSPC, Jefferson County, Kentucky, Louisville, Ward 3, 1860, image 103, ancestry.com; USMSSC, Jefferson County, Kentucky, Louisville, Ward 3, 1860, image 11, ancestry.com.

82. Petition of Wesley Brown to the Chancery Court of Jefferson County, Kentucky, 3 August 1841, in Records of the Circuit Court, Case Files, *Wesley Brown v. Thomas J. Godwin, Francis Brumaker, and T. L. Huff*, Box/Drawer 2-54, Document/Case 3150, KDLA; Related Documents: Amended Bills, 17 September 1841, 18 October 1842, 1 October 1844; Answer, Thomas Godman, 24 January 1842; Copy of Last Will and Testament, Stephen Donaldson, 13 February 1815; Decree, 14 October 1845, with *Brown v. Godwin et al.* PAR 20784113. Granted.

83. As was the case for many African Americans who appeared in freedom suits, it is unclear what happened to Wesley Brown after he was released from slavery. It appears, however, that he did not remain in Kentucky.

Chapter 13

1. Records of the County Court, Halifax County, Virginia, Last Will and Testament of Philip E. Vass, 8 August 1831, Will Bk 16, 340–345; sections of the will are illegible; for a better copy (the one quoted here) see Copy of Last Will and Testament of Philip E. Vass, 8 August 1831, in General Assembly, Session Records, Petition of Jacob, Mary, Patsey, Meriwether, and Matilda to the Legislature of North Carolina, 20 December 1844, in Senate Committee Reports, November 1844–January 1845, Box 4, NCDAH. Vass's father migrated from North Carolina to Halifax County during the mid-1790s; he gradually acquired land, purchased a tobacco plantation, and built up a slave labor force. At the time of his death in 1825, he possessed thirty-six slaves. The slaves were passed on as a life estate to his wife Elizabeth who died about 1830; see US Bureau of the Census, Department of Commerce and Labor, *Heads of Families at the First Census of the United States Taken in the Year 1790: North Carolina* (Washington, DC: Government Printing Office 1908), 80; Records of the County Court, Halifax County, Virginia, Last Will and Testament of Philip Vass the Elder, 13 December 1816, Will Book 14, 185–187; sections of the will are illegible; for better copies (the ones quoted here and henceforth) see Copy of Last Will and Testament of Philip Vass the Elder, 13 December 1816, in Records of the Circuit Superior Court, Halifax County, Virginia, Chancery Causes, *John and Elizabeth Shepard, formerly Elizabeth Vass, Richard and Mary E. Carter, formerly Mary E. Shepard, Samuel V. Shepard, Emily B. Shererd, Phillip P. Shepard and Martha T. Shepard, children of Elizabeth Shepard, by their next friend John Shepard v. Isaac Medley,* 23 January 1832, Case 1832-001, CCH, Halifax, Virginia; and in Records of the Circuit Superior Court, Halifax County, Virginia, Chancery Causes, *John Shepard and Elizabeth Shepard his wife, formerly Elizabeth Vass, Richard Carter and his wife, Samuel V. Shepard, Joseph Haden and Emily B. Haden his wife, Philip P. Sheperd and Martha Shepard, minors, by John Shepard, their next friend, all children of Elizabeth Shepard v. John C. Cabanis, Administrator of Samuel Carter, deceased,* 5 September 1839, Case 1840-015; Inventory and Appraisement, Estate of Philip Vass the Elder, 24 February 1827, Will Book 14, 243–247; Account, Estate of Philip Vass the Elder, 26 February 1827, Will Book 14, 221–222; Records of the County Court, Halifax County, Virginia, Last Will and Testament of Elizabeth Vass, Widow of Philip Vass, 1 December 1828, Will Book 15, 123–124; Account, 6 October 1832, Will Book 16, 238–239, CCH, Halifax, Virginia.

2. Last Will and Testament of Philip E. Vass, 8 August 1831, cited above.

3. Louis P. Masur, "Nat Turner and the Sectional Crisis," in *Nat Turner: A Slave Rebellion in History and Memory,* ed. Kenneth Greenberg (New York: Oxford University Press, 2003), 148–161; William Sidney Drewry, *The Southampton Insurrection* (Washington, DC: Neale, 1900; reprint, Murfreesboro, NC: Johnson, 1968); Thomas C. Parramore, *Southampton County, Virginia* (Charlottesville: University of Virginia Press, 1978); Herbert Aptheker, *Nat Turner's Slave Rebellion* (New York: Grove, 1966); Scot French, *The Rebellious Slave: Nat Turner in American Memory* (Boston: Houghton Mifflin, 2004).

4. The literature on the sectional crisis is immense. See Eric Foner, *The Fiery Trial: Abraham Lincoln and American Slavery* (New York: W. W. Norton, 2010); Elizabeth R. Varon, *Disunion! The Coming of the American Civil War, 1789–1859* (Chapel Hill: University of North Carolina Press, 2009); Richard Sewell, *A House Divided: Sectionalism and the Civil War, 1848–1865* (Baltimore: Johns Hopkins University Press, 1998); Charles Dew,

Apostles of Disunion: Southern Secession Commissioners and the Causes of the Civil War (Charlottesville: University Press of Virginia, 2001); Don E. Fehrenbacher, *The Slaveholding Republic: An Account of the United States Government's Relations to Slavery* (New York: Oxford University Press, 2001).

5. For Virginia, see: William A Link, *Roots of Secession: Slavery and Politics in Antebellum Virginia* (Chapel Hill: University of North Carolina Press, 2003); Luther Porter Jackson, *Free Negro Labor and Property Holding in Virginia, 1830-1860* (Washington, DC: American historical Association, 1942); John Russell, *The Free Negro in Virginia, 1619-1865* (Baltimore: Johns Hopkins University Press, 1913); Michael L. Nicholls, "'The squint of freedom': African American Freedom Suits in Post-Revolutionary Virginia," *Slavery and Abolition: A Journal of Comparative Studies* 20, no. 2 (August 1999): 47-62; Philip J. Schwarz, *Slave Laws in Virginia* (Athens: University of Georgia Press, 1996).

6. Copy of Commissioners' Report, Division of the Slaves of Philip Vass the Elder, deceased, 29 December 1832, Records of the County Court, Halifax County, Virginia, found with General Assembly, Session Records, Petition of Jacob, Mary, Patsey, Meriweather, and Matilda to the Legislature of North Carolina, 20 December 1844, in Senate Committee Reports, November 1844-January 1845, Box 4, NCDAH. In various documents, Meriweather is spelled in a variety of ways. Prior to his death, Philip Vass the Elder owned all six slaves. The elder Vass made special arrangements for only one of his slaves, Ann B. Rachel, and any children she might have in the future. He stipulated that she should not be sold nor removed from the county without the consent of a majority of his heirs. If any attempt were made to sell or remove her, she should revert to the estate. He loaned Rachel to his daughter Mary Boyd and her husband Alexander Boyd during their lives. After their deaths, she was to revert to his estate. Records of the County Court, Halifax County, Virginia, Last Will and Testament of Philip Vass the Elder, 13 December 1816, Will Book 14, 185-187; Inventory and Appraisement, Estate of Philip Vass the Elder, 24 February 1827, Will Book 14, 243-247; Account, Estate of Philip Vass the Elder, 26 February 1827, Will Book 14, 221-222, CCH, Halifax, Virginia. In some sections, Vass's original will is illegible. The author relied on two different copies of the will found in Records of the Circuit Superior Court, Halifax County, Virginia, Chancery Causes, *John and Elizabeth Shepard, formerly Elizabeth Vass, Richard and Mary E. Carter, formerly Mary E. Shepard, Samuel V. Shepard, Emily B. Shepard, Phillip P. Shepard and Martha T. Shepard, children of Elizabeth Shepard, by their next friend John Shepard v. Isaac Medley*, 23 January 1832, Case 1832-001, CCH, Halifax, Virginia.

7. USMSPC, Halifax County, Virginia, 1830, p. 446; Records of the Circuit Superior Court, Halifax County, Virginia, Supplemental Bill of Complaint, *Henry Edmunds v. Isaac Medley, George Ewing, Elizabeth Ewing*, 4 September 1833, included with *Vass, et al., v. Parker*, Case 1834-002, CCH, Halifax, Virginia. For Elizabeth Vass's will and estate, see Records of the County Court, Halifax Co., Virginia, Will Book 15 (1 December 1828), 123-124, and Account, Will Book 16 (6 October 1832), 237-238, in CCH, Halifax, Virginia.

8. Records of the County Court, Halifax Co., Virginia, Minutes, Vol. 4 (November 1830), 276-77, 291 and (August 1831), 424-425; Register of Marriages, Book 1 (September 1792), 24; "Inventory & Appraisement of the Estate of Henry Polly," Will Book 15 (7 December 1830), 431; Account (28 December 1840), 398-400, CCH, Halifax, Virginia.

9. Records of the Circuit Superior Court, Halifax County, Virginia, Chancery Causes, *John and Elizabeth Shepard, formerly Elizabeth Vass, Richard and Mary E. Carter, formerly Mary E. Shepard, Samuel V. Shepard, Emily B. Shepard, Phillip P. Shepard and Martha T. Shepard, children of Elizabeth Shepard, by their next friend John Shepard v. Isaac Medley*, 23 January 1832, Case 1832-001, CCH, Halifax, Virginia; Answer, Isaac Medley, 5 September 1832, and Copy of the Last Will and Testament of Philip Vass the Elder, 13 December 1816, with *Shepard v. Medley*.

10. Copy of Commissioners' Report, Division of the Slaves of Philip Vass the Elder, deceased, 29 December 1832, Records of the County Court, Halifax County, Virginia, found with General Assembly, Session Records, Petition of Jacob, Mary, Patsey, Meriweather, and Matilda to the Legislature of North Carolina, 20 December 1844, in Senate Committee Reports, November 1844-January 1845, Box 4, NCDAH.

11. Records of the Halifax Circuit Superior Court, *William McCabaniss, Executor of James P. Vass, deceased v. Isaac Medley Sr., Executor of Philip E. Vass, deceased,* April 1833, copy in General Assembly, Session Records, Petition of Jacob, Mary, Patsey, Meriwether, and Matilda to the Legislature of North Carolina, 20 December 1844, in Senate Committee Reports, November 1844-January 1845, Box 4, NCDAH.

12. John Hope Franklin, *The Free Negro in North Carolina, 1790–1860* (Chapel Hill: University of North Carolina Press, 1943), p. 43. The anti-free black immigration law was passed in 1827. *Acts Passed by the General Assembly of the State of North Carolina at Its Session Commencing the 25 of December 1825* (Raleigh, NC: Lawrence & Lemay, 1827), 13–16.

13. Records of the County Court, Halifax County, Virginia, Land Deeds, Bargain and Sale, Book 16 (26 April 1796), 621; Book 34 (4 March 1827), 291–292; Surveys 1 (April 1802), 299; Last Will and Testament of Isaac Medley,15 May 1851, Will Book A1, 175–182; Inventory of the Estate of Isaac Medley, 14 July 1854, Will Book A1, 183–191; Accounts, Estate of Isaac Medley, 8 December 1854, 1 May 1855, Will Book A1, 202–212, 215–222. In 1856, Medley's son observed that his father, from "a very remote period down to his death," owned a ferry on the Dan River, crossing from his land on the north bank of the river and to the public road on the opposite side. Records of the Circuit Superior Court, Chancery Causes, *James Medley v. Oliver,* 188 January 1856, Case 1857-34, CCH, Halifax, Virginia.

14. USMSPC, Halifax County, Virginia, 1830, 418.

15. USMSPC, Halifax County, Virginia, Southern District, 1840, 38. By 1840, forty-one of his slaves under were age ten and fourteen were over the age of fifty-five.

16. Certificate, Isaac Medley Sr., 23 November 1841, found with Legislative Petitions, Petition of Jacob, Mary, and Patsey to the Virginia House of Delegates, Halifax County, 15 December 1841, LV.

17. Copy of the Estate of Philip E. Vass decided in Account, 2 September 1832 [Samuel's hire for twenty dollars] and 28 May 1832 [Jacob and Mary's hire], in Records of the Circuit Superior Court in Chancery, Chancery Causes, Halifax County, Virginia, *George B. Ewing and wife v. Executor of the Estate of Philip E. Vass,* October 1858, Case 1858-0161, CCH, Halifax, Virginia. Also see: Legislative Petitions, Petition of Patty Daniel to the Virginia General Assembly, Halifax County, 14 December 1842, LV; Certificate, James Young, et al., 30 November 1842, with *Ewing v. Vass.* For slave hiring in the area, see Lynda J. Morgan, *Emancipation in Virginia's Tobacco Belt, 1850–1870* (Athens: University of Georgia Press, 1992), chap. 3.

18. Records of the Circuit Superior Court, Halifax County, Virginia, Chancery Causes, *Jacob, Mary, Sam, Meriweather, Patty, Matilda v. Isaac Medley,* Administrator of the Estate of Philip E. Vass, 29 April 1840, Case 1841-010, CCH, Halifax, Virginia; Answer, Isaac Medley, 17 June 1840; Decree, 12 April 1841; Copy of Court Order [permitting slaves except Jacob to sue in forma pauperis], 3 April 1840; Summons, Isaac Medley, 25 April 1840, with *Jacob et al. v. Medley,* CCH, Halifax, Virginia. A copy of the court record can be found in General Assembly, Session Records, 20 December 1844, in Senate Committee Reports, November 1844–January 1845, Box 4, NCDAH.

19. Records of the Circuit Superior Court, Halifax County, Virginia, Court Order, 3 April 1840, in General Assembly, Session Records, Petition of Jacob, Mary, Patsey, Meriwether, and Matilda to the Legislature of North Carolina, 20 December 1844, in Senate Committee Reports, November 1844–January 1845, Box 4, NCDAH.

20. Subpoena to Isaac Medley, 25 April 1840, in Records of the Circuit Superior Court, Chancery Causes, Halifax County, Virginia, *Jacob, Mary, Sam, Meriweather, Patty, Matilda vs. Isaac Medley,* 29 April 1840, Case 1841-010, CCH, Halifax, Virginia; Records of the Circuit Superior Court, Halifax County, Virginia, Chancery Order Book 1, 3 April 1840, p. 290, with *Jacob et al. v. Medley.*

21. Records of the Circuit Superior Court, Halifax County, Virginia, *Jacob, Mary, Sam, Meriweather, Patty, and Matilda v. Isaac Medley Sr.,* 29 April 1840, with in General Assembly, Session Records, Petition of Jacob, Mary, Sam, Patty, Meriwether, and Matilda to the Legislature of North Carolina, 20 December 1844, in Senate Committee Reports, November 1844–January 1845, Box 4, NCDAH.

22. Records of the Circuit Superior Court, Halifax County, Virginia, Answer of Isaac Medley Sr. to bill of complaint of Jacob, Mary, Sam, Patty, Meriwether, Matilda, 17 June 1840, General Assembly, Session Records, Petition of Jacob, Mary, Patsey, Meriwether, and Matilda to the Legislature of North Carolina, 20 December 1844, in Senate Committee Reports, November 1844–January 1845, Box 4, NCDAH.

23. *Acts Passed at a General Assembly of the Commonwealth of Virginia, Begun and Held at the Capitol, in the City of Richmond, on Tuesday, the Tenth Day of November, One Thousand Seven Hundred and Ninety-Five* (Richmond, VA: Augustine Davis, 1796), 16–17; John Codman Hurd, *The Law of Freedom and Bondage in the United States*, 2 vols (Boston: Little, Brown, 1862; reprint, New York: Negro Universities Press, 1968): 2:6; *Acts Passed at a General Assembly of the Commonwealth of Virginia, Begun and Held at the Capitol, in the City of Richmond, on Monday the Fourth Day of December One Thousand Seven Hundred and Ninety-Seven* (Richmond, VA: Augustine Davis, 1798), 5; *Digest of the Laws of Virginia, Which Are of a Permanent Character and General Operation; Illustrated by Judicial Decisions* (Richmond, VA: Smith and Palmer, 1841), 869–871.

24. For how these statutes worked during an earlier period see Michael L. Nicholls, "Strangers Setting among Us: The Sources and Challenge of the Urban Free Black Population of Early Virginia," *Virginia Magazine of History and Biography*, 108, no. 2 (Spring 2000): 160–161.

25. Records of the Circuit Superior Court, Halifax County, Virginia, Decree of Judge William Leigh, 12 April 1841, in General Assembly, Session Records, Petition of Jacob, Mary, Patsey, Meriwether, and Matilda to the Legislature of North Carolina, 20 December 1844, in Senate Committee Reports, November 1844–January 1845, Box 4, NCDAH; Records of the Circuit Superior Court, Halifax County, Virginia, Chancery Order Book 1, April 1841, n.p., CCH, Halifax, Virginia.

26. June Purcell Guild, ed., *Black Laws of Virginia: A Summary of the Legislative Acts of Virginia Concerning Negroes from Earliest Times to the Present* (Richmond, VA: Whittet & Shepperson, 1936; reprint, New York: Negro Universities Press, 1969), 72, 106. In 1831, the 1806 law was updated.

27. Legislative Petitions, Petition of Jacob, Mary, and Patsy to the Virginia House of Delegates, Halifax County, 15 December 1841, LV; Certificate, Isaac Medley Sr., 23 November 1841, with petition of Mary et al.; Records of the Circuit Superior Court, Halifax County, Virginia, Answer of Isaac Medley Sr. to the Bill of Complaint of Jacob, et al., 17 June 1840, in General Assembly, Session Records, Petition of Jacob, Mary, Patsey, Meriwether, and Matilda to the Legislature of North Carolina, 20 December 1844, in Senate Committee Reports, November 1844-January 1845, Box 4, NCDAH.

28. Legislative Petitions, Petition of Jacob, Mary, and Patsy to the Virginia House of Delegates, Halifax County, 15 December 1841, LV. The petition was written in November 1841, referred to the Committee of the Judiciary on 15 December and rejected on 20 December 1841; Certificate, Isaac Medley Sr., 23 November 1841, with petition of Jacob et al; Records of the Circuit Superior Court, Halifax County, Virginia, Answer of Isaac Medley Sr. to the Bill of Complaint of Jacob, et al., 17 June 1840, in General Assembly, Session Records, Petition of Jacob, Mary, Patsey, Meriwether, and Matilda to the Legislature of North Carolina, 20 December 1844, in Senate Committee Reports, November 1844–January 1845, Box 4, NCDAH.

29. Terry Daniel's mother Fanny Daniel was freed at age seven in 1785 by her owner William P. Martin. Daniel was born in 1797; he was later described as a person of dark complexion and about 5'5" tall. Fanny had a number of children, all born free, between the mid-1790s and the second decade of the nineteenth century. By the time Patty presented her petition, she also had numerous grandchildren. She died in 1849. See Register of Free Negroes No. 2 Commencing in 1831, Records of the Circuit Court, Halifax, County, Virginia, CCH, Halifax, Virginia; "Register of Free Negroes No. 1 1802–1831," CCH, Halifax County Virginia; USMSPC, Halifax County, Virginia, 1850, printed p. 129; Records of the Chancery Court, Halifax County, Virginia, "Alphabetical List of the Negroes & Mulattoes within the District of Joseph Landford Commissr for the year 1802 Agreeable to an act of Assembly Passd the 21st day of January 1801," Loose Papers, CCH, Halifax, Virginia; "List of Free Negroes delinquent for the nonpayment of Taxes & Levies for the year 1862 in the County of Halifax Va duly

advertised for Sale," Loose Papers, CCH, Halifax, Virginia; Records of the Circuit Superior Court of Chancery, Halifax County, Virginia, Petition of William Daniel, John Williams, Agnes Daniel, Hilliard Daniel, Nathaniel Daniel, Opha Daniel to the Judge of the Circuit Court, 3 October 1855, in Case 1866-008, in *Anderson v. Miller, et al.*, CCH, Halifax, Virginia. The author wishes to thank local historian Faye Royster Tuck for her assistance in uncovering the genealogy of the Daniel family.

30. Legislative Petitions, Petition of Patty Daniel to the Virginia General Assembly, Halifax County, 14 December 1842, LV; Certificate, James Young, et al., 30 November 1842, LV.

31. Legislative Petitions, Petition of Patty Daniel to the Virginia General Assembly, Halifax County, 14 December 1842, LV; Certificate, James Young, R. M. Guillard [?], Thomas H. Averett, William Easley, J. A. Easley, John Conner, et al., 30 November 1842, Petition of Daniel. In the 1840 census, James Young was listed as a head of household, the only white person at the residence, with eleven slaves residing with him, including two males under two years of age, three males between ten and twenty-four, and with two females under ten, two between ten and twenty-four, and one between thirty-six and fifty-five. Also listed as heads of households with slaves at the same residence were Thomas H. Averett and John Conner. USMSPC, Halifax County, Virginia, Eastern District, 1840, printed p. 64 [Young]; printed p. 81 [Averett]; South District, printed p. 63 [Conner].

32. Records of the Circuit Superior Court, Halifax County, Virginia, Finals, *George B. and Apphia Ewing, Mary Boyd, Elizabeth Shepard and John Shepard v. Isaac Medley*, 16 December 1843, Box 27, CCH, Halifax, Virginia; Decree of Judge William Leigh, 13 September 1847, with *Ewing et al. v. Medley*.

33. General Assembly, Session Records, Petition of Jacob, Mary, Patsey, Meriwether, and Matilda to the Legislature of North Carolina, 20 December 1844, in Senate Committee Reports, November 1844–January 1845, Box 4, NCDAH.

34. General Assembly, Session Records, Report of the Committee of Propositions and Grievances, 20 December 1844, in Senate Committee Reports, November 1844-January 1845, Box 4, NCDAH. The House concurred on 26 December 1844.

35. For other suits concerning various members of the Vass family, see Records of the Circuit Superior Court, Halifax County, Virginia, Chancery Causes, *Preston Parker v. Isaac Medley, administrator of the estate of Philip Vass, James P. Vass, Edward Womack and Sarah L. Womack, his wife, George B. Ewing and Aphia, his wife formerly Aphia Vass, and Isaac Medley, Trustee of Philip E. Vass*, 28 November 1832, Case 1833-006, CCH, Halifax, Virginia. Dismissed by Plaintiff, 4 September 1833, *Shepard et al. v. Medley*; Copy of Records of the Circuit Superior Court, Halifax County, Virginia, Chancery Causes, *John Shepard and Elizabeth his wife, formerly Elizabeth Vass, Richard Carter and Mary his wife, Samuel V. Shepard, Emily B. Shepard, Philip P. Shepard and Shepard children of Elizabeth Shepard v. Isaac Medley in his own right and as administrator of Philip Vass, deceased, and Henry Edmunds*, 8 September 1832, found with Case 1840-015, CCH, Halifax, Virginia.

36. Single women could, of course, obtain a prenuptial agreement placing their land and slaves in the hands of a trustee rather than turning property over to their husbands. Such agreements, however, were not common. Most women who possessed a comfortable estate prior to their marriage turned their property over to their husbands when they took their marital vows.

37. In 1836, she obtained a restraining order to prohibit him from selling or conveying away the slaves Caleb, Shadrack, Lucy, Amanda, Abednego, Griffin, Jacob, Jackson, John, Jefferson, or William, Records of the Circuit Superior Court, Halifax County, Virginia, Chancery Causes, *Sarah L. Womack by her next friend John Dunkerley v. Eduard Womack*, 15 October 1836, Case 1839-015, CCH, Halifax, Virginia; Writ, 15 October 1836; Sheriff's Return, 19 October 1836; List of Negroes in Mr. Womack's Possession, ca. 1836; Negroes Sold by Womack, ca. 1836, with *Womack v. Womack*; Land and other Property sold by Mr. Womack, ca. 1836; Deposition of Julius Hudson, 22 April 1837; Deposition of Beverly Flemming, 22 April 1837; Answer, Edward Womack, 28 August 1837, with *Womack v. Womack*. On 4 April 1839, the suit was dismissed by the plaintiff's counsel. Some years later McCargo was sued in Kentucky (on his way to New Orleans) for fraudulently selling Willa Viley two babies who were sickly and probably would not live. Records of the Circuit Court, Scott County, Kentucky, *Willa Viley v. Thomas McCargo*, 17 November 1845, Case Files, Box 12, Case 3169, KDLA.

38. Records of the County Court, Halifax County, Virginia, Deposition of Isaac Medley, 4 September 1841, with *Sarah L. Womack by her next friend Daniel F. Morris v. Edward Womack*, 7 April 1841, in Legislative Petitions, Halifax County, Virginia, 1 March 1848, LV; Loren Schweninger, *Families in Crisis: Divorce, Slavery, and the Law in the Old South* (Chapel Hill: University of North Carolina Press, 2012), 50.

39. In 1850, census takers counted 534 free blacks, 14,452 slaves, and 19,976 whites, for a total of 25,962 inhabitants in the county. *The Seventh Census of the United States: 1850* (Washington, DC: Robert Armstrong, 1853), 256.

40. "Register of Free Negroes No. 1 1802-1831," in Records of the Circuit Court, Halifax, County, Virginia; "Register of Free Negroes No. 2 Commencing in 1831," CCH, Halifax, Virginia.

41. USMSPC, Halifax County, Virginia, Southern District, 1850, 264; USMSSC, Halifax County, Virginia, Southern District, 1850, 995. See also USMSPC, Halifax County, Virginia, Eastern District, 1840, printed 54; US Manuscript Agricultural Census, Halifax County, Virginia, Southern District 1850, printed 639.

42. Records of the Circuit Superior Court, Halifax County, Virginia, Finals, *James Young, trustee and Jacob, Patsey, Meriwether, Mary, and Matilda, free persons of color, v. Isaac Medley, executor of Philip E. Vass, deceased*, Copy of Decree of Special Court of Appeals, Richmond, 16 January 1855, Box 22, Circuit Court Building, South Boston, Virginia. The original appeals court decree and most of the other appeals court records burned when Confederate soldiers set fire to Richmond as they retreated from the city in early April 1865; this was found in the circuit court records of Halifax County. William Hamilton Bryson, *Legal Education in Virginia, 1779-1979* (Charlottesville: University Press of Virginia, 1982), 596-599; Richmond *Dispatch*, 25 April, 1866.

43. USMSSC, Halifax County, Virginia, Southern District, 1850, holograph, 881-883; J. D. B. DeBow, *Statistical View of the United States . . . Being a Compendium of the Seventh Census* (Washington, DC: Beverley Tucker, 1854), 95.

44. USMSPC, Halifax County, Virginia, Northern District, 1850, image 113, ancestry.com; USMSSC, Halifax County, Virginia, Northern District, 1850, image 71, ancestry.com.

45. Records of the Circuit Superior Court, Halifax County, Virginia, Finals, *James Young, trustee and Jacob, Patsey, Meriwether, Mary, and Matilda, free persons of color, v. Isaac Medley, executor of Philip E. Vass, deceased*, Decree of Special Court of Appeals, Richmond, 16 January 1855, Box 22, Circuit Court Building, Halifax, Virginia.

46. Records of the County Court, Halifax County, Virginia, Estate of Philip E. Vass, Account, Bk 1A (5 December 1856), 264, CCH, Halifax, Virginia.

47. Records of the County Court, Halifax County, Virginia, Minutes No. 18, November Term 1858, 204, CCH, Halifax, Virginia.

48. The departure date could have been 15 April 1859. In the estate of James Young, who died in 1864, there was an account of the interest due Mary, Matilda, Harriet Matilda, and Peter Vass; the account for each of them was similar to the one for Mary Vass: 1859 April 15 By amt due Mary Vass to date $377.94; By Interest to 26 Dec. 1864 $129.08 and $506.76; Records of the County Court, Halifax County, Virginia, Estate of James Young, Account, Will Book 29 (March 1867), 262-267, CCH, Halifax, Virginia. During the Civil War, Young paid taxes on the trust. He died with nearly $142,000 in virtually worthless Confederate currency, thirty-five slaves, and his wheat, cotton, and tobacco crops under cultivation. Records of the County Court, Halifax County, Virginia, Estate of James Young, Inventory, Will Book 28 (15 July 1864), 612-618; Accounts, Will Book 28 (23 October 1865), 72-73; Will Book 29 (28 May 1866), 235-238; Will Book 29 (24 September 1866), 307-308; Will Book 29 (28 January 1867), 333-334; Will Book 29 (28 September 1868), Will Book 34 (24 April 1886), 388-390, CCH, Halifax, Virginia. Despite its black codes and anti-free black attitudes, Ohio was a popular destination for Virginia's black emigrants. Philip J. Schwarz, *Migrants against Slavery: Virginians and the Nation* (Charlottesville and London: University Press of Virginia, 2001), 10, chaps. 6 and 7.

49. Legislative Petitions, Petition of Philip Vass and Emily B. Haden to the Virginia Senate and House of Delegates, 1860, Halifax County, LV. In 1850, Philip P. Vass was listed as a tailor who owned no real estate but possessed a single fifteen-year-old slave. USMSPC, Halifax County, Virginia, Southern District, 1850, holograph p. 234; USMSSC, Halifax County, Virginia,

Southern District, 1850, holograph p. 594; Jacob Vass, a relative, was listed as a "ditcher" in 1850 with no real estate and no slaves. USMSPC, Halifax County, Virginia, Northern District, 1850, holograph p. 100.

50. Among the "List of Debts" due James Young at the time of his death in 1864 was $2.00 borrowed 1 March 1861 by Meriweather Vass, and $4.58 borrowed 1 September 1861 by lawyer Richard Logan. Records of the County Court, Halifax County, Virginia, Inventory, Estate of James Young, Will Book 28 (15 July 1864), 617–618, CCH, Halifax, Virginia. Meriweather Vass remained in Halifax County during and after the war. In 1870, he was listed in the census as a fifty-year-old black farm laborer living with his wife, age forty-five, and their twenty-one-year old daughter Sophia, also listed as a black farm laborer. They were illiterate. USMSPC, Halifax County, Virginia, Bannister Township, 1870, printed p. 432. See also Records of the County Court, Halifax County, Virginia, L. F. Deitrick v. Meriweather Vass, Judgments, Book 4 (27 November 1885), 82.

51. Ted Maris-Wolf, Family Bonds: Free Blacks and Re-Enslavement Law in Antebellum Virginia (Chapel Hill: University of North Carolina Press, 2015), 4–5, 89.

52. John H. Russell, The Free Negro in Virginia, 1619–1865 (Baltimore: Johns Hopkins University Press, 1913), 156.

Conclusion

1. Besides perusing the literature, the author sent this section to a dozen scholars of different slave societies in the Americas. Special thanks to David Berry Gaspar of Duke University, Marcela Echeverri of Yale University, and Omar Ali of the University of North Carolina Greensboro for their helpful suggestions.

2. A. E. Keir Nash, "A More Equitable Past? Southern Supreme Courts and the Protection of the Antebellum Negro," North Carolina Law Review 48 (1979): 197–241; A. E. Keir Nash, "Fairness and Formalism in the Trials of Blacks in the State Supreme Courts of the Old South," Virginia Law Review 56, no. 1 (1970): 65–100; A. E. Keir Nash, "Reason and Slavery: Understanding the Judicial Role in the Peculiar Institution," Vanderbilt Law Review 32, no. 1 (January 1979):7–218; Charles C. Trabue, "The Voluntary Emancipation of Slaves in Tennessee as Reflected in the State's Legislation and Judicial Decisions," Tennessee Historical Magazine 4, no. 1 (March 1918): 50–68; William E. Wiethoff, A Peculiar Humanism: The Judicial Advocacy of Slavery in High Courts of the Old South, 1820–1850 (Athens: University of Georgia Press, 1996).

3. Carl N. Degler, "Slavery in Brazil and the United States: An Essay in Comparative History," American Historical Review 75, no. 4 (April 1970): 1006. "No slave in Brazil could enter a complaint himself," Degler explained; "it has to be done by his master or by the public authority." The custom of permitting self-purchase was not codified until 1871. Sidney Chalhoub, "Slaves, Freedmen and the Politics of Freedom in Brazil: The Experience of Blacks in the City of Rio," Slavery & Abolition 10, no. 3 (December 1989): 65; Keila Grinberg, "Freedom Suits and Civil Law in Brazil and the United States," Slavery and Abolition 22 (December 2001): 66–82; Sidney Chalhoub, "The Politics of Silence: Race and Citizenship in Nineteenth-Century Brazil," Slavery & Abolition 27, no. 1 (April 2006): 73–87.

4. R. R. Madden, The Island of Cuba: Its Resources, Progress, and Prospects, Considered in Relation Especially of the Influence of the Prosperity on the Interests of the British West Indies Colonies (London: J. Unwin, 1849), 128, 137; Alejandro de la Fuente, "Slave Law and Claims-Making in Cuba: The Tennenbaum Debate Revisited," Law and History Review 22 (Summer 2004): 12. Syndics were legal advocates "officially charged with acting in the best interest of the slaves." They were primarily planters and slave owners. For other Spanish societies and coartación, see Luis A. Figueroa, Sugar, Slavery, and Freedom in Nineteenth-Century Puerto Rico (Chapel Hill: University of North Carolina Press, 2005), 85; Alejandro de la Fuente, "Slaves and the Creation of Legal Rights in Cuba: Coartación and Papel," Hispanic American Historical Review 87, no. 4 (November 2007): 659–660, 659–692; Gloria García Rodríguez, Voices of the Enslaved in Nineteenth-Century Cuba: A Documentary History (Chapel Hill: University of North Carolina Press, 2011), 41 [arriendo], 3, 42, 43, 48 [syndic].

5. Maribel Arrelucea Barrantes, "Slavery, Writing, and Female Resistance: Black Women Litigants in Lima's Tribunals of the 1780s," in *Afro-Latino Voices: Narratives from the Early Modern Ibero-Atlantic World, 1550–1812,* ed. Kathryn Joy McKnight and Leo J. Garofalo (Philadelphia: University of Pennsylvania Press, 2009), 286–288. Between 1760 and 1820, forty-five complaints among 173 cases involved free status.

6. Bernard Moitt, "Freedom from Bondage at a Price: Women and Redemption from Slavery in the French Caribbean in the Nineteenth Century," *Slavery and Abolition* 26, no. 2 (August 2005): 247–248; Myriam Cottias, "Gender and Republican Citizenship in the French West Indies, 1848–1945," *Slavery & Abolition* 26, no. 2 (August 2005): 233–245.

7. JCCASN, *Whiteford v. Smith (a pauper)*, Va., 6 Randolph 612, December 1828, 1:157. D GARev. *Cases Argued and Determined in the Court of Appeals of Virginia: To Which Are Added Cases Decided in the General Court of Virginia*, vol. 11, comp. Peyton Randolph (Richmond, VA: Samuel Shepherd, 1829), 612–617.

8. *Being a Series of the Most Important Law Cases Argued and Determined in the General Court and Court of Appeals of the State of Maryland, from October, 1790, to May, 1797,* 3 vols., comp. Thomas Harris Jr. and Tom McHenry (New York: I. Riley, 1813), 3:193.

9. John Codman Hurd, *Topics of Jurisprudence Connected with Conditions of Freedom and Bondage* (New York: D. Van Nostrad, 1856), 43.

10. Thomas R. R. Cobb, *An Inquiry into the Law of Negro Slavery to Which Is Prefixed an Historical Sketch of Slavery*, 2 vols. (Philadelphia: T. & J. W. Johnson, 1858), 1:247–259.

11. Petition of G. Mason, John A. Washington, and Dennis Johnston to the Virginia General Assembly, Fairfax County, 14 January 1851, in *The Southern Debate over Slavery*, vol. 1: *Petitions to Southern Legislatures, 1778–1864*, ed. Loren Schweninger (Urbana: University of Illinois Press, 2001), 210–15. PAR 11685109. Rejected.

12. Court Opinion, 30 September 1833, in *Thomas v. Hunt*; see note 47, chap. 6, this volume.

13. For citation, see note 47, chap. 12, this volume.

SELECTED BIBLIOGRAPHY

Ablavsky, Gregory. "'Making Indians White': The Judicial Abolitions of Native Slavery in Revolutionary Virginia and Its Racial Legacy." *University of Pennsylvania Law Review* 159 (2011): 1457–531.

Adams, Catherine, and Elizabeth H. Pleck. *Love of Freedom: Black Women in Colonial and Revolutionary New England.* New York: Oxford University Press, 2010.

Ambrose, Douglass. "Of Stations and Relations: Proslavery Debates in Early National Virginia." In *Religion and the Antebellum Debate Over Slavery,* edited by John R. McKivigan and Michael Snay, 35–67. Athens: University of Georgia Press, 1998.

Aslakson, Kenneth R. *Making Race in the Courtroom: The Legal Construction of Three Races in Early New Orleans.* New York: New York University Press, 2014.

Bancroft, Frederic. *Slave-Trading in the Old South.* Baltimore: J. H. Furst Company, 1931.

Bardaglio, Peter W. *Reconstructing the Household: Families, Sex, and the Law in the Nineteenth-Century South.* Chapel Hill: University of North Carolina Press, 1995.

Barrantes, Maribel Arrelucea. "Slavery, Writing, and Female Resistance: Black Women Litigants in Lima's Tribunals of the 1780s." In *Afro-Latino Voices: Narratives from the Early Modern Ibero-Atlantic World, 1550–1812,* edited by Kathryn Joy McKnight and Leo J. Garofalo, 285–301. Indianapolis, IN: Hackett, 2009.

Berlin, Ira. *Many Thousands Gone: The First Two Centuries of Slavery in North America.* Cambridge: Harvard University Press, 1998.

Berlin, Ira. *Slaves without Masters: The Free Negro in the Antebellum South.* New York: Pantheon, 1974.

Billings, Warren M. "The Cases of Fernando and Elizabeth Key: A Note on the Status of Blacks in Seventeenth-Century Virginia." *William and Mary Quarterly* 30, no. 3 (July 1973): 467–474.

Billings, Warren M., ed. *The Historic Rules of the Supreme Court of Louisiana, 1813–1879.* Lafayette: University of Southwestern Louisiana, 1985.

Blassingame, John W., ed. *Slave Testimony, Two Centuries of Letters, Speeches, Interviews, and Autobiographies.* Baton Rouge: Louisiana State University Press, 1977.

Bogen, David Skillen. "The Maryland Context of Dred Scott: The Decline in the Legal Status of Maryland Free Blacks, 1776–1810." *The American Journal of Legal History* 34 (October 1990): 381–411.

Bogger, Tommy L. *Free Blacks in Norfolk, Virginia, 1790–1860: The Darker Side of Freedom.* Charlottesville: University Press of Virginia, 1997.

Brown, Kathleen M. *Good Wives, Nasty Wenches, Anxious Patriarchs: Gender, Race and Power in Colonial Virginia.* Chapel Hill: University of North Carolina Press, 1996.

Brown, Letitia Woods. *Free Negroes in the District of Columbia, 1790–1846.* New York: Oxford University Press, 1974.

Brown, Theodore, Jr. "The Formative Period in the History of the Supreme Court of Tennessee, 1796–1835." In *A History of the Tennesee Supreme Court*, edited by James W. Ely Jr., 1–60. Knoxville: University of Tennessee Press, 2002.

Brown, Thomas F., and Leah C. Sims. "'To Swear Him Free,' Ethnic Memory as Social Capital in Eighteenth Century Freedom Petitions." In *Colonial Chesapeake: New Perspectives*, edited by Debra Myers and Melanie Perrault, 81–106. Lanham, MD: Lexington, 2006.

Burke, Joseph C. "What Did the Prigg Decision Really Decide?" *Pennsylvania Magazine of History and Biography* 93, no. 1 (January 1969): 73–85.

Calderhead, William L. "Slavery in Maryland in the Age of the Revolution, 1775–1790." *Maryland Historical Magazine* 98 (Fall 2003): 302–324.

Catterall, Helen, ed. *Judicial Cases Concerning American Slavery and the Negro.* 5 vols. Washington, DC: Carnegie Institution, 1926–1937; reprint, New York: Octagon Books, 1968.

Catterall, Helen. "Some Antecedents of the Dred Scott Case." *American Historical Review* 30, no. 1 (1924): 56–71.

Chenault, Alexander J. "*Jones v. Bennet*: The Bifurcated Legal Status of Early Nineteenth Century Free Blacks in Kentucky." *The Modern American* 5 (Spring 2009): 32–36.

Clegg, Claude A., III. *The Price of Liberty: African Americans and the Making of Liberia.* Chapel Hill: University of North Carolina Press, 2004.

Clinton, Catherine, and Michelle Gillespie, eds. *The Devil's Lane: Sex and Race in the Early South.* New York: Oxford University Press, 1997.

Condon, Sean. "The Significance of Group Manumissions in Post-Revolutionary Rural Maryland." *Slavery & Abolition* 32 (2011): 75–89.

Cover, Robert. *Justice Accused: Antislavery and the Judicial Process.* New Haven, CT: Yale University Press, 1975.

Davis, Adrienne. "The Private Law of Race and Sex: An Antebellum Perspective." *Stanford Law Review* 51, no. 2 (1999): 221–288.

de la Fuente, Alejandro. "Slave Law and Claims-Making in Cuba: The Tennenbaum Debate Revisited." *Law and History Review* 22, no. 2 (Summer 2004): 339–369.

de la Fuente, Alejandro. "Slaves and the Creation of Legal Rights in Cuba: *Coartación* and Papel." *Hispanic American Historical Review* 87, no. 4 (November 2007): 659–692.

de la Fuente, Alejandro, and Ariela Gross. "Slaves, Free Blacks and Race in the Legal Regimes of Cuba, Louisiana, and Virginia: A Comparison." *North Carolina Law Review* 91, no. 7 (2013): 1699–1756.

Deyle, Steven. *Carry Me Back: The Domestic Slave Trade in American Life.* New York: Oxford University Press, 2005.

Douglass, Frederick. *My Bondage and My Freedom.* New York: Miller, Orton and Milligan, 1855.

Down, Harry. "Unlikely Abolitionist: William Cushing and the Struggle against Slavery." *Journal of Supreme Court History* 29, no. 2 (June 2004):123–135.

Doyle, Christopher. "Judge St. George Tucker and the Case of *Tom v. Roberts*: Blunting the Revolution's Radicalism from Virginia's District Courts." *Virginia Magazine of History and Biography* 106 (Autumn 1998): 419–442.

Dumbauld, Edward. "A Manuscript from Monticello: Jefferson's Law Library and Legal History." *American Bar Association Journal* 38, no. 5 (May 1952): 389–392, 446–447.

Edwards, Laura. "Law, Domestic Violence, and the Limits of Patriarchal Authority in the Antebellum South." *Journal of Southern History* 65, no. 4 (November 1999): 733–770.

Edwards, Laura. *The People and Their Peace: Legal Culture and the Transformation of Inequality in the Post-Revolutionary South.* Chapel Hill: University of North Carolina Press, 2009.

Edwards, Laura. "Status without Rights: African Americans and the Tangled History of Law and Governance in the Nineteenth-Century U.S. South." *The American Historical Review* 112, no. 2 (April 2007): 365–393.

Eisgruber, Christopher L. M. "Justice Story, Slavery, and the Natural Law Foundations of American Constitutionalism." *University of Chicago Law Review* 55, no. 1 (Winter 1988): 273–327.

Ely, Melvin Patrick. *Israel on the Appomattox: A Southern Experiment in Black Freedom from the 1790s through the Civil War*. New York: Knopf, 2004.

Essah, Patience. *A House Divided: Slavery and Emancipation in Delaware, 1638–1865*. Charlottesville: University of Virginia Press, 1996.

Essig, James. *The Bonds of Wickedness: American Evangelicals Against Slavery, 1770–1808*. Philadelphia: Temple University Press, 1982.

Everett, C. S. "'They shalbe Slaves for Their Lives': Indian Slavery in Colonial Virginia." In *Indian Slavery in Colonial America*, edited by Allan Gallay, 67–108. Lincoln: University of Nebraska Press, 2009.

Farnam, Henry W. *Chapters in the History of Social Legislation in the United States to 1860*. Washington, DC: Carnegie Institution, 1938.

Fawver, Kathleen, "The Black Family in the Chesapeake: New Evidence, New Perspectives." In *Colonial Chesapeake: New Perspectives*, edited by Debra Myers and Melanie Perrault, 51–80. Lanham, MD: Lexington, 2006.

Fede, Andrew. *People without Rights: An Interpretation of the Fundamentals of the Law of Slavery in the U.S. South*. New York: Garland, 1992.

Fede, Andrew. *Roadblocks to Freedom: Slavery and Manumission in the United States South*. New Orleans, LA: Quid Pro Books, 2011.

Fehrenbacher, Don E. *Slavery, Law, and Politics: The Dred Scott Case in Historical Perspective*. New York: Oxford University Press, 1981.

Fernandez, Mark F. *From Chaos to Continuity: The Evolution of Louisiana's Judicial System, 1712–1862*. Baton Rouge: Louisiana State University Press, 2001.

Finkelman, Paul. *An Imperfect Union: Slavery, Federalism, and Comity*. Chapel Hill: University of North Carolina Press, 1981.

Finkelman, Paul. "*Prigg v. Pennsylvania*: Understanding Justice Story's Pro-Slavery Nationalism." *Journal of Supreme Court History* 2 (1997): 51–64.

Finkelman, Paul. *Slavery and the Founders: Race and Liberty in the Age of Jefferson*. 3d ed. Armonk, New York: M. E. Sharp, 2014.

Finnie, Gordon E. "The Antislavery Movement in the Upper South before 1840." *Journal of Southern History* 35, no. 3 (November 1969): 319–42.

Foley, William E. "Slave Freedom Suits before Dred Scott: The Case of Marie Jean Scypion's Descendants." *Missouri Historical Review* 79 (1984–1985):1–23.

Foner, Eric. *Gateway to Freedom: The Hidden History of the Underground Railroad*. New York: W. W. Norton, 2015.

Foner, Laura. "The Free People of Color in Louisiana and St. Domingue: A Comparative Portrait of Two Three-Caste Slave Societies." *Journal of Social History* 3, no. 4 (Summer 1970): 406–430.

Fox-Genovese, Elizabeth. *Within the Plantation Household: Black and White Women of the Old South*. Chapel Hill: University of North Carolina Press, 1988.

Fox-Genovese, Elizabeth, and Eugene Genovese. *The Mind of the Master Class: History and Faith in the Southern Slaveholders' Worldview*. Cambridge: Cambridge University Press, 2005.

Franklin, John Hope. *The Free Negro in North Carolina, 1790–1860*. Chapel Hill: University of North Carolina Press, 1943.

Franklin, John Hope. *The Militant South, 1800–1861*. Cambridge: Harvard University Press, 1956.

Franklin, John Hope, and Loren Schweninger. *Runaway Slaves: Rebels on the Plantation*. New York: Oxford University Press, 1999.

Gardner, Eric. "'You Have No Business to Whip Me': The Freedom Suits of Polly Walsh and Lucy Ann Delaney." *African American Review* 41, no. 1 (Spring 2007): 33–50.

Geggus, David. *Slavery, War, and Revolution: The British Occupation of Saint Domingue, 1793–1798*. New York: Oxford University Press, 1982.

Gellman, David Nathaniel. *Emancipating New York: The Politics of Slavery and Freedom, 1777–1827*. Baton Rouge: Louisiana State University Press, 2006.

Gillmer, Jason A. "Suing for Freedom: Interracial Sex, Slave Law, and Racial Identity in the Post-Revolutionary and Antebellum South." *North Carolina Law Review* 82, Part 2 (January 2004): 535–620.

Graber, Mark. *Dred Scott and the Problem of Constitutional Evil.* Cambridge: Cambridge University Press, 2008.

Greene, Lorenzo Johnston. *The Negro in Colonial New England, 1620–1776.* New York: Columbia University Press, 1942.

Grinberg, Keila. "Freedom Suits and Civil Law in Brazil and the United States." *Slavery and Abolition* 22, no. 3 (2001): 66–82.

Grivno, Max. *Gleanings of Freedom: Free and Slave Labor along the Mason-Dixon Line, 1790–1860.* Urbana: University of Illinois Press, 2011.

Gross, Ariela J. "Litigating Whiteness: Trials of Racial Determination in the Nineteenth Century South." *Yale Law Journal* 108, no. 1 (1998): 109–188.

Gross, Ariela J. "Slavery, Anti-Slavery, and the Coming of the Civil War." In *The Cambridge History of Law in America. Volume II: The Long Nineteenth Century (1789–1920),* edited by Michael Grossberg and Christopher Tomlins, 280–312. Cambridge: Cambridge University Press, 2008.

Gross, Ariela J. *What Blood Won't Tell: A History of Race on Trial in America.* Cambridge, MA: Harvard University Press, 2008.

Hall, Kermit L., Paul Finkelman, and James W. Ely, Jr., eds. *American Legal History: Cases and Materials.* 3d ed. New York: Oxford University Press, 2005.

Harrold, Stanley. *Border War: Fighting over Slavery before the Civil War.* Chapel Hill: University of North Carolina Press, 2010.

Harrold, Stanley. *Subversives: Antislavery Community in Washington, D.C., 1828–1865.* Baton Rouge: Louisiana State University Press, 2003.

Higginbotham, A. Leon, Jr. *In the Matter of Color: Race and the American Legal Process; The Colonial Period.* New York: Oxford University Press, 1978.

Hodes, Martha. *White Women, Black Men: Illicit Sex in the Nineteenth-Century South.* New Haven, CT: Yale University Press, 1997.

Hodges, Graham Russell. *Root and Branch: African Americans in New York and East Jersey, 1613–1863.* Chapel Hill: University of North Carolina Press, 1999.

Holton, Woody. *Black Americans in the Revolutionary Era: A Brief History with Documents.* New York: Bedford/St. Martin's, 2009.

Howington, Arthur. "'Not in the Condition of a Horse or an Ox': *Ford v. Ford,* the Law and Testamentary Manumission, and the Tennessee Courts' Recognitions of Slave Humanity." *Tennessee Historical Quarterly* 34, no. 3 (1975): 249–263.

Howington, Arthur. "'A Property of Special and Peculiar Value': The Tennessee Supreme Court and the Law of Manumission." *Tennessee Historical Quarterly* 44, no. 3 (Fall 1985): 302–317.

Hudson, J. Blaine. "In Pursuit of Freedom: Slave Law and Emancipation in Louisville and Jefferson County, Kentucky." *The Filson History Quarterly* 76 (Summer 2002): 287–326.

Huebner, Timothy S. "Judicial Independence in an Age of Democracy, Sectionalism, and War, 1835–1865." In *A History of the Tennessee Supreme Court,* edited by James W. Ely, 61–98. Knoxville: University of Tennessee, 2002.

Huebner, Timothy S. "The Roots of Fairness: *State v. Caesar* and Slave Justice in Antebellum North Carolina." In *Local Matters: Race, Crime and Justice in the Nineteenth-Century South,* edited by Christopher Waldrep and Donald G. Neiman, 29–52. Athens: University of Georgia Press, 2001.

Huebner, Timothy S. *The Southern Judicial Tradition: State Judges and Sectional Distinctiveness, 1790–1890.* Athens: University of Georgia Press, 1999.

Hunter, Tera W. *Bound in Wedlock: Slave and Free Black Marriage in the Nineteenth Century.* Cambridge, MA: Harvard University Press, 2017.

Hurd, John Codman. *The Law of Freedom and Bondage in the United States.* 2 vols. Boston: Little, Brown, 1862; reprint, New York: Negro Universities Press, 1968.

Ingersoll, Thomas N. "Free Blacks in a Slave Society: New Orleans, 1718–1812." In *The Louisiana Purchase Bicentennial Series in Louisiana History. Volume 11, The African American Experience in Louisiana, Part A: From Africa to the Civil War*, edited by Charles Vincent, 123–153. Lafayette: Center for Louisiana Studies, 1999.

Ireland, Robert. *The Legal Career of William Pinkney, 1764–1822*. New York: Garland, 1986.

Johnson, Guion Griffis. *Ante-Bellum North Carolina: A Social History*. Chapel Hill: University of North Carolina Press, 1937.

Johnson, Walter. "The Slave Trader, the White Slave, and the Politics of Racial Determination in the 1850s." *The Journal of American History* 87, Part 1 (June 2000): 13–38.

Johnson, Walter. *Soul by Soul: Life inside the Antebellum Slave Market*. Cambridge, MA: Harvard University Press, 1999.

Jones, Bernie D. *Fathers of Conscience: Mixed-Race Inheritance in the Antebellum South*. Athens: University of Georgia Press, 2009.

Jordan, Winthrop. *White over Black: American Attitudes toward the Negro 1550–1812*. Chapel Hill: University of North Carolina Press, 1967.

Kelly Marie. "Law, Geography, and Mobility: Suing for Freedom in Antebellum St. Louis." *Journal of Southern History* 80, no. 3 (August 2014): 575–604.

Kennington, Kelly M. *In the Shadow of Dred Scott: St. Louis Freedom Suits and the Legal Culture of Slavery in Antebellum America*. Athens: University of Georgia Press, 2017.

Kennington, Kelly Marie. "River of Injustice: St. Louis's Freedom Suits and the Changing Nature of Legal Slavery in Antebellum America." PhD diss., Duke University, 2009.

Kettner, James H. "Persons or Property? The Pleasants Slaves in the Virginia Courts, 1792–1799." In *Launching the "Extended Republic": The Federalist Era*, edited by Ronald Hoffman and Peter J. Albert, 136–55. Charlottesville: University Press of Virginia, 1996.

King, Wilma. *Stolen Childhood: Slave Youth in Nineteenth-Century America*. Bloomington: Indiana University Press, 1995.

Koger, Larry. *Black Slaveowners: Free Blacks Slave Masters in South Carolina, 1790–1860*. Jefferson, NC: McFarland and Company, 1985.

Konefsky, Alfred S. "The Legal Profession: From the Revolution to the Civil War." In *The Cambridge History of Law in America, Volume 2: The Long Nineteenth Century (1789–1920)*, edited by Michael Grossberg and Christopher Tomlins, 68–105. Cambridge, MA: Cambridge University Press, 2008.

Lachance, Paul F. "The Politics of Fear: French Louisianians and the Slave Trade, 1706–1809." In *The Louisiana Purchase Bicentennial Series in Louisiana History, Volume XI, The African American Experience in Louisiana, Part A: From Africa to the Civil War*, edited by Charles Vincent, 123–153. Lafayette: Center for Louisiana Studies, 1999.

Lightner, David. *Slavery and the Commerce Power: How the Struggle against the Interstate Slave Trade Led to the Civil War*. New Haven, CT: Yale University Press, 2006.

Litwack, Leon. *North of Slavery: The Negro in the Free States, 1790–1860*. Chicago: University of Chicago Press, 1961.

McMillen, Sally G. *Southern Women: Black and White in the Old South*. Arlington Heights, IL: Harlan Davidson, 1992.

Maltz, Earle M. "Slavery, Federalism and the Structure of the Constitution." *The American Journal of Legal History* 36 (October 1992): 466–498.

Maris-Wolf, Ted. *Family Bonds: Free Black and Re-enslavement Law in Antebellum Virginia*. Chapel Hill: University of North Carolina Press, 2015.

Martin, Jonathan D. *Divided Mastery: Slave Hiring in the American South*. Cambridge, MA: Harvard University Press, 2004.

Mason, Matthew. "Necessary but Not Sufficient: Revolutionary Ideology and Anti-Slavery Action in the Early Republic." In *Contesting Slavery: The Politics of Bondage and Freedom in the New American Nation*, edited by John Craig Hammond and Matthew Mason, 13–31. Charlottesville: University of Virginia Press, 2011.

Mason, Matthew. *Slavery and Politics in the Early American Republic*. Chapel Hill: University of North Carolina Press, 2006.

Menard, Russell. "The Maryland Slave Population, 1658–1730: A Demographic Profile of Blacks in Four Counties." *William and Mary Quarterly* 32, 3rd ser. (January 1975): 29–54.

Millward, Jessica. "'That All Her Increase Shall Be Free': Enslaved Women's Bodies and the Maryland 1809 Law of Manumission." *Women's History Review* 21, no. 3 (June 2012), 363–378.

Moitt, Bernard. "Slave Women and Resistance in the French Caribbean." In *More Than Chattel: Black Women and Slavery in the Americas*, edited by Darlene Clarke Hine and David Barry Gaspar, 239–258. Bloomington: Indiana University Press, 1996.

Morgan, Edmund S. *American Slavery American Freedom: The Ordeal of Colonial Virginia*. New York: W. W. Norton, 1975.

Morgan, Lynda J. *Emancipation in Virginia's Tobacco Belt, 1850–1870*. Athens: University of Georgia Press, 1992.

Morris, Thomas D. *Free Men All: The Personal Liberty Laws of the North, 1780–1861*. Baltimore: Johns Hopkins University Press, 1974.

Morris, Thomas D. *Southern Slavery and the Law, 1619–1860*. Chapel Hill: University of North Carolina Press, 1996.

Myers, Amrita Chakrabarti. *Forging Freedom: Black Women and the Pursuit of Liberty in Antebellum Charleston*. Chapel Hill: University of North Carolina Press, 2011.

Najar, Monica. "'Meddling with Emancipation': Baptist, Authority, and the Rift over Slavery in the Upper South." *The Journal of the Early Republic* 25, no. 2 (Summer 2005): 157–186.

Nash, A. E. Keir. "Fairness and Formalism in the Trials of Blacks in the State Supreme Courts of the Old South." *Virginia Law Review* 56, no. 1 (1970): 65–100.

Nash, A. E. Keir. "A More Equitable Past? Southern Supreme Courts and the Protection of the Antebellum Negro." *North Carolina Law Review* 48 (1970): 197–241.

Nash, A. E. Keir. "Reason and Slavery: Understanding the Judicial Role in the Peculiar Institution." *Vanderbilt Law Review* 32, no. 1 (January 1979): 7–218.

Nash, Gary B., and Jean R. Soderlund. *Freedom by Degrees: Emancipation in Pennsylvania and its Aftermath*. New York: Oxford University Press, 1991.

Nicholls, Michael L. "'The Squint of Freedom': African-American Freedom Suits in Post-Revolutionary Virginia." *Slavery and Abolition* 20, no. 2 (August 1999): 47–62.

Nicholls, Michael L. "Strangers Setting among Us: The Sources and Challenge of the Urban Free Black Population of Early Virginia." *The Virginia Magazine of History and Biography* 108, no. 2 (Spring 2000): 155–179.

Nogee, Joseph. "The Prigg Case and Fugitive Slavery, 1842–1850: Part I." *Journal of Negro History* 39, no. 3 (July 1954): 185–205.

Oshatz, Molly. *Slavery and Sin: The Fight against Slavery and the Rise of Liberal Protestantism*. New York: Oxford University Press, 2012.

Papenfuse, Eric Robert. "From Recompense to Revolution: *Mahoney v. Ashton* and the Transfiguration of Maryland Culture, 1791–1802." *Slavery and Abolition* 15 (December 1994): 38–62.

Patton, John W. "The Progress of Emancipation in Tennessee." *The Journal of Negro History* 17, no. 1 (January 1932): 67–102.

Peabody, Sue. *"There Are No Slaves in France": The Political Culture of Race and Slavery in the Ancien Regime*. New York: Oxford University Press, 1996.

Peabody, Sue. "'Free upon Higher Ground,': Saint Domingue Slaves' Suits for Freedom in U.S. Courts." In *The World of the Haitian Revolution*, edited by David Geggus and Norman Fiering, 261–283. Bloomington: Indiana University Press, 2009.

Phillips, Christopher. *Freedom's Port: The African American Community of Baltimore, 1790–1860*. Urbana: University of Illinois Press, 1997.

Phillips, Christopher. "The Roots of Quasi-Freedom: Manumission and Term Slavery in Early National Baltimore." *Southern Studies*, new series 4 (Spring 1993): 39–66.

Post, Edward M. "Kentucky Law Concerning Emancipation and Freedom of Slaves." *The Filson Club History Quarterly* 59 (July 1985): 344–367.

Quarles, Benjamin. *The Negro in the American Revolution.* Chapel Hill: University of North Carolina Press, 1961.

Reid, Patricia A. "Margaret Morgan's Story: A Threshold between Slavery and Freedom, 1820–1842." *Slavery & Abolition* 33, no. 3 (September 2012): 359–380.

Robinson, Charles F., II. *Dangerous Liaisons: Sex and Love in the Segregated South.* Fayetteville: University of Arkansas Press, 2003

Rockman, Seth. *Scraping By: Wage Labor, Slavery, and Survival in Early Baltimore.* Baltimore: Johns Hopkins University Press, 2009.

Rothman, Joshua D. *Notorious in the Neighborhood: Sex and Families across the Color Line in Virginia, 1787–1861.* Chapel Hill: University of North Carolina Press, 2003.

Russell, Marion J. "American Slave Discontent in Records of the High Courts." *Journal of Negro History* 31, no. 4 (October 1946): 411–434.

Salafia, Matthew. *Slavery's Borderlands: Freedom and Bondage along the Ohio River.* Philadelphia: University of Pennsylvania Press, 2013.

Schafer, Judith Kelleher. *Becoming Free, Remaining Free: Manumission and Enslavement in New Orleans, 1846–1862.* Baton Rouge: Louisiana State University Press, 2003.

Schafer, Judith Kelleher. "'Open and Notorious Concubinage': The Emancipation of Slave Mistresses by Will and the Supreme Court in Antebellum Louisiana." *Louisiana History* 28 (Spring 1987): 165–182.

Schafer, Judith Kelleher. *Slavery, the Civil Law, and the Supreme Court of Louisiana.* Baton Rouge: Louisiana State University Press, 1994.

Schermerhorn, Calvin. *Money over Mastery, Family over Freedom: Slavery in the Antebellum Upper South.* Baltimore: Johns Hopkins University Press, 2011.

Schwarz, Philip J. *Slave Laws in Virginia.* Athens: University of Georgia Press, 1996.

Scott, Rebecca, and Jean M. Hébrard. *Freedom Papers: An Atlantic Odyssey in the Age of Emancipation.* Cambridge, MA: Harvard University, 2014.

Shalon, Trevor J. "A Plea for Freedom: Enslaved Independence through Petitions for Freedom in Washington DC, between 1810 and 1830." MA diss., University of Nebraska-Lincoln, 2012.

Smith, David G. *On the Edge of Freedom: The Fugitive Slave Issue in South Central Pennsylvania, 1820–1870.* New York: Fordham University Press, 2013.

Sommerville, Diane Miller. *Rape & Race in the Nineteenth Century South.* Chapel Hill: University of North Carolina Press, 2004.

Stampp, Kenneth M. *The Peculiar Institution: Slavery in the Ante-Bellum South.* New York: Knopf, 1956.

Sterkx, Herbert E. *The Free Negro in Antebellum Louisiana.* Rutherford, NJ: Fairleigh Dickinson University Press, 1972.

Story, Joseph. *Commentaries on Equity Jurisprudence as Administered in England and America.* Boston: Hilliard, Gray and Co., 1836; reprint ed., Washington, DC, Beard Books, 2000.

Sullivan, Ronald S., Jr. "Classical Racism, Justice Story, and Margaret Morgan's Journey from Freedom to Slavery: The Story of Prigg v. Pennsylvania." In *Race Law Stories,* edited by Rachel F. Moran and John D. Carbado, 59–88. New York: Foundation Press, 2008.

Sweet, Frank W. *The Legal History of the Color Line: The Rise and Triumph of the One-Drop Rule.* Palm Coast, FL: Backintyme, 2005.

Sweet, John Wood. *Bodies Politic: Negotiating Race in the American North, 1730–1830.* Baltimore: Johns Hopkins University Press, 2003.

Tadman, Michael. *Speculators and Slaves: Masters, Traders, and Slaves in the Old South.* Madison: University of Wisconsin Press, 1989.

Taylor, Arnold. *Rose, a Woman of Colour: A Slave's Struggle for Freedom in the Courts of Kentucky.* New York: iUniverse, 2008.

Taylor, Arnold. *Suing for Freedom in Kentucky.* Bangor, ME: BookLocker.com, 2010.

Tedesco, Marie. "A Free Black Slave Owner in East Tennessee: The Strange Case of Adam Waterford." In *Appalachians and Race: The Mountain South from Slavery to Segregation,* edited by John Inscoe, 133–153. Lexington: University of Kentucky Press, 2001.

Tomlins, Christopher. *Freedom Bound: Law, Labor, and Civic Identity in Colonizing English America, 1580–1865*. Cambridge: Cambridge University Press, 2010.

Tushnet, Mark. *The American Law of Slavery, 1810–1860: Considerations of Humanity and Interest*. Princeton, NJ: Princeton University Press, 1981.

Twitty, Anne. *Before Dred Scott: Slavery and Legal Culture in the American Confluence, 1787–1857*. New York: Cambridge University Press, 2016.

Urofsky, Melvin, and Paul Finkelman. *A March of Liberty: A Constitutional History of the United States*. Vol. 1, *From the Founding to 1890*. New York: Oxford University Press, 2002.

Van Cleve, George William. *A Slaveholders' Union: Slavery, Politics, and the Constitution in the Early American Republic*. Chicago: University of Chicago Press, 2010.

VanderVelde, Lea. *Redemption Songs: Suing for Freedom before Dred Scott*. New York: Oxford University Press, 2014.

Wallenstein, Peter. "Indian Foremothers: Race, Sex, Slavery and Freedom in Early Virginia." In *The Devil's Lane: Sex and Race in the Early South*, edited by Catherine Clinton and Michele Gillespie, 57–73. New York: Oxford University Press, 1997.

Wallenstein, Peter. *Tell the Court I Love My Wife: Race, Marriage, and Law—An American History*. New York: Palgrave Macmillan, 2002.

Walsh, Lorena. "Rural African Americans in the Constitutional Era in Maryland, 1776–1810." *Maryland Historical Magazine* 84 (1989): 327–341.

Welch, Kimberly. *Black Litigants in the Antebellum American South*. Chapel Hill: University of North Carolina Press, 2018.

West, Emily. *Family or Freedom: People of Color in the Antebellum South*. Lexington: University Press of Kentucky, 2012.

West, Emily. "'She Is Dissatisfied with Her Present Condition': Requests for Voluntary Enslavement in the Antebellum American South." *Slavery and Abolition* 28, no. 3 (December 2007): 329–350.

Whitman, T. Stephen. *Challenging Slavery in the Chesapeake: Black and White Resistance to Human Bondage, 1775–1865*. Baltimore: Maryland Historical Society, 2007.

Whitman, T. Stephen. *The Price of Freedom: Slavery and Manumission in Baltimore and Early National Maryland*. Lexington: University of Kentucky Press, 1997.

Wiethoff, William E. *A Peculiar Humanism: The Judicial Advocacy of Slavery in High Courts of the Old South, 1820–1850*. Athens: University of Georgia Press, 1996.

Williams, William H. *Slavery and Freedom in Delaware, 1639–1865*. Wilmington, Delaware: Scholarly Resources, 1996.

Wilson, Carol. *Freedom at Risk: The Kidnapping of Free Blacks in America, 1780–1865*. Lexington: University of Kentucky Press, 1994.

Wilson, Carol. *The Two Lives of Sally Miller: A Case of Mistaken Racial Identity in Antebellum New Orleans*. New Brunswick, NJ: Rutgers University Press, 2007.

Wolf, Eva Sheppard. *Race and Liberty in the New Nation: Emancipation in Virginia from the American Revolution to Nat Turner's Rebellion*. Baton Rouge: Louisiana State University Press, 2006.

Wong, Edlie L. *Neither Fugitive nor Free: Atlantic Slavery, Freedom Suits, and the Legal Culture of Travel*. New York: New York University Press, 2009.

Woodson, Carter G. "The Beginnings of the Miscegenation of the Whites and Blacks." *Journal of Negro History* 3, no. 4 (October 1918): 335–353.

Wright, Donald R. *African Americans in the Early Republic, 1789–1831*. Arlington Heights, IL: Harlan Davidson, 1993.

Zilversmit, Arthur. *The First Emancipation: The Abolition of Slavery in the North*. Chicago: University of Chicago Press, 1967.

Zilversmit, Arthur. "Quok Walker, Mumbet, and the Abolition of Slavery in Massachusetts." *William and Mary Quarterly* 25, no. 4 (October 1968): 614–624.

INDEX